ESSENTIAL ITALY

1st Edition

**Where to Stay and Eat
for All Budgets**

**Must-See Sights
and Local Secrets**

Ratings You Can Trust

Excerpted from *Fodor's Italy*
Fodor's Travel Publications   New York, Toronto, London, Sydney, Auckland
www.fodors.com

FODOR'S ESSENTIAL ITALY
Editor: Matthew Lombardi

Editorial Production: Eric B. Wechter

Editorial Contributors: Peter Blackman, Jeff Booth, Linda Cabasin, Robin S. Goldstein, Cristina Gregorin, Madeleine Johnson, Dana Klitzberg, Ann Reavis, Patricia Rucidlo, Pamela Santini, Megan K. Williams

Maps: David Lindroth, *cartographer;* Bob Blake and Rebecca Baer, *map editors.* Additional cartography provided by Henry Colomb, Mark Stroud, and Ali Baird, Moon Street Cartography; and by Mapping Specialists Ltd.

Design: Fabrizio La Rocca, *creative director,* Guido Caroti, *art director,* Chie Ushio, Siobhan O'Hare, Ann McBride, Tina Malaney, Brian Ponto

Photography: Melanie Marin, *senior picture editor*

Production/Manufacturing: Robert Shields

Cover Photo: Gondolier hat, Peter Adams/Alamy; Colosseum, Nic Cleave Photography/Alamy; Glass of red wine, Alain Proust/Alamy; Spaghetti, Campania Tourism; Shoe, Bobo/Alamy; Coffee, Jochem Wijnands/Alamy.

ISBN 978-1-4000-1746-1

ISSN 1934-5550

SPECIAL SALES
This book is available for special discounts for bulk purchases for sales promotions or premiums. Special editions, including personalized covers, excerpts of existing books, and corporate imprints, can be created in large quantities for special needs. For more information, write to Special Markets/Premium Sales, 1745 Broadway, MD 6-2, New York, NY 10019, or e-mail specialmarkets@randomhouse.com.

AN IMPORTANT TIP & AN INVITATION
Although all prices, opening times, and other details in this book are based on information supplied to us at press time, changes occur all the time in the travel world, and Fodor's cannot accept responsibility for facts that become outdated or for inadvertent errors or omissions. So **always confirm information when it matters**, especially if you're making a detour to visit a specific place. Your experiences—positive and negative—matter to us. If we have missed or misstated something, **please write to us.** We follow up on all suggestions. Contact the Italy editor at editors@fodors.com or c/o Fodor's at 1745 Broadway, New York, NY 10019.

PRINTED IN THE UNITED STATES OF AMERICA

10 9 8 7 6 5 4 3 2 1

ITALY IN FOCUS

CLOSEUPS

CONTENTS

ABOUT THIS BOOK

Organization

The first part of this book is designed to give you the lay of the land and help you decide where and when to go. The Great Itinerary section has our suggestions for the best approach to seeing the best of Italy. If You Like . . . identifies some classic Italian experiences and tells you where you can have them.

Jump to the back pages for Smart Travel Tips, a section of nuts-and-bolts planning information. Topics are arranged in alphabetical order. Some won't apply to you, but many will.

The remainder of the book consists of our region-by-region listings—the places to go and things to do—interlaced with history, background, and tips from our on-the-spot writers. Chapters appear in geographical order, beginning in Rome and ending in Venice.

Our Ratings

Anything we list in this guide, whether it's a museum, a ruin, or a restaurant, has our recommendation. Naturally, not every place is going to be for everyone. Our goal is to provide the information you need to make choices that are right for you.

A black star next to a listing means it's Highly Recommended. Year in and year out, travelers of all stripes

have great experiences at these spots.

Orange stars indicate our highest rating, Fodor's Choice. These are the places we think you'll be telling your friends about when you return home—places where you stand a good chance of making a memory. Some selections you'll expect, but others might surprise you. They're all truly special and uniquely Italian. When you have your own Fodor's Choice experience, let us know about it at www. fodors.com/feedback.

Deciphering the Listings

For the most part, our listings are self-explanatory, but a few details are worth mentioning.

For attractions, we give standard adult admission fees; reductions for children, students, and senior citizens are rare (unless you're an EU citizen). Hotel- and restaurant-price categories are defined on the charts found in each chapter. Unless otherwise indicated, restaurants are open for lunch and dinner daily. We mention dress at restaurants only when there's a specific requirement and reservations only when they're essential or not accepted. Hotels have private bath, phone, TV, and air-conditioning unless other-

wise indicated. We list facilities but not whether you'll be charged extra to use them, so when pricing accommodations, find out what's included.

Want to pay with plastic? AE, DC, MC, V following restaurant and hotel listings indicate whether American Express, Diner's Club, MasterCard, and Visa are accepted.

Many Listings	
★	Fodor's Choice
★	Highly recommended
☾	Family-friendly
⊠	Physical address
⊠	Branch address
⊹	Directions
⌂	Mailing address
☏	Telephone
🖷	Fax
⊕	On the Web
✍	E-mail
🎟	Admission fee
☉	Open/closed times
Ⓜ	Metro stations
▭	Credit cards
⇨	See also

Hotels & Restaurants	
🏨	Hotel
⇛	Number of rooms
☊	Facilities
¶◎¶	Meal plans
✕	Restaurant
⌂	Reservations
🏛	Dress code
↘	Smoking
₲♀	BYOB
✕🏨	Hotel with restaurant that warrants a visit

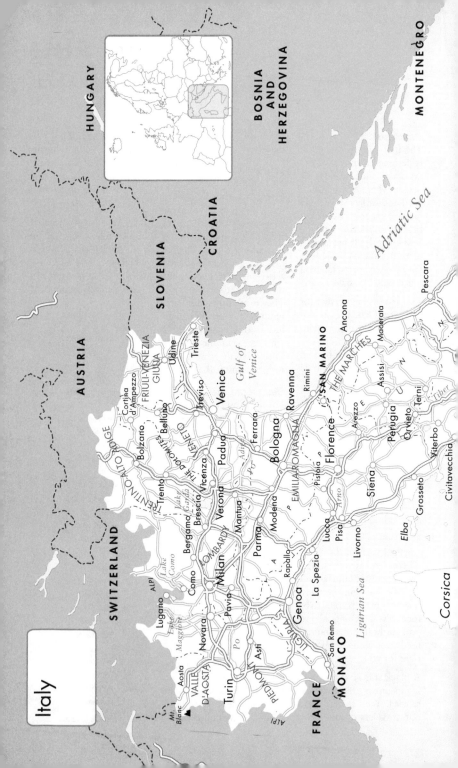

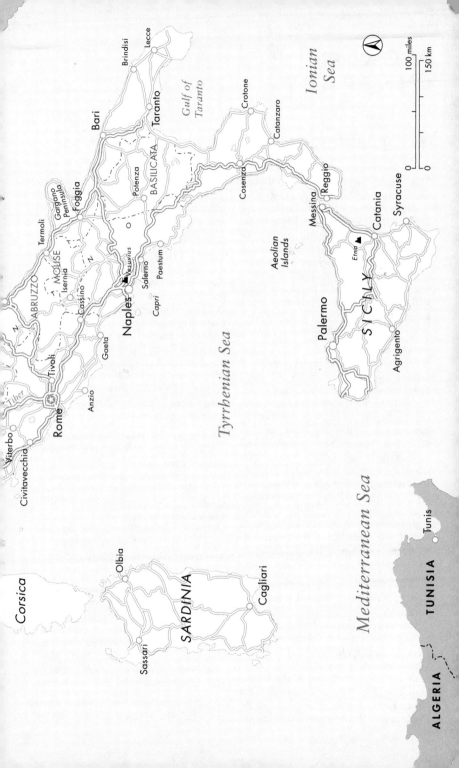

A GREAT ITINERARY

ITALY'S HIGHLIGHTS IN 2 WEEKS (MORE OR LESS)

This itinerary works like an accordion: it can expand or contract, depending on the amount of time you have and where your interests lie. If your top priority is seeing Italy's most famous sights, extend your visits to the great cities of Rome, Florence, and Venice. If you're more drawn by beautiful landscapes, exceptional food and wine, and the Italians' knack for living well, then devote a good part of your trip to the other stops along the way, where the pace of life is more relaxed.

Getting There

Rome and Milan have Italy's busiest international airports, but there are also direct flights between the United States and Venice. To follow the itinerary outlined here, look into "open-jaw" tickets, with which you fly into one city (in this case Rome) and out of another (Venice). You could also finish up your trip by making the three-hour train ride from Venice to Milan, where you'll have more return-flight options (and you can see yet another side of Italy). Or you could go back to Rome (one-way plane tickets for flights within Italy are reasonably priced), and fly home from there. For transportation details, ⇨ Smart Travel Tips at the end of this book.

Getting Around

Your main decision is whether to rent a car or to use Italy's efficient, reasonably priced railway system. The smartest strategy may be to do some of both. Within the cities, a car is a liability: both driving and parking are generally worse in Italian cities than anything you'll find in the United States. Outside of the cities, though, a car has its clear advantages: it gives you the freedom and flexibility to go places not served (or poorly served) by public transit. Particularly in Tuscany, there are significant limits on what you'll be able to see and do without a car.

Stop 1: Rome (2–4 Days)

Rome is a large, bustling city that lives in the here and now, yet there's no other place on earth where you'll encounter such powerful evocations of a long and spectacular past. Take a few steps from Piazza del Campidoglio, designed by Michelangelo, and you're looking down upon the ruins of ancient Rome—smack dab in the middle of the city. Exit a baroque church housing a masterpiece by Caravaggio, turn the corner, and find yourself face-to-face with the Pantheon. Such mind-bending juxtapositions are everywhere.

If you're arriving on an international flight, you'll settle into your hotel in the afternoon. Resist the temptation to nap; instead head outside and spend some time getting to know the surrounding neighborhood. In the evening, check out Piazza Navona and the Trevi Fountain—the energy of the city at night will perk you up like a shot of good espresso. For your first dinner, you can't miss one of Rome's exceptional pizzerias.

In the morning, head to the Vatican to see St. Peter's Basilica and Michelangelo's glorious Sistine Chapel at the Vatican Museums. Have lunch back in Rome proper in the area around the Pantheon, then visit the Pantheon itself and spend the afternoon wandering the cobblestone streets of the neighborhood, taking time for a break at one of the famous coffee shops in the area.

Begin the next day at Campo de' Fiori, where you'll find Rome's most colorful open-air

market in full swing. Then head to the **Campidolgio,** and from there explore the ruins of ancient Rome, topped off by a visit to the **Colosseum.** In the afternoon, hop across town to **Piazza di Spagna,** a good place to shop, lick gelato, and watch the sunset.

On further days here, follow the same basic strategy: devote mornings to significant sights (**Galleria Borghese** is a great choice; note that it requires a reservation) and afternoons to exploring neighborhoods (such as **Trastevere** and the **Jewish Ghetto**). In the evening, do as the Romans do: make a long, relaxed dinner the main event.

Extend your stay if: you're fascinated by Rome's mix of the ancient and the modern, and you love city life. You won't encounter such an intensely urban environment anywhere else on this trip.

Keep your visit short if: an urban environment is what you're on vacation to get away from.

Stop 2: Perugia (1–2 Days)

Perugia is about 2½ hours north of Rome by car or train, but consider a short detour along the way to **Orvieto,** a town with an impressive hilltop setting and one of Italy's great Gothic cathedrals. Both towns are in the largely rural **Umbria** region. The more

relaxed pace of life makes a nice contrast to the energy of Rome.

Perugia is Umbria's largest city, but with a population of about 150,000 it's far from overwhelming, and it has a well-preserved medieval core. The pedestrian-only street through the heart of town, **Corso Vannucci,** is a classic place for a *passeggiata* (evening stroll), and there's a cluster of sights along the street that are worth checking out the next morning—particularly the **Collegio del Cambio,** a Renaissance guild hall frescoed by Perugia's greatest artist, Perugino.

Extend your stay if: you want to make a day trip to **Assisi,** the city of St. Francis, which is about half an hour (by car or train) east of Perugia.

Keep your visit short if: you're a thrill-seeker. Umbria is a beautiful region, but it's not as likely to quicken your pulse as much as some of the other stops on the itinerary.

Stop 3: Chianti (1–2 Days)

To the northwest of Umbria is the region of **Tuscany,** which is rightly famous for having Italy's most gorgeous landscapes. Most beautiful of all is the Chianti district, between Florence and Siena, where vineyards and olive groves blanket rolling hills as far

A GREAT ITINERARY

as the eye can see. To make the most of the experience, stay in the countryside at a converted villa or *agriturismo* (a farm taking overnight guests). Though Chianti is Tuscany's most idyllic location, you can hardly go wrong in the surrounding districts as well—particularly outside Siena and in the hills to its west.

Siena itself is a magnificent hill town that shouldn't be missed. With the exception of Florence, it has more to see than anywhere else in Tuscany, and its **Piazza del Campo** is one of Italy's most appealing town squares. If you leave Perugia in the morning, you can make the 1½ hour drive west to Siena and spend the afternoon there. Tuscany is also a great place for winery tours; the **Strada Chiantigiana**, the beautiful road through the heart of Chianti, takes you past visitor-friendly vineyards and *enoteche* (wineshops).

Extend your stay if: *il dolce far niente* (the sweetness of doing nothing) is a concept you find appealing. Tuscany has some spectacular sights, but the greatest pleasure here is relaxing and unwinding.

Keep your visit short if: you're dead-set against driving. The only town south of Florence that's easily accessible by train is **Arezzo**, which is worth a visit but won't give you the full Tuscan experience.

Stop 4: Florence (2–4 Days)

It's hard to think of a place that's more closely linked to one specific historical period than Florence. In the 15th century the city was at the center of the artistic revolution that would come to be known as the Renaissance. Five hundred years later, the Renaissance remains the main reason people visit Florence—the abundance of art treasures is mind-boggling.

Begin your first day here at the heart of the city, the **Piazza del Duomo.** Check out Ghiberti's famous bronze doors on the **Battistero,** then climb the 463 steps to the top of Brunelleschi's splendid cathedral dome, from where you have an unbeatable view of the entire city and the hills beyond. Back on solid ground, take some time to visit the **Museo dell'Opera del Duomo,** which now holds much of the art that was once in the Duomo. Following lunch, spend the afternoon at the **Gallleria degli Uffizi** (reserve your ticket in advance), which houses one of the world's greatest art collections. When you're through, step outside into the neighboring **Piazza della Signoria,** Florence's most impressive square. You'll find there a copy of Michelangelo's *David,* standing in the spot that was occupied by the original for centuries.

The following morning, visit the real *David* at his indoor home, the **Galleria dell'Accademia.** (Reserve your ticket here as well.) A few steps down the street are the works of another, completely different Renaissance master: the **Museo di San Marco,** a former convent, is decorated with simple, ethereal, occasionally bizarre frescoes of Fra Angelico. You can get another dose of Michangelo before lunch a few blocks away at the **Capelle Medici.** After a day and a half of walking and art-gazing, if a post-lunch nap appeals to you, don't resist. Later in the afternoon, use your revived energy to make the trip up to the **Piazzale Michelangelo,** high on a hill above Florence, from which you have a sweeping view of the city. Stick around for sunset, then head down to the Oltrarno neighborhood below and feast on a famed *bistecca alla fiorentina* (grilled T-bone steak with olive oil).

You'll have seen a lot by this point, but you've still just scratched the surface.

"Must-sees" for additional days are the **Santa Croce** and **Santa Maria Novella** cathedrals and the **Bargello** sculpture museum. And Florence isn't exclusively about art; some visitors come just for the shopping, from the food stalls of the **Mercato Centrale** to the showrooms of the exclusive boutiques along **Via Tournabuoni.**

Extend your stay if: you want to make a side trip to towns of **Lucca** and **Pisa** (home of the leaning tower), west of Florence.

Keep your visit short if: you put a premium on getting off the beaten path. After several hundred years of steady tourism, almost every path in Florence has been pretty well beaten.

Stop 5: Bologna (1–2 Days)

A 1-hour trip by train north from Florence, or 1½ hours by car, brings you to Bologna, a city that doesn't have Florence's abundance of sights, but will give you more of a taste of the pleasures of day-to-day life in Italy. With a population of about 375,000, Bologna is the largest city in **Emilia-Romagna,** a region famed for its cuisine. Many of Italy's signature food products originate here, including Parmigiano-Reggiano cheese (aka Parmesan), prosciutto di Parma, and balsamic vinegar. The pasta is considered Italy's finest—a reputation the region's chefs earn every day. If you're going to splurge on one over-the-top meal, this is the place to do it.

But a visit here is about more than food: Bologna is home to Europe's oldest university, making it a cultural and intellectual center, and it has rows of street arcades winding through grandiose towers. After you've settled into your hotel, take a walk around **Piazza Maggiore** at the heart of the city. Following dinner, you can check out some of northern Italy's best nightlife—one

of the by-products of the university. The next day, continue your exploration of the city center, including a visit to the basilica of **Santo Stefano** and a climb up Bologna's own leaning tower, the **Torre degli Asinelli.**

Extend your stay if: you're lured by a day trip east to see the glorious Byzantine mosaics in **Ravenna,** or west to the foodie meccas of **Parma** and **Modena.**

Keep your visit short if: your priority is seeing Italy's most spectacular sights. Bologna's sights *are* impressive—they just don't rank with the treasures of Rome, Florence, and Venice.

Stop 6: Verona (1–2 Days)

North from Bologna (1½ hours by train, 1¾ hours by car) is Verona, a charming midsize city with a distinctly northern Italian air. Standing alongside the fast-flowing River Adige, gazing at the rows of old palazzi along its banks and the rolling hills of cypress and beyond, it's easy to fall for this city of Romeo and Juliet. Spend your time here wandering the medieval piazzas; skip the touristy so-called "House of Juliet," but don't miss the stunning ancient Roman **Arena,** the **Castelvecchio** (old castle), and **San Zeno Maggiore,** possibly Italy's finest Romanesque church.

Verona is often mentioned in the same breath with **Vicenza** and **Padua,** two other cities of similar size in the **Veneto** region, on the green plains to the west of Venice. Vicenza is best known for its palaces designed by Andrea Palladio, one of history's most influential architects; Padua's star attraction is the **Cappella degli Scrovegni,** a chapel decorated with landmark Giotto frescoes. Both towns are well worth a visit as you make your way toward Venice.

A GREAT ITINERARY

Extend your stay if: you're here in the summer and have a chance to see an opera at Verona's Arena—a truly grand spectacle.

Keep your visit short if: you're impatient to see Venice.

Stop 7: Venice (2–4 Days)

Venice is one of the world's most novel cities, with canals where roads should be and an atmosphere of faded splendor that practically defines the word *decadent*. Once a great seafaring power, Venice now lives for tourism, prompting cynics to compare it to Disneyland. It's true that Piazza San Marco, the magnificent main square, is frequently packed with sightseers, and there are plenty of kitschy souvenirs for sale in the heavily trafficked area around the Rialto Bridge. But Venice is no Mickey Mouse affair: it has a rich history, it's packed with artistic treasures accumulated over a thousand years, and despite the crowds it remains inescapably romantic.

Allow yourself some time to get acclimated. If you have a rental car, return it at the offices on the city's western edge, then find your hotel (be sure to get directions in advance), and if all goes well, you'll have time left in the day for sightseeing. Rather than making a beeline for Piazza San Marco, check out some of the other spectacular attractions, such as the church of Santa Maria Gloriosa dei Frari and the Scuola Grande di San Rocco, or just spend a couple of hours getting lost along the city's back canals before finding your way to a seafood dinner. Afterward, consider a nightcap around the Campo San Luca or Campo Santa Margarita.

Begin the next morning with a *vaporetto* (water bus) cruise along the Grand Canal, then make your visit to Piazza San Marco, the Byzantine splendor of the Basilica di San Marco, and the imposing Palazzo Ducale. After lunch, perhaps at a traditional Venetian *bacaro* (wine bar), take the Accademia footbridge across the Grand Canal and see the Gallerie dell'Accademia, Venice's most important art gallery. Wander through the Dorsoduro neighborhood, finishing up with a romantic sunset stroll along the Zattere boardwalk before proceeding to dinner.

On subsequent days, make your sightseeing priorities the Rialto fish market (a foodie highlight), Ca' Rezzonico and Ca' d'Oro (classic Venetian palaces), and Santa Maria dei Miracoli and Santi Giovanni e Paolo (two spectacular churches).

Extend your stay if: you want to discover Venice beyond the crowds. Exploring the neighborhoods east of Piazza San Marco and the quieter outer islands will take you to another world.

Keep your visit short if: you don't have a tolerance for getting lost. Navigating the streets of Venice can feel like working through a maze.

WHEN TO GO

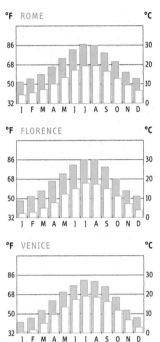

The main tourist season in Italy runs from April to mid-October. The so-called low season from fall to early spring is cooler and rainier, but if you're serious about seeing the sights and not so concerned about weather, you'll reap rewards from visiting at this time: flights are cheaper, hotel rooms are often discounted, crowds at sights are smaller, and locals are less likely to be experiencing "tourist fatigue."

If you *do* care about the weather, aim for a visit in late spring, early summer, or early fall. July is hot and crowded; August is even hotter, and because it's the month when most Italians go on vacation, the cities can feel like they're occupied exclusively by tourists. If you visit at this time of the year, it's smart to adopt the siesta mentality: get up and out early, nap during the afternoon, and head back out in the evening. Be sure to confirm that your hotel has air-conditioning; it has become increasingly prevalent in recent years, but it's still not a given.

Climate

Winters throughout the territory covered here are rainy and cool, but temperatures seldom drop below freezing. The region of Emilia–Romagna is notorious for its winter fog, which can make driving an impossibility. In Venice, spring and fall are the seasons for *acqua alta,* the short-term flooding that can engulf low-lying parts of the city, including the Piazza San Marco, at high tide.

Summers are dry and hot—the past decade has seen some of the hottest on record. May through early June and mid-September through mid-October are the idyllic times to be here: temperatures are mild, and rains have either tapered off (in the spring) or not yet started in earnest (in the fall).

🇮 Forecasts **Weather Channel Connection** (☎ 900/9328437, 95¢ per min ⊕ www.weather.com).

QUINTESSENTIAL ITALY

Il Caffè (Coffee)

The Italian day begins and ends with coffee, and more cups of coffee punctuate the time in between. To live like the Italians do, drink as they drink, standing at the counter or sitting at an outdoor table of the corner bar. (In Italy, a "bar" is a coffee bar.) A primer: *caffè* means coffee, and Italian standard issue is what Americans call espresso—short, strong, and usually taken very sweet. *Cappuccino* is a foamy half-and-half of espresso and steamed milk; cocoa powder *(cacao)* on top is acceptable, cinnamon is not. If you're thinking of having a cappuccino for dessert, think again—Italians drink only caffè or caffè *macchiato* (with a spot of steamed milk) after lunchtime. Confused? Homesick? Order caffè *americano* for a reasonable facsimile of good old filtered joe.

Il Calcio (Soccer)

Imagine the most rabid American football fans—the ones who paint their faces on game day and sleep in pajamas emblazoned with the logo of their favorite team. Throw in a dose of melodrama along the lines of a tear-jerking soap opera. Ratchet up the intensity by a factor of 10, and you'll start to get a sense of how Italians feel about their national game, soccer—known in the mother tongue as *calcio*. On Sunday afternoons throughout the long September-to-May season, stadiums are packed throughout Italy from tip to toe. Those who don't get to games in person tend to congregate around television sets in restaurants and bars, rooting for the home team with a passion that feels like a last vestige of the days when the country was a series of warring medieval city-states. How calcio mania affects your stay in Italy depends on how eager you are to get involved. At the very least, you may notice an eerie Sunday-af-

If you want to get a sense of contemporary Italian culture and indulge in some of its pleasures, start by familiarizing yourself with the rituals of daily life. These are a few highlights—things you can take part in with relative ease.

ternoon silence on the city streets, or erratic restaurant service around the same time, accompanied by occasional cheers and groans from a neighboring room. If you want a memorable, truly Italian experience, attend a game yourself. Availability of tickets may depend on the current fortunes of the team in the town where you're staying, but they often can be acquired with some help from your hotel concierge.

Il Gelato (Ice Cream)

During warmer months, *gelato*—the Italian equivalent of ice cream—is a national obsession. It's considered a snack rather than a dessert, bought at stands and shops in piazzas and on street corners, and consumed on foot, usually at a leisurely stroll. (⇨ La Passeggiata, *below.*) Gelato is softer, less creamy, and more intensely flavored than its American counterpart. It comes in simple flavors that capture the essence of

the main ingredient. (You won't find Chunky Monkey or Cookies 'n' Cream.) At most gelaterias standard choices include pistachio, nocciola (hazelnut), caffè, and numerous fresh-fruit varieties. Quality varies; the surest sign that you've hit on a good spot is a line at the counter.

La Passeggiata (Strolling)

A favorite Italian pastime is the *passeggiata* (literally, the promenade). In the late afternoon and early evening, especially on weekends, couples, families, and packs of teenagers stroll the main streets and piazzas of Italy's towns. It's a ritual of exchanged news and gossip, window-shopping, flirting, and gelato eating that adds up to a uniquely Italian experience. To join in, simply hit the streets for a bit of wandering. You may feel more like an observer than a participant, until you realize that observing is what la passeggiata is all about.

IF YOU LIKE . . .

Renaissance Art

Travel veterans will tell you that the seemingly countless masterpieces of Italian art can cause first-time visitors—eyes glazed over from a heavy downpour of images, dates, and names—to lean, Pisa-like, on their companions for support. After a surfeit of Botticellis and Raphaels, even the miracle of the High Renaissance may begin to pall. The secret is to act like a tortoise, not a hare, and take your sweet time.

Instead of trotting after brisk tour guides, allow the splendors of the age to unfold slowly. Don't stop at the museums; get out and explore the chapels, palaces, and town squares for which Italy's marvelous art was conceived centuries ago and where much of it remains. Take in Michelangelo's *David* in Florence's Accademia, but then meander down the nearby 15th-century street where the sculptor was born.

Those caveats aside, here are the places to go when you're ready for an art feast:

- **Galleria degli Uffizi, Florence.** Allow the better part of a day to explore the world's greatest collection of Italian Renaissance art.

- **Musei Vaticani, Rome.** To gaze up at the impossible brushstrokes forming Michelangelo's Adam into muscular perfection at the zenith of the Sistine Chapel is to confront the divine— however you define it.

- **Basilica di San Francesco, Arezzo.** Piero della Francesa's *True Cross* frescoes merit a pilgrimage to this Tuscan town.

- **Galleria dell'Accademia, Venice.** Come here to experience the rich colors that are the trademark of the Venetian Renaissance.

Monumental Churches

Few images are more identifiable with Italy than the country's great churches, stunning works of architecture that often took centuries to build. Across the boot you'll find churches in styles ranging from flying-buttressed medieval Gothic to rococo and fanciful baroque.

The name duomo (derived from the Latin for house, "domus," and the root of the English "dome") is used to refer to the principal church of a town or city. Generally speaking, the bigger the city, the more splendid its duomo. Still, some impressive churches inhabit some unlikely places—in the Umbrian hill towns of Assisi and Orvieto, for example.

- **Basilica di San Pietro, Rome.** You've probably seen the Catholic Church's mother ship a thousand times on TV, but the imposing splendor of the Vatican can't be captured by the small screen.

- **Duomo, Orvieto.** Few cathedrals can claim masterpieces inside and out, but here you'll find Italy's most perfect Gothic facade matched with Luca Signorelli's phenomenal frescoes in the Cappella di San Brizio.

- **Duomo, Florence.** Brunelleschi's beautiful dome is the most recognizable in Italy, an unequaled feat of 15th-century engineering.

- **Santo Stefano, Bologna.** A splendid basilica is also an archaeological phenomenon: you can see here remnants of numerous churches that have stood on the same spot through the ages.

- **Basilica di San Marco, Venice.** This one building above all others captures the East-meets-West character of Venice.

Traditional Cooking

Italian cuisine all comes back to *la cucina di casa* (home cooking). From Tuscany's *ribollita* (bread soup) to a simply grilled whole fish from along the Adriatic coastline, the finest plates are often the simplest. The emphasis is on exceptionally good *materie prime* (primary ingredients) handled with skill and with respect for the foods themselves and for the traditional methods of preparing them.

Each region of Italy has its own distinct, time-tested cuisine that's a source of local pride, and even sophisticated restaurants often maintain an orthodox focus on generations-old recipes. Chefs revere the most humble ingredients, devoting the same attention to day-old bread that they do to costly truffles. Here are a few places where the simplest food will take your breath away:

- **Dar Poeta, Rome.** Pizza in Italy is in a different class than what you get anywhere else. This popular pizzeria is open-minded enough to serve both Roman (thin-crusted) and Neapolitan (slightly thicker) varieties.

- **Bucadisantantonio, Lucca.** Simple, traditional Tuscan cuisine is created here with exceptional grace.

- **Antico Noe, Florence.** If Florence had diners, this unpretentious restaurant would be the best diner in town. What's on the menu depends on what's best that day at the market.

- **Cantinone Già Schiavi, Venice.** Venetian wine bars are known as *bacari,* and at the best of them, such as this one, you can make a simple meal of the sumptuous *cicchetti* (snacks).

Il Dolce Far Niente

"The sweetness of doing nothing" has long been an art form in Italy. This is a country in which life's pleasures are warmly celebrated, not guiltily indulged. Of course, doing "nothing" doesn't really mean nothing. It means doing things differently. It means lingering over a glass of wine for the better part of an evening just to watch the sun slowly set. It means coming home from wherever you are at midday, whether you're a suited businessman or a third-grade schoolgirl, just to have lunch at the family table.

It means savoring a slow and flirtatious evening passeggiata along the main street of a little town, a procession with no destination other than the town and its streets. And it means making a commitment—however temporary—to thinking, feeling, and believing that there is nowhere that you have to be next, that there is no other time than the magical present.

- **Sunset, Piazzale Michelangelo, Florence.** The view looking down over the great city of the Renaissance takes on an added glow at twilight.

- **Piazza del Campo, Siena.** Perhaps it's the sloping shell shape that makes this one of Italy's most pleasing town squares. Have a gelato, take a seat, and watch the world go by.

- **Gondola ride, Venice.** There is still nothing more romantic than a glide along Venice's canals in a gondola, your escorted trip to nowhere, watched over by Gothic palaces with delicately arched eyebrows.

ON THE CALENDAR

	The Italian calendar is filled with festivals and holidays. These are the biggest ones—those that could play a part in your trip planning.
WINTER Feb. 12– Feb. 21	A big do in the 18th century and revived in the latter part of the 20th century, Carnevale in Venice includes concerts, plays, masked balls, fireworks, and indoor and outdoor happenings of every sort. It is probably Italy's most famous festival, bringing in hundreds of thousands.
SPRING Apr. 8	Needless to say, the Messa di Pasqua al Vaticana (Easter Mass at the Vatican) in Rome is long, intense, and packed, with many people attending in elaborate holiday costumes.
Late Apr.– early July	Maggio Musicale Fiorentino (Florence May Music Festival) is the oldest and most prestigious Italian festival of the performing arts.
SUMMER/FALL Mid-June–Nov.	In odd-numbered years, the Biennale Exhibition of Contemporary Art dominates Venice's cultural scene throughout summer and into fall.
Mid-June– Mid-July	The Festival dei Due Mondi (Festival of Two Worlds), in Spoleto, is Italy's most internationally renowned performing-arts festival, bringing in a worldwide audience for concerts, operas, ballets, film screenings, and crafts fairs. Plan well in advance.
July 2 & Aug. 16	The world-famous Palio in Siena is a bareback horse race with ancient Sienese factions showing their colors and participants competing for a prized *palio* (banner).
Early July– late Aug.	The Arena di Verona Stagione Lirica (Verona Arena Outdoor Opera Season) heralds spectacular productions in Verona's 16,000-seat Roman amphitheater.
July	The Umbria Jazz Festival, in Perugia, brings in many of the biggest names in jazz each summer.
3rd Sat. in July	Venice's Festa del Redentore (Feast of the Redeemer) is a procession of gondolas and other craft commemorating the end of the plague of 1575. The fireworks over the lagoon are spectacular.
Late Aug.– early Sept.	The Festival di Venezia (Venice Film Festival), the oldest of the international film festivals, takes place mostly on the Lido.

Rome

Forum

WORD OF MOUTH

"There's something very powerful to being surrounded by all that history (and I'm not a history buff). It's not a place where you walk up, snap a picture, and say, 'All right I've seen it.' It's an imposing experience (in a good way). The effect is very strong. There are other beautiful scenic places in the world, but there's only one Rome."

—flatfeet

WELCOME TO ROME

TOP REASONS TO GO

★ **The Pantheon:** Of ancient Rome's remains, this is the best preserved and most impressive.

★ **St. Peter's Square and Basilica:** The primary church of the Catholic faith is truly awe-inspiring.

★ **Galleria Borghese:** With a setting as exquisite as its collection, this small, elegant museum showcases some of the finest baroque and Renaissance art in Italy.

★ **A morning walk through Campo de' Fiori:** The city comes alive in this wonderful square.

★ **Roman pizza:** Maybe it's the ovens, maybe the crust, maybe the cheese, but they just don't make it like this back home.

St. Peter's Basilica

1 At the Vatican, headquarters of the Roman Catholic Church, everything is done in bold measures, from **St. Peter's Basilica** to the ceiling of the **Sistine Chapel.**

2 From Via del Corso to the Tiber, the cobblestone streets of Baroque Rome lead from one landmark to another, including the **Pantheon, Piazza Navona,** and **Campo de' Fiori.**

3 Trastevere residents pride themselves on being the most authentic Romans, and though the neighborhood has become trendy, it retains a tight-knit feel.

4 The center of the present-day city was once the heart of Ancient Rome. The area of the forums and the **Colosseum** has been preserved as an archaeological treasure.

5 Piazza Venezia, at the southern end of Via del Corso, is Rome's busiest crossroads.

6 The Monti and San Giovanni neighborhoods are home to several art-rich churches.

7 The Quirinale area is filled with palaces, including the home of the Italian president, as well as several works by the baroque master Bernini.

Villa Borghese

Botanical Gardens

Galleria Borghese ◆

9

Pincio

Galoppatoio

V. del Babuino

V. del Corso

V.d. Ripetta

Spanish Steps ◆
Pza.di Spagna

8

V. Condotti

avour

V. d. Due Macelli

V. Vitt. Veneto

V. XX Settembre

7

V. del Quirinale
V. d. Quattro Fontane

QUIRINALE
Giardini del Quirinale

V. del Corso

V. Nazionale

◆ **Pantheon**

5

Pza. Venezia

Via d. S. Maria Maggiore

Stazione Termini

MONTI

V. Cavour

6

V. dei Fori Imperiali

Campidoglio

4

San Pietro in Vincoli

Roman Forum

Colosseum

SAN GIOVAN

V. di S. Gregorio

V. S. Giovanni in Laterano

Palatino

San Giovanni Basilica

Tiber

Parco di Porta Capena

Terme di Caracalla

0 ——— 1/2 mi
0 ——— 1/2 km

GETTING ORIENTED

Rome is a sprawling city, but you'll likely spend all your time in and around the historic center. The area is split by the River Tiber (Tevere in Italian). To its west are the Vatican and the Trastevere neighborhood. To its east is everything else you've come to see: the Colosseum, the Pantheon, and scores of other exceptional sights, not to mention piazzas, fountains, shops, and restaurants. This is one of the most culturally rich plots of land in the world.

8 The Spanish Steps have been a popular gathering place for centuries. Radiating out from them is Rome's toniest shopping district.

9 Villa Borghese is Rome's answer to Central Park. Within it is the exceptional **Galleria Borghese** art museum.

Above: St. Peter's
Left: Villa Borghese

ROME
PLANNER

Making the Most of Your Time

"Roma, non basta una vita" (Rome, a lifetime is not enough): this famous saying should be stamped on the passport of every first-time visitor to the Eternal City. On the one hand, it's a warning: Rome is so packed with sights that it's impossible to take them all in; it's easy to run yourself ragged trying to check off the items on your "must-see" list. At the same time, the saying is a celebration of the city's abundance. There's so much here, you're bound to make discoveries you hadn't anticipated.

To conquer Rome, strike a balance between visits to major sights and leisurely neighborhood strolls. In the first category, the Vatican and the remains of ancient Rome loom the largest. Both require at least half a day; a good strategy is to devote your first morning to one and your second to the other. Leave the afternoons for exploring the neighborhood we label "Baroque Rome" and the shopping district around the Spanish Steps and Via del Corso.

If you have more days at your disposal, continue with the same approach. Among the sights, Galleria Borghese and the multilayered church of San Clemente are particularly worthwhile, and the neighborhoods of Trastevere and the Jewish Ghetto make for great wandering.

Getting Around

Most of Rome's sights are concentrated in the city center, but the area is too large to cover exclusively on foot. Transportation options are the metro (subway), bus, tram, and taxi—the pros and cons of each are detailed in the "Essentials" section at the end of the chapter. No matter what method you use to get around, try to avoid rush hours (8–9, 1–2:30, 7–8). Driving is always a mistake.

Expect to do lots of walking. Cobblestone streets call for comfortable shoes (though some natives seem willing to endure any pain in the name of fashion). Try to avoid the congestion and noise of major thoroughfares; plan routes along parallel side streets instead. Most hotels will give you a functional city map, and you can also pick maps up for free at tourist information booths. If you crave greater detail, purchase better maps at newsstands.

Safety Tips

Chances are your visit will be incident-free, but it's smart to be alert to the following:

■ The young pickpockets described under "Safety" in the Smart Travel Tips section at the back of this book are a common presence around Rome's major sights.

■ Pickpockets like to work public transit, particularly bus lines 64 and 40 Express between Termini station and St. Peter's. Gropers are also a presence on buses and subways. If you encounter one, react like the locals: forcefully and loudly.

■ Termini station is the site of numerous scams. Keep an eye on your belongings at all times.

■ They may not qualify as criminals, but the men who linger around the Colosseum in gladiator costume are con artists. They'll happily pose for a photograph with you, then demand a ridiculous fee.

Piazza Navona

Roman Hours

■ Most churches open at 8 or 9 in the morning, close from noon to 3 or 4, then reopen until 6:30 or 7. The notable exception is St. Peter's, which has continuous hours from 7 to 7 (6 in the fall and winter).

■ Many museums are closed on Monday, including the Galleria Borghese, the Etruscan Museum at Villa Giulia, and the museums of the Campidoglio.

■ The Vatican Museums are open on Monday but closed on Sunday, except for the last Sunday of the month (when admission is free and crowds are large). From November through mid-March, the museums close for the day at 1:45.

How's the Weather?

Not surprisingly, spring and fall are the best times to visit, with mild temperatures and many sunny days; the famous Roman sunsets are also at their best.

Summers are often sweltering. In July and August, come if you like, but learn to do as the Romans do—get up and out early, seek refuge from the afternoon heat (nap if you can), resume activities in early evening, and stay up late to enjoy the nighttime breeze. Come August, many shops and restaurants close as natives head for the beach or the countryside. Roman winters are relatively mild, with persistent rainy spells.

Reservations Required

You should reserve tickets for the following sights. See the listings within the chapter for contact information:

■ **Galleria Borghese** requires reservations. Visitors are admitted in two-hour shifts, and prime time slots can sell out days in advance, so it pays to plan ahead. You can reserve by phone or through the gallery's Web site.

■ In the ancient Rome archaeological area, reservations for the **Colosseum** save you from standing in a ticket line that sometimes takes upward of an hour. You can reserve tickets either by phone (reservation agents speak English) or on the Web.

■ At the **Vatican**, you need to reserve several days in advance to see the necropolis and the gardens. For information about attending a papal audience, see the CloseUp box "A Morning with the Pope" several pages into this chapter.

Sistine Chapel

Updated by
Megan K.
Williams &
Dana Klitzberg

ROME IS A HEADY BLEND of artistic and architectural masterpieces, classical ruins, and extravagant baroque churches and piazzas—all of which serve as the backdrop to a joyful and frenetic street life. The city's 2,700-year-old history is on display wherever you look; the ancient rubs shoulders with the medieval, the modern runs into the Renaissance, and the result is a bustling open-air museum. Julius Caesar and Nero, the Vandals and the Popes, Raphael and Caravaggio, Napoléon and Mussolini—these and countless other political, cultural, and spiritual luminaries have left their mark on the city. More than Florence, more than Venice, Rome is Italy's treasure trove, packed with masterpieces from more than two millennia of artistic achievement. This is where a metropolis once bustled around the carved marble monuments of the Roman Forum, where centuries later Michelangelo painted Christian history in the Sistine Chapel, where Gian Lorenzo Bernini's nymphs and naiads dance in their fountains, and where an empire of gold was worked into the crowns of centuries of rulers.

Today Rome's formidable legacy is kept alive by its people, their history knit into the fabric of their everyday lives. Students walk dogs in the park that was once the mausoleum of the family of the emperor Augustus; Raphaelesque teenage girls zip through traffic on their *motorini*; priests in flowing robes walk through medieval piazzas talking on cell phones. Modern Rome has one foot in the past, one in the present—a fascinating stance that allows you to tip back an espresso in a square designed by Bernini, then hop on the metro to your hotel room in a renovated Renaissance palace. "When you first come here you assume that you must burrow about in ruins and prowl in museums to get back to the days of Numa Pompilius or Mark Antony," Maud Howe observes in her book *Roma Beata*. "It is not necessary; you only have to live, and the common happenings of daily life—yes, even the trolley car and your bicycle—carry you back in turn to the Dark Ages, to the early Christians, even to prehistoric Rome."

EXPLORING ROME

Updated by
Megan K.
Williams

Plan your day taking into account the varying opening hours of the sights you want to visit, which usually means mixing the ancient, classical, and baroque, museums and parks, the center and the environs. Keep in mind that an uncharted ramble through the heart of the old city can be just as satisfying as the quiet contemplation of a chapel or a trek through marbled museum corridors. The Rome Archeologia Card, a combination ticket for the Colosseum, Palatine, and the various branches of the Museo Nazionale Romano (Palazzo Altemps, Crypta Balbi, Terme di Diocleziano, Terme di Caracalla, Villa dei Quintili, the Tomba di Cecilia Metella, and Palazzo Massimo alle Terme), valid for seven consecutive days, is available at each participant's ticket office for €20—a good deal for ancient-history buffs.

The Vatican: Rome of the Popes

This tiny walled city-state, capital of the Catholic Church, draws millions every year to its wealth of treasures and spiritual monuments. You might visit the Vatican for its exceptional art holdings—Michelangelo's frescoes, rare archaeological marbles, and Bernini's statues—or you may want to appreciate the singular and grandiose architecture of St. Peter's Square. Many come here on pilgrimage, spiritual or otherwise, to see the seat of world Catholicism and the most overwhelming architectural achievement of the Renaissance, St. Peter's Basilica. At the Vatican Museums there are magnificent rooms decorated by Raphael, sculptures such as the *Apollo Belvedere* and the *Laocoön,* frescoes by Fra Angelico, paintings by Giotto and Leonardo, and the celebrated ceiling of the Sistine Chapel. The Church power that emerged as the Rome of the emperors declined gave impetus to a profusion of artistic expression and shaped the destiny of the city for a thousand years.

Allow yourself an hour to see St. Peter's Basilica, 30 minutes for the Museo Storico, 15 minutes for the Vatican Grottoes, an hour for Castel Sant'Angelo, and an hour to climb to the top of the dome. Ushers at the entrance of St. Peter's Basilica and the Vatican Museums bar entry to people with "inappropriate" clothing—which means no bare knees or shoulders.

The Main Attractions

★ ❸ **Basilica di San Pietro.** The physical proportions of the sublime St. Peter's Basilica are staggering: it covers about 18,100 square yards, extends 212 yards in length, and carries a dome that rises 435 feet and measures 138 feet across its base. The church's history dates back to the year AD 319, when the emperor Constantine built a basilica over the site of the tomb of St. Peter (died AD 64). This early church stood for more than 1,000 years, undergoing a number of restorations, until it was on the verge of collapse.

In 1506 Pope Julius II (1443–1513) commissioned the architect Bramante to build a new and greater basilica, but construction would take more than 170 years. In 1546 Michelangelo was persuaded to take over the job, but the magnificent cupola was finally completed by Giacomo della Porta (circa 1537–1602) and Domenico Fontana (1543–1607). The new church wasn't dedicated until 1626; by that time Renaissance had given way to baroque, and many of the plan's original elements had gone the way of their designers. At the entrance, the 15th-century bronze doors by Filarete (circa 1400–69) fill the central portal. Off the entry portico, architect and sculptor Gianlorenzo Bernini's famous *Scala Regia,* the ceremonial entry to the Vatican Palace, is one of the most magnificent staircases in the world and is graced with Bernini's dramatic statue of Constantine the Great.

Entering the sanctuary, take a moment to adjust to the enormity of the space stretching in front of you. The cherubs over the holy-water fonts have feet as long as the distance from your fingertips to your elbow. It is because the proportions are in such perfect harmony that the vastness may escape you at first. The megascale was inspired by the size of the ancient Roman ruins.

Over an altar in a side chapel near the entrance is Michelangelo's *Pietà,* a sculpture of Mary holding her son Jesus's body after crucifix-

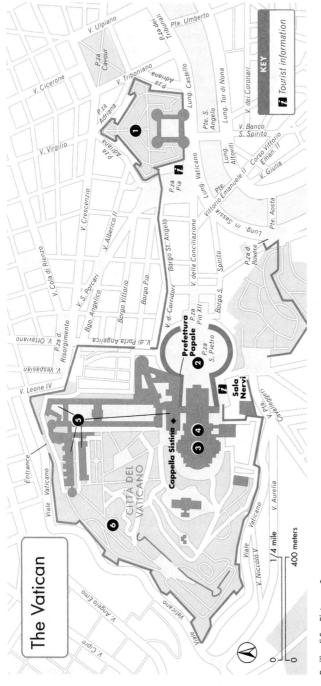

The Vatican

KEY

🛈 Tourist information

0 — 1/4 mile
0 — 400 meters

CITTÀ DEL VATICANO

ion—the star attraction here other than the basilica itself. Legend has it that the artist, only 22 at the time the work was completed, overheard passersby expressing skepticism that such a young man could have executed such a sophisticated and moving piece. It's said that his offense at the implication was why he crept back that night and signed the piece—in big letters, on a ribbon falling from the Virgin's left shoulder across her breast.

Inlaid in the gorgeous marble pavement of the nave's central aisles are the names of the world's great cathedrals organized by church size—the message is clear, St. Peter's has them all beaten. At the crossing of the aisles four massive piers support the dome, and the mighty Bernini **baldacchino** (canopy) rises high above the papal altar, where the pope celebrates Mass. "What the barbarians didn't do, the Barberini did," 17th-century wags quipped when Barberini Pope Urban VIII had the bronze stripped from the Pantheon's portico and melted down to make the baldacchino (using what was left over for cannonballs). The bronze throne behind the main altar in the apse, the *Cathedra Petri* (Chair of St. Peter), is Bernini's work (1656), and it covers a wooden-and-ivory chair that St. Peter himself is said to have used. However, scholars contend that this throne probably dates only from the Middle Ages. See how the adoration of a million kisses has completely worn down the bronze on the right foot of the statue of St. Peter in front of the near-right pillar in the transept. Free one-hour English-language tours of the basilica depart Monday–Saturday at 10 and 3, Sunday at 2:30 (sign up at the little desk under the portico). St. Peter's is closed during ceremonies in the piazza. ⊠ *Piazza San Pietro* ⊕ *www.vatican.va* ☉ *Apr.–Sept., daily 7–7; Oct.–Mar., daily 7–6.*

The **Grotte Vaticane** (Vatican Grottoes) in the basilica contain the tombs of many popes, including John Paul II, and the Tomb of St. Peter. The entrance is opposite the baldacchino, near a pillar where the dome begins. The only exit leads outside the church, so don't go down until you're finished elsewhere. ☎ *Free* ☉ *Apr.–Sept., daily 7–6; Oct.–Mar., daily 7–5.*

A small but rich collection of Vatican treasures is housed in the **Museo Storico** in St. Peter's Sacristy, among them precious antique chalices and the massive 15th-century sculptured bronze tomb of Pope Sixtus V (1520–90) by Antonio del Pollaiuolo (1431–98). ☎ €9 ☉ *Daily 8–5.*

The **roof** of St. Peter's Basilica, reached by elevator or stairs, provides a view among a landscape of domes and towers. An interior staircase (170 steps) leads to the base of the dome for a dove's-eye look at the interior of St. Peter's. Then, only if you are stout of heart and sound of lung should you attempt the taxing and claustrophobic climb up the remaining 330 steps to the balcony of the lantern, where the view embraces the Vatican Gardens and all of Rome. The up and down staircases are one-way; once you commit to climbing, there's no turning back. ☎ 06/69883462 ☎ *Elevator €7, stairs €4* ☉ *Daily 8–5.*

Castel Sant'Angelo. For hundreds of years this fortress guarded the Vatican, to which it is linked by the **Passetto,** an arcaded passageway. According to legend, Castel Sant'Angelo got its name during the plague of

A Morning with the Pope

THE POPE HOLDS AUDIENCES in a large, modern hall (or in St. Peter's Square in summer) on Wednesday morning at 10. To attend, you must get tickets; apply in writing at least 10 days in advance to the **Papal Prefecture** (Prefettura della Casa Pontificia; 🏛 00120 Vatican City ☎ 06/69883273 🖷 06/69885863), indicating the date you prefer, your language, and your hotel. Or go to the prefecture, through the Porta di Bronzo, the bronze door at the end of the colonnade on the right side of the piazza; the office is open Monday–Saturday 9–1, and last-minute tickets may be available. You can also arrange to pick up free tickets on Tuesday from 5 to 6:45 at the **Santa Susanna American Church** (✉ Via XX Settembre 15, near Termini ☎ 06/42014554); call first. For a fee, travel agencies make arrangements that include transportation. Arrive early, as security is tight and the best places fill up fast.

590, when Pope Gregory the Great (circa 540–604), passing by in a religious procession, had a vision of an angel sheathing its sword atop the stone ramparts. Though it may look like a stronghold, Castel Sant'Angelo was in fact built as a tomb for the emperor Hadrian (76–138) in AD 135. By the 6th century it had been transformed into a fortress, and it remained a refuge for the popes for almost 1,000 years. It has dungeons, battlements, cannon and cannonballs, and a collection of antique weaponry and armor. The lower levels formed the base of Hadrian's mausoleum; ancient ramps and narrow staircases climb through the castle's core to courtyards and frescoed halls, where temporary exhibits are held. Off the loggia is a café.

The upper terrace, with the massive angel statue commemorating Gregory's vision, evokes memories of Tosca, Puccini's poignant heroine in the opera of the same name, who threw herself off these ramparts with the cry, *"Scarpia, avanti a Dio!"* ("Scarpia, we meet before God"). On summer evenings a book fair with musical events and food stalls surrounds the castle. One of Rome's most beautiful pedestrian bridges, **Ponte Sant'Angelo** spans the Tiber in front of the fortress and is studded with graceful angels designed by Bernini. ✉ *Lungotevere Castello 50, San Pietro* ☎ *06/39967700* ⊕ *www.pierreci.it* 🎟 *€5* ☉ *Tues.–Sun. 9–8.*

⑤ **Musei Vaticani** (The Vatican Museums). The Vatican Palace has been the papal residence since 1377; it's a collection of buildings covering more than 13 acres, with an estimated 1,400 rooms, chapels, and galleries. Other than the pope and his court, the occupant is the Musei Vaticani (Vatican Museums), containing some of art's greatest masterpieces. The Sistine Chapel is the headliner here, but in your haste to get there, don't overlook the Museo Egizio, with its fine Egyptian collection; the famed classical sculptures of the Chiaramonti and the Museo Pio Clementino; and the Stanze di Raffaello (Raphael Rooms), a suite of halls covered floor-to-ceiling in some of the master's greatest works.

FodorśChoice
★

On a first visit to the Vatican Museums, you may just want to see the highlights—even that will take several hours and a good, long walk. In peak tourist season, be prepared for at least an hour's wait to get into the museums and large crowds once inside. Getting there first thing in the morning is highly recommended. The collection is divided among different galleries, halls, and wings connected end to end. Pick up a leaflet at the main entrance to the museums to see the overall layout. The Sistine Chapel is at the far end of the complex, and the leaflet charts two abbreviated itineraries through other collections to reach it. An audio guide (€5.50, about 90 minutes) for the Sistine Chapel, the Stanze di Raffaello, and 350 other works and locations is worth the added expense. Phone at least a day in advance to book a guided tour (€16.50) through the Guided Visit to Vatican Museums.

The main entrance to the museums, on Viale Vaticano, is a long walk from Piazza San Pietro along a busy thoroughfare. Some city buses stop near the main entrance: Bus 49 from Piazza Cavour stops right in front; Buses 81 and 492 and Tram 19 stop at Piazza Risorgimento, halfway between St. Peter's and the museums. The Ottaviano–S. Pietro and the Cipro–Musei Vaticani stops on Metro A also are in the vicinity. Entry is free the first Sunday of the month, and the museum is closed on Catholic holidays, of which there are many. Last admission is an hour before closing. ⊠ *Main museum entrance, Viale Vaticano; guided visit office, Piazza San Pietro* ☎ *06/69883332, 06/69884676 guided visit reservations* 🖷 *06/69885100 guided visit reservations* ⊕ *www.vatican.va* ✉ *€12* ☉ *Mid-Mar.–Oct., weekdays 8:45–4:45, Sat. 8:45–2:45, last Sun. of month 8:45–1:45; Nov.–mid-Mar., Mon.–Sat. and last Sun. of month 8:45–1:45.*

Besides the galleries mentioned here, there are many other wings along your way—full of maps, tapestries, classical sculpture, Egyptian mummies, Etruscan statues, and even Aztec treasures. From the main entrance of the Vatican Museums take the escalator up to the **Pinacoteca** (Picture Gallery) on your right. This is a self-contained section, and it's worth visiting first for works by such artists as Leonardo, Giotto (circa 1266–1337), Fra Angelico (1387–1455), and Filippo Lippi (circa 1406–69), and Raphael's exceptional *Transfiguration, Coronation* and *Foligno Madonna.*

The **Cortile Ottagano** (Octagonal Courtyard) of the Vatican Museums displays some of sculpture's most famous works, including the 4th century BC *Apollo Belvedere* (and Canova's 1801 *Perseus,* heavily influenced by it) and the 2nd-century *Laocoön.*

The **Stanze di Raffaello** (Raphael Rooms) are second only to the Sistine Chapel in artistic interest—and draw crowds comparable. In 1508 Pope Julius II employed Raphael, on the recommendation of Bramante, to decorate the rooms with biblical scenes. The result is a Renaissance tour de force. Of the four rooms, the second and third were decorated mainly by Raphael. The others were decorated by Giulio Romano (circa 1499–1546) and other assistants of Raphael; the first room is known as the Stanza dell'Incendio, with frescoes by Romano of the *incendio* (fire) in the Borgo neighborhood.

The frescoed **Stanza della Segnatura** (Room of the Signature), where papal bulls were signed, is indeed one of Raphael's finest works; indeed, they are thought by many to be some of the finest paintings in the history of Western art. This was Julius's private library, and the room's use is reflected in the frescoes' themes, philosophy and enlightenment. A paradigm of High Renaissance painting, the works demonstrate the revolutionary ideals of naturalism (Raphael's figures lack the awkwardness of those painted only a few years earlier); humanism (the idea that human beings are the noblest and most admirable of God's creations); and a profound interest in the ancient world, the result of the 15th-century rediscovery of classical antiquity. The *School of Athens* glorifies some of philosophy's greats, including Plato (pointing to Heaven) and Aristotle (pointing to Earth) at the fresco's center. The pensive figure on the stairs is thought to be modeled after Michelangelo, who was painting the Sistine ceiling at the same time Raphael was working here. Michelangelo does not appear in preparatory drawings, so Raphael may have added his fellow artist's portrait after admiring his work.

> **WORD OF MOUTH**
>
> "At the Vatican Museums, we did the audio tour, and took our time looking at the Map Room, the tapestries, trompe l'oeil ceilings, the stunning Borgia Papal Apartments, and the Raphael Rooms. Finally, we got to the Sistine Chapel. Wow! We just sat on the benches along the wall for 30 minutes, looking at the Old and New Testament friezes." —Bardo

The tiny **Cappella di Nicholas V** (Chapel of Nicholas V) is aglow with frescoes by Fra Angelico, the Florentine monk whose sensitive paintings were guiding lights for the Renaissance. The **Appartamento Borgia** (Borgia Apartment) is worth seeing for the elaborately painted ceilings, designed and partially executed by Pinturicchio. Among the frescoes, look for the Borgia's family emblem, the bull, and for the blond Lucrezia, the Borgia pope's daughter, posing piously as St. Catherine.

In 1508, just before Raphael started work on his rooms, the redoubtable Pope Julius II commissioned Michelangelo to paint singlehandedly the more-than-10,000-square-foot ceiling of the **Cappella Sistina** (Sistine Chapel). The task cost the artist four years of mental and physical anguish. It's said that for years afterward Michelangelo couldn't read anything without holding it up over his head. The result, however, was the masterpiece that you now see, its colors cool and brilliant after restoration. Bring a pair of binoculars to get a better look at this incredible work (unfortunately, you're not allowed to lie down on the floor to study the frescoes above, the viewing position of choice in decades past). Tourists in the 19th century used pocket mirrors so as not to strain their necks.

The exhibition halls of the **Biblioteca Vaticana** (Vatican Library) are bright with frescoes and contain a sampling of the library's rich collections of precious manuscripts. The **Room of the Aldobrandini Marriage** (Room X) holds a beautiful Roman fresco of a nuptial rite, which deserves a look after you've seen the rest of the museum.

NEED A BREAK? You don't have to snack at the touristy joints outside the Vatican Museums; a short walk away are neighborhood restaurants catering to locals. Among them is the Il Mozzicone (⊠ Borgo Pio 180, near San Pietro), where you can fill up on solid Roman fare at moderate prices. La Caravella (⊠ Via degli Scipioni 32, at Via Vespasiano, off Piazza Risorgimento, near San Pietro) serves pizza at lunch every day but Thursday, when it's closed.

2 **Piazza San Pietro.** As you enter St. Peter's Square you are officially entering Vatican territory. The piazza is one of Bernini's most spectacular masterpieces. It was completed in 1667 after 11 years' work, a relatively short time, considering the vastness of the task. The piazza can hold 400,000 people—as it did in the days following the death of Pope John Paul II. The piazza is surrounded by a curving pair of quadruple colonnades, topped by a balustrade and statues of 140 saints. Look for the two disks set into the pavement on either side of the obelisk at the center of the piazza. When you stand on either disk, a trick of perspective makes the colonnades seem to consist of a single row of columns. Bernini had an even grander visual effect in mind when he designed the square: the surprise of stepping into an immense, airy space after approaching it through a neighborhood of narrow, shadowy streets. The contrast was intended to evoke the metaphor of moving from darkness to light. But in the 1930s Mussolini spoiled the effect. To celebrate the "conciliation" between the Vatican and the Italian government under the Lateran Pact of 1929, he conceived of the Via della Conciliazione, the broad avenue that now forms the main approach to St. Peter's.

Remember to look for the Swiss Guards in their colorful uniforms; they've been standing at the Vatican entrances for the past 500 years.

Also Worth Seeing

6 **Giardini Vaticani** (Vatican Gardens). Generations of popes have strolled in these beautifully manicured gardens, originally laid out in the 16th century. A two-hour guided tour, half by bus and half on foot, takes you through a haven of shady walkways, elaborate fountains, and exotic plants. Make reservations two or three days in advance and pick up your tickets in the Guided Visit to Vatican Museums Office at the museum entrance. If you have a reservation, you can skip the line (go in through the "Exit" door); the office window is inside the atrium. ⊠ *Viale Vaticano* ☎ *06/69884466 reservations* ⊕ *www.vatican.va* ✆ *€9* ⊙ *Tours Mon. Sat. 10 AM, office Mon.–Sat. 8:30–7.*

4 **Vatican Necropolis.** Visit the pre-Constantine necropolis under St. Peter's for a fascinating glimpse of the underpinnings of the great basilica, which was built over the cemetery where archaeologists believe they have found St. Peter's tomb. Apply in advance by sending a fax or e-mail with the name of each visitor, language spoken, proposed days for the visit, and a local phone number. Reservations will be confirmed a few days in advance. No children under 15 are admitted. Tickets are sometimes available for same-day tours; apply at the Ufficio Scavi (Excavations Office), on the right beyond the Arco delle Campane entrance to the Vatican, to the left of the basilica. Tell the Swiss Guard you want the Ufficio Scavi, and he will let you by. ⊠ *Piazza San Pietro* ☎ *06/69885318* 🖷 *06/69873017* ✆ *€10* ⊙ *Ufficio Scavi Mon.–Sat. 9–5.*

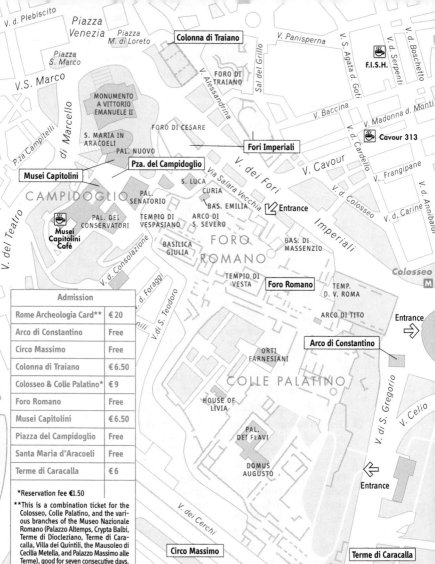

Admission	
Rome Archeologia Card**	€ 20
Arco di Constantino	Free
Circo Massimo	Free
Colonna di Traiano	€ 6.50
Colosseo & Colle Palatino*	€ 9
Foro Romano	Free
Musei Capitolini	€ 6.50
Piazza del Campidoglio	Free
Santa Maria d'Aracoeli	Free
Terme di Caracalla	€ 6

*Reservation fee €1.50

**This is a combination ticket for the Colosseo, Colle Palatino, and the various branches of the Museo Nazionale Romano (Palazzo Altemps, Crypta Balbi, Terme di Diocleziano, Terme di Caracalla, Villa dei Quintili, il Mausoleo di Cecilia Metella, and Palazzo Massimo alle Terme), good for seven consecutive days.

CAPITOLINE HILL: The original capitol hill. The seat of government in Rome since its founding now also holds the Capitoline Museums, chock-full of the treasures of antiquity.

ROMAN FORUM: Downtown Ancient Rome. People from all corners of the empire crowded into the Forum to do business, to hear the latest news, and to worship.

PALATINE HILL: Home of the empire's rich and famous. Luxurious villas lined Palatine Hill; emperors held court on its heights and vied with their predecessors for lasting renown.

CAMPIDOGLIO

FORO ROMANO

COLLE PALATINO

ANCIENT ROME
GLORIES OF
THE CAESARS

Time has reduced ancient Rome to fields of silent ruins, but the powerful impact of what happened here, of the genius and power that made Rome the center of the Western world, echoes across the millennia.

In this one compact area of the city, you can step back into the Rome of Cicero, Julius Caesar, and Virgil. Walk along the streets they knew, cool off in the shade of the Colosseum that towered over their city, see the sculptures that watched over their piazzas. At the end of a day of exploring, climb one of the famous seven hills and watch the sun set over what was once the heart of the civilized world.

Today, this part of Rome, more than any other, is a perfect example of that layering of historic eras, the overlapping of ages, of religions, of a past that is very much a part of the present. Christian churches rise from the foundations of ancient pagan temples. An immense marble monument to a 19th-century king shares a square with a medieval palace built by a pope. Still, the history and memory of ancient Rome dominate the area. It's fitting that in the aftermath of centuries of such pageantry Percy Bysshe Shelley and Edward Gibbon reflected here on the meaning of *sic transit gloria mundi* (so passes away the glory of the world).

Domus Aurea

Viale del Monte Oppio

Parco Traiano

V. Terme di Tito

V. Nicola Salvi

COLOSSEO

Colosseo

V. d. Domus Aurea

V. Labicana

Pza. del Colosseo

Ristoro della Salute

Pasqualino

V. S. Giov. in Laterano

V. dei S. Quattro Coronati

Vibenna

KEY

Cafe | Restaurant

0   100 yards

0   100 meters

Villa Celimontana

V. Claudia

Cl. d. Scauro

COLOSSEUM: Gladiators fought for the chance to live another day on the floor of the Colosseum, iconic symbol of ancient Rome.

CAMPIDOGLIO

The Capitoline Museums are closed on Monday; admission is free on the last Sunday of the month. Late evening is an option for this area. Though the church is closed, the museums are open until 9 PM, and the views of the city lights and the illuminated Victor Emmanuel II monument and the Foro Romano are striking.

CLIMB MICHELANGELO'S DRAMATIC RAMP TO THE SUMMIT OF ONE OF Rome's seven hills, the Campidoglio (also known as Capitoline Hill), for views across the rooftops of modern Rome in one direction and across the ruins of ancient Rome in the other. Check out the stellar Musei Capitolini, crammed with a collection of masterpieces rivaled only by the Vatican museums.

★ **Piazza del Campidoglio.** In Michelangelo's piazza at the top of the Campidoglio stands a bronze equestrian statue of Marcus Aurelius (AD 121–180). A legend foretells that some day the statue's original gold surface will return, heralding the end of the world. Pending the arrival of that day, the original 2nd-century statue was moved inside the Musei Capitolini; a copy sits on the piazza. Stand with your back to it to survey central Rome.

The Campidoglio, the site of the Roman Empire's first and holiest temples, had fallen into ruin by the Middle Ages and was called *Monte Caprino* (Goat Hill). In 1536 Pope Paul III (1468–1549) decided to restore its grandeur for the triumphal entry into the city of Charles V (1500–1558), the Holy Roman Emperor. He called upon Michelangelo to create the staircase ramp, the buildings and facades

on the square, the pavement decoration, and the pedestal for the bronze statue.

The two buildings that make up the **Musei Capitolini** are on the piazza, flanking the **Palazzo Senatorio**. The Campidoglio has always been the seat of Rome's government; its Latin name is the root for the word *capitol*. Today, Rome's city hall occupies the Palazzo Senatorio. Head to the vantage points in the belvederes on the sides of the palazzo for great views of the ruins of ancient Rome.

★ **Musei Capitolini** (Capitoline Museums). This immense collection, housed in the twin Palazzi del Museo Capitolino and Palazzo dei Conservatori buildings, is a greatest hits collection of Roman art through the ages, from the ancients to the baroque.

The **Palazzi del Museo Capitolino** contains hundreds of Roman busts of philoso-

AN EMPEROR CHEAT SHEET

OCTAVIAN/AUGUSTUS (27 BC–AD 14)

After the death of Julius Caesar, Octavian gained control of Rome after a series of battles that culminated with the defeat of Antony and Cleopatra at Actium. Later known as Caesar Augustus, he was Rome's first emperor. His rule began a 200-year period of peace known as the Pax Romana.

Colle Palatino

CALIGULA (AD 37–41)

Caligula was tremendously popular when he came to power at the age of 25, but he very soon became infamous for his excessive cruelty, immorality, and erratic behavior. His contemporaries universally considered him to be insane. He was murdered by his own guard within four years.

phers and emperors—a fascinating Who's Who of the ancient world. Forty-eight Roman emperors are represented. Unlike the Greeks, whose portraits are idealized, the Romans preferred the warts-and-all school of representation. Other notable sculptures include the poignant *Dying Gaul* and the regal *Capitoline Venus*. In the Capitolino courtyard is a gigantic, reclining sculpture of Oceanus, found in the Roman Forum and later dubbed *Marforio*. This was one of Rome's talking statues to which citizens from the 1500s to the 1900s affixed anonymous satirical verses and notes of political protest. (Another talking statue still in use today sits at Piazza Pasquino, near Piazza Navona.)

Lining the courtyard of the **Palazzo dei Conservatori** are the colossal fragments of a head, leg, foot, and hand—all that remains of the famous statue of the emperor Constantine the Great, who believed that Rome's future lay with Christianity. These immense effigies were much in vogue in the later days of the Roman Empire. The renowned symbol of Rome, the *Capitoline Wolf*, a 6th-century

BC Etruscan bronze, holds a place of honor in the museum; the suckling twins were added during the Renaissance to adapt the statue to the legend of Romulus and Remus. The Palazzo also contains some of baroque painting's great masterpieces, including Caravaggio's *La Buona Ventura* (1595) and *San Giovanni Battista* (1602), Peter Paul Rubens's *Romulus and Remus* (1614), and Pietro da Cortona's sumptuous portrait of Pope Urban VIII (1627). When museum fatigue sets in, enjoy the view and refreshments on a large open terrace in the Palazzo dei Conservatoria. ☎ *06/39967800 or 06/67102475* ⊕ *www.pierreci.it* ⊙ *Tues.–Sun. 9–8.*

Santa Maria d'Aracoeli. Seemingly endless, steep stairs climb from Piazza Venezia to the Santa Maria. There are 15th-century frescoes by Pinturicchio (1454–1513) in the first chapel on the right. ⊙ *Oct.–May, daily 7–noon and 4–6; June–Sept., daily 7–noon and 4–6:30.*

	NERO (AD 54–68) Nero is infamous as a violent persecutor of Christians. He also murdered his wife, his mother, and countless others. Although it's not certain whether he actually fiddled as Rome burned in AD 64, he was well known as a singer and a composer of music.
	Domus Aurea

	DOMITIAN (AD 81–96) The first emperor to declare himself "Dominus et Deus" (Lord and God), he stripped away power from the Senate. After his death, the Senate retaliated by declaring him "Damnatio Memoriae" (his name and image were erased from all public records).
	Colle Palatino

FORO ROMANO

It takes about an hour to explore the Roman Forum. There are entrances on the Via dei Fori Imperiali and near the Colosseum. Another hour's walk will cover the Imperial Fora. With the exception of the overpriced stands along the avenue and cafés on Largo Corrado Ricci, there are few places nearby for food and drink, so bring a snack and water.

EXPERIENCE THE ENDURING ROMANCE OF THE FORUM. WANDER AMONG its lonely columns and great, broken fragments of sculpted marble and stone— once temples, palaces, and shops crowded with people from all corners of the known world. This was the heart of ancient Rome and a symbol of the values that inspired Rome's conquest of an empire.

★ **Foro Romano** (Roman Forum). Built in a marshy valley between the Capitoline and Palatine hills, the Forum was the civic core of Republican Rome, the austere era that preceded the hedonism of the emperors. The Forum was the political, commercial, and religious center of Roman life. Hundreds of years of plunder and the tendency of later Romans to carry off what was left of the better building materials reduced it to the series of ruins you see today. Archaeological digs continue to uncover more about the sight; bear in mind that what you see are the ruins not of one period but of almost 900 years, from about 500 BC to AD 400.

The **Basilica Giulia**, which owes its name to Julius Caesar, who had it built, was where the Centumviri, the hundred-or-so judges forming the civil court, met to hear cases. The open space before it was the core of the forum proper and prototype of Italy's famous piazzas. Let your imagination dwell on Mark Antony (circa 81 BC–30 BC), who delivered the funeral address in Julius Caesar's honor from the rostrum left of the **Arco di Settimio Severo**. This arch, one of the grandest of all antiquity, was built hundreds of years later in AD 203 to celebrate the victory of the emperor Severus (AD 146–211) over the Parthians, and was topped by a bronze equestrian statuary group with six horses. You can explore the reconstruction of the large brick senate hall, the **Curia**; three Corinthian columns (a favorite of 19th-century poets) are all that remains of the **Tempio di Vespasiano**. In the **Tempio di Vesta**, six highly privileged vestal virgins kept the sacred fire, a tradition that dated back to the very earliest days of Rome, when guarding the community's precious fire was essential to its well-being. The cleaned and restored

AN EMPEROR CHEAT SHEET

TRAJAN (AD 98–117)

Trajan, from southern Spain, was the first Roman emperor not born in Italy. He enlarged the empire's boundaries to include modern-day Romania, Armenia, and Upper Mesopotamia.

Colonna di Traiano

HADRIAN (AD 117–138)

He expanded the empire in Asia and the Middle East. He's best known for designing and rebuilding the Pantheon, constructing a majestic villa at Tivoli, and initiating myriad other constructions across the empire, including the famed wall across Britain.

Pantheon, in Baroque Rome

Arco di Tito, which stands in a slightly elevated position on a spur of the Palatine Hill, was erected in AD 81 to celebrate the sack of Jerusalem 10 years earlier, after the great Jewish revolt. A famous relief shows the captured contents of Herod's Temple—including its huge seven-branched menorah—being carried in triumph down Rome's Via Sacra. Making sense of the ruins isn't always easy; consider renting an audio guide (€4) or buying a booklet that superimposes an image of the Forum in its heyday over a picture of it today. Guided tours in English usually begin at 10:30 AM. In summer the Forum is sometimes open for midnight (guided) tours—look for signs at the entrance or ask at your hotel. ☎ 06/39967700 ⊕ www.pierreci.it ⊘ Daily 9–1 hr before sunset.

THE OTHER FORA

Fori Imperiali (Imperial Fora). These five grandly conceived squares flanked with columnades and temples were built by the emperors Caesar, Augustus, Vespasian, Nerva, and Trajan. The original Roman Forum, built up over 500 years of Republican Rome, had grown crowded, and Julius Caesar was the first to attempt to rival it.

He built the **Foro di Cesare** (Forum of Caesar), including a temple dedicated to himself and the goddess Minerva. Four later emperors followed his lead, creating their own fora. The grandest was the **Foro di Traiano** (Forum of Trajan) a veritable city unto itself built by Trajan (AD 53–117). The adjoining Mercati Traianei (Trajan's Markets), a huge multilevel brick complex of shops, walkways, and terraces, was one of the marvels of the ancient world. In the 20th century, Benito Mussolini built the Via dei Fori Imperiali directly through the Imperial Fora area. Marble and bronze maps on the wall along the avenue portray the extent of the Roman Empire and Republic, and many of the remains of the Imperial Fora lay buried beneath its surface.

Colonna di Traiano (Trajan's Column). The ashes of Trajan were buried inside the base of this column (the ashes have since been removed). Remarkable reliefs spiral up its sides, celebrating his military campaigns in Dacia (Romania). The column has stood in what was once the Forum of Trajan since AD 113. ☎ 06/69780532 ⊘ Tues.–Sun. 9–4:30.

MARCUS AURELIUS (AD 161–180)

Remembered as a humanitarian emperor, Marcus Aurelius was a Stoic philosopher and his *Meditations* are still read today. Nonetheless, he was an aggressive leader devoted to expanding the empire.

Piazza del Campidoglia

CONSTANTINE I (AD 306–337)

Constantine changed the course of history by legalizing Christianity. He legitimized the once-banned religion and paved the way for the papacy in Rome. Constantine also founded Constantinople, an Imperial capital in the East.

Arco di Constantino

COLLE PALATINO

A stroll on the Palatino, with a visit to the Museo Palatino, takes about two hours. You can reserve tickets online or by phone—operators speak English. If you are buying tickets in person, remember that there are often shorter lines here than at the Colosseum and the ticket is good for both sights. The entrances are in the Roman Forum and on Via S. Gregorio.

IT ALL BEGAN HERE. IT IS BELIEVED THAT ROMULUS, THE FOUNDER OF ROME, lived on the Colle Palatino (Palatine Hill). It was an exclusive address in ancient Rome, and emperors built palaces upon its slopes. Tour the Palatine's hidden corners and shady lanes, take a welcome break from the heat in its peaceful gardens, and enjoy a view of the Circo Massimo fit for an emperor.

★ **Colle Palatino** (Palatine Hill). A lane known as the Clivus Palatinus, paved with worn stones that were once trod by emperors and their slaves, climbs from the Forum area to a site that historians identify with Rome's earliest settlement. The legend goes that the infant twins Romulus and Remus were nursed by a she-wolf on the banks of the Tiber and adopted by a shepherd. Encouraged by the gods to build a city, the twins chose this site in 735 BC, fortifying it with a wall that archaeologist Rudolfo Lanciani identified in the late 19th century when digging on Palatine Hill.

During the Republican era the hill was an important religious center, housing the Temple of Cybele and the Temple of Victory, as well as an exclusive residential area. Cicero, Catiline, Crassus, and Agrippa all had homes here. Augustus was born on the hill, and as he rose in power, he built libraries, halls, and temples here; the **House of Livia,** reserved for his wife, is best preserved. Emperor Tiberius was the first to build a palace here; others followed. The structures most visible today date back to the late 1st century AD, when the Palatine experienced an extensive remodeling under Emperor Domitian. His architects put up two separate palaces, the **Domus Augustana** and the **Domus Livia.** During the Renaissance, the powerful Farnese family built gardens atop the ruins overlooking the Forum. Known as the **Orti Farnesiani,** they were Europe's first botanical gardens. The **Museo Palatino** charts the history of the hill. Splendid sculptures, frescoes, and mosaic intarsia from various imperial buildings are on display. ☎ *06/39967700* ⊕ *www.pierreci.it* ⏱ *Tues.–Sun. 9–1 hr before sunset.*

THE RISE AND FALL OF ANCIENT ROME

218 BC

ca. 800 BC	Rise of Etruscan city-states.
510	Foundation of the Roman republic; expulsion of Etruscans from Roman territory.
343	Roman conquest of Greek colonies in Campania.
264–241	First Punic War (with Carthage): increased naval power helps Rome gain control of southern Italy and then Sicily.
218–200	Second Punic War: Hannibal's attempted conquest of Italy, using elephants, is eventually crushed.

NEAR THE COLLE PALATINO

Circo Massimo (Circus Maximus). Ancient Rome's oldest and largest racetrack lies in the natural hollow between Palatine and Aventine hills. From the imperial box in the palace on Palatine Hill, emperors could look out over the oval course. Stretching about 650 yards from end to end, the Circus Maximus could hold more than 300,000 spectators. On certain occasions there were as many as 24 chariot races a day, and competitions could last for 15 days. The central ridge was the sight of two Egyptian obelisks (now in the Piazza del Popolo and Piazza San Giovanni in Laterano). Check out the panoramic views of the Circus Maximus from the Palatine Hill's Belvedere. You can also see the green slopes of the Aventine and Celian hills, as well as the bell tower of Santa Maria in Cosmedin.

Terme di Caracalla (Baths of Caracalla). For the Romans, public baths were much more than places to wash. The baths also had recital halls, art galleries, libraries, massage rooms, sports grounds, and gardens. Even the smallest public baths had at least some of these amenities, and in the capital of the Roman Empire, they were provided on a lavish scale. Ancient Rome's most beautiful and luxurious public baths were opened by the emperor Caracalla in AD 217 and were used until the 6th century.

Taking a bath was a long and complex process, and a social activity first and foremost. Remember, too, that for all their sophistication, the Romans didn't have soap. You began by sweating in the *sudatoria*, small rooms resembling saunas. From these you moved on to the *calidarium* for the actual business of washing, using a *strigil*, or scraper, to get the dirt off. Next was the *tepidarium*, where you gradually cooled down. Finally, you splashed around in the *frigidarium*, the only actual "bath" in the place, in essence a cold-water swimming pool. There was a nominal admission fee, often waived by officials and emperors wishing to curry favor with the plebeians. The baths' functioning depended on the slaves who cared for the clients and stoked the fires that heated the water. ☎ 06/39967700 ⊕ *www.pierreci.it* ⊗ *Tues.–Sun. 9–1 hr hour before sunset, Mon. 9–2.*

44 BC

150 BC	Roman Forum begins to take shape as the principal civic center in Italy.
146	Third Punic War: Rome razes city of Carthage and emerges as the dominant Mediterranean force.
133	Rome rules entire Mediterranean Basin except Egypt.
49	Julius Caesar conquers Gaul.
44	Julius Caesar is assassinated.
27	Rome's Imperial Age begins; Octavian (now named Augustus) becomes the first emperor and is later deified. The Augustan Age is celebrated in the works of Virgil (70 BC–AD 19), Ovid (43 BC–AD 17), Livy (59 BC–AD 17), and Horace (65–8 BC).

COLOSSEO

You can give the Colosseum a cursory look in about 30 minutes, but it deserves at least an hour. Make reservations by phone (there are English-speaking operators) or online at least a day in advance to avoid long lines. Or buy your ticket for the Colosseum at Palatine Hill, where the lines are usually shorter.

LEGEND HAS IT THAT AS LONG AS THE COLOSSEUM STANDS, ROME WILL stand; and when Rome falls, so will the world. No visit to Rome is complete without a trip to the crumbling oval that has been the iconic symbol of the city for centuries.

★ **Colosseo.** A program of games and shows lasting 100 days celebrated the opening of the massive and majestic Colosseum in AD 80. On the opening day alone, 5,000 wild beasts perished. More than 70,000 spectators could sit within the arena's 573-yard circumference, which had marble facing, hundreds of statues for decoration, and a *velarium*—an ingenious system of sail-like awnings rigged on ropes manned by imperial sailors—to protect the audience from the sun and rain. Before the imperial box, gladiators would salute the emperor and cry, "*Ave, imperator, morituri te salutant*" ("Hail, emperor, men soon to die salute you"); it is said that when one day they heard the emperor Claudius respond, "Or maybe not," they were so offended that they called a strike.

Originally known as the Flavian Amphitheater, it took the name Colosseum after a truly colossal gilt bronze statue of Nero that stood nearby. Gladiator combat and staged animal hunts ended by the 6th century. The arena later served as a quarry from which materials were looted to build Renaissance churches and palaces. Finally, it was declared sacred by the Vatican in memory of the many Christians believed martyred here. (Scholars now maintain that Christians met their death elsewhere.) During the 19th century, romantic poets lauded the glories of the ruins when viewed by moonlight. Now its arches glow at night with mellow golden spotlights—less romantic, perhaps, but still impressive.

Expect long lines at the entrance and actors dressed as gladiators who charge a hefty fee to pose for pictures. Once inside you can walk around much of the outer ring of the structure and look down into the exposed passages under what was once the arena floor, now represented by a thin gangway and a small stage at one end. Climb the steep stairs for panoramic views in the Colosseum and out to the Forum and Arch of Constantine. A museum space on

THE RISE AND FALL OF ANCIENT ROME

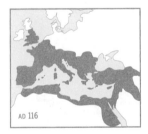

AD 116

43 AD	Rome invades Britain.
50	Rome is the largest city in the world, with a population of a million.
65	Emperor Nero begins the persecution of Christians in the Empire; Saints Peter and Paul are executed.
70–80	Vespasian builds the Colosseum.
98–117	Trajan's military successes are celebrated with his Baths (98), Forum (110), and Column (113); the Roman Empire reaches its apogee.

the upper floor holds temporary archaeological exhibits. ☎ 06/7005469, 06/39967700 *reservations* ⊕ *www.pierreci.it* ⊗ *Daily. 8:30–1 hr before sunset.*

Arco di Costantino. The largest (69 feet high, 85 feet long, 23 feet wide) and the best preserved of Rome's triumphal arches was erected in AD 315 to celebrate the victory of the emperor Constantine (280–337) over Maxentius (died 312). It was just before this battle that Constantine, the emperor who converted Rome to Christianity, had a vision of a cross in the heavens and heard the words "In this sign, thou shalt conquer."

NEAR THE COLOSSEO

Domus Aurea. Nero's "Golden House" is closed to visitors until at least late 2007, and possibly much longer, as preservationists struggle with how to slow its deterioration. The closure's unfortunate because the site gives a good sense of the excesses of Imperial Rome. After fire destroyed much of the city in AD 64, Nero took advantage of the resulting open space to construct a lavish palace so large that it spread over four of Rome's seven hills. It had a fa-cade of pure gold, seawater piped into the baths, decorations of mother-of-pearl, and vast gardens. Not much has survived of all this; a good portion of the building and grounds was buried under the public works with which subsequent emperors sought to make reparation to the Roman people for Nero's phenomenal greed. As a result, the site of the Domus Aurea itself remained unknown for many centuries. A few of Nero's original halls were discovered underground at the end of the 15th century. Raphael (1483–1520) was one of the artists who had themselves lowered into the rubble-filled rooms, which resembled grottoes. The artists copied the original painted Roman decorations, barely visible by torchlight, and scratched their names on the ceilings. Raphael later used these models—known as *grotesques* because they were found in the so-called grottoes—in his decorative motifs for the Vatican Loggia.

The palace remains impressive in scale, even if a bit of imagination is required to envision the original. ⊕ *www.pierreci.it.*

AD 450

238 AD	The first wave of Germanic invasions penetrates Italy.
293	Diocletian reorganizes the Empire into West and East.
330	Constantine founds a new Imperial capital (Constantinople) in the East.
410	Rome is sacked by Visigoths.
476	The last Roman emperor, Romulus Augustus, is deposed. The Roman Empire falls.

Baroque Rome: Gold & Grandeur

The area between the Corso and the Tiber bend is one of Rome's most beautiful districts, filled with narrow streets bearing curious names, airy piazzas, and half-hidden courtyards. Some of Rome's most coveted residential addresses are nestled here. So, too, are the ancient Pantheon and the medieval square of Campo de' Fiori, but baroque design of the 16th and 17th centuries predominates.

Occupying the horn of land that pushes the Tiber westward toward the Vatican, this district has been an integral part of the city since ancient times, and its position between the Vatican and Lateran palaces, both seats of papal rule, put it in the mainstream of Rome's development from the Middle Ages onward. Craftsmen and shopkeepers toiled in the shadow of the huge palaces built to consolidate the power of leading figures in the papal court. Writers and artists, such as the satirist Aretino and the goldsmith-sculptor Cellini, made sarcastic comments on the alternate fortunes of the courtiers and courtesans who populated the area. Artisans and artists still live here, but their numbers are diminishing as the district becomes gentrified. Two of the liveliest piazzas in Rome, Piazza Navona and Piazza del Pantheon, are the lodestars in a constellation of cafés, trendy stores, restaurants, and wine bars.

The Main Attractions

★ ⑱ **Campo de' Fiori.** This bustling square is home to a famed market. Each morning, vendors fill temporary stalls with all manner of local produce, nuts, cheese, spices, flowers, and seafood; by early afternoon it's all gone, to reappear in the city's homes and restaurants at dinnertime. Cafés and bars where the city's hip, young professionals hang out at night border the market. Overseeing the action is a brooding statue of philosopher-monk Giordano Bruno (1548–1600), who, along with many others from the Middle Ages, was burned alive in the square.

NEED A BREAK? Some of Rome's best pizza comes out of the ovens of **Il Forno di Campo de' Fiori** (☎ 06/68806662 ✉ Campo de' Fiori). Choose pizza *bianca*, topped with olive oil, or *rossa*, with tomato sauce. Move to the annex next door to have your warm pizza filled with prosciutto and figs, or other mouthwatering combinations.

⑨ **Largo di Torre Argentina.** In the middle of this busy piazza lies Rome's largest fully excavated Republican-era ruins. The **area sacra** (sacred area) has columns, altars, and foundations from four temples dating as far back as the 1st century BC. On the west side of the square lies the **Curia Pompeii,** the site where Caesar was slain in 44 BC. The frescoes on the taller brickwork are from the 12th-century church of San Nicola de' Cesarini, which was built into

WORD OF MOUTH

"My 'magic moment' had to be rounding the corner and coming upon the Pantheon without knowing it was coming up. I can't even describe it. This spot ended up becoming my favorite even after a month in Italy. The building just simply strikes me speechless."
–reedpaints

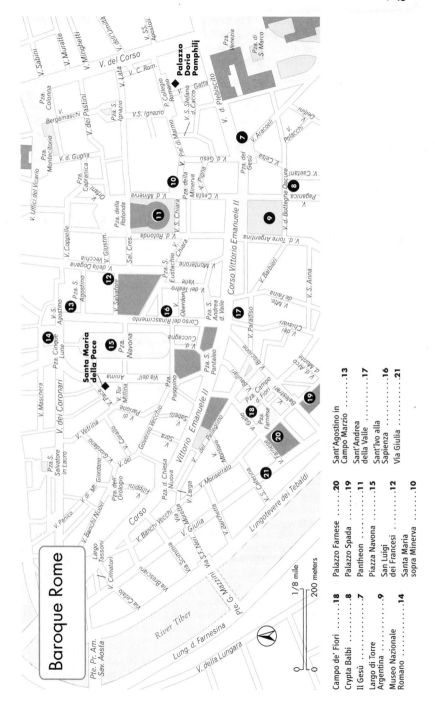

Baroque Rome

1/8 mile

200 meters

one of the temples. The ruins serve as a cat sanctuary for hundreds of the city's strays: take the staircase down to visit the cats and the cat ladies who look after them. Volunteer cat tenders are welcome, even for a few hours. ⊠ *Near Piazza Venezia.*

⓮ Museo Nazionale Romano. The ancient Roman and Egyptian sculptures in the **Palazzo Altemps,** part of the Museo Nazionale Romano, make up a terrific antiquities collection. Look for two works in the famed Ludovisi collection: the large, intricately carved Ludovisi Sarcophagus and *Galata,* a poignant work portraying a barbarian warrior who chooses death for himself and his wife rather than humiliation by the enemy. The 16th-century palazzo, with gorgeously frescoed ceilings and loggia, is an impressive home for the sculptures. This is a must-see for serious art buffs. ⊠ *Piazza Sant'Apollinare 46, near Piazza Navona* ☎ *06/39967700* 💶 *€6* ⊗ *Tues.–Sun. 9–7:45.*

⓫ Pantheon. One of Rome's most impressive and best-preserved ancient mon-
Fodor'sChoice uments, the Pantheon is particularly close to the hearts of Romans. The
★ emperor Hadrian designed it around AD 120 and had it built on the site of an earlier temple that had been damaged by fire. Although the sheer size of the Pantheon is impressive (until 1960 the dome was the largest ever built), what's most striking is its tangible sense of harmony. In large part this feeling is the result of the building's symmetrical design: the height of the dome is equal to the diameter of the circular interior. The oculus, or opening in the dome, is meant to symbolize the all-seeing eye of heaven; in practice, it illuminates the building and lightens the heavy stone ceiling. The original bronze doors have survived more than 1,800 years, centuries longer than the interior's rich gold ornamentation, which was plundered by popes and emperors. Art lovers can pay homage to the tomb of Raphael, who is buried in an ancient sarcophagus under the altar of Madonna del Sasso. ⊠ *Piazza della Rotonda, Pantheon* ☎ *06/68300230* 💶 *Free* ⊗ *Mon.–Sat. 9–7:30, Sun. 9–5:30.*

★ ☾ **⓯ Piazza Navona.** This famed piazza has the carefree air of the days when it was the scene of Roman circus games, medieval jousts, and 17th-century carnivals. Today it often attracts fashion photographers on shoots and Romans out for their *passeggiata* (evening stroll). Bernini's splashing **Fontana dei Quattro Fiumi** (Fountain of the Four Rivers), with an enormous rock squared off by statues representing the four corners of the world, makes a fitting centerpiece. Behind the fountain is the church of **Sant'Agnese in Agone,** an outstanding example of baroque architecture built by the Pamphilj Pope Innocent X. The facade—a wonderfully rich mélange of bell towers, concave spaces, and dovetailed stone and marble—is by Borromini, a contemporary and rival of Bernini, and by Carlo Rainaldi (1611–91). One story has it that the Bernini statue nearest the church, which represents the River Plate, has its hand up before its eye because it can't bear the sight of the Borromini facade. Though often repeated, the story is fiction: the facade was built after the fountain.

From early December through January 6 a Christmas market fills the square with games, Nativity scenes (some well crafted, many not), and multiple versions of the Befana, the ugly but good witch who brings candy

Roman Baroque

1

FLAGRANTLY EMOTIONAL, heavily expressive, and visually sensuous, the 17th-century artistic movement known as the baroque was born in Rome. It was the creation of three geniuses: the sculptor and architect Gianlorenzo Bernini (1598–1680), the painter and architect Pietro da Cortona (1596–1669), and the architect and sculptor Francesco Borromini (1599–1667). From the drama found in the artists' paintings to the jewel-laden, gold-on-gold detail of 17th-century Roman palaces, baroque style was intended both to shock and delight by upsetting the placid, "correct" rules of proportion and scale in the Renaissance. If a building looks theatrical—like a stage or a theater, especially with curtains being drawn back—it is usually baroque. Look for over-the-top, curvaceous marble work, tromp l'oeil, allusions to other art, and high drama to identify the style. Baroque's appeal to the emotions made it a powerful weapon in the hands of the Counter-Reformation.

and toys to Italian children on Epiphany. (Her name is a corruption of the Italian word for "epiphany," *Epifania*.)

⑫ **San Luigi dei Francesi.** The clergy of San Luigi considered Caravaggio's roisterous and unruly lifestyle scandalous enough, but his realistic treatment of sacred subjects—seen in three paintings depicting the life of St. Matthew in the last chapel—was too much for them. They rejected outright his first version of the altarpiece, and they weren't especially happy with the other two works. Thanks to the intercession of Caravaggio's patron, the influential Cardinal Francesco del Monte, the clergy were persuaded to keep them—a lucky thing, since the works are now thought to be among the artist's finest paintings. Have a few one-euro coins handy for the light machine. ⊠ *Piazza San Luigi dei Francesi, near Piazza Navona* ☎ *06/688271* ☺ *Fri.–Wed. 7–12:30 and 3:30–7.*

⑬ **Sant'Agostino in Campo Marzio.** Caravaggio's celebrated *Madonna of the Pilgrims*—which scandalized all Rome because it pictured pilgrims with dirt on the soles of their feet—can be found on the left over the first altar in this small church. Also of interest are Raphael's *Prophet*, on the first pilaster on the left, and the dozens of heart-shape ex-votos to *Madonna del Parto* (Mary of Childbirth) at the entrance. ⊠ *Piazza di Sant'Agostino, near Piazza Navona* ☎ *06/68801962* ☺ *Daily 7:45–12:30 and 4–7:30.*

Also Worth Seeing

❽ **Crypta Balbi** (Crypt of Balbus). After 20 years of excavation and restoration, these fascinating remains of a courtyard with a portico and theater built in 13 BC afford a unique look at Roman history. Rather than focus on one era, the crypt is displayed in such a way that it peels back the layers of the site, following the latest techniques in conservation. The well-explained exhibits (with text in English and Italian) give you a tangible sense of the sweeping changes that this spot—and Rome—underwent from antiquity to the 20th century. A partially restored wall provides an example of what marble and tufa constructions looked like before weather took its toll and medieval builders stripped the marble off for reuse. Copies of documents and reconstructed coins and other everyday objects found in drains, rubbish dumps, and tombs are a window into the world of the people who lived and worked here over the ages. ⊠ *Via Delle Botteghe Oscure 31, near Piazza Venezia* ☏ *06/39967700* ⊕ *www.pierreci.it* 🎫 *€6* ⊙ *Tues.–Sun. 9–7:45.*

❼ Il Gesù. Grandmother of all baroque churches, this huge structure was designed by the architect Vignola (1507–73) to be the tangible symbol of the Jesuits, a major force in the Counter-Reformation in Europe. It remained unadorned for about 100 years, but when it finally was decorated, no expense was spared: the interior drips with lapis lazuli, precious marbles, gold, and more gold. A fantastically painted ceiling by Baciccia (1639–1709) seems to merge with the painted stucco figures at its base. St. Ignatius's apartments, reached from the side entrance of the church, are also worth a visit (afternoons only) for the trompe-l'oeil frescoes and relics of the saint. ⊠ *Piazza del Gesù, near Piazza Venezia* ☏ *06/3613717* ⊙ *Sun.–Fri. 8:30–12:15 and 4–7:30, Sat. 8:30–12:15 and 4–10.*

⓴ Palazzo Farnese. The Farnese family rose to great power during the Renaissance, in part due to the favor Pope Alexander VI showed to the beautiful Giulia Farnese. The large palace was begun when, with Alexander's aid, Giulia's brother became cardinal; it was further enlarged on his election as Pope Paul III in 1534. The uppermost frieze decorations and main window overlooking the piazza are the work of Michelangelo, who also designed part of the courtyard (viewable through windows on Via Giulia), as well as the graceful arch over Via Giulia at the back. The facade on Piazza Farnese has geometrical brick configurations that have long been thought to hold occult meaning. When looking up at the palace from outside you can catch a glimpse of the splendid frescoed ceilings, including the **Galleria Carracci** vault painted by Annibale Carracci between 1597 and 1604—the second-greatest ceiling in Rome. For permission to view it from the inside, write several months ahead of time to the French Embassy, which now occupies the palace. Specify

---

A GOOD WALK: CARAVAGGIO'S ROME

Michelangelo Merisi—better known by the name of his birthplace, Caravaggio—may have been Rome's greatest painter. He certainly was one of its most notorious: he cultivated a reputation as a rebel, keeping company with prostitutes and local gangs. His nonconformist spirit found its way into his painting: his vibrant work was a major innovation in Western art. This walk introduces you to Caravaggio's art and his world. It covers about 1½ km (1 mi), including the final stretch to Piazza del Popolo.

Start at the **Palazzo Doria Pamphilj** ㉕, home to some of Caravaggio's most famous early works, including *Rest on the Flight to Egypt* and *Penitent Magdalene*, both from 1595. The latter created a scandal: Caravaggio used a real model for Mary Magdalene, something prohibited by the Church. To compound the sin, the model was his lover, the prostitute Maddalena Antonietti. It wouldn't be the last time Caravaggio used profane models for sacred subjects—later, his patrons drew the line at the *Death of Mary*, the model for which was said to be the drowned body of a prostitute.

the number in your party, when you wish to visit, and a local phone number for confirmation a few days before the visit. ☒ *French Embassy, Servizio Culturale, Piazza Farnese 67, 00186* ☎ *06/686011* ✆ *Free* ☉ *By appointment only.*

⑲ Palazzo Spada. A dazzling stuccoed facade on Piazza Capo di Ferro, west of Piazza Farnese, fronts an equally magnificent inner courtyard. On the southeast side of the inner courtyard, the gallery designed by Borromini creates an elaborate optical illusion, appearing to be much longer than it really is. On the first floor there are paintings and sculptures that belonged to Cardinale Bernardino Spada, an art connoisseur who collected works by Italian and Flemish masters. ☒ *Piazza Capo di Ferro 13, near Campo de' Fiori* ☎ *06/6832409* ⊕ *www.galleriaborghese.it* ✆ *€5* ☉ *Tues.–Sun. 9:30–7:30.*

⑩ Santa Maria sopra Minerva. Michelangelo's *Risen Christ* and the tomb of the gentle 15th-century artist Fra Angelico are in practically the only Gothic-style church in Rome. Have some coins handy to light up the **Cappella Carafa** in the right transept, where exquisite 15th-century frescoes by Filippino Lippi (circa 1457–1504) are well worth the small investment. (Lippi's most famous student was Botticelli.) In front of the church, Bernini's charming elephant bearing an Egyptian obelisk has an inscription on the base saying that it takes a strong mind to sustain solid wisdom. ☒ *Piazza della Minerva, Pantheon* ☎ *06/6793926* ☉ *Daily 7–noon and 4–7.*

⑰ Sant'Andrea della Valle. This huge 17th-century church looms mightily over a busy intersection. Puccini set the first act of his opera *Tosca* here; fans have been known to hire a horse-drawn carriage at night to trace the course of the opera from Sant'Andrea up Via Giulia to Palazzo Farnese—Scarpia's headquarters—to the locale of the opera's climax, Castel Sant'Angelo. Inside, above the apse are striking frescoes depicting scenes from St. Andrew's life by the Bolognese painter Domenichino (1581–1641). ☒ *Corso Vittorio Emanuele II, near Campo de' Fiori* ☎ *06/6861339* ☉ *Daily 7:30–noon and 4:30–7:30.*

⑯ Sant'Ivo alla Sapienza. Borromini's eccentric church has what must surely be Rome's most unusual dome—topped by a golden spiral said

---

Exit the gallery and walk left along Piazza Collegio Romano, continuing on Via Piè di Marmo. The street bends right through Piazza Minerva, with its elephant obelisk, and continues alongside the Pantheon. In front of the Pantheon, walk around the fountain and take Via Giustiniani, extending left from the far left corner of the piazza. Follow it to the church **San Luigi dei Francesi** ⑫. Inside is the painting cycle of the Life of St. Matthew (1600), which shocked the public with its contemporary depiction of sacred subjects and thrilled the art world with its realism and use of light.

Leave the church, turn left along the piazza, then take the third right, Vicolo Vaccarella. Follow it until it ends, then turn left onto Vicolo Coppelle. This alley soon opens into Piazza Campo Marzio, with the entrance to the church of **Sant'Agostino** ⑬ on the right. Inside is the *Madonna of the Pilgrims* (1605), which caused another sensation for its depiction of filthy, ragged pilgrims, and for its model, once again the formidable Maddalena, dressed as the Mother of God. Exit the church and continue up Via Metastasio to Vicolo Divino Amore. At its corner with Vicolo San Biato have been inspired by a bee's stinger. ⊠ *Corso Rinascimento 40, near Piazza Navona* ☺ *Sun. 10–noon.*

㉑ Via Giulia. Named after Pope Julius II and serving for more than four centuries as the "salon of Rome," this street is still the address of choice for Roman aristocrats and rich foreigners. Built with funds garnered by taxing prostitutes, the street is lined with elegant palaces, including the Palazzo Falconieri, and old churches (one, San Eligio, reputedly designed by Raphael himself). The area around Via Giulia is a wonderful place to wander in to get the feeling of daily life as carried on in a centuries-old setting—an experience enhanced by the dozens of antiques shops in the neighborhood.

Piazza Venezia to the Spanish Steps: Vistas & Views

Though it has a bustling commercial air, this part of the city also holds great visual allure, from the gaudy marble confection that is the monument to Vittorio Emanuele II to the theatrical Piazza di Sant'Ignazio. Among the things to look for are stately palaces, baroque ballrooms, and the greatest example of portraiture in Rome, Velázquez's incomparable *Innocent X* at the Galleria Doria Pamphilj. Highlights are the Trevi Fountain and the Spanish Steps, 18th-century Rome's most famous example of city planning.

The Main Attractions

★ **㉘ Fontana di Trevi** (Trevi Fountain). The huge fountain designed by Nicola Salvi (1697–1751) is a whimsical rendition of mythical sea creatures amid cascades of splashing water. The fountain is the world's most spectacular wishing well: legend has it that you can ensure your return to Rome by tossing a coin into the fountain. It was featured in the 1954 film *Three Coins in the Fountain* and was the scene of Anita Ekberg's aquatic frolic in Fellini's *La Dolce Vita*. By day this is one of the most crowded sites in town; at night the spotlighted piazza feels festive. ⊠ *Off Via del Tritone, Piazza di Trevi.*

㉒ Monumento a Vittorio Emanuele II. Known as the Vittoriano, this vast marble monument was erected in the late 19th century to honor Italy's first king, Vittorio Emanuele II (1820–78), and the unification of Italy. Aes-

---

gio is the apartment where Caravaggio lived. It was here, on a mission from the irate landlady, that a debt collector discovered Caravaggio's secret method—he arranged glass and mirrors in order to create intense, focused light and shadow on subjects, which he then would view with a mirror as he painted.

Continue on Vicolo Divino Amore one block to Via Fontanella Borghese and turn left, then left again on to Via Pallacorda. The street was the site of a duel that changed Caravaggio's life. On May 29, 1606, the artist fought with and killed Ranuccio Tomassoni, a gang-

ster said to have been a contender for the favors of Maddalena. Condemned to death for the deed, Caravaggio fled Rome, never to return. He first went to Naples, then to Malta. He died near Porto Ercole, a coastal town in southern Tuscany, in 1610. From Via Pallacorda, continue north up Via Ripetta about 1 km (½ mi) to Piazza del Popolo and the church of **Santa Maria del Popolo** ㊾, at the far end of the piazza. The Cappella Cerasi there holds two more masterpieces.

thetically minded Romans have derided the oversize structure, visible from many parts of the city, calling it "the typewriter," "the wedding cake," or even "the urinal." Whatever you think of its design, the views from the top are unforgettable. Here also is the **Tomb of the Unknown Soldier** with its eternal flame. A side entrance in the monument leads to the rather somber **Museo del Risorgimento,** which charts Italy's struggle for nationhood. The red shirt and boots of revolutionary hero Giuseppe Garibaldi (1807–82) are among the mementos. Opposite the Vittoriano, note the name "Bonaparte" still visible on the enclosed wooden veranda fronting the palace on the corner of Via del Plebiscito and Via Corso. Napoléon's mother had a fine view from here of the local goings-on for the many years that she lived in Rome. ⊠ *Entrance at Piazza Ara Coeli, near Piazza Venezia* ☎ *06/6991718* ⊕ *www.ambienterm. arti.beniculturali.it/vittoriano/index.html* 🖃 *Monument free, museum €5* ⊗ *Tues.–Sun. 10–4.*

㉔ Palazzo Colonna. Inside the fabulous, private Palazzo Colonna, the 17th-century **Sala Grande**—more than 300 feet long, with bedazzling chandeliers, colored marble, and enormous paintings—is best known as the site where Audrey Hepburn met the press in *Roman Holiday.* The entrance to the picture gallery, the **Galleria Colonna,** hides behind a plain, inconspicuous door. The private palace is open to the public Saturday only; reserve ahead to get a free guided tour in English. ⊠ *Via della Pilotta 17, near Piazza di Trevi* ☎ *06/6784350* ⊕ *www.galleriacolonna. it* 🖃 *€7* ⊗ *Sept.–July, Sat. 9–1.*

㉖ Sant'Ignazio. The interior dome in this sumptuous 17th-century church is a trompe-l'oeil oddity: the cupola is painted as, well, a cupola—but open at the top, and full of flying angels, saints, and heavenly dignitaries who float about in what appears to be a rosy sky above. To get the full effect of the illusionistic ceiling painted by Andrea del Pozzo (1642–1709), stand on the small disk set into the floor of the nave. The church also contains some of Rome's most splendid, jewel-encrusted altars. If you're lucky, you might catch an evening concert performed here (check with the tourist office). Step outside the church to look at it from Filippo Raguzzini's 18th-century piazza, where the buildings, as in much baroque art, are arranged resembling a stage set. ⊠ *Piazza Sant'Ignazio, near Pantheon* ☎ *06/6794406* ⊗ *Daily 7:30–12:15 and 3–7:15.*

★ ㉚ Spanish Steps. Both the steps and the Piazza di Spagna get their names from the Spanish Embassy to the Vatican on the piazza, though the staircase was actually built with French funds in 1723. In an allusion to the church of *Trinità dei Monti* (Trinity of the Mount), at the top of the hill, the staircase is divided by three landings (beautifully banked with azaleas from mid-April to mid-May). This area has always welcomed tourists: 18th-century dukes and duchesses on their Grand Tour, 19th-century artists and writers in search of inspiration—among them Stendhal, Balzac, Thackeray, and Byron—and today's enthusiastic hordes. The **Fontana della Barcaccia** (Fountain of the Old Boat) at the base of the steps is by Pietro Bernini, father of the famous Gianlorenzo. ⊠ *Piazza di Spagna.*

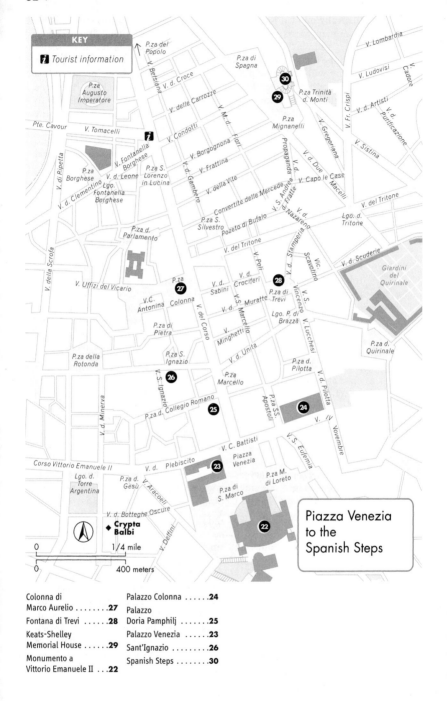

KEY

i Tourist information

Piazza Venezia
to the
Spanish Steps

Also Worth Seeing

27 Colonna di Marco Aurelio. This ancient column, like the Colonna di Traiano, is an extraordinary stone history book. Its detailed reliefs spiraling up to the top illustrate the victorious campaigns of emperor Marcus Aurelius against the barbarians. It stands in front of a different kind of monument to power: the offices of the prime minister. ⊠ *Piazza Colonna, near Piazza di Spagna.*

29 Keats-Shelley Memorial House. English Romantic poet John Keats (1795–1821) once lived in what is now a (very small) museum dedicated to him and his great contemporary and friend Percy Bysshe Shelley (1792–1822). You can visit his tiny rooms, preserved as they were when he died here. ⊠ *Piazza di Spagna 26, next to the Spanish Steps* ☎ *06/ 6784235* ⊕ *www.keats-shelley-house.org* ⊡ *€3.50* ☉ *Weekdays 9–1 and 3–6, Sat. 11–2 and 3–6.*

25 Palazzo Doria Pamphilj. This bona fide patrician palace is still home to a princely family, which rents out many of its 1,000 rooms. You can visit the remarkably well-preserved **Galleria Doria Pamphilj** (pronounced pom-*fee*-lee), a picture-and-sculpture gallery that gives you a sense of the sumptuous living quarters. Numbered paintings (the bookshop's museum catalog comes in handy) are packed onto every available inch of wall space. Pride of place is given to the famous and strikingly modern portrait of the 17th-century Pamphilj pope Innocent X by Diego Velázquez (1599–1660), but don't overlook Caravaggio's affecting *Rest on the Flight into Egypt* or the formidable bust of Olympia, the powerful woman whose political brilliance launched the dynasty. The audio guide (included in admission) is narrated by the current Doria Pamphilj prince himself and gives a fascinating personal history of the palace. ⊠ *Piazza del Collegio Romano 2, near Piazza Venezia* ☎ *06/6797323* ⊕ *www.doriapamphilj.it* ⊡ *€8* ☉ *Fri.–Wed. 10–5.*

23 Palazzo Venezia. A Roman landmark on the city's busiest square, this palace is best known for the balcony over the main portal, from which Mussolini gave public addresses to crowds in Piazza Venezia during the dark days of Fascism. Today it's home to a haphazard collection of mostly early-Renaissance weapons, ivories, and paintings in its grand salons, some of which Il Duce used as his offices. The palace also hosts major touring art exhibits, so check to see what's currently showing. ⊠ *Piazza San Marco 49, near Piazza Venezia* ☎ *06/32810* ⊕ *www.ticketeria. it/palazzovenezia-eng.asp* ⊡ *€4* ☉ *Tues.–Sun. 8:30–7:30.*

Monti & San Giovanni: Centuries of Worship

Through the centuries, the development of Christian worship has shaped Rome's history; these monuments to Christianity, though less frequented today, are a living record of the faith and its expression in Rome. The city is home to hundreds of old churches, each with something unique to offer visitors. Monti and San Giovanni, adjoining neighborhoods east of Rome's historic center, are packed with some of Rome's greatest art and architecture, executed for the glory of the Roman Catholic Church.

The Main Attractions

★ ㉛ **San Clemente.** A 12th-century church built on top of a 4th-century church, which in turn was constructed over a 2nd-century pagan temple to the god Mithras, San Clemente is an extraordinary archaeological site. The upper church, which you enter from street level, holds a beautiful early-12th-century mosaic showing a cross on a gold background, surrounded by swirling green acanthus leaves teeming with little scenes of everyday life. The marble choir screens, salvaged from the 4th-century church, are decorated with early Christian symbols: doves, vines, and fish. The **Cappella Castiglioni,** off the left aisle, holds frescos painted around 1400 by the Florentine artist Masolino da Panicale (1383–1440), a key figure in the introduction of realism and one-point perspective into Renaissance painting. Note the large Crucifixion and scenes from the lives of Sts. Catherine, Ambrose, and Christopher, plus an Annunciation (over the entrance). Before you leave the upper church, take a look at the pretty cloister— evening concerts are held here in summer.

From the right aisle, stairs lead down to the remains of the **4th-century church,** which was active until 1084, when it was damaged beyond repair during a siege of the neighborhood by the Norman prince Robert Guiscard. Its remains are largely intact, in part because it wasn't unearthed until the 19th century. (It was discovered by Irish Dominican monks; members of the order still live in the adjacent monastery.) The vestibule is decorated with marble fragments found during the excavations (which are still under way), and in the nave are colorful 11th-century frescoes depicting stories from the life of St. Clement. Another level down is the **Mythraeum,** a shrine dedicated to the god Mithras, whose cult spread from Persia and gained a hold in Rome during the 2nd and 3rd centuries. ✉ *Via San Giovanni in Laterano 108, San Giovanni* ☎ *06/70451018* 💶 *€3* ☉ *Mon.–Sat. 9–noon and 3–6, Sun. 10–12:30 and 3–6.*

㉛ **Santa Maria Maggiore.** One of Rome's four great pilgrimage churches was built on the spot where a 3rd-century pope witnessed a miraculous midsummer snowfall (reenacted every August 15). The gleaming mosaics on the arch in front of the main altar date from the 5th century, and the opulently carved wood ceiling is believed to have been gilded with the first gold brought from the New World. To view the elaborate 14th-century facade mosaics, inquire at the souvenir shop. ✉ *Piazza Santa Maria Maggiore, off Via Cavour* ☎ *06/483195* ☉ *Daily 7 AM–8 PM.*

㉝ **Santi Quattro Coronati.** The 12th-century church of the Four Crowned Martyrs, part of a fortified abbey that provided refuge to early popes and emperors, is in an unusual corner of Rome, a quiet island that has resisted the tide of time and traffic flowing beneath its ramparts. Few places are so reminiscent of the Middle Ages. Don't miss the cloister with its well-tended gardens and 12th-century fountain. The entrance is the door in the left aisle; ring the bell if it's not open. You can also ring at the adjacent convent for the key to the **Oratorio di San Silvestro** (Oratory of St. Sylvester), with 13th-century frescoes. ✉ *Largo Santi Quattro Coronati, San Giovanni* ☎ *06/70475427* ☉ *Easter–Christmas, daily 9:30–12:30 and 3:30–6; Christmas–Easter, daily 9:30–12:30.*

Also Worth Seeing

34 **San Giovanni in Laterano.** You may be surprised to discover that the cathedral of Rome is not St. Peter's but this church. (St. Peter's is in Vatican City, hence not technically part of Rome.) Dominating the piazza whose name it shares, this immense building is where the pope officiates in his capacity as bishop of Rome. The towering facade and Borromini's cool baroque interior emphasize the majesty of its proportions. The **cloister** is one of the city's finest, with beautifully carved columns surrounding a peaceful garden.

The adjoining **Palazzo Laterano** was the official papal residence until the 13th century, and is still technically part of the Vatican. It houses the offices of the Rome Diocese and the rather bland **Museo Storico Laterano** (Lateran Historical Museum). Behind the palace are the 4th-century octagonal **Battistero di San Giovanni** (St. John's Baptistery), forerunner of many similar buildings throughout Italy, and Rome's oldest and tallest obelisk, brought from Thebes and dating from the 15th century BC. ⊠ *Piazza San Giovanni in Laterano* ☎ *06/69886433* ⊡ *Church free, cloister €2.50, museum €4* ☉ *Church Apr.–Sept., daily 7–7; Oct.–Mar., daily 7–6. Cloister 9–½ hr before church closing. Museum Sat. guided tours at 9:15, 10:30, and noon; 1st Sun. of each month 8:45–1. Baptistery daily 9–1 and 5 PM–1 hr before sunset.*

㉟ Scala Santa (Sacred Stairs). A small building opposite the Palazzo Laterano houses what is claimed to be the staircase from Pilate's palace in Jerusalem. The faithful climb it on their knees. ⊠ *Piazza San Giovanni in Laterano* ☉ *Daily 6:15–noon and 3:30–6:30.*

Il Quirinale to Piazza della Repubblica: Palaces & Fountains

Near the Piazza della Repubblica you can see ancient Roman sculptures, early Christian churches, and highlights from the 16th and 17th centuries, when Rome was conquered by the baroque—and by Bernini. Il Quirinale is the highest of Rome's seven hills, and was once home to the popes, housed in the massive Palazzo Quirinale, now Italy's presidential palace.

The Main Attractions

㊵ Fontana del Tritone (Triton Fountain). The centerpiece of busy Piazza Barberini is Bernini's graceful fountain designed in 1637 for the sculptor's patron, Pope Urban VIII. The pope's Barberini family coat of arms, featuring bees, is at the base of the large shell. Close by is the **Fontana delle Api** (Fountain of the Bees), the last fountain designed by Bernini. ⊠ *Piazza Barberini, near Via Veneto.*

㊹ Palazzo Massimo alle Terme. This 19th-century palace in neobaroque style holds part of the collections of antiquities belonging to the Museo Nazionale Romano (also exhibited in the Palazzo Altemps). Here you can see extraordinary examples of the fine mosaics and masterful paintings that decorated ancient Rome's palaces and villas. Don't miss the fresco—depicting a lush garden in bloom—that came from the villa that Livia, wife of Emperor Augustus, owned outside Rome. ⊠ *Largo Villa Peretti 1, near Termini* ☎ *06/480201* ⊕ *www.pierreci.it* 🎟 *€6* ☉ *Tues.–Sun. 9–7:45.*

㊱ Il Quirinale. The highest of ancient Rome's seven hills, this is where ancient Romans, and later popes, built their residences in order to escape the deadly miasmas and malaria of the low-lying area around the Forum. The fountain in the square has ancient statues of Castor and Pollux reining in their unruly steeds and a basin salvaged from the Roman Forum. The **Palazzo del Quirinale** passed from the popes to Italy's kings in the 19th century; it's now the official residence of the nation's president. Every day at 4 PM the ceremony of the changing of the guard at the portal includes a miniparade complete with band. ⊠ *Piazza del Quirinale, near Piazza di Trevi* ☎ *06/46991* 🎟 *€5* ☉ *Sept.–June, Sun. 8:30–noon.*

Directly opposite the main entrance of the Palazzo del Quirinale sits Le **Scuderie Papale al Quirinale** (the Quirinal Stables), which once housed more than 120 horses for the exclusive use of the pope and his guests. The low-lying building was designed by Alessandro Specchi (1668–1729) in 1722 and was among the major achievements of baroque Rome. The stables were remodeled in the late 1990s by eminent architect Gae Aulenti and now serve as a venue for touring art exhibits. ⊠ *Piazza del Quirinale, near Piazza di Trevi* ☎ *06/39967500 or 06/696271* ⊕ *www.scuderiequirinale.it* 🎟 *€10* ☉ *Sun.–Thurs. 10–7, Fri. and Sat. 10–9:30.*

Il Quirinale
to Piazza della
Repubblica

KEY

Tourist information

0 ——— 1/4 mile

0 ——— 400 meters

🕑 **④①** **Santa Maria della Concezione.** In the crypt under the main Capuchin church, the bones of some 4,000 dead Capuchin monks are arranged in peculiar decorative designs around the shriveled and decayed skeletons of their kinsmen, a macabre reminder of the impermanence of earthly life. Signs declare WHAT YOU ARE, WE ONCE WERE. WHAT WE ARE, YOU SOMEDAY WILL BE. Although not for the easily spooked, the crypt is oddly beautiful. ⊠ *Via Veneto 27, Piazza di Spagna* ☎ *06/4871185* 💳 *Donation expected* ⊘ *Fri.–Wed. 9–noon and 3–6.*

④② **Santa Maria della Vittoria.** The most famous feature here is Bernini's baroque decoration of the **Cappella Cornaro,** an exceptional fusion of architecture, painting, and sculpture in which the *Ecstasy of St. Teresa* is the focal point. Bernini's audacious conceit was to model the chapel after a theater: members of the Cornaro family—sculpted in white marble—watch from theater boxes as, center stage, St. Teresa, in the throes of mystical rapture, is pierced by an angel's gilded arrow. To quote one 18th-century observer, President de Brosses: "If this is divine love, I know it well." ⊠ *Via XX Settembre 17, Termini* ☎ *06/42740571* ⊘ *Mon.–Sat. 9–noon and 3–6, Sun. 3–6.*

Also Worth Seeing

③⑨ Palazzo Barberini. Along with architect Carlo Maderno (1556–1629), Borromini helped make the splendid 17th-century Palazzo Barberini a residence worthy of Rome's leading art patron, Pope Urban VIII, who began the palace for his family in 1625. Inside, the **Galleria Nazionale d'Arte Antica** has some fine works by Caravaggio and Raphael, including the latter's portrait of his lover, *La Fornarina*. Rome's biggest ballroom is here; its ceiling, painted by Pietro da Cortona, depicts Immortality bestowing a crown upon Divine Providence escorted by a "bomber squadron"—to quote Sir Michael Levey—of mutant bees. (Bees featured prominently in the heraldic device of the Barberini.) ⊠ *Via Barberini 18, near Via Veneto* ☎ *06/328101* ⊕ *www.galleriaborghese.it* ⊠ *€6* ⊙ *Tues.–Sun. 8:30–7:30.*

④③ Piazza della Repubblica. Smog-blackened porticoes, a subway station, and a McDonald's make this grand piazza feel a bit derelict. The racy **Fontana delle Naiadi** (Fountain of the Naiads), an 1870 addition to the square, depicts voluptuous bronze ladies wrestling happily with marine monsters. In ancient times, the Piazza della Repubblica served as the entrance to the immense **Terme di Diocleziano** (Baths of Diocletian), an archaeological site today. Built in the 4th century AD, these were the largest and most impressive of the baths of ancient Rome, with vast halls, pools, and gardens that could accommodate 3,000 people at a time. The *aula ottagonale* (octagonal hall) now holds a sampling of the ancient sculptures unearthed here, including two beautiful bronzes. ⊠ *Via Romita 8, near Termini* ☎ *06/4870690* ⊠ *Free* ⊙ *Tues.–Sat. 9–2, Sun. 9–1.*

The curving ancient Roman brick facade on one side of the Piazza della Repubblica marks the church of **Santa Maria degli Angeli,** adapted by Michelangelo from the vast central chamber of the colossal baths. Look for the sundial carved on the floor. ⊠ *Via Cernaia 9* ☎ *064880812* ⊕ *www. santamariadegliangeliroma.it* ⊙ *Mon.–Sat. 7–6:30, Sun. 7 AM–7:30 PM.*

③⑧ San Carlino alle Quattro Fontane. In a church no larger than the base of one of the piers of St. Peter's, Borromini attained geometric architectural perfection. Characteristically, he chose a subdued white stucco for the interior decoration, so as not to distract from the form. Don't miss the cloister, which you reach through the door to the right of the altar. The exterior of the church is Borromini at his bizarre best, all curves and rippling movement. (Keep an eye out for cars whipping around the corner as you're looking.) Outside, the *quattro fontane* (four fountains) frame views in four directions. ⊠ *Via del Quirinale 23, near Piazza di Trevi* ☎ *06/4883261* ⊙ *Daily 10–noon and 3–6 (closed Sat. afternoon).*

③⑦ Sant'Andrea al Quirinale. This small but imposing baroque church was designed and decorated by Bernini, who considered it one of his finest works. ⊠ *Via del Quirinale, Piazza di Trevi* ☎ *06/4740807* ⊙ *Mon.–Sat. 8–noon and 3:30–7, Sun. 9–noon and 3:30–7.*

Villa Borghese to the Ara Pacis: Amid Sylvan Glades

Touring Rome's artistic masterpieces while staying clear of its hustle and bustle can be, quite literally, a walk in the park. Some of the city's finest

sights are tucked away in or next to green lawns and pedestrian piazzas, offering a breath of fresh air for weary sightseers. Villa Borghese,
one of Rome's largest parks, can alleviate gallery gout by offering an
oasis in which to cool off under the ilex trees. If you feel like a picnic,
have an *alimentare* (food shop) make you some *panini* (sandwiches) before you go; food carts within the park are overpriced.

The Main Attractions

51 Ara Pacis Augustae (Altar of Augustan Peace). This magnificent classical monument, with an exquisitely detailed frieze, was erected in 13 BC
to celebrate Emperor Augustus's triumphant return from military conflicts in Gaul and Spain. It's housed in one of Rome's newest landmarks,
a glass and travertine structure designed by American architect Richard
Meier. The building was opened in 2006, after 10 years of delays and
controversy, and early indications are that it's a triumph. Along the altar
itself, the building holds a luminous museum overlooking the Tiber on
one side and the imposing ruins of the marble-clad Mausoleo di Augusto
(Mausoleum of Augustus) on the other. The result is a gloriously tranquil oasis in the center of Rome. ⊠ *Lungotevere in Augusta, near Piazza di Spagna* ☎ *06/82059127* ⊕ *www.arapacis.it* ⊠ *€6.50*
⊙ *Tues.–Sun. 9–6.*

45 Galleria Borghese. The palace that was completed in 1613 for Cardinal Scipione Borghese (1576–1633) is a monument to 18th-century
Roman interior decoration at its most luxurious, dripping with porphyry and alabaster. Today it contains the art collection of the cardinal. The grand salons have ancient Roman mosaic pavements and
statues of various deities, including one officially known as *Venus Vic-
trix*. There has never been any doubt, however, as to the statue's real
subject: Pauline Bonaparte, Napoléon's sister, who married Prince
Camillo Borghese in one of the storied matches of the 19th century.
Sculpted by Canova (1757–1822), the princess reclines on a chaise,
bare-bosomed, her hips swathed in classical drapery, the very model
of haughty detachment and sly come-hither. Pauline is known to
have been shocked that her husband took pleasure in showing off the
work to his guests. This coyness seems curious given the reply she is
supposed to have made to a lady who asked her how she could have
posed for the work: "Oh, but the studio was heated." Other rooms
hold important sculptures by Bernini, including *David* and the breathtaking *Apollo and Daphne*. The picture collection has splendid works
by Titian, Caravaggio, and
Raphael, among others. Reservations are required, and the most
popular time slots can sell out days
in advance; you can book by phone
or online. ⊠ *Piazza Scipione
Borghese 5, off Via Pinciana, Villa
Borghese* ☎ *06/8513979 information, 06/32810 reservations*
⊕ *www.galleriaborghese.it*
⊠ *€10.50, audio guide or English
guided tour €5* ⊙ *Tues.–Sun. 9–7.*

FodorśChoice
★

> ### WORD OF MOUTH
>
> "The Borghese Gallery is one of
> the most precious places I have
> ever had the good fortune to visit—
> twice. The Bernini Statues bring
> tears to my eyes. The building is
> gorgeous. Just a little jewel box of
> a museum."   –bugswife1

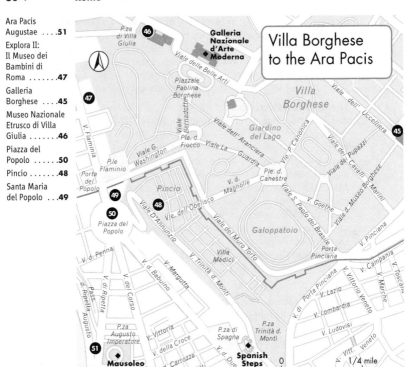

Villa Borghese
to the Ara Pacis

50 Piazza del Popolo. Designed by neoclassical architect Giuseppe Valadier (1762–1839) in the early 1800s, this piazza is one of the largest in Rome, and it has a 3,000-year-old obelisk in the middle. Always a favorite spot for café-sitting and people-watching, the piazza is closed to motorized traffic. The bookend baroque churches **Santa Maria dei Miracoli** and **Santa Maria in Montesanto** are not, first appearances to the contrary, twins. On the piazza's eastern side, stairs lead uphill to the ⇨ **Pincio.** To the north, at the end of the square, is the 400-year-old **Porta del Popolo,** Rome's northern city gate, and next to it the church of Santa Maria del Popolo. The city gate was designed by Bernini to welcome the Catholic convert Queen Christina of Sweden to Rome in 1605. ⊠ *Near Villa Borghese.*

49 Santa Maria del Popolo. This church next to the Porta del Popolo goes almost unnoticed, but it has one of the richest art collections of any church in Rome. Here is Raphael's High Renaissance masterpiece the **Cappella Chigi,** as well as two stunning Caravaggios in the **Cappella Cerasi.** Each December an exhibit of Christmas Nativity scenes is held in the adjacent building. ⊠ *Piazza del Popolo, near Villa Borghese* ☎ *06/3610836* ☉ *Mon.–Sat. 7–noon and 4–7, Sun. 7:30–1:30 and 4:30–7:30.*

Also Worth Seeing

Explora: Il Museo dei Bambini di Roma. Explore: the Museum for the Children of Rome is one of the few sights in the city geared specifically to kids. There are two floors of open space filled with hands-on activities and games for toddlers to 12-year-olds, and a child-friendly pizzeria. Steps from the car-free Piazza del Popolo and a short hike downhill from the playground in Villa Borghese, the museum is well suited to a kids' day in the neighborhood. Reservations are essential on weekends. You're let in for two-hour shifts. ⊠ *Via Flaminia 82, near Villa Borghese* ☎ *06/3613776* ⊕ *www.mdbr.it/inglese* 🎟 *€7 for children 3 and up, €6 for adults* ☼ *Tues.–Fri. admission at 9:30, 11:30, 3, and 5; weekend admission at 10, noon, 3, and 5.*

Museo Nazionale Etrusco di Villa Giulia (National Etruscan Museum at Villa Giulia). Known for their sophisticated art and design, the Etruscans left a legacy of sarcophagi, bronze sculptures, terra-cotta vases, and stunning jewelry. (Unlike the Greeks, Etruscan women sat at the banquet tables with men and enjoyed displaying their wealth on their bodies.) Acclaimed pieces of statuary in the gallery include the *Goddess with Infant* and the *Sarcophagus of the Married Couple*. In the villa's courtyard visit the atmospheric underground **Ninfeo,** the remains of the Virgin's Aqueduct from the Augustan period. ⊠ *Piazzale Villa Giulia 9, near Villa Borghese* ☎ *06/3226571* ⊕ *www.beniculturali.it* 🎟 *€4* ☼ *Tues.–Sun. 8:30–7:30.*

NEED A BREAK?

Caffè delle Arti (⊠ Viale delle Belle Arti 131, near Villa Borghese ☎ 06/32651236), an exquisite, light-filled space with towering ceilings and bronze statues, is inside the not-so-noteworthy Galleria Nazionale d'Arte Moderna, across the street from Villa Giulia. The menu includes tea with a variety of homemade pastries as well as Roman and Neapolitan dishes. In warm weather sit out on the huge terrace and take in the splendor of the surrounding Villa Borghese.

Pincio. At the southwestern corner of Villa Borghese, the Pincio belvedere and gardens were laid out by architect Giuseppe Valadier as part of his overall plan for Piazza del Popolo. Nineteenth-century counts and countesses liked to take their evening passeggiata here in the hope of meeting Pius IX (1792–1878), the last pope to go about Rome on foot. Nowadays you're more likely to see runners and in-line skaters, as well as throngs of Romans dressed in their best, out for a stroll. It's a good place to take in the summer concerts and New Year's fireworks staged in Piazza del Popolo below. ⊠ *Piazza del Popolo.*

Crossing the Tiber: The Ghetto, Tiberina Island & Trastevere

Despite rampant gentrification, Trastevere remains about the most tightly knit community in the city, its natives proudly proclaiming their descent from the ancient Romans. The old Jewish Ghetto is a warren of twisting, narrow streets, where Rome's Jewish community was once confined, then deported, and now, barely, persists. Ancient bridges, the Ponte Fabricio and Ponte Cestio, link the Ghetto and Trastevere to Tiberina Island; this area is Rome's medieval heart.

The Main Attractions

56 **Fontana delle Tartarughe.** The 16th-century Fountain of the Turtles in Piazza Mattei is one of Rome's loveliest. Designed by Giacomo della Porta (1539–1602) in 1581 and sculpted by Taddeo Landini (1550–96), the piece revolves around four bronze boys, each clutching a dolphin that jets water into marble shells. Several bronze tortoises, thought to have been added by Bernini, are held in each of the boys' hands and drink from the fountain's upper basin. The piazza is lined by a few interesting cafés and shops. It was named for the Mattei family, who built the **Palazzo Mattei** on Via Caetani. (The palace is not open to the public, but it's worth a peek at the sculpture-rich courtyard and staircase if the door is open.) ⊠ *Piazza Mattei, Ghetto.*

59 **Isola Tiberina** (Tiberina Island) is where a city hospital stands on a site that has been dedicated to healing ever since a temple to Aesculapius was erected here in 291 BC. If you have time, and if the river's not too high, walk down the stairs for a different perspective on the island and the Tiber River. Every July, the city's Estate Romana hosts an open-air cinema on the island's paved shores. ⊠ *Ponte Fabricio and Ponte Cestio, near Ghetto.*

Jewish Ghetto. Rome has had a Jewish community since the 1st century BC, and from that time until the present its living conditions have varied widely according to its relations with the city's rulers. In 1555 Pope Paul II established Rome's Jewish Ghetto in the neighborhood marked off by the Portico d'Ottavia, the Tiber, and Via Arenula. The area quickly became Rome's most squalid and densely populated. At one point, Jews—who had engaged in many businesses and professions in Trastevere—were limited to the sale of used iron and clothing as a trade. The laws were rescinded around the time of the Italian unifications in the 1870s. German troops occupied Rome during World War II, and on October 16, 1943, many of Rome's Jews were rounded up and deported to Nazi concentration camps. In 1982 the synagogue here was attacked with grenades and machine guns by Palestinian terrorists, and in 1986, as a gesture of reconciliation, Pope John Paul II paid a visit to Rabbi Elio Toaff, becoming the first pope ever to pray in a Jewish synagogue. Today some of Rome's 15,000 Jewish residents still live in the area; there are a few Judaica shops and kosher groceries, bakeries, and restaurants—as well as linen and shoe stores run by Jewish families—especially on Via di Portico d'Ottavia. **Tours of the Ghetto** (€8, about two hours) that explore Rome's Jewish history can be booked through the SIDIC historical society. ⊠ *SIDIC Office, Via Garibaldi 28, Ghetto* 🕾 *06/ 58333615* ⊕ *www.sidic.org.*

★ **62** **Piazza di Santa Maria in Trastevere.** This piazza is a popular spot for afternoon coffee and evening cocktails at its outdoor cafés. But the showpiece of the Piazza di Santa Maria is the 12th-century church of **Santa Maria in Trastevere.** The 13th-century mosaics on the church's facade—which add light and color to the piazza, especially at night when they are in spotlight—are believed to represent the Wise and Foolish Virgins. Inside, the enormous golden mosaic in the apse is the city's finest, a shining burst of Byzantine color and light set off by giant columns filched

from an ancient Roman building. Make sure to look down at the splendid Cosmati work, a mosaic style from the 12th and 13th centuries in which tiny squares and triangles were laid with larger stones to form geometric patterns, in the church floors. In August, processions honoring the Virgin Mary gather at the church as part of Trastevere's traditional feast, called *Festa de Noantri* (Our Own Feast). ⊠ *Piazza di Santa Maria, Trastevere* ☎ *06/5814802* ⊙ *Daily 7:30–1 and 4–7.*

❺❽ Sinagoga. The imposing, square-dome synagogue on the Tiber is a Roman landmark. The **Museo Ebraico** documents the history of the Jewish community in Rome. Most of the decorative crowns, prayer books, holy chairs, and tapestries dating from the 17th century were donated by prominent Jewish families whose ancestors once lived in the Ghetto. The collection is a change of pace from the predominantly Christian art found elsewhere in Rome. ⊠ *Lungotevere Cenci 15, Ghetto* ☎ *06/ 68400661* ⊠ *€7.50* ⊙ *Oct.–May, Mon.–Thurs. 9–5, Fri. 9–2, Sun. 9–noon; June–Sept., Mon.–Thurs. 9–7:30, Fri. 9–4, Sun. 9–noon.*

❺❺ Teatro di Marcello. The Teatro, hardly recognizable as a theater today, was originally designed to hold 20,000 spectators. It was begun by Julius Caesar; today, the 16th-century apartment building that sprouted out of its remains has become one of Rome's most prestigious residential addresses. The area south of the theater makes a grand stage for chamber music concerts in summer. ✉ *Via del Teatro di Marcello, Ghetto* ☎ *06/87131590 concert information* ⊕ *www.tempietto.it* ⊙ *Open during concerts only.*

Trastevere. This area consists of a maze of narrow streets that is still, despite evident gentrification, one of the city's most authentically Roman neighborhoods. Literally translated, its name means "across the Tiber," and indeed Trastevere and the Trasteverini—the neighborhood's natives—are a breed apart. The area is hardly undiscovered, but among its self-consciously picturesque trattorias and trendy tearooms you can also find old shops and dusty artisans' workshops in alleys festooned with laundry hung out to dry. Stroll along Via dell'Arco dei Tolomei and Via dei Salumi, shadowy streets showing the patina of the ages. One of the least affected parts of Trastevere centers on Piazza in Piscinula, north of Via dei Salumi and south of the Ponte Cestio Fabricio, where the smallest medieval church in the city, San Benedetto, stands opposite the restored medieval Casa dei Mattei.

57 **Via del Portico d'Ottavia.** Along this street in the heart of the Jewish Ghetto are buildings where medieval inscriptions, ancient friezes, and half-buried classical monuments attest to the venerable history of the neighborhood. The old **Chiesa di Sant'Angelo in Pescheria** was built right into the ruins of the Portico d'Ottavia, which was a monumental area enclosing a temple, library, and other buildings within colonnaded porticoes. ✉ *Ghetto.*

★ **64** **Villa Farnesina.** Money was no object to extravagant patron Agostino Chigi, a Sienese banker who financed many a papal project. His munificence is evident in his elegant villa, built about 1511. When Raphael could steal some precious time from his work on the Vatican Stanze and wooing Fornarina, he executed some of the frescoes, notably a luminous *Galatea.* Chigi delighted in impressing guests by having his servants cast precious dinnerware into the Tiber when it was time to clear the table. The guests didn't know of the nets he had stretched under the waterline to catch everything. ✉ *Via della Lungara 230, Trastevere* ☎ *06/68027268* ⊕ *www.lincei.it/informazioni/villafarnesina/index.php* 💳 *€5* ⊙ *Mon.–Sat. and 1st Sun. of month 9–1.*

Also Worth Seeing

65 **Palazzo Corsini.** This elegant palace holds the 16th- and 17th-century painting collection of the **Galleria Nazionale d'Arte Antica;** even if you're not interested in the paintings, stop in to climb the extraordinary 17th-century stone staircase, itself a drama of architectural shadows and sculptural voids. The adjacent Corsini gardens, now Rome's **Giardino Botanico,** offer delightful tranquillity, with native and exotic plants and a marvelous view at the top. ✉ *Via della Lungara 10, Trastevere* ☎ *06/68802323* ⊕ *www.galleriaborghese.it* 💳 *€4* ⊙ *Tues.–Sun. 8:30–1:30.*

52 **Piazza Bocca della Verità.** On the site of the Forum Boarium, ancient Rome's cattle market, this square was later used for public executions. Its name is derived from the marble Bocca della Verità (Mouth of Truth), a huge medieval drain cover in the form of an open-mouth face that is now set

VOICES OF ITALY

Dana Prescott
Artist/Arts Director, American Academy in Rome

For nearly two decades, Rome has been American artist Dana Prescott's home—and her muse. Between her painting and her work as Andrew Heiskell Arts Director of the venerable American Academy in Rome, she's immersed in the Eternal City's creative life. Dana shares some thoughts on the pleasures of her adopted hometown:

On Rome as inspiration: "I love Rome's ability to continue to surprise me. I bicycle around and keep falling in love with the shapes of things, the proportions, the sheer unfussy beauty of a city living and working amidst its monuments.

"As a painter, I tend to respond to things visually but somewhat randomly, so Rome is a perfect companion. From braided loaves of bread on a bakery shelf to the clutter of Porta Portese, from the polish on a Bernini sculpture to Italian moms wheeling kids around in baby carriages, from peeling facades to *ragazzi* on *motorini*, how ice cream is stacked in a gelateria, the twists on the end of a *bocconcino* of mozzarella, it's all a constant bombardment of visual stimulation."

On connecting with the ancient city: "Above all, take time in the Pantheon—not taking pictures there, just sitting. Feel the vast proportions, the amazing light, the swell of the floor. Move around; reconsider your position in time and space."

On her neighborhood, the Jewish Ghetto: "Its mesh of history, of humanity, of great food, its charming Turtle Fountain, *spoglie* (pieces of ancient stonework) tucked into facades, and its stories and legends all make the city instantly accessible."

On her favorite places: "I have so many. Sant'Ignazio, with its amazing anamorphic frescoes by Pozzo, how they change while you walk through the room. I love the botanical gardens (off Via della Lungara in Trastevere), especially the unmanicured edges of the park with bamboo and wildflowers sprawled all over the lawn. By far my favorite church is Santa Maria sopra Minerva, for its Filippino Lippi frescoes, the tomb of Saint Catherine, the Madonna of the Dowery by Antoniaccio Romano, the tomb of Fra Angelico—the patron saint for artists—and two-two!—Berninis and one Michelangelo. The list goes on and on: the Pantheon, Raphael's *Galatea* in the Villa Farnesina in Trastevere, Cavallino's scenes from the life of St. Mary at Santa Maria in Trastevere . . ."

On Rome's artistic spirit: "Every street corner reveals another trace of history or of a hand at work, a carving, a construction, a beautiful view. I don't need to go to a museum to see art and to feel its presence on a daily basis. Every fountain, church, roadway, facade—everything reveals the skill and labor of an artist or artisan. Rome humbles me."

into the entry portico of the 12th-century church of **Santa Maria in Cosmedin**. In the Middle Ages, legend had it that any person who told a lie with his hand in the mouth would have it chomped off. Today tour groups line up in this noisy, traffic-jammed piazza to give this ancient lie detector a go. ⊠ *Ghetto.*

⓺ **San Francesco a Ripa.** Ask the sacristan to show you the cell where St. Francis slept when he came to seek the pope's approval for his new order. Also in this church is one of Bernini's most dramatic sculptures, the figure of the *Blessed Ludovica Albertoni*, ecstatic at the prospect of entering heaven. ⊠ *Piazza San Francesco d'Assisi, Trastevere* ☎ *06/5819020* ⊙ *Daily 7–noon and 4–7:30.*

⓺ **San Pietro in Montorio.** One of Rome's key Renaissance buildings, the **Tempietto,** stands in the cloister of this church built by order of Ferdinand and Isabella of Spain in 1481. Bramante built the Tempietto over the spot where St. Peter was thought to have been crucified. It's an architectural gem and was one of his earliest and most successful attempts to design a building in an entirely classical style. ⊠ *Via Garibaldi, Gianicolo, Trastevere* ☎ *06/5813940* ⊙ *Church daily 8:30–noon and 1:30–5:30. Tempietto daily 8:30–noon and 3:30–5:30.*

⓺ **Santa Cecilia in Trastevere.** Mothers and children love to dally in the delightful little garden in front of this church. Duck inside for a look at the 9th-century mosaics and the languid statue of St. Cecilia under the altar. Fragments of a *Last Judgment* fresco cycle by Pietro Cavallini (circa 1250–1330), dating from the late 13th century, remain one of his most important works. Though the Byzantine-influenced fragments are obscured by the structure, what's left reveals a rich luminosity in the seated apostles' drapery and a remarkable depth in their expressions. A pretty cloister and remains of Roman houses are visible under the church. To see them, ask at the booth to the left of the main nave. ⊠ *Piazza Santa Cecilia, Trastevere* ☎ *06/5899289* 🎟 *Church free, frescoes €2.50* ⊙ *Daily 9:30–12:30 and 4–6:30; frescoes Mon.–Sat. 10:15–12:15, Sun. 11:15–noon.*

⓾ **Tempio della Fortuna Virilis.** This rectangular temple devoted to "manly fortune" dates from the 2nd century BC and is built in the Greek style, as was the norm in the early years of Rome. For its age, its remains are remarkably well preserved, in part due to its subsequent consecration as a Christian church. ⊠ *Piazza Bocca della Verità, near Piazza Venezia.*

⓾ **Tempio di Vesta.** All but 1 of the 20 original Corinthian columns in Rome's most evocative small ruin remain intact. It was built in the 2nd century BC. Researchers now believe the temple was devoted to Hercules by a successful olive merchant. ⊠ *Piazza Bocca dell Verità, near Piazza Venezia.*

Off the Beaten Path

Colle Aventino (Aventine Hill). One of the seven hills of ancient Rome, Aventino is now a quiet residential neighborhood that most tourists don't see. It's home to some of the city's oldest and least visited churches and some appealing views. There's a wide panorama of the city from the walled park next to the church of **Santa Sabina,** off Via Santa Sabina. Peek through the keyhole in the gate to the **Garden of the Knights of Malta** for a surprise perspective of the dome of St. Peter's. ⊠ *Piazza Cavalieri di Malta, Colle Aventino.*

The Catacombs & Via Appia Antica

The early Christian sites on the ancient Appian Way are some of the religion's oldest. Catacombs, where early Christians (whose religion prohibited cremation) buried their dead and gathered to worship in secret, lie below the very road where tradition says Christ appeared to St. Peter. The Via Appia Antica, built 400 years before, is a quiet, green place to walk and ponder the ancient world. The Rome APT office provides an informative free pamphlet for this itinerary.

Resist any temptation to undertake the 1½-km (1-mi) walk between Porta San Sebastiano and the catacombs; it's a dull and tiring hike on a heavily trafficked cobblestone road, with stone walls the only scenery. Instead, hop on Bus 660 from the Colli Albani metro stop on Line A to the end of the line, at Via Appia Antica. (Bus 218 from San Giovanni in Laterano also passes near the catacombs, but you have to walk about ½ km [¼ mi] east from Via Ardeatina to Via Appia Antica.) A slightly more-expensive but hassle-free option is to take Bus 110 from Piazza Venezia; it's air-conditioned and allows you to hop on and off as you please.

The Main Attractions

67 **San Callisto.** A friar will guide you through the crypts and galleries of the well-preserved San Callisto catacombs. ⊠ *Via Appia Antica 110* ☎*06/ 4465610* ⌨ €5 ☉ *Mar.–Jan., Thurs.–Tues. 8:30–12:30 and 2:30–5.*

68 **San Sebastiano.** The 4th-century catacomb, named for the saint who was buried here, burrows underground on four levels. The only one of the catacombs to remain accessible during the Middle Ages, it's the origin of the term *catacomb,* for it was in a spot where the road dips into a hollow, a place the Romans called *catacumbas* ("near the hollow"). Eventually the Christian cemetery that had existed here since the 2nd century came to be known by the same name, which was applied to all underground cemeteries discovered in Rome in later centuries. ⊠ *Via Appia Antica 136* ☎ *06/7850350* ⌨ €5 ☉ *Mid-Nov.–mid-Oct., Mon.–Sat. 9–noon and 2–5.*

70 **Tomba di Cecilia Metella.** The circular mausoleum of a Roman noblewoman, who lived at the time of Julius Caesar, was transformed into a fortress in the 14th century. The tomb houses a tiny museum with sculptures from the Via Appia Antica and an interesting reconstruction of the area's geological and historical past. ⊠ *Via Appia Antica 161* ☎ *06/ 78021465 or 06/39967700* ⊕ *www.pierreci.it* ⌨ €2 ☉ *Mon.–Sat. 9 –1hr before sunset.*

The Catacombs
& Via Appia Antica

★ **66** **Via Appia Antica.** This Queen of Roads, "Regina Viarium," was the most important of the extensive network of roads that traversed the Roman Empire, a masterful feat of engineering that made possible Roman control of a vast area by allowing for the efficient transport of armies and commercial goods. Completed in 312 BC by Appius Claudius, the road was ancient Europe's first highway, connecting Rome with Brindisi, 584 km (365 mi) away on the Adriatic coast. Part of the route exists as Via Appia (SS7), but it is a paved, modern highway. The stretch indicated here is closed to traffic; the ancient roadway passes through grassy fields and shady groves and by the villas of movie stars (Marcello Mastroianni and Gina Lollobrigida had homes here) and other VIPs. This part is still paved with the ancient *basoli* (basalt stones) over which the Romans drove their carriages—look for the wheel ruts. Taverns, houses, temples, and tombs flanked the ancient road, and the occasional lone statue, crumbling wall, or column is still visible, draped in ivy or alone in a patch of wildflowers. Pick a sunny day for your visit, wear comfortable shoes, and bring a bottle of water. You can take Bus 660 from the Colli Albani metro station Line A for Via Cecilia Metella at Via Appia Antica. ✉ *Exit Via Cristoforo Colombo at Circonvallazione Ardeatina, follow signs to Appia Antica parking lot.*

Also Worth Seeing

69 **Circo di Massenzio.** On the east side of Via Appia Antica are the ruins where the obelisk now in Piazza Navona once stood. ⊠ *Via Appia Antica 153* ☎ *06/7801324* ⊠ *€3* ⊙ *Tues.–Sun. 9–1.*

WHERE TO EAT

Updated by Dana Klitzberg

Rome has been known since ancient times for its great feasts and banquets, and though the days of the triclinium and the Saturnalia are long past, dining out is still the Romans' favorite pastime. The city is distinguished more by its good attitude toward eating out than by a multitude of world-class restaurants; simple, traditional cuisine reigns, although things are slowly changing as talented young chefs explore new culinary frontiers. Many of the city's restaurants cater to a clientele of regulars, and atmosphere and attitude are usually friendly and informal. The flip side is that in Rome the customer is not always right—the chef and waiters are in charge, and no one will beg forgiveness if you wanted *skim* milk in that cappuccino. Be flexible and you're sure to *mangiar bene* (eat well). Lunch is served from 12:30 to 2:30 and dinner from 8 until about 11, though some restaurants stay open later, especially in summer, when patrons linger at sidewalk tables to enjoy the parade of people and the *ponentino* (evening breeze).

WHAT IT COSTS In euros					
	$$$$	$$$	$$	$	¢
AT DINNER	over €45	€35–€45	€25–€35	€15–€25	under €15

Prices are for a first course *(primo)*, second course *(secondo)*, and dessert *(dolce)*.

Campo de' Fiori

★ **$$–$$$$** ✕ **Osteria del Pesce.** The entrance to this restaurant looks like an upscale *pescheria* (fish market). Awaiting you inside is seafood from the coast south of Rome that's beautiful enough to display like aquatic jewels: from starters such as tuna or sea bass carpaccio, to seafood pasta dishes, to secondi of grilled or sautéed fish and crustaceans, all is simply prepared and of the highest quality. The space—hardwood floors, subtle lighting, and walls in royal blue and chili-pepper red—brims with energy. The extensive wine list has mostly whites; there are numerous after-dinner liqueurs available. ⊠ *Via di Monserrato 32, near Campo de' Fiori* ☎ *06/6865617* ⊟ *AE, DC, MC, V* ⊙ *Closed Sun. and 2 wks in Aug. No lunch.*

$–$$$ ✕ **Roscioli.** Marco Roscioli opened this restaurant (with an upscale deli counter and wineshop) around the corner from his famous *forno* (bakery). The menu has a mix of tasty and often uncommon Italian meats and cheeses, as well as pasta and fish dishes, all of which are meant to be paired with one of the 800 wines. Try the homemade pasta with duck prosciutto or the potato gnocchi with sea-urchin sauce, or splurge on the foie gras. If you book ahead you can get a table in the cozy, appealing wine cellar. ⊠ *Via dei Giubbonari 21/22, near Campo de' Fiori* ☎ *06/6875287* ⊟ *AE, DC, MC, V* ⊙ *Closed Sun.*

$-$$ ╳ **Grappolo d'Oro Zampanò.** This Campo-area favorite has both a pizzeria and a restaurant, which serves eclectic regional Italian cuisine such as an eggplant flan with Gorgonzola sauce. Second courses include beef stewed in Sangiovese wine and a delicate grouper fillet oven-baked in foil with potatoes, tomatoes, and oregano. There's a well-selected (though not bargain-priced) wine list. ⊠ *Piazza della Cancelleria 80, near Campo de' Fiori* ☎ *06/6897080* ☱ *AE, MC, V* ☉ *Closed Mon. and Aug.*

¢-$ ╳ **Acchiapafantasmi.** The name translates as "ghostbusters," after the restaurant's award-winning pizza shaped like a ghost with mozzarella, cherry tomatoes, and oregano. But the menu extends beyond pizza to spicy treats of the Commisso brothers' native Calabria, such as the spreadable *'nduja* sausage (half pork, half hot peppers) and an innovative version of eggplant parmigiana. The gelato, brought up from the southern town of Pizzo Calabria, is considered by some the best in Italy. ⊠ *Via dei Cappellari 66, near Campo de' Fiori* ☎ *06/6873462* ⩘ *Reservations not accepted* ☱ *AE, DC, MC, V* ☉ *Closed Tues. and 1 wk in Aug.*

¢-$ ╳ **Le Piramidi.** Come here for great falafel, *schewerma* (spit-roasted meat, in this case veal), and other to-go Middle Eastern specialties. Sundry desserts are sure to include phyllo pastry, honey, and nuts. ⊠ *Vicolo del Gallo 11, Campo de' Fiori* ☎ *06/6879061* ☱ *No credit cards* ☉ *Closed Mon.*

¢ ╳ **Il Forno di Campo de' Fiori.** Crowds fill this counter-service pizzeria throughout the day. Try the *farcita* (stuffed) pizza, filled with meats, cheeses, vegetables—even prosciutto and warm figs in season—at their adjacent sandwich bar. ⊠ *Piazza Campo de' Fiori 22* ☎ *06/66806662* ⩘ *Reservations not accepted* ☱ *No credit cards* ☉ *Closed Sun.*

Piazza di Spagna

$-$$$ ╳ **Dal Bolognese.** The classic Dal Bolognese is both a convenient shopping-spree lunch spot and an in-crowd dinner destination. The tables on the expansive pedestrian piazza are prime people-watching real estate, and tables inside are perfectly spaced for table-hopping and lots of two-cheek kisses. As the name promises, the cooking here adheres to the hearty tradition of Bologna, with delicious homemade tortellini *in brodo* (in broth), fresh pastas in creamy sauces, and steaming trays of boiled meats. Among the desserts, try the *dolce della mamma* (a concoction of gelato, zabaglione, and chocolate sauce) and the fruit-shape gelato. ⊠ *Piazza del Popolo 1, near Piazza di Spagna* ☎ *06/3611426* ☱ *AE, DC, MC, V* ☉ *Closed Mon. and Aug.*

$$ ╳ **Il Palazzetto.** At this small restaurant by the Spanish Steps is part of the International Wine Academy of Rome. Chef Antonio Martucci creates seasonal menus using traditional Roman ingredients, to which he gives a unique "twist" in preparation and flavor pairings. Stuffed calamari on an eggplant puree with sautéed baby peppers is a study in contrasting flavor and texture; homemade ricotta-filled gnocchi with sausage and asparagus hits all the right notes. It's wise to call in advance, both for reservations and to find out about regular prix-fixe dinners, sometimes with guest chefs, focusing on wine-food pairings. ⊠ *Vicolo del Bottino 8, Piazza di Spagna* ☎ *06/6990878* ☱ *AE, DC, MC, V.*

$-$$ ╳ **GINA.** "Homey minimalism" isn't a contradiction at this whitewashed café with a modern edge (block seats, single flowers in mason jars, white chandeliers, mirrors). With a reasonable menu of salads, sandwiches, pastas, and American-style desserts, this is the perfect spot for a late lunch or a light dinner that won't break the bank despite the high-end neighborhood. Upscale picnic baskets are stocked and ready to pick up on the way to nearby Villa Borghese. For a relaxed Saturday evening, join the friendly owners for live jazz from 9:30 to midnight. ⊠ *Via San Sebastianello 7A, near Piazza di Spagna* ☎ *06/6780251* ▤ *AE, MC, V* ⊙ *Closed Sun. and Aug.*

★ **$-$$**   ✕ **Osteria della Frezza.** You can get regular tavern fare and service at this member of the 'Gusto restaurant empire (which dominates the surrounding block), or you can sample *cicchetti* (Venetian dialect for bar snacks). These are miniature portions of what's on the regular menu: cured meats and a head-spinning selection of cheeses; cooked meats like lamb chops and meatballs in tomato sauce; and pastas, including thick spaghetti with octopus, tomato, and pecorino cheese. Homemade desserts are also available in tiny portions. The wine list is full of interesting choices; trust the knowledgable staff to point you in the right direction. ⊠ *Via della Frezza 16, near Piazza di Spagna* ☎ *06/3226273* ▤ *AE, DC, MC, V.*

Piazza Navona & the Pantheon

$$$$ ✕ **Il Convivio.** The Troiani brothers came to Rome in the late 1980s; since
Fodor'sChoice   then they've been the leaders of a small circle of top Italian food elite.
★   Their inventive fare can be characterized as Italian cuisine revisited—classic dishes made from the best ingredients, given a unique, elegant tweak. The raw "lacquered" tuna and the foie gras are luscious starters, and a delicious squid ink risotto has Asian touches of lemongrass and Thai basil. For secondi, the pigeon is exquisitely cooked, and the fish are all first-rate. Desserts are delicious, if a bit restrained, service is excellent, and the wine selection, although pricey, would impress any connoisseur. ⊠ *Vicolo dei Soldati 31, near Piazza Navona* ☎ *06/6869432* ⌲ *Reservations essential* ▤ *AE, DC, MC, V* ⊙ *Closed Sun., 1 wk in Jan., and 2 wks in Aug. No lunch.*

★ **$$$-$$$$**   ✕ **Myosotis.** Don't overlook the traditional Myosotis in favor of trendier choices in the area. Secondi include a hearty veal chop *alla Milanese*, breaded and panfried, as well as a delicate catch of the day in a garlic, olive oil, and tomato broth. A soup of whitefish, fava beans, and chicory is a study in bittersweet. The chocolate mousse in chocolate raspberry sauce is elegant in its simplicity. Bright and fresh, the space has parquet floors, creamy table linens, and walls sponge-painted the color of fresh fettuccine. Service is sometimes slow, but owners and staff obviously care about the food. ⊠ *Vicolo della Vaccarella 3/5, near Piazza Navona* ☎ *06/6865554* ▤ *AE, DC, MC, V* ⊙ *Closed 2 wks in Aug.*

$$$-$$$$ ✕ **Romilo.** The name represents three locations where the owner wants to open a restaurant: Rome, Milan, and London. So far it's one out of three. Despite the cosmopolitan ambitions, Romilo does best with traditional Roman cuisine—the more-gimmicky dishes from chef Vito Specchia (formerly of Hotel de Russie and La Pergola) can fall flat. So stick to a delicious mushroom risotto, or a basic-but-satisfying fillet of beef with red-wine reduction and potato gratin. Desserts (almost exclusively frozen) are tasty, and the wine list has some interesting offerings

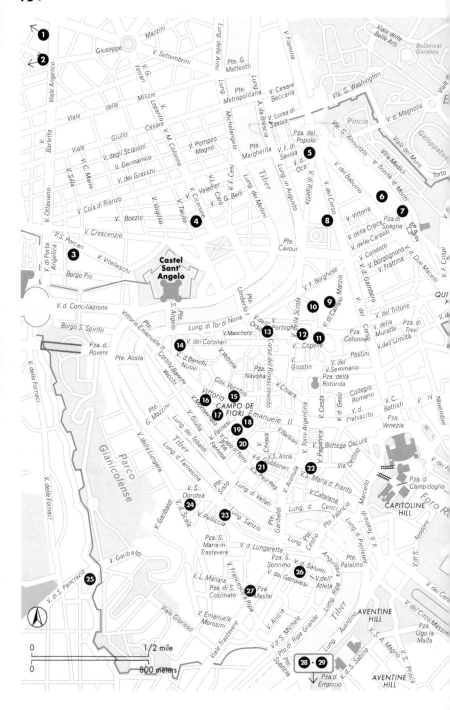

Where to Eat in Rome

EATING WELL IN ROME

ROMAN COOKING IS SIMPLE, rustic cuisine, perfected over centuries. Dishes rarely have more than a few ingredients, and meat and fish are most often roasted, baked, or grilled. The best meat is often *abbacchio* (milk-fed lamb)–legs are usually roasted with rosemary and potatoes, and chops served *alla scottadito* (literally "burn your finger"–hot off the grill). Most Mediterranean fish are light yet flavorful, among them *spigola* (the Roman name for sea bass, more commonly called *branzino* elsewhere), *orata* (gilthead bream), and *rombo* (turbot). Romans swoon for batter-fried *baccalà* (cod).

The quintessential Roman pasta dishes are made with *guanciale* (cured pork cheek) and pecorino Romano cheese. *All'amatriciana* adds onion and tomato to the mix and is classically served with *bucatini* (a thick, hollow spaghetti); *alla carbonara* tosses the pork and cheese with egg yolk and black pepper; and *alla gricia* is amatriciana without tomatoes. Potato gnocchi with a tomato sauce and Parmesan or pecorino is a favorite for Thursday dinner.

Seasonal vegetables may not appear on the menu but are usually available. Romans love their greens–*cicoria* and *spinaci ripassati* (sautéed chicory and spinach) are perennial favorites–and many restaurants specialize in vegetable *fritto misto* (literally "mixed fried"). Rome is famous for *carciofi* (artichokes)–available from November to April–prepared *alla romana* (stuffed with garlic and mint and braised) or *alla giudia*

(fried whole, making each petal crisp). A springtime treat is *vignarola*, a mixture of tender peas, fava beans, artichokes, and guanciale.

Typical wines of Rome are from the Castelli Romani, the towns in the hills to the southeast: Frascati, Colli Albani, Marino, and Velletri. Though Roman tap water is the best in Italy, restaurants usually offer bottled water, either *gassata* or *frizzante* (sparkling) or *liscia* (still).

It was not so long ago that wine in Rome (and other towns) was strictly local; you didn't have to walk far to find an *osteria*, a tavernlike establishment where you could buy wine straight from the barrel or sit down to drink and nibble a bit, chat, or play cards. The tradition continues today, as many Roman wineshops are also open as *enoteche* (wine bars). Most have done away with the folding chairs and rickety tables in favor of designer interiors, chic ambience, and excellent menus. Shelves are lined with hundreds of bottles from all over the country, representing the best in Italian wine making, and many selections are available by the glass. Behind the bar you'll usually find a sommelier or at least a serious wine enthusiast.

at a fair markup. ✉ *Via di Campo Marzio 13* ☎ *06/6893499* 🍴 *AE, DC, MC, V* 🕙 *Closed Sun.*

$$$–$$$$ ✗ **Sangallo.** This quiet and intimate restaurant snuggled between Piazza Navona and the Pantheon serves high-quality seafood. The owner hails from Anzio, a coastal town south of Rome. The menu has some sophisticated touches, such as oysters tartare, snapper with foie gras, and pasta dishes made with toothsome *Gragnano* pasta (made in Gragnano of 100% Italian wheat, and dried to strict specifications). There are precious few tables in the tiny dining room, so make sure to book ahead. ✉ *Vicolo della Vaccarella 11/a, near Piazza Navona* ☎ *06/6865549* 🍴 *Reservations essential* 🍴 *AE, DC, MC, V* 🕙 *Closed Sun., 1 wk in Jan., and 2 wks in Aug. No lunch Mon.*

$–$$ ✗ **Ōbikā.** The owners of this concept restaurant are trying something original: a "mozzarella bar," with choices ranging from the familiar cow's-milk variety to delectable buffalo-milk mozzarella to sinfully rich *burrata* (fresh cow's-milk mozzarella encasing a creamy center of unspun curds). You can get cured meats, vegetables, sauces, and breads to accompany your cheese, and salads and pasta dishes, including interesting lasagnas, are also on the menu. The wines, like the mozzarella, tend to come from the southern Italian regions. ✉ *Piazza di Firenze and Via dei Prefetti, near Pantheon* ☎ *06/6832630* 🍴 *AE, DC, MC, V.*

★ $ ✗ **Cul de Sac.** This is a classic Roman *enoteca* (wine bar), frequented by everyone from local soccer fans to the Fendi sisters. Quarters are cramped, both inside and out on the small piazza, but once you begin sipping the wine and sampling the food, you realize it's worth any discomfort. The selection of Italian regional cheeses and cured meats is vast, and the soups, pastas, and salads have homemade appeal. Especially refreshing are the international dishes: hummus, Greek salad, and pâtés that can be difficult to find in these parts. The wine list is tremendous and constantly changing. ✉ *Piazza Pasquino 73, near Piazza Navona* ☎ *06/68801094* 🍴 *AE, MC, V* 🕙 *Closed 2 wks in Aug.*

San Pietro

$$$$ ✗ **La Pergola.** High atop Monte Mario, the Cavalieri Hilton's rooftop restaurant has a commanding view of the city below. Trompe-l'oeil ceilings and handsome wood paneling combine with low lighting to enhance the intimate dining experience. Celebrated wunder-chef Heinz Beck brings Rome its most polished example of Mediterranean *alta cucina* (haute cuisine): dishes are balanced and light (a perfectly cooked lobster) and presentation is striking (a plate of spiraling sea scallops and black truffles, each one the exact same size). For a window table reserve a month in advance; for others, two weeks. ✉ *Cavalieri Hilton, Via Cadlolo 101, Monte Mario* ☎ *06/3509221* 🍴 *Reservations essential* 🍴 *Jacket and tie* 🍴 *AE, DC, MC, V* 🕙 *Closed Sun. and Mon., and 2 wks in Dec. No lunch.*

Fodor's Choice
★

$$–$$$$ ✗ **Il Simposio di Costantini.** The most sophisticated wine bar in town is done in wood paneling and velvet, and has sculptured iron vines as decoration. Here you can choose from about 30 wines by the glass. Food is appropriately fancy: marinated and smoked fish, composed salads, top-quality salami and other cured meats, terrines and pâtés, vegetable dishes, and several inventive secondi, mostly meat-game selections. Finish off with a plate from an assortment of 80 cheeses grouped according to origin or type, and a well-balanced dessert menu. ⊠ *Piazza Cavour 16, near San Pietro* ☎ *06/3211502* ⊟ *AE, DC, MC, V* ☉ *Closed Sun. and last 2 wks of Aug. No lunch Sat.*

$$ ✕ **Alfredo e Ada.** Squeeze into a table at this lovable hole-in-the-wall and make yourself at home. There's no menu, just plate after plate of whatever Ada thinks you should try, from hearty, classic pastas to *involtini di vitello* (savory veal rolls with tomato) and homemade sausage. Sit back, relax, and enjoy—it's all good. By the time you leave you may have made some new friends, too. The cost depends on how many courses you eat and how much wine you consume, but an average meal might run around €25. Alfredo e Ada is across the river from Castel Sant'Angelo. ⊠ *Via dei Banchi Nuovi 14, near San Pietro* ☎ *06/6878842* ⊟ *No credit cards* ☉ *Closed weekends.*

$$ ✕ **Taverna Angelica.** The area surrounding St. Peter's Basilica isn't known for culinary excellence, but Taverna Angelica is an exception to the rule. The chef takes care with each dish, and the results are impressive: lentil soup with pigeon breast, duck in balsamic vinegar, and warm octopus salad on a bed of mashed potatoes with a basil-parsley pesto drizzle are all exquisitely executed. The narrow, candlelit dining room has plenty of space between tables; excellent service is icing on the cake. ⊠ *Piazza A. Capponi 6, near San Pietro* ☎ *06/6874514* ⌂ *Reservations essential* ⊟ *AE, V.*

★ **$–$$**   ✕ **Siciliainbocca.** Looking for a straight-up, no-nonsense Sicilian restaurant? The owners, both Sicily natives, decided to open up Siciliainbocca after years of frustration at not finding a decent pasta *alla norma,* with eggplant, tomato sauce, and aged ricotta cheese. Try the risotto *ai profumi di Sicilia,* with lemon, orange, mozzarella, and zucchini. You might also opt for the delicious grilled swordfish, shrimp, or squid. Even in the dead of winter, Siciliainbocca's yellow walls and brightly colored ceramic plates are warming. There's outdoor seating in summer. ⊠ *Via E. Faà di Bruno 26, near San Pietro* ☎ *06/37358400* ⊟ *AE, DC, MC, V* ☉ *Closed Sun.*

Near Termini & San Lorenzo

★ **$$$$**   ✕ **Agata e Romeo.** The husband-and-wife team of Agata Parisella and Romeo Caraccio runs one of Rome's top restaurants. Agata puts an inspired twist on Roman cuisine with dishes such as crepes with chestnut flour and ewe's-milk ricotta, and breaded lamp chops. Romeo acts as maître d' and expert sommelier. The tasting menu, complete with wine, changes monthly to reflect seasonal dishes and allows you to try a range of specialties. Desserts are scrumptious and the wine list is excellent. ⊠ *Via Carlo Alberto 45, near Termini* ☎ *06/4466115* ⊟ *AE, DC, MC, V* ☉ *Closed weekends, 2 wks in July, and 2 wks in Aug.*

$$$–$$$$ ✕ **F.I.S.H.** The name stands for Fine International Seafood House, which sums up the kitchen's approach. This is fresh, fresh fish in capable and creative hands—from Italian fish-based pastas to a Thai mollusk soup with lemongrass and coconut milk that's a party for the senses. The menu is divided into three sections: sushi, Asian, and Mediterranean. Seating is limited, so book ahead. ⊠ *Via dei Serpenti 16, Monti* ☎ *06/47824962* ⌂ *Reservations essential* ⊟ *AE, D, MC, V* ☉ *Closed Mon. and 2 wks in Aug.*

$$–$$$ ✕ **Bistro.** The high, pale-yellow arched ceilings, immense gilt mirrors, rich oak paneling, and wrought-iron bar counter here are all true to the art nouveau style. Chef Emanuele Vizzini serves fusion dishes such as fettuccine *al cabernet con scampi* (with red wine, shrimp, and vegetables) and *Nasdaq taglionini* (dollar-green pasta made with curaçao liqueur) topped with lobster. The wine list has 300 labels to choose from (12 available by the glass). ⊠ *Via Palestro 40, Termini* ☎ *06/44702868* ⊟ *AE, DC, MC, V* ⊘ *No lunch Sun.*

$$–$$$ ✕ **Trattoria Monti.** The cuisine of the Marches region is underrepresented in Rome, especially considering that more Marchegiani live here than in the region itself. Trattoria Monti fulfills their desire for home cooking. The hearty dishes include soups and roasted meats and game. A selection of soufflés and timbales, generally vegetarian, changes seasonally. For dessert there are cheeses with dried fruits, nuts, and honey. The brothers who run the place are always welcoming. ⊠ *Via San Vito 13/a, Esquilino* ☎ *06/4466573* ⊟ *AE, DC, MC, V* ⊘ *Closed Aug., 2 wks at Easter, and 10 days at Christmas.*

★ **$$** ✕ **Uno e Bino.** This restaurant in an artsy corner of the San Lorenzo neighborhood is popular with Romans from all over town. The kitchen turns out inventive cuisine inspired by the owner's Umbrian and Sicilian roots. Octopus salad with asparagus and carrots is a specialty, and perfectly prepared pigeon can satisfy the most critical foodies on an autumn night. ⊠ *Via degli Equi 58, San Lorenzo* ☎ *06/4460702* ⊟ *AE, D, MC, V* ⊘ *Closed Mon. and Aug. No lunch.*

$ ✕ **Arancia Blu.** Owner-chef Fabio Passan has a mission—to prove that "vegetarian cuisine" isn't an oxymoron. He succeeds, with creative dishes that have won him a devoted omnivorous clientele. Start with a leek-and-almond quiche or lemon-ricotta ravioli with squash and sage, and move on to *polpettine vegetali* (meatless meatballs) with a tomato-and-coriander-seed sauce. For dessert you might tickle your palate with a chocolate tasting: 14 chocolate wafers of different flavors and origins. Vegan and wheat-free dishes are available on request. ⊠ *Via dei Latini 65, San Lorenzo* ☎ *06/4454105* ⊟ *No credit cards* ⊘ *No lunch.*

$ ✕ **Pommidoro.** Mamma's in the kitchen and the rest of the family greets, serves, and keeps you happy and well fed at this trattoria popular with artists, filmmakers, and actors. It's near Rome's main university in the countercultural San Lorenzo neighborhood, a short cab ride east of the Termini train station. The menu has especially good grilled meats and game birds as well as classic home-style *cucina*. You can dine outside in warm weather. ⊠ *Piazza dei Sanniti 44, San Lorenzo* ☎ *06/4452692* ⊟ *AE, DC, MC, V* ⊘ *Closed Sun. and Aug.*

$ ✕ **La Soffitta.** This is Rome's hottest spot for classic Neapolitan pizza (thick-crusted, though crunchy on the bottom, rather than paper-thin and crispy like the Roman kind); it's one of the few pizzerias in town certified by the True Neapolitan Pizza Association. Desserts are brought in daily from Naples. You pay more here, but hey, it's imported. ⊠ *Via dei Villini 1/e, Termini* ☎ *06/4404642* ⌖ *Reservations not accepted* ⊟ *AE, DC, MC, V* ⊘ *Closed Aug. 10–31. No lunch.*

★ **¢–$** ✕ **Cavour 313.** Wine bars are popping up all over the city, but Cavour 313 has been around for a while, and it's easy to understand its stay-

Pizza, Roman Style

CLOSE UP

PIZZA MAY HAVE BEEN invented somewhere else, but in Rome it's hard to walk a block without encountering it in one form or another. You'll see it in bakeries, usually made without cheese—either pizza bianca (just olive oil and salt) or pizza rossa (with tomato sauce). Many small shops specialize in pizza al taglio (by the slice), priced by the etto (100 grams, about 1/4 pound), according to the kind of topping. These places are great for a snack on the go any time of day.

But don't leave Rome without sitting down to a classic, wafer-thin, crispy Roman pizza in a lively, no-frills pizzeria. Most are open only for dinner, usually from 8 PM to midnight. Look for a place with a *forno a legna* (wood-burning oven), a must for a good thin crust on your plate-size Roman pizza. Standard models are the margherita (tomato, mozzarella, and basil) and the capricciosa (a little bit of everything, depending upon the "caprices" of the pizza chef: tomato, mozzarella, sausage, olives, artichoke hearts, prosciutto, even egg), and most pizzerias have a long list of additional options, including tasty mozzarella *di bufala* (made from buffalo milk).

---

ing power. Well-prepared food options include cured meats, cheeses, and salads. Choose from about 25 wines by the glass or uncork a bottle (there are more than 1,200) and linger. ⊠ *Via Cavour 313, Colosseo* ☎ *06/ 6785496* ⊟ *AE, DC, MC, V* ⊗ *Closed Aug. No lunch weekends. No dinner Sun. June 15–Sept.*

Trastevere, Testaccio & the Ghetto

$$-$$$$ ✕ **Ferrara.** What used to be a well-stocked wine bar with a few nibbles has expanded to become a full-fledged restaurant, wine bar, and gastronomic boutique—known as the "Ferrara block." It's a modernist destination with a frequently changing menu and tasty antipasti and primi. Consistency is neither the kitchen's nor the servers' strong point: you can have a wonderful experience one visit and a drawn-out, disappointing meal the next. The wine list never lets you down though, and the sinful desserts end things on a positive note. ⊠ *Via del Moro 1A, Trastevere* ☎ *06/58333920* ⊟ *DC, MC, V* ⊗ *Closed Tues. and 2 wks in Aug.*

$$$ ✕ **Il Sanpietrino.** Tucked away in a tiny corner of the Jewish Ghetto, this historic restaurant (named for the cobblestones that line its floors) serves fresh, simple preparations of Roman staples and a few more-distinctive dishes. Appetizers like the local Jewish-style fried artichokes are lip-smacking good, and homemade gnocchi with a white (tomatoless) rabbit ragu are light, fluffy pillows of potato heaven. ⊠ *Piazza Costaguti 15, Ghetto* ☎ *06/68806471* ⊟ *AE, DC, MC, V* ⊗ *Closed Sun. No lunch.*

$$-$$$ ✕ **Antico Arco.** Founded by three friends with a passion for wine and fine food, Antico Arco has won the hearts of foodies from Rome and beyond with its culinary inventiveness and high style. The menu changes

with the season, but you may find such delights as *flan di taleggio con salsa di funghi* (cheese flan with mushrooms), or a *carré d'agnello* (rack of lamb) with foie-gras sauce and pears in port wine. Don't miss the chocolate soufflé with melted chocolate center: it's justly famous among chocoholics all over the city. ✉ *Piazzale Aurelio 7, Trastevere* ☎ *06/5815274* ⟐ *Reservations essential* ▤ *AE, DC, MC, V* ⊘ *Closed Sun. and 2 wks in Aug. No lunch.*

$$–$$$ ✕ **Spirito di Vino.** At this restaurant on the less-traveled side of Viale Trastevere, the food ranges from inventive (mini meatballs seasoned with coriander) to traditional (spaghetti with *cacio,* an aged sheep's milk cheese) to ancient (braised pork shoulder with apple and leeks—from a recipe by Apicius, Rome's first cookbook author). The dining room is welcoming and refined, with walls in tomato-red and dark wood. The proud owner is happy to explain every dish on the menu and give you the history of his wine cellar, where several ancient sculptures, now in the Vatican and Capitoline museums, were unearthed. ✉ *Via dei Genovesi 31 A/B, Trastevere* ☎ *06/5896689* ▤ *AE, MC, V* ⊘ *Closed Sun. and 2 wks in Aug.*

★ $–$$ ✕ **Alle Fratte.** Here staple Roman trattoria fare shares the menu with dishes that have a Neapolitan slant: spaghetti carbonara, as well as penne *alla Sorrentina,* with tomato, basil, and fresh mozzarella, for example. Try the pressed octopus carpaccio with arugula to start, followed by a mixed seafood pasta or a grilled sea bass with oven-roasted potatoes. Ask about daily specials, too—always worth a try. Boisterous owner Francesco, his American relatives, and their trusted waiter Peppe make you feel at home. ✉ *Via delle Fratte di Trastevere 49/50* ☎ *06/5835775* ▤ *AE, DC, MC, V* ⊘ *Closed Wed. and 2 wks in Aug.*

$–$$ ✕ **Perilli.** A bastion of authentic Roman cooking since 1911 (the decor has changed little), this trattoria is the place to go to try rigatoni *con pajata* (with calves' intestines)—if you're into that sort of thing. The pasta carbonara is also a classic. House wine is a hearty white from the Castelli Romani estate. ✉ *Via Marmorata 39, Testaccio* ☎ *06/5742415* ▤ *AE, DC, MC, V* ⊘ *Closed Wed.*

★ ¢–$ ✕ **Dar Poeta.** It's always crowded and lively at this innovative pizzeria, which serves both Roman-style (paper-thin) and the thicker Neapolitan variety. Topping choices go beyond the usual: try the house specialty with sautéed zucchini, sausage, and hot pepper. There are several types of *bruschette* (grilled breads with toppings) and salads. A must-try: the dessert calzone, filled with ricotta cheese and chocolate-hazelnut Nutella. ✉ *Vicolo del Bologna, Trastevere* ☎ *06/5880516* ▤ *AE, MC, V.*

¢–$ ✕ **Remo.** Expect a wait at this perennial favorite in Testaccio frequented by students and neighborhood locals. You won't find tablecloths or other nonessentials, just classic Roman pizza and boisterous conversation. ✉ *Piazza Santa Maria Liberatrice 44, Testaccio* ☎ *06/5746270* ⟐ *Reservations not accepted* ▤ *No credit cards* ⊘ *Closed Sun., Aug., and Christmas wk. No lunch.*

Via Veneto

$$$$ ✕ **La Terrazza dell'Eden.** The Hotel Eden's La Terrazza restaurant has an unparalleled view of Rome's seven hills and food that's just as spectacular. The culinary expertise of the well-traveled young chef is reflected in his refined touch with Mediterranean dishes and his pairing the finest primary ingredients with unusual accents like candied celery and pearl barley. If you're a wine enthusiast, ask the maître d' to let you view the restaurant's showcase cellar. ⊠ *Hotel Eden, Via Ludovisi 49, near Via Veneto* ☎ *06/47812752* ⌁ *Reservations essential* 🏛 *Jacket and tie* ⊟ *AE, DC, MC, V.*

★ **$$$–$$$$** ✕ **Papá Baccus.** Italo Cipriani takes his meat as seriously as any Tuscan; in fact he imports what he serves here from his home region. Prized Chianina beef is used for the house-specialty *bistecca alla fiorentina,* a thick grilled steak left rare in the middle. Try the sweet and delicate prosciutto from Pratomagno or the *ribollita* (a traditional bread-based, minestrone-like soup). The welcome is warm, the service excellent. ⊠ *Via Toscana 36, near Via Veneto* ☎ *06/42742808* ⊟ *AE, DC, MC, V* ⊗ *Closed Sun. and 2 wks in Aug. No lunch Sat.*

$$$–$$$$ ✕ **Tullio.** For years members of the international business and the entertainment industries have frequented this upscale trattoria. The decor is basic—wood paneling and white linens—with the requisite older, often grumpy, waiters. But fresh seafood is available in abundance, as are greens such as *brocoletti* (broccoli florets), sautéed to perfection with garlic and olive oil. The menu is heavy on Tuscan classics such as ribollita and grilled steak; the wild-hare sauce, served over flat noodles, is delectable. The wine list favors robust Tuscan reds (for which you pay a hefty markup). ⊠ *Via San Nicola da Tolentino 26, off Piazza Barberini, near Via Veneto* ☎ *06/4745560* ⊟ *AE, DC, MC, V* ⊗ *Closed Aug.*

Cafés

Café-sitting is the most popular leisure-time activity in Rome, practiced by all and involving nothing more strenuous than gesturing to catch the waiter's eye. Cafés are meant for relaxing, chatting with a companion, and watching the passing parade, possibly within view of one of the city's spectacular fountains or churches. Part of the pleasure is resting your tired feet; you won't be rushed, even when the cafés are most crowded, just before lunch and dinner. (Be aware, though, that you pay for your seat—prices are higher at tables than at the counter.) Nearly every corner in Rome holds a faster-paced coffee bar, where locals stop for a quick caffeine hit at the counter. You can get coffee drinks, fruit juices, pastries, sandwiches, liquor, and beer there, too.

Pricey **Antico Caffè Greco** (⊠ Via Condotti 86, near Piazza di Spagna ☎ 06/6791700) is a national landmark popular with tourists; its red-velvet chairs and marble tables have hosted the likes of Byron, Shelley, Keats, Goethe, and Casanova. **Rosati** (⊠ Piazza del Popolo 5, near Piazza di Spagna ☎ 06/3225859) is Piazza del Popolo's premier people-watching spot. Tables on the car-free square fill up quickly on weekends, when it seems the whole city is here. **Ciampini** (⊠ Piazza San Lorenzo in Lucina 29, near Piazza di Spagna ☎ 06/6876606), in a jewel of a piazza off Via del Corso, is a prime spot for a predinner aperitivo. Be sure to ask for the free *assaggini* (Italian hors d'oeuvres). **Zoe Caffè** (⊠ Via della Colonna Antonina 42, near Pantheon ☎ 06/69380930) offers the usual café fare but also a lovely selection of sweets.

Antico Caffè della Pace (⊠ Via della Pace 3, near Piazza Navona ☎ 06/6861216) is ornate and old-fashioned. Inside, cozy candlelight is a treat, or you can sit outside by ivy-lined walls in warm weather. **Caffè Sant'Eustachio** (⊠ Piazza Sant'Eustachio 82, near Pantheon ☎ 06/6861309) makes one of the smoothest cappuccinos anywhere. The secret? *Crema di caffè* (coffee cream)—a rich, homemade addition slipped into each cup. If you want your *caffè* (espresso) without sugar, ask for it *amaro*. **Tazza d'Oro** (⊠ Via degli Orfani 84, near Pantheon ☎ 06/6789792) serves some of the best coffee in the city, as well as decadent *granita di caffè* (iced espresso) with a thick dollop of whipped cream mixed in.

Gelato & Pastry

For Italians, gelato is more a snack than a dessert. Romans are not known for having a sweet tooth, but there are a few *pasticcerie* (pastry shops) in town that distinguish themselves with particularly good examples of regional desserts.

Gelateria Duomo (⊠ Largo Arenula 27, near Campo de' Fiori ☎ 320/1633871) specializes in artisanal, all-natural gelato. **Il Gelato di San Crispino** (⊠ Via della Panetteria 42, near Piazza di Trevi ☎ 06/6793924), closed Tuesday, is perhaps the most celebrated gelato in all of Italy, made without artificial colors or flavors. It's worth crossing town for.

Giolitti (⊠ Via Uffici del Vicario 40, near Pantheon ☎ 06/6991243), off Via Campo Marzio, has a quaint tearoom and delicious fruit-flavor gelato. **Fiocco di Neve** (⊠ Via del Pantheon 51 ☎ 06/6786025) is renowned for its zabaglione and *riso bianco* (white rice) ice cream.

Fonte della Salute (⊠ Via Cardinal Marmaggi 2, Trastevere ☎ 06/5897471), literally "fountain of health," serves frozen yogurt as well as traditional gelato. It's closed Tuesday in winter. **Forno del Ghetto** (⊠ Via del Portico d'Ottavia 1, Ghetto ☎ 06/6878637) preserves a tradition of Italian-Jewish sweets that cannot be found anywhere else. The ricotta cake (with sour-cherry jam or chocolate) is unforgettable. This hole-in-the-wall—no sign, no tables, just a take-out counter—is a neighborhood fixture. It's closed Friday at sundown, Saturday, and Jewish holidays. The apple strudel and Sacher torte at **Dolceroma** (⊠ Via del Portico d'Ottavia 20/b, Ghetto ☎ 06/6892196) may not be Italian, but this is a popular spot just the same. Prices have become a bit outrageous. It's closed Sunday afternoon, Monday, and four weeks in July and August.

Dagnino (⊠ Galleria Esedra, Via Vittorio Emanuele Orlando 75, near Termini ☎ 06/4818660) is an outpost of Sicilian sweets. The pastries, such as ricotta-filled cannoli and *cassata* (sponge cake with sheep's ricotta and candied fruit), as well as colorful marzipan candies, are exquisite. For decades, **Muse** (⊠ Via Eleanora Duse 1E, Parioli ☎ 06/8079300), popularly known as da Giovanni (after the owner), has been a mecca for Romans in the know. Winter flavors include chestnut and almond. It's closed Sunday.

WHERE TO STAY

Updated by
Dana Klitzberg

Appearances can be misleading in Rome: crumbling stucco facades may promise little from the outside, but they often hide interiors of considerable elegance. By the same token, elaborate reception areas may lead to surprisingly plain, even dilapidated, rooms. Generally, rooms tend to be small by U.S. standards. Many of the lower-priced hotels are actually old-fashioned *pensioni* (boardinghouses) set on one or several floors of a large building. One disadvantage of staying in central hotels in lower categories is noise; you can ask for an inside room if you are a light sleeper, but you may end up looking out on a dark courtyard. The grand monuments to luxury and elegance are around the major piazzas and Via Veneto.

Rome is a year-round destination, so you should always try to make reservations, even if only a few days in advance. Always ask about special rates, often available in both winter and summer if occupancy is low. If you arrive in Rome without reservations, try **Hotel Reservation Service** (☎ 06/6991000), with an English-speaking operator available daily 7 AM–10 PM, and with desks at Aeroporto Fiumicino and Stazione Termini. A list of all the hotels in Rome, with prices and facilities, is available from the main **APT information office** (⊠ Via Parigi 5, Termini ☎ 06/48899255 ⊕ www.romaturismo.it).

WHAT IT COSTS In euros				
$$$$	**$$$**	**$$**	**$**	**¢**
FOR 2 PEOPLE over €290	€210–€290	€140–€210	€80–€140	under €80

Prices are for two people in a standard double room in high season.

Campo de' Fiori

$$$–$$$$ 🏨 **Hotel Ponte Sisto.** Staying near the pedestrian bridge that connects the Campo de' Fiori neighborhood to Trastevere provides the convenience of the city center and access to the trattorias and bars of Trastevere, an area popular with both Romans and expats. Once the palazzo of the noble Venetian Palottini family, the hotel now has clean and bright, if basic, rooms. Wall-to-wall carpeting and green-marble bathrooms add refinement, but the real draw is the large internal courtyard, where you can get sun, read beneath the shade of the enormous palms, and sip cocktails under the stars. ⊠ *Off Ponte Sisto, Via dei Pettinari 64, Campo de' Fiori, 00186* ☎ *06/686310* 🖷 *06/68301712* ⊕ *www.hotelpontesisto. it* ➭ *103 rooms, 4 suites* ⚭ *Dining room, in-room safes, minibars, cable TV, bar, meeting rooms, parking (fee)* ☰ *AE, DC, MC, V* ⧖ *BP.*

★ **$$–$$$**   🏨 **Residenza Farnese.** The Renaissance charm of this former priests' convent has been preserved—its landmark status prevents the owners from making too many changes. Room 309, believed to be a former chapel, has a ceiling fresco found during renovations; it's been professionally restored. Furnishings run from understated antiques and deep-blue fabrics to more-ornate hand-painted floral dressers and original artwork. All have hardwood floors and modern bathrooms with showers. There is a billiards room with a bar for socializing, and a large breakfast room where home-made breads and organic marmalades are served. ☒ *Via del Mascherone 59, Campo de' Fiori, 00186* ☎ *06/68891388* 🖷 *06/68210980* ✉ *residenzafarnese@libero.it* ➷ *31 rooms* ₺ *In-room safes, minibars, cable TV, billiards, bar, meeting room, in-room data ports* ▤ *AE, MC, V* ❮◯❯ *BP.*

$ 🖭 **Hotel In Parione.** Smeraldo's sister hotel shines with marble—cream in the staircases and hallways, deeper reddish tones in the guest-room bathrooms. Celery-green fabrics and cherry-stain wood decorate the rooms, which are smallish but very neat. Five floors above one of the bustling *vicoli* (small side streets) near the Campo de' Fiori, the roof garden provides a peek into the residential side of Roman living. ☒ *Via dei Chiavari 32, near Campo de' Fiori, 00186* ☎ *06/6892330* 🖷 *06/ 6834094* ⊕ *www.inparione.com* ₺ *Minibars, cable TV, in-room data ports, bar* ▤ *AE, DC, MC, V* ❮◯❯ *EP.*

$ 🖭 **Smeraldo.** The location, on a quiet side street a stone's throw from Campo de' Fiori, makes this an excellent choice in its price category. White marble floors, salmon-color bedding and curtains, and wooden bed frames and furniture decorate the guest rooms. Shiny bathrooms in green marble have showers or a combination bath and shower. The roof terrace has a nice view of the surrounding neighborhood. ☒ *Vicolo dei Chiodaroli 9, Campo de' Fiori, 00186* ☎ *06/6875929 or 06/ 6892121* 🖷*06/68805495* ⊕*www.smeraldoroma.com* ➷*25 rooms* ₺*In-room safes, cable TV, bar* ▤ *AE, DC, MC, V* ❮◯❯ *BP.*

Colosseo

$$$–$$$$ 🖭 **47 Hotel.** The location of this office-building-turned-four-star-hotel is central to much of ancient Rome, and it offers a good quality-to-price ratio for the heart of the city, with fine service and modern amenities. The style of the place is comfortable modern-deco; muted earth tones and brickwork give it added warmth. The rooftop bar and restaurant offer excellent views over the Circus Maximus, Bocca della Verita, Teatro di Marcello, and the heart of *Roma antica.* ☒ *Via Petroselli 47, 00186* ☎ *06/6787816* 🖷 *06/69190726* ⊕ *www.fortysevenhotel.com* ➷ *61 rooms* ₺ *Restaurant, in-room safes, minibars, cable TV, in-room data ports, bar, laundry, concierge, meeting rooms, no-smoking rooms* ▤ *AE, DC, MC, V* ❮◯❯ *BP.*

$$$–$$$$ 🖭 **Hotel Capo d'Africa.** Designed on a boutique hotel model, the Capo d'Africa has '60s-style furnishings in bright purple and orange, commissioned artwork on the walls, and quirky light fixtures. The 1903 building was originally a school, and as a result rooms are different sizes; all are done in earth tones and saffron, with marble-and-tile bathrooms. Two rooftop terraces, connected by the breakfast room, are a delightful bonus in warmer weather. ☒ *Via Capo d'Africa 54, near Colosseo, 00184* ☎ *06/772801* 🖷 *06/77280801* ⊕ *www.hotelcapodafrica.com* ➷ *64 rooms, 1 suite* ₺ *In-room safes, minibars, cable TV, gym, bar, meeting rooms, parking (fee), no-smoking rooms, in-room data ports,* ▤ *AE, DC, MC, V* ❮◯❯ *BP.*

$$ 🖭 **Duca d'Alba.** This elegant hotel has made a stylish contribution to the ongoing gentrification of the Suburra neighborhood, near the Colosseum and the Roman Forum. The tasteful neoclassical decor includes custom

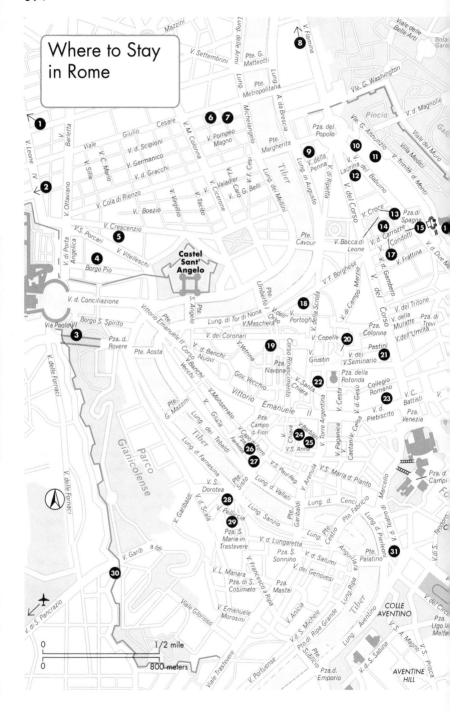

Where to Stay in Rome

furnishings such as inlaid wood headboards. All rooms are entirely soundproof. The breakfast buffet is ample. With its attentive staff and reasonable rates, Duca d'Alba is an exceptional value. ☒ *Via Leonina 14, near Colosseo, 00184* ☎ *06/484471* 🖷 *06/4884840* ⊕ *www. hotelducadalba.com* 📞 *27 rooms, 1 suite* ♿ *In-room safes, some kitchenettes, minibars, cable TV, in-room data ports, bar* ⊟ *AE, DC, MC, V* 🍽 *BP.*

Piazza di Spagna

$$$$ 🏨 **D'Inghilterra.** Legendary names like Liszt, Mendelssohn, Hans Christian Andersen, Mark Twain, and Hemingway litter the guest book here. With a residential feel and a staff that is as warm as the surroundings are velvety, this hotel near the Spanish Steps was once the guesthouse of the fabulously rich Prince Torlonia. Rooms are so full of carpets, giltframe mirrors, and cozy bergères, you hardly notice the snug dimensions. The chic Café Romano, with ocher walls and vaulted ceilings, serves eclectic cuisine and has tables on Via Borgogna. ☒ *Via Bocca di Leone 14, near Piazza di Spagna, 00187* ☎ *06/699811* 🖷 *06/69922243* ⊕ *www.hoteldinghilterraroma.it* 📞 *90 rooms, 8 suites* ♿ *Restaurant, in-room safes, minibars, cable TV, bar, laundry service, parking (fee), no-smoking rooms* ⊟ *AE, DC, MC, V* 🍽 *EP.*

$$$$
Fodor'sChoice
★
🏨 **Hassler.** Enjoy sweeping views of Rome from the front rooms and the roof restaurant of the enchanting Hassler hotel, itself at the top of the Spanish Steps; other rooms overlook the gardens of the Villa Medici. An extravagant 1950s elegance pervades the public spaces—especially the clubby winter bar and the summer garden bar. Luxe guest rooms are decorated in classic styles with rich fabrics and some ornate, handpainted furniture; the fifth floor has stylized art deco rooms done in black and white. The penthouse suite, resplendent with antiques, has a huge terrace. ☒ *Piazza Trinità dei Monti 6, near Piazza di Spagna, 00187* ☎ *06/699340* 🖷 *06/6789991* ⊕ *www.lhw.com* 📞 *85 rooms, 15 suites* ♿ *Restaurant, in-room safes, minibars, cable TV, gym, hair salon, bar, laundry service, concierge, in-room data ports, Wi-Fi, parking (fee), no-smoking rooms* ⊟ *AE, DC, MC, V* 🍽 *EP.*

$$$$ 🏨 **Hotel Art.** Via Margutta has long been an artists' enclave, so it's fitting that this modern hotel is a favorite of creative types. In the futuristic lobby the check-in staff works within a glowing white, podlike fixture. Arches, vaults, and columns are painted in contrasting deep blue and white, defining the café-bar space. Each of the four floors has a corridor color (yellow, green, orange, and blue) that is mirrored in the guest rooms' bathroom tiles. Otherwise, the rooms—clean-line furnishings, high-quality linens, and sleek parquet floors—have a neutral palette. A central courtyard is a good lounging spot in warmer months. ☒ *Via Margutta 56, near Piazza di Spagna, 00187* ☎ *06/328711* 🖷 *06/36003995* ⊕ *www.hotelart.it* 📞 *44 rooms, 2 suites* ♿ *In-room safes, minibars, cable TV, gym, sauna, steam room, bar* ⊟ *AE, DC, MC, V* 🍽 *EP.*

$$$$ 🏨 **Hotel de Russie.** In the 19th century this hotel counted Russian princes among its guests; later Picasso and Cocteau leaned out the windows to pick oranges from the trees in the lush terraced garden. Famed hotelier Sir Rocco Forte has brought the de Russie to a superlative standard of accommodations and service today. Rooms are chic Italian contemporary in style, with Roman mosaic motifs in bathrooms. Many have garden views, and several suites have panoramic terraces. The spa is luxurious, but be warned: you have to dole out an extra €11 for health club privileges, an absurdity given the room cost. ⊠ *Via del Babuino 9, off Piazza del Popolo, near Piazza di Spagna, 00187* ☎ *06/328881* 🖷 *06/32888888* ⊕ *www.rfhotels.com* 🛏 *130 rooms, 27 suites* ⚖ *Restaurant, in-room safes, minibars, cable TV, in-room data ports, health club, hair salon, spa, bar, meeting rooms* ☰ *AE, DC, MC, V* ¶ *EP.*

$$$$ ⌺ **Inn at the Spanish Steps.** The name of this small, exclusive hotel tells it all. Staying here is like having your own little place on fabled Via Condotti, the elegant shopping street crowned by the Spanish Steps. The hotel occupies the upper floors of a centuries-old palazzo it shares with Caffè Greco. Rooms, all junior suites, are handsomely decorated with damask fabrics and antiques. ⊠ *Via Condotti 85, near Piazza di Spagna, 00187* ☎ *06/69925657* 🖷 *06/6786470* ⊕ *www.atspanishsteps.com* 🛏 *22 suites* ⚖ *In-room safes, minibars, cable TV, airport shuttle, no-smoking rooms* ☰ *AE, DC, MC, V* ¶ *BP.*

★ **$$–$$$$** ⌺ **Locarno.** Art aficionados and people in the cinema have long appreciated this hotel's preserved fin de siècle charm, intimate feel, and central location off Piazza del Popolo. Wallpaper and fabric prints are coordinated in the rooms, and some rooms have antiques. Everything is lovingly supervised by the owners, a mother-daughter duo. The buffet breakfast is ample, there's bar service on the panoramic roof garden, and complimentary bicycles are available if you feel like braving the traffic. ⊠ *Via della Penna 22, near Piazza di Spagna, 00186* ☎ *06/3610841* 🖷 *06/3215249* ⊕ *www.hotellocarno.com* 🛏 *64 rooms, 2 suites* ⚖ *Restaurant, in-room safes, minibars, cable TV, in-room data ports, bar, laundry service, no-smoking rooms* ☰ *AE, DC, MC, V* ¶ *BP.*

$$$ ⌺ **Carriage.** The Carriage's location is its main appeal: it's two blocks from the Spanish Steps, in the heart of Rome. The decor of subdued baroque accents, richly colored wallpaper, and antique reproductions lends a touch of old-world charm. Some furniture has seen better days, and rooms can be pint-size, but several have small terraces. A roof garden adds to the appeal. ⊠ *Via delle Carrozze 36, near Piazza di Spagna, 00187* ☎ *06/6990124* 🖷 *06/6788279* ⊕ *www.hotelcarriage.net* 🛏 *24 rooms, 3 suites* ☰ *AE, DC, MC, V* ¶ *BP.*

$–$$ ⌺ **Margutta.** Looking for a decent value and friendly owner-managers? The Margutta's your place. The lobby and halls in this small hotel are unassuming, but rooms are a pleasant surprise, with tall windows, attractive wrought-iron bedsteads, and modern baths. Three rooms have private terraces. Though it's in an old building, there's an elevator. The location is on a quiet side street between the Spanish Steps and Piazza del Popolo. ⊠ *Via Laurina 34, near Piazza di Spagna, 00187* ☎ *06/3223674* 🖷 *06/3200395* ⊕ *www.hotelmargutta.it* 🛏 *24 rooms* ⚖ *Cable TV, in-room data ports* ☰ *AE, DC, MC, V* ¶ *BP.*

$ ⌺ **Panda.** Via della Croce is one of Piazza di Spagna's chic shopping streets, so it's refreshing to find a budget option (with an old pensione feel) in this decidedly nonbudget neighborhood. Guest rooms are outfitted in terra-cotta and wrought iron; they're smallish, but spotless and quiet, thanks to double-glaze windows. You can pay even less by sharing a bath—in low season, you may have it to yourself anyway. ⊠ *Via della Croce 35, Piazza di Spagna, 00187* ☎ *06/6780179* 📠 *06/69942151* ⊕ *www.hotelpanda.it* ↵ *20 rooms, 14 with bath* ♻ *No a/c in some rooms, no room TVs* ⊟ *MC, V* ⊨ *BP.*

Trastevere

$$–$$$ ⊡ **Hotel Santa Maria.** All the ground-floor rooms at this lovely former convent surround a pebbled courtyard shaded by orange trees. Room furniture leans towards the standard American hotel style, with two double beds, but there are terra-cotta tile floors and a tub with shower in the bathrooms. In fair weather, breakfast or a drink in the courtyard is a real treat, with a backdrop of old Trastevere that seems more opera set than reality. ⊠ *Vicolo del Piede 2, behind Piazza Santa Maria, Trastevere, 00153* ☎ *06/5894626* 📠 *06/5894815* ⊕ *www.htlsantamaria. com* ↵ *18 rooms, 2 suites* ♻ *In-room safes, minibars, cable TV, bar* ⊟ *AE, DC, MC, V* ⊨ *BP.*

$$ ⊡ **Grand Hotel Gianicolo.** Atop Janiculum Hill, one of the famed seven
Fodor'sChoice hills of Rome, the Grand Hotel feels removed from the urban chaos.
★ It's a bargain, with many of the trappings standard at higher prices: beautifully manicured gardens, a pool, a rooftop terrace, conference rooms, and a clubby bar. Comfortable guest rooms have patterned wallpaper and draperies. The viewing point on the drive up has breathtaking, encompassing views of the Eternal City. ⊠ *Via delle Mura Gianicolensi 107, Trastevere, 00152* ☎ *06/58333405* 📠 *06/58179434* ⊕ *www. grandhotelgianicolo.it* ♻ *Café, in-room safes, some in-room hot tubs, minibars, cable TV, in-room data ports, pool, bar, babysitting, laundry service, concierge, meeting rooms, free parking, some pets allowed, no-smoking rooms* ⊟ *AE, DC, MC, V* ⊨ *BP.*

$ ⊡ **Hotel Trastevere House.** Close to the pizzerias and bars of Viale Trastevere, yet off the beaten path in an 18th-century house tucked onto a tiny street, this bed-and-breakfast is a find. The cozy rooms are done in traditional dark wood and deep-blue fabric, with wood-beam ceilings and terra-cotta floors. The owners have another hotel, Domus Tiberina, around the corner, complete with a suite with balcony. ⊠ *Vicolo del Buco 7, Trastevere, 00153* ☎ *06/5883774* ⊕ *www.trasteverehouse.it* ↵ *10 rooms, 7 with bath* ♻ *Cable TV; no a/c* ⊟ *MC, V* ⊨ *BP.*

Piazza Navona

$$$$ ⊡ **Raphaël.** Old-world European luxury is alive and well behind the vine-covered facade of Raphaël. An array of sculpture, hand-carved wood antiques, and original Picasso ceramics grace the lobby. Rooms—a few with minuscule proportions—are individually decorated, some with tapestries and columns. Bathrooms are finished with travertine marble or hand-painted tiles. A Richard Meier–designed wing adds a modern touch to this classic space. Arrange to have your meal on the bi-level Bramante Terrace for great city views. ⊠ *Largo Febo 2, near Piazza Navona, 00186* ☎ *06/682831* 📠 *06/6878993* ⊕ *www. raphaelhotel.com* ↵ *51 rooms, 7 suites, 10 apartments* ♻ *Restaurant,* *cable TV, gym, sauna, bar, laundry service, parking (fee), in-room data ports* ▤ *AE, DC, MC, V* ⦿ *EP.*

$$ ▦ **Abruzzi.** Look out from the windows of this little hostelry and the Pantheon is literally in your face. Though location is the main selling point, basic rooms are modern, and all have bathrooms with a shower or tub. The rooftop terrace has a great view over the remarkable dome and the piazza it dominates. ⊠ *Piazza della Rotonda 69, near Pantheon, 00186* ☎ *06/6792021* ⛁ *06/69788076* ⊕ *www.hotelabruzzi.it* ⤵ *26 rooms* ⚒ *In-room safes, minibars, cable TV* ▤ *AE, MC, V* ⦿ *BP.*

★ $$ ▦ **Cesàri.** The exterior of this 1787 hotel looks much as it did when Stendhal stayed here in the 1800s. Old prints of Rome embellish the cream-color guest room walls; soft-green drapes and bedspreads create comfort and serenity. Bathrooms are done in smart two-tone blue marble. Overall, Cesàri exudes a quiet elegance in a very central location on a traffic-free street. ⊠ *Via di Pietra 89a, near Pantheon, 00186* ☎ *06/6749701* ⛁ *06/67497030* ⊕ *www.albergocesari.it* ⤵ *47 rooms* ⚒ *Some in-room safes, some minibars, cable TV, bar, laundry service, parking (fee), some pets allowed, no-smoking floor* ▤ *AE, DC, MC, V* ⦿ *BP.*

★ $$ ▦ **Santa Chiara.** Three ancient buildings form a gracious hotel that has been in the same family for 200 years. The personal attention shows in meticulously decorated and maintained lounges and rooms. Each room has built-in oak headboards, a marble-top desk, and an elegant travertine bath. Double-glaze windows look out over the Piazza della Minerva. There are three apartments, for two to five people, with full kitchens. ⊠ *Via Santa Chiara 21, near Pantheon, 00186* ☎ *06/6872979* ⛁ *06/6873144* ⊕ *www.albergosantachiara.com* ⤵ *100 rooms, 4 suites, 3 apartments* ⚒ *Some kitchens, cable TV, bar* ▤ *AE, DC, MC, V* ⦿ *BP.*

$–$$ ▦ **Coronet.** This small hotel occupies part of a floor in one wing of the vast Palazzo Doria Pamphilj; seven interior rooms overlook the family's lovely private garden court. Don't expect palatial ambience, but elaborate moldings in the carpeted halls and wood-beam ceilings in several rooms do lend a sense of age. The good-size rooms have oldish baths, some very small. Several rooms can accommodate three or four beds. ⊠ *Piazza Grazioli 5, near Piazza Venezia, 00186* ☎ *06/6792341* ⛁ *06/69922705* ⊕ *www.hotelcoronet.com* ⤵ *13 rooms, 10 with bath* ▤ *AE, MC, V* ⦿ *BP.*

¢ ▦ **Fraterna Domus.** On a byway near Piazza Navona sits a guesthouse run by nuns, though you might not realize it because they don't wear religious habits. Rooms are spare, with single beds, but they have small private bathrooms. Three hearty meals a day are served in the dining room (dinner €12), and the curfew is 11 PM. ⊠ *Vicolo del Leonetto 16, Piazza Navona, 00186* ☎ *06/68802727* ⛁ *06/6832691* ✍ *domusrm@tin.it* ⤵ *20 rooms* ⚒ *Dining room; no a/c in some rooms, no room TVs* ▤ *DC, MC, V* ⦿ *BP.*

San Pietro

$$$–$$$$ ▦ **Giulio Cesare.** An aristocratic town house with a garden in the residential but central Prati district, the Giulio Cesare is a 10-minute walk across the Tiber from Piazza del Popolo. It's beautifully run, with a friendly

staff and a quiet luxury. The rooms are elegant, with chandeliers, thick rugs, floor-length drapes, and rich damasks in soft colors. Public rooms have Oriental carpets, old prints and paintings, marble fireplaces, and a grand piano. The buffet breakfast is a veritable banquet. ⊠ *Via degli Scipioni 287, near San Pietro, 00192* ☎ *06/3210751* 🖷 *06/3211736* ➡ *90 rooms* ⟡ *Dining room, in-room safes, minibars, cable TV, in-room data ports* ▭ *AE, DC, MC, V* ⑪ *BP.*

$$–$$$$ 🏨 **Atlante Star.** The lush rooftop-terrace garden café and the restaurant of this hotel have a knockout view of the basilica and the rest of Rome. The rooms in the distinguished 19th-century building are attractive, in striped silks and prints; many bathrooms have hot tubs. The friendly family management is attentive to your needs and takes pride in selling extra-virgin olive oil produced from their own trees in the country. A sister hotel around the corner, Atlante Garden, has larger rooms at slightly lower rates. ⊠ *Via Vitelleschi 34, near San Pietro, 00193* ☎ *06/ 6873233* 🖷 *06/6872300* ⊕ *www.atlantehotels.com* ➡ *65 rooms, 10 suites* ⟡ *Restaurant, in-room safes, some in-room hot tubs, minibars, cable TV, bar, laundry service, concierge, parking (fee), no-smoking rooms* ▭ *AE, DC, MC, V* ⑪ *BP.*

★ $$$ 🏨 **Hotel Farnese.** The intimate Farnese began life as a late-19th-century mansion. Today it's furnished with great attention to detail in belle epoque style: marble-top tables and curvaceous-wood or scrolled-iron headboards, for example. Fresco embellishments are lively, and the modern baths sparkle. A roof garden has tall hedges and umbrella-shaded tables for two. The hotel is not far from the metro. ⊠ *Via Alessandro Farnese 30, near San Pietro, 00192* ☎ *06/3212553* 🖷 *06/3215129* ⊕ *www. hotelfarnese.com* ➡ *23 rooms, 2 suites* ⟡ *Minibars, cable TV, bar, laundry service, concierge, free parking* ▭ *AE, DC, MC, V* ⑪ *EP.*

$$–$$$ 🏨 **Residenza Paolo VI.** The Paolo Sesto (Italian for Paul VI) is within the Vatican walls. Rooms in this former monastery are simple, with wood furniture, marble floors, and Persian rugs. The roof terrace, however, has a spectacular view of St. Peter's. Breakfast is an American-style buffet. ⊠ *Via Paolo VI 29, near San Pietro, 00193* ☎ *06/68134108* 🖷 *06/ 6867428* ⊕ *www.residenzapaolovi.com* ➡ *29 rooms* ⟡ *In-room safes, minibars, cable TV, bar, laundry service, parking (fee), no-smoking rooms* ▭ *AE, D, MC, V* ⑪ *BP.*

$$ 🏨 **Sant'Anna.** In the quiet Borgo neighborhood surrounding St. Peter's, this small hotel has done much with its limited size. The spacious attic rooms have their own tiny terraces, and some of the large bedrooms have coffered ceilings. Design accents are in navy, gold, and rose. Frescoes enliven the breakfast room, and the fountain in the courtyard is typically Roman. ⊠ *Borgo Pio 134, near San Pietro, 00193* ☎ *06/68801602* 🖷 *06/68308717* ⊕ *www.hotelsantanna.com* ➡ *20 rooms* ⟡ *Minibars, cable TV, parking (fee)* ▭ *AE, DC, MC, V* ⑪ *BP.*

¢ 🏨 **San Giuseppe della Montagna.** This convent is right outside the Vatican walls, near the entrance to the Vatican Museums. It's run by Catalan nuns, so unless you speak Italian or Spanish, you may have to work at communicating with the staff. The rooms are immaculate (no pun intended), though spare; some have three beds. Unusual for a convent is that there's no curfew; you are given keys. ⊠ *Viale Vaticano 87, near*

San Pietro, 00165 ☎ *06/39723807* 🖨 *06/3972104*
♨ *No a/c, no room TVs* 🖃 *No credit cards* ⚬ *BP.*

Termini & Via Nazionale

★ **$$$$** 🏨 **Exedra.** The opening of the luxurious, stately Exed
2002 transformed a dilapidated piazza into a vibrant mee
struction also unearthed additional baths of Diocletian,
glass outside the conference rooms on the lower floor. A red carpet leads
to the arched entry; inside an attentive staff waits to attend your every
need. Chandeliers hang from high ceilings that are detailed with stepped
moldings or timbers, and king-size beds rest atop deep, soft carpets in neoclassical rooms. Marble adorns all bathrooms. A rooftop terrace contains
the pool and a bar, and there's a world-class spa on-site. ⊠ *Piazza della
Repubblica 47, near Via Nazionale, 00185* ☎ *06/489381* 🖨 *06/48938000*
⊕ *www.boscolohotels.com* ⤵ *262 rooms, 6 suites* ♨ *3 restaurants, in-
room safes, minibars, cable TV, pool, health club, spa, 2 bars, babysitting, dry cleaning, laundry service, concierge, meeting rooms, parking (fee),
no-smoking rooms, Web TV, in-room data ports, Internet room* 🖃 *AE,
DC, MC, V* ⚬ *BP.*

$$$–$$$$ 🏨 **Mediterraneo.** Constructed in 1935—and operated as a hotel since
1940—the Mediterraneo is a service-oriented charmer. Though it lacks
the slick modernities of a newly renovated hotel, it has clubby 1940s
character. The lobby has a fireplace, and the breakfast room is done in
green tile. Either parquet floors with Persian rugs or deep wall-to-wall
carpeting lies underfoot in guest rooms, and velvet easy chairs wait for
you to sink in. Double-glaze windows keep things surprisingly quiet.
The rooftop terrace bar is open May–September. ⊠ *Via Cavour 15, near
Termini, 00184* ☎ *06/4884051 or 800/2239832* 🖨 *06/4744105* ⊕ *www.
romehotelmediterraneo.it* ♨ *Restaurant, room service, in-room safes,
minibars, cable TV, bar, laundry service, meeting rooms* 🖃 *AE, DC, MC,
V* ⚬ *BP.*

$$$ 🏨 **Britannia.** Owner Pier Paolo Biorgi has created a very special small
Fodor'sChoice hotel. His influence is evident: the caring staff provides English-language
★ newspapers daily, and local weather reports are delivered to your room
each morning. Planted palms and fluted columns adorn frescoed halls.
Each guest room has a unique layout and is furnished with lush fabrics and original artwork. A heat lamp warms marble bathrooms. On
the top floor, a light-filled suite opens onto a private terrace. ⊠ *Via
Napoli 64, near Via Nazionale, 00184* ☎ *06/4883153* 🖨 *06/4882343*
⊕ *www.hotelbritannia.it* ⤵ *32 rooms, 1 suite* ♨ *In-room safes, minibars, cable TV, babysitting, laundry service, free parking* 🖃 *AE, DC,
MC, V* ⚬ *BP.*

$$ 🏨 **Hotel Venezia.** Here's an old-fashioned, side-street hotel that's charm-
ing and, well, *pretty*, with 16th-century wood tables and sideboards set
off by cozy matching armchairs and tapestries. Guest rooms are some-
what simpler but still a cut above many of the other hotels near the Ter-
mini station. There's even a "pillow menu" from which you can order
the type of bed pillow you want. ⊠ *Via Varese 18, near Termini, 00185*
☎ *06/4457101* 🖨 *06/4957687* ⊕ *www.hotelvenezia.com* ⤵ *60 rooms*
♨ *In-room safes, minibars, cable TV; no a/c in some rooms* 🖃 *AE, D,
MC, V* ⚬ *BP.*

$$ ☷ **Morgana.** Apart from the fact it's near the central train station, nothing about this refurbished hotel screams Roman. Still, plaid wallcoverings, upholstered sofas, and soft chairs in the lobby reading room and the TV lounge are welcoming. The cozy public spaces belie the guest-room decor, which could be mistaken for that of a boutique hotel—slick and modern, in gray, black, and burgundy. Everything about the place (including the elevator) is compact, except for the breakfast room, where there's a big, full buffet. ☒ *Via Filippo Turati 33, near Termini, 00185* ☎ *06/4467230* 🖷 *06/4469142* ⊕ *www.hotelmorgana.com* ↩ *103 rooms, 2 suites* ⚭ *In-room safes, minibars, cable TV, bar, laundry service, concierge, no-smoking rooms* ▭ *AE, DC, MC, V* ⏏ *BP.*

$–$$ ☷ **Des Artistes.** The three personable Riccioni brothers have transformed their hotel into one of the best for its price range in the Termini train station neighborhood. They've lavished rooms with paintings, mahogany furnishings, and marble baths. The breakfast room doubles as a TV lounge with Internet access. One floor has 10 dorm-style rooms (six to eight beds per room, €20 per bed). ☒ *Via Villafranca 20, near Termini, 00185* ☎ *06/4454365* 🖷 *06/4462368* ⊕ *www.hoteldesartistes. com* ↩ *40 rooms, 27 with bath* ⚭ *In-room safes, minibars, cable TV, in-room data ports, bar, concierge, parking (fee); no a/c in some rooms, no smoking* ▭ *AE, DC, MC, V* ⏏ *BP.*

$–$$ ☷ **Montreal.** On a central avenue, three blocks from Stazione Termini, the compact Montreal occupies three floors of an older building. It's been totally renovated and has fresh-looking, though small, rooms. The owner-managers are pleasant and helpful, and the neighborhood has plenty of reasonably priced restaurants. ☒ *Via Carlo Alberto 4, across from Santa Maria Maggiore, near Termini, 00185* ☎ *06/4457797* 🖷 *06/ 4465522* ⊕ *www.hotelmontrealroma.com* ↩ *27 rooms* ⚭ *In-room safes, minibars, cable TV, parking (fee)* ▭ *AE, DC, MC, V* ⏏ *BP.*

$ ☷ **Adler.** This tiny pensione run by the same family for more than three decades provides a comfortable stay on a quiet street near the station for a very good price. Ideal for families, the Adler has six spacious rooms that sleep three, four, or five, as well as a single and a double. Rooms are basic but impeccably clean (owner Serena Biancalana sees to that). Worn but cozy chairs line the lobby, and in summer, breakfast can be taken on the leafy courtyard balcony. ☒ *Via Modena 5, near Termini, 00184* ☎ *06/484466* 🖷 *06/4880940* ↩ *8 rooms* ⚭ *Cable TV, bar* ▭ *AE, DC, MC, V* ⏏ *BP.*

$ ☷ **Tempio di Pallade.** This small hotel near Porta Maggiore is a good deal. Rooms are simple but elegant, done in blue and gold. The owners, Ranieri siblings, will be happy to make arrangements for you, from airport taxis to tours of the city to opera tickets. Triples and quads are available on request, as are group meals. ☒ *Via Giolitti 425–427, near Termini, 00185* ☎ *06/70451521* 🖷 *06/70452758* ⊕ *www. hoteltempiodipallade.com* ↩ *50 rooms* ⚭ *In-room safes, minibars, cable TV, concierge* ▭ *AE, DC, MC, V* ⏏ *BP.*

★ ¢–$ ☷ **The Beehive.** Linda Martinez-Brenner and Steve Brenner are the friendly American couple who run this funky B&B—as well as apartment rentals. Bright, clean rooms have ultramodern furniture and colorful artwork. One hostel-style room with eight bunk beds costs a mere

€20 per person. Downstairs, a café-lounge serves drinks, light meals, and snacks. There's free Internet access and concierge service; have them book you a dinner reservation while you sit in the lobby's Philippe Starck chairs and wonder how something so good can cost so little. ⊠ *Via Marghera 8, near Termini, 00185* ☎ *06/44704553* ⊕ *www.the-beehive. com* ↪ *9 rooms without bath, 10 apartments* ↺ *Café, fans, concierge, Internet; no a/c, no room TVs, no smoking* ⊟ *No credit cards* ¶⊙¶ *EP.*

Via Veneto

★ **$$$$** 🏨 **Aleph.** Adam Tihany's upscale, boutique hotel design plays with the themes of heaven and hell: in the Paradiso spa, in the Angel lobby bar, in the flaming red Maremeto seafood restaurant. Guest rooms are done in a whimsical, modern Venetian style, with Murano-glass light fixtures, cream-and-deep-blue color schemes, and black-and-white accents—including full-wall photo blowups. ⊠ *Via San Basilio 15, near Via Veneto, 00187* ☎ *06/422901* 🖷 *06/42290000* ⊕ *www.boscolohotels.com* ↪ *94 rooms, 2 suites* ↺ *Restaurant, in-room safes, minibars, cable TV, gym, spa, 2 bars, laundry service, concierge, no-smoking rooms, in-room data ports* ⊟ *AE, DC, MC, V* ¶⊙¶ *EP.*

★ **$$$$** 🏨 **Eden.** This superlative hotel combines dashing elegance and stunning vistas of Rome with the warmth of Italian hospitality. The Eden was once a preferred haunt of Hemingway, Ingrid Bergman, and Federico Fellini. Antiques, sumptuous Italian fabrics, linen sheets, and marble baths are the essence of good taste. Views from the rooftop bar and terrace can take your breath away (as can the bill). The hotel's top-floor restaurant, La Terrazza dell'Eden, is one of the city's best. ⊠ *Via Ludovisi 49, near Via Veneto, 00187* ☎ *06/478121* 🖷 *06/4821584* ⊕ *www. hotel-eden.it* ↪ *112 rooms, 14 suites* ↺ *Restaurant, in-room safes, minibars, cable TV, gym, bar, laundry service, concierge, parking (fee), no-smoking rooms* ⊟ *AE, DC, MC, V* ¶⊙¶ *EP.*

$$$$ 🏨 **Rose Garden Palace.** The elegant Rose Garden Palace is a marriage of the classic (marble floors, velvet sofas, patterned curtains) and the contemporary (clean lines, modern wood). Guest rooms are done in calming tones of beige, slate blue, and terra-cotta. A state-of-the-art fitness room, pool, and sauna and steam room below ground are small but ideal. Friday nights, jazz musicians play in the bar, and in warm weather the bar opens into the rose garden. The hotel is behind the American Embassy. ⊠ *Via Boncompagni 19, near Via Veneto, 00187* ☎ *06/ 421741* 🖷 *06/4815608* ⊕ *www.rosegardenpalace.com* ↪ *59 rooms, 6 suites* ↺ *Restaurant, in-room safes, minibars, cable TV, indoor pool, gym, spa, bar, meeting rooms, parking (fee), no-smoking rooms* ⊟ *AE, DC, MC, V* ¶⊙¶ *BP.*

$$$$ 🏨 **Westin Excelsior.** Next door to the American Embassy, the Excelsior is the hotel of choice for visiting diplomats, American business conferences, and celebrities. It's of the breed that put the *luxe* in deluxe: every corner is lavished with mirrors, moldings, Oriental rugs, crystal chandeliers, and huge, baroque floral arrangements. Guest rooms have elegant drapery, marble baths, top-quality linens, and big, firm beds. ⊠ *Via Veneto 125, 00187* ☎ *06/47081* 🖷 *06/4826205* ⊕ *www.westin.com* ↪ *286 rooms, 35 suites* ↺ *Restaurant, in-room safes, minibars, cable*

TV, indoor pool, gym, bar, laundry service, concierge, no-smoking rooms ▤ *AE, DC, MC, V* ⦿| *EP.*

$$ ⊡ **La Residenza.** Mainly Americans frequent this cozy hotel in a converted town house near Via Veneto. Rooms are basic and comfortable (although singles are windowless). The real charm is at the bar, on the terrace, and in the lounges (smoking and no-smoking), which have warm-colored wallpaper and love seats, a big-screen TV, a piano, and card tables. Rates include a generous American-style buffet breakfast and an in-house movie every night. ⊠ *Via Emilia 22, near Via Veneto, 00187* ☎ *06/4880789* ⊟ *06/485721* ⊕ *www.thegiannettihotelsgroup. com* ↩ *29 rooms* ⟁ *In-room safes, minibars, cable TV, bar, laundry service, parking (fee)* ▤ *AE, MC, V* ⦿| *BP.*

Beyond the City Center

$$$$ ⊡ **Cavalieri Hilton.** Though the Cavalieri is outside the city center, distance has its advantages, including the magnificent view from the hotel's hilltop position (ask for a room facing the city). This hotel is an island of quiet good taste with a distinctive Italian flair. If you can tear yourself away from the gardens and pools, a courtesy shuttle bus to downtown Rome leaves every hour. Don't miss the acclaimed rooftop restaurant, La Pergola. ⊠ *Via Cadlolo 101, Monte Mario, 00136* ☎ *06/ 35091* ⊟ *06/35092241* ⊕ *www.cavalieri-hilton.com* ↩ *357 rooms, 17 suites* ⟁ *2 restaurants, cable TV, tennis court, 2 pools (1 indoor), health club, hair salon, spa, bar* ▤ *AE, DC, MC, V* ⦿| *EP.*

★ **$$$–$$$$** ⊡ **Castello della Castelluccia.** Removed from the hustle and bustle of Rome's city center, this beautifully renovated 12th-century castle is surrounded by a small wooded park. The original structure has been preserved, complete with watchtower (now a three-level suite); all that's missing is a medieval knight clinking down the echoing stone halls. Guest rooms are luxuriously appointed, with inlaid-wood antiques and four-poster beds; a few have marble fireplaces, and two have giant, tiled hot-tub alcoves. There's shuttle-bus service to central Rome. ⊠ *Via Carlo Cavina, Località La Castelluccia, 00123, 16 km (10 mi) north of center* ☎ *06/ 30207041* ⊟ *06/30207110* ⊕ *www.lacastelluccia.com* ↩ *18 rooms, 6 suites* ⟁ *Restaurant, room service, some in-room hot tubs, minibars, cable TV, in-room data ports, pool, spa, horseback riding, bar, laundry service, meeting room, free parking, some pets allowed* ▤ *AE, D, MC, V* ⦿| *BP.*

NIGHTLIFE & THE ARTS

The Arts

Rome lacks the level of culture in some of Italy's other cities, but it is the capital, so performances from the worlds of music, dance, theater, and film are to be found. Consult one of the local publications for listings: in the back of the weekly *roma c'è* magazine (published Wednesday) there are comprehensive listings in English, along with handy bus and metro information. The monthly *Time Out Roma* gives event schedules, as well as editors' picks, that are mainly in Italian (with a small summary in English) but are easy to decipher. The monthly *Where* mag-

Entertainment Alfresco

ROMAN NIGHTLIFE MOVES outdoors in summertime, and that goes not only for pubs and discos but for higher culture as well. Open-air opera in particular is a venerable Italian tradition; competing companies commandeer church courtyards, ancient villas, and soccer stadiums for performances that range from student-run mom-and-poperas to full-scale extravaganzas. The same goes for dance and for concerts covering the spectrum of pop, classical, and jazz. Look for performances at the Baths of Caracalla, site of the famous televised "Three Tenors" concert; regardless of the production quality, it's a breathtaking setting. In general, though, you can count on performances being quite good, even if small productions often resort to school-play scenery and folding chairs to cut costs. Tickets run about €15–€40. The more-sophisticated productions may be listed in newspapers and magazines such as *roma c'è* and *Wanted in Rome*, but your best sources for information are old-fashioned posters plastered all over the city, advertising classics such as *Tosca* and *La Traviata*.

---

azine is distributed free at hotels and restaurants. An English-language biweekly, *Wanted in Rome* (www.wantedinrome.com), is sold at central newsstands and has good listings of events and museum exhibitions. *Trovaroma* is the weekly entertainment guide published in Italian every Thursday as a supplement to the daily newspaper *La Repubblica*.

Concerts

Christmastime is an especially busy classical concert season in Rome. Many small classical concert groups perform in cultural centers and churches year-round; all performances in Catholic churches are religious music and are free. Look for posters outside the churches. Pop, jazz, and world music concerts are frequent, especially in summer, although they may not be well advertised. Many of the bigger-name acts perform outside the center, so it's worth asking about transportation *before* you buy your tickets (about €8–€30).

CLASSICAL A year-round classical concert series is organized by the **Accademia di Santa Cecilia** (Concert hall and box office ⊠ Via della Conciliazione 4, near San Pietro ☎ 06/684391). The **Accademia Filarmonica Romana** (⊠ Via Flaminia 118, near Stadio Olimpico ☎ 06/3201752, 06/3265991 tickets) has concerts at the Teatro Olimpico. **Istituzione Universitaria dei Concerti** (⊠ Aula Magna, Piazzale Aldo Moro 5, near San Lorenzo ☎ 06/3610051 ⊕ www.concertiiuc.it) presents small concerts with music ranging from swing to Bach. The internationally respected **Oratorio del Gonfalone series** (⊠ Via del Gonfalone 32/a, Campo de' Fiori ☎ 06/6875952) focuses on baroque music. **Il Tempietto** (☎ 06/87131590 ⊕ www.tempietto.it) organizes classical music concerts indoors in winter and in the atmospheric settings of Teatro di Marcello and Villa Torlonia in summer.

The church of **Sant'Ignazio** (✉ Piazza Sant'Ignazio, near Pantheon ☎ 06/6794560) often hosts classical concerts in its spectacularly frescoed setting.

ROCK, POP &
JAZZ

Tickets for major music events are usually handled by **Orbis** (✉ Piazza Esquilino 37, near Santa Maria Maggiore ☎ 06/4744776). **Box Office** (✉ Viale Giulio Cesare 88, near San Pietro ☎ 06/37500375 ⊕ www.ticket.it/boxoffice.htm) sells rock, pop, and jazz concert tickets from Monday to Saturday. **Hello Ticket** (✉ At Termini train station ☎ 06/47825710 ⊕ www.helloticket.it) sells tickets to concerts as well as theater and other cultural events. **Messaggerie Musicale** (✉ Via del Corso 473, Piazza di Spagna ☎ 06/684401) is a huge, centrally located store that sells music, DVDs, books, and international magazines as well as concert tickets.

Dance

Modern dance and classical ballet companies from Russia, the United States, and Europe sporadically visit Rome; performances are at the Teatro dell'Opera, Teatro Olimpico, or one of the open-air venues in summer. Small dance companies from Italy and abroad perform in numerous venues.

The **Rome Opera Ballet** (☎ 06/48160255 tickets ⊕ www.opera.roma.it) performs at the Teatro dell'Opera, often with international guest stars.

Film

Movie tickets range in price from €4.50 for matinees and some weeknights up to €10 for reserved seats on weekend evenings. Check listings in *roma c'è* or *Trovaroma* (www.trovacinema.it). The **Metropolitan** (✉ Via del Corso 7, off Piazza del Popolo, near Piazza di Spagna ☎ 06/32600500) has four screens, one dedicated to English-language films September–June. The five-screen **Warner Village Moderno** (✉ Piazza della Repubblica 45–46, near Via Nazionale ☎ 06/47779202), close to the train station, usually has one theater with an English-language film.

Opera

The season for the **Opera Theater of Rome** (☎ 06/4817515 ⊕ www.opera.roma.it) runs from November or December to May. Main performances are staged at the Teatro dell'Opera in cooler weather and at outdoor locations, such as Piazza del Popolo, in summer.

A GOOD WALK: TRASTEVERE BY NIGHT

For centuries home to Rome's artists and beggars, Trastevere has parlayed its bohemian appeal into a new life, as the place where Romans—and many visitors—step out at night. After dark, you'll have your choice of restaurants, bars, street performances, and the best people-watching in town. The neighborhood is a mix of the sacred and profane; follow this route in early evening for gelato, dinner, and a stroll—or stick around at night for a pub crawl with a cultural chaser. It covers about three-quarters of a mile.

From Piazza Sonnino, enter Trastevere by walking past the pharmacy on your right down Via Lungaretta. This street is Trastevere's main artery, jammed after dark with restaurants, bars, jewelry shops, street vendors, and revelers partying until the early hours. Continue on Via Lungaretta until it ends in **Piazza Santa Maria in Trastevere** 62. Bordered by two cafés and the swanky Sabatini restaurant (at No. 13), the piazza has a fountain in the center ringed by steps on which passersby join neo-hippies, grimy punks, and fresh-faced tourists for a front-row seat. On summer nights and weekends, jug-

Theater

Theater performances are staged throughout the year in Italian, English, and several other languages, depending on who is sponsoring the performance.

For comic theater in English, check out the **Miracle Players** (☎ 06/70393427 ⊕ www.miracleplayers.org), a group of English-speaking actors who write and produce free public performances every summer in the Roman Forum, presenting a perfectly balanced mix of the historical and the hilarious.

Venues

★ Rome's state-of-the-art **Auditorium-Parco della Musica** (✉ Via de Coubertin 15, Flaminio ☎ 06/80241350 ⊕ www.musicaperroma.it), a 10-minute tram ride from Piazza del Popolo, has three halls with excellent acoustics and a large courtyard used for concerts and other events—everything from chamber music to jazz to big-name pop, even film screenings and art exhibits.

Teatro Argentina (✉ Largo Argentina 52, near Campo de' Fiori ☎ 06/68804601), built in 1732 by the architect Theoldi, has been the home of the Teatro Sabile theater company since 1994. The theater has been renovated several times over the centuries, most recently in 2001. It's a beautiful, ornate structure, with velvet seats and chandeliers. The layout is more vertical than horizontal, creating a surprising number of seats, some at vertiginous heights. Teatro Argentina plays host to many plays, classical music performances, operas, and dance performances.

Both the city's ballet and opera companies, as well as visiting international performers, appear at the **Teatro dell'Opera** (✉ Piazza Beniamino Gigli 8, near Termini ☎ 06/481601, 06/48160255 tickets ⊕ www.opera.roma.it).

Teatro Valle (✉ Via del Teatro Valle 23A, near Pantheon ☎ 06/68803794) hosts dramatic performances of the same caliber as its neighbor, Teatro Argentina, but often with a more-experimental bent, particularly in fall. Dance and classical music are also presented here.

---

glers, flame-eaters, and magicians take turns wowing the crowds here. Bar del Marzio, next to Sabatini, has excellent gelato you can take with you out to the square. While you're there, stop into the church of Santa Maria in Trastevere, often open well into the evening in summer, for a look at the magnificent golden-tiled apse mosaic. Even if the church is closed, take a look at the fragments of ancient Roman graffiti salvaged from the city and plastered into the walls of the outer entryway.

Facing the church, follow the street leaving the piazza from the far right corner. It curves around to the right past several open-air restaurants, opening into Piazza Sant'Egidio. This lovely square is home to Rome's English-language Cinema Pasquino, a favorite with foreign residents. Next door are the outdoor tables of Ombre Rosse, where you'll find light meals, coffee, cocktails, the *International Herald Tribune*, and live music long, long into the night. Across the piazza, the Museo di Roma in Trastevere, open until 8, hosts Roman and international photography shows.

The ancient **Terme di Caracalla** (⊠ Via delle Terme di Caracalla 52, Aventino ☎ No phone) has one of the most spectacular and enchanting outdoor stages in the world.

Teatro Olimpico (⊠ Piazza Gentile da Fabriano 17, Stadio Olimpico ☎ 06/3265991) hosts both concerts and dance performances.

Nightlife

Rome's nightlife is decidedly more happening for locals and insiders who know whose palms to grease and when to go where. The "flavor of the month" factor is at work here, and many places fade into oblivion after their 15 minutes of fame. Smoking has been banned in all public areas in Italy (that's right, it actually happened); Roman aversion to clean air has meant a decrease in crowds at bars and clubs. The best sources for an up-to-date list of nightspots are the *roma c'è* booklet and *Where* magazine. Trastevere and the area around Piazza Navona are both filled with bars, restaurants, and, after dark, people. In summer, discos and many bars close to beat the heat (although some simply relocate to the beach, where many Romans spend their summer nights). The city-sponsored Estate Romana (Rome Summer) festival takes over, lighting up hot city nights with open-air concerts, bars, and discos. Pick up the event guide at newsstands.

Bars

So where do you go for a cocktail? **Bar della Pace** (⊠ Via della Pace 5, near Piazza Navona ☎ 06/6861216) has been the chic people-watching cocktail bar of choice since time immemorial. **Acqua Negra** (⊠ Largo Teatro Valle 9, Piazza Navona ☎ 06/97606025) packs in the twenty- to fortysomething crowd for aperitif, dinner, and postdinner drinks in a sexy, minimalist space. A hangout for scruffy-chic Romans sipping cocktails is **Société Lutéce** (⊠ Piazza di Montevecchio 17, off Via dei Coronari, Piazza Navona ☎ 06/6832361). **Freni e Frizioni** (⊠ Via de Politeama 4-6, Trastevere ☎ 06/58334210), another hot spot by the same owners, spills out onto its Trastevere piazza and down the stairs, filling the area around Piazza Trilussa with an attractive crowd of local mojito-sippers.

Continue on Via della Scala (with your back to Ombre Rosse, the street leaving from the piazza's far right corner). This narrow, pedestrian-only street has more bars and restaurants, all with street-side seating. At the end of Via della Scala, you'll see the Porta Settimiana, one of the city's ancient gates. Turning right here, follow Via San Dorotea to No. 19, once the home of La Fornarina, Raphael's Trasteverina lover. Continue on Via San Dorotea across Piazza San Giovanni Malva to Piazza Trilussa and have a look at the Ponte Sisto crossing the Tiber. The original bridge dates to the 2nd century BC, although most of what you see now dates from a 15th-century renovation (and a 1999 cleanup). Heading back through Piazza Trilussa, follow Vicolo del Cinque past more bars and restaurants. If it's after midnight, you can stop at No. 40, Daniela Orecchia, for *cornetti caldi*, hot, sweet pastries fresh out of the oven. Continue up Vicolo del Cinque, leading back to Piazza Sant'Egidio. Here you can have a nightcap and then retrace your steps across Piazza Santa Maria in Trastevere and down Via Lungaretta to Piazza Sonnino, where there's a taxi stand.

Salotto 42 (✉ Piazza di Pietra 42, near Pantheon ☎ 06/6785804) is open morning until late; the cozy-sleek room reflects its owners' Roman–New York–Swedish pedigrees as it moves from daylight bar with smorgasbord to cocktail lounge–design den, complete with art books and local sophisticates.

English- and Irish-style pubs have long been a prominent part of the bar scene in Rome, among Italians and foreigners alike. **Trinity College** (✉ Via del Collegio Romano 6, near Piazza Venezia ☎ 06/6786472) is one of the best of these drinking halls.

Following the modern-design-bar trend, **Fluid** (✉ Via Governo Vecchio 46/47, near Campo de' Fiori ☎ 06/6832361) serves drinks to cool patrons seated on glowing ice cube–like chairs as water streams down the walls. (As Fluid has gotten older, its clientele have gotten younger.) **La Vineria** (✉ Campo de' Fiori 15 ☎ 06/68803268) is the original bar on a square that's now full of them. It remains the truest example of an old-school Roman enoteca, always in style and great for watching the "scenery." **Crudo** (✉ Via Degli Specchi 6, Campo de' Fiori ☎ 06/6838989 ⊕ www.crudoroma.it) is a spacious, modern, New York–style lounge serving cocktails and *crudo* (raw) nibbles such as sushi and carpaccio. **Sloppy Sam's** (✉ Campo de' Fiori 10 ☎ 06/68802637) is an American-run pub on one of the city's busiest piazzas. Look for happy-hour specials and student discounts. For that essential predinner aperitivo, head for the buzzing **Friends** (✉ Piazza Trilussa 34, Trastevere ☎ 06/5816111) across the Tiber from the historic center. Late in the evening, head to **Stardust** (✉ Vicolo de' Renzi 4, Trastevere ☎ 06/58320875) for cocktails mixed up by an international bar staff and an ambience provided by eclectic music and local characters.

Music Clubs

Jazz, folk, pop, and Latin-music clubs are flourishing in Rome, particularly in Trastevere and Testaccio. Jazz clubs are especially popular, and talented local groups may be joined by visiting musicians from other countries. As admission, many clubs require that you buy a membership card, often valid for a month, at a cost of €6 and up. On weekend nights it's a good idea to reserve a table in advance no matter where you're going.

Behind the Vatican Museums, **Alexanderplatz** (✉ Via Ostia 9, near San Pietro ☎ 06/39742171), Rome's most famous jazz and blues club, has a bar and a restaurant. Local and internationally known musicians play nightly. **La Palma** (✉ Via Giuseppe Mirri 35, Tiburtina ☎ 06/43599029) is the venue favored by experimental jazz musicians. It's near the Tiburtina metro stop. **Big Mama** (✉ Vicolo San Francesco a Ripa 18, Trastevere ☎ 06/5812551) presents live blues, R&B, African, jazz, and rock. Latin rhythms are the specialty at **No Stress Brasil** (✉ Via degli Stradivari 35, Trastevere ☎ 06/5813249), where there's a Brazilian orchestra from Tuesday to Saturday. Monday is karaoke night.

Il Locale (✉ Vicolo del Fico 3, near Piazza Navona ☎ 06/6879075), closed Monday, pulls in a lively crowd for Italian rock. **The Place** (✉ Via Al-berico II 27–29, near San Pietro ☎ 06/68307137) has a mixture of live funk, Latin, and jazz sounds, accompanied by tasty fusion cuisine. In trendy Testaccio, **Caffè Latino** (✉ Via Monte Testaccio 96 ☎ 06/57288556) is a vibrant Roman locale that has live music (mainly Latin) almost every night, followed by recorded soul, funk, and '70s and '80s revival; it's closed Monday.

Nightclubs

Most dance clubs open about 10:30 PM and charge an entrance fee of about €20, which may include the first drink (subsequent drinks cost about €10). Clubs are usually closed Monday, and all those listed here close in summer, some opening instead at the beaches of Ostia or Fregene. The liveliest areas for clubs with a younger clientele are the grittier working-class districts of Testaccio and Ostiense. Any of the clubs lining Via Galvani, leading up to Monte Testaccio, are fair game for a trendy, crowded dance-floor experience—names and ownership of clubs change frequently, but the overall scene has shown some staying power.

The large **Art Café** (✉ Via del Galoppatoio 33, near Piazza di Spagna ☎ 06/36006578) has multiple levels, and there are theme nights (Tuesday fashion night, Thursday live jazz and dinner, Friday hip-hop), and *privé* (private) areas with a wading pool. **Supperclub** (✉ Via dei Nari 14, near Piazza di Spagna ☎ 06/68807207) is not only a place for reclined dining, but also a trendy club where DJs and live entertainment draw a sexy crowd. Most rooms are lined with big white beds and fluffy pillows, complete with roaming masseurs. Monday night is a laid-back hip-hop party organized by a former L.A. club promoter.

La Maison (✉ Vicolo dei Granari 4, near Piazza Navona ☎ 06/6833312), bedecked in purple velvet and chandeliers, has two distinct spaces and one main dance floor, with DJs dishing up the latest dance tunes. **Bloom** (✉ Via del Teatro Pace 29, near Piazza Navona ☎ 06/68802029) is a lounge-club in the city center, where Romans and visiting celebrities go to swill cocktails and dance in tight quarters. **Cabala** (✉ Via dei Soldati 23c, Piazza Navona ☎ 06/68301192), a multilevel disco–piano bar inside a gorgeous palazzo, can be uncomfortably packed on weekends. One of Rome's first discos, **Piper** (✉ Via Tagliamento 9, near Piazza Fiume ☎ 06/8414459), is still a magnet for young movers and shakers who favor disco and house beats and spectacular light effects. It's open Saturday and Sunday nights only.

Alibi (✉ Via di Monte Testaccio 39 ☎ 06/5743448) is a multilevel complex that caters to a mixed gay and straight crowd. The **Ex Magazzini** (✉ Via dei Magazzini Generali 8bis, Ostiense ☎ 06/5758040) is a happening disco bar that has a mix of live and DJ sets and hosts a vintage market on Sunday. **Goa** (✉ Via Libetta 13, Testaccio ☎ 06/5748277) is among Rome's trendiest clubs. In a Southeast Asian–inspired space you can listen to hip-hop, tribal, and house music played by some of Europe's most touted DJs.

SPORTS & THE OUTDOORS

Biking

You can rent a bike at **Collalti** (✉ Via del Pellegrino 82, Campo de' Fiori ☎ 06/68801084), which is also a reliable bike-repair shop; it's closed Monday. **St. Peter Moto** (✉ Via di Porta Castello 43, near San Pietro ☎ 06/6875714) is a good place to rent scooters as well as bikes.

Running

The best bet for running in central Rome is the **Villa Borghese** park, with a ⅔-km (½-mi) circuit of the Pincio, among the marble statuary. A longer run in the park itself might include a loop around Piazza di Siena, a grass riding arena. Although most traffic is barred from Villa Borghese, government and police cars sometimes speed through. Be careful to stick to the sides of the roads. For a long run away from all traffic, try the hilly and majestic **Villa Ada** in northern Rome, in the upscale Parioli neighborhood. **Villa Doria Pamphilj** on Janiculum Hill is a beautiful spot for a run south of the city. History-loving runners should do as the chariot horses did and run at the old **Circus Maximus**. A standard oval track (dubbed "il biscotto," as it's shaped like a cookie) is in the park flanked by the **Via delle Terme di Caracalla.**

Soccer

Italy's favorite spectator sport stirs passionate enthusiasm. Games are usually held on Sunday afternoons fall–spring and can be seen at many sports bars around the city: just follow the fans' screams.

The two city soccer teams, Roma and Lazio, are both in Series A (the top division); they play home games at the **Stadio Olimpico** (✉ Viale dello Stadio Olimpico ☎ 06/3237333), part of the Foro Italico complex built by Mussolini on the banks of the Tiber. There's a chance of Lazio soccer tickets being on sale at the box office before game time, but it's a better idea to buy them in advance from **Lazio Point** (✉ Via Farini 34, near Termini ☎ 06/4826688) to see the Lazio team play. Go to **Orbis** (✉ Piazza Esquilino 37, near Santa Maria Maggiore ☎ 06/4744776) to buy tickets to see the Roma play.

SHOPPING

Updated by
Dana Klitzberg

They say when in Rome to do as the Romans do—and the Romans love to shop. Stores are generally open from 9 or 9:30 to 1 and from 3:30 or 4 to 7 or 7:30. There's a tendency for shops in central districts to stay open all day, and hours are becoming more flexible throughout the city. Many places close Sunday, though this is changing, too, especially in the city center. With the exception of food stores, many stores also close Monday morning from September to mid-June and Saturday afternoon from mid-June through August. Stores selling food are usually closed Thursday afternoon.

You can stretch your euros by taking advantage of the Tax-Free for Tourists V.A.T. tax refunds, available at most large stores for purchases over €155. Or hit Rome in January and early February or in late July, when stores clean house with the justly famous biannual sales. There are so many hole-in-the-wall boutiques selling top-quality merchandise in Rome's center that even just wandering you're sure to find something that catches your eye.

Shopping Districts

★ The city's most famous shopping district, **Piazza di Spagna,** is conveniently compact, fanning out at the foot of the Spanish Steps in a galaxy of boutiques selling gorgeous wares with glamorous labels. Here you can ricochet from Gucci to Prada to Valentino to Versace with less effort than it takes to pull out your credit card. If your budget is designed for lower altitudes, you also can find great clothes and accessories at less-extravagant prices. But here, buying is not necessarily the point—window displays can be works of art, and dreaming may be satisfaction enough. Via Condotti is the neighborhood's central axis, but there are shops on every street in the area bordered by Piazza di Spagna on the east, Via del Corso on the west, between Piazza San Silvestro and Via della Croce, and extending along Via del Babuino to Piazza del Popolo.

Shops along **Via Campo Marzio,** and adjoining Piazza San Lorenzo in Lucina, stock eclectic, high-quality clothes and accessories—without the big names and at slightly lower prices. Running from Piazza Venezia to Piazza del Popolo lies **Via del Corso,** a main shopping avenue that has more than a mile of clothing, shoes, leather goods, and home furnishings from classic to cutting-edge. Running west from Piazza Navona, **Via del Governo Vecchio** has numerous women's boutiques and secondhand-clothing stores. **Via Cola di Rienzo,** across the Tiber from Piazza del Popolo, is block after block of boutiques, shoe stores, and department stores, as well as street stalls and upscale food shops. **Via dei Coronari,** across the Tiber from Castel Sant'Angelo, has quirky antiques and home furnishings. Via Giulia and other surrounding streets are good bets for decorative arts. Should your gift list include religious souvenirs, look for everything from rosaries to Vatican golf balls at the shops between Piazza San Pietro and **Borgo Pio.** Liturgical vestments and statues of saints make for good window-shopping on **Via dei Cestari,** near the Pantheon. On **Via Cola di Rienzo,** near San Pietro, there are stands selling everything from CDs to handicrafts, as well as many mid-level chain stores. **Via Nazionale** is a good bet for affordable stores of the Benetton ilk, and for shoes, bags, and gloves. The **Termini** train station has become a good one-stop place for many shopping needs. Its 60-plus shops are open until 10 PM and include a Nike store, the Body Shop, Sephora, Mango (women's clothes), a UPIM department store, and a grocery store.

Bargains

The market at **Via Sannio** (⊠ Near San Giovanni) has lots of designer shoes and stalls selling new and used clothing at bargain prices; hours are weekdays 8–2, Saturday 8–5. The **Borghetto Flaminio** (⊠ Piazza della Marina, Flaminio) market sells good-quality vintage clothing Sunday 9–2. The morning market in **Piazza Testaccio,** in the heart of the neighborhood of the same name, is known for stands selling last season's designer shoes at a third of the original price or less.

Romans and visitors alike flock to the **McArthurGlen Designer Outlet** (⊠ Via Ponte di Piscina Cupa, Castel Romano ☎ 06/5050050 ⊕ www. mcarthurglen.it), 10 km (6 mi) east of the city. Housed in a mock ancient Roman setting, the complex has more than 90 stores that sell major labels at prices 30% to 70% less than retail, from inexpensive Italian chains to designers such as Versace, Etro, and D & G. To get there, get on the Grande Raccordo Anulare ring road, take Exit 26 onto the Via Pontina (SS148) toward Pomezia, exit at Castel Romano, and follow the signs. The mall is open daily 10–10.

Department Stores & Malls

Italian department stores have little in common with their American cousins; most of them are much smaller and do not carry the same variety of merchandise, nor the recognizable brands. **Galleria Alberto Sordi** (⊠ Via del Corso and Viale Tritone, near Piazza di Spagna) is a mall with a café in the center of two corridors lined with shops. The star attractions are a large branch of Feltrinelli (a book and media store like Barnes & Noble), JAM (clothing and accessories, gifts and gadgets), and the women's affordable fashion mecca from Spain, Zara. **Rinascente** (⊠ Via del Corso 189, near Piazza di Trevi ☎ 06/6797691 ⊠ Piazza Fiume, Salario ☎ 06/8841231) sells only clothing and accessories in its main store. The Piazza Fiume branch also has furniture and housewares. Both stores are open seven days a week. **Oviesse** (⊠ Via Candia 74, near San Pietro ☎ 06/39743518 ☞ Other locations throughout the city) has moderately priced goods ranging from bathing suits to children's clothes.

Coin (⊠ Piazzale Appio 7, near San Giovanni ☎ 06/7080020 ⊠ Via Mantova 1/b, Salario ☎ 06/8416279) is somewhat trendier than other department stores; it carries a large collection of housewares as well as fashions for men and women. The mid-range chain store **UPIM** (⊠ Piazza Santa Maria Maggiore ☎ 06/4465579) is an institution in Italy; it sells clothing, bed linen, and contemporary kitchenware at reasonable prices. **Cinecittà Due** (⊠ Viale Palmiro Togliatti 2 ☎ 06/7220910) was the first of Rome's several megamalls (100 stores); take Metro A to the Subaugusta or Cinecittà stops.

Markets

Outdoor markets are open Monday–Saturday from early morning to about 1 PM (a bit later on Saturday), but get there early for the best selection. Remember to keep an eye on your wallet—the money changing hands draws Rome's most skillful pickpockets. And don't go if you can't stand crowds. Downtown Rome's most colorful outdoor food market is at **Campo de' Fiori**, south of Piazza Navona. The **Trionfale market** (⊠ Via Andrea Doria, near San Pietro) is big and bustling; it's about a five-minute walk north of the entrance to the Vatican Museums. There's room for bargaining at the Sunday-morning flea market at **Porta Portese**

(⊠ Via Ippolito Nievo, Trastevere). Seemingly endless rows of merchandise includes new and secondhand clothing, bootleg CDs, old furniture, car stereos of suspicious origin, and all manner of old junk and hidden treasures.

Specialty Stores

Antiques & Prints

For old prints and antiques, **Tanca** (⊠ Salita dei Crescenzi 12, near Pantheon ☎ 06/6875272) is a good hunting ground. Early photographs of Rome and views of Italy from **Alinari** (⊠ Via Alibert 16/a, near Piazza di Spagna ☎ 06/69941998) make memorable souvenirs. **Nardecchia** (⊠ Piazza Navona 25 ☎ 06/6869318) is reliable for prints. Stands in **Piazza della Fontanella Borghese** (⊠ Near Via del Corso) sell prints and old books.

Designer Clothing

All of Italy's top fashion houses and many international designers have stores near Piazza di Spagna. Buying clothes can be a bit tricky for American women, as sizes tend to be cut for a petite Italian frame. A size 12 (European 46) is not always easy to find, but the more-expensive stores should carry it. Target less-expensive stores for accessories if this is an issue.

D & G (⊠ Piazza di Spagna 82 ☎ 06/69924999), a spin-off of the top-of-the-line Dolce & Gabbana, shows trendy casual wear and accessories for men and women. The flagship store for **Fendi** (⊠ Largo Carlo Goldoni 419-421, near Piazza di Spagna ☎ 06/696661) is in the former Palazzo Boncompagni, renamed "Palazzo Fendi." It overlooks the intersection of famed Via Condotti and Via del Corso, and it's the quintessential Roman fashion house, presided over by the Fendi sisters. Their signature baguette bags, furs, accessories, and sexy separates are all found here. The **Giorgio Armani** (⊠ Via Condotti 77, near Piazza di Spagna ☎ 06/6991460) shop is as understated and elegant as its designs. **Gucci** (⊠ Via Condotti 8, near Piazza di Spagna ☎ 06/6783762) often has lines out the door of its two-story shop, testament to the continuing popularity of its colorful bags, wallets, and shoes in rich leathers. Edgy clothes designs are also available. Sleek, vaguely futuristic **Prada** (⊠ Via Condotti 92, near Piazza di Spagna ☎ 06/6790897) has two entrances: the one for the men's boutique is to the left of the women's.

Rome's leading local couturier, **Valentino** (Valentino Donna ⊠ Via Condotti 13, near Piazza di Spagna ☎ 06/6795862 ⊠ Valentino Uomo ⊠ Via Bocca di Leone 15, near Piazza di Spagna ☎ 06/6783656), is recognized the world over by the "V" logo. The designer has shops for the *donna* (woman) and the *uomo* (man) not far from his headquarters in Piazza Mignanelli beside the Spanish Steps. **Gianni Versace** (Versace Uomo ⊠ Via Borgognona 24–25, near Piazza di Spagna ☎ 06/6795037 ⊠ Versace Donna ⊠ Via Bocca di Leone 26–27, near Piazza di Spagna ☎ 06/6780521) sells the rock-star styles that made the house's name.

Degli Effetti (⊠ Piazza Capranica, near Pantheon ☎ 06/6791650) is a top-of-the-line boutique with men's and women's avant-garde fashion from the likes of Dries Van Noten, Miu Miu, Jil Sander, Martin Margiela, and Helmut Lang.

MEN'S CLOTHING **Ermenegildo Zegna** (✉ Via Borgognona 7/e, near Piazza di Spagna ☎ 06/6789143) has the finest in men's elegant styles and accessories. **Il Portone** (✉ Via delle Carrozze 71, near Piazza di Spagna ☎ 06/69925170) embodies a tradition in custom shirt making. **Brioni** (✉ Via Condotti 21, near Piazza di Spagna ☎ 06/6783428 ✉ Via Barberini 79, near Piazza di Trevi ☎ 06/6783635) has a well-deserved reputation as one of Italy's top tailors. There are ready-to-wear garments in addition to impeccable custom-made apparel. **Davide Cenci** (✉ Via Campo Marzio 1-7, near Pantheon ☎ 06/6990681) is famed for conservative clothing of exquisite craftsmanship. For something a little funkier, employing unusual cuts and lively colors, try Bologna designer **Daniele Alessandrini** (✉ Corso Rinascimento 58, near Piazza Navona ☎ 06/6879664).

WOMEN'S Come to the **Dress Agency** (✉ 1B Via del Vantaggio, Piazza di Spagna
CLOTHING ☎ 06/3210898) for designer-label consignment shopping: finds have included Prada sweaters and Gucci dresses, some pieces as low as €20. Although you never know exactly when you'll hit pay dirt, try right after the season changes and Roman women have cleaned out their closets to make room for new goodies. **Galassia** (✉ Via Frattina 21, near Piazza di Spagna ☎ 06/6797896) has expensive, extreme, and extravagant women's styles by Gaultier, Westwood, and Yamamoto—this is the place for feather boas and hats with ostrich plumes. If you're in the market for luxurious lingerie, **La Perla** (✉ Via Condotti 79, near Piazza di Spagna ☎ 06/69941934) is the place to shop.

If you're feeling flush, try **Nuyorica** (✉ Piazza Pollarolla 36, Campo de' Fiori ☎ 06/68891243), which sells expensive, superchic designer pieces from Balenciaga, Chloe, and American favorite Marc Jacobs, among others. **Josephine de Huertas & Co.** (✉ Via del Governo Vecchio 68, near Piazza Navona ☎ 06/6876586) is a precious little boutique with colorful, high-end stock from the likes of Paul Smith and lesser-known designers. **Ethic** (✉ Via del Pantheon 46/47 ☎ 06/68803167) is a great reasonably priced stop for funky fashions in this season's color palette, from knits to leather jackets. The boutique **rose d.** (✉ Corso Rinascimento 60, Piazza Navona ☎ 06/6867641) showcases upbeat urban fashions. (The unusual display racks can give taller customers a case of "shopper's crouch.")

The garments at **Luisa Spagnoli** (✉ Via del Tritone 30, near Piazza di Trevi ☎ 06/69202220) are elegant but contemporary, and they go to large sizes. **Alternative** (✉ Piazza Mattei 5, Jewish Ghetto ☎ 06/68309505) is a gorgeous addition to a beautiful piazza. Amid sparkling floor-to-ceiling crystal chandeliers, black walls, and colorful plush seating, you'll find select styles from cutting-edge designers such as Antonio Berardi, Alessandro dell-Acqua, Michael Kors, and Catherine Malandrino.

Embroidery & Linens

Frette (✉ Piazza di Spagna 11 ☎ 06/6790673) is a Roman institution for luxurious linens. **Venier Colombo** (✉ Via Frattina 79, near Piazza di Spagna ☎ 06/6787705) has a selection of exquisite lace goods, including lingerie and linens. **Lavori Artigianali Femminili** (✉ Via Capo le Case

6, near Piazza di Spagna ☎ 06/6781100) sells delicately embroidered household linens, infants' and children's clothing, and blouses.

Food

There are several hundred *salumerie* (gourmet food shops specializing in fresh and cured meats and cheeses) in town, but a few stand out for a particularly ample selection and items of rare, superior quality. Foodies should head straight for **Franchi** (✉ Via Cola di Rienzo 200, near San Pietro ☎ 06/6864576) to check out the sliced meats and cheeses that you can have vacuum-packed for safe transport home. They also sell the city's best take-out treats, including salmon mousse, roast beef, and vegetable fritters. **Castroni** (✉ Via Cola di Rienzo 196, near San Pietro ☎ 06/6864383) is an excellent general food shop with lots of imported items. **Volpetti** (✉ Via Marmorata 47, Testaccio ☎ 06/5742352) has high-quality meats and aged cheeses from small producers. The men behind the counter will be happy to let you take a taste.

A bottle of liqueur, jar of marmalade, or bar of chocolate made by Cistercian monks at Italian monasteries makes an unusual and tasty treat to take home. Choose from the goodies at **Ai Monasteri** (✉ Corso Rinascimento 72, near Piazza Navona ☎ 06/68802783). Drop into **Panella** (✉ Via Merulana 54, near Santa Maria Maggiore ☎ 06/4872344), one of Rome's most spectacular bakeries, for exquisite bread sculptures and a fine selection of pastas, oils, and preserves to take home.

Housewares

The kitchen shop at **'Gusto** (✉ Piazza Augusto Imperatore 9, near Piazza di Spagna ☎ 06/3226273) has a great selection of cookbooks, including some in English. Pricey **C.u.c.i.n.a.** (✉ Via Mario de' Fiori 65, near Piazza di Spagna ☎ 06/6791275) is one of the best kitchen-supply stores in town. **D Cube** (✉ Via della Pace 38, near Piazza Navona ☎ 06/6861218) is a kitschy boutique with colorful, architectural gadgets for the home. From within a striking frescoed 17th-century palazzo, **Spazio Sette** (✉ Via dei Barbieri 7, near Campo de' Fiori ☎ 06/6869747) sells gadgets and furniture created by the biggest names in Italian and international design. **Leone Limentani** (✉ Via Portico d'Ottavia 47, Ghetto ☎ 06/68806686) is a warehouse full of discounted kitchenware, by such names as Richard Ginori, Bernardaud, Reidel, and Baccarat.

Jewelry & Silver Objects

★ **Fornari & Fornari** (✉ Via Frattina 133, Piazza di Spagna ☎ 06/6980105) has a vast selection of silver pieces, as well as fine crystal and china. What Cartier is to Paris, **Bulgari** (✉ Via Condotti 10, near Piazza di Spagna ☎ 06/6793876) is to Rome; the shop's elegant display windows hint at what's beyond the guard at the door. **Buccellati** (✉ Via Condotti 31, near Piazza di Spagna ☎ 06/6790329) is a tradition-rich Florentine jewelry house renowned for its silver work; it ranks with Bulgari for quality and reliability.

At **Liliana Michilli** (✉ Via Dei Banchi Vecchi 37, near Campo de' Fiori ☎ 06/68392154) you can buy convincing copies of Bulgari and Gucci rings for a fraction of the price. The craftswomen of **Danae** (✉ Via della Maddalena 40, near Pantheon ☎ 06/6791881) make original jewelry pieces, working with metals and chunky stones like amber, milky aqua-marine, and turquoise. **Quattrocolo** (⊠ Via della Scrofa 54, near Pantheon ☎ 06/68801367) has been specializing in antique micro-mosaic jewelry and baubles from centuries past since 1938.

Shoes & Leather Accessories

It's the women's accessories—Luella bags to Marc Jacobs shoes—that bring shoppers back to the **Tad Concept Store** (⊠ Via del Babuino 155a, near Piazza di Spagna ☎ 06/32695131). Also sold are fabulous home-decorating items and *the* music you should be listening to; there's even a café. For gloves as pretty as Holly Golightly's, shop at **Sermoneta** (⊠ Piazza di Spagna 61 ☎ 06/6791960). Any color or style one might de-sire, from elbow-length black leather to scallop-edged lace-cut lilac suede, is available at this glove institution. For the latest, Italian-made styles in mid-range handbags, shoes, scarves, and costume jewelry, go to **Furla** (⊠ Piazza di Spagna 22 ☎ 06/69200363), which has a num-ber of stores in the city center.

Ferragamo Uomo (⊠ Via Condotti 65, near Piazza di Spagna ☎ 06/6781130) sells classic shoes for men. **Di Cori** (⊠ Piazza di Spagna 53 ☎ 06/6784439) has gloves in every color of the spectrum. **Bruno Magli** (⊠ Via del Gambero 1, near Piazza di Spagna ☎ 06/6793802 ⊠ Via Veneto 70 ☎ 06/42011671) is known for well-made shoes and match-ing handbags at both moderate and high prices. **Campanile** (⊠ Via Con-dotti 58, near Piazza di Spagna ☎ 06/6790731) has two floors of shoes in classic styles; they also sell other leather goods. The **Tod's** (⊠ Via Foontanella di Borghese 56 a/c, near Piazza di Spagna ☎ 06/68210066) central boutique sells signature button-sole moccasins made by Ital-ian shoe maestro Diego della Valle, as well as a line of handmade bags.

Federico Polidori (⊠ Via Pie di Marmo 7, near Pantheon ☎ 06/6797191) crafts custom-made leather bags and briefcases complete with mono-grams. For original, handcrafted bags and purses (some based on styles from names like YSL), **Sirni** (⊠ Via della Stelletta 33, near Pantheon ☎ 06/68805248) is worth seeking out.

For a vast selection of affordable, high-quality Italian bags and acces-sories, head for **Regal** (⊠ Via Nazionale 254, near Termini ☎ 06/4884893). **Calzature Fausto Santini** (⊠ Via Santa Maria Maggiore 165, near Santa Maria Maggiore ☎ 06/6784114) is the place for colorful, offbeat Santini shoes at half price. (The flagship store is on upmarket Via Frattina.)

Silks & Fabrics

Fratelli Bassetti (⊠ Corso Vittorio Emanuele II 73, near Campo de' Fiori ☎ 06/6892326) has a vast selection of world-famous Italian silks and fashion fabrics in a rambling palazzo. **Aston** (⊠ Via Boncompagni 27, near Via Veneto ☎ 06/42871227) stocks couture-level fabrics for men and women. You can find some real bargains if there are *scampoli* (rem-nants).

Stationery & Gifts

Fabriano (⊠ Via del Babuino 173, near Piazza di Spagna ☎ 06/6864268) sells stylish stationery, organized by color, as well as leather albums and pens of every description. Present your gifts with Italian flair: **Daniela Rosati** (⊠ Via della Stelletta 27, Pantheon ☎ 06/68802053) has beautifully handmade gift boxes covered in colorful paper.

ROME ESSENTIALS

Transportation

BY AIR

Most international flights and all domestic flights arrive at Aeroporto Leonardo da Vinci, also known as Fiumicino, 30 km (19 mi) southwest of Rome. Some international and charter flights and most low-cost carriers land at Ciampino, a civil and military airport 15 km (9 mi) southeast of Rome. To get to the city from Fiumicino by car, follow the signs for Rome on the expressway from the airport, which links with the GRA, the beltway around Rome. The direction you take on the GRA depends on where your hotel is, so get directions from the car-rental people at the airport. A taxi from Fiumicino to the center of town costs about €50, including *supplementi* (extra charges) for airport service and luggage, and the ride takes 30–40 minutes, depending on traffic. Private limousines can be hired at booths in the arrivals hall; they charge a little more than taxis but can take more passengers. Ignore gypsy drivers who approach you inside the terminal; stick to the licensed cabs, yellow or white, that wait by the curb. A booth inside the arrivals hall provides taxi information.

You have a choice of two trains to get to downtown Rome from Fiumicino Airport. Ask at the airport (at APT or train information counters) which train takes you closer to your hotel. The nonstop Airport–Termini Leonardo Express takes you directly to Track 22 at Stazione Termini, Rome's main train station, which is well served by taxis and is the hub of metro and bus lines. The ride takes 30 minutes; departures are every half hour beginning at 6:37 AM from the airport, with a final departure at 11:37 PM. From Termini to the airport, trains leave at 21 and 51 minutes past the hour. Tickets cost €9.50 at the main ticket counters in the station, or €10.50 if purchased at the little booth beside Track 22.

FM1, the other airport train, runs from the airport to Rome and beyond, terminating in Monterotondo, a suburban town to the east. The main stops in Rome are at Trastevere, Ostiense, and Tiburtina stations; at each you can find taxis and bus and/or metro connections to other parts of Rome. This train runs from Fiumicino from 6:35 AM to 12:15 AM, with departures every 20 minutes, a little less frequently in off-hours. The ride to Tiburtina takes 40 minutes. Tickets cost €5. For either train buy your ticket at automatic vending machines. There are ticket counters at some stations (at Termini/Track 22, Trastevere, Tiburtina). Date-stamp the ticket at the gate before you board.

🚩 Airport Information **Aeroporto Leonardo da Vinci** (also known as Fiumicino) ☎ 06/65951, 06/65953640 English-language flight information ⊕ www.adr.it. **Ciampino** ⊠ Via Appia Nuova ☎ 06/794941.

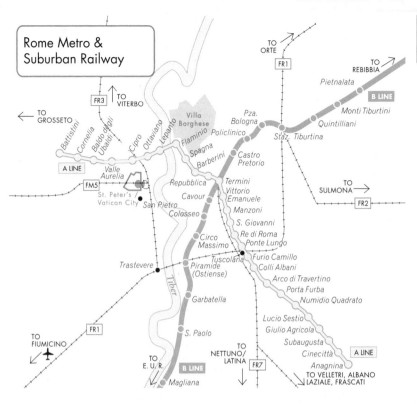

Rome Metro &
Suburban Railway

BY BUS, METRO & TRAM

There's no central bus terminal in Rome. COTRAL is the suburban bus company that connects Rome with outlying areas and other cities in the Lazio region. Long-distance and suburban buses terminate either near Tiburtina Station or near outlying metro stops such as Rebbibia and Anagnina. For COTRAL bus information, call weekdays 8 AM–6 PM.

Rome's metro (subway) is somewhat limited, but it's a quick, safe, and relatively low-stress way to get around town if there's a stop where you're going. The public bus and tram system is the opposite—routes are extensive, but the city's narrow streets and chronic traffic can make street-level transport slow. Metro service begins at 5:30 AM, and the last trains leave the most distant station at 11:30 PM (on Saturday night, trains run until 12:30 AM). Buses run day and night, although some routes change after 10 PM or midnight. Stops are marked by high white signs on yellow poles listing bus numbers and upcoming stops, but for serious exploring, a bus map (available at newsstands) is invaluable. The compact electric buses of Lines 117 and 119 take routes through the center of Rome that can save lots of walking. Routes change frequently; if you know a little Italian, you can plan itineraries and download maps before you go at ATAC's Web site.

ATAC city buses and tram lines run from about 6 AM to midnight, with night buses (indicated N) on some lines. A ticket valid for 75 minutes on any combination of buses and trams and one entrance to the metro costs €1. You are expected to date-stamp your ticket when you board the first vehicle, stamping it again when boarding for the last time within 75 minutes (the important thing is to stamp it the first time). Tickets for the public transit system are sold at tobacconists, newsstands, some coffee bars, green machines positioned in metro stations and some bus stops, and at ATAC and COTRAL ticket booths (in some metro stations, on the lower concourse at Stazione Termini, and at a few main bus terminals). A BIG tourist ticket, valid for one day on all public transport, costs €4. A weekly ticket (Settimanale, also known as CIS) costs €16 and can be purchased only at ATAC booths.

🚌 Bus & Metro Information **ATAC** ☎ 800/431784 toll-free ⊕ www.atac.roma.it. **COTRAL** ☎ 800/150008 toll-free.

BY CAR

The main access routes from the north are A1 (Autostrada del Sole) from Milan and Florence and the A12–E80 highway from Genoa. The principal route to or from points south, including Naples, is the A2. All highways connect with the Grande Raccordo Anulare (GRA), which channels traffic into the city center. As elsewhere in Italy, road signs for the center of town are marked with a bull's-eye. Signs on the GRA are confusing: take time to study the route you need.

Romans park wherever they find space, and sidewalk, double-, and triple-parking is common. Parking spaces outlined in blue are paid by buying a ticket from a small gray machine, located along the street. Leave the ticket, which shows how long you've paid to park, visible on the dashboard. Spaces outlined in yellow are not parking spaces at all—stay away to avoid being towed. If you rent a car in the city, make sure the rental desk gives you specific directions for getting out of town, and invest in a detailed city map (available at most newsstands).

BY MOPED

Zipping and careening through traffic on a *motorino* (moped) in downtown Rome is an attractive way to visit the city for some, but if you're averse to risk, pass on it. If your impulses—and reflexes—are fast, you can join the craziness of Roman traffic by renting a moped and the mandatory helmet at numerous rental spots throughout the city. Be extremely careful of pedestrians when riding: Romans are casual jaywalkers and pop out frequently from between parked cars.

🛵 Moped Rentals **Enjoy Rome** ⊠ Via Marghera 8A, Termini, 00185 ☎ 06/4451843 ⊕ www.enjoyrome.com. **Scoot-a-Long** ⊠ Via Cavour 302, Termini ☎ 06/6780206. **St. Peter Moto** ⊠ Via di Porta Castello 43, San Pietro ☎ 06/5757063. **Trevi Tourist Service** ⊠ Via dei Lucchesi 2, Piazza di Spagna ☎ 06/69200799.

BY TAXI

Taxis in Rome do not cruise, but if empty (look for an illuminated TAXI sign on the roof) they will stop if you flag them down. There is a taxi shortage in the city, so your best bet—especially during peak hours—is to wait at one of the city's many taxis stands or call by phone, in which case the meter starts when the taxi receives the request for a pickup. The meter price begins at €2.33 from 7 AM to 10 PM, at €3.36 on Sundays and holidays, and at €4.91 after 10 PM. Each piece of baggage will add an extra €2.03 to your fare. There are two different fare systems, one for outside the city and one for inside, shown on the LED meter display. Make sure your cab is charging you *tariffa uno*—the cheaper one—when you're in town. Use only licensed, metered yellow or white cabs, identified by a numbered shield on the side, an illuminated taxi sign on the roof, and a plaque next to the license plate reading SERVIZIO PUBBLICO. Avoid unmarked, unauthorized, unmetered cabs (common at airports and train stations), whose renegade drivers actively solicit your trade and often demand astronomical fares. Most taxis accept credit cards, but make sure to specify when calling that you will pay that way.

Taxi Companies Taxi ☎ 06/5551, 06/3570, 06/4994, or 06/88177.

BY TRAIN

Stazione Termini is Rome's main train terminal; the Tiburtina and Ostiense stations serve some long-distance trains, many commuter trains, and the FM1 line to Fiumicino Airport. Some trains for Pisa and Genoa leave Rome from, or pass through, the Trastevere Station. You can find English-speaking staff at the information office at Stazione Termini, or ask for information at travel agencies. You can purchase tickets up to two months in advance at the main stations or at most travel agencies. Lines at station ticket windows may be very long: you can save time by using the electronic ticket machines, which have instructions in English, or by buying your ticket at a travel agency. You can reserve a seat up to one day in advance at a travel agency or up to an hour in advance at a train station. Tickets for train rides within a radius of 100 km (62 mi) of Rome can be purchased at tobacco shops and at some newsstands, as well as at ticket machines on the main concourse. All train tickets must be date-stamped before you board, at the machine near the track, or you may be fined.

Train Information Trenitalia ☎ 892021 (a small service charge applies) ⊕ www.trenitalia.it.

Contacts & Resources

EMERGENCIES

Farmacia Internazionale Apotheke, Farmacia Trinità dei Monti, and Laltrafarmacia are pharmacies that have some English-speaking staff. Most pharmacies are open 8:30–1 and 4–8; some are open all night. A schedule posted outside each pharmacy indicates the nearest pharmacy open during off-hours (afternoons, through the night, and Sunday). Dial ☎ 1100 for an automated list of three open pharmacies closest to the telephone from which you call. The hospitals listed below have English-speaking doctors. Rome American Hospital is about 30 minutes by cab from the center of town.

Emergency Services Ambulance ☎ 118. **Police** ☎ 112 or 113. **Red Cross** ☎ 06/5510.
Hospitals Rome American Hospital ✉ Via Emilio Longoni 69, Via Prenestina ☎ 06/22551 ⊕ www.rah.it. **Salvator Mundi International Hospital** ✉ Viale delle Mura Gianicolensi 67, Trastevere ☎ 06/588961 ⊕ www.smih.pcn.net.

⚑ Pharmacies **Farmacia Internazionale Apotheke** ⊠ Piazza Barberini 49, near Via Veneto ☎ 06/4825456. **Farmacia Trinità dei Monti** ⊠ Piazza di Spagna 30 ☎ 06/6790626. **Laltrafarmacia** ⊠ Via Torino 21, near Termini ☎ 06/4881625.

TOURS

BIKE TOURS Enjoy Rome organizes all-day bike tours of Rome for small groups covering major sights and some hidden ones. Remember, Rome is famous for its seven hills; be prepared for a workout.

⚑ Fees & Schedules **Enjoy Rome** ⊠ Via Marghera 8A, near Termini ☎ 06/4451843 ⊕ www.enjoyrome.com.

BUS TOURS American Express and CIT offer general orientation tours of the city, as well as specialized tours of particular areas such as the Vatican or Ancient Rome. Stop-'n'-go City Tours has English-speaking guides and the option of getting off and on at 14 key sites in the city. A day pass costs €12.

⚑ Fees & Schedules **American Express** ☎ 06/67641. **Appian Line** ☎ 06/487861. **CIT** ⊠ Piazza della Repubblica 64, near Termini ☎ 06/4620311. **Stop-'n'-go City Tours** ☎ 06/47826379 ⊕ www.romecitytours.com.

WALKING TOURS All About Rome, American Express, Context: Rome, Enjoy Rome, Through Eternity, and Walks of Rome offer walking tours of the city and its sites.

⚑ Fees & Schedules **All About Rome** ☎ 06/7100823 ⊕ www.allaboutromewalks.netfirms.com. **American Express** ☎ 06/67641. **Context: Rome** ⊠ Via Baccina 40, near Termini ☎ 06/4820911 or 888/4671986 ⊕ www.contextrome.com. **Enjoy Rome** ⊠ Via Marghera 8A, near Termini ☎ 06/4451843 ⊕ www.enjoyrome.com. **Through Eternity** ☎ 06/7009336 ⊕ www.througheternity.com. **Walks of Rome** ⊠ Via Urbana 38, Quirinale ☎ 06/484853.

VISITOR INFORMATION

⚑ Tourist Information **Tourist office** (Azienda di Promozione Turistica di Roma/APT) ⊠ Via Parigi 5, near Termini ☎ 06/488991 ⊗ Mon.-Sat. 9-7 ⊠ Aeroporto Leonardo da Vinci ☎ 06/65956074 ⊗ Daily 8:15-7.

Between Rome & Florence

HIGHLIGHTS OF UMBRIA & TUSCANY

Norcia

WORD OF MOUTH

"Siena is not for a daytime, 'hit the highlights' tour. It is deeper than that. I think it is Italy's most enchanting medieval city. Give it a go!"

—jtrandolph

WELCOME TO UMBRIA & TUSCANY

TOP REASONS TO GO

★ **Assisi, shrine to St. Francis:** Recharge your soul in this rose-color hill town with a visit to the gentle saint's majestic Basilica.

★ **Orvieto's Duomo:** Arresting visions of heaven and hell on the façade and brilliant frescoes within make this Gothic cathedral a dazzler.

★ **Piazza del Campo, Siena:** Sip a cappuccino, lick some gelato, and take in this spectacular piazza.

★ **Piero della Francesca's** *True Cross* **frescoes, Arezzo:** If your holy grail is great Renaissance art, seek out these 12 silently enigmatic scenes.

★ **Sunset, San Gimignano:** Grab a spot on the steps of the Collegiata church as flocks of swallows swoop in and out of the famous medieval towers.

★ **Wine tasting in Chianti:** Sample the fruits of the region's gorgeous vineyards, at either the wineries themselves or the towns' wine bars.

The Tuscan countryside

1 Central Tuscany. The privileged hilltop site that helped **Siena** flourish in the Middle Ages keeps it one of Italy's most enchanting medieval towns today. To the west, **San Gimignano** bristles with 15th-century stone towers. To the north, the hills of the **Chianti** district present a rolling pageant of vineyards and villas.

2 Eastern Tuscany. The ancient stone town of **Cortona** sits high above the perfectly flat Valdichiana valley, offering great views of beautiful countryside. **Arezzo**, to the north, is best known for its sublime frescoes by Piero della Francesca.

3 **Northern Umbria. Assisi**—sanctified by St. Francis—doubles as a beautiful medieval village and a major pilgrimage site. Umbria's largest town, **Perugia,** is home to some of Perugino's great frescoes and a hilltop *centro storico*. It's also beloved by chocoholics: hazelnut Baci candies were born here.

Duomo, Orvieto

4 **Southern Umbria.** The town of **Orvieto** is famed for its cathedral, its dry white wines, and its spectacular hilltop location. Farther east, **Spoleto** offers Filippo Lippi frescoes, a massive castle towering over the town, and one of the world's great summer music festivals.

2

GETTING ORIENTED

The path between Rome and Florence runs along the Apennine mountain range through the hilly regions of Tuscany and Umbria. A mix of forests, vineyards, olive groves, and poppy fields adds up the Italian countryside at its most beautiful. The hillside towns, many dating from the days of ancient Rome, are rich with history: you'll encounter towering Gothic cathedrals, glowing Renaissance frescoes, and cobblestone streets worn smooth by a thousand years of strollers. When people close their eyes and dream of Italy, this is what they see.

Chianti

UMBRIA & TUSCANY PLANNER

The Strada Chiantigiana

Making the Most of Your Time

The best strategy for visiting Umbria and Tuscany is to choose one town as your base for several nights and then take day trips through the surrounding region. The beauty of such a plan is that it's virtually impossible to choose the wrong base: every town listed in this chapter has countless adherents who have fallen in love with it. Even the places with the heaviest tourist traffic—Assisi, Siena, San Gimignano—seem to breathe a sigh and relax in the evening after the day-trippers have departed.

Wherever you settle, keep in mind that this isn't the place for a jam-packed sightseeing agenda. One of the greatest pleasures here is indulging in rustic hedonism, marked by long lunches and showstopping sunsets.

Sample Travel Times

	HOURS BY CAR/TRAIN
Rome–Florence	3:00/1:45
Rome–Orvieto	1:30/1:00
Rome–Assisi	2:15/2:00
Rome–Siena	2:45/3:30
Florence–Assisi	1:45/2:30
Florence–Siena	1:00/1:30
Florence–Arezzo	1:00/0:30

Getting Around

A crucial thing to know when you're traveling through the hilly terrain of Umbria and Tuscany is that the valleys primarily run north–south. That means you can move in a north–south direction, following a valley, with relative ease, but when you're going east–west, you're climbing over hills, which involves slow, winding roads.

Getting around by Car: The major highway through the regions is the north–south A1 superstrada, which runs a 277-km (172-mi) course between Rome and Florence. It passes through western Umbria, skirting the hill town of Orvieto, and eastern Tuscany, passing close to Arezzo.

For more than a fleeting glance at these two regions, you need to get off the superstrada. Fortunately, the quality of the secondary roads is good, and driving them is a pleasure in itself. In Umbria, a loop of highway (made up of road nos. 204, 3, and 75) takes you off A1 to Spoleto, Assisi, and Perugia. In Tuscany, the A14 is the major highway between Siena and Florence, whereas road no. 222, know as the Strada Chiantigiana, is the slower, more picturesque, alternative.

Getting around by Train: Like the main highway, the direct train line from Rome to Florence runs through Orvieto and Arezzo. Other towns in Umbria are accessible by regional trains, but in Tuscany, the towns of the Chianti region aren't; there's train service to Siena, but the station isn't near the center of the old city—you need to take a taxi between the two.

For more information about car and train travel, as well as getting around by bus, see the "Essentials" section at the end of the chapter.

What's on the Menu

The foods of central Italy are a celebration of simple goodness: cooks pride themselves on using exceptional ingredients and letting the high quality shine through without a lot of culinary razzmatazz. Here are some dishes to look for:

Antipasti (appetizers): *Affettati misti:* Cured meats. *Crostini:* Toasted slices of bread with toppings. *Verdure sott' olio:* Vegetables cured in olive oil.

Primi (first courses): *Ribollita:* A vegetable soup thickened with cannellini beans and bread. *Panzanella:* A salad of bread, tomatoes, basil, cucumbers, and olive oil. *Pappardelle col sugo di cinghiale:* Fresh pasta with wild boar sauce. *Ravioli di ricotta e spinaci:* Spinach and cheese ravioli. *Strangozzi al tartufo:* Thin pasta with olive oil and truffles.

Secondi (second courses): *Bistecca alla fiorentina:* An extra-thick T-bone steak, grilled rare. *Arista di maiale:* Roast pork loin with rosemary. *Salsiccia e fagioli:* Pork sausage with beans. *Tagliata di manzo:* Thin slices of roasted beef, drizzled with oil.

The classic dessert is *cantuccini con vin santo*—very hard, little almond cookies dipped into a sherry-like dessert wine.

Finding a Place to Stay

It's a common practice in Umbria and Tuscany to convert old villas, farms, and monasteries into first-class hotels. The natural beauty of the countryside more than compensates for being located outside of town—provided you have a car. Hotels in towns tend to be simpler than their country cousins, with a few notable exceptions. Though it's tempting to think of this as an area where you can wander the hills and then stumble upon a charming little hotel at the end of the day, you're better off not testing your luck. Reservations are the way to go.

How's the Weather?

Spring and fall are the best times to visit Umbria and Tuscany, when the weather is mild and the volume of tourists comparatively low. In summer, try to start your days early and hit major sights first—that way you'll beat the crowds and the midday heat. Rising early isn't hard; Umbria and Tuscany aren't about late nights—most restaurants and bars close well before midnight.

Come winter, you'll meet with rain and chill. It's not a bad time to visit the cities—museums and monuments are uncrowded, and locals fill the restaurants. In the countryside, though, many restaurants and hotels close in November and reopen in the spring.

TOP PASSEGGIATA

Perugia's stately, palace-lined Corso Vannucci is where residents of Umbria's capital stretch their legs in style before dinner.

Perugia

	$$$$	$$$	$$	$	¢
Restaurants	over €45	€35–45	€25–35	€15–25	under €15
Hotels	over €220	€160–220	€110–160	€70–110	under €80

Restaurant prices are for a first course (*primo*), second course (*secondo*), and dessert (*dolce*). Hotel prices are for two people in a standard double room in high season, including tax and service.

UMBRIA

Updated by
Peter Blackman **UMBRIA CONTAINS A SERIES OF CHARACTER-RICH** hill towns, all within
an hour or two drive of one another; you can choose one as your base,
then explore the others, and the countryside and forest in between, on
day trips. The towns may not have the extravagant wealth of art and
architecture of Florence, Rome, or Venice, but this can work in their
favor: the towns feel knowable, not overwhelming. And there's plenty
to admire: Orvieto's cathedral and Assisi's basilica are two of the most
important sights in Italy, and Perugia and Spoleto are rich in art and architecture. While you're here, keep an eye out for remnants of ancient
Rome, which crop up all over—expect to see Roman villas, aqueducts,
theaters, walls, and temples.

ORVIETO

30 km (19 mi) west of Todi, 81 km (51 mi) west of Spoleto.

Carved out of an enormous plateau of volcanic rock high above a green
valley, Orvieto has natural defenses that made the high walls seen in many
Umbrian towns unnecessary. The Etruscans were the first to settle here,
digging a honeycombed network of more than 1,200 wells and storage
caves out of the soft stone. The Romans attacked, sacked, and destroyed the city in 283 BC; since then, it has grown up out of the rock
into an enchanting maze of alleys and squares. Orvieto was solidly
Guelph in the Middle Ages, and for several hundred years popes sought
refuge in the city, at times needing protection from their enemies, at times
from the summer heat of Rome.

When painting his frescoes inside the Duomo, Luca Signorelli asked that
part of his contract be paid in Orvietan wine, and he was neither the
first nor the last to appreciate the region's popular white. In past times
the caves carved underneath the town were used to ferment the Trebbiano grapes used in making Orvieto Classico; now local wine production has moved out to more traditional vineyards, but you can still while
away the afternoon in tastings at any number of shops in town.

Exploring Orvieto

Orvieto is well connected by train to Rome, Florence, and Perugia. It's
also adjacent to the A1 superstrada that runs between Florence and Rome.
Parking areas in the upper town tend to be crowded—a safer option is
to follow the signs to the Porta Orvetiana parking lot, then take the free
funicular up the hill.

If you're arriving by train, take another funicular that runs from the station up the side of the hill and through the fortress to Piazzale Cahen. It
runs every 20 minutes, daily 7:15 AM–8:30 PM, and costs €1. Although

Orvieto

Funicular

La Rocca

Tempio del
Belvedere

1

2

Giardino
Pubblico

Piazzale
Cahen

Porta
Rocca

SS71

Strada Statale Umbro Casentinese

Via Carducci

V. Quattro Cantone

V. Roma

Santa
Maria dei
Servi

V. U.
d'Ilario

V. Postierla

San
Domenico

Piazza
XXIX
Marzo

V. A di Cambio

V. Felice Cavallotti

V. Angelo
da Orvieto

V. Sta. Stefano

V. S.: Porcari

V. di piazza del Popolo

V. d. Orti

Crocefisso
del Tufo

Corso Cavour

V. C.
Nebbia

Sant'
Agostino

Piazza G.
Gonzaga

Piazza d.
Repubblica

V. dell'Olmo

Piazza
del Popolo

Vic di
Maurizio

3

San Giovenale

V.
Filippeschi

V. del Duomo

6

5

4

San
Bernardino

V. Malabranca

Palazzo
Comunale

Sant'
Andrea

Via Garibaldi

S.S.
Apostoli

Via
Maitani

Pozzo
della
Cava

San
Giovanni

Piazza
di Febei

Piazza
del Duomo

Porta
Maggiore

SS71

Piazza
Campo della
Fiera

V. D. Alberici

Porta
Romana

San
Francesco

San Lorenzo
di Arari

SS71

0   200 yards

0   200 meters

ORVIETO

the workings have been modernized, there are a few pictures in each station of the old cog railcars, which were once run hydraulically. Keep your funicular ticket, as it will get you a discount on admission to the Museo Claudio Faina. Bus 1 makes the same trip from 8 AM to 11 PM. From Piazzale Cahen, Bus A runs to Piazza del Duomo in the town center.

A *biglietto unico* (single ticket) is a great deal; for €12.50, you get admission to four major sights in town—Cappella di San Brizio (at the Duomo), Museo Claudio Faina, Torre del Moro, and Orvieto Underground—plus a combination bus-funicular pass or five hours of free parking.

The main sights in town can be seen in a full day; allow plenty of time for the Duomo and the Cappella di San Brizio. A day and a half might do better to enjoy Orvieto at a more leisurely pace, explore the local cuisine and perhaps pop into a winery. Thursday and Saturday are market days in Piazza del Popolo.

The Main Attractions

★ ❸ **Duomo.** Orvieto's cathedral is a dazzling triumph of Romanesque-Gothic architecture. It was built to commemorate a local miracle: a priest in the nearby town of Bolsena suddenly found himself assailed by doubts about the transubstantiation—he could not bring himself to believe that the body of Christ was contained in the consecrated communion host. His doubts were put to rest, however, when a wafer he had just blessed suddenly started to drip blood onto the linen covering the altar. The pope certified the miracle and declared a new religious holiday— the Feast of Corpus Christi.

The stunning carved-stone church facade is the work of some of Italy's finest artists and took 300 years to complete. The bas-reliefs on the lower parts of the pillars by Lorenzo Maitani (circa 1275–1330), one of the Duomo's architects, show scenes from the Old Testament and some scary renderings of the *Last Judgment and Hell,* as well as a more tranquil *Paradise.*

Inside the cathedral you must cross a vast expanse to reach the major works, at the far end of the church in the transepts. To the left is the **Cappella del Corporale,** where the famous stained altar cloth is displayed in a modern casing. The cloth is carried outside the cathedral, for festive viewings, on Easter and on Corpus Christi (the ninth Sunday after Easter). It was originally stored in the golden reliquary that is also on display. Though often ignored, the old container, modeled after the cathedral and inlaid with transparent enamel images, deserves a closer look—it's one of the finest examples of this kind of 14th-century Italian workmanship in existence today. On the nearby chapel walls, frescoes executed by a trio of local artists depict the miracle. In the right transept, Signorelli's *Stories of the Antichrist and of the Last Judgement,* the artistic jewels of the Duomo, deck the walls of the **Cappella Nuova** (or Cappella di San Brizio; buy tickets in the tourist office across the square). In these delightfully gruesome works, the damned fall to hell, and lascivious demons bite off ears, step on heads, and spirit away young girls. Dante would surely have approved; his portrait accompanies *Scenes from Purgatorio.* Signorelli and Fra Angelico, who also worked

UMBRIA THROUGH THE AGES

THE EARLIEST INHABITANTS of Umbria, the Umbri, were thought by the Romans to be the most ancient inhabitants of Italy. Little is known about them; with the coming of Etruscan culture the tribe fled into the mountains in the eastern portion of the region. The Etruscans, who founded some of the great cities of Umbria, were in turn supplanted by the Romans. Unlike Tuscany and other regions of central Italy, Umbria had few powerful medieval families to exert control over the cities in the Middle Ages—its proximity to Rome ensured that it would always be more or less under papal domination.

In the center of the country, Umbria has for much of its history been a battlefield where armies from north and south clashed. Hannibal destroyed a Roman army on the shores of Lake Trasimeno, and the bloody course of the interminable Guelph-Ghibelline conflict of the Middle Ages was played out here. Dante considered Umbria the most violent place in Italy. Trophies of war still decorate the Palazzo dei Priori in Perugia, and the little town of Gubbio continues a warlike rivalry begun in the Middle Ages—every year it challenges the Tuscan town of Sansepolcro to a crossbow tournament. Today the bowmen shoot at targets, but neither side has forgotten that 500 years ago its ancestors shot at each other. In spite of—or perhaps because of—this bloodshed, Umbria has produced more than its share of Christian saints. The most famous is St. Francis, the decidedly pacifist saint whose life shaped the Church of his time. His great shrine at Assisi is visited by hundreds of thousands of pilgrims each year. St. Clare, his devoted follower, was Umbria-born, as were St. Benedict, St. Rita of Cascia, and the patron saint of lovers, St. Valentine.

on the chapel, witness the gory scene. ✉ *Piazza del Duomo* ☎ *0763/ 341167 Duomo, 0763/342477 Capella Nuova* ⊕ *www.opsm.it* 🎫 *Duomo free, Cappella Nuova €3* ⊗ *Duomo, Nov.–Feb., daily 7:30–12:45 and 2:30–5:15; Mar. and Oct., daily 7:30–12:45 and 2:30–6:15; Apr.–Sept., daily 7:30–12:45 and 2:30–7:15. Capella Nuova, Nov.–Feb., Mon.–Sat. 9–12:45 and 2:30–5:15; Mar. and Oct., Mon.–Sat. 9–12:45 and 2:30–6:15; Apr.–Sept., Mon.–Sat. 9–12:45 and 2:30–7:15; Oct.–June, Sun. 2:30–5:45; July–Sept., Sun. 2:30–6:45.*

❹ **Museo Claudio Faina.** This superb private collection, beautifully arranged and presented, goes far beyond the usual museum offerings of a scattering of local remains. The collection is particularly rich in Greek- and Etruscan-era pottery, from large Attic amphorae (6th–4th century BC) to Attic black- and red-figure pieces to Etruscan *bucchero* (dark, reddish clay) vases. Other interesting pieces in the collection include a 6th-century sarcophagus and a substantial display of Roman-era coins. ✉ *Piazza del Duomo 29* ☎ *0763/341511* ⊕ *www.museofaina.it* 🎫 *€4.50* ⊗ *Apr.–Sept., daily 9:30–6; Oct. and Mar., daily 10–5; Nov.–Feb., Tues.–Sun. 10–5.*

★ ❺ **Orvieto Underground.** There is no better way to get a sense of Orvieto's multilayered history than to take a tour of the maze of tunnels and chambers that make up Orvieto Underground. Members of an Umbrian speleological club lead small groups down below street level to explain the origins of the tufa plateau on which Orvieto sits and to reveal the fascinating purposes to which these hidden caverns were put. Tickets and information are available from the Orvieto

Tourist Office, which also serves as the meeting place for tour groups. ⊠ *Piazza Duomo 24* ☎ *0763/344891* ⊕ *www.orvietounderground.it* ⊠ *€5.50* ☉ *Visits daily at 11, 12:30, 4, and 5:15.*

Also Worth Seeing

❷ **Fortezza.** On Piazza Cahen, this fortress, built in the mid-14th century, encloses a public park with benches, shade, and an incredible view.

❶ **Pozzo di San Patrizio** (Well of St. Patrick). When Pope Clement VII (1478–1534) took shelter in Orvieto during the Sack of Rome in 1527, he had to ensure a safe water supply should Orvieto come under siege. Many wells and cisterns were built, and the pope commissioned one of the great architects of the day, Antonio da Sangallo the Younger (1493–1546), to build the well adjacent to the Rocca. After nearly a decade of digging, water was found at a depth of 203 feet. Two one-way spiral stairways allowed donkey-driven carts to descend and return without running into one another. Windows open onto the shaft, providing natural light in the stairwells. There are 248 steps down to the bottom, but you'll probably get the idea after just a few. The well was once compared to St. Patrick's Well in Ireland. The name stuck, and the Italian *pozzo di san patrizio* has come to represent an inexhaustible source of wealth. ⊠ *Viale Sangallo, off Piazza Cahen* ☎ *0763/343768* ⊠ *€4.50* ☉ *Oct.–Mar., daily 10–5:45; Apr.–Sept., daily 10–6:45.*

❻ **Torre del Morro.** It's hard to imagine a simpler, duller affair than this tower in the center of town. It took on a little more character in the 19th century, when the large, white-faced clock was added along with the fine 14th-century bell, marked with the symbols of the 24 arts and craft guilds then operating in the city. The views, however, are worth the climb. ⊠ *Corso Cavour at Via del Duomo* ☎ *0763/344567* ⊠ *€2.80* ☉ *May–Aug., daily 10–8; Mar.–Apr. and Sept.–Oct., daily 10–7; Nov.–Feb., daily 10–1 and 2:30–5.*

Where to Stay & Eat

$$$$ ✗ **Osteria dell'Angelo.** Come here for a decidedly nouvelle alternative to heavy Umbrian cuisine, in which tempting ingredients are delicately spiced and thoughtfully prepared. From the changing menu you might try the

animelle di carciofi con mousse di mele al calvados (artichoke hearts with an apple-and-Calvados mousse) as a starter, and continue with the *umbrichelli al sedano, limone, e burro del chianti* (local handmade spaghetti with a celery, lemon, and butter sauce). Desserts are spectacular, and the book-length wine list details an intoxicating array of producers and vintages. ✉ *Piazza XXIX Marzo 8/a* ☎ *0763/341805* ⌂ *Reservations essential* ☰ *AE, DC, MC, V* ⊗ *No dinner Sun.; no lunch Mon. and Tues.; closed 2 wks in Jan. and in July.*

$$ ✕ **Le Grotte del Funaro.** This restaurant has an extraordinary location, deep in a series of caves within the volcanic rock beneath Orvieto. Once you have negotiated the steep steps, typical Umbrian specialties like tagliatelle *al vino rosso* (with red wine sauce) and grilled beef with truffles await. Sample the fine Orvieto wines, either the whites or the lesser-known reds. ✉ *Via Ripa Serancia 41* ☎ *0763/343276* ⊕ *www.ristorantiorvieto.it* ⌂ *Reservations essential* ☰ *AE, DC, MC, V* ⊗ *Closed Mon. and 1 wk in July.*

¢ ✕ **Cantina Foresi.** For a light lunch of cheese, salami, bread, and salad accompanied by a glass of cool white wine, this small *enoteca* (wine bar) is hard to beat. The umbrella-shaded tables have one of the best views of the cathedral facade in town. ✉ *Piazza del Duomo 2* ☎ *0763/341611* ☰ *AE, DC, MC, V* ⊗ *Closed Tues. Nov.–Mar.*

$$ ✕⌂ **Villa Bellago.** Three farmhouses overlooking Lake Corbara have been completely renovated, resulting in a lodging with bright, spacious guest rooms and ample facilities. The hotel's fine restaurant ($$) specializes in imaginatively prepared Umbrian and Tuscan dishes, such as *umbrichelli alla norcina* (local handmade spaghetti with a cream-and-sausage sauce), and fresh fish is always on the menu. ✉ *On S448, 05023 Baschi, 7 km (4½ mi) south of Orvieto* ☎ *0744/950521* 🖨 *0744/ 950524* ⊕ *www.argoweb.it/hotel_villabellago* ⌂ *19 rooms* ⌂ *Restaurant, minibars, tennis court, pool, gym, sauna, bar* ☰ *AE, DC, MC, V* ⊗ *Restaurant closed Mon. and 3 wks in Feb.* ⍾ *BP.*

★ $$$$ ⌂ **Hotel La Badia.** One of the best-known country hotels in Umbria occupies a 12th-century building—a former monastery. Vaulted ceilings and exposed stone walls establish the rustic elegance in the guest rooms, which have hand-knotted rugs and upholstered furniture. The rolling park around the hotel provides wonderful views of the valley and the town of Orvieto in the distance. ✉ *Località La Badia, 05018 Orvieto Scalo, 4 km (2½ mi) south of Orvieto* ☎ *0763/301959* 🖨 *0763/305396* ⊕ *www.labadiahotel.it* ⌂ *21 rooms, 7 suites* ⌂ *Restaurant, 2 tennis courts, pool, bar, Internet room, meeting rooms* ☰ *AE, MC, V* ⊗ *Closed Jan. and Feb.* ⍾ *BP.*

$$ ⌂ **Palazzo Piccolomini.** Once a 16th-century palace, this is perhaps your best bet in central Orvieto for a pleasant stay. Though the entrance hall and bar are austere, the guest rooms, which vary in size, are modern and comfortable. Try for one of the larger rooms on an upper floor. Service is friendly and efficient. ✉ *Piazza Ranieri 36, 05018* ☎ *0763/ 341743* 🖨 *0763/391046* ⊕ *www.hotelpiccolomini.it* ⌂ *29 rooms, 2 suites* ⌂ *Bar, Internet room* ☰ *AE, DC, MC, V* ⊗ *Closed Jan. 15–31* ⍾ *BP.*

Shopping

Excellent Orvieto wines are justly prized throughout Italy and the world. The whites pressed from the region's Trebbiano grapes are fruity, with a tart finish. Orvieto also produces its own version of the Tuscan dessert wine *vin santo*. It's darker than its Tuscan cousin and is aged five years before bottling. You can stop for a glass of vino at the **Wine Bar Nazzaretto** (⊠ Corso Cavour 40 ☎ 0763/340868), where there's also a good selection of sandwiches and snacks, and vin santo is for sale.

With a few small tables, a cheese counter that is second to none, a short menu, and a carefully chosen wine list, the specialty store **Carraro** (⊠ Corso Cavour 101 ☎ 0763/342870) is an excellent place for either a *degustazione* (tasting) of Orvietan cheese or a light lunch.

Orvieto artisans do particularly fine inlay and veneer woodwork. The Corso Cavour has a number of shops, the best known being the **Michelangeli family studio** (⊠ Via Michelangeli 3, at Corso Cavour ☎ 0763/ 342377), chock-full of imaginatively designed creations ranging in size from a giant *armadio* (wardrobe) to a simple wooden spoon.

Embroidery and lace making are not lost arts; **Duranti** (⊠ Corso Cavour 105 ☎ 0763/342222) is a good shop in which to find handmade *merletto* (lace).

SPOLETO

For most of the year Spoleto is one in a pleasant succession of sleepy hill towns. But for three weeks every summer it shifts into high gear for its turn in the spotlight: the Festival dei Due Mondi, a world-class extravaganza of theater, opera, music, painting, and sculpture, where the world's top artists vie for honors and throngs of art aficionados vie for hotel rooms.

But there is good reason to visit Spoleto any time of the year. Roman and medieval attractions and superb natural surroundings make it one of Umbria's most inviting towns. From the churches set among silvery olive groves on the outskirts of town to the soaring Ponte delle Torri behind it, Spoleto has sublime views in every direction.

Exploring Spoleto

Spoleto is small, and its sights are clustered in the upper part of town, so it's best explored on foot. Several walkways cut down the hill, crossing the Corso Mazzini, which turns up the hill. Parking in Spoleto is always difficult; park outside the walls in Piazza della Vittoria. One day in Spoleto allows you to see the highlights and still have time for a leisurely lunch and a walk across the Ponte delle Torri.

The Main Attractions

❸ **Duomo.** A Renaissance loggia, eight rose windows, and an early-13th-century gold mosaic of the Benedictory Christ lightens the church's rather dour 12th-century Romanesque facade. The contrast makes this

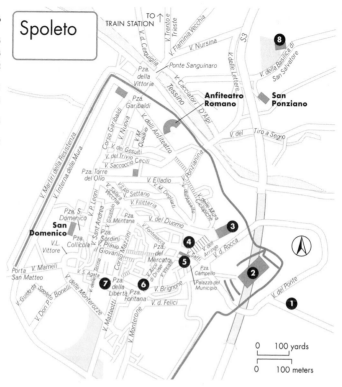

one of the finest church exteriors in the region. Inside, the Duomo holds the most notable art in town, including the immaculately restored frescoes in the apse by Fra Filippo Lippi (1406–69), depicting the *Annunciation,* the *Nativity,* and the *Dormition of Mary,* with a marvelous *Coronation of the Virgin* adorning the dome. Be ready with a €0.50 coin to illuminate the masterpiece. The Florentine artist died shortly after completing the work, and his tomb—designed by his son, Filippino Lippi (1457–1504)—lies in the right transept. Another fresco cycle, including work by Pinturicchio, is in the **Cappella Eroli** off the right aisle. ⊠ *Piazza Duomo* ☎ *0743/44307* ⊙ *Mar.–Oct., daily 8:30–12:30 and 3:30–7; Nov.–Feb., daily 8:30–12:30 and 3:30–6.*

★ ❶ **Ponte delle Torri.** Spanning massively and gracefully across the gorge that separates Spoleto from Monteluco, this 14th-century bridge is one of Umbria's most-photographed sights, and justifiably so. Built by Gattapone over the foundations of a Roman-era aqueduct, it's 750 feet long and soars up to 262 feet above the forested gorge. Postcard valley views make a walk across the bridge a must, particularly on a starry night. Beyond are the slopes of Monteluco, where well-marked trails invite further exploration on foot. ⊠ *Via del Ponte.*

Hiking the Umbrian Hills

MAGNIFICENT SCENERY makes the heart of Italy excellent walking, hiking, and mountaineering country. In Umbria, the area around Spoleto is particularly good; several pleasant, easy, and well-signed trails begin at the far end of the Ponte delle Torri bridge over Monteluco. From Cannara an easy half-hour walk leads to the fields of Pian d'Arca, the site of St. Francis's sermon to the birds. For slightly more arduous walks, you can follow the saint's path, uphill from Assisi to the Eremo delle Carceri, and then continue along the trails that crisscross Monte Subasio. At 4,250 feet, the Subasio's treeless summit affords views of Assisi, Perugia, far-off Gubbio, and the distant mountain ranges of Abruzzo.

For even more challenging hiking, the northern reaches of the Valnerina are exceptional; the mountains around Norcia should not to be missed. Throughout Umbria and the Marches, you'll find that most recognized walking and hiking trails are marked with the distinctive red-and-white blazes of the Club Alpino Italiano (CAI). Tourist offices are a good source for walking and climbing itineraries to suit all ages and levels of ability, and bookstores, *tabacchi* (tobacconists), and *edicole* (newsstands) often have maps and hiking guides that detail the best routes in their area. Depending on the length and location of your walk, it can be important that you have comfortable walking shoes or boots, appropriate attire, and plenty of water to drink.

Also Worth Seeing

❻ Arco di Druso. This arch was built in the 1st century AD by the Senate of Spoleto to honor the Roman general Drusus (circa 13 BC–AD 23), son of the emperor Tiberius. It once marked the entrance to the Foro Romano (Roman Forum). ⊠ *Piazza del Mercato.*

❺ Casa Romana. The house excavated at the end of the 19th century is thought to have belonged to Vespasia Polla, the mother of the Roman emperor Vespasian. The design is typical for houses of the 1st century AD, and some of the original decoration is still intact, including geometrically patterned marble mosaics and plaster moldings. ⊠ *Palazzo del Municipio, Via Visiale 9* ☎ *0743/224656* ⊠ *€2.50* ☉ *June–Oct. 15, daily 10–8; Oct. 16–May, daily 10–6.*

❷ La Rocca. The fortress built in 1359–63 by the Gubbio-born architect Gattapone dominates Spoleto. The structure served as a prison between 1860 and 1982 and now houses a small museum dedicated to medieval Spoleto. Plans for future development include an open-air theater and an international school for book restoration. You can admire the formidable exterior from the road that circles the extensive park beneath the castle. Tickets include a shuttle up to the entrance. Guided visits start on the hour; the last tour starts an hour before closing. ⊠ *Via del Ponte* ☎ *0743/46434* ⊠ *€6.50* ☉ *Apr.–Oct. 15, daily 10–7; Oct. 16–Mar., weekdays 10–noon and 3–5, weekends 10–5.*

4 **Sant'Eufemia.** Ancient and austere, this 11th-century church sits in the courtyard of the archbishop's palace. Its most interesting feature is the gallery, unique in Umbria, where female worshippers were required to sit. Enter through the attached **Museo Diocesano,** which contains paintings including a Madonna by Fra Filippo Lippi. ☒ *Via Saffi between Piazza del Duomo and Piazza del Mercato* ☎ *0743/23101* 🎫 *€3* ☉ *Oct.–Mar., Wed.–Sat. and Mon. 10–12:30 and 3–6, Sun. 11–5; Apr.–Sept., Wed.–Sat. and Mon. 10–1 and 4–7, Sun. 10:30–1 and 3–6.*

7 **Teatro Romano.** The small but well-preserved Roman theater was the site of a gruesome episode in Spoleto's history. During the medieval struggle between Guelph (papal) and Ghibelline (imperial) factions for control of central and northern Italy, Spoleto took the side of the Holy Roman Emperor. And woe to those who disagreed: 400 Guelph supporters were massacred in the theater, their bodies burned in an enormous pyre. In the end, however, the Guelphs were triumphant, and Spoleto was incorporated into the states of the Church in 1354. Through a door in the west portico, the **Museo Archeologico** displays assorted artifacts and the *Lex Spoletina* (Spoleto Law) tablets dating from 315 BC. This ancient legal document prohibited the destruction of the *Bosco Sacro* (Sacred Forest), south of town on Monteluco, a pagan prayer site later frequented by St. Francis. The theater is used in summer for Spoleto's arts festival. ☒*Piazza della Libertà* ☎*0743/223277* 🎫*€4* ☉*Daily 8:30–7:30.*

Off the Beaten Path

8 **San Salvatore.** The church and cemetery of San Salvatore seem very much forgotten, ensconced in solitude and cypress trees on a peaceful hillside, with the motorway rumbling below. One of the oldest churches in the world, it was built by eastern monks in the 4th century, largely of Roman-era materials. The highlight is the facade, with three exquisite marble doorways and windows, one of the earliest and best preserved in Umbria. It dates from a restoration in the 9th century and has hardly been touched since. ☒ *Via della Basilica di San Salvatore, 1 km (½ mi) northeast of town, off Via Flaminia* ☉ *Nov.–Feb., daily 7–5; Mar., Apr., Sept., and Oct., daily 7–6; May–Aug., daily 7–7.*

Where to Stay & Eat

$$–$$$ ✕ **Il Tartufo.** As the name, the Truffle, indicates, dishes prepared with truffles are the specialty here—don't miss the risotto al tartufo—but there are also choices not perfumed with this expensive delicacy. Traditional fare is spiced up to appeal to the cosmopolitan crowd attending (or performing in) the summertime Festival dei Due Mondi. Incorporating the ruins of a Roman villa, the restaurant's decor is rustic on the ground floor; furnishings are more modern upstairs, and there's outdoor seating in warm weather. ☒ *Piazza Garibaldi 24* ☎ *0743/40236* 🍴 *Reservations essential* 🖃 *AE, DC, MC, V* ☉ *Closed Mon. and last 2 wks in July. No dinner Sun.*

$$ ✕ **Osteria del Trivio.** At this friendly trattoria serving up traditional Umbrian fare, everything is homemade and changes daily depending on what's in season. Dishes might include stuffed artichokes, pasta with *funghi* *sanguinosi* (a local mushroom) sauce, or chicken with artichokes. The homemade biscotti, for dunking in sweet wine, are a great dessert choice. There is a printed menu, but your effusive host will gladly explain the dishes in a number of languages. ⊠ *Via del Trivio 16* ☎ *0743/ 44349* ▭ *AE, DC, MC, V.*

$$ ✕ **Il Pentagramma.** A stable-turned-restaurant serves fresh local dishes such as *tortelli ai carciofi e noci* (artichoke-filled pasta with a hazelnut sauce) and lamb in a truffle sauce. It's quite central, off the Piazza della Libertà. ⊠ *Via Martani 4* ☎ *0743/223141* ▭ *DC, MC, V* ⊘ *Closed Mon. No dinner Sun.*

$$ ✕ **Ristorante Panciolle.** In the heart of Spoleto's medieval quarter, this restaurant has one of the most appealing settings you could wish for: a small piazza filled with lemon trees. Dishes change throughout the year, and may include pastas served with asparagus or mushrooms, as well as grilled meats. When in season, more expensive dishes prepared with fresh truffles are also available. ⊠ *Vicolo degli Eroli 1* ☎ *0743/221241* ⊕ *www. ristoranteilpanciollespoleto.com* ⌂ *Reservations essential* ▭ *AE, DC, MC, V* ⊘ *Closed Wed.*

★ $$ ▦ **Cavaliere Palace Hotel.** Turn into an arched passage off one of Spoleto's busy shopping streets and enter an elegant world through a quiet courtyard. Built in the 17th century for an influential cardinal, the rooms, particularly on the second floor, retain their sumptuously frescoed ceilings; care has been taken to retain a sense of old-world comfort throughout. In warm weather enjoy breakfast on a terrace and in a peaceful garden at the back of the hotel. ⊠ *Corso Garibaldi 49, 06049* ☎ *0743/220350* 📠 *0743/224505* ⊕ *www.cavalierehotels.com* ⇨ *29 rooms, 2 suites* ⌂ *Restaurant, in-room safes, minibars, cable TV, bar, meeting rooms* ▭ *AE, DC, MC, V* ⦿ *BP.*

$$ ▦ **Hotel San Luca.** The elegant San Luca is Spoleto's finest hotel, thanks

to its commendable attention to detail: hand-painted friezes decorate guest-room walls, linen sheets cover firm beds, and some of the spacious rooms are wheelchair accessible. Enjoy an ample breakfast buffet, including homemade cakes, which is served in a pleasant room facing the central courtyard. You can sip afternoon tea in oversize armchairs by the fireplace, and the hotel's rose garden provides a sweet-smelling backdrop for a walk or a nap. Service is cordial and prices are surprisingly modest. ⊠ *Via Interna delle Mura 21, 06049* ☎ *0743/223399* 📠 *0743/223800* ⊕ *www.hotelsanluca.com* ⇨ *33 rooms, 2 suites* ⌂ *In-room safes, some in-room hot tubs, bar, laundry service, Internet room, parking (fee)* ▭ *AE, DC, MC, V* ⦿ *BP.*

$$ ▦ **Palazzo Dragoni.** Housed in the 15th-century palazzo of a Spoleto noble and decorated with antiques and frescoes, all the rooms of this hotel differ in size and aspect. Room 8 with a canopied bed and Room 10 with elegant picture windows are particularly beautiful. The plain tile bathrooms, although simple and functional, lack the charm of the rest of the building. Look out at the cathedral and the sloping rooftops of the town from the guest rooms that face the valley and from the loggia, where the buffet breakfast is served. ⊠ *Via del Duomo 13, 06049* ☎ *0743/222220* 📠 *0743/222225* ⊕ *www.palazzodragoni.it* ⇨ *15 rooms* ⌂ *Wi-Fi, bar, meeting rooms, parking (fee), some pets allowed; no a/c in some rooms* ▭ *MC, V* ⦿ *BP.*

Bernini's giant canopy, beneath Michelangelo's even larger dome, in the Basilica di San Pietro, the Vatican, Rome.

(top left) Rome's Bocca della Verità. *(top right)* Monumento Vittorio Emanuele II, one of Rome's most conspicuous landmarks. *(bottom)* A hall in the great Vatican Museums, Rome. *(opposite page, top)* The Tuscan countryside, near Siena. *(opposite page, bottom)* The arcaded streets of Bologna.

(top) A copy of Michelangelo's *David* braves the elements in Florence's Piazza della Signoria, on the spot where for centuries the original stood. *(bottom)* The Piazza del Duomo, in the heart of Florence.

(top) Assisi, one of Umbria's definitive hill towns. (bottom) The café scene outside Verona's ancient arena.

(top) Young priests stroll along Venice's Grand Canal. *(bottom)* The Regata Storica, a race of traditional Venetian boats, held the first weekend in September. *(opposite page, top)* Fashion is a passion in Milan. *(opposite page, bottom)* Sixth-century Byzantine mosaics in the church of Sant'Apollinare Nuovo, Ravenna.

The church of Santa Maria della Salute, perched above Venice's Grand Canal.

$ ▣ **Hotel Clitunno.** A renovated 18th-century building houses this pleasant hotel in the center of town. Cozy bedrooms and intimate public rooms, some with timbered ceilings, have the sense of a traditional Umbrian home—albeit one with a good restaurant. The hotel staff is glad to light the fireplace in Room 212 in advance of winter arrivals. Upper-floor rooms look over Spoleto's rooftops. ⊠ *Piazza Sordini 6, 06049* ☎ *0743/223340* 🖷 *0743/222663* ⊕ *www.hotelclitunno.com* ☎ *47 rooms* ♿ *Restaurant, minibars, bar, library, babysitting, laundry service, Internet room, meeting rooms; no a/c in some rooms* ▭ *AE, DC, MC, V* ⦿ *BP.*

Nightlife & the Arts

★ Thousands of spectators flock to the **Festival dei Due Mondi** (Festival of Two Worlds ⊠ Box office, Piazza Duomo 8 ☎ 800/565600 ⊕ www. spoletofestival.it), held mid-June–mid-July, to watch music, opera, and theater artists perform. Order tickets as far in advance as possible; full program information is available starting in February.

ASSISI

Assisi, 47 km (30 mi) north of Spoleto and 25 km (16 mi) east of Perugia, began as an Umbri settlement in the 7th century BC and was conquered by the Romans 400 years later. It was Christianized by St. Rufino, its patron saint, in AD 238, but it is the spirit of St. Francis, patron saint of Italy, that is felt throughout the narrow medieval streets. Basilica di San Francesco, the famous 13th-century church built in his honor, was decorated by the greatest artists of the period. Assisi is pristinely medieval in architecture and appearance, due in large part to relative neglect from the 16th century until 1926, when the celebration of the 700th anniversary of St. Francis's death brought more than 2 million visitors. Since then, Assisi has become one of the most important pilgrimage destinations in the Christian world.

Exploring Assisi

The train station is 4 km (2½ mi) from town, with bus service about every half hour. The walled town is closed to outside traffic, so cars must be left in the parking lots at Porta San Pietro, near Porta Nuova, or beneath Piazza Matteotti. Frequent minibuses run between the parking lots and the center of town. You can see the major sights in Assisi in half a day, but set aside more time if you want to fully explore the town.

The Main Attractions
Eremo delle Carceri. In the caves on the slope of Monte Subasio, Francis and his followers established their first home, to which he returned often. The church and monastery—in dense woodlands—retain a tranquil, contemplative air. A narrow set of steps leads through the building to the areas where Francis slept and prayed. True to their Franciscan heritage, the friars here are entirely dependent on alms from visitors. ⊠ *Via Santuario delle Carceri, 4 km (2½ mi) east of Assisi* ☎ *075/812301* 🖾 *Donations accepted* ⊗ *Nov.–Easter, daily 6:30–sunset; Easter–Oct., daily 6:30 AM–7:15 PM.*

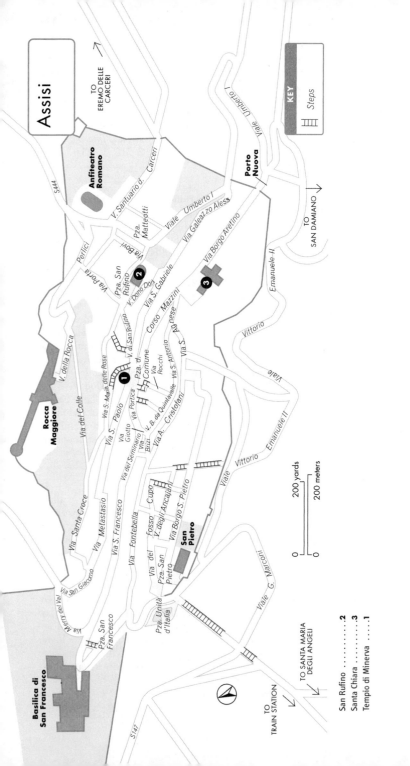

Assisi

TO
EREMO DELLE
CARCERI

Anfiteatro
Romano

Rocca
Maggiore

Basilica di
San Francesco

San Pietro

Porto
Nuova

TO
SAN DAMIANO

KEY

Steps

0   200 yards
0   200 meters

TO
TRAIN STATION

TO SANTA MARIA
DEGLI ANGELI

San Rufino **2**
Santa Chiara **3**
Tempio di Minerva **1**

❸ Santa Chiara. This striking red-striped 13th-century church is dedicated to St. Clare, one of the earliest and most fervent of St. Francis's followers and the founder of the Order of Poor Clares, in imitation of the Franciscans. The church contains the body of the saint, and in the **Cappella del Crocifisso** is the crucifix that spoke to St. Francis and led him to a life of piety. A heavily veiled member of St. Clare's order is stationed before the cross in perpetual adoration of the image. ⊠ *Piazza Santa Chiara* ☎ *075/812282* ☉ *Mar. 21–Oct., daily 6:30–noon and 2–7; Nov.–Mar. 20, daily 6:30–noon and 2–6.*

❶ Tempio di Minerva. Pieces of a Roman temple dating from the time of Augustus (63 BC–AD 14) make up this sanctuary, once dedicated to the goddess of wisdom, that was transformed into a Catholic church in the 16th century. The expectations raised by the perfect classical facade are not met by the interior, subjected to a thorough baroque assault in the 17th century, but both are worth a look. ⊠ *Piazza del Comune* ☎ *075/ 812268* ☉ *Mon., Wed., Thurs., and Sat. 7:15–7; Tues. and Fri. 7:15–2 and 5:15–7; Sun. 8:15–7.*

Also Worth Seeing

❷ San Rufino. St. Francis and St. Clare were among those baptized in Assisi's Duomo, the principal church in town until the 12th century. The baptismal font has since been redecorated, but it is possible to see the crypt of San Rufino, the martyred 3rd-century bishop who brought Christianity to Assisi. Admission to the crypt includes a look at the small **Museo Capitolare** and its detached frescoes and artifacts. ⊠ *Piazza San Rufino* ☎ *075/812283* 🎫 *Duomo free, crypt and museum €2.50* ☉ *Mar. 21–Oct., daily 8–1 and 3–7; Nov.–Mar. 20, daily 8–1 and 2–6.*

Santa Maria degli Angeli. The shrine here is much venerated because it was in the **Cappella del Transito,** then a humble cell, that St. Francis died in 1226. This baroque church is built over the **Porziuncola,** a chapel restored by St. Francis. It's on the outskirts of town, near the train station. ⊠ *Località Santa Maria degli Angeli* ☎ *075/80511* ☉ *Mar. 21–June and Oct., daily 6:15–7:45 PM; July–Sept., daily 6:15–7:45 PM and 9 PM–11 PM; Nov.–Mar. 20, daily 6:30–noon and 2–6.*

| OFF THE BEATEN PATH

CANNARA – A pleasant excursion 16 km (10 mi) southwest of Assisi leads to this tiny town; a half-hour walk then brings you to the fields of Pian d'Arca, the legendary site of St. Francis's sermon to the birds. The first week of September the town's *Sagra della Cipolla* (Onion Festival) is in full swing, with everything from soup to ice cream flavored with the town's favorite vegetable. *Pro Loco tourist office* ⊠ *Piazza Umberto I* ☎ *0742/72177.*

Where to Stay & Eat

Advance room reservations are absolutely essential if you are visiting Assisi between Easter and October or during Christmastime; latecomers are often left to choose from lodging in modern Santa Maria degli

Angeli, 8 km (5 mi) out of town. Ask at the Assisi **tourist office** for a list of pilgrim hostels, an interesting and economical alternative to conventional lodgings. Private convents, churches, or other Catholic organizations run these *ostelli* (hostels) or *conventi* (convents). Rooms are on the spartan side, but you are virtually assured of a peaceful night's stay (€36–€68). ⊠ *Piazza del Comune 22, 06081* ☎ *075/812534* ☉ *Oct.–June, Mon.–Sat. 8–2 and 3–6, Sun. 9–1; July–Sept., Mon.–Sat. 8–2 and 3–6, Sun. 10–1 and 2–5* ⊕ *www.umbria2000.it.*

$$ ✕ **Buca di San Francesco.** In summer dine in a cool green garden; in winter under the low brick arches of the restaurant's cozy cellars: no wonder this central restaurant is Assisi's busiest. The food is first-rate, too. Try spaghetti *alla buca*, homemade pasta served with a roasted mushroom sauce. ⊠ *Via Brizi 1* ☎ *075/812204* ▭ *AE, DC, MC, V* ☉ *Closed Mon. and July.*

$–$$ ✕ **La Fortezza.** Romans built parts of the walls that make up this family-run restaurant. The service is personable and the kitchen reliable. A particular standout is *anatra al finocchio selvatico* (duck with wild fennel). La Fortezza also has seven simple but clean guest rooms available. ⊠ *Vicolo della Fortezza 2/b* ☎ *075/812418* ⌲ *Reservations essential* ▭ *AE, DC, MC, V* ☉ *Closed Thurs. and Feb.*

★ $ ✕ **Osteria Piazzetta dell'Erba.** Avoid stodgy tourist eateries and come here for an informal meal or a light snack. There are two different *primi piatti* (first courses) every day, along with various salads and a good selection of fillings to go in the ever-present *torta al testo* (flat, pitalike bread that can be filled to order with various combinations of meat, cheese, and vegetables). The goat cheese is from Sardinia and is a delicious surprise. ⊠ *Via San Gabriele dell'Addolorata 15/b* ☎ *075/815352* ▭ *MC, V* ☉ *Closed Mon. and 3 wks late Jan.–mid Feb.*

¢ ✕ **La Stalla.** In a converted stable, a simple and rustic restaurant turns out hearty country fare. Meats grill and potatoes and onions bake on an open fire; for something light, try the torta al testo with your choice of local cheeses, salami, sausages, and vegetables. In summer take your meal outside under a trellis of vines and flowers. Though it's very popular with bus tours, the atmosphere and food make this an excellent stopover on your way to or from the Eremo delle Carceri. ⊠ *Via Santuario delle Carceri 8, 1 km (½ mi) east of center* ☎ *075/812317* ▭ *No credit cards* ☉ *Closed Mon. Oct.–June.*

¢ ✕ ▣ **La Pallotta.** One of the best hotels in its category and a great family-run restaurant are found here under one roof. Upstairs, the beds are **Fodor's Choice** firm, and some of the upper-floor rooms look out across the rooftops **★** of town. Downstairs, with a separate entrance on the alley around the corner, Vicolo della Volta Pinta ($–$$) is a cozy trattoria with a fireplace and stone walls. The *menu di degustazione* (tasting menu) is a good way to sample the tasty local dishes, such as *strangozzi* (a long, thin pasta also spelled *stringozzi* and *strengozzi*) with *salsa di funghi* (mushroom sauce). ⊠ *Via San Rufino 6, 06081* ☎ *075/812307 hotel* ☎ *075/812649 restaurant* ⊕ *www.pallottaassisi.it* ⇥ *8 rooms* ⌂ *Restaurant, bar, Internet room; no a/c* ▭ *AE, DC, MC, V* ⊙│ *BP.*

Continued on page 137

Basilica di San Francesco

ASSISI'S BASILICA DI SAN FRANCESCO

The legacy of St. Francis, founder of the Franciscan monastic order, pervades Assisi. Each year the town hosts several million pilgrims, but the steady flow of visitors does nothing to diminish the singular beauty of one of Italy's most important religious centers. The pilgrims' ultimate destination is the massive Basilica di San Francesco, which sits halfway up Assisi's hill, supported by graceful arches.

The basilica is not one church but two. The Romanesque **Lower Church** came first; construction began in 1228, just two years after St. Francis's death, and was completed within a few years. The low ceilings and candlelit interior make an appropriately solemn setting for St. Francis's tomb, found in the crypt below the main altar. The Gothic **Upper Church**, built only half a century later, sits on top of the lower one, and is strikingly different, with soaring arches and tall stained-glass windows (the first in Italy). Inside, both churches are covered floor to ceiling with some of Europe's finest frescoes: the Lower Church is dim and full of candlelit shadows, and the Upper Church is bright and airy.

VISITING THE BASILICA

THE LOWER CHURCH

The most evocative way to experience the basilica is to begin with the dark Lower Church. As you enter, give your eyes a moment to adjust. Keep in mind that the artists at work here were conscious of the shadowy environment—they knew this was how their frescoes would be seen.

In the first chapel to the left, a superb fresco cycle by Simone Martini depicts scenes from the life of St. Martin. As you approach the main altar, the vaulting above you is decorated with the *Three Virtues of St. Francis* (poverty, chastity, and obedience) and *St. Francis's Triumph*, frescoes attributed to Giotto's followers. In the transept to your left, Pietro Lorenzetti's *Madonna and Child with St. Francis and St. John* sparkles when the sun hits it. Notice Mary's thumb; legend has it Jesus is asking which saint to bless, and Mary is pointing to Francis. Across the way in the right transept, Cimabue's *Madonna Enthroned Among Angels and St. Francis* is a famous portrait of the saint. Surrounding the portrait are painted scenes from the childhood of Christ, done by the assis-

tants of Giotto. Nearby is a painting of the crucifixion attributed to Giotto himself.

You reach the crypt via stairs midway along the nave—on the crypt's altar, a stone coffin holds the saint's body. Steps up from the transepts lead to the cloister, where there's a gift shop, and the treasury, which contains holy objects.

THE UPPER CHURCH

The St. Francis fresco cycle is the highlight of the Upper Church. (See facing page.) Also worth special note is the 16th-century choir, with its remarkably delicate inlaid wood. When a 1997 earthquake rocked the basilica, the St. Francis cycle sustained little damage, but portions of the ceiling above the entrance and altar collapsed, reducing their frescoes (attributed to Cimabue and Giotto) to rubble. The painstaking restoration is ongoing. ⚠ The dress code is strictly enforced—no bare shoulders or bare knees. Piazza di San Francesco, 075/819001, Lower Church Easter–Oct., Mon.–Sat. 6:30 AM–6:50 PM, Sun. 6:30 AM–7:15 PM; Nov.–Easter, daily 6:30–5:40. Upper Church Easter–Oct., Mon.–Sat. 8:30–6:50, Sun. 8:30–7:15; Nov.–Easter, daily 8:30–5:40.

FRANCIS, ITALY'S PATRON SAINT

PREGANDO ASPETTERO CHE TORNI

St. Francis was born in Assisi in 1181, the son of a noblewoman and a well-to-do merchant. His troubled youth included a year in prison. He planned a military career, but after a long illness Francis heard the voice of God, renounced his father's wealth, and began a life of austerity. His mystical embrace of poverty, asceticism, and the beauty of man and nature struck a responsive chord in the medieval mind; he quickly attracted a vast number of followers. Francis was the first saint to receive the stigmata (wounds in his hands, feet, and side corresponding to those of Christ on the cross). He died on October 4, 1226, in the Porziuncola, the secluded chapel in the woods where he had first preached the virtue of poverty to his disciples. St. Francis was declared patron saint of Italy in 1939, and today the Franciscans make up the largest of the Catholic orders.

THE UPPER CHURCH'S ST. FRANCIS FRESCO CYCLE

The 28 frescoes in the Upper Church depicting the life of St. Francis are the most admired works in the entire basilica. They're also the subject of one of art history's biggest controversies. For centuries they were thought to be by Giotto (1267–1337), the great early-Renaissance innovator, but inconsistencies in style, both within this series and in comparison to later Giotto works, have thrown their origin into question. Some scholars now say Giotto was the brains behind the cycle, but that assistants helped with the execution; others claim he couldn't have been involved at all.

Two things are certain. First, the style is revolutionary, which argues for Giotto's involve-

ment. The tangible weight of the figures, the emotion they show, and the use of perspective all look familiar to modern eyes, but in the art of the time there was nothing like it. Second, these images have played a major part in shaping how the world sees St. Francis. In that respect, who painted them hardly matters.

Starting at the transept, the frescoes circle the church, showing events in the saint's life (and afterlife). Some of the best are grouped near the church's entrance—look for the nativity at Greccio, the miracle of the spring, the death of the knight at Celano, and, most famously, the sermon to the birds.

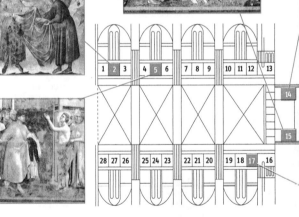

The St. Francis fresco cycle	10. Chasing devils from Arezzo	20. Death of St. Francis
1. Homage of a simple man	11. Before the sultan	21. Apparition before Bishop Guido
2. Giving cloak to a poor man	12. Ecstasy of St. Francis	and Fra Agostino
3. Dream of the palace	13. Nativity at Greccio	22. Verification of the stigmata
4. Hearing the voice of God	14. Miracle of the spring	23. Mourning of St. Clare
5. Rejection of worldly goods	15. Sermon to the birds	24. Canonization
6. Dream of Innocent III	16. Death of knight at Celano	25. Apparition before Gregory IX
7. Confirmation of the rules	17. Preaching to Honorius III	26. Healing of a devotee
8. Vision of flaming chariot	18. Apparition at Arles	27. Confession of a woman
9. Vision of celestial thrones	19. Receiving the stigmata	28. Repentant heretic freed

Basilica di San Francesco

VOICES OF ITALY

Sister Marcellina,
Order of St. Bridget

Sister Marcellina of the Order of St. Bridget talks about her life in Assisi, where she and 11 other sisters live in a convent and guesthouse on the outskirts of the town:

"Before coming to Assisi, I lived in various countries. I've lived in India, and in England, and been to Holland, to Sweden, and to Finland, as well as lived in Rome. But Assisi is the place that I would never want to change for any other. I don't know; I think there is something very special about this place. I've been here 13 years now, and each year I pray that I won't be sent somewhere else. I'm very happy here.

"I like the atmosphere of Assisi. It's very friendly, and of course with St. Francis and St. Clare, but especially St. Francis, there is a simplicity to life that I like very much. Even though I'm in the Order of St. Bridget, living here I feel very much a part of Franciscan spirituality. There is also a very strong ecumenical feeling to Assisi and this is very nice. There are over 60 different religious communities, with people from all over the world. And even though they come from different religious backgrounds they still feel a part of Assisi. Living here, you don't see the people of Assisi, you see people who have come from all over the world.

"There is something you feel when you come to Assisi, something you feel in your heart that makes you want to come back. And people do return! They feel the peacefulness and tranquillity. Not that there aren't other aspects, like the commercialism—but these things happen. People return for the simplicity of this place. People feel attracted to Assisi. There's always something that people feel when they come here—even the hard-hearted ones!"

Asked if she thinks Assisi is changing, Sister Marcellina answers, with laughter in her voice, "When they wanted to make all the changes in the year 2000, the Jubilee Year, our Lord said, 'I must stop everything.' They had lots of projects to build new accommodations to house the people coming for the Jubilee Year, but the Lord said, 'No!'"

$$$ ⊡ **Castello di Petrata.** Built as a fortress in the 14th century, the Petrata

rightfully dominates its position—with Monte Subasio, Assisi, and the

★ distant hills and valleys of Perugia all in view. Every room is different from the last: wood beams and sections of exposed medieval stonework make up the background and comfortable couches and upholstered chairs turn each room into a delightful retreat. The bathrooms with tubs are considerably more spacious than those with showers. ⊠ *Località Petrata 22, 06081, 6 km (4 mi) east of Assisi* ☎ *075/815451* 🖷 *075/8043026* ⊕ *www.castellopetrata.com* ↘ *21 rooms, 2 suites* ⚒ *Restaurant, minibars, pool, bar, Internet room, meeting rooms, some pets allowed; no a/c* ⊟ *AE, DC, MC, V* ☺ *Closed Jan.–Mar.* ⦿⦿ *BP.*

$$$ ⊡ **Hotel Subasio.** The Subasio, housed in a converted monastery, has counted Marlene Dietrich and Charlie Chaplin among its guests. Some of the rooms remain a little monastic, but the splendid views, comfortable old-fashioned sitting rooms, flower-decked terraces, and lovely garden more than balance out a certain austerity in the furnishings. Ask for a room overlooking the valley. The hotel is close to the Basilica di San Francesco. ⊠ *Via Frate Elia 2, 06082* ☎ *075/812206* 🖷 *075/816691* ⊕ *www.hotelsubasio.com* ↘ *54 rooms, 8 suites* ⚒ *Restaurant, bar, parking (fee)* ⊟ *AE, DC, MC, V* ⦿⦿ *BP.*

$$–$$$ ⊡ **San Francesco.** You can't beat the location—the roof terrace and some of the rooms look out onto the Basilica di San Francesco, which is opposite the hotel. Rooms and facilities range from simple to homely, but you may be reminded that looks aren't everything by the nice touches like slippers, a good-night piece of chocolate, and soundproofing. Fruit, homemade tarts, and fresh ricotta make for a first-rate breakfast. ⊠ *Via San Francesco 48, 06082* ☎ *075/812281* 🖷 *075/816237* ⊕ *www.hotelsanfrancescoassisi.it* ↘ *44 rooms* ⚒ *Restaurant, minibars, bar, Internet room, some pets allowed* ⊟ *AE, DC, MC, V* ⦿⦿ *BP.*

$$ ⊡ **Hotel Umbra.** A 16th-century town house is the setting for this charming hotel in a tranquil part of the city, an area closed to traffic and near Piazza del Comune. The rooms are arranged as small suites, each with tiny living room and balcony. Ask for an upper room with a view over the Assisi rooftops to the valley below. The restaurant, closed for lunch on Tuesday and Wednesday, has a charming vine-covered terrace leading to a secluded garden. ⊠ *Via degli Archi 6, 06081* ☎ *075/812240* 🖷 *075/813653* ⊕ *www.hotelumbra.it* ↘ *25 suites* ⚒ *Restaurant, minibars, bar* ⊟ *AE, DC, MC, V* ☺ *Closed mid-Jan.–mid-Mar.* ⦿⦿ *BP.*

PERUGIA

The painter Perugino (the Perugian) filled his work with images of his home: soft hills with sparse trees, wide plains dotted with lakes. Despite the development of undistinguished modern suburbs, this peaceful landscape still survives, and venerable Perugia's medieval hilltop city remains almost completely intact. Perugia is the best-preserved hill town of its size; there are few better examples of the self-contained city-state that so shaped the course of Italian history. Little remains of Perugia's earliest ancestors, although the Arco di Augusto (Arch of Augustus) in Piazza Fortebraccio, the northern entrance to the city, is of Etruscan origin.

Exploring Perugia

The best approach to the city is by train—the station is in the unlovely suburbs, but there are frequent buses running directly to Piazza d'Italia, the heart of the old town. If you are driving, leave your car in one of the parking lots near the station and then take the bus or the escalator, which passes through subterranean excavations of the city's Roman foundations, from Piazza Partigiani to the Rocca Paolina. A half day is sufficient to visit the major sights in the center of town.

The Main Attractions

★ ❹ **Collegio del Cambio.** The series of elaborate rooms at Bankers' Guild Hall housed the meeting hall and chapel of the guild of bankers and money changers. The walls were frescoed from 1496 to 1500 by the most important Perugian painter of the Renaissance, Pietro Vannucci, better known as Perugino (circa 1450–1523). The iconography prevalent in the works includes common religious themes, like the Nativity and the Transfiguration (on the end walls), but also figures intended to inspire the businessmen who congregated here. On the left wall are female figures representing the Virtues, beneath them the heroes and sages of antiquity. On the right wall are the prophets and sibyls. Perugino's most famous pupil, Raffaello Sanzio, or Raphael (1483–1520), is said to have painted here; experts say his hand is most apparent in the figure of Fortitude. On one of the pilasters is a remarkably honest self-portrait of Perugino, surmounted by a Latin inscription. The Collegio is on the ground floor of the Palazzo dei Priori, and is entered from Corso Vannucci. ⌧ *Corso Vannucci 25* ☎ *075/5728599* ⌨ *€2.60* ☉ *Mon.–Sat. 9–12:30 and 2:30–5:30, Sun. 9–1.*

Corso Vannucci. The heart of the city is the broad stately pedestrian street that runs from Piazza d'Italia to Piazza IV Novembre. As evening falls, Corso Vannucci is filled with Perugians out for their evening *passeggiata,* a pleasant predinner stroll that may include a pause for an *aperitivo* (aperitif) at one of the many cafés that line the street.

❸ **Galleria Nazionale dell'Umbria.** On the fourth floor of the ⇨ **Palazzo dei Priori** is the region's most comprehensive art gallery. Well-placed information panels (in Italian and English) describe work by native artists—most notably Pinturicchio (1454–1513) and Perugino—along with others of the Umbrian and Tuscan schools. The gallery also exhibits frescoes, sculptures, and several superb painted crucifixes from the 13th and 14th centuries; other rooms are dedicated to Perugia itself, illustrating the evolution of the medieval city. The last entry is a half hour before closing. ⌧ *Corso Vannucci 19, Piazza IV Novembre* ☎ *075/5721009* ⊕ *www.gallerianazionaledellumbria.it* ⌨ *€6.50* ☉ *Daily 8:30–7:30; closed first Mon. of month.*

★ ❷ **Palazzo dei Priori.** The imposing palace, begun in the 13th century, has an unusual staircase that fans out into Piazza IV Novembre. The facade is decorated with symbols of Perugia's former power: the griffin is the city's symbol; the lion denotes Perugia's allegiance to the medieval Guelph (or papal) cause. Both figures support the heavy chains of the gates of Siena, which fell to Perugian forces in 1358. Most of the build-

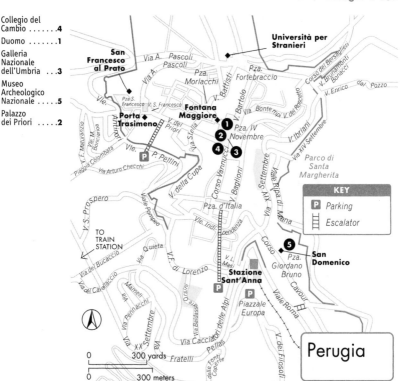

ing now houses the town's municipal offices, which are not open to tourists, with access permitted only to the fourth floor ⇨ **Galleria Nazionale dell'Umbria.** ⊠ *Corso Vannucci 19* ☎ *075/5771.*

Also Worth Seeing

❶ **Duomo.** This church's prize relic is the Virgin Mary's wedding ring, stolen in 1488 from the nearby town of Chiusi. The ring, kept in a chapel on the left aisle, is the size of a large bangle and is kept under lock—15 locks actually—and key year-round except July 30 and the second-to-last Sunday in January. The first date commemorates the day the ring was brought to Perugia, the second, Mary's wedding anniversary. The cathedral itself is large and rather plain, dating from the Middle Ages but with many additions from the 15th and 16th centuries. There are some elaborately carved choir stalls, executed by Giovanni Battista Bastone in 1520. Precious objects associated with the cathedral are on display at the associated **Museo Capitolare,** including vestments, vessels, manuscripts, and gold work. An early masterpiece by Luca Signorelli (circa 1450–1523) is the altarpiece showing the Madonna with St. John the Baptist, St. Onophrio, and St. Lawrence (1484). Note that sections of the church may be closed to visitors during religious services and the last admission is a half hour before closing. ⊠ *Piazza IV Novembre*

☎ *075/5723832* 🖃 *Duomo free, museum €3.50* ⊘ *Duomo Mon.–Sat. 7–12:30 and 4–6:45, Sun. 8–12:30 and 4–6:45; museum daily 10–1 and 2:30–5:30.*

❺ Museo Archeologico Nazionale. Perugia was a flourishing Etruscan site long before it fell under Roman domination in 310 BC. This museum next to the imposing church of San Domenico contains an excellent collection of Etruscan artifacts from throughout the region. 🖃 *Piazza G. Bruno 10* ☎ *075/5727141* ⊕ *www.archeopg.arti.beniculturali.it* 🖃 *€4* ⊘ *Mon. 2:30–7:30, Tues.–Sun. 8:30–7:30.*

Where to Stay & Eat

$$ ✕ La Taverna. Medieval steps lead to a rustic two-story restaurant where wine bottles and artful clutter decorate the walls. Good choices from the regional menu include *caramelle al gorgonzola* (pasta rolls filled with red cabbage and mozzarella with a Gorgonzola sauce) and grilled meat dishes, such as the *medaglioni di vitello al tartufo* (grilled veal with truffles). 🖃 *Via delle Streghe 8, off Corso Vannucci* ☎ *075/5724128* 🖃 *AE, DC, MC, V* ⊘ *Closed Mon.*

$ ✕ Il Falchetto. Exceptional food at reasonable prices makes this Perugia's best bargain. Service is smart but relaxed in the two medieval dining rooms that put the kitchen and chef on view. The house specialty is *falchetti* (homemade gnocchi with spinach and ricotta cheese). 🖃 *Via Bartolo 20* ☎ *075/5731775* 🖃 *AE, DC, MC, V* ⊘ *Closed Mon. and last 2 wks in Jan.*

★ ¢ ✕ Dal Mi' Cocco. A great favorite with Perugia's university students, this is a fun, crowded, and truly inexpensive place to enjoy a multicourse fixed-price meal (€13). You may find yourself seated at a long table with other diners, but some language help from your neighbors could come in handy—the menu is in pure Perugian dialect. Meals change with the seasons, and each day of the week brings some new creation *dal cocco* (from the "coconut," or head) of the chef. 🖃 *Corso Garibaldi 12* ☎ *075/5732511* 🖃 *Reservations essential* 🖃 *No credit cards* ⊘ *Closed Mon. and July 20–Aug. 15.*

$$$$ 🏨 Brufani Palace. A 19th-century palazzo has been turned into an elegant lodging choice, where public rooms and first-floor guest rooms have high ceilings and are done in grand belle epoque style. Second-floor rooms are more modern; many on both floors have a marvelous view of the Umbrian countryside or the city, as does the extensive rooftop terrace. Linen bedsheets and luxuriously equipped bathrooms make for a particularly comfortable stay, but breakfast (€32 per person) is not normally included in the price of a room. 🖃 *Piazza d'Italia 12, 06121* ☎ *075/ 5732541* 🖃 *075/5720210* ⊕ *www.brufanipalace.com* 🏨 *63 rooms, 31 suites* ⚖ *Restaurant, in-room safes, cable TV, in-room data ports, Wi-Fi, indoor pool, gym, sauna, Turkish bath, bar, concierge, Internet room, meeting rooms, parking (fee)* 🖃 *AE, DC, MC, V* ⦿I *EP.*

$$$ 🏨 Castello di Oscano. A splendid neo-Gothic castle, a late-19th-century villa, and a converted farmhouse hidden in the tranquil hills north of Perugia offer a range of accommodations. Step back in time in the castle, where spacious suites and junior suites, all with high oak-beam ceilings, and some with panoramic views, are decorated with 18th- and

Truffle Talk

UMBRIA IS RICH with truffles—more are found here than anywhere else in Italy—and those not consumed fresh are processed into pastes or flavored oils. The primary truffle areas are around the tiny town of Norcia, which holds a truffle festival every February, and near Spoleto, where signs warn against unlicensed truffle hunting at the base of the Ponte delle Torri. Although grown locally, the rare delicacy can cost a small fortune, up to $200 for a quarter pound—fortunately, a little goes a long way. At such a price there's great competition among the nearly 10,000 registered truffle hunters in the province, who use specially trained dogs to sniff them out among the roots of several types of trees, including oak and ilex. Despite one or two incidences of poisoning truffle-hunting dogs and importing inferior tubers from China, you can be reasonably assured that the truffle shaved onto your pasta has been unearthed locally.

19th-century antiques. Standard rooms in the villa annex are smaller and more modern than those in the main building, and the apartments of the farmhouse, in the valley below the castle, provide kitchens and simple accommodation for two to five people. ⊠ *Strada Palaretta 19, 06134 Località Cenerente Oscano, 5 km (3 mi) north of Perugia* ☎ *075/ 584371* 🖷 *075/690666* ⊕ *www.oscano.it* ☞ *24 rooms, 8 suites, 13 apartments* ♤ *Restaurant, cable TV, pool, gym, bicycles, bar, library, Internet room, meeting rooms; no a/c in some rooms* ⊟ *AE, DC, V* ❘⊖❘ *BP.*

$$$ 🏨 **Locanda della Posta.** Reside at the center of Perugia's old district in an 18th-century palazzo. Renovation has left the reception and other public areas rather bland, but the rooms, all of which are carpeted, are tastefully and soothingly decorated in muted colors. Though sound-proofed, rooms at the front of the hotel face the busy Corso Vannucci and should be avoided in favor of those on the upper floors at the back of the building, which also have great views. ⊠ *Corso Vannucci 97, 06121* ☎ *075/5728925* 🖷 *075/5732562* ☞ *38 rooms, 1 suite* ♤ *Minibars, bar, Internet room, parking (fee)* ⊟ *AE, DC, MC, V* ❘⊖❘ *BP.*

$$ 🏨 **Hotel Fortuna.** The elegant furnishings in this friendly hotel comple-

Fodor's Choice ment the 18th-century frescoes that decorate several of the rooms. Some
★ guest rooms have balconies, and a pleasant rooftop terrace affords panoramic views of the city. The building itself, just out of sight of Corso Vannucci, dates back to the 1300s, and the sections of medieval walls exposed here and there throughout the structure are a fascinating feature. A three-night stay is required during the Umbria Jazz and Euro-chocolate festivals and during a number of public holidays, including Christmas, New Year, and Easter. ⊠ *Via Bonazzi 19, 06123* ☎ *075/ 5722845* 🖷 *075/5735040* ⊕ *www.umbriahotels.com* ☞ *51 rooms* ♤ *Some in-room hot tubs, minibars, in room safes, cable TV, bar, Internet room, meeting rooms, some free parking* ⊟ *AE, DC, MC, V* ❘⊖❘ *BP.*

Nightlife & the Arts

The monthly *Viva Perugia* (sold at newsstands), with a section in English, is a good source of information about what's going on in town. Summer sees several music festivals in Perugia. The **Festival delle Nazioni di Musica da Camera** (International Chamber Music Festival ✉ On S3bis, 80 km [50 mi] north of Perugia, Città di Castello ☎ 075/8521142 🖷 075/8552461) is a two-week event held in late August and early September. **Sagra Musicale Umbra** (☎ 075/5732800 ⊕ www.umbria.org/eng/eventi) celebrates the traditional music of the region at performances ★ during 10 days in September. The **Umbria Jazz Festival** (☎ 075/5732432 🖷 075/572256 ⊕ www.umbriajazz.com), a world-famous concert series, lasts for 10 days in July.

The third week in October is especially sweet, when Perugia hosts the **Eurochocolate Festival** (☎ 075/5732670 ⊕ www.eurochocolate.perugia. it) and the streets are filled with stands, sculptures, and—best of all—tastings.

Shopping

Judging by the expensive shops around the Corso Vannucci, Perugians are not afraid to part with their euros. Clothing shops selling Italian designers such as Gucci, Ferragamo, Armani, and Fendi line the streets. The town is also known for its famous Perugina chocolate, although the brand (a Nestlé company since the early 1990s) is easily found throughout Italy. *Cioccolato al latte* (milk chocolate) and *fondente* (dark chocolate) are sold in tiny jewel-like containers, and in giant boxes the size of serving trays, all over town. Round hazelnut-filled chocolate candies, *baci* (literally, "kisses"), come wrapped in silver foil and, like fortune cookies, contain romantic sayings in several languages, English included.

TUSCANY

Updated by
Patricia Rucidlo

THERE'S A MAGIC ABOUT TUSCANY: the right elements have all fallen into place here. The art and the culture, the food and the wine, are justly famous. The gorgeous countryside and the picture-book towns take on a certain glow in the late-afternoon sun. And the people mix warmth, modesty, and pride in a way that honors their glorious past without bowing down to it.

Tuscany isn't the place for a jam-packed itinerary. One of the great pleasures here is indulging in rustic hedonism, marked by long lunches and spectacular sunsets. Whether by car, bike, or foot, you'll want to get out into the glorious landscape, but it's smart to keep your plans modest. Set a church or a hill town or an out-of-the-way restaurant as your destination, knowing that half the pleasure is in getting there—admiring as you go the stately palazzos, the tidy geometry of row upon row of grape vines, the fields vibrant with red poppies and yellow broom.

You'll need to devise a Siena strategy. The town shouldn't be missed; it's compact enough that you can see the major sights on a day trip, and that's exactly what most people do. Spend the night, and you'll get to witness the town breathe a sigh and relax once the day-trippers depart. The flip side is, your favorite place to stay in Tuscany is more likely to be out in the country than in town.

SIENA

One of Italy's most enchanting medieval cities, Siena is the one place in Tuscany you should visit if you see no other. Florence's great historical rival was in all likelihood founded by the Etruscans. During the late Middle Ages it was both wealthy and powerful, for it saw the birth of the world's oldest bank, the Monte dei Paschi, still very much in business. It was bitterly envied by Florence, which in 1254 sent forces that besieged the city for more than a year, reducing its population by half and laying waste to the countryside. The city was finally absorbed by the grand duchy of Tuscany, ruled by Florence, in 1559.

Sienese identity is still defined by its 17 medieval *contrade* (neighborhoods), each with its own church, museum, and emblem. Look for streetlights painted in the contrada's colors, plaques displaying its symbol, and statues embodying the spirit of the neighborhood. The various contrade uphold ancient rivalries during the centuries-old Palio, a twice-yearly horse race (held in July and August) in the main piazza.

Exploring Siena

Practically unchanged since medieval times, Siena stretches over the slopes of three steep hills. The most interesting sights are in a fairly compact

TUSCANY THROUGH THE AGES

Etruscans & Romans. Tuscany was populated, at least by the 7th century BC, by the Etruscans, a mysterious lot who chose to live on hills—the better to see the approaching enemy—in such places as present-day Arezzo, Chiusi, Cortona, Fiesole, and Volterra. Some 500 years later, the Romans came, saw, and conquered; by 241 BC they had built the Aurelia, a road from Rome to Pisa that is still in use today. The crumbling of the Roman Empire and subsequent invasions by marauding Lombards, Byzantines, and Holy Roman Emperors meant centuries of turmoil. By the 12th century city-states were being formed throughout Tuscany in part, perhaps, because it was unclear exactly who was in charge.

Guelphs & Ghibellines. The two groups vying for power were the Guelphs and the Ghibellines, champions of the pope and the Holy Roman Emperor, respectively. They jostled for control of individual cities and of the region as a whole. Florence was more or less Guelph, and Siena more often than not Ghibelline. This led to bloody battles, most notably the 1260 battle of Montaperti, in which the Ghibellines roundly defeated the Guelphs.

Eventually—by the 14th century—the Guelphs became the dominant force. But this did not mean that the warring Tuscan cities settled down to a period of relative peace and tranquillity. The age in which Dante wrote his *Divine Comedy* and Giotto and Piero della Francesca created their incomparable frescoes was one of internecine strife.

Florentines & Sienese. Florence was the power to be reckoned with; it coveted its main rival, Siena, which it conquered, lost, and reconquered during the 15th and 16th centuries. Finally, in 1555, following in the footsteps of Volterra, Pisa, Prato, and Arezzo, Siena fell for good. They were all united under Florence to form the grand duchy of Tuscany. The only city to escape Florence's dominion was Lucca, which remained fiercely independent until the arrival of Napoléon. Eventually, however, even Florence's influence waned, and the 17th and 18th centuries saw the decline of the entire region as various armies swept across it.

pedestrian-only *centro storico* (historic town center), but leave some time to wander off the main streets.

If you have only one day in Siena, see the Piazza del Campo, the Duomo, the Cripta, and the Palazzo Pubblico. If you are seeing more sights, it's usually worthwhile to buy a combination ticket (valid for three days, €10), good for entrance to the Duomo's Biblioteca Piccolomini, the Battistero, and the Museo dell'Opera Metropolitana. ■ TIP→ **If you can overnight here, by all means do so: the city is filled with day-trippers and tour buses, and in the late afternoon and evening it empties out.** The *passeggiata* (evening stroll) along the main shopping streets should not be missed: Siena's medieval charm and narrow streets are thrown into high relief,

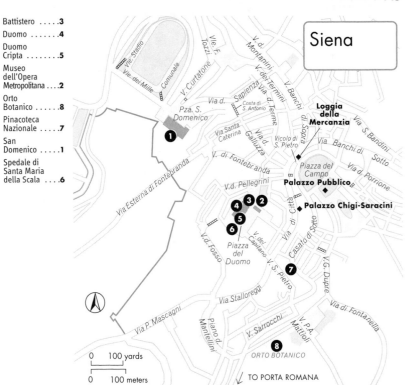

and Piazza del Campo positively glows. Keep in mind that most shops are closed Sunday and museums have variable hours.

Siena is 69 km (43 mi) south of Florence; there are two basic routes. The speedy, modern SS2 is good if you're making a day trip from Florence, as it's a four-lane divided highway. For a jaunt through Chianti, take the narrower and more meandering SS222, known as the Strada Chiantigiana. It's a gorgeous ride on only two lanes—patience is a necessity.

The Main Attractions

★ ❹ **Duomo.** A few minutes' walk west of Piazza del Campo, Siena's Duomo is beyond question one of the finest Gothic cathedrals in Italy. The facade, with its multicolor marbles and painted decoration, is typical of the Italian approach to Gothic architecture, lighter and much less austere than the French. The cathedral as it now stands was completed in the 14th century, but at the time the Sienese had even bigger plans. They had decided to enlarge the building by using the existing church as a transept for a new one, with a new nave running toward the southeast. But in 1348 the Black Death decimated Siena's population, the city fell into decline, funds dried up, and the plans were never carried out. The

Continued on page 150

Climbing the 500 narrow steps of the **Torre del Mangia** rewards you with unparalleled views of Siena's rooftops and the countryside beyond.

The **Palazzo Pubblico**, Siena's town hall since the 14th century.

Something about the fan-shape, sloping design of **Il Campo** encourages people to sit and relax (except during the Palio, when they stand and scream). The communal atmosphere here is unlike that of any other Italian piazza.

PIAZZA DEL CAMPO

Fodor'sChoice The fan-shape **Piazza del Campo,** known simply as il Campo (The
★ Field), is one of the finest squares in Italy. Constructed toward the end
of the 12th century on a market area unclaimed by any contrada, it's still the heart of town. The bricks of
the Campo are patterned in nine different
sections—representing each member of
the medieval Government of Nine. At
the top of the Campo is a copy of the
Fonte Gaia, decorated in the early
15th century by Siena's greatest
sculptor, Jacopo della Quercia,
with 13 sculpted reliefs of biblical events and virtues. Those lining the rectangular fountain are
19th-century copies; the originals are in the Spedale di Santa
Maria della Scala. On Palio horse
race days (July 2 and August 16),
the Campo and all its surrounding
buildings are packed with cheering,
frenzied locals and tourists craning
their necks to take it all in.

The Gothic **Palazzo Pubblico,** the focal point of the Piazza del Campo,
has served as Siena's town hall since the 1300s. It now also contains
the **Museo Civico,** with walls covered in early Renaissance frescoes. The
nine governors of Siena once met in the Sala della Pace, famous for Ambrogio Lorenzetti's frescoes called *Allegories of Good and Bad Government,* painted in the late 1330s to demonstrate the dangers of
tyranny. The good government side depicts utopia, showing first the
virtuous ruling council surrounded by angels and then scenes of a perfectly running city and countryside. Conversely, the bad government
fresco tells a tale straight out of Dante. The evil ruler and his advisers
have horns and fondle strange animals, and the town scene depicts the
seven mortal sins in action. Interestingly, the bad government fresco is
severely damaged, and the good government fresco is in terrific condition. The **Torre del Mangia,** the palazzo's famous bell tower, is named
after one of its first bell ringers, Giovanni di Duccio (called Man-
giaguadagni, or earnings eater). The climb up to the top is long and
steep, but the view makes it worth every step. ⊠ *Piazza del Campo 1,
Città* ☎ *0577/41169* ⊡ *Museo €7, Torre €6, combined ticket €10*
⊙ *Museo Nov.–Mar. 15, daily 10–6:30; Mar. 16–Oct., daily 10–7.
Torre Nov.–Mar. 15, daily 10–4; Mar. 16–Oct., daily 10–7.*

THE PALIO

The three laps around a makeshift racetrack in Piazza del Campo are over in less than two minutes, but the spirit of Siena's Palio—a horse race held every July 2 and August 16—lives all year long.

The Palio is contested between Siena's contrade, the 17 neighborhoods that have divided the city since the Middle Ages. Loyalties are fiercely felt. At any time of year you'll see on the streets contrada symbols—Tartuca (turtle), Oca (goose), Istrice (porcupine), Torre (tower)—emblazoned on banners and engraved on building walls. At Palio time, simmering rivalries come to a boil.

It's been that way since at least August 16, 1310, the date of the first recorded running of the Palio. At that time, and for centuries to follow, the race went through the streets of the city. The additional July 2 running was instituted in 1649; soon thereafter the location was moved to the Campo and the current system for selecting the race entrants established. Ten of the contrade are chosen at random to run in the July Palio. The August race is then contested between the 7 contrade left out in July, plus 3 of the 10 July participants, again chosen at random. Although the races are in theory of equal importance, Sienese will tell you that it's better to win the second and have bragging rights for the rest of the year.

The race itself has a raw and arbitrary character—it's no Kentucky Derby. There's barely room for the 10 horses on the makeshift Campo course, so falls and collisions are inevitable. Horses are chosen at random three days before the race, and jockeys (who ride bareback) are mercenaries hired from surrounding towns. Almost no tactic is considered too underhanded. Bribery, secret plots, and betrayal are commonplace—so much so that the word for "jockey," *fantino,* has come to mean "untrustworthy" in Siena. There have been incidents of drugging (the horses) and kidnapping (the jockeys); only sabotaging a horse's reins remains taboo.

Above: The tension of the starting line. Top left: The frenzy of the race. Bottom left: A solemn flag bearer follows in the footsteps of his ancestors.

AQUILA

BRUCO

CHIOCCIOLA

17 MEDIEVAL CONTRADE

Festivities kick off three days prior to the Palio, with the selection and blessing of the horses, trial runs, ceremonial banquets, betting, and late-night celebrations. Residents don their contrada's colors and march through the streets in medieval costumes. The Campo is transformed into a racetrack lined with a thick layer of sand. On race day, each horse is brought to the church of the contrada for which it will run, where it's blessed and told, "Go, little horse and return a winner." The Campo fills through the afternoon, with spectators crowding into every available space until bells ring and the piazza is sealed off. Processions of flag wavers in traditional dress march to the beat of tambourines and drums and the roar of the crowds. The *palio* itself—a banner for which the race is named, dedicated to the Virgin Mary—makes an appearance, followed by the horses and their jockeys.

The race begins when one horse, chosen to ride up from behind the rest of the field, crosses the starting line. There are always false starts, adding to the frenzied mood. Once under way, the race is over in a matter of minutes. The victorious rider is carried off through the streets of the winning contrada (where in the past tradition dictated he was entitled to the local girl of his choice) while winning and losing sides use television replay to analyze the race from every possible angle. The winning contrada will celebrate into the night, at long tables piled high with food and drink. The champion horse is guest of honor.

Reserved seating in the stands is sold out months in advance of the races; contact the Siena Tourist Office (✉ Piazza del Campo 56 ☎ 0577/280551) to find out about availability, and ask your hotel if it can procure you a seat. The entire area in the center is free and unreserved, but you need to show up early in order to get a prime spot against the barriers.

CIVETTA | DRAGO
GIRAFFA | ISTRICE
LEOCORNO | LUPA
NICCHIO | OCA
ONDA | PANTERA
SELVA | TARTUCA
TORRE | VALDIMONTONE

beginnings of the new nave can be seen from the steps outside the Duomo's right transept.

The Duomo's interior, with its coffered and gilded dome, is striking. The magnificent inlaid marble floors took almost 200 years to complete (beginning around 1370); more than 40 artists contributed to the work, made up of 56 separate compositions depicting biblical scenes, allegories, religious symbols, and civic emblems. They are covered for most of the year for conservation purposes but are usually un-

veiled every September for the entire month. The Duomo's pulpit, also much appreciated, was carved by Nicola Pisano between 1266 and 1268; the life of Christ is depicted on the rostrum frieze. In the **Biblioteca Piccolomini,** a room painted by Pinturicchio (circa 1454–1513) between 1502 and 1509, frescoes show scenes from the life of native son Aeneas Sylvius Piccolomini (1405–64), who became Pope Pius II in 1458. They are in excellent condition and reveal a freshness rarely seen in Renaissance frescoes. ⊠ *Piazza del Duomo, Città* ☎ *0577/283048* 🔁 *Church free, Biblioteca Piccolomini €3* ☉ *Mar.–May, Mon.–Sat. 10:30–7:30, Sun. 1:30–5:30; June–Aug., Mon.–Sat. 10:30–8, Sun. 1:30–6:30; Sept. and Oct., Mon.–Sat. 10:30–7:30, Sun. 10:30–7:30; Nov.–Feb., Mon.–Sat. 10:30–6:30, Sun. 1:30–5:30.*

❺ **Duomo Cripta.** Rediscovered during routine excavation work, the crypt—
FodorśChoice under the grand *pavimento* (floor) of the Duomo upstairs—was opened to
★ the public in fall of 2003. An unknown master executed the breathtakingly beautiful frescoes here sometime between 1270 and 1280; they retain their original colors and pack an emotional punch even given the sporadic paint loss. The *Deposition/Lamentation* gives strong evidence that the Sienese school could paint emotion just as well as the Florentine school, some 20 years before Giotto. Guided tours in English take place more or less every half hour and are limited to no more than 35 persons. ⊠ *Piazza del Duomo, Città* ☎ *0577/283048* 🔁 *€6* ☉ *Mar.–May, daily 9:30–7; June–Aug., daily 9:30–8; Sept. and Oct., daily 9:30–7; Nov.–Feb., daily 10–5.*

Also Worth Seeing

❸ **Battistero.** The Duomo's 14th-century Gothic Baptistery was built to prop up one side of the Duomo. There are frescoes throughout, but the highlight is a large bronze 15th-century baptismal font designed by Jacopo della Quercia and adorned with bas-reliefs by various artists, including two by Renaissance masters: the *Baptism of Christ* by Lorenzo Ghiberti (1378–1455) and the *Feast of Herod* by Donatello. ⊠ *Piazza San Giovanni, Duomo* 🔁 *€3* ☉ *Mar.–May, daily 9:30–7; June–Aug., daily 9:30–8; Sept. and Oct., daily 9:30–7; Nov.–Feb., daily 10–5.*

❷ **Museo dell'Opera Metropolitana.** Built into part of the unfinished new cathedral's nave, the museum contains a small but important collection of Sienese art and the cathedral treasury. Its masterpiece is unquestionably the

Maestà by Duccio (circa 1255–1318), painted around 1310 and magnificently displayed in a room devoted entirely to the artist's work. The tower inside the museum has a splendid view. ⊠ *Piazza del Duomo, next to Duomo, Città* ☎ *0577/283048* 🖺 *€6* ☉ *Mar.–May, daily 9:30–7; June–Aug., daily 9:30–8; Sept. and Oct., daily 9:30–7; Nov.–Feb., daily 10–5.*

❼ **Pinacoteca Nazionale.** The national picture gallery contains an excellent collection of Sienese art, including works by native sons Ambrogio Lorenzetti (active 1319–48), Duccio, and Domenico Beccafumi (1486–1551). ⊠ *Via San Pietro 29, Città* ☎ *0577/281161* 🖺 *€4* ☉ *Sun. and Mon. 8:30–1:30, Tues.–Sat. 8:15–7.*

❶ **San Domenico.** In the church of San Domenico is the **Cappella di Santa Caterina,** with frescoes by Sodoma portraying scenes from the life of St. Catherine of Siena. Catherine was a much-respected diplomat, noted for ending the Great Schism by persuading the pope to return to Rome from Avignon. The saint's preserved head and finger are on display in the chapel. ⊠ *Costa di Sant'Antonio, Camollia* ☎ *0577/280893* ☉ *Nov.–mid-Mar., daily 9–6; mid-Mar.–Oct., daily 7–7.*

❻ **Spedale di Santa Maria della Scala.** A former *ospedale* (hospital) and hostel for weary pilgrims, built beginning in the late 9th century, continues to evolve into a grand exhibition space, hosting major contemporary art shows and housing, among other gems, some of the Fonte Gaia sculpted reliefs by Jacopo della Quercia (1371/74–1438). Even if you are not particularly taken with Etruscan objects, the subterranean archaeological museum contained within is not to be missed. Its interior design is sheer brilliance—it's beautifully lighted, eerily quiet, and an oasis of cool on hot summer days. ⊠ *Piazza del Duomo, opposite front of Duomo, Città* ☎ *0577/224811* 🖺 *€5.20* ☉ *Mar. 17–Oct., daily 10–6; Nov.–Dec. 23, daily 10:30–4:30; Dec. 24–Jan. 6, daily 10–6; Jan. 7–Mar. 16, daily 10:30–4:30.*

Off the Beaten Path

❽ **Orto Botanico.** Not far from the Duomo and the Pinacoteca, Siena's botanical garden is a great place to relax and enjoy views of the countryside. Guided tours in English are available with a reservation. ⊠ *Via Pier Andrea Mattioli 4, Città* ☎ *0577/232874* 🖺 *€8* ☉ *Weekdays 8–12:30 and 2:30–5:30, Sat. 8–noon.*

Where to Stay & Eat

$$$ ✕ **Antica Trattoria Botteganova.** Chef Michele Sorrentino's cooking is all about clean flavors, balanced combinations, and inviting presentation. Look for inspiring dishes such as spaghetti *alla chitarra in salsa di astice piccante* (with a spicy lobster sauce). The dining room's interior, with high vaulting, is relaxed yet classy, and there's a small room for nonsmokers. Service is first rate. ⊠ *Strada per Montevarchi (SS408) 29, 2 km (1 mi) north of Siena along road to Chianti* ☎ *0577/284230* ▤ *AE, DC, MC, V* ☉ *Closed Sun.*

$$–$$$ ✕ **Le Logge.** Bright flowers add a dash of color in this classic Tuscan dining room with stenciled ceilings. The wooden cupboards (now filled with wine bottles) recall the turn-of-the-19th-century food store it once was. A small menu, with four or five primi and secondi, changes regularly, but almost always includes *malfatti all'osteria,* ricotta-and-spinach dumplings in a cream sauce. Try inventive desserts such as *coni con mousse al cioccolato e gelato allo zafferano,* which is two diminutive ice-cream cones with chocolate mousse and saffron ice cream. ⊠ *Via del Porrione 33, San Martino* ☎ *0577/48013* ▭ *AE, DC, MC, V* ☉ *Closed Sun. and 3 wks in Jan.*

★ $-$$ ✕**Osteria del Coro.** Chef-owner Stefano Azzi promotes local fare, uses age-old Sienese recipes, and backs up all his creations with a stellar wine list. His *pici con le briciole alla mio modo* (thick spaghetti with bread crumbs), liberally dressed with fried *cinta senese* (a local bacon), dazzles. The place was once a pizzeria, and it retains its unadorned, unpretentious nature—you certainly wouldn't come because of the decor. ⊠ *Via Pantaneto 85–87, San Martino* ☎ *0577/222482* ⛤ *Reservations essential* ▭ *No credit cards.*

$ ✕**La Taverna del Capitano.** Not far from the Duomo you can step into a comfortable little taverna that is simplicity itself. The *pici al pomodoro fresco,* thick noodles topped with a lively fresh tomato sauce and a bit of cheese dusted on top, proves that less can indeed be more. Tuscan specialties and flavorful primi are strong suits here. Waiters dash between the closely spaced tables and can speak knowledgeably about the fine wine list. ⊠ *Via del Capitano 8, Città* ☎ *0577/288094* ▭ *AE, DC, MC, V* ☉ *Closed Tues.*

¢ ✕**da Trombicche.** Wiped out from too much sightseeing? Consider an invigorating snack at this one-room eatery. Here they do tasty things with eggs (the frittata is exceptional), plates of cured meats, and made-to-order *panini* (sandwiches). The list of daily specials reflects the season, and the collection of *verdure sott'olio* (marinated vegetables) is refreshing. Anything you choose can be washed down with the inexpensive, eminently drinkable, house red. ⊠ *Via delle Terme 66, Camollia* ☎ *0577/288089* ▭ *No credit cards* ☉ *Closed Sun.*

$$$$ ▦ **Certosa di Maggiano.** A former 14th-century monastery has been converted into an exquisite country hotel. The officious staff is a drawback, but rooms have the style and comfort of an aristocratic villa—with classic prints and bold colors such as a happy daffodil yellow. Common spaces are luxurious, with fine woods and leather. In warm weather, breakfast is served on the patio next to the garden ablaze with flowers. Half board is required in high season. ⊠ *Strada di Certosa 82, take the Siena Sud exit off superstrada, 53100* ☎ *0577/288180* 🖷 *0577/288189* ⊕ *www.certosadimaggiano.it* ⇄ *9 rooms, 8 suites* ⌂ *Restaurant, minibars, cable TV, in-room data ports, tennis court, pool, exercise equipment, dry cleaning, laundry service, concierge, helipad, no-smoking rooms; no kids under 12* ▭ *AE, MC, V* ☉ *Closed mid.-Jan–mid Mar.* ❏ *MAP.*

★ $$-$$$ ▦ **Palazzo Ravizza.** There might not be a more romantic place in the center of Siena than this quietly charming pension, a 10-minute walk to the Duomo. Rooms exude a faded gentility, with high ceilings, antique furniture, big windows, and bathrooms done in hand-painted tiles. The restaurant serves Tuscan favorites, which, when it's warm, can be enjoyed outside in a lovely, tranquil garden complete with trickling fountain. ⊠ *Pian dei Mantellini 34, near Porto San Marco, Città, 53100* ☎ *0577/280462* 🖷 *0577/221597* ⊕ *www.palazzoravizza.it* 🛏 *40 rooms, 4 suites* ⏶ *Restaurant, some in-room safes, some minibars, cable TV, bar, laundry service, concierge, free parking, some pets allowed* ⊟ *AE, DC, MC, V* ❘❘❘ *BP.*

$$ ⌂ **Antica Torre.** An old stone staircase, wooden beams, and original brick vaults here and there are reminders that the building is a 16th-century tower. The lodging is the work of a cordial couple who have carefully evoked a private home, with only eight simple but tasteful guest rooms. Antica Torre is a 10-minute walk from Piazza del Campo. ⊠ *Via Fieravecchia 7, San Martino, 53100* ☎ *0577/226102* 🖷 *0577/222255* ⊕ *www.anticatorresiena.it* 🛏 *8 rooms* ⏶ *Cable TV, parking (fee)* ⊟ *AE, DC, MC, V* ❘❘❘ *EP.*

¢ ⌂ **Alma Domus.** If you're after a contemplative, utilitarian experience, seek refuge at the former convent run by the committed parishioners of the Santurario Santa Caterina (Sanctuary of St. Catherine); it's around the corner from the church of San Domenico. Rooms are spartan and very clean. Many have a view of the Duomo and the rest of Siena, which might make the 11:30 curfew livable. A two-night minimum stay is required; the best way to reserve is by fax. ⊠ *Via Camporeggio 37, Camollìa, 53100* ☎ *0577/44177* 🖷 *0577/47601* 🛏 *31 rooms* ⏶ *No-smoking floors; no room phones, no room TVs* ⊟ *No credit cards* ❘❘❘ *EP.*

Nightlife & the Arts

Music

During two weeks in July, Siena hosts the **Settimane Musicali Senesi,** a series of classical concerts held in churches and courtyards. The event is arranged by the **Accademia Musicale Chigiana** (⊠ Via di Città 89, Città ☎ 0577/22091 ⊕ www.chigiana.it), which also conducts master classes and workshops in July and August and sponsors concerts from November through April. Age-old venues such as Santa Maria della Scala and the church of Sant'Agostino provide the setting.

Shopping

Siena is known for its cakes and cookies, made from recipes of medieval origin—look for *cavallucci* (sweet spice biscuits), *panforte* (a densely packed concoction of honey, hazelnuts, almonds, and spices), and *ricciarelli* (almond-paste cookies). The best place in town to find Sienese baked goods, as well as to grab a cappuccino, is **Nannini,** located on the main drag north of the Campo (⊠ Banchi di Sopra 24, Camollìa ☎ 0577/236009).

Siena has excellent specialty wine and food shops. **La Bottega dei Sapori Antichi** (⊠ Via delle Terme 41, Camollìa ☎ 0577/285501) is a good option for local products. Italy's only state-sponsored enoteca, **Enoteca Italiana** (⊠ Fortezza Medicea, Camollìa ☎ 0577/288497), sells wines from all across Italy.

Siena Ricama (⊠ Via di Città 61, Duomo ☎ 0577/288339) has embroidered linens and other housewares for sale. Chiara Perinetti Casoni at

Bottega dell'Arte (✉ Via Stalloreggi 47, Città ☎ 0577/40755) creates high-quality copies of 14th- and 15th-century Sienese panel paintings using tempera and gold leaf.

AREZZO & CORTONA

The hill towns of Arezzo and Cortona carry on age-old local traditions—in June and September, for example, Arezzo's Romanesque and Gothic churches are enlivened by the Giostra del Saracino, a costumed medieval joust. Arezzo has been home to important artists since ancient times, when Etruscan potters produced their fiery-red vessels here. Fine examples of the work of Luca Signorelli are preserved in Cortona, his hometown.

Arezzo

63 km (39 mi) northeast of Siena, 81 km (50 mi) southeast of Florence.

The birthplace of the poet Petrarch (1304–74) and the Renaissance artist and art historian Giorgio Vasari, Arezzo is today best known for the magnificent Piero della Francesca frescoes in the church of San Francesco. The city dates from pre-Etruscan times and thrived as an Etruscan capital from the 7th to the 4th century BC. During the Middle Ages it was fully embroiled in the conflict between the Ghibellines (pro-emperor) and the Guelphs (pro-pope), losing its independence to Florence at the end of the 14th century after many decades of doing battle.

Urban sprawl testifies to the fact that Arezzo (population 90,000) is the third-largest city in Tuscany (after Florence and Pisa). But the old town, set on a low hill, is relatively small, and almost completely closed to traffic. Look for parking along the roads that circle the lower part of town, near the train station, and walk into town from there. You can explore the most interesting sights in a few hours, adding time to linger for some window-shopping at Arezzo's many antiques shops.

FodorśChoice
★

The remarkable frescoes by Piero della Francesca (circa 1420–92) in the **Basilica di San Francesco** were painted between 1452 and 1466. They depict scenes from the *Legend of the True Cross* on three walls of the *cappella maggiore,* or high altar choir. What Sir Kenneth Clark called "the most perfect morning light in all Renaissance painting" may be seen in the lowest section of the right wall, where the troops of the emperor Maxentius flee before the sign of the cross. A 15-year project restored the works to their original brilliance. Reservations are required to see the choir area with the frescoes. ✉ *Piazza San Francesco 6* ☎ *0575/ 352727* ⊕ *www.pierodellafrancesca.it* 🎫 *Church free, choir €6* ⊙ *Apr.–Oct., weekdays 9–6:30, Sat. 9–5:30, Sun. 1–5:30; Nov.–Mar., weekdays 9–5:30, Sat. 9–5, Sun. 1–5.*

Some historians maintain that Arezzo's oddly shaped, sloping **Piazza Grande** was once the site of an ancient Roman forum. Now it hosts a first-Sunday-of-the-month antiques fair as well as the **Giostra del Saracino** (Joust of the Saracen), featuring medieval costumes and competition, held here in the middle of June and on the first Sunday of September.

Check out the 16th-century loggia designed by native son Giorgio Vasari on the northeast side of the piazza.

The curving, tiered apse on Piazza Grande belongs to **Pieve di Santa Maria,** one of Tuscany's finest Romanesque churches, built in the 12th century. Don't miss the Portale Maggiore (great door) with its polychrome figures representing the months; restored in 2002, they are remarkably vibrant. ⊠ *Corso Italia* ☎ *0575/377678* ⊙ *Daily 8–noon and 3–6:30.*

Arezzo's medieval **Duomo** (at the top of the hill) contains a fresco of a somber *Magdalen* by Piero della Francesca; look for it next to the large marble tomb near the organ. ⊠ *Piazza del Duomo 1* ☎ *0575/23991* ⊙ *Daily 7–12:30 and 3–6:30.*

Italy's most famous art historian designed and decorated his private home, **Casa di Giorgio Vasari,** in about the year 1540. ⊠ *Via XX Settembre 55* ☎ *0575/409040* ⊠ *€2* ⊙ *Mon. and Wed.–Sat. 8:30–6:30, Sun. 8:30–1:30.*

Where to Stay & Eat

¢ ✕ **La Torre di Gnicche.** Looking for Italian home cooking? Eating *ribollita* (a hearty, traditional Tuscan soup) here is a heightened experience, especially when accompanied by an affordable glass of red. The short menu includes assorted crostini, sensational vegetables marinated in oil, cheese plates, and an earthy *polpettone* (meat loaf). This one-room restaurant, seating about 30, is part of a Renaissance palazzo. ⊠ *Piaggia San Martino 8* ☎ *0575/352035* ⊟ *MC, V* ⊙ *Closed Wed.*

$$ ✕▥ **Castello di Gargonza.** Enchantment reigns at this tiny 13th-century hamlet in the countryside near Monte San Savino, part of the fiefdom of the aristocratic Florentine Guicciardini and restored by the modern Count Roberto Guicciardini as a way to rescue a dying village. A castle, church, and cobbled streets set the stage. A minimum two-night stay in any of the rooms is appreciated; apartments (sleeping 2–10 people) rent Saturday to Saturday. La Torre restaurant serves local fare, such as *zuppa di porcini* (a thick puree of porcini mushrooms). Follow with any of the superb grilled meats. Regional wines are well represented. ⊠ *52048 Monte San Savino* ☎ *0575/847021* ⊟ *0575/847054* ⊕ *www.gargonza. it* ⊃ *18 rooms, 11 apartments, 1 suite* ☾ *Restaurant, minibars, pool, meeting room; no a/c, no room TVs* ⊟ *AE, DC, MC, V* ⊙ *Closed 3 wks in Jan. and 3 wks in Nov. Restaurant closed Tues.* ⊺⊙⊺ *BP.*

★ $ ▥ **Calcione Castle and Country.** The elegant Marchesa Olivella Lotteringhi della Stufa has turned her six-centuries-old family homestead into comfortable rental apartments. Think sophisticated rustic: many of the apartments have open fireplaces. The houses have a private pool (the apartments share the estate pool), and there are two nearby lakes for fishing and swimming. A stay here is restorative, since it's blissfully quiet. Calcione is convenient to Arezzo, Siena, San Gimignano, and the delights of Umbria. A one-week minimum stay is mandatory. ⊠ *Lucignano, 52046* ☎ *0575/837100* ⊟ *0575/837153* ⊕ *www.calcione.com* ⊃ *2 houses, 7 apartments* ☾ *BBQ, 3 pools, lake, babysitting, some pets allowed; no a/c, no fans in some rooms, no room TVs, no room phones* ⊟ *No credit cards* ⊙ *Closed Nov.–Mar.* ⊺⊙⊺ *EP.*

Shopping

On the first Sunday of each month a colorful flea market with antiques and other less-precious objects for sale takes place in the **Piazza Grande**.

GOLD Gold production here is on an industrial scale. Uno-A-Erre is the largest of several factories supplying local shops. **Prosperi** (⊠ Corso Italia 76 ☎ 0575/20746) works wonders in gold, silver, and platinum.

OUTLET MALLS Savvy shoppers head to the **Prada outlet** (⊠ Località Levanella, SS69, Montevarchi, 29 km [18 mi] west of Arezzo ☎ 055/91901) for discounted Prada products. Go during the week—if a weekend is your only option, remember that patience is a virtue. If you're on an outlet roll, continue north to **The Mall** (⊠ Via Europa 8, Leccio Reggello, 52 km [33 mi] northwest of Arezzo ☎ 055/8657775 ⊕ www.outlet-firenze.com), where discounts on lines such as Gucci, Yves Saint Laurent, Armani, Sergio Rossi—to name but a few—abound.

TEXTILES At **Busatti** (⊠ Corso Italia 48 ☎ 0575/355295 ⊕ www.busatti.com), the Busatti-Sassolini family has been making sumptuous handwoven linen, wool, hemp, and cotton since 1842. Look for hand-stitched hems, embroideries, and lace.

Cortona

29 km (18 mi) south of Arezzo, 79 km (44 mi) east of Siena, 117 km (73 mi) southeast of Florence.

With olive trees and vineyards creeping up to its walls, pretty Cortona—popularized by Frances Mayes's *Under the Tuscan Sun*—commands sweeping views over Lake Trasimeno and the plain of the Valdichiana. Its two galleries and churches are rarely visited; its delightful medieval streets are a pleasure to wander for their own sake. The heart of town is formed by Piazza della Repubblica and the adjacent Piazza Signorelli, which both contain pleasant shops to browse through.

Cortona is considered one of Italy's oldest towns—popularly known as the "Mother of Troy and Grandmother of Rome." Tradition claims that it was founded by Dardanus, also the founder of Troy (after whom the Dardanelles were named). He was fighting a local tribe, so the story goes, when he lost his helmet (*corythos* in Greek) on Cortona's hill. In time a town grew up that took its name (Corito) from the missing headgear. By the 5th century BC the Etruscans had built the first set of town walls, whose cyclopean traces can still be seen in the 3-km (2-mi) sweep of the present fortifications.

The **Museo Diocesano** (Diocesan Museum) houses an impressive number of large and splendid paintings by native son Luca Signorelli, as well as a stunning *Annunciation* by Fra Angelico, a delightful surprise in this small town. ⊠ *Piazza del Duomo 1* ☎ *0575/637235* 💶 €5 ⊙ *Nov.–Mar., Tues.–Sun. 10–5; Apr.–Oct., Tues.–Sun. 10–7.*

Where to Stay & Eat

$ ✕ **Osteria del Teatro.** Walls filled with photographs of theater stars provide the backdrop for a two-room restaurant much frequented by locals. They come for good reason: the food here is tasty and abundant.

2

If you're lucky enough to be around during truffle season (fall and early winter), start with the *fonduta al tartufo* (truffle fondue), in this case made with melted pecorino served with little toast squares. The *fagottini di pollo con carciofi* (chicken-stuffed pasta) proves that it's possible to have divine, dairy-free filled pasta. ☒ *Via Maffei 2, off Piazza del Teatro* ☎ *0575/630556* ▭ *AE, DC, MC, V* ⊗ *Closed Wed. and 2 wks in Nov.*

$$$$
Fodor'sChoice
★

☓▥ **Il Falconiere.** The husband-and-wife team of Riccardo and Silvia Baracchi run a hotel with rooms in an 18th-century villa, just minutes outside Cortona. Suites are in the *chiesetta* (little church) that once belonging to an obscure 19th-century Italian poet and hunter. You can also stay in the very private Le Vigne del Falco building at the end of the property, where suites have individual entrances and grand views of the plain. The restaurant's inventive menu is complemented by a wine list that's the product of Silvia's sommelier training. By all means sample their estate-produced olive oil. Weeklong cooking classes are available. ☒ *Località San Martino 370, 52044* ☎ *0575/612679* ⊟ *0575/612927* ⊕ *www.ilfalconiere.com* ⤳ *13 rooms, 6 suites* ⟐ *Restaurant, room service, in-room safes, minibars, cable TV, in-room data ports, 2 pools, bar, babysitting, dry cleaning, laundry service, concierge, free parking, some pets allowed (fee), no-smoking rooms* ▭ *AE, MC, V* ⊗ *Closed 3 wks in Jan. Restaurant closed Mon. Nov.–Mar.* ¶⊙¶ *BP.*

HILL TOWNS WEST OF SIENA

Submit to the draw of Tuscany's enchanting fortified cities that crown the hills west of Siena, many dating to the Etruscan period. San Gimignano, known as the "medieval Manhattan" because of its forest of stout medieval towers built by rival families, is the most heavily visited. This one-time Roman outpost, with its tilted cobbled streets and ancient buildings, can make the days of Guelph-Ghibelline conflicts palpable. Rising from a series of bleak gullied hills and valleys, Volterra has always been popular for its minerals and stones, particularly alabaster, which was used by the Etruscans for many implements. Examples are now displayed in the exceptional and unwieldy Museo Etrusco Guarnacci.

Volterra

❶ *48 km (30 mi) south of San Miniato, 75 km (47 mi) southwest of Florence.*

Unlike other Tuscan hill towns rising above sprawling vineyards and rolling fields of green, Volterra is surrounded by desolate terrain marred with industry and mining equipment. D. H. Lawrence described it as "somber and chilly alone on her rock" in his *Etruscan Places.* The fortress, walls, and gates still stand mightily over Le Balze, a distinctive series of gullied hills and valleys to the west that were formed by irregular erosion. The town has long been known for its alabaster, which has been mined since Etruscan times; today the Volterrans use it to make ornaments and souvenirs sold all over town. An €8 combined ticket is your only option for visiting the Museo Etrusco Guarnacci and the Pinacoteca e Museo Civico.

Volterra has some of Italy's best small museums. The extraordinarily large and unique collection of Etruscan artifacts at the **Museo Etrusco Guarnacci** is a treasure in the region. (Many of the other Etruscan finds from the area have been shipped off to state museums or the Vatican.) If only a curator had thought to cull the best of the 700 funerary urns rather than to display every last one of them. ⊠ *Via Don Minzoni 15* ☎ *0588/ 86347* ⊕ *www.comune.volterra.pi.it* ⊠ *Combined ticket €8* ⊘ *Mar. 16–Nov. 3, daily 9–7; Nov. 4–Mar. 15, daily 9–1:30.*

The **Pinacoteca e Museo Civico** houses a highly acclaimed collection of religious art, including a *Madonna and Child with Saints* by Luca Signorelli (1445/50–1523) and a *Deposition* by Rosso Fiorentino (1494–1541) that is reason enough to visit Volterra. ⊠ *Via dei Sarti 1* ☎ *0588/87580* ⊕ *www.comune.volterra.pi.it* ⊠ *Combined ticket €8* ⊘ *Mar. 16–Nov. 3, daily 9–7; Nov. 4–Mar. 15, daily 9–1:30.*

Next to the altar in the town's unfinished **Duomo** is a magnificent 13th-century carved-wood *Deposition*. Note the fresco by Benozzo Gozzoli (1420–97) in the Cappella della Addolorata. Along the left wall of the nave you can see the arrival of the Magi. ⊠ *Piazza San Giovanni* ☎ *0588/86192* ⊘ *Daily 9–1 and 3–6.*

Among Volterra's best-preserved ancient remains is the Etruscan **Porta all'Arco,** an arch dating from the 4th century BC now incorporated into the city walls. The ruins of the 1st-century BC **Teatro Romano,** a beautifully preserved Roman theater, are worth a visit. Adjacent to the theater are the remains of the **terme** (baths). The complex is outside the town walls past Porta Fiorentina. ⊠ *Viale Francesco Ferrucci* ☎ *0588/ 86347* ⊠ *€2* ⊘ *Mar.–May and Sept.–Nov., daily 10–1 and 2–4; June–Aug., daily 10–6:45; Dec.–Feb., weekends 10–1 and 2–4.*

Where to Stay & Eat

$ ✕ **Il Sacco Fiorentino.** Start with the *porcini e fegatini di pollo saltati*—a medley of sautéed chicken liver and porcini mushrooms drizzled with balsamic vinegar. The meal just gets better when you move on to a dish like *filetto di maiale e cipolline,* pork medallions with pearl onions in a tangy mustard sauce. The wine list is a marvel, both long and affordably priced. Unremarkable white walls, tile floors, and red tablecloths are easily forgiven once the food starts arriving. ⊠ *Piazza XX Settembre 18* ☎ *0588/ 88537* ⊟ *AE, DC, MC, V* ⊘ *Closed Wed. and Jan. and Feb.*

$ ▦ **Il Giardino di Venzano.** Terraced gardens bloom with native and exotic specimens: this agriturismo is run by two transplanted Australians with serious green thumbs. The grounds and buildings are what remains of an Augustinian monastery complete with Romanesque chapel. Three apartments, each sleeping two to four people, have high ceilings with light-color timbers, white walls and linens, and terra-cotta tile floors. Windows provide sweeping views of the surrounding countryside. A minimum one-week stay is required. ⊠ *Località Venzano, 56048 Mazzolla, 10 km (6 mi) south of Volterra* ☎ *0588/39095* ⊕ *www. venzanogardens.com* ⇨ *3 apartments* ⚭ *BBQs, fans, kitchens; no a/c, no room phones, no room TVs* ⊟ *No credit cards* ⊘ *Closed Nov. 1–Apr. 14* ⦿ *EP.*

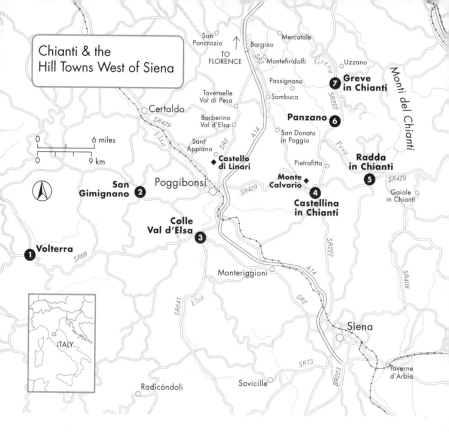

$ 🏨 **San Lino.** Within Volterra's medieval walls, a convent-turned-hotel pairs wood-beam ceilings, archways, and terra-cotta floors in public spaces with modern-day comforts in your private domain. Hair dryers and some carpeting in the guest rooms accompany contemporary wood laminate furnishings and straight-line ironwork pieces. Sip a drink on the small terrace with tables, umbrellas, and potted geraniums; the pool area is framed on one side by a church with a stained-glass window of the Last Supper. The restaurant serves Tuscan classics and local specialties such as *zuppa alla volteranna*, a thick vegetable soup. ⊠ *Via San Lino 26, 56048* ☎ *0588/85250* 🖶 *0588/80620* ⊕ *www.hotelsanlino.com* 🛏 *43 rooms* ⚑ *Dining room, minibars, cable TV, pool, bar, dry cleaning, laundry service, concierge, parking (fee), some pets allowed, no-smoking rooms* ⊟ *AE, DC, MC, V* ☺ *Closed Nov.–Jan.* ⍾ *BP.*

Shopping

A number of shops in Volterra sell boxes, jewelry, and other objects made of alabaster. The **Cooperativa Artieri Alabastro** (⊠ Piazza dei Priori 5 ☎ 0588/87590) has two large showrooms of alabaster pieces. At **Camillo Rossi** (⊠ Via Lungo le Mura del Mandorlo 7 ☎ 0588/86133) you can actually see craftspeople at work, creating alabaster objects for all tastes and budgets.

Anna Maria Molesini (✉ Via Gramsci 45 ☎ 0588/88411) weaves scarves, shawls, jackets, throws, and jackets—mostly in mohair—on her loom in her small shop.

San Gimignano

❷ *27 km (17 mi) east of Volterra, 57 km (35 mi) southwest of Florence.*

When you're high on its hill surrounded by centuries-old towers silhouetted against the blue sky, it's difficult not to fall under the medieval spell of San Gimignano. Today 15 towers remain, but at the height of the Guelph-Ghibelline conflict there was a forest of more than 70, and it was possible to cross the town by rooftop rather than street. The towers were built partly to defend the town—they provided a safe refuge and were useful for pouring boiling oil on attacking enemies—and partly to bolster the egos of their owners, who competed with deadly seriousness to build the highest tower in town. When the Black Death devastated the population in 1348, power and independence faded fast and civic autonomy was ultimately surrendered to Florence.

Today San Gimignano isn't much more than a gentrified walled city, amply prepared for its booming tourist trade but still very much worth exploring. Despite the remarkable profusion of chintzy souvenir shops lining its main drag, there's some serious Renaissance art to be seen here and an equally important local wine (Vernaccia, a light white) to be savored. Escape at midday to the uninhabited areas outside the city walls for a hike and a picnic, and return to explore the town in the afternoon and evening, when things quiet down and the long shadows cast by the imposing towers take on fascinating shapes. A €7.50 combination ticket covers the sights, except for the private Museo di Criminologia Medievale.

San Gimignano's most noteworthy medieval buildings are clustered around the central **Piazza del Duomo.** The imposing **Torre Grossa** is the tallest tower in town (177 feet), with views that are well worth the climb. ✉ *Piazza del Duomo 1* ☎ *0577/940008* ✉ *€5 (includes Palazzo del Popolo)* ۞ *Mar.–Oct., daily 9:30–7; Nov.–Feb., daily 10–5:30.*

The **Palazzo del Popolo** houses the **Museo Civico,** featuring Taddeo di Bartolo's celebratory scenes from the life of San Gimignano. The town's namesake, a bishop of Modena, achieved sainthood by driving hordes of barbarians out of the city in the 10th century. Dante visited San Gimignano as an ambassador from Florence for only a single day in 1300, but it was long enough to get a room named after him, which now holds a *Maestà* by 14th-century artist Lippo Memmi. A small room (probably the private domain of the commune's chief magistrate) contains frescoes by Memmo di Filippuccio (active 1288–1324) depicting a young couple's courtship. ✉ *Piazza del Duomo* ☎ *0577/940008* ✉ *€5 (includes Torre Grossa)* ۞ *Mar.–Oct., daily 9:30–7:30; Nov.–Feb., daily 10–5:30.*

★ The Romanesque **Collegiata** is a treasure trove of frescoes, including Bartolo di Fredi's cycle of scenes from the Old Testament on the left nave wall dating from 1367. Taddeo di Bartolo's otherworldly *Last Judgment,* on the arch inside the facade, depicts distorted and suffering nudes—

avant-garde stuff for the 1390s. The New Testament scenes on the right wall, which may have been executed by Barna da Siena in the 1330s, suggest a more reserved, balanced Renaissance manner. The **Cappella di Santa Fina** contains glorious frescoes by Domenico Ghirlandaio (1449–94) depicting the story of this local saint. ⊠ *Piazza del Duomo* ☎ *0577/940316* ≊ *€3.50* ☼ *Apr.–Oct., weekdays 9:30–7:10, Sat. 9:30–5:10, Sun. 12:30–5:10; Nov.–Jan. 20 and Mar., Mon.–Sat. 9:30–4:40, Sun. 12:30–4:40.*

The **Museo di Criminologia Medievale** (Museum of Medieval Criminology) exhibits reproductions of medieval torture technology, along with operating instructions and a clear description of the intended effect. Though scholars dispute the historical accuracy of many of the instruments, the final, very contemporary object—an electric chair imported from the United States—does give pause. ⊠ *Via del Castello 1–3* ☎ *0577/942243* ≊ *€8* ☼ *Apr.–Sept, daily 10–8; Oct.–Mar., Mon.–Sat. 10–6, Sun. 10–7.*

Before leaving San Gimignano, be sure to see its most revered work of art: Benozzo Gozzoli's utterly stunning 15th-century fresco cycle depicts scenes from the life of St. Augustine in the church of **Sant'Agostino.** ⊠ *Piazza Sant'Agostino, north end of town* ☎ *0577/907012* ☼ *Nov.–Mar., daily 7–noon and 3–6; Apr.–Oct., daily 7–noon and 3–7.*

Where to Stay & Eat

$$ ✕ **La Mangiatoia.** Bright-color gingham tablecloths provide an interesting contrast to the 13th-century, rib-vault ceilings here—the lighthearted feminine touch might be explained by chef Susi Cuomo, who has been presiding over her kitchen for more than 20 years. The menu is seasonal: in autumn, don't miss her *sacottino di pecorino al tartufo* (little packages of pasta stuffed with sheep's cheese and truffles), and in summer enjoy lighter fare on the intimate, flower-bedecked terrace in the back. ⊠ *Via Mainardi 5, off Via San Matteo* ☎ *0577/941528* ⊟ *MC, V* ☼ *Closed Tues., 3 wks in Nov., and Jan. and Feb.*

★ ¢ ✕ **Enoteca Gustavo.** The ebullient Maristella Becucci reigns supreme in this tiny wine bar (three small tables in the back, two in the bar, two bar stools) serving divine, and ample, crostini. The *crostino con carciofini e pecorino* (toasted bread with artichokes topped with semi-aged pecorino) packs a punch. The changing list of wines by the glass has about 16 reds and whites, mostly local, all good. The cheese plate is a bit more expensive than the crostini, but it's worth it. ⊠ *Via San Matteo 29* ☎ *0577/940057* ⌂ *Reservations not accepted* ⊟ *AE, DC, MC, V* ☼ *Closed Tues. Oct.–Mar.*

$$$$ ▥ **La Collegiata.** After serving as a Franciscan convent and then residence of the noble Strozzi family, the Collegiata has been transformed into a fine hotel. Antiques and precious tapestries furnish the rooms, and bathrooms have whirlpool tubs. A park surrounds the building: ask for a room with a private balcony to enjoy the view more closely. The restaurant occupies the deconsecrated church. ⊠ *Località Strada 27, 53037, 1 km (½ mi) north of town center* ☎ *0577/943201* ▤ *0577/940566* ⊕ *www.relaischateaux.com* ⇥ *20 rooms, 1 suite* ⌂ *Restaurant, room service, in-room safes, some in-room hot tubs, cable TV, pool, bar, wine* *bar, meeting room, free parking, some pets allowed* ▤ *AE, DC, MC, V* ☺ *Closed Jan. 7–Mar. 12* †○| *EP.*

$–$$ ▥ **Pescille.** A rambling farmhouse 4 km (2½ mi) outside San Gimignano has been transformed into a handsome hotel with understated contemporary furniture in the bedrooms. Country-classic motifs, such as farm implements hanging on the walls, dominate in the bar. From this charming spot you get a splendid view of San Gimignano and its towers. ✉ *Località Pescille, Strada Castel San Gimignano, 53037* ☎ *0577/940186* 🖷 *0577/943165* ⊕ *www.pescille.it* ↪ *38 rooms, 12 suites* ⚐ *Cable TV, Wi-Fi in some rooms, tennis court, pool, gym, bar, free parking; no a/c in some rooms* ▤ *AE, DC, MC, V* ☺ *Closed Nov.–Mar.* †○| *BP.*

Colle Val d'Elsa

❸ *15 km (9 mi) southeast of San Gimignano, 50 km (31 mi) southwest of Florence.*

On the road from Florence to Siena, Colle Val d'Elsa rises dramatically along a winding road, its narrow streets lined with palazzi dating from the 15th and 16th centuries. For art enthusiasts, it's perhaps best known as the birthplace of Arnolfo di Cambio (circa 1245–1310), architect of Florence's Duomo. Once a formidable producer of wool, the town now produces glass and crystal sold in local shops. Colle has two distinct parts: the relatively modern and less-interesting lower town, Colle Bassa, and the older, upper town, Colle Alta.

Where to Stay & Eat

★ **$$$$** ✕ **Ristorante Arnolfo.** Food lovers with some money to spend should not miss Arnolfo, one of Tuscany's most highly regarded restaurants. Chef Gaetano Trovato sets high standards of creativity; his dishes straddle the line between innovation and tradition, almost always with spectacular results. The menu changes frequently and has two fixed-price options, but there are always plenty of fresh vegetables and herbs. You're in for a treat if *medaglioni di sogliola e gamberi rossi con finocchi allo zafferano* (sole and shrimp with fennel, flavored with saffron) is on the list. The restaurant is in a tranquil spot at the center of town. ✉ *Piazza XX Settembre 52* ☎🖷 *0577/920549* ▤ *AE, DC, MC, V* ☺ *Closed Tues. and Wed., mid-Jan.–mid-Feb., and 2 wks in Aug.*

★ **$$$$** ▥ **La Suvera.** Pope Julius II once owned this luxurious estate in the valley of the River Elsa. The papal villa and adjacent building have magnificently furnished guest rooms and suites appointed with antiques and modern comforts. La Suvera's first-rate facilities, including drawing rooms, a library, an Italian garden, a park, and the Oliviera restaurant (serving organic estate wines), make it hard to tear yourself away. ✉ *Pievescola (Casola d'Elsa) off SS541, 15 km (9 mi) south of Colle di Val d'Elsa, 53030* ☎ *0577/960300* 🖷 *0577/960220* ⊕ *www.lasuvera. it* ↪ *16 rooms, 16 suites* ⚐ *Restaurant, room service, in-room safes, minibars, cable TV, in-room broadband, tennis court, pool, exercise equipment, massage, Turkish bath, mountain bikes, bar, library, dry cleaning, laundry service, concierge, meeting room; no kids under 12* ▤ *AE, DC, MC, V* ☺ *Closed Nov.–Easter* †○| *BP.*

2

$ ▦ **Villa Belvedere.** The Conti-Iannone family, who have run this place since 1984, provide the intimacy that you might find in a family home. Some of the 17th-century villa's rooms have three beds (with an option for adding a fourth), making this a good choice for families. A classic garden provides a place to read or have a drink, and an on-site restaurant serves Tuscan specialties. On a good day you can glimpse San Gimignano from here, but there's a fair amount of traffic that goes by on the road in front of the hotel. Half board is available. ✉ *Località Belvedere, 53034, 1½ km (1 mi) south on SS2* ☎ *0577/920966* 🖷 *0577/ 92412* ⊕ *www.villabelvedere.com* ⟿ *15 rooms* ⚭ *Restaurant, cable TV, Wi-Fi, tennis court, pool, bar, free parking, some pets allowed; no a/c* ▭ *AE, DC, MC, V* ⦿| *EP.*

CHIANTI

Directly south of Florence is Chianti, one of Italy's most famous wine-producing areas; its hill towns, olive groves, and vineyards are quintessential Tuscany. Many British and northern Europeans have relocated here, drawn by the unhurried life, balmy climate, and charming villages; there are so many Britons, in fact, that the area has been nicknamed Chiantishire. Still, it remains strongly Tuscan in character, with drop-dead views of vine-quilted hills and elegantly elongated cypress trees.

The sinuous SS222 highway, known as the Strada Chiantigiana, runs from Florence through the heart of Chianti. Its most scenic section connects Strada in Chianti, 16 km (10 mi) south of Florence, and Greve in Chianti, whose triangular central piazza is surrounded by restaurants and vintners offering *degustazioni* (wine tastings), 11 km (7 mi) farther south.

Castellina in Chianti

❹ *14 km (8 mi) west of Radda, 42 km (26 mi) south of Florence.*

Castellina in Chianti, or simply Castellina, is on a ridge above the Val di Pesa, Val d'Arbia, and Val d'Elsa, with beautiful panoramas in every direction. The imposing 15th-century tower in the central piazza hints at the history of this village, which was an outpost during the continuing wars between Florence and Siena.

Where to Stay & Eat

$$$–$$$$ ✕ **Alberghaccio.** The simple interior, with whitewashed walls and cypress-beam ceilings, stands in high contrast to the sophisticated meals that come from the kitchen at Alberghaccio. The chef pays attention to the seasons, with the menu reflecting what's freshest at the market. The *sformato di cavolo nero* (creamy polenta with Tuscan kale) is a highlight in fall and winter; the outstanding *arista* (roast pork with rosemary and sage) should not be missed. A comprehensive wine list has selections from all over the world. This upscale trattoria is a short walk from Castellina's tiny center. ✉ *Via Fiorentina 63* ☎ *0577/741042* ⚐ *Reservations essential* ▭ *MC, V* ⊗ *Closed Sun.*

$$ 🏠 **Collelungo.** One of the loveliest agriturismi in the area, Collelungo consists of a series of once-abandoned farmhouses that have been carefully remodeled. Set amid a notable vineyard (it produces internationally recognized Chianti Classico), the apartments—all with cooking facilities and dining areas—have exposed stone walls and typical Tuscan tile floors. The *salone* (lounge), which possibly dates from the 14th century, has satellite TV; adjacent to it is an honor bar. In high season a minimum three-night stay is required. ✉ *Podere Collungo, 53011* 🕾 *0577/740489* 🖷 *0577/741330* ⊕ *www.collelungo.com* ⇆ *12 apartments* ⚴ *BBQs, pool, bar, laundry service, free parking; no a/c, no room phones, no room TVs* ☰ *MC, V* ☻ *Closed Nov.–Mar.* ⦿ *EP.*

$$ 🏠 **Palazzo Squarcialupi.** This refurbished 15th-century palace on the main street in town is a pleasant, restful place to stay. Rooms have high ceilings, white walls, and tile floors; bathrooms are tiled in local stone. Many of the rooms have a view of the valley below. Common areas are elegant but comfortable, and the breakfast buffet is ample. The multilingual staff goes out of its way to be helpful. Though there's no restaurant, the hotel will arrange for a light lunch in the warmer months. ✉ *Via Ferruccio 22, 53011* 🕾 *0577/741186* 🖷 *0577/740386* ⊕ *www.palazzosquarcialupi.com* ⇆ *17 rooms* ⚴ *Minibars, cable TV, Wi-Fi, bar, babysitting, dry cleaning, laundry service, free parking, some pets allowed* ☰ *AE, DC, MC, V* ☻ *Closed Nov.–Mar.* ⦿ *BP.*

Radda in Chianti

★ ❺ *26 km (15 mi) south of Panzano, 52 km (32 mi) south of Florence.*

Radda in Chianti sits on a hill separating two valleys, Val di Pesa and Val d'Arbia. It's one of many tiny Chianti villages that invite you to stroll their steep streets; follow the signs pointing you toward the *camminamento,* a covered medieval passageway circling part of the city inside the walls. In Piazza Ferrucci, is the **Palazzo del Podestà** (or Palazzo Comunale), the city hall that has served the people of Radda for more than four centuries. It has 51 coats of arms embedded in its facade.

OFF THE BEATEN PATH

VOLPAIA – Perched atop a hill 10 km (6 mi) north of Radda is Volpaia, a fairy-tale hamlet that was a military outpost from the 10th to the 16th century and once a shelter for religious pilgrims. Every August, for the Festa di San Lorenzo, people come to Volpaia to watch for falling stars and a traditional fireworks display put on by the family that owns the adjacent wine estate and agriturismo lodging, **Castello di Volpaia** (✉ Piazza della Cisterna 1, 53017 🕾 0577/738066).

Where to Stay & Eat

¢ ✕ **Osteria Le Panzanelle.** Nada Michelassi and Silvia Bonechi combined their accumulated wisdom in the hospitality industry to create this welcoming restaurant a few minutes outside Radda. The small but carefully crafted menu has typical tastes of Tuscany, such as the exquisite *trippa alla fiorentina* (tripe Florentine, with tomatoes, onions, and bay leaves), and unexpected treats like *crostone con salsiccia fresca* (toasted bread with fresh sausage). The wine list, equally well thought out, is particularly strong on the local Chianti Classicos and Super Tuscans. Two

CLOSE UP

Bacchus in Tuscany

2

TUSCANY PRODUCES SOME of Italy's finest wines. Here's a primer to help you navigate the region's wine lists, as well as its wine roads.

VARIETIES

The name **Chianti** evokes Tuscany as readily as gondolas evoke Venice, but if you think Chianti is about straw-covered jugs and deadly headaches, think again. This firm, full-bodied wine pressed from mostly Sangiovese grapes is the region's most popular, and it's easy to taste why. More difficult to understand is the difference between the many kinds of Chianti: there are seven subregions, including Chianti Classico, the oldest, whose wines have a *gallo nero* (black rooster) on the label. Each subregion has its own peculiarities, but the most noticeable—and costly—difference is between regular Chianti and the *riserva* stock, aged at least four years.

Beginning in the 1970s, some winemakers, chafing at the strict regulations for making Chianti, chose to buck tradition and blend their wines in innovative ways. Thus was born the **Super Tuscan** (a name coined by American journalists). These pricey, French oak-aged wines continue to be the toast of Tuscany.

The Etruscans were making wine in Montepulciano before the days of ancient Rome. **Vino Nobile di Montepulciano,** the "Noble Wine," gained its title by virtue of royal patronage: in 1669, England's William III sent a delegation to procure the highly regarded wine. Less noble but no less popular is **Rosso di Montepulciano,** a light, fruity red.

With its velvety black berries and structured tannins, **Brunello di Montalcino** is just as sophisticated as Vino Nobile. The strain of Sangiovese grape used to make it was developed in 1870 by a winemaker in need of vines that could cope with windy weather. The resulting wine was a hit. Brunello has a younger sibling, **Rosso di Montepulciano.**

Not all of Tuscany's great wines are reds; in fact, many give top honors to a white wine, **Vernaccia di San Gimignano.** This golden wine is made from grapes native to Liguria. Its name is thought to be a corruption of Vernazza, one of the Cinque Terre villages.

WINERY VISITS

The SS222 (aka the Strada Chiantigiana) running through the heart of Chianti and other Strade del Vino (Wine Roads) throughout the region will lead you to an abundance of producers. You can do preliminary research at www.terreditoscana.region.toscana.it (click on "Strade del Vino"). When you're on the ground, visit any tourist information center in wine country (Greve, Montalcino, and Montepulciano are the best places to start) for maps and guidance. Then hit the road. Many wineries—especially smaller producers—offer free tastings without an appointment. Larger producers usually charge a small fee for a three-glass tasting, and sometimes require a reservation for a tour. Remember: always have a designated driver. Vineyards are usually off narrow, curving roads. Sobriety is a must.

small, simple rooms and tables outdoors provide the setting for your meal. ⊠ *Località Lucarellia 29* ☎ *0577/733511* ▤ *MC, V* ⊙ *Closed Mon. and Nov.–Mar.*

★ **$$$–$$$$** ✕▦ **Relais Fattoria Vignale.** On the outside it's an unadorned manor house with an annex across the street. Inside it's refined country-house comfortable, with terra-cotta floors, sitting rooms, and nice stone- and woodwork. White rooms with exposed brick and wood beams contain simple wooden bed frames and furniture, charming rugs and prints, and modern white-tile bathrooms. The grounds, flanked by vineyards and olive trees, are equally inviting, with lawns, terraces, and a pool. The sophisticated Ristorante Vignale ($$$–$$$$) serves excellent wines and Tuscan specialties, such as Chianina beef; the *taverna* (wine bar) serves less-expensive fare. ⊠ *Via Panigiani 9, 53017* ☎ *0577/738300 hotel, 0577/738094 restaurant, 0577/738012 enoteca* ▤ *0577/738592* ⊕ *www. vignale.it* ⇨ *35 rooms, 5 suites* ⚒ *2 restaurants, in-room safes, minibars, cable TV, pool, bar, library, laundry service, concierge, free parking, no-smoking rooms* ▤ *AE, DC, MC, V* ⊙ *Closed Jan.–Mar. Restaurant closed Thurs. and Jan.–Mar. Taverna closed Wed. and Jan.–Mar.* ⍾⚬⍾ *BP.*

$$$ ▦ **Palazzo Leopoldo.** A contemporary interpretation of neoclassicism predominates at Palazzo Leopoldo. The former 15th-century palazzo on Radda's main street is now an invitingly intimate small hotel. Rooms have high ceilings and chandeliers—in the suites and in public rooms some are handcrafted 19th-century reproductions of Venetian Renaissance originals. The staff speaks English, and there's an inviting terrace. The tasty breads served at breakfast are made locally, and the restaurant has mostly Tuscan food; full and half board are options. ⊠ *Via Roma 33, 53017* ☎ *0577/735605* ▤ *0577/738031* ⊕ *www.palazzoleopoldo. it* ⇨ *8 rooms, 9 suites* ⚒ *Restaurant, room service, in-room safes, some kitchenettes, minibars, refrigerators, cable TV, Wi-Fi, indoor pool, hot tub, massage, sauna, spa, bar, babysitting, dry cleaning, laundry service, concierge, meeting room, free parking, some pets allowed, no-smoking rooms* ▤ *AE, DC, MC, V* ⊙ *Closed Jan. and Feb.* ⍾⚬⍾ *BP.*

¢ ▦ **La Bottega di Giovannino.** The name is actually that of the wine bar run by Giovannino Bernardoni; rentals are run by his children Monica and David in the house next door. This is a fantastic place for the budget-conscious traveler, as rooms are immaculate and beds comfortable. Most rooms have a stunning view of the surrounding hills. All have their own baths, though most of them necessitate taking a short trip outside one's room. ⊠ *Via Roma 6–8, 53017* ☎ *0577/738056* ⊕ *www. labottegadigiovannino.it* ⇨ *10 rooms* ⚒ *Bar; no a/c, no room phones* ▤ *MC, V* ⍾⚬⍾ *EP.*

Panzano

❻ *7 km (4½ mi) south of Greve, 29 km (18 mi) south of Florence.*

The little town of Panzano, between Greve in Chianti and Castellina in Chianti, has inviting shops, and enoteche offering tastes of the local wine (in this case, Chianti). A walk up a steep incline brings you to the town's showpiece, the church of **Santa Maria Assunta,** where you can see an *Annunciation* attributed to Michele di Ridolfo del Ghirlandaio (1503–77).

VOICES OF ITALY

Dario Cecchini
Butcher, Panzano

Dario Cecchini loves meat. At the half-century mark and standing more than 6 feet tall, he could be a poster boy for the beef industry. He breathes health, vitality, vigor.

By trade, Dario is a butcher, but his Antica Macelleria Cecchini is not your typical butcher shop. From its intimate confines at Via XX Luglio 11 in Panzano, he holds forth behind a counter teeming with luscious meats. Opera plays in the background; sometimes customers sing along. Dario quotes Dante as he offers up samples of his wares.

Dario calls himself *un artigiano* (an artisan)—an indication of the pride he takes in his work. His shop has been in the family since the late 1700s, and his father trained Dario in the craft. "At 13," he says, "my grandmother made me a butcher's jacket. My mother began to cry. I guess she hoped I'd choose something else." The same grandmother is responsible for Dario's habit of offering wine to his customers. "She said a glass of wine brings people together, and I like to bring people together."

In March 2001, when beef cuts near the spine were banned by the European Union due to fears of mad cow disease, he held a funeral for such cuts, and most of the town turned out to watch. A beef auction was part of the solemnities, with Sir Elton John the high bidder; proceeds went to a nearby children's hospital.

Dario is perhaps the world's greatest devotee of *bistecca fiorentina*, the definitive Tuscan steak. To get one of his *bistecche*, you must request it seven days in advance. Ask him to halve its width, and you will incur this genial man's scorn. About its preparation, Dario brooks no compromises. "It must be very thick, seared on both sides, and very, very rare in the middle." If you prefer your steak well done? "You shouldn't order it." This is not to say that Dario is an unwavering traditionalist. One of his prized creations is sushi del Chianti, which took him five years to develop. After a taste of the coarsely ground raw beef, it can be difficult to stop eating.

What wine does Dario pair with his bistecca? "A young, simple, unstructured Chianti." If—heaven forbid—such a Chianti is not on the wine list? "Any young, honest red will do—no dallying in oak casks. Anything disliked by the *Wine Spectator*."

Where does Dario like to eat out these days? "Il Cipresso in Loro Ciuffenna (some 20 minutes northwest of Arezzo). Top-notch cooking with good seasonal ingredients."

As a lifelong resident of Chianti, Dario has a firm view on views. After a good meal, where should you go to contemplate the finest vista in Tuscany? "If I had only a short time, I'd say the hills around Volpaia (just outside Radda in Chianti). If I had more time, the Crete Senesi. It's *un luogo dell'anima*—a place to feed your soul."

Your climb will also reward you with breathtaking views. ⊠ *Panzano Alto* ⊙ *Daily 7–noon and 4–6.*

Where to Stay & Eat

$$ ✕ **Oltre il Giardino.** An ancient stone farmhouse has been converted into a cozy dining area with a large terrace and spectacular views of the valley. Terra-cotta–color, stenciled walls, and simple wood tables provide the background for very tasty Tuscan food. The *peposo* (a beef stew laced with black pepper) is particularly piquant, the tagliatelle *sul piccione* (with a delicate squab sauce) delightfully fragrant. The wine list is particularly strong on the local variety, which in this case is Chianti Classico. ⊠ *Piazza G. Bucciarelli 42* ☎ *055/852828* ▤ *AE, DC, MC, V* ⊙ *Closed Mon. and mid-Nov.–mid-Dec.*

$–$$ ▥ **Villa La Barone.** Formerly the home of the Viviani della Robbia family, this 16th-century villa retains many aspects of a private home. The honor bar allows you to enjoy an aperitivo in the tile barroom or on the terrace while admiring the view, and there are views here in abundance, from the pool to the rose garden to the back of the villa. Guest rooms have tile floors, white walls, and timber ceilings. ⊠ *Via San Leolino 19, 50020* ☎ *055/852621* ▤ *055/852277* ↴ *30 rooms* ⚬ *Dining room, Wi-Fi, tennis court, pool, babysitting, laundry service, concierge; no a/c in some rooms, no room TVs* ▤ *AE, MC, V* ⊙ *Closed Nov.–Easter* ▯ *BP.*

Greve in Chianti

❼ *40 km (25 mi) northeast of Colle Val d'Elsa, 27 km (17 mi) south of Florence.*

If there is a capital of Chianti, it is Greve, a friendly market town with no shortage of cafés, *enoteche* (wine bars), and crafts shops lining its main square. The sloping, asymmetrical **Piazza Matteotti** is attractively arcaded and has a statue of Giovanni da Verrazano (circa 1480–1528), the explorer who discovered New York harbor, in the center. At one end of the piazza is the **Chiesa di Santa Croce.** The church contains works from the school of Fra Angelico (circa 1400–55). ⊠ *Piazza Matteotti* ⊙ *Daily 9–1 and 3–7.*

OFF THE
BEATEN
PATH

MONTEFIORALLE – Just 2 km (1 mi) west of Greve, in the tiny hilltop town of Montefioralle, you'll find the ancestral home of Amerigo Vespucci (1454–1512), the navigator and mapmaker who named America and whose niece Simonetta may have been the model for Venus in Sandro Botticelli's (1445–1510) *Primavera.* Chianti's annual mid-September wine festival, **Rassegna del Chianti Classico,** takes place here.

Where to Stay & Eat

★ $$$ ✕ **Osteria di Passignano.** Sophisticated country dining may not get better than at this deceptively simple restaurant next to a Vallombrosan abbey. A tiny sampling (maybe *sformatino di pecorino di fosso,* a flan made with aged pecorino) whets the appetite for what's to come. The young chefs in the kitchen can do traditional as well as whimsical Tuscan—and then divine things such as the *maccheroni del Martelli al ragù bianco di agnelli e carciofi morellini* (tubular pasta with a lamb and artichoke sauce), which really isn't Tuscan at all. The wine list is unbeatable, as is the service. ⊠ *Via Passignano 33, Località Badia a Passignano, 15 km (9 mi) east of Greve in Chianti* ☎ *055/8011278* ▭ *AE, DC, MC, V* ⊘ *Closed Sun., Jan. 7–Feb. 1, and 15 days in Aug.*

★ $$ ✕ **Ristoro di Lamole.** Although off the beaten path (in this case, the SS222), this place is worth the effort to find—up a winding hill road lined with olive trees and vineyards. The view from the outdoor terrace is divine, as is the simple, exquisitely prepared Tuscan cuisine. Start with the bruschetta drizzled with olive oil or the sublime *verdure sott'olio* (vegetables marinated in oil) before moving on to any of the fine secondi. The kitchen has a way with *coniglio* (rabbit); don't pass it up if it's on the menu. ⊠ *Off SS222, Lamole in Chianti* ☎ *055/8547050* ▭ *AE, DC, MC, V* ⊘ *Closed Jan. 6–Feb. 28.*

★ $ ✕ **Enoteca Fuoripiazza.** Detour off Greve's flower-strewn main square for food that relies heavily on local ingredients (especially those produced by nearby makers of cheese and salami). The lengthy wine list provides a bewildering array of choices to pair with *affettati misti* (a plate of cured meats) or one of their primi—the *pici* (a thick, short noodle) is deftly prepared here. All the dishes are made with great care. ⊠ *Via I Maggio 2, Piazza Trenta* ☎ *055/8546313* ▭ *AE, DC, MC, V* ⊘ *Closed Mon.*

$$$$ ▦ **Villa Bordoni.** David and Catherine Gardner, expat Scots, have transformed a ramshackle 16th-century villa into a stunning little hotel nestled in the hills above Greve. Elaborate care has been given in decorating the rooms, no two of which are the same. All have stenciled walls; some have four-poster beds, others small mezzanines. Bathrooms are a riot of color, with tiles from Vietri. A public sitting room on the second floor, with comforting fireplace, is the perfect place for a cup of tea or a glass of wine. The hotel's restaurant has a young chef of notable talent. ⊠ *Via San Cresci 31/32, Località Mezzuola, Greve* ☎ *055/8840004* ▤ *055/8840005* ⊕ *www.villabordoni.com* ⊸ *8 rooms, 3 suites* ⌂ *Restaurant, minibars, in-room safes, in-room data ports, cable TV, Wi-Fi, pool, exercise equipment, mountain bikes (fee), babysitting, laundry service, free parking* ▭ *AE, DC, MC, V* ⊘ *Closed Jan. and Feb.* ⍭ *BP.*

FodorśChoice
★

★ $$$ ▦ **Fonte de' Medici.** The Antinori family has been making wine since 1180, and in 2001 they extended their efforts into an agriturismo—appropriately, each of the individually decorated rooms and apartments bears the name of a grape. All are decorated with sponged walls, some with canopy beds, most with fireplaces and deep bathtubs, and nearly all with views of the tranquil countryside. Rooms are scattered among three structures, the busiest being Santa Maria a Macerata, and the most remote Podere Vivaio. If you're after bliss in the middle of Chianti, look no further. ⊠ *Via Santa Maria a Macerata 31, 50020 Montefiridolfi* ☎ *055/8244700* ▤ *055/8244701* ⊕ *www.fontedemedici.com* ⊸ *7 rooms, 21 apartments* ⌂ *Restaurant, picnic area, BBQs, some fans, in-room safes, some kitchens, some microwaves, refrigerators, cable TV, in-room data ports, tennis court, pool, wading pool, exercise equipment, massage, sauna, steam room, mountain bikes, soccer, wine bar, babysitting, laundry facilities, laundry service, meeting rooms, free parking, some pets allowed (fee); no a/c in some rooms* ▭ *AE, DC, MC, V* ⊘ *Restaurant closed Nov. and mid-Jan.–mid-Feb.* ⍭ *BP.*

$$–$$$ ⌂ **Villa Vignamaggio.** The villa, surrounded by manicured classical Italian gardens, dates from the 14th century but was restored in the 16th. It's reputedly the birthplace of Mona Lisa, the woman later made famous by Leonardo da Vinci. There are guest rooms, suites, and apartments in the villa and other buildings, and a cottage on the grounds. The place also hosts tastings of its very fine wines: inquire at reception to organize one. Dinner can also be arranged sometimes. ⊠ *Via Petriolo 5, 50022* ☎ *055/854661* 🖷 *055/8544468* ⊕ *www.vignamaggio.com* ⥅ *3 rooms, 4 suites, 13 apartments, 1 cottage* ⊘ *Dining room, minibars, cable TV, tennis court, 2 pools, mountain bikes, bar, babysitting, playground, laundry service, some pets allowed, no-smoking rooms* ⊟ *AE, DC, MC, V* ⊘ *Closed mid-Nov.–mid-Mar.* ⑩ *BP.*

UMBRIA & TUSCANY ESSENTIALS

Transportation

BY AIR

The largest airports in the region are Pisa's Aeroporto Galileo Galilei and Florence's Aeroporto Amerigo Vespucci, known as Peretola, which connects to Amsterdam, Brussels, Frankfurt, London, Munich, and Paris. Perugia's tiny Aeroporto Sant'Egidio has daily flights to and from Milan, and seasonally scheduled flights to Paris, Copenhagen, and a small number of vacation destinations in the Mediterranean.

🛈 Airport Information **Aeroporto Galileo Galilei** ☎ 050/849300 ⊕ www.pisa-airport.com. **Aeroporto Sant'Egidio** ☎ 075/592141 ⊕ www.airport.umbria.it. **Peretola** ⊠ 10 km [6 mi] northwest of Florence ☎ 055/315874 ⊕ www.airport.florence.it.

BY BUS

Perugia is served by the Sulga Line, with daily departures from Rome's Stazione Tiburtina and from Piazza Adua in Florence. Connections between Rome and Spoleto are provided by the associated bus companies Bucci and Soget. These same companies operate local bus service between all the major and minor towns within Umbria.

SENA connects Rome with Siena on several scheduled daily trips. Within Tuscany, bus service between towns is conducted primarily by two private companies, Tra-In and Lazzi. Bus information is available from local tourist information offices or directly from area bus companies.

🛈 Bus Information **Bucci-Soget** ⊠ Strada delle Marche 56, Pesaro ☎ 0721/32401 ⊕ www.autolineebucci.com. **Lazzi Eurolines** ⊠ Via Mercante 2, Florence ☎ 055/363041 ⊕ www.lazzi.it. **SENA** ⊠ Piazza Gramsci, Siena ☎ 0577/283203 🖷 0577/40731 ⊕ www.sena.it. **Sulga Line** ⊠ Stazione Tiburtina, Rome ☎ 075/5009641 ⊕ www.sulga. it. **Tra-In** ⊠ Statale 73, Levante 23, Due Ponti, Siena ☎ 0577/204111.

BY CAR

The Autostrada del Sole (A1), northern and central Italy's major north–south highway, runs a 277-km (172-mi) course between Rome and Florence. It passes through western Umbria, skirting Orvieto, and eastern Tuscany, passing close to Arezzo. When you venture off the A1,

2

the hills and valleys that make Umbria and Tuscany so attractive also make for challenging driving. Fortunately, the area has an excellent, modern road network, though you should expect slow, winding mountain roads if your explorations take you far from beaten track.

Central Umbria is served by a major highway, the S75bis, which passes along the shore of Lake Trasimeno and ends in Perugia. Assisi is served by the modern highway S75; S75 connects to S3 and S3bis, which cover the heart of the region.

Within Tuscany, Siena and Florence are connected by a superstrada and also the panoramic SS222, which threads through Chianti wine country. The hill towns west of Siena lie along superstrade and winding local roads. Roads in the regions are well marked, but you should arm yourself with a good map nonetheless, as well as a flashlight, and, if possible, a cell phone in case of a breakdown.

Drivers should be prepared to navigate through suburban sprawl around some of the larger towns, such as Arezzo. To reach the historic centers where most sights are, look for the CENTRO signs. In many small towns you must park outside the city walls.

BY TRAIN

Italy's main rail line, which runs from Milan in the north to Calabria in the toe of the boot, links Florence to Rome. Within Tuscany, trains on this line stop in Prato, Arezzo, and Chiusi as well as Florence. To visit other areas of Tuscany—such as Siena and Chianti—you are better off going by car or by bus. Train stations in these towns, when they exist, are far from the historic centers, run infrequently, and are slow.

Umbria is more train-friendly. Trains on the line running between Rome and Florence stop in Orvieto. The main Rome–Ancona line passes through Spoleto, and there are also frequent intercity trains linking Florence and Rome with Perugia and Assisi.

Visit the Web site of FS, the Italian State Railway, for schedules and booking.

🚆 Train Information **FS** ☎ 892021 ⊕ www.trenitalia.com.

Contacts & Resources

EMERGENCIES

For first aid, dial the general emergency number (118), which is the same throughout Italy, and ask for *pronto soccorso* (first aid). Be prepared to give your address. If you can find a concierge or some other Italian-speaker to call on your behalf, do so, as not all operators speak English. All pharmacies post signs on the door with addresses of pharmacies that stay open in off-hours (at night, on Saturday afternoon, and on Sunday).

For car emergencies, call ACI for towing and repairs—you can ask to be transferred to an English-speaking operator; be prepared to tell the operator which road you're on, the direction you're going (e.g., "*verso* [in the direction of] Perugia") and the *targa* (license plate number) of your car. The great majority of Italians carry cellular phones, so if you don't have one, for help, flag down someone who does.

🔁 **ACI** ☎ 803/116. **Medical emergencies** ☎ 118. **Police** ☎ 113. **Fire** ☎ 115.

VISITOR INFORMATION

🔁 Tourist Information Offices, Umbria **Assisi** ✉ Piazza del Comune 22, 06081 ☎ 075/812534 ⊕ www.assisi.umbria2000.it. **Orvieto** ✉ Piazza Duomo 24, 05018 ☎ 0763/341772 ⊕ www.orvieto.umbria2000.it. **Perugia** ✉ Piazza Matteotti 18, 06123 ☎ 075/5736458 ⊕ www.perugia.umbria2000.it. **Spoleto** ✉ Piazza della Libertà 7, 06049 ☎ 0743/238920 ⊕ www.spoleto.umbria2000.it. **Turismo Verde** ✉ Via Maria Angeloni 1, 06124 Perugia ☎ 075/5002953 🖶 075/5002956 ⊕ www.turismoverde.it.

🔁 Tourist Information Offices, Tuscany **Arezzo** ✉ Piazza della Repubblica 28 ☎ 0575/377678 ⊕ www.apt.arezzo.it. **Colle Val d'Elsa** ✉ Via F. Campana 43 ☎ 0577/922791. **Cortona** ✉ Via Nazionale 42 ☎ 0575/630352 ⊕ www.cortonaweb.net. **Greve in Chianti** ✉ Piazza Ferrante Mori 1 ☎ 055/8546299 ⊕ www.chiantislowtravel.it. **Radda in Chianti** ✉ Piazza Castello 1 ☎ 0577/738494. **San Gimignano** ✉ Piazza del Duomo 1 ☎ 0577/940008 ⊕ www.sangimignano.com. **Siena** ✉ Piazza del Campo 56 ☎ 0577/280551 ⊕ www.terresiena.it; www.comune.siena.it. **Volterra** ✉ Piazza dei Priori 20 ☎ 0588/87257 ⊕ www.volterratour.it.

Florence

Piazza della Signoria

WORD OF MOUTH

"Michaelangelo, Dante, Galileo. Gelato, red wine, amazing food. Some of the most wonderful art and architecture. Firenze is a magical city (and where my fiancé and I got engaged). It is an absolute gem."

—Kristin

WELCOME TO FLORENCE

TOP REASONS TO GO

★ **Galleria degli Uffizi:** Italian Renaissance art doesn't get much better than this vast collection bequeathed to the city by the last Medici.

★ **The dome of the Duomo:** Brunelleschi's work of engineering genius is the city's undisputed centerpiece.

★ **Michelangelo's *David*:** One look and you'll know why this is the Western world's most famous sculpture.

★ **The view from Piazzale Michelangelo:** From this perch the city is laid out before you. Being there at sunset heightens the experience.

★ **Piazza Santa Croce:** After you've had your fill of Renaissance masterpieces, hang out here and watch the world go by.

1 The area from the Duomo to the Ponte Vecchio is the heart of Florence. Among the numerous highlights are the city's greatest museum (**the Uffizi**) and its most impressive square (**Piazza della Signoria**).

2 The blocks from the church of San Lorenzo to the Accademia gallery bear the imprints of the Medici family and of Michelangelo, culminating in his masterful *David*. Just to the north, the former convent of San Marco is an oasis decorated with ethereal frescoes.

3 The quarter from Santa Maria Novella to the Arno includes the train station, 15th-century palaces, and the city's most chic shopping street, **Via Tornabuoni**.

Piazza del Duomo

4 The Santa Croce district centers around its namesake church, which is filled with the tombs of Renaissance luminaries. The area is also known for its leather shops, some of which have been in operation since the 16th century.

5 The **Oltrarno** contrasts the massive Palazzo Pitti and the narrow streets of the **Santo Spirito** district, which is filled with artisans' workshops and antiques stores. A climb up to the **Piazzale Michelangelo** gives you a spectacular view of the city.

Sante Croce basilica

GETTING ORIENTED

The historic center of Florence is flat and compact—you could walk from one end to the other in half an hour. In the middle of everything is the Duomo, with its huge dome towering over the city's terracotta rooftops. Radiating out from the Duomo are Renaissance-era neighborhoods identified by their central churches and piazzas. Though the majority of sights are north of the Arno River, the area to the south, known as the Oltrarno, has its charms as well.

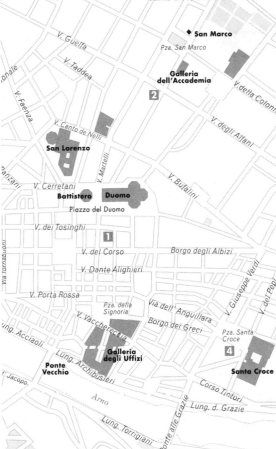

♦ San Marco

Pza. San Marco

Galleria dell'Accademia

2

V. Guelfa

V. Taddea

V. Faenza

V.della Colonna

V. degli Alfani

V. Canto de Nelli

San Lorenzo

V. Martelli

V. Cerretani

Battistero **Duomo**

Piazza del Duomo

V. dei Tosinghi

V. Bufalini

V. del Corso

Borgo degli Albizi

V. Dante Alighieri

V. Porta Rossa

Via dell'Anguillara

Pza. della Signoria

Borgo dei Greci

V. Vaccherrecia

V. Giuseppe Verdi

V. del Pepi

Pza. Santa Croce

4

V. dell'Agnolo

SANTA CROCE

Lung. Acciaoli

Galleria degli Uffizi

Ponte Vecchio

Lung. Archibusieri

Santa Croce

V. Ghibellina

Jacopo

Arno

Corso Tintori

Lung. d. Grazie

Ponte alle Grazie

Lung. Torrigiani

Lung. Serristori

OLTRARNO

5

0 ¼ mile

0 400 meters

To Piazzale Michelangelo

FLORENCE PLANNER

Getting Around

Florence's flat, compact city center is made for walking, but when your feet get weary, you can use the efficient bus system, which includes small electric buses making the rounds in the center. Buses also climb to Piazzale Michelangelo and San Miniato south of the Arno.

An automobile in Florence is a liability. If your itinerary includes parts of Italy where you'll want a car (such as Tuscany), pick the vehicle up on your way out of town. For more information on getting into, out of, and around Florence, see "Essentials" at the end of this chapter.

Avoiding an Art Hangover

Trying to take in Florence's amazing art can be a headache—there's just too much to see. Especially if you're not a dedicated art enthusiast, remember to pace yourself. Allow time to wander and follow your whims, and ignore any pangs of guilt if you'd rather relax in a café and watch the world go by than trudge on sore feet through another breathtaking palace or church.

Florence isn't a city that can be "done." It's a place you can return to again and again, confident there will always be more treasures to discover.

Titian's *Venus of Urbino*

Making the Most of Your Time

With some planning, you can see Florence's most famous sights in a couple of days. Start off at the city's most awe-inspiring work of architecture, the Duomo, climbing to the top of the dome if you have the stamina. On the same piazza, check out Ghiberti's bronze doors at the Battistero. (They're actually high-quality copies; the Museo dell'-Opera del Duomo has the originals.) Set aside the afternoon for the Galleria degli Uffizi, making sure to reserve tickets in advance.

On day two, visit Michelangelo's *David* in the Galleria dell'Accademia—reserve tickets here too. Linger in the Piazza della Signoria, Florence's central square, where a copy of *David* stands in the spot the original occupied for centuries, then head east a couple of blocks to Santa Croce, the city's most artistically rich church. Double back and walk across Florence's landmark bridge, the Ponte Vecchio.

Do all that, and you'll have seen some great art, but you've just scratched the surface. If you have more time, put the Bargello, the Museo di San Marco, and the Cappelle Medicee at the top of your list. When you're ready for an art break, stroll through the Boboli Gardens or explore Florence's lively shopping scene, from the food stalls of the Mercato Centrale to the chic boutiques of the Via Tornabuoni.

Florentine Hours

Florence's sights keep tricky hours. Some are closed on Wednesday, some on Monday, some on every other Monday. Quite a few shut their doors each day (or on most days) by 2 in the afternoon. Things get even more confusing on weekends. Make it a general rule to check the hours closely for any place you're planning to visit; if it's somewhere you have your heart set on seeing, call to confirm.

Here's a selection of major sights that might not be open when you'd expect—consult the sight listings within this chapter for the full details. And be aware that, as always, hours can and do change.

■ The **Uffizi** and the **Accademia** are both closed Monday. All but a few of the galleries at Palazzo Pitti are closed Monday as well.

■ The **Duomo** closes at 3:30 on Thursday (as opposed to 5:30 on other weekdays, 4:45 on weekends). The dome of the Duomo is closed on Sunday.

■ The **Battistero** is open from noon until 7, Monday through Saturday, and on Sunday from 8:30 to 2.

■ The **Bargello** closes at 1:50 in the afternoon, and is closed entirely on alternating Sundays and Mondays.

■ The **Cappelle Medicee** are closed on alternating Sundays and Mondays.

■ **Museo di San Marco** closes at 1:50 on weekdays but stays open till 7 on weekends—except for alternating Sundays and Mondays, when it's closed entirely.

■ **Palazzo Medici-Riccardi** is closed Wednesday.

How's the Weather?

The best times to visit Florence are spring and fall. Days are warm, nights are cool, and the city is crowded, but not overly so. Avoid July and August: the heat is unbearable, mosquitoes are rampant, and so are tour groups. You'll find the city at its emptiest in November or January. It rains quite a bit and can get cold, but you'll avoid waits at museums and competition for restaurant tables.

With Reservations

At most times of day you'll see a line of people snaking around the Uffizi. They're waiting to buy tickets, and you don't want to be one of them. Instead, call ahead for a reservation (055/294883; reservationists speak English). You'll be given a reservation number and a time of admission—the further in advance you call, the more time slots you'll have to choose from. Go to the museum's reservation door at the appointed hour, give the clerk your number, pick up your ticket, and go inside. You'll pay €3 for this privilege, but it's money well spent.

Use the same reservation service to book tickets for the Galleria dell'Accademia, where lines rival those of the Uffizi. (Reservations can also be made for the Palazzo Pitti, the Bargello, and several other sights, but they aren't needed.) An alternative strategy is to check with your hotel—many will handle reservations.

TOP PASSEGGIATA

Via dei Calzaiuoli, between Piazza del Duomo and Piazza della Signoria, is where Florence comes out for its evening stroll.

Piazza della Signoria

Updated by
Patricia Rucidlo **FLORENCE, THE CITY OF THE LILY,** gave birth to the Renaissance and changed the way we see the world. For centuries it has captured the imagination of travelers, who come here to walk in the footsteps of Dante, Donatello, Botticelli, and Michelangelo. You'll find sublime art at almost every turn, but Florence (Firenze in Italian) isn't simply one large museum. Even if *David* and the Duomo didn't exist, you could still fall in love with the city for its winding streets, its earthy yet sophisticated food and wine, or the way the natives manage to lead thoroughly modern lives in a place that hasn't changed all that much since the 16th century.

Florence was "discovered" in the 1700s by upper-class northerners making the grand tour. It became a mecca for travelers, particularly the Romantics, who were inspired by the elegance of its palazzi and its artistic wealth. Today millions of modern visitors follow in their footsteps. When the sun sets over the Arno and, as Mark Twain described it, "overwhelms Florence with tides of color that make all the sharp lines dim and faint and turn the solid city to a city of dreams," it's hard not to fall under the city's spell.

EXPLORING FLORENCE

Most sights in Florence are concentrated in the relatively small historic center, and walking through its streets and alleyways is a discovery in itself. Today a handful of the more than 200 towers built in the 12th and 13th centuries survive; look for them as you explore. The town has managed to preserve its predominantly medieval street plan and mostly Renaissance infrastructure while successfully adapting to the insistent demands of 21st-century life.

Centro Storico: The Duomo to the Ponte Vecchio

Florence's *centro storico* (historic center), stretching from the Piazza del Duomo south to the Arno, is as dense with artistic treasures as anyplace in the world. The churches, medieval towers, Renaissance palaces, and world-class museums and galleries contain some of the most outstanding aesthetic achievements of Western history.

Much of the centro storico is closed to automobile traffic, but you still must dodge mopeds, cyclists, and masses of fellow tourists as you walk the narrow streets, especially in the area bounded by the Duomo, Piazza della Signoria, Galleria degli Uffizi, and Ponte Vecchio.

The Main Attractions

★ **⑦** **Bargello.** During the Renaissance, this building was headquarters for the *podestà,* or chief magistrate. It was also used as a prison, and the exterior served as a "most wanted" billboard: effigies of notorious criminals and Medici enemies were painted on its walls. Today it houses the **Museo Nazionale,** containing what is probably the finest collection of Renaissance sculpture in

WORD OF MOUTH

"I think the Bargello might be the most underrated museum in Florence, if not Italy."   –Jess

FLORENCE THROUGH THE AGES

Guelph vs. Ghibelline. Though Florence can lay claim to a modest importance in the ancient world, it didn't come into its own until the Middle Ages. In the early 1200s, the city, like most of the rest of Italy, was rent by civic unrest. Two factions, the Guelphs and the Ghibellines, competed for power. The Guelphs supported the papacy, the Ghibellines the Holy Roman Empire. Bloody battles—most notably at Montaperti in 1260—tore Florence and other Italian cities apart. By the end of the 13th century the Guelphs ruled securely and the Ghibellines had been vanquished. This didn't end civic strife, however: the Guelphs split into the Whites and the Blacks for reasons still debated by historians. Dante was banished from Florence in 1301 because he was a White.

The Guilded Age. Local merchants had organized themselves into guilds by 1250. In that year they proclaimed themselves the "*primo popolo*" (literally, "first people"), and made an attempt at elective, republican rule. Though the episode lasted only 10 years, it constituted a breakthrough in Western history. Such a daring stance by the merchant class was a by-product of Florence's emerging economic power. Florentines were papal bankers; they instituted the system of international letters of credit; and the gold florin became the international standard currency. With this economic strength came a building boom. Palaces and basilicas were erected or enlarged. Sculptors such as Donatello and Ghiberti decorated them; painters such as Giotto and Botticelli frescoed their walls.

Mighty Medici. Though ostensibly a republic, Florence was blessed (or cursed) with one very powerful family, the Medici, who came to prominence in the 1430s and were the de facto rulers of Florence for several hundred years. It was under patriarch Cosimo il Vecchio (1389–1464) that the Medici's position in Florence was securely established. Florence's golden age occurred during the reign of his grandson Lorenzo de' Medici (1449–92). Lorenzo was not only an astute politician but also a highly educated man and a great patron of the arts. Called "Il Magnifico" (the Magnificent), he gathered around him poets, artists, philosophers, architects, and musicians.

Lorenzo's son, Piero (1471–1503), proved inept at handling the city's affairs. He was run out of town in 1494, and Florence briefly enjoyed its status as a republic while dominated by the Dominican friar Girolamo Savonarola (1452–98). After a decade of internal unrest, the republic fell and the Medici were recalled to power, but Florence never regained its former prestige. By the 1530s most of the major artistic talent had left the city—Michelangelo, for one, had settled in Rome. The now-ineffectual Medici, eventually attaining the title of grand dukes, remained nominally in power until the death of heirless Gian Gastone in 1737. (The last of the Medicis, Gian Gastone's sister Anna Maria Luisa, died equally childless in 1743.) With the demise of the Medicis, Florence passed from the Austrians to the French and back again until the unification of Italy (1865–70), when it briefly became the capital under King Vittorio Emanuele II.

Italy. The concentration of masterworks by Michelangelo (1475–1564), Donatello (circa 1386–1466), and Benvenuto Cellini (1500–71) is remarkable; they're distributed among an eclectic array of arms, ceramics, and enamels. For Renaissance-art lovers, the Bargello is to sculpture what the Uffizi is to painting.

In 1401 Filippo Brunelleschi (1377–1446) and Lorenzo Ghiberti (circa 1378–1455) vied for the most prestigious commission of the day: the decoration of the north doors of the baptistery in Piazza del Duomo. For the competition, each designed a bronze bas-relief panel depicting the Sacrifice of Isaac; both panels are displayed, together, in the room devoted to the sculpture of Donatello on the upper floor. The judges chose Ghiberti for the commission; see if you agree with their choice. ⊠ *Via del Proconsolo 4, Bargello* ☎ *055/2388606* ⊕ *www.polomuseale. firenze.it* 🎫 *€4* ☉ *Daily 8:15–1:50. Closed 2nd and 4th Mon. of month and 1st, 3rd, and 5th Sun. of month.*

★ ❷ **Battistero** (Baptistery). The octagonal Baptistery is one of the supreme monuments of the Italian Romanesque style and one of Florence's oldest structures. Local legend has it that it was once a Roman temple of Mars; modern excavations, however, suggest that its foundations date from the 4th to 5th and the 8th to 9th century AD, well after the collapse of the Roman Empire. The round-arch Romanesque decoration on the exterior probably dates from the 11th century. The interior dome mosaics from the early 14th century are justly renowned, but—glittering beauties though they are—they could never outshine the building's famed bronze Renaissance doors decorated with panels crafted by Lorenzo Ghiberti. The doors—or at least copies of them—on which Ghiberti spent most of his adult life (1403–52) are on the north and east sides of the Baptistery, and the Gothic panels on the south door were designed by Andrea Pisano (active circa 1290–1348) in 1330. The original Ghiberti doors were removed to protect them from the effects of pollution and have been beautifully restored; some of the panels are now on display in the Museo dell'Opera del Duomo.

Ghiberti's north doors depict scenes from the life of Christ; his later east doors (dating 1425–52), facing the Duomo facade, render scenes from the Old Testament. Very different in style, they illustrate the artistic changes that marked the beginning of the Renaissance. Look at the far right panel of the middle row on the earlier (1403–24) north doors (*Jesus Calming the Waters*). Ghiberti captured the chaos of a storm at sea with great skill and economy, but the artistic conventions he used are basically pre-Renaissance: Jesus is the most important figure, so he is the largest; the disciples are next in size, being next in importance; the ship on which they founder looks like a mere toy.

The exquisitely rendered panels on the east doors are larger, more expansive, more sweeping—and more convincing. Look at the middle panel on the left-hand door. It tells the story of Jacob and Esau, and the various episodes—the selling of the birthright, Isaac ordering Esau to go hunting, the blessing of Jacob, and so forth—have been merged into a single beautifully realized street scene. Ghiberti's use of perspective suggests depth: the background architecture looks far more credible than on the north door panels, the figures in the foreground are grouped realistically, and the naturalism and grace of the poses (look at Esau's left leg and the dog next to him) have nothing to do with the sacred message being conveyed. Although the religious content remains, the figures and their place in the natural world are given unprecedented prominence and are portrayed with a realism not seen in art since the fall of the Roman Empire more than a thousand years before.

As a footnote to Ghiberti's panels, one small detail of the east doors is worth a special look. To the lower left of the Jacob and Esau panel, Ghiberti placed a tiny self-portrait bust. From either side, the portrait is extremely appealing—Ghiberti looks like everyone's favorite uncle—but the bust is carefully placed so that there is a single spot from which you can make direct eye contact with the tiny head. When that contact is made, the impression of intelligent life is astonishing. It is no wonder that these doors received one of the most famous compliments in the history of art from an artist known to be notoriously stingy with praise: Michelangelo himself declared them so beautiful that they could serve as the Gates of Paradise. ⊠ *Piazza del Duomo* ☎ *055/2302885* ⊕ *www. operaduomo.firenze.it* ⌸ *€3* ⊘ *Mon.–Sat. noon–7, Sun. 8:30–2.*

❸ **Campanile.** The Gothic bell tower designed by Giotto (1266–1337) is a soaring structure of multicolor marble originally decorated with reliefs that are now in the Museo dell'Opera del Duomo. They have been replaced with copies. A climb of 414 steps rewards you with a close-up of Brunelleschi's cupola on the Duomo next door and a sweeping view of the city. ⊠ *Piazza del Duomo* ☎ *055/2302885* ⊕ *www.operaduomo. firenze.it* ⌸ *€6* ⊘ *Daily 8:30–7:30.*

★ ❶ **Duomo** (Cattedrale di Santa Maria del Fiore). In 1296 Arnolfo di Cambio (circa 1245–circa 1310) was commissioned to build "the loftiest, most sumptuous edifice human invention could devise" in the Romanesque style on the site of the old church of Santa Reparata. The immense Duomo was not completed until 1436, the year it was consecrated. The imposing facade dates only from the 19th century; its neo-Gothic style complements Giotto's genuine Gothic 14th-century campanile. The real glory of the Duomo, however, is Filippo Brunelleschi's dome, presiding over the cathedral with a dignity and grace that few domes to this day can match.

> ### WORD OF MOUTH
>
> "The Duomo was a truly amazing cathedral. We visited it twice, once to attend mass (in English, which we appreciated), and once to look at its architecture and art and to climb up to the top. Although the climb is definitely a bit tiring, it was well worth it—the view from the top was incredible."   —Gina

Brunelleschi's **cupola** was an ingenious engineering feat. The space to be enclosed by the dome was so large and so high above the ground that traditional methods of dome construction—wooden centering and scaffolding—were of no use whatsoever. So Brunelleschi developed en-

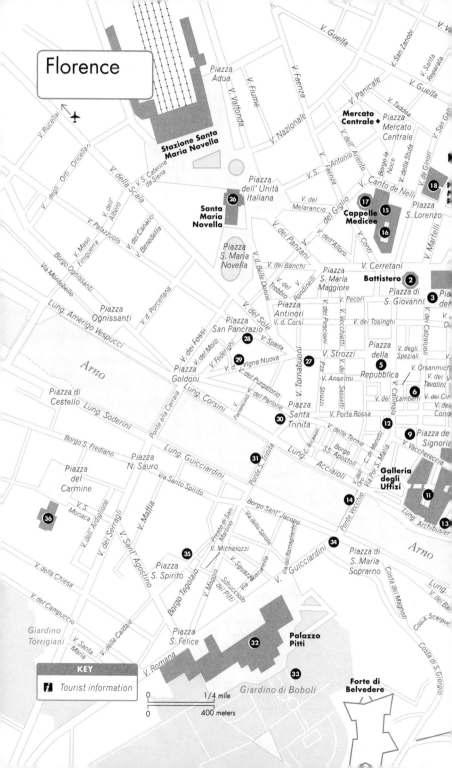

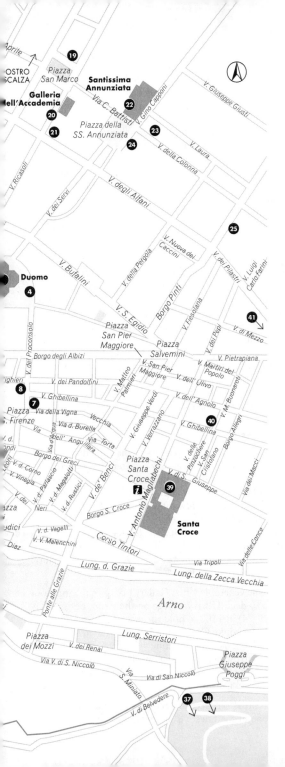

tirely new building methods, which he implemented with equipment of his own design (including a novel scaffolding method). Beginning work in 1420, he built not one dome but two, one inside the other, and connected them with common ribbing that stretched across the intervening empty space, thereby considerably lessening the crushing weight of the structure. He also employed a new method of bricklaying, based on an ancient Roman herringbone pattern, interlocking each course of bricks with the course below in a way that made the growing structure self-supporting. The result was one of the great engineering breakthroughs of all time: most of Europe's later domes, including that of St. Peter's in Rome, were built employing Brunelleschi's methods, and today the Duomo has come to symbolize Florence in the same way that the Eiffel Tower symbolizes Paris. The Florentines are justly proud, and to this day the Florentine phrase for "homesick" is *nostalgia del cupolone* (homesick for the dome).

The interior is a fine example of Florentine Gothic. Much of the cathedral's best-known art has been moved to the nearby Museo dell'Opera del Duomo. Notable among the works that remain, however, are two towering equestrian frescoes honoring famous soldiers: *Niccolò da Tolentino*, painted in 1456 by Andrea del Castagno (circa 1419–57), and *Sir John Hawkwood,* painted 20 years earlier by Paolo Uccello (1397–1475); both are on the left-hand wall of the nave. A 10-year restoration, completed in 1995, repaired the dome and cleaned the vast and crowded fresco of the *Last Judgment,* executed by Vasari and Zuccaro, on its interior. Originally Brunelleschi wanted mosaics to cover the interior of the great ribbed cupola, but by the time the Florentines got around to commissioning the decoration, 150 years later, tastes had changed. Too bad: it's a fairly dreadful *Last Judgment* and hardly worth the effort of craning your neck to see it.

You can explore the upper and lower reaches of the cathedral. The remains of a Roman wall and an 11th-century cemetery have been excavated beneath the nave; the way down is near the first pier on the right. The **climb to the top of the dome** (463 steps) is not for the faint of heart, but the view is superb. ⊠ *Piazza del Duomo* ☎ *055/2302885* ⊕ *www. operaduomo.firenze.it* 🕾 *Church free, crypt €3, cupola €6* 🕙 *Church Mon.–Wed. and Fri. 10–5, Thurs. 10–3:30, Sat. 10–4:45, Sun. 1:30–4:45, 1st Sat. of month 10–3:30. Crypt Mon.–Wed. and Fri. 10–5, Thurs. 10–3:30, Sat. 10–5:45, 1st Sat. of month 10–3:30. Cupola weekdays 8:30–7, Sat. 8:30–5:40, 1st Sat. of month 8:30–4.*

⓫ **Galleria degli Uffizi.** The venerable Uffizi Gallery occupies the top floor of the U-shape **Palazzo degli Uffizi** fronting on the Arno, designed by Giorgio Vasari (1511–74) in 1560 to hold the *uffizi* (administrative offices) of the Medici grand duke Cosimo I (1519–74). Later, the Medici installed their art collections here, creating what was Europe's first modern museum, open to the public (at first only by request) since 1591. Hard-core museum aficionados can pick up a complete guide to the collections at bookshops and newsstands.

FodorśChoice
★

Among the highlights are Paolo Uccello's *Battle of San Romano,* its brutal chaos of lances one of the finest visual metaphors for warfare ever captured in paint; the *Madonna and Child with Two Angels,* by Fra Filippo Lippi (1406–69), in which the impudent eye contact established by the angel would have been unthinkable prior to the Renaissance; the *Birth of Venus* and *Primavera* by Sandro Botticelli (1445–1510), the goddess of the former seeming to float on air and the fairy-tale charm of the latter exhibiting the painter's idiosyncratic genius at its zenith; the portraits of the Renaissance duke Federico da Montefeltro and his wife, Battista Sforza, by Piero della Francesca (circa 1420–92); the *Madonna of the Goldfinch* by Raphael (1483–1520), which, though darkened by time, captures an aching tenderness between

> ## WORD OF MOUTH
>
> "The Uffizi has gorgeous high Renaissance art, but in my experience it is a user-unfriendly museum: lots of stairs, no captions or signs to speak of, no a/c. I was glad I went but I was also glad to leave. I'll go again, but with a headache tablet in hand."   –elaine

mother and child; Michelangelo's *Doni Tondo* (the only panel painting that can be securely attributed to him); a *Self-Portrait as an Old Man* by Rembrandt (1606–69); the *Venus of Urbino* by Titian (circa 1488/90–1576); and the splendid *Bacchus* by Caravaggio (circa 1571/72–1610). In the last two works, the approaches to myth and sexuality are diametrically opposed, to put it mildly. Six additional exhibition rooms opened in 2004, convoluting the way you exit the museum. Many of the more than 400 works now displayed would have been better left in storage.

Late in the afternoon is the least crowded time to visit. For a fee, advance tickets can be reserved by phone or, once in Florence, at the Uffizi reservation booth at least one day in advance of your visit. If you book by phone, remember to keep the confirmation number and take it with you to the door at the museum marked "Reservations." Usually you're ushered in almost immediately. Come with cash, because credit cards are not accepted. When there's a special exhibit on, which is often, the base ticket price goes up to €9.50. ⊠ *Piazzale degli Uffizi 6, near Piazza della Signoria* ☎ *055/2388651* ⊠ *Advance tickets* ⊠ *Consorzio ITA, Piazza Pitti 1, 50121* ☎ *055/294883* ⊕ *www.uffizi.firenze. it* 🎟 *€6.50, reservation fee €3* ☉ *Tues.–Sun. 8:15–6:50.*

NEED A BREAK? Calling itself a "zupperia," **La Canova di GustaVino** (⊠ Via della Condotta 29/r, near Piazza della Signoria ☎ 055/2399806) keeps several hearty, restorative soups on hand. Solid fare includes mixed cheese plates (both French and Italian), as well as *tomino con prosciutto* (mild cow's cheese, topped with thin slices of prosciutto) run under the broiler.

★ ❾ **Piazza della Signoria.** This is by far the most striking square in Florence. It was here, in 1497, that the famous "bonfire of the vanities" took place, when the fanatical friar Savonarola induced his followers to hurl their worldly goods into the flames; it was also here, a year later, that he was hanged as a heretic and, ironically, burned. A bronze plaque in the pavement marks the exact spot of his execution.

The statues in the square and in the 14th-century **Loggia dei Lanzi** on the south side vary in quality. Cellini's famous bronze *Perseus* holding the severed head of Medusa is certainly the most important sculpture in the loggia. Other works include *The Rape of the Sabine* and *Hercules and the Centaur,* both late-16th-century works by Giambologna (1529–1608), and, in the back, a row of sober matrons dating to ancient Roman times.

In the square, the Neptune Fountain, dating from between 1550 and 1575, wins the booby prize. It was created by Bartolomeo Ammannati (1511–92), who considered it a failure himself. The Florentines call it *Il Biancone,* which may be translated as "the big white one" or "the big white thing." Giambologna's equestrian statue to the left of the fountain pays tribute to Grand Duke Cosimo I. Occupying the steps of the Palazzo Vecchio are a copy of Donatello's heraldic lion of Florence, known as the *Marzocco* (the original is in the Bargello); a copy of Donatello's *Judith and Holofernes* (the original is inside the Palazzo Vecchio); a copy of Michelangelo's *David* (the original is now in the Galleria dell'Accademia); and Baccio Bandinelli's insipid *Hercules* (1534).

⑭ Ponte Vecchio (Old Bridge). This charming bridge was built in 1345 to replace an earlier bridge that was swept away by a flood, and its shops housed first butchers, then grocers, blacksmiths, and other merchants. But in 1593 the Medici grand duke Ferdinand I (1549–1609), whose private corridor linking the Medici palace (Palazzo Pitti) with the Medici offices (the Uffizi) crossed the bridge atop the shops, decided that all this plebeian commerce under his feet was unseemly. So he threw out the butchers and blacksmiths and installed 41 goldsmiths and eight jewelers. The bridge has been devoted solely to these two trades ever since.

Also Worth Seeing

❽ Badia Fiorentina. This ancient church was rebuilt in 1285; its graceful bell tower, best seen from the interior courtyard, is beautiful for its unusual construction—a hexagonal tower built on a quadrangular base. The interior of the church was halfheartedly remodeled in the baroque style during the 17th century; its best-known work of art is the delicate *Vision of St. Bernard* by Filippino Lippi (circa 1457–1504), on the left as you enter. The painting—one of Lippi's finest—is in superb condition; note the Virgin Mary's beautifully rendered hands. ⊠ *Via Dante Alighieri 1, near Bargello* ☎ *055/264402* ☞ *Free.*

⑬ Istituto e Museo di Storia della Scienza (Institute and Museum of the History of Science). Though it tends to be obscured by the glamour of the Uffizi, this science museum has much to recommend it: Galileo's own instruments, antique armillary spheres—some of them real works of art—and other reminders that the Renaissance made not only artistic but also scientific history. ⊠ *Piazza dei Giudici 1, near Piazza della Signoria* ☎ *055/265311* ⊕ *www.imss.fi.it* ☞ *€5* ⊙ *Oct.–May, Mon., Wed.–Sat. 9:30–5, Tues. 9:30–1; 2nd Sun. of month 10–1; June–Sept., Mon. and Wed.–Fri. 9:30–5, Tues. and Sat. 9:30–1; last Thurs. of June and Aug. 8–11, 1st Thurs. of July and Sept. 8–11.*

⑫ Mercato Nuovo (New Market). This open-air loggia was new in 1551. Beyond its slew of souvenir stands, its main attraction is a copy of

Pietro Tacca's bronze *Porcellino* (which translates as "little pig," despite the fact that the animal is, in fact, a wild boar) on the south side, dating from around 1612 and copied from an earlier Roman work now in the Uffizi. The Porcellino is Florence's equivalent of the Trevi Fountain: put a coin in his mouth, and if it falls through the grate below (according to one interpretation), it means that one day you'll return to Florence. ⊠ *Corner of Via Por Santa Maria and Via Porta Rossa, near Piazza della Repubblica* ☉ *Tues.–Sat. 8–7, Mon. 1–7.*

❹ Museo dell'Opera del Duomo (Cathedral Museum). Ghiberti's original Baptistery door panels and the *cantorie* (choir loft) reliefs by Donatello and Luca della Robbia (1400–82) keep company with Donatello's *Mary Magdalen* and Michelangelo's *Pietà* (not to be confused with his more famous *Pietà* in St. Peter's in Rome). Renaissance sculpture is in part defined by its revolutionary realism, but in its palpable suffering Donatello's *Magdalen* goes beyond realism. Michelangelo's heart-wrenching *Pietà* was unfinished at his death; the female figure on the left was added by one Tiberio Calcagni (1532–65), and never has the difference between competence and genius been manifested so clearly. ⊠ *Piazza del Duomo 9* ☎ *055/2302885* ⊕ *www.operaduomo.firenze. it* ☑ *€6* ☉ *Mon.–Sat. 9–7:30, Sun. 9–1:40.*

❻ Orsanmichele. This multipurpose structure began as an 8th-century oratory, then in 1290 was turned into an open-air loggia for selling grain. Destroyed by fire in 1304, it was rebuilt as a loggia-market. Between 1367 and 1380 the arcades were closed and two stories added above; finally, at century's end it was turned into a church. Within the church is a beautifully detailed 14th-century Gothic tabernacle by Andrea Orcagna (1320–68). The exterior niches contain copies of sculptures dating from the early 1400s to the early 1600s by Donatello and Verrocchio (1435–88), among others, that were paid for by the guilds. Though it is a copy, Verrocchio's *Doubting Thomas* (circa 1470) is particularly deserving of attention. Here Christ, like the building's other figures, is entirely framed within the niche, and St. Thomas stands on its bottom ledge, with his right foot outside the niche frame. This one detail, the positioning of a single foot, brings the whole composition to life. You can see the original sculptures inside, in the **Museo di Orsanmichele,** accessed via its own flight of stairs. ⊠ *Via dei Calzaiuoli (museum entrance at Via Arte della Lana), near Piazza della Repubblica* ☎ *055/ 284944* ☑ *Free* ☉ *Weekdays 9–noon and 4–6, weekends 9–1 and 4–6. Closed 1st and last Mon. of month.*

❿ Palazzo Vecchio (Old Palace). Florence's forbidding, fortresslike city hall, presumed to have been designed by Arnolfo di Cambio, was begun in 1299, and its massive bulk and towering campanile dominate the Piazza della Signoria. It was built as a meeting place for the elected guildsmen who governed the city at the time; over the centuries it has served lesser purposes, but today it is once again City Hall. The interior courtyard is a good deal less severe, having been remodeled by Michelozzo (1396–1472) in 1453; the copy of Verrocchio's bronze *puttino* (little child), topping the central fountain, softens the space.

Two adjoining rooms on the second floor supply one of the starkest contrasts in Florence. The vast **Sala dei Cinquecento** (Room of the Five Hundred) is named for the 500-member Great Council, the people's assembly established by Savonarola, which met here. The Sala was later decorated by Giorgio Vasari, around 1563–65, with huge—almost grotesquely huge—frescoes celebrating Florentine history; depictions of battles with nearby cities predominate. Continuing the martial theme, the Sala also contains Michelangelo's *Victory* group, intended for the never-completed tomb of Pope Julius II (1443–1513), plus other lesser sculptures.

The little **Studiolo** is to the right of the Sala's entrance. The study of Cosimo I's son, the melancholy Francesco I (1541–87), was designed by Vasari and decorated by Vasari and Bronzino (1503–72). It's intimate, civilized, and filled with allegorical art. ⊠ *Piazza della Signoria* ☎ *055/2768465* ▭ *€6* ☽ *By reservation Mon.–Wed. and Fri.–Sun. 9–7, Thurs. 9–2.*

❺ **Piazza della Repubblica.** This was the site of the ancient forum at the core of the original Roman settlement. The street plan in the area around the piazza still reflects the carefully plotted grid of the Roman military encampment. The Mercato Vecchio (Old Market), dating from the Middle Ages, was demolished and the piazza you see now was constructed between 1885 and 1895 as a neoclassical showpiece. The piazza is lined with outdoor cafés affording excellent spots to people-watch.

In Michelangelo's Footsteps: San Lorenzo to the Accademia

A sculptor, painter, architect, and even a poet, Florentine native son Michelangelo was a consummate genius, and some of his finest creations remain in his hometown. The Biblioteca Medicea Laurenziana is perhaps his most fanciful work of architecture. A key to understanding Michelangelo's genius can be found in the magnificent Cappelle Medicee, where both his sculptural and architectural prowess can be clearly seen. Planned frescoes were never completed, sadly, for they would have shown in one space the

> ### WORD OF MOUTH
>
> "Seeing *David* is a must. It is one of those magical moments in life."
> –JandaO

artistic triple threat that he certainly was. The towering yet graceful *David,* his most famous work, resides in the Galleria dell'Accademia.

After visiting San Lorenzo, resist the temptation to explore the market that surrounds the church. You can always come back later, after the churches and museums have closed; the market is open until 7 PM. Note that the Museo di San Marco closes at 1:50 on weekdays.

The Main Attractions

★ ⑰ **Cappelle Medicee** (Medici Chapels). This magnificent complex includes the **Cappella dei Principi,** the Medici chapel and mausoleum that was begun in 1605 and kept marble workers busy for several hundred years, and the **Sagrestia Nuova** (New Sacristy), designed by Michelangelo and so called to distinguish it from Brunelleschi's *Sagrestia Vecchia* (Old Sacristy).

Continued on page 195

3

WHO'S WHO OF RENAISSANCE ART

Michelangelo. Leonardo da Vinci. Raphael. The heady triumvirate of the Italian Renaissance is synonymous with artistic genius. Yet they are only three of the remarkable cast of characters whose work inspired the Renaissance, that extraordinary flourishing of art and culture in Italy, especially in Florence, as the Middle Ages drew to a close. The artists were visionaries, who redefined painting, sculpture, architecture, and even what it means to be an artist.

THE PIONEER. In the mid-14th century, a few artists began to move away from the flat, two-dimensional painting of the Middle Ages. **Giotto**, who painted seemingly three-dimensional figures who show emotion, had a major impact on the artists of the next century.

THE GROUNDBREAKERS. The generations of **Brunelleschi** and **Botticelli** took center stage in the 15th century. **Ghiberti, Donatello, Uccello, Fra Angelico, Masaccio,** and **Filippo Lippi** were other major players. Part of the Renaissance (or "rebirth") was a renewed interest in classical sources—the texts, monuments, and sculpture of Ancient Greece and Rome. Perspective and the illusion of three-dimensional space in painting was another theme of this era, known as the Early Renaissance. Suddenly the art appearing on the walls looked real, or more realistic than it used to.

Roman ruins were not the only thing to inspire these artists. There was an incredible exchange of ideas going on. In Santa Maria del Carmine, Filippo Lippi was inspired by the work of Masaccio, who in turn was a friend of Brunelleschi. Young artists also learned from the masters via the apprentice system. Ghiberti's workshop (*bottega* in Italian) included, at one time or another, Donatello, Masaccio, and Uccello. Botticelli was apprenticed to Filippo Lippi.

THE BIG THREE. The mathematical rationality and precision of 15th-century art gave way to what is known as the High Renaissance. **Leonardo, Michelangelo,** and **Raphael** were much more concerned with portraying the body in all its glory and with achieving harmony and grandeur in their work. Oil paint, used sparingly and unknowingly up until this time, became more widely employed: as a result, Leonardo's colors are deeper, more sensual, more alive. For one brief time, all three were in Florence at the same time. Michelangelo and Leonardo surely knew each other, as they were simultaneously working on frescoes (never completed) inside Palazzo Vecchio.

When Michelangelo left Florence for Rome in 1508, he began the slow drain of artistic exodus from Florence, which never really recovered her previous glory.

A RENAISSANCE TIMELINE

IN THE WORLD

Black Death in Europe kills one-third of the population, 1347–50.

Joan of Arc burned at the stake, 1431.

IN FLORENCE

Dante, a native of Florence, writes *The Divine Comedy*, 1302–21.

Founding of the Medici bank, 1397.

Medici family made official papal bankers.

1434, Cosimo il Vecchio becomes de facto ruler of Florence. The Medici family will dominate the city until 1494.

1300

1400

IN ART

EARLY RENAISSANCE

Giotto frescoes in Santa Croce, 1320–25.

Masaccio and Masolino fresco Santa Maria del Carmine, 1424–28.

GIOTTO (ca. 1267–1337)

BRUNELLESCHI (1377–1446)

LORENZO GHIBERTI (ca. 1381–1455)

DONATELLO (ca. 1386–1466)

PAOLO UCCELLO (1397–1475)

FRA ANGELICO (ca. 1400–1455)

MASACCIO (1401–1428)

FILIPPO LIPPI (ca. 1406–1469)

Donatello sculpts his bronze *David*, ca. 1440.

Fra Angelico frescoes monks'cells in San Marco, ca. 1438–45.

Uccello's *Sir John Hawkwood*, ca. 1436.

1334, 67-year-old Giotto is appointed chief architect of Santa Maria del Fiore, Florence's Duomo (above). He begins to work on the Campanile, which will be completed in 1359, after his death.

Ghiberti wins the competition for the Baptistery doors (above) in Florence, 1401.

Brunelleschi wins the competition for the Duomo's cupola (below), 1418.

Gutenberg Bible is
printed, 1455.

Columbus discovers
America, 1492.

Martin Luther posts his 95 theses on
the door at Wittenberg, kicking off the
Protestant Reformation, 1517.

Constantinople falls
to the Turks, 1453.

Machiavelli's *Prince*
appears, 1513.

Copernicus proves that the
earth is not the center of
the universe, 1530–43.

Lorenzo "il Magnifico"
(right), the Medici patron
of the arts, rules in
Florence, 1449–92.

Two Medici popes Leo X
(1513–21) and Clement VII
(1523–34) in Rome.

Catherine de'Medici
becomes Queen of France,
1547.

1450   **1500**   **1550**

HIGH RENAISSANCE   MANNERISM

Botticelli paints the
Birth of Venus, ca. 1482.

1508, Raphael begins
work on the chambers
in the Vatican, Rome.

Giorgio Vasari
publishes his first
edition of *Lives of
the Artists*, 1550.

1504, Michelangelo's
David is put on display
in Piazza della
Signoria, where it
remains until 1873.

Leonardo paints
The Last Supper in
Milan, 1495–98.

Michelangelo
begins to
fresco the
Sistine Chapel
ceiling, 1508.

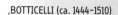

BOTTICELLI (ca. 1444–1510)

LEONARDO DA VINCI (1452–1519)

RAPHAEL (1483–1520)

MICHELANGELO (1475–1564)

Fra Filippo Lippi's
*Madonna and
Child*, ca. 1452.

Giotto's *Death of St. Francis*

Donatello's *St. John the Baptist*

Ghiberti's *Gates of Paradise*

GIOTTO (CA. 1267–1337)

Painter/architect from a small town north of Florence.

He unequivocally set Italian painting on the course that led to the triumphs of the Renaissance masters. Unlike the rather flat, two-dimensional forms found in then prevailing Byzantine art, Giotto's figures have a fresh, lifelike quality. The people in his paintings have bulk, and they show emotion, which you can see on their faces and in their gestures. This was something new in the late Middle Ages. Without Giotto, there wouldn't have been a Raphael.

In Florence: Santa Croce; Uffizi; Campanile; Santa Maria Novella
Elsewhere in Italy: Scrovegni Chapel, Padua; Vatican Museums, Rome

FILIPPO BRUNELLESCHI (1377–1446)

Architect/engineer from Florence.

If Brunelleschi had beaten Ghiberti in the Baptistery doors competition in Florence, the city's Duomo most likely would not have the striking appearance and authority that it has today. After his loss, he sulked off to Rome, where he studied the ancient Roman structures firsthand. Brunelleschi figured out how to vault the Duomo's dome, a structure unprecedented in its colossal size and great height. His Ospedale degli Innocenti employs classical elements in the creation of a stunning, new architectural statement; it is the first truly Renaissance structure.

In Florence: Duomo; Ospedale degli Innocenti; San Lorenzo; Santo Spirito; Baptistery Doors Competition Entry, Bargello; Santa Croce

LORENZO GHIBERTI (CA. 1381–1455)

Sculptor from Florence.

Ghiberti won a competition—besting his chief rival, Brunelleschi—to cast the gilded bronze North Doors of the Baptistery in Florence. These doors, and the East Doors that he subsequently executed, took up the next 50 years of his life. He created intricately worked figures that are more true-to-life than any since antiquity, and he was one of the first Renaissance sculptors to work in bronze. Ghiberti taught the next generation of artists; Donatello, Uccello, and Masaccio all passed through his studio.

In Florence: Door Copies, Baptistery; Original Doors, Museo dell'Opera del Duomo; Baptistry Door Competition Entry, Bargello; Orsanmichele

DONATELLO (CA. 1386–1466)

Sculptor from Florence.

Donatello was an innovator who, like his good friend Brunelleschi, spent most of his long life in Florence. Consumed with the science of optics, he used light and shadow to create the effects of nearness and distance. He made an essentially flat slab look like a three-dimensional scene. His bronze *David* is probably the first free-standing male nude since antiquity. Not only technically brilliant, his work is also emotionally resonant; few sculptors are as expressive.

In Florence: *David*, Bargello; *St. Mark*, Orsanmichele; Palazzo Vecchio; Museo dell'Opera del Duomo; San Lorenzo; Santa Croce
Elsewhere in Italy: Padua; Prato; Venice

Fra Angelico's *The Deposition*

Masaccio's *Trinity*

Filippo Lippi's *Madonna and Child*

PAOLO UCCELLO (1397–1475)
Painter from Florence.

Renaissance chronicler Vasari once observed that had Uccello not been so obsessed with the mathematical problems posed by perspective, he would have been a very good painter. The struggle to master single-point perspective and to render motion in two dimensions is nowhere more apparent than in his battle scenes. His first major commission in Florence was the gargantuan fresco of the English mercenary Sir John Hawkwood (the Italians called him Giovanni Acuto) in Florence's Duomo.

In Florence: **Sir John Hawkwood, Duomo; Battle of San Romano, Uffizi; Santa Maria Novella**

Elsewhere in Italy: **Urbino**

FRA ANGELICO (CA. 1400–1455)
Painter from a small town north of Florence.

A Dominican friar, who eventually made his way to the convent of San Marco, Fra Angelico and his assistants painted frescoes for aid in prayer and meditation. He was known for his piety; Vasari wrote that Fra Angelico could never paint a crucifix without a tear running down his face. Perhaps no other painter so successfully translated the mysteries of faith and the sacred into painting. And yet his figures emote, his command of perspective is superb, and his use of color startles even today.

In Florence: **Museo di San Marco; Uffizi**

Elsewhere in Italy: **Vatican Museums, Rome**

MASACCIO (1401–1428)
Painter from San Giovanni Valdarno, southeast of Florence.

Masaccio and Masolino, a frequent collaborator, worked most famously together at Santa Maria del Carmine. Their frescoes of the life of St. Peter use light to mold figures in the painting by imitating the way light falls on figures in real life. Masaccio also pioneered the use of single-point perspective, masterfully rendered in his *Trinity*. His friend Brunelleschi probably introduced him to the technique, yet another step forward in rendering things the way the eye sees them. Masaccio died young and under mysterious circumstances.

In Florence: **Santa Maria del Carmine; Trinity, Santa Maria Novella**

FILIPPO LIPPI (CA. 1406–1469)
Painter from Prato.

At a young age, Filippo Lippi entered the friary of Santa Maria del Carmine, where he was highly influenced by Masaccio and Masolino's frescoes. His religious vows appear to have made less of an impact; his affair with a young nun produced a son, Filippino (Little Philip, who later apprenticed with Botticelli), and a daughter. His religious paintings often have a playful, humorous note; some of his angels are downright impish and look directly out at the viewer. Lippi links the earlier painters of the 15th century with those who follow; Botticelli apprenticed with him.

In Florence: **Uffizi; Palazzo Medici Riccardi; San Lorenzo; Palazzo Pitti**

Elsewhere in Italy: **Prato**

Botticelli's *Primavera*

Leonardo's *Portrait of a Young Woman*

Raphael's *Madonna on the Meadow*

BOTTICELLI (CA. 1444–1510)
Painter from Florence.
Botticelli's work is characterized by stunning, elongated blondes, cherubic angels (something he undoubtedly learned from his time with Filippo Lippi), and tender Christs. Though he did many religious paintings, he also painted monumental, nonreligious panels—his *Birth of Venus* and *Primavera* being the two most famous of these. A brief sojourn took him to Rome, where he and a number of other artists frescoed the Sistine Chapel walls.
In Florence: **Birth of Venus, Primavera, Uffizi; Palazzo Pitti**
Elsewhere in Italy: **Vatican Museums, Rome**

LEONARDO DA VINCI (1452–1519)
Painter/sculptor/engineer from Anchiano, a small town outside Vinci.
Leonardo never lingered long in any place; his restless nature and his international reputation led to commissions throughout Italy, and took him to Milan, Vigevano, Pavia, Rome, and, ultimately, France. Though he is most famous for his mysterious *Mona Lisa* (at the Louvre in Paris), he painted other penetrating, psychological portraits in addition to his scientific experiments: his design for a flying machine (never built) predates Kitty Hawk by nearly 500 years. The greatest collection of Leonardo's work in Italy can be seen on one wall in the Uffizi.
In Florence: **Adoration of the Magi, Uffizi**
Elsewhere in Italy: **Last Supper, Santa Maria delle Grazie, Milan**

RAPHAEL (1483–1520)
Painter/architect from Urbino.
Raphael spent only four highly productive years of his short life in Florence, where he turned out made-to-order panel paintings of the Madonna and Child for a hungry public; he also executed a number of portraits of Florentine aristocrats. Perhaps no other artist had such a fine command of line and color, and could render it, seemingly effortlessly, in paint. His painting acquired new authority after he came up against Michelangelo toiling away on the Sistine ceiling. Raphael worked nearly next door in the Vatican, where his figures take on an epic, Michelangelesque scale.
In Florence: **Uffizi; Palazzo Pitti**
Elsewhere in Italy: **Vatican Museums, Rome**

MICHELANGELO (1475–1564)
Painter/sculptor/architect from Caprese.
Although Florentine and proud of it (he famously signed his St. Peter's *Pietà* to avoid confusion about where he was from), he spent most of his 90 years outside his native city. He painted and sculpted the male body on an epic scale and glorified it while doing so. Though he complained throughout the proceedings that he was really a sculptor, Michelangelo's Sistine Chapel ceiling is arguably the greatest fresco cycle ever painted (and the massive figures owe no small debt to Giotto).
In Florence: **David, Galleria dell'Accademia; Uffizi; Casa Buonarroti; Bargello**
Elsewhere in Italy: **St. Peter's Basilica, Vatican Museums, and Piazza del Campidoglio in Rome**

Michelangelo received the commission for the New Sacristy in 1520 from Cardinal Giulio de' Medici (1478–1534), who later became Pope Clement VII and who wanted a new burial chapel for his cousins Giuliano (1478–1534) and Lorenzo (1492–1519). The result was a tour de force of architecture and sculpture. Architecturally, Michelangelo was as original and inventive here as ever, but it is, quite properly, the powerful sculpture that dominates the room. The scheme is allegorical: on the tomb to the right are figures representing Day and Night, and on the tomb to the left are figures representing Dawn and Dusk; above them are idealized sculptures of the two Medici men, usually interpreted to represent the active life and the contemplative life. But the allegorical meanings are secondary; what is most important is the intense presence of the sculptural figures. ⊠ *Piazza di Madonna degli Aldobrandini, near San Lorenzo* ☏ *055/294883 reservations* ⊕ *www.polomuseale.firenze.it* 🎫 *€6* ⊗ *Daily 8:15–5. Closed 1st, 3rd, and 5th Mon. and 2nd and 4th Sun. of month.*

★ ⓴ **Galleria dell'Accademia** (Accademia Gallery). The collection of Florentine paintings here, dating from the 13th to the 18th century, is largely unremarkable, but the sculptures by Michelangelo are worth the price of admission. The unfinished *Slaves,* fighting their way out of their marble prisons, were meant for the tomb of Michelangelo's overly demanding patron, Pope Julius II (1443–1513). But the focal point is the original *David,* moved here from Piazza della Signoria in 1873. The *David* was commissioned in 1501 by the Opera del Duomo (Cathedral Works Committee), which gave the 26-year-old sculptor a leftover block of marble that had been ruined by another artist. Michelangelo's success with the block was so dramatic that the city showered him with honors, and the Opera del Duomo voted to build him a house and a studio in which to live and work.

Today *David* is beset not by Goliath but by tourists, and seeing the statue at all—much less really studying

> **WORD OF MOUTH**
>
> "I strongly recommend making reservations for both the Accademia and the Uffizi. We saved ourselves a ton of time. We walked right into the Accademia and right past the line of unreserved people."   –Ivy

it—can be a trial, as it is surrounded by a Plexiglas barrier. Anxious Florentine art custodians determined not to limit the number of tourists (whose entrance fees help preservation) have suggested installing an "air blaster" behind *David* that would remove the dust and humidity that each tourist brings in. A two-year study is under way, and a decision will probably be reached sometime in 2007. The statue is not quite what it seems. It is so poised and graceful and alert—so miraculously alive—that it is often considered the definitive embodiment of the ideals of the High Renaissance in sculpture. But its true place in the history of art is a bit more complicated.

As Michelangelo well knew, the Renaissance painting and sculpture that preceded his work were deeply concerned with ideal form. Perfection of proportion was the ever-sought Holy Grail; during the Renaissance, ideal proportion was equated with ideal beauty, and ideal beauty was equated with spiritual perfection. But *David,* despite its supremely calm and dignified pose, departs from these ideals. Michelangelo did not give the statue perfect proportions. The head is slightly too large for the body, the arms are too large for the torso, and the hands are dramatically large for the arms. The work was originally commissioned to adorn the facade of the Duomo and was intended to be seen from below at a distance. Michelangelo knew exactly what he was doing, calculating that the perspective of the viewer would be such that, in order for the statue to appear properly proportioned, the upper body, head, and arms would have to be bigger, as they are farther away from the viewer's line of vision. But he also did it to express and embody, as powerfully as possible in a single figure, an entire biblical story. David's hands *are* big, but so was Goliath, and these are the hands that slew him. Save yourself a long and tiresome wait at the museum entrance by reserving your tickets in advance. ⊠ *Via Ricasoli 60, near San Marco* ☎ *055/294883 reservations, 055/2388609 gallery* ⊕ *www.polomuseale.firenze.it* ⊠ *€6.50, reservation fee €3* ⊙ *Tues.–Sun. 8:15–6:50.*

★ ⑲ **Museo di San Marco.** A former Dominican convent adjacent to the church of San Marco houses this museum, which contains many stunning works by Fra Angelico (circa 1400–55), the Dominican friar famous for his piety as well as for his painting. When the friars' cells were restructured between 1439 and 1444, he decorated many of them with frescoes meant to spur religious contemplation. His paintings are simple and direct and furnish a compelling contrast to those in the Palazzo Medici-Riccardi chapel. Whereas Gozzoli's frescoes celebrate the splendors of the Medici, Fra Angelico's exalt the simple beauties of the contemplative life and quiet reflection. Fra Angelico's works are everywhere in this complex, from the friars' cells to the superb panel paintings on view in the museum. Don't miss the famous *Annunciation* on the upper floor and the works in the gallery off the cloister as you enter. Here you can see his beautiful *Last Judgment*; as usual, the tortures of the damned are far more inventive and interesting than the pleasures of the redeemed. ⊠ *Piazza San Marco 1* ☎ *055/2388608* ⊕ *www.polomuseale. firenze.it* ⊠ *€4* ⊙ *Weekdays 8:15–1:50, weekends 8:15–6:15. Closed 1st, 3rd, and 5th Sun., and 2nd and 4th Mon. of month.*

⑮ **San Lorenzo.** The interior of this church, like that of Santo Spirito on the other side of the Arno, was designed by Filippo Brunelleschi around 1420. Both proclaim with ringing clarity the beginning of the Renaissance in architecture (neither was completed by Brunelleschi, and which he worked on first is unknown). San Lorenzo's most dramatic element is its floor grid of dark, inlaid marble lines. The grid makes the rigorous geometry of the interior immediately visible and is an illuminating lesson on the laws of perspective. If you stand in the middle of the nave at the church entrance, on the line that stretches to the high altar, every element in the church—the grid, the nave columns, the side aisles, the coffered nave ceiling—seems to march inexorably toward a hypothetical vanishing point beyond the high altar, exactly as in a single-point-perspective painting. Brunelleschi's **Sagrestia Vecchia** (Old Sacristy) has stucco decorations by Donatello; it's at the end of the left transept. The

Florence's Trial by Fire

ONE OF THE MOST striking figures of Renaissance Florence was Girolamo Savonarola, a Dominican friar who, for a moment, captured the conscience of the city. In 1491 he became prior of the convent of San Marco, where he adopted a life of austerity and delivered sermons condemning Florence's excesses and the immorality of his fellow clergy. Following the death of Lorenzo de' Medici, Savonarola was instrumental in the formation of the Grand Council, a representative body of 3,000 men, modeled after the council in Venice. In one of his most memorable acts, he urged Florentines to toss worldly possessions—from frilly dresses to Botticelli paintings—onto a "bonfire of the vanities" in Piazza della Signoria. Savonarola's antagonism toward church hierarchy led to his undoing: he was excommunicated in 1497, and the following year was hanged and burned on charges of heresy. Today, at the Museo di San Marco, you can visit Savonarola's cell and see his arresting portrait.

3

facade of the church was never finished. ⊠ *Piazza San Lorenzo* ☎ *055/ 290184* ✉ *€2.50* ☾ *Mon.–Sat. 10–5.*

Also Worth Seeing

16 **Biblioteca Medicea Laurenziana** (Laurentian Library). Begun in 1524 and finished in 1568, the Laurentian Library and its famous **vestibolo** (anteroom) and staircase express the idiosyncratic personal vision of Michelangelo the architect, who was every bit as original as Michelangelo the sculptor. Unlike Brunelleschi (the architect of San Lorenzo), he was obsessed not with proportion and perfect geometry but with experimentation and invention.

At this writing, the library was open only to scholars and the vestibule and stairs were temporarily closed. The strangely shaped anteroom has had experts scratching their heads for centuries. In a space more than two stories high, why did Michelangelo limit his use of columns and pilasters to the upper two-thirds of the wall? Why didn't he rest them on strong pedestals instead of on huge, decorative curlicue scrolls, which rob them of all visual support? Why did he recess them into the wall, which makes them look weaker still? The architectural elements here do not stand firm and strong and tall, like those inside the church next door; instead, they seem to be pressed into the wall as if into putty, giving the room a soft, rubbery look that is one of the strangest effects ever achieved by aping classical architecture. It is almost as if Michelangelo purposely set out to defy his predecessors, intentionally flouting the conventions of the High Renaissance to see what kind of bizarre, mannered effect might result. His innovations were tremendously influential and produced a period of architectural experimentation. As his contemporary Giorgio Vasari put it, "Artisans have been infinitely and perpetually indebted to him because he broke the bonds and chains of a way of working that had become habitual by common usage."

Nobody has ever complained about the anteroom's staircase (best viewed head-on), which emerges from the library with the visual force of an unstoppable lava flow. In its highly sculptural conception and execution, it's quite simply one of the most original and fluid staircases in the world. ✉ *Piazza San Lorenzo 9, entrance to left of San Lorenzo* ☎ *055/210760* ⊕ *www.bml.firenze.sbn.it* 🖾 *Library free, special exhibitions* €5 ⊗ *Daily 8:30–1:30.*

㉓ Museo Archeologico. Of the Etruscan, Egyptian, and Greco-Roman antiquities in this museum, the Etruscan collection is particularly notable—one of the largest in Italy. The famous bronze *Chimera* was discovered (without the tail, a reconstruction) in the 16th century. ✉ *Via della Colonna 38, near Santissima Annunziata* ☎ *055/23575* ⊕ *www.comune. firenze.it/soggetti/sat/didattica/museo.html* 🖾 €4 ⊗ *Mon. 2–7, Tues. and Thurs. 8:30–7, Wed. and Fri.–Sun. 8:30–2.*

㉑ Museo dell'Opificio delle Pietre Dure. Ferdinand I established a workshop in 1588 to train craftsmen in the art of working with precious and semiprecious stones and marble. Four hundred–plus years later, the workshop is renowned as a center for the restoration of mosaics and inlays in semiprecious stones. The little museum is highly informative and includes some magnificent antique examples of this highly specialized and beautiful craft. ✉ *Via degli Alfani 78, near San Marco* ☎ *055/26511* 🖾 €2 ⊗ *Mon.–Sat. 8:15–1:50.*

⑱ Palazzo Medici-Riccardi. The upper floor **Cappella dei Magi** is the main attraction of this palace begun in 1444 by Michelozzo for Cosimo il Vecchio. Benozzo Gozzoli's famous *Procession of the Magi* (finished in 1460) adorns the walls. It celebrates both the birth of Christ and the splendor of the Medici family. Gozzoli's gift was for entrancing the eye, not challenging the mind, and on those terms his success here is beyond question. The paintings are full of activity yet somehow frozen in time in a way that fails utterly as realism but succeeds triumphantly when the demand for realism is set aside. Entering the chapel is like walking into the middle of a magnificently illustrated children's storybook, and this beauty makes it one of the most enjoyable rooms in the entire city. ✉ *Via Cavour 1, near San Lorenzo* ☎ *055/2760340* 🖾 €4 ⊗ *Thurs.–Tues. 9–7.*

㉕ Santa Maria Maddalena dei Pazzi. One of Florence's hidden treasures, Perugino's (circa 1445/50–1523) cool and composed *Crucifixion* is in the chapter house of the monastery below this church. Here you can see the Virgin Mary and St. John the Evangelist with Mary Magdalen and Sts. Benedict and Bernard of Clairvaux posed against a simple but haunting landscape. The figure of Christ crucified occupies the center of this brilliantly hued fresco. Perugino's colors radiate—note the juxtaposition of the yellow-green cuff against the orange tones of Mary Magdalen's robe. ✉ *Borgo Pinti 58, near Santissima Annunziata* ☎ *055/2478420* 🖾 *Donation requested* ⊗ *Mon.–Sat. 9–noon, 5–5:20, and 6–7; Sun. 9–noon and 5–6:20.*

㉒ Santissima Annunziata. Dating from the mid-13th century, this church was restructured in 1447 by Michelozzo, who gave it an uncommon (and lovely) entrance cloister with frescoes by Andrea del Sarto (1486–1530),

Pontormo (1494–1556), and Rosso Fiorentino (1494–1540). The interior is a rarity for Florence: an over-the-top baroque design. But it's not really a fair example, since it is merely 17th-century baroque decoration applied willy-nilly to an earlier structure—exactly the sort of violent remodeling exercise that has given baroque a bad name. The **Cappella dell'Annuziata,** immediately inside the entrance to the left, illustrates the point. The lower half, with its stately Corinthian columns and carved frieze bearing the Medici arms, was commissioned by Piero de' Medici in 1447; the upper half, with its erupting curves and impish sculpted cherubs, was added 200 years later. Each is effective in its own way, but together they serve only to prove that dignity is rarely comfortable wearing a party hat. ⊠ *Piazza di Santissima Annunziata* ☎ *055/266186* ☼ *Daily 7:30–12:30 and 4–6:30.*

㉔ **Spedale degli Innocenti.** Brunelleschi designed this foundling hospital in 1419; it takes the prize for the very first Renaissance construction employing the two shapes he considered mathematically (and therefore philosophically and aesthetically) perfect—the square and the circle. Below the level of the arches the portico encloses a row of perfect cubes; above the arch level the portico encloses a row of intersecting hemispheres. The whole geometric scheme is articulated with Corinthian columns, capitals, and arches borrowed directly from antiquity. At the same time Brunelleschi was also designing the interior of San Lorenzo, using the same basic ideas, but the portico here was finished before the church. As exterior decoration, there are 10 ceramic medallions that depict swaddled infants, done in about 1487 by Andrea della Robbia (1435–1525/28). Inside there's a small museum devoted to lesser-known Renaissance works. ⊠ *Piazza di Santissima Annunziata 12* ☎ *055/20371* ▨ *€4* ☼ *Mon.–Sat. 8:30–7, Sun. 8:30–2.*

Santa Maria Novella to the Arno

Piazza Santa Maria Novella, near the train station, suffers a degree of squalor, especially at night. Nevertheless, the streets in and around the piazza have their share of architectural treasures, including some of Florence's most tasteful palaces. Between Santa Maria Novella and the Arno is Via Tornabuoni, Florence's finest shopping street.

The Main Attractions
㉗ **Palazzo Strozzi.** The Strozzi family built this imposing palazzo in an attempt to outshine the Palazzo Medici. The design is based on a circa 1489 model by Giuliano da Sangallo (circa 1452–1516). Construction took place between 1489 and 1504 under Il Cronaca (1457–1508) and Benedetto da Maiaino (1442–97). The exterior is simple, severe, and massive: it's a testament to the wealth of a patrician, 15th-century Florentine family. The interior courtyard is another matter altogether. It is here that the classical vocabulary—columns, capitals, pilasters, arches, and cornices—is given uninhibited and powerful expression. Blockbuster art shows frequently take place here. ⊠ *Via Tornabuoni, near Piazza della Repubblica* ☎ *055/2776461* ⊕ *www.firenzemostre.com* ▨ *Free except during exhibitions* ☼ *Daily 10–7.*

㉖ Santa Maria Novella. The facade of Santa Maria Novella looks distinctly clumsy by later Renaissance standards, and with good reason: it is an architectural hybrid. The lower half was completed mostly in the 14th century; its pointed-arch niches and decorative marble patterns reflect the Gothic style of the day. About a hundred years later (around 1456), architect Leon Battista Alberti was called in to complete the job. The marble decoration of his upper story clearly defers to the already existing work below, but the architectural motifs he added evince an entirely different style. The problem was to soften the abrupt transition between a wide ground floor and the narrow upper story. Alberti designed S-curve scrolls surmounting the decorative circles on either side of the upper story: this had no precedent in antiquity but set one in his time. Once you start to look for them, you see scrolls such as these (or sculptural variations of them) on churches all over Italy, and every one of them derives from Alberti's example here.

The architecture of the interior is, like the Duomo, a dignified but somber example of Florentine Gothic. Exploration is essential, however, because the church's store of art treasures is remarkable. Of special interest for its great historical importance and beauty is Masaccio's *Trinity,* on the left-hand wall, almost halfway down the nave. Painted around 1426–27 (at the same time he was working on his frescoes in Santa Maria del Carmine), it unequivocally announced the arrival of the Renaissance in painting. The realism of the figure of Christ was revolutionary in itself, but what was probably even more startling to contemporary Florentines was the barrel vault in the background. The mathematical rules for employing perspective in painting had just been discovered (probably by Brunelleschi), and this was one of the first works of art to employ them with utterly convincing success.

Other highlights include the 14th-century stained-glass rose window depicting the *Coronation of the Virgin* (above the central entrance); the Cappella Filippo Strozzi (to the right of the altar), containing late-15th-century frescoes and stained glass by Filippino Lippi; the Cappella Maggiore (the area around the high altar), displaying frescoes by Domenico Ghirlandaio (1449–94); and the Cappella Gondi (to the left of the altar), containing Filippo Brunelleschi's famous wood crucifix, carved around 1410 and said to have so stunned the great Donatello when he first saw it that he dropped a basket of eggs. Early, well-preserved frescoes painted between 1348 and 1355 by Andrea da Firenze are in the chapter house, or the **Cappellone degli Spagnoli** (Spanish Chapel). ✉ *Piazza Santa Maria Novella* ☎ *055/210113* ✆ *Church €2.50, chapel €2.50* ◷ *Mon.–Thurs. and Sat. 9–5, Sun. 9–2.*

In the cloisters of the **Museo di Santa Maria Novella,** to the left of Santa Maria Novella, is a faded fresco cycle by Paolo Uccello depicting tales from Genesis, with a dramatic vision of the Flood. ✉ *Piazza Santa Maria Novella 19* ☎ *055/282187* ✆ *€2.70* ◷ *Mon.–Thurs. and Sat. 9–5, Sun. 9–2.*

㉛ Ponte Santa Trinita. Take a moment to study the bridge downriver from the Ponte Vecchio: it was designed by Bartolomeo Ammannati in 1567 (possibly from sketches by Michelangelo), blown up by the retreating Germans during World War II, and painstakingly reconstructed after the war. The view from Ponte Santa Trinita is beautiful, which might explain why so many young lovers hang out there. ⊠ *Near Ponte Vecchio.*

30 **Santa Trinita.** Started in the 11th century by Vallombrosan monks in Romanesque style, this church underwent a Gothic remodeling during the 14th century. (Remains of the Romanesque construction are visible on the interior front wall.) Its major work is the cycle of frescoes and the altarpiece in the Cappella Sassetti, the second to the high altar's right, painted by Domenico Ghirlandaio between 1480 and 1485. Ghirlandaio was a wildly popular but conservative painter for his day, and generally his paintings show little interest in the laws of perspective that other Florentine painters had been experimenting with for more than 50 years. But his work here has such graceful decorative appeal it hardly seems to matter. The frescoes illustrate the life of St. Francis, and the altarpiece, depicting the Adoration of the Shepherds, veritably glows. ⊠ *Piazza Santa Trinita, near Santa Maria Novella* ☏ *055/216912* ☉ *Mon.–Sat. 8–noon and 4–6.*

Also Worth Seeing

28 **Museo Marino Marini.** One of the few 20th-century art museums in Florence is dedicated to Marino Marini's (1901–80) paintings, sculptures, drawings, and engravings. A 21-foot-tall Etruscanesque bronze of a horse and rider dominates the main gallery. The museum itself is an eruption of contemporary space in a deconsecrated 9th-century church, designed with a series of open stairways, walkways, and balconies that allow you to peer at Marini's work from all angles. ⊠ *Piazza San Pancrazio, near Santa Maria Novella* ☏ *055/219432* 🎟 *€4* ☉ *Mon. and Wed.–Sat. 10–5; closed Sat. June–Aug.*

29 **Palazzo Rucellai.** Architect Leon Battista Alberti (1404–72) designed what is perhaps the very first private residence (built between 1455 and 1470) that was inspired by antiquity. A comparison between the Palazzo Rucellai's facade and that of the severe Palazzo Strozzi is illuminating. An ordered arrangement of elements is seen on both, but Alberti devoted a larger proportion of his wall space to windows, which lightens the appearance. He filled in the space with rigorously ordered classical details. Though still severe, the result is less fortresslike (Alberti is on record as saying that only tyrants need fortresses). Ironically, the Palazzo Rucellai was built some 30 years *before* the Palazzo Strozzi. Alberti's civilizing ideas had little influence on the Florentine palaces that followed. To Renaissance Florentines, power—in architecture, as in life—was as impressive as beauty. ⊠ *Via della Vigna Nuova, near Santa Maria Novella.*

The Oltrarno

A walk through the Oltrarno (literally "the other side of the Arno") takes in two very different aspects of Florence: the splendor of the Medici, manifest in the riches of the mammoth Palazzo Pitti and the gracious Giardino di Boboli; and the charm of the Oltrarno, a slightly gentrified but still fiercely proud working-class neighborhood with artisans' and antiques shops.

Farther east across the Arno, a series of ramps and stairs climbs to Piazzale Michelangelo, where the city lies before you in all its glory (skip this trip if it's a hazy day). More stairs (behind La Loggia restaurant) lead to the church of San Miniato al Monte. You can avoid the long walk by taking Bus 12 or 13 at the west end of Ponte alle Grazie and getting off at Piazzale Michelangelo; you still have to climb the monumental stairs to and from San Miniato, but you can then take the bus from Piazzale Michelangelo back to the center of town. If you decide to take a bus, remember to buy your ticket before you board.

WORD OF MOUTH

"A good idea for Oltrarno: get lost between Borgo San Jacopo and Santo Spirito for wonderful antiques and restoration workshops. Extremely charming."   –lcquinn2

The Main Attractions

③ ㉝ **Giardino di Boboli** (Boboli Garden). The Italian gift for landscaping—less formal than the French but still full of sweeping drama—is displayed here at its best. The garden began to take shape in 1549, when the Pitti family sold the palazzo to Eleanora da Toledo, wife of the Medici grand duke Cosimo I. The initial horticultural plans were laid out by Niccolò Tribolo (1500–50). After his death, Vasari, Ammannati, Giambologna, Bernardo Buontalenti (circa 1536–1608), Giulio (1571–1635), and Alfonso Parigi (1606–56), among others, continued the work. The result was the most spectacular backyard in Florence. A copy of the famous *Morgante* statue, Cosimo I's favorite dwarf astride a particularly unhappy tortoise, is near the exit. Sculpted by Valerio Cioli (circa 1529–99), the work shows a perfectly executed potbelly. ⊠ *Enter through Palazzo Pitti* ☎ *055/294883* ⊕ *www.polomuseale.firenze.it* ⊠ *€4 combined ticket with Museo degli Argenti* ⊙ *Jan., Feb., Nov., Dec., daily 8:15–4:30; Mar. daily 8:15–5:30; Apr., May, Sept., Oct., daily 8:15–6:30; June, July, Aug., daily 8:15–7:30. Closed 1st and last Mon. of month.*

㉜ **Palazzo Pitti.** This palace is one of Florence's largest—if not one of its best—architectural set pieces. The original palazzo, built for the Pitti family around 1460, comprised only the main entrance and the three windows on either side. In 1549 the property was sold to the Medici, and Bartolomeo Ammannati was called in to make substantial additions. Although he apparently operated on the principle that more is better, he succeeded only in proving that more is just that: more. Today the palace houses several museums. The **Galleria Palatina** contains a collection of paintings from the 15th to the 17th century. High points include a number of portraits by Titian and an unparalleled group of paintings by Raphael, notably the double portraits of Angelo Doni and his wife, the sullen Maddalena Strozzi. The rooms here remain much as the Medici left them. The floor-to-ceiling paintings are considered by some to be Italy's most egregious exercise in conspicuous consumption, aesthetic overkill, and trumpery. Admission to the Galleria Palatina also allows you to explore the former **Appartamenti Reali,** containing furnishings from a remodel done in the 19th century. The **Museo degli Argenti** displays a vast collection of Medici household treasures; the **Galleria del Costume** showcases fashions from the past 300 years. In the **Galleria d'Arte Moderna** there's a collection of 19th- and 20th-century paintings, mostly Tuscan. ⊠ *Piazza Pitti* ☎ *055/2388616* ⊠ *Galleria Palatina*

€6.50, Museo degli Argenti combined with Giardino di Boboli €5, Galleria del Costume combined with Galleria d'Arte Moderna €5 ⊙ Tues.–Sun. 8:15–6:50. All but Galleria Palatina closed 2nd and 4th Sun. and 1st, 3rd, and 5th Mon. of month.

㊳ Piazzale Michelangelo. From this lookout you have a marvelous view of Florence and the hills around it, rivaling the vista from the Forte di Belvedere. It has a copy of Michelangelo's *David* and outdoor cafés packed with tourists during the day and with Florentines in the evening. The **Giardino dell'Iris** (Iris Garden) off the piazza is in full flower in May. The **Giardino delle Rose** (Rose Garden) on the terraces below the piazza is only open when it blooms in May and June. ⊠ *Lungarno South.*

㊱ Santa Maria del Carmine. Within the **Cappella Brancacci,** at the end of the right transept of this church, is a fresco cycle that forever changed the course of Western art. This masterpiece of Renaissance painting is the creation of three artists: Masaccio and Masolino (1383–circa 1440/47), who began it around 1424, and Filippino Lippi, who finished it some 50 years later, after a long interruption during which the sponsoring Brancacci family was exiled.

It was Masaccio's work that opened a new frontier for painting, as he was among the first to employ single-point perspective. He painted the *Tribute Money* on the upper-left wall; *St. Peter Baptizing* on the upper altar wall; the *Distribution of Goods* on the lower altar wall; and, most famous, the *Expulsion of Adam and Eve* on the chapel's upper-left entrance pier. If you look closely at the last painting and compare it with some of the chapel's other works, you see a pronounced difference. The figures of Adam and Eve have a startling presence, primarily due to the dramatic way in which their bodies seem to reflect light. Masaccio here shaded his figures consistently, so as to suggest a single, strong source of light within the world of the painting but outside its frame. In so doing, he succeeded in imitating with paint the real-world effect of light on mass, and he thereby imparted to his figures a sculptural reality unprecedented in his day. But his skill went beyond mere technical innovation. In the faces of Adam and Eve you see more than finely modeled figures. You see terrible shame and suffering depicted with a humanity rarely achieved in art. Tragically, Masaccio did not live to experience the revolution his innovations caused—he died in 1428 at the age of 27. Fire nearly destroyed the church in the 18th century; miraculously, the Cappella Brancacci survived almost intact.

Reservations to visit the church are mandatory, but can be booked on the same day. Your time inside is limited to 15 minutes—a frustration that's only partly mitigated by the 40-minute DVD about the history of the chapel you can watch either before or after your visit. ⊠ *Piazza del Carmine, near Santo Spirito* ☎ *055/2768224 reservations* ▦ *€4* ⊙ *Mon. and Wed.–Sat. 10–5, Sun. 1–5.*

㊲ San Miniato al Monte. A fine example of Romanesque architecture, San Miniato al Monte dates from the 11th century. The lively green-and-white marble facade has a 12th-century mosaic topped by a gilt bronze eagle, emblem of San Miniato's sponsors, the Calimala (cloth merchants' guild). Inside are a 13th-century marble floor and apse mosaic. Spinello Aretino (1350–1410) covered the walls of the **Sagrestia** with frescoes on the life of St. Benedict. The adjacent **Cappella del Cardinale del Portogallo** is one of the richest Renaissance works in Florence. Built to hold the tomb of a Portuguese cardinal, Prince James of Lusitania, who died young in Florence in 1459, it has a glorious ceiling by Luca della Robbia, a sculptured tomb by Antonio Rossellino (1427–79), and inlaid pavement in multicolor marble. ⊠ *Viale Galileo Galilei, Piazzale Michelangelo, Lungarno South* ☎ *055/2342731* ⊙ *Apr.–Oct., daily 8:30–7; Nov.–Mar., Mon.–Sat. 8–noon and 3–5, Sun. 3–5.*

Also Worth Seeing

❸④ Santa Felicita. This late-baroque church (its facade was remodeled 1736–39) contains the Mannerist Jacopo Pontormo's (1494–1556) tour de force, the *Deposition* (executed 1525–28), which is a masterpiece of 16th-century Florentine art and the centerpiece of the **Cappella Capponi.** The remote figures, which transcend the realm of Renaissance classical form, are portrayed in tangled shapes and intense pastel colors (well preserved because of the low lights in the chapel), in a space and depth that defy reality. Note, too, the exquisitely frescoed *Annunciation,* also by Pontormo, at a right angle to the *Deposition.* The granite column in the piazza was erected in 1381 and marks a Christian cemetery. ⊠ *Piazza Santa Felicita, Via Guicciardini, near Palazzo Pitti* ⊙ *Mon.–Sat. 9–noon and 3–6, Sun. 9–1.*

❸⑤ Santo Spirito. The plain, unfinished facade gives nothing away, but the interior is one of a pair designed in Florence by Filippo Brunelleschi in the early 15th century (the other is San Lorenzo). It was here that Brunelleschi supplied definitive solutions to the two main problems of interior Renaissance church design: how to build a cross shape using architectural elements borrowed from antiquity, and how to reflect the order and regularity that Renaissance scientists (including himself) were discovering in the natural world around them at the time. Brunelleschi's solution to the first problem was brilliantly simple: turn a Greek temple inside out. To see this clearly, look at one of the stately arch-top arcades that separate the side aisles from the central nave. Whereas ancient Greek temples were walled buildings surrounded by classical colonnades, Brunelleschi's churches were classical arcades within walled buildings. This brilliant architectural idea overthrew the previous era's religious taboo against pagan architecture once and for all, triumphantly reclaiming that architecture for Christian use.

Brunelleschi's solution to the second problem—making the entire interior orderly and regular—was mathematically precise: he designed the church so that all its parts were proportionally related. The transepts and nave have exactly the same width; the side aisles are precisely half as wide as the nave; the little chapels off the side aisles are exactly half as deep as the side aisles; the chancel and transepts are exactly one-eighth the depth of the nave; and so on, with dizzying exactitude. For Brunelleschi, such a design technique would have been a matter of passionate conviction. Like most theoreticians of his day, he believed that mathematical regularity and aesthetic beauty were flip sides of the same coin, that one was not possible without the other. In the **refectory of Santo Spirito,** adjacent to the church, you can see the remains of Andrea Orcagna's fresco of the *Crucifixion.* ⊠ *Piazza Santo Spirito* ☎ *055/210030 church, 055/287043 refectory* 🖃 *Church free, refectory* €2.20 🕙 *Thurs.–Tues. 10–noon and 4–5:30, Sun. 11:30–noon.*

NEED A BREAK?

Cabiria (⊠ Piazza Santo Spirito 4/r ☎ 055/215732), across the piazza from the church of Santo Spirito, draws a funky crowd in search of a cappuccino or a drink. When it's warm, sit outside on the terrace. Snacks and light lunches are also available.

3

Santa Croce

The Santa Croce quarter, on the southeast fringe of the historic center, was built up in the Middle Ages outside the second set of medieval city walls. The centerpiece of the neighborhood was the basilica of Santa Croce, which could hold great numbers of worshippers; the vast piazza could accommodate any overflow and also served as a fairground and, allegedly since the middle of the 16th century, as a playing field for no-holds-barred soccer games. A center of leather working since the Middle Ages, the neighborhood is still packed with leather craftsmen and leather shops.

> **WORD OF MOUTH**
>
> "You can walk *anywhere* in Florence easily–it's one of my favorite cities because it is so compact. Every time I go I am surprised by how close all the major sights are."   –Travelday

On June 24 each year, around the Festa di San Giovanni, the piazza hosts Calcio Storico, a medieval-style soccer tournament. Teams dress in costumes that represent the six Florence neighborhoods.

The Main Attractions

39

Fodor's Choice
★

Santa Croce. Like the Duomo, this church is Gothic, but, also like the Duomo, its facade dates from the 19th century. As a burial place, the church probably contains more skeletons of Renaissance celebrities than any other in Italy. The tomb of Michelangelo is immediately to the right as you enter; he is said to have chosen this spot so that the first thing he would see on Judgment Day, when the graves of the dead fly open, would be Brunelleschi's dome through Santa Croce's open doors. The tomb of Galileo Galilei (1564–1642) is on the left wall; he was not granted a Christian burial until 100 years after his death because he produced evidence that Earth is not the center of the universe. The tomb of Niccolò Machiavelli (1469–1527), the political theoretician whose brutally pragmatic philosophy so influenced the Medici, is halfway down the nave on the right. The grave of Lorenzo Ghiberti, creator of the Baptistery doors, is halfway down the nave on the left. Composer Gioacchino Rossini (1792–1868) is entombed at the end of the nave on the right. The monument to Dante Alighieri (1265–1321), the greatest Italian poet, is a memorial rather than a tomb (he is buried in Ravenna); it's on the right wall near the tomb of Michelangelo.

The collection of art within the complex is by far the most important of any church in Florence. The most famous works are probably the Giotto frescoes in the two chapels immediately to the right of the high altar. They illustrate scenes from the lives of St. John the Evangelist and St. John the Baptist (in the right-hand chapel) and scenes from the life of St. Francis (in the left-hand chapel). Time has not been kind to these frescoes; through the centuries, wall tombs were placed in the middle of them, they were whitewashed and plastered over, and in the 19th century they suffered a clumsy restoration. But the reality that Giotto introduced into painting can still be seen. He did not paint beautifully stylized religious icons, as the Byzantine style that preceded him prescribed; he instead painted drama—St. Francis surrounded by grieving friars at the very moment of his death. This was a radical shift in emphasis: before Giotto, painting's role was to symbolize the attributes of God; after him, it was to imitate life. His work is indeed primitive compared with later painting, but in the early 14th century it caused a sensation that was not equaled for another 100 years. He was, for his time, the equal of both Masaccio and Michelangelo.

Among the church's other highlights are Donatello's *Annunciation,* a moving expression of surprise (on the right wall two-thirds of the way down the nave); 14th-century frescoes by Taddeo Gaddi (circa 1300–66) illustrating scenes from the life of the Virgin Mary, clearly showing the influence of Giotto (in the chapel at the end of the right transept); and Donatello's *Crucifix,* criticized by Brunelleschi for making Christ look like a peasant (in the chapel at the end of the left transept). Outside the church proper, in the **Museo dell'Opera di Santa Croce** off the cloister, is the 13th-century *Triumphal Cross* by Cimabue (circa 1240–1302), badly damaged by the flood of 1966. A model of architectural geometry, the Cappella Pazzi, at the end of the cloister, is the work of Brunelleschi. ⊠ *Piazza Santa Croce 16* ☏*055/2466105* 💳*€4 combined admission to church and museum* ☉ *Mon.–Sat. 9:30–5:30, Sun. 1–5:30.*

❹ Sinagoga. Jews were already well settled in Florence by 1396, when the first money-lending operations were officially sanctioned. Medici patronage initially helped Jewish banking houses to flourish. Then in 1570, by decree of Pope Pius V (1504–72), Jews were required to live within

A GOOD WALK: FLORENTINE PIAZZAS

You may come to Florence for the art, but once here you're likely to be won over by the vibrant, pedestrian-friendly street life played out on its numerous and wonderfully varied piazzas—which are often works of art themselves. This walk, designed for a beautiful day, takes you through many of them (but bypasses some of the most prominent ones you'll inevitably encounter while sightseeing). Stopping along the way for gelato, a caffè, or an aperitivo isn't mandatory, but when the urge strikes you, don't resist.

Start off in **Piazza Santa Maria Novella,** by the train station; note the glorious facade by Leon Battista Alberti decorating the square's church. Take Via delle Belle Donne, a narrow street running southeast from the piazza, and go left heading toward Via del Trebbio. Here you'll see a cross marking the site of a 13th-century street scuffle between Dominican friars and Patarene heretics. (The Dominicans won.) A right on Via Tornabuoni takes you to tiny **Piazza Antinori**; the 15th-century Antinori palace has been in the hands of its wine-producing namesake family for generations.

the large ghetto, near today's Piazza della Repubblica. Construction of the modern Moorish-style synagogue, with its lovely garden, began in 1874 as a bequest of David Levi, who wished to endow a synagogue "worthy of the city." Falcini, Micheli, and Treves designed the building on a domed Greek-cross plan with galleries in the transept and a roofline bearing three distinctive copper cupolas. The exterior has alternating bands of tan travertine and pink granite, reflecting an Islamic style repeated in Giovanni Panti's ornate interior. Of particular interest are the cast-iron gates by Pasquale Franci, the eternal light by Francesco Morini, and the Murano glass mosaics by Giacomo dal Medico. The gilded doors of the Moorish ark, which fronts the pulpit and is flanked by extravagant candelabra, are decorated with symbols of the ancient Temple of Jerusalem and bear bayonet marks from vandals. The synagogue was used as a garage by the Nazis, who failed to inflict much damage in spite of one attempt to blow up the place with dynamite. Only the columns on the left side were destroyed, and, even then the women's balcony above did not collapse. Note the Star of David in black and yellow marble inlaid in the floor. The original capitals can be seen in the garden.

Some of the oldest and most beautiful Jewish ritual artifacts in all of Europe are displayed in the small **Museo Ebraico,** accessible by stairs or elevator. Exhibits document the Florentine Jewish community and the building of the synagogue. The donated objects all belonged to local families and date from as early as the late 16th century. Take special note of the exquisite needlework and silver objects. A small but well-stocked gift shop is downstairs. ⊠ *Via Farini 4, near Santa Croce* ☎ *055/2346654* ✉ *€4* ☉ *Apr., May, Sept., and Oct., Sun.–Thurs. 10–5, Fri. 10–2; June–Aug., Sun.–Thurs. 10–6, Fri. 10–2; Nov.–Mar., Sun.–Thurs. 10–3, Fri. 10–2. English-guided tours 10:10, 11, noon, 1, 2 (no tour at 2 on Fri.).*

Also Worth Seeing

❹ **Casa Buonarroti.** Michelangelo Buonarroti the Younger, the grandnephew of the famed Michelangelo, turned his family house into a shrine honoring the life of his great-uncle. It's full of works executed by Michelangelo, including a marble bas-relief, the *Madonna of the Steps,* carved

Continue south on Via Tornabuoni, stopping in **Piazza Strozzi** to admire (or recoil at) the gargantuan Palazzo Strozzi, a 15th-century palace designed specifically to dwarf Palazzo Medici. Step into the courtyard, which is as graceful as the facade is not. Next stop on Via Tornabuoni is lovely little **Piazza Santa Trinita.** Take a look into the church of Santa Trinita; in its Sassetti Chapel (right of the high altar), Ghirlandaio's 15th-century frescoes neatly depict the square where you were just standing.

Continue south to the Arno and cross it on the Ponte Santa Trinita, which affords an excellent view of the Ponte Vecchio upriver. Go south on Via Maggio, then make a right on Via Michelozzi, which leads to **Piazza Santo Spirito,** one of the loveliest—and liveliest—squares in Florence. Walking away from the piazza's church (heading south), make a left on Via Sant'Agostino, which quickly turns into Via Mazzetta. Stop briefly in **Piazza San Felice** and note Number 8, home of the English poets Elizabeth Barrett Browning and Robert Browning from 1849 to 1861.

From here Via Guicciardini takes you to the massive

when Michelangelo was a teenager, and his wooden model for the facade of San Lorenzo. ⊠ *Via Ghibellina 70, near Santa Croce* ☎ *055/241752* ⊕ *www.casabuonarroti.it* ✉ *€6.50* ☉ *Fri.–Wed. 9:30–2.*

WHERE TO EAT

Dining hours start at around 1 for the midday meal and at 8 for dinner. Many of Florence's restaurants are small, so reservations are a must. You can sample such specialties as creamy *fegatini* (a chicken-liver spread) and *ribollita* (minestrone thickened with bread and beans and swirled with extra-virgin olive oil) in a bustling, convivial trattoria, where you share long wooden tables set with paper place mats, or in an upscale *ristorante* with linen tablecloths and napkins. Follow the Florentines' lead and take a break at an *enoteca* (wine bar) during the day and discover some excellent Chiantis and Super Tuscans from small producers who rarely export.

WHAT IT COSTS In euros					
	$$$$	**$$$**	**$$**	**$**	**¢**
AT DINNER	over €45	€35–€45	€25–€35	€15–€25	under €15

Prices are for three courses (*primo*, *secondo*, and dessert).

The Duomo to the Ponte Vecchio

$–$$ ✕ **Frescobaldi Wine Bar.** Right around the corner from Palazzo Vecchio, this wine bar/restaurant showcases Frescobaldi wine, which the family has been making for centuries. Serious meals may be had in the lively color dining rooms with trompe l'oeil adorning the walls. Frescobaldino, the wine bar, serves lighter fare such as sumptuous salads and lovely cheese plates. Wine afficionados might like to try a flight or two from their wine tasting list. ⊠ *Via de'Magazzini 2–4/r, near Piazza della Signoria* ☎ *055/284724* ▭ *MC, V* ☉ *Closed Sun. No lunch Mon.*

$ ✕ **Coquinarius.** After seeing the Duomo, you can rest and replenish at this tranquil enoteca one block away. They serve tasty salads and sandwiches here, as well as clever pastas such as the *crespelle di farina di castagne con ricotta e radicchio* (chestnut pancakes stuffed with ricotta

---

Piazza dei Pitti. Palazzo Pitti was intended to outstrip Palazzo Strozzi in size and ostentatiousness, and it certainly succeeds. Behind the palazzo is the Giardino di Boboli. Walking the straight axis to its top, you'll pass man-made lakes, waterfalls, and grottoes. Head for the 18th-century Giardino dei Cavalieri, then pause and admire the view. It's hard to believe the pastoral scene, complete with olive groves, is in the city center.

If you have a climb left in you, head back toward the Arno along Via Guicciardini. Just before the Ponte Vecchio, turn right onto Via de' Bardi. Stop for a moment

in **Piazza Maria Sopr'Arno** and check out the eerie 20th-century sculpture of John the Baptist, patron saint of Florence. Continue along Via de' Bardi until it becomes Via San Niccolò. Make a right on Via San Miniato, passing through the city walls at Porta San Niccolò. Head up, steeply, on Via Monte alle Croci, and veer left, taking the steps of Via di San Salvatore al Monte. At the top is **Piazzale Michelangelo,** where your effort is rewarded with a breathtaking view of Florence below. Don't forget your camera.

and radicchio). ✉ *Via delle Oche 15/r, near Duomo* ☎ *055/2302153* ⊟ *MC, V* ⊘ *Closed Sun.*

San Lorenzo & Beyond

★ **$$$–$$$$** ✕ **Taverna del Bronzino.** Want to have a sophisticated meal in a 16th-century Renaissance artist's studio? The former workshop of Santi di Tito, a student of Bronzino's, is now a restaurant with simple formality and white tablecloths. Lots of classic, superb Tuscan food graces the artful menu, and the presentation is often dramatic. Try the *i cappellacci al cedro* (round pasta pillows stuffed with ricotta and served in a citrus sauce). The wine list has solid, affordable choices. Book far ahead if you want to dine at the wine cellar's only table; the service is outstanding. ✉ *Via delle Ruote 25/r, near San Marco* ☎ *055/495220* ⚹ *Reservations essential* ⊟ *AE, DC, MC, V* ⊘ *Closed Sun. and 3 wks in Aug.*

$–$$ ✕ **Le Fonticine.** Owner Silvano Bruci is from Tuscany, his wife, Gianna, from Emilia-Romagna; their ristorante near the train station combines the best of two Italian cuisines. Start with the mixed-vegetable antipasto plate and then move on to any of their house-made pastas. The feathery light *tortelloni nostro modo* is large stuffed tortellini with fresh ricotta, served with a tomato-and-cream sauce. The dining room, filled with the Brucis' painting collection, provides an upbeat space for this soul-satisfying food. Note that a 12% service charge may be automatically added to the bill. ✉ *Via Nazionale 79/r, near San Lorenzo* ☎ *055/282106* ⊟ *AE, DC, MC, V* ⊘ *Closed Sun. and Mon., Nov. 24–Jan. 5, and July 25–Aug. 25.*

★ **¢–$** ✕ **Mario.** Florentines flock to this narrow family-run trattoria to feast on Tuscan favorites served at simple tables under a wooden ceiling dating from 1536. Genuine Florentine hospitality prevails: you're seated wherever there's room, which often means with strangers. Yes, there's a bit of extra oil in most dishes, which imparts calories as well as taste, but aren't you on vacation in Italy? Worth the splurge is *riso al ragù* (rice with ground beef and tomatoes). ✉ *Via Rosina 2/r, at Piazza del Mercato Centrale, near San Lorenzo* ☎ *055/218550* ⚹ *Reservations not accepted* ⊟ *No credit cards* ⊘ *Closed Sun. and Aug. No dinner.*

¢ ✕ **Casa del Vino.** Most customers come here for the creative *panini* (sandwiches), such as *sgrombri e carciofini sott'olio* (mackerel and marinated baby artichokes), and the ever-changing list of significant wines by the glass. There's also a well-stocked collection of bottles to-go, at more than fair prices. ✉ *Via dell'Ariento 16/r, near San Lorenzo* ☎ *055/215609* ⊟ *MC, V* ⊘ *Closed Sun.*

Santa Maria Novella to the Arno

$$$ ✕ **Cantinetta Antinori.** After a rough morning of shopping on Via Tornabuoni, stop in this 15th-century palazzo and dine in the company of Florentine ladies (and men) who lunch. The kitchen reliably turns out Tuscan standards and a few unusual dishes like the *insalata di gamberoni con carciofi freschi* (shrimp salad with shaved raw artichokes). Most selections on the stellar wine list can be had by the glass, so that sampling Tignanello, the Super Tuscan that kicked off the entire Italian wine revolution, becomes affordable. ✉ *Piazza Antinori 3, near Santa Maria*

EATING WELL IN FLORENCE

A TYPICAL FLORENTINE meal starts with an antipasto of *crostini* (grilled bread spread with various savory toppings) or cured meats such as prosciutto *crudo* (ham thinly sliced) and *finocchiona* (salami seasoned with fennel). *Primi piatti* (first courses) can consist of local versions of pasta dishes available throughout Italy. More distinctly Florentine are the vegetable-and-bread soups such as *pappa al pomodoro* (bread and tomato soup) and *ribollita* (minestrone thickened with bread and beans and swirled with extra-virgin olive oil), and, in summer, a salad called *panzanella* (tomatoes, onions, vinegar, oil, basil, and bread). Before they are eaten, these dishes are often christened with *un "C" d'olio*, a generous C-shape drizzle of the sumptuous local olive oil.

Unparalleled among the *secondi piatti* (second courses) is *bistecca alla fiorentina*–a thick slab of local Chianina beef, often grilled over charcoal, seasoned with olive oil, salt, and pepper, and served rare. Arista (roast loin of pork seasoned with rosemary) is also a local specialty, as are many other roasted meats that pair especially well with Chianti. A *secondo* is usually served with a *contorno* (side dish) of white beans, sautéed greens, or artichokes in season, all of which can be drizzled with more of that fruity olive oil.

Desserts in Florence are more or less an afterthought. The meal often ends with a glass of *vin santo* (literally, "holy wine"), an ocher-color dessert wine that pairs beautifully with *biscotti* ("twice-cooked" cookies).

Novella ☎ *055/292234* ⊟ *AE, DC, MC, V* ⊘ *Closed weekends, 20 days in Aug., and Dec. 25–Jan. 6.*

🕒 **$-$$** ✕ **Il Latini.** Although Il Latini may well be the noisiest, most crowded trattoria in Florence, it's also one of the most fun, precisely because of the liveliness. A genial Torello ("little bull") Latini presides over his four big, homey dining rooms. Ample portions of ribollita prepare the palate for the hearty meat dishes that follow. Florentines and tourists alike praise the *agnello fritto* (fried lamb), and the ravioli *con ricotta e spinaci* (stuffed with spinach and cheese) is so tasty that kids don't even realize they're eating greens. Though reservations are advised, there's always a wait anyway. ⊠ *Via dei Palchetti 6/r, near Santa Maria Novella* ☎ *055/210916* ⌂ *Reservations essential* ⊟ *AE, DC, MC, V* ⊘ *Closed Mon. and 15 days at Christmas.*

Oltrarno

$-$$$ ✕ **Quattro Leoni.** The eclectic staff at this trattoria is an appropriate match for the diverse menu. Classics such as *taglierini con porcini* (long, thin, flat pasta with porcini mushrooms) are on the list, but so, too, are less-typical dishes such as the earthy cabbage salad with avocado, pine nuts, and drops of *olio di tartufo* (truffle oil). In cold weather, dine in one of two rooms with high ceilings; in summer you can sit outside. ⊠ *Piazza della Passera, Via dei Vellutini 1/r, near Palazzo Pitti* ☎ *055/218562* ⌂ *Reservations essential* ⊟ *AE, DC, MC, V* ⊘ *No lunch Wed.*

$$ ✕ **Borgo Antico.** Perched on the beautiful piazza of Santo Spirito, this pizzeria-trattoria is almost always crowded with Florentines and tourists alike, seated outdoors in warm weather and at closely spaced indoor tables when it's chilly. The young staff expertly navigates this maze to bring tasty €7 pizzas (such as *prosciutto con funghi*) and large salads to the table. Plenty of grilled meats are on offer, as well as a *menu del giorno* (a menu of the day). ✉ *Piazza Santo Spirito 6/r* ☎ *055/210437* ▭ *AE, MC, V.*

¢–$ ✕ **La Casalinga.** The nostalgic charm of a 1950s kitchen pervades "The Housewife" restaurant, and it has the Tuscan comfort food to match. If you eat ribollita anywhere in Florence, do so here—the soup couldn't be more authentic. The menu is long, portions are plentiful, and service is prompt and friendly. Save room for dessert: the *sorbetto al limoncello* (lemon sorbet) perfectly caps off the meal. Mediocre paintings clutter the semipaneled walls and tables are set close together in a place that is usually jammed. ✉ *Via Michelozzi 9/r, near Santo Spirito* ☎ *055/218624* ▭ *AE, DC, MC, V* ☾ *Closed Sun., 1 wk at Christmas, and 3 wks in Aug.*

¢–$ ✕ **Osteria Antica Mescita San Niccolò.** Always crowded, always good, and always cheap: this is simple Tuscan at its best. If you sit in the lower dining area, you're in what was once a chapel dating from the 11th century (the osteria is next to the church of San Niccolò). Such subtle but dramatic background plays off nicely with the food, such as *pollo con limone,* tasty pieces of chicken in a lemon-scented broth. In winter try the *spezzatino di cinghiale con aromi* (wild boar stew with herbs). ✉ *Via San Niccolò 60/r,* ☎ *055/2342836* ⚱ *Reservations essential* ▭ *AE, MC, V* ☾ *Closed Sun. and Aug.*

★ **¢** ✕ **Fuori Porta.** One of the oldest and best wine bars in Florence serves cured meats and cheeses, as well as daily specials such as the sublime spaghetti *al curry. Crostini* and *crostoni*—grilled breads topped with a mélange of cheeses and meats—are the house specialty; the *verdure sott' olio* (vegetables with oil) are divine. The friendly staff who wait on the rustic wooden tables set with paper place mats are only too happy to pour delicious wines by the glass or to discuss the beauties of the lengthy, comprehensive wine list. ✉ *Via Monte alle Croci 10/r, near San Niccolò* ☎ *055/2342483* ▭ *AE, MC, V.*

¢ ✕ **Le Volpi e l'Uva.** Just off Piazza Santa Trinita is an oenophile's dream: a little bar with a few stools, served by well-informed barmen who pour well-priced wine by the glass from lesser-known Italian vineyards and local favorites. Equally impressive are the cheeses and savory delights such as tiny truffled sandwiches. Something of a rarity among Florentine bars, this one offers wines and cheeses from France. The outdoor terrace opens in warmer weather. ✉ *Piazza de'Rossi 1, near Palazzo Pitti* ☎ *055/2398132* ▭ *AE, MC, V* ☾ *Closed Sun.*

Santa Croce

$$$$ ✕ **Alle Murate.** Few restaurants can boast that their staff includes an on-site art historian, but at this high-end eatery an expert will walk you around the site's medieval ruins and point out the building's lovely 14th-century frescoes. Along with a 2005 relocation to this space came a fresh new menu that's strong on Tuscan food with sophisticated variations: try the *tagliatelle all'olio nuovo, tonno fresco, e timo* (wide noo-

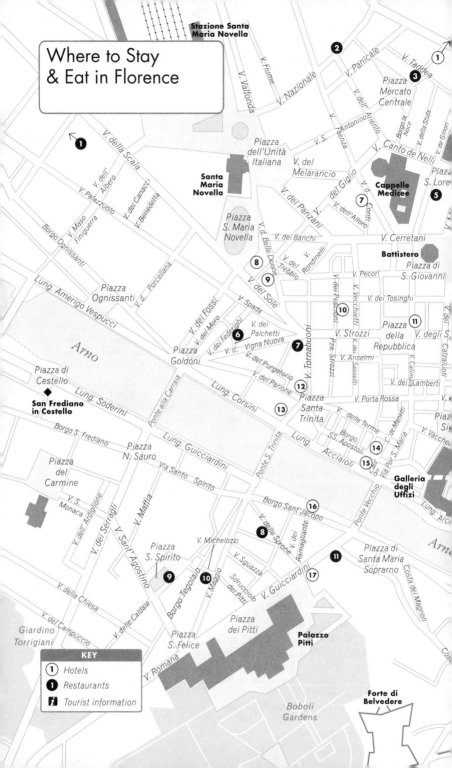

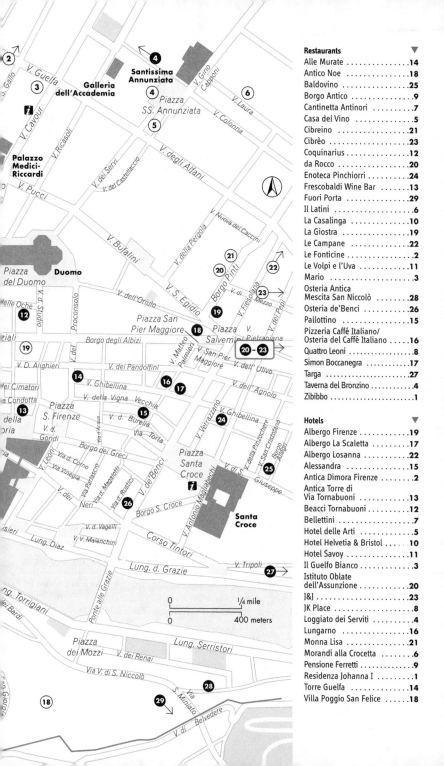

dles with freshly pressed olive oil, tuna, and thyme). ✉ *Via del Proconsolo near Santa Croce* ☎ *055/240 618* ⌕ *Reservations essential.* ▭ *MC, V* ⊙ *Closed Mon.*

$$$$
Fodor'sChoice
★
✕ **Cibrèo.** From the crostini with a savory chicken-liver spread to the melt-in-your-mouth desserts, the food at this upscale trattoria is fantastic and creative. If you thought you'd never try tripe—let alone like it—this is the place to lay any doubts to rest: the *trippa in insalata* (cold tripe salad) with parsley and garlic is an epiphany. If chef Fabio Picchi provides unsolicited advice, take it as a sign of his enthusiasm for cooking. Around the corner is Cibreino, Cibrèo's budget sibling. ✉ *Via A. del Verrocchio 8/r, near Santa Croce* ☎ *055/2341100* ⌕ *Reservations essential* ▭ *AE, DC, MC, V* ⊙ *Closed Sun. and Mon., July 25–Sept. 5, and Dec. 31–Jan. 7.*

$$$$
✕ **Enoteca Pinchiorri.** A sumptuous Renaissance palace—with high, frescoed ceilings and floral bouquets in silver vases—provides the backdrop for one of the most expensive restaurants in Italy. Some consider it one of the best, and others consider it a non-Italian rip-off; the kitchen is presided over by a Frenchwoman with sophisticated, yet internationalist, leanings. Interesting pasta combinations such as the *ignudi* (ricotta-and-spinach dumplings with a lobster-and-coxcomb fricassee) are always on the menu. Though portions are small, the holdings of the wine cellar are vast and service is top-notch. ✉ *Via Ghibellina 87, near Santa Croce* ☎ *055/242777* ⌕ *Reservations essential* ▭ *AE, MC, V* ⊙ *Closed Sun. and Mon., and Aug. No lunch Tues. or Wed.*

$$$$
✕ **Simon Boccanegra.** Florentine food cognoscenti flock to this place named for a *condottiere* (mercenary) hero in a Verdi opera. Under high ceilings, candles on every table cast a rosy glow; the fine wine list and superb service make a meal here a true pleasure. The young chef has a deft hand with fish dishes, as well as an inventive sense when it comes to reinterpreting such classics as risotto with chicken liver—he adds leek and saffron to give it a lift. Remember to save room for dessert. A less-expensive, less-formal wine bar serving a basic Tuscan menu is also on the premises. ✉ *Via Ghibellina 124/r, near Santa Croce* ☎ *055/2001098* ⌕ *Reservations essential* ▭ *AE, DC, MC, V* ⊙ *Closed Sun. No lunch.*

★ **$$$**
✕ **La Giostra.** The clubby La Giostra ("carousel") is owned and run by Prince Dimitri Kunz d'Asburgo Lorena, whose way with mushrooms is as remarkable as his charm. If you ask for an explanation of any of the unusually good pasta on the menu, Soldano, one of the prince's twin sons, will answer in perfect English. One favorite dish, *taglierini con tartufo bianco,* is a decadently rich, ribbonlike pasta with white truffles. To pair with the food, choose from the well-culled wine list. Do leave room for sweets, as this is the only show in town serving a sublime tiramisu *and* a wonderfully gooey Sacher torte. ✉ *Borgo Pinti 12/r, near Santa Croce* ☎ *055/241341* ▭ *AE, DC, MC, V.*

★ **$-$$$**
✕ **Antico Noe.** If Florence had diners (it doesn't), this would be the best diner in town. The short menu at the one-room eatery relies heavily on seasonal ingredients picked up daily at the market. The menu comes alive particularly during truffle and artichoke season (don't miss the grilled artichokes if they're on the menu). Locals rave about the tagliatelle *ai porcini* (with mushrooms); the fried eggs liberally laced with truffle might

be the greatest truffle bargain in town. The wine list is short but has some great bargains. ⊠ *Volta di San Piero 6/r, Santa Croce* ☎ *055/ 2340838* ▤ *AE, DC, MC, V* ⊘ *Closed Sun. and 2 wks in Aug.*

★ **$$** ✕ **Osteria de'Benci.** A few minutes from Santa Croce, this charming osteria serves grilled meats that are justifiably famous; the *carbonata* is a succulent piece of grilled beefsteak served rare. You might also try the *eliche del profeta* (a short pasta served with fresh ricotta, oregano, olive oil, tomatoes, and grated pecorino Romano cheese). When it's warm, you can dine outside with a view of the 13th-century tower belonging to the prestigious Alberti family. Next door, the Osteria de'Benci Caffè (¢) serves coffee, aperitifs, salads, and sandwiches 8 AM–midnight, as well as the osteria's menu. ⊠ *Via de'Benci 11–13/r, near Santa Croce* ☎ *055/2344923* ▤ *AE, DC, MC, V* ⊘ *No lunch Sun.*

☺ **$–$$** ✕ **Baldovino.** Here the standard pizzas delight the kids, and to satisfy the parents, there are pizzas with more sophisticated toppings, such as the *lombarda,* with potatoes, *taleggio* (soft, whole-milk cheese), and truffles. If pizza doesn't appeal, *primi* and *secondi* are available, including a taste bud–pleasing *petto di pollo ai broccoli e mandorle* (chicken breast with broccoli and almonds). ⊠ *Via San Giuseppe 22/r, near Santa Croce* ☎ *055/241773* ▤ *MC, V* ⊘ *Closed Mon.*

$ ✕ **Cibreino.** This intimate little trattoria, known affectionately to locals as "Cibreo povero" (loosely, the poor man's Cibrèo) shares its kitchen with that famed Florentine culinary institution. They share the same menu, too, though Cibreino's is much shorter. Start with *il gelatina di pomodoro* (tomato gelatine) liberally laced with basil, garlic, and a pinch of hot pepper, and then sample the justifiably renowned *passato in zucca gialla* (purèed yellow pepper soup) before moving on to any of the succulent second courses. Save room for dessert, as the pastry chef has a dangerous hand with chocolate tarts. To avoid sometimes agonizingly long waits, come early (7 pm) or late (after 9:30). ⊠ *Via dei Macci 118 near Santa Croce* ☎ *055/2341100* ⚬ *Reservations not accepted* ▤ *No credit cards* ⊘ *Closed Sun. and Mon. Closed July 25–Sept. 5 and Dec. 31–Jan. 7.*

☺ **¢–$** ✕ **Pallottino.** With its tiled floor, photograph-filled walls, and wooden tables, Pallottino is the quintessential Tuscan trattoria. Hearty, heart-warming classics include *peposa alla toscana* (a beef stew laced with black pepper). The menu changes frequently to reflect what's seasonal; the staff is friendly, as are the diners, who often share a table and, eventually, conversation. They also do pizza here, as well as great lunch specials. ⊠ *Via Isola delle Stinche 1/r, near Santa Croce* ☎ *055/289573* ▤ *AE, DC, MC, V* ⊘ *Closed Mon. and 2–3 wks in Aug.*

¢ ✕ **Pizzeria Caffè Italiano.** Locals swear by the pizzeria associated with the Osteria del Caffè Italiano, two doors down. Come early to grab one of the few tables, and ignore the intentionally rushed service. ⊠ *Via Isole delle Stinche, near Santa Croce* ☎ *055/289368* ▤ *No credit cards* ⊘ *Closed Mon.*

¢ ✕ **da Rocco.** At one of Florence's biggest markets you can grab lunch to go, or you could cram yourself into one of the booths and pour from the straw-cloaked flask (wine here is *da consumo,* which means they charge you for how much you drink). Food is abundant, Tuscan, and

What Tripe!

WHILE IN FLORENCE, those with a sense of culinary adventure should seek out a tripe sandwich, which is just about as revered by local gourmands as the *bistecca alla fiorentina*—a thick slab of local Chianina beef, often grilled over charcoal, seasoned with olive oil, salt, and pepper, and served rare. In this case, however, the treasure comes on the cheap—sandwiches are sold from small stands found in the city center, topped with a fragrant green sauce or a piquant red hot sauce, or both. *Bagnato* means that the hard, crusty roll is first dipped in the tripe's cooking liquid; it's advisable to say *"sì"* when asked if that's how you like it. Sandwiches are usually taken with a glass of red wine poured from the tripe seller's *fiasco* (flask). If you find the tripe to your liking, you might also enjoy *lampredotto*, another, some say

better, cut of stomach. For an exalted, high-end tripe treat, try Fabio Picchi's cold tripe salad, served gratis as an *amuse-bouche* at the restaurant Cibrèo. It could make a convert of even the staunchest "I'd never try *that*" kind of eater.

Tripe carts are lunchtime favorites of Florentine working men—it's uncommon, but not unheard of, to see a woman at a tripe stand. Aficionados will argue which sandwich purveyor is best; here are three that frequently get mentioned: **La Trippaia** (⊠ Via dell'Ariento, near Santa Maria Novella ☎ No phone ☉ Closed Sun.). **Il Trippaio** (⊠ Via de'Macci, at Borgo La Croce, near Santa Croce ☎ No phone ☉ Closed Sun.). **Nerbone** (⊠ Inside the Mercato Centrale, near Santa Maria Novella ☎ No phone ☉ Closed Sun.)

fast; locals pack in. The menu changes daily, and the prices are so right. ⊠ *In Mercato Sant'Ambrogio, Piazza Ghiberti, near Santa Croce* ☎ *No phone* ⌘ *Reservations not accepted* ▭ *No credit cards* ☉ *Closed Sun. No dinner.*

Beyond the City Center

\$\$–\$\$\$\$ ✕ **Targa.** It looks and feels like California on the Arno at this sleek, airy restaurant a short ride from the city center. Owner-chef Gabriele Tarchiani has spent time in the United States, which shows in the plant-decorated interior. Creative touches on the frequently changing menu include combinations such as fusilli *al ragù di anatra e finferli* (with a minced duck and wild-mushroom sauce). The desserts are culinary masterpieces. ⊠ *Lungarno Colombo 7, east of center* ☎ *055/677377* ⌘ *Reservations essential* ▭ *AE, DC, MC, V* ☉ *Closed Sun.*

\$\$–\$\$\$ ✕ **Zibibbo.** Benedetta Vitali, formerly of Florence's famed Cibrèo, has a restaurant of her very own. It's a welcome addition to the sometimes claustrophobic Florentine dining scene—particularly as you have to drive a few minutes out of town to get here. Off a quiet piazza, it has two intimate rooms with rustic, maroon-painted wood floors and a sloped ceiling. *Tagliatelle al sugo d'anatra* (wide pasta ribbons with duck sauce) are aromatic and flavorful, and *crocchette di fave con salsa di yogurt* (fava bean croquettes with a lively yogurt sauce) are innovative and tasty. ⊠ *Via di Terzollina 3/r, northwest of city center* ☎ *055/433383* ▭ *AE, DC, MC, V* ☉ *Closed Sun.*

Cafés

Cafés in Italy serve not only coffee concoctions and pastries but also drinks and some light lunches as well. They open early in the morning and usually close around 8 PM.

The always-crowded **Caffè Giacosa/Roberto Cavalli** (✉ Via della Spada 10, near Santa Maria Novella ☎ 055/2776328), joined at the hip with a Florentine fashion designer's shop, is open for breakfast, lunch, tea, and cocktails—except on Sunday. Classy **Procacci** (✉ Via Tornabuoni 64/r, near Santa Maria Novella ☎ 055/211656) is a Florentine institution dating back to 1885; try one of the panini *tartufati* (a small roll with truffled butter) and swish it down with a glass of *prosecco* (a dry, sparkling white wine). It's closed Sunday.

Gran Caffè (✉ Piazza San Marco 11/r ☎ 055/215833) is down the street from the Accademia, so it's a perfect stop for a marvelous *panino* (sandwich) or sweet while raving about the majesty of Michelangelo's *David*. Perhaps the best café for people-watching is **Rivoire** (✉ Piazza della Signoria, Via Vacchereccia 4/r ☎ 055/214412). Stellar service, light snacks, and terrific *aperitivi* (aperitifs) are the norm. Think twice, however, before ordering the more substantial fare, which is pricier than it is tasty.

Gelaterie & Pasticcerie

The convenient **Caffè delle Carrozze** (✉ Piazza del Pesce 3–5/r, near Piazza Signoria ☎ 055/2396810) is around the corner from the Uffizi; their gelati, according to some, are the best in the historic center. **Gelateria Carabe** (✉ Via Ricasoli 60/r, San Marco ☎ 055/289476) specializes in desserts Sicilian (including cannoli). Its *granità* (granular, flavored ices), made only in summer, are tart and flavorful—perfect thirst-quenchers.

Dolci e Dolcezze (✉ Piazza C. Beccaria 8/r, near Santa Croce ☎ 055/2345458), a *pasticceria* (bakery) in Borgo La Croce, probably has the prettiest and tastiest cakes, sweets, and tarts in town. It's closed Monday. Most visitors consider **Vivoli** (✉ Via Isola delle Stinche 7/r, near Santa Croce ☎ 055/292334) the best gelateria in town; Florentines find it highly overrated. It is closed Sunday. **Vestri** (✉ Borgo Albizi 11/r, near Santa Croce ☎ 055/2340374) is devoted to chocolate in all its guises, every day but Sunday. The small but sublime selection of chocolate-based gelati includes one with hot peppers.

Salumerie

Delicatessens and gourmet food shops specializing in fresh and cured meats and cheeses, *salumerie,* can be a great places to assemble a picnic or purchase dinner. Most are closed Sunday.

Looking for some cheddar cheese to pile in your panino? **Pegna** (✉ Via dello Studio 8, near Duomo ☎ 055/282701) has been selling both Italian and non-Italian food since 1860. The cheese collection at **Baroni** (✉ Mercato Centrale, enter at Via Signa, near San Lorenzo ☎ 055/289576) may be the most comprehensive in Florence. **Perini** (✉ Mercato Centrale, enter at Via dell'Ariento, near San Lorenzo ☎ 055/2398306) sells everything from cured meats to sumptuous pasta sauces. They're generous with free samples. Hungry for lunch or a snack in the

Oltrarno? Drop into **Azzarri Delicatesse** (⊠ Borgo S. Jacopo 27b/cr, near Santo Spirito ☎ 055/2381714) for a sandwich, meat for the grill, wine, or French cheeses.

WHERE TO STAY

Whether you are in a five-star hotel or a more modest establishment, one of the greatest pleasures of all is a room with a view, like the one made famous by E. M. Forster. Florence has so many famous landmarks that it's not hard to find lodgings with a panoramic vista. And the equivalent of the genteel pensions of yesteryear still exists, with the benefit of modern plumbing.

Florence's importance not only as a tourist city but as a convention center and site of the Pitti fashion collections throughout the year means a high demand for rooms. If you want to come during Pitti Uomo (early January), book well in advance, or you will be out of luck. Conversely, Florentine hotels often offer substantial deals in July, August, and February. If you find yourself in Florence with no reservations, go in person to **Consorzio ITA** (⊠ Stazione Centrale, near Santa Maria Novella ☎ 055/282893) to make a booking.

WHAT IT COSTS In euros					
	$$$$	$$$	$$	$	¢
FOR 2 PEOPLE	over €290	€210–€290	€140–€210	€80–€140	under €80

Prices are for a standard double room in high season.

Centro Storico

★ **$$$$** 🏨 **Hotel Helvetia & Bristol.** Painstaking care has gone into making this hotel in the center of town one of the prettiest and most intimate in Florence. From the cozy-yet-sophisticated lobby with its *pietra serena* (gray sandstone) columns to the guest rooms each decorated differently with antiques, the impression is one of a sophisticated manor house where you're spending the night. Osteria Bibendum, the restaurant ($$$$), serves sumptuous fare amid romantically tomato-red walls and cascading chandeliers. Top-notch staff make a stay here a real treat. ⊠ *Via dei Pescioni 2, Piazza della Repubblica, 50123* ☎ *055/26651* 📠 *055/288353* ⊕ *www.hbf.royaldemeure.com* ⬿ *54 rooms, 13 suites* ♨ *Restaurant, room service, in-room safes, some in-room hot tubs, minibars, cable TV, in-room VCRs, Wi-Fi, bar, babysitting, dry cleaning, laundry service, concierge, meeting room, parking (fee), some pets allowed* ▤ *AE, DC, MC, V* 🍽 *EP.*

$$$$ 🏨 **Hotel Savoy.** On the outside, the Savoy is a paragon of the baroque style prevalent in Italian architecture at the turn of the 19th century. Inside, sleek minimalism and up-to-the-minute amenities prevail. Sitting rooms have a funky edge, their cream-color walls dotted with contemporary prints. Streamlined furniture and muted colors predominate in the guest rooms, many of which look out at the Duomo's cupola or Piazza della Repubblica. The deep marble tubs might be reason enough to stay here—but you may also appreciate the efficient and courteous staff. ✉ *Piazza della Repubblica 7, 50123* ☎ *055/27351* 🖷 *2735888* ⊕*www.roccofortehotels.com* ⮡*92 rooms, 11 suites* ⚒ *R rant, room service, in-room fax, in-room safes, minibars, cable TV with movies and video games, in-room VCRs, in-room data ports, Wi-Fi, exercise equipment, bar, children's programs (ages infant–12), dry cleaning, laundry service, concierge, business services, meeting rooms, parking (fee)* ▤ *AE, DC, MC, V* ❢❙ *EP.*

¢–$ 🖼 **Albergo Firenze.** A block from the Duomo, Albergo Firenze is on one of the oldest piazzas in Florence, and for the location, the place is a great bargain. Though the reception area and hallways have all the charm of a dormitory, the similarity ends when you enter the spotlessly clean rooms with tile floors and wood veneer. A good number of singles, triples, and quads make this an attractive alternative for families and budget travelers. ✉ *Piazza Donati 4, near Duomo, 50122* ☎ *055/214203* 🖷 *055/ 212370* ⊕ *www.hotelfirenze-fi.it* ⮡ *58 rooms* ⚒ *In-room safes, cable TV, parking (fee)* ▤ *No credit cards* ❢❙ *BP.*

San Lorenzo & Beyond

$$$ 🖼 **Morandi alla Crocetta.** Near Piazza Santissima Annunziata is a charm-
Fodor'sChoice ing and distinguished residence in which you're made to feel like priv-
★ ileged friends of the family. The former convent is close to the sights but very quiet, and is furnished comfortably in the classic style of a gracious Florentine home. One room retains original 17th-century fresco fragments, and two others have small private terraces. The Morandi is not only an exceptional hotel but also a good value. It's very small, so try to book well in advance. ✉ *Via Laura 50, near Santissima Annunziata, 50121* ☎ *055/2344747* 🖷 *055/2480954* ⊕ *www.hotelmorandi.it* ⮡ *10 rooms* ⚒ *In-room safes, minibars, cable TV, in-room data ports, Wi-Fi, dry cleaning, laundry service, concierge, parking (fee), some pets allowed* ▤ *AE, DC, MC, V* ❢❙ *EP.*

$$–$$$ 🖼 **Il Guelfo Bianco.** Though the 15th-century building has been retrofitted with all the modern conveniences, its Renaissance charm still shines, and though it is in the centro storico, it still feels somewhat off the beaten path. Rooms have high ceilings (some are coffered), and windows are triple-glazed to ensure quiet. Contemporary prints and paintings on the walls contrast nicely with classic furnishings. Larger-than-usual single rooms with French-style beds are a good choice if you are traveling alone. Take breakfast in the small outdoor garden when weather permits. ✉ *Via Cavour 29, San Marco, 50129* ☎ *055/288330* 🖷 *055/295203* ⊕*www.ilguelfobianco.it* ⮡ *40 rooms* ⚒ *In-room safes, minibars, cable TV, in-room data ports, Wi-Fi, babysitting, dry cleaning, laundry service, concierge, Internet room, business services, parking (fee), some pets allowed* ▤ *AE, DC, MC, V* ❢❙ *BP.*

$$ 🖼 **Hotel delle Arti.** If you're looking for a small hotel with lots of character, this place is perfect. Just down the street from Piazza Santissima Annunziata, one of Florence's prettiest Renaissance squares, the unobtrusive entrance (it looks like a well-appointed town house) leads to a reception room that feels like a small, intimate living room. Rooms are simply but elegantly furnished with pale, pastel walls, muted fabrics, and polished hardwood floors. Breakfast is taken on the top floor, and a small

terrace provides city views. The highly capable staff is completely fluent in English. ⊠ *Via dei Servi 38/a, near Santissima Annunziata, 50122* ☎ *055/2645307* 🖷 *055/290140* ⊕ *www.hoteldellearti.it* 🛏 *9 rooms* ⚷ *Minibars, cable TV, dry cleaning, laundry service, business services, some pets allowed (fee)* 🖃 *AE, DC, MC, V* ❘❂❘ *BP.*

$$ 🏨 **Loggiato dei Serviti.** Though the hotel was not designed by Brunelleschi, it might as well have been; it's a mirror image of the architect's famous Spedale degli Innocenti across the way. Occupying a 16th-century former convent building, this was once an inn for traveling priests. Vaulted ceilings, tester canopy beds, and rich fabrics help make this spare Renaissance building with modern comforts a find. The Loggiato is on one of the city's loveliest squares. ⊠ *Piazza Santissima Annunziata 3, 50122* ☎ *055/289592* 🖷 *055/289595* ⊕ *www.loggiatodeiservitihotel.it* 🛏 *38 rooms* ⚷ *In-room safes, minibars, cable TV, in-room data ports, bar, babysitting, dry cleaning, laundry service, parking (fee), some pets allowed* 🖃 *AE, DC, MC, V* ❘❂❘ *BP.*

$-$$ 🏨 **Antica Dimora Firenze.** Each room in the intimate *residenza* (a residence property, this one opened in May 2004) is painted a different pastel color—peach, rose, powder blue. Simple, homey furnishings (that could be your grandmother's handmade quilt on the bed) and double-glazed windows ensure a peaceful night's sleep. You might ask for one of the rooms that has a small private terrace; if you contemplate a longer stay, one of their well-located apartments might suit. Coffee and tea, available all day in the sitting room, are on the house. Note that the staff goes home at 7 PM. ⊠ *Via San Gallo 72, near San Marco, 50129* ☎ *055/4627296* 🖷 *055/4634450* ⊕ *www.anticadimorafirenze.it* 🛏 *6 rooms* ⚷ *In-room safes, minibars, refrigerators, cable TV, in-room data ports, Wi-Fi* 🖃 *No credit cards* ❘❂❘ *BP.*

$ 🏨 **Residenza Johanna I.** Savvy travelers and those on a budget know the Johanna I has a tremendous price-to-location ratio. Here you're very much in the centro storico. Rooms have high ceilings, traditional furniture (iron beds, wooden desks), and bedspreads done in pastel floral prints. Morning tea and coffee (but no breakfast) are taken in one's room. You're given a large set of keys to let yourself in, as the staff goes home at 7 PM. ⊠ *Via Bonifacio Lupi 14, near San Marco, 50129* ☎ *055/481896* 🖷 *055/482721* ⊕ *www.johanna.it* 🛏 *11 rooms* ⚷ *Fans, parking (fee); no a/c, no room phones, no room TVs* 🖃 *No credit cards* ❘❂❘ *EP.*

FodorsChoice
★

Santa Maria Novella to the Arno

$$$$ 🏨 **JK Place.** Ori Kafri, the manager of this boutique hotel, refers to it as a house, and indeed it is a sumptuously appointed home away from home. A library serves as the reception room; buffet breakfast is laid out on a gleaming chestnut table in an interior atrium. Soothing earth tones prevail in the rooms, some of which have chandeliers, others canopied beds. A secluded rooftop terrace makes a perfect setting for an aperitivo, as do the ground-floor sitting rooms with large, pillow-piled couches. The Lounge restaurant ($$$–$$$$) offers Tuscan classics with a dash of fantasy. A stellar staff caters to every need. ⊠ *Piazza Santa Maria Novella 7, Santa Maria Novella 50123* ☎ *055/2645181* 🖷 *055/2658387* ⊕ *www.jkplace.com* 🛏 *14 doubles, 6 suites* ⚷ *In-room safes, minibars, cable TV, in-room VCRs, in-room data ports, Wi-Fi,*

FodorsChoice
★

bar, babysitting, dry cleaning, laundry service, concierge, parking (fee), some pets allowed ⊟ AE, DC, MC, V ⫟⦿⫟ BP.

$$$ ⊞ **Antica Torre di Via Tornabuoni.** If you're looking for the proverbial view, stop here, where just about every room has a window that frames the awe-inspiring Duomo or the Arno (some even have small terraces). When it's warm, you can sit on the rooftop terrace with a glass of wine and enjoy a 360-degree panorama. The tastefully furnished rooms, with their high ceilings and sweeping draperies, create a fine backdrop for historic Florence. This is the perfect place if you desire luxe privacy; since it's a residenza, the staff goes home at 7 PM. Charming host Jacopo d'Albasio strives to ensure that all his guests are not only happy, but yearn to come back. ⊠ *Via Tornabuoni 1, near Santa Maria Novella, 50122* ☎ *055/2658161* 🖷 *055/218841* ⊕ *www.tornabuoni1.com* ⫟ *11 rooms, 1 suite* ♿ *In-room safes, minibars, cable TV, in-room data ports, bar, meeting rooms, parking (fee), some pets allowed* ⊟*AE, DC, MC, V* ⫟⦿⫟*EP.*

★ $$–$$$ ⊞ **Beacci Tornabuoni.** Florentine pensioni do not come any more classic than this one in a 14th-century palazzo. There's an old-fashioned grace, and enough modern comforts. Wallpaper or tapestry-like wall hangings make rooms inviting. The sitting room has a large fireplace, and the terrace has a tremendous view of some major Florentine monuments, such as the church of Santa Trinita. On Monday, Wednesday, and Friday nights May–October, the dining room ($$–$$$) opens to serve Tuscan specialties on a lovely, flower-strewn terrace. ⊠ *Via Tornabuoni 3, near Santa Maria Novella, 50123* ☎ *055/212645* 🖷 *055/283594* ⊕ *www.tornabuonihotels.com* ⫟ *28 rooms* ♿ *Dining room, minibars, cable TV, bar, babysitting, dry cleaning, laundry service, Internet room, parking (fee), some pets allowed* ⊟ *AE, DC, MC, V* ⫟⦿⫟ *BP.*

$$ ⊞ **Torre Guelfa.** Enter this hidden hotel through an immense wooden door on a narrow street, and continue through the iron gate and up a few steps to an elevator that takes you to the third floor. A few more steps and you're in a 13th-century Florentine *torre* (tower) that once protected the fabulously wealthy Acciaiuoli family. Now it's one of the best-located small hotels in Florence. Each guest room is different—some with canopied beds, some with balconies. Those on a budget might want to consider one of the six less-expensive rooms on the second floor that have no TVs. ⊠*Borgo Santi Apostoli 8, near Santa Maria Novella, 50123.* ☎ *055/2396338* 🖷 *055/2398577* ⊕ *www.hoteltorreguelfa.com* ⫟ *24 rooms, 2 suites* ♿ *Some in-room safes, Wi-Fi, babysitting, dry cleaning, laundry service, parking (fee), some pets allowed; no TV in some rooms* ⊟ *AE, MC, V* ⫟⦿⫟ *BP.*

$–$$ ⊞ **Alessandra.** The building, known as the Palazzo Roselli del Turco, was designed in 1507 by Baccio d'Agnolo, a contemporary of Michelangelo's. Though little remains of the original design save for the high wood ceilings, there's still an aura of grandeur in the ample rooms. Several have views of the Arno; the sole suite is spacious. Friendly hosts Anna and Andrea Gennarini speak fluent English. The location, a block from the Ponte Vecchio, helps make this a good choice. ⊠ *Borgo Santi Apostoli 17, near Santa Maria Novella, 50123* ☎ *055/283438* 🖷 *055/210619* ⊕*www.hotelalessandra.com* ⫟*26 rooms, 19 with bath; 1 suite; 1 apartment* ♿ *In-room safes, some minibars, cable TV, in-room data* ports, Wi-Fi, babysitting, dry cleaning, laundry service, parking (fee) 🚫 AE, MC, V ☺ Closed Dec. 10–26 ⦿ BP.

$–$$ 🏨 **Bellettini.** You're in good hands at this small, three-floor pensione run by sisters Marzia and Gina Naldini and their husbands. Public rooms are simple but comfortable; the good-size guest rooms have Venetian or Tuscan provincial decor; bathrooms are bright and modern. The top floor has two rooms with a view, and a handful of triples and quadruples make this the perfect place for families or friends traveling together. There's an ample buffet breakfast, including tasty homemade cakes. ✉ Via dei Conti 7, near Santa Maria Novella, 50123 ☎ 055/213561 🖷 055/283551 ⊕ www.hotelbellettini.com ⇨ 28 rooms ⚘ In-room safes, minibars, cable TV, in-room broadband, bar, parking (fee), some pets allowed 🚫 AE, DC, MC, V ⦿ BP.

$ 🏨 **Pensione Ferretti.** Minutes away from Piazza Santa Maria Novella, this pensione has views onto the tiny piazza containing the Croce al Trebbio, as well as easy access to the historic center. English-speaking owner Luciano Michel and his South Africa–born wife, Sue, do just about anything to make you feel at home (including providing 24-hour, free Internet access). Ceiling fans make warmer months more bearable. Though it's housed in a 16th-century palazzo, accommodations are no-frills. ✉ Via delle Belle Donne 17, near Santa Maria Novella, 50123 ☎ 055/2381328 🖷 055/219288 ⊕ www.emmeti.it/Hferretti ⇨ 16 rooms, 6 with bath; 1 apartment ⚘ Fans, Internet room, parking (fee), some pets allowed; no a/c, no room TVs 🚫 AE, DC, MC, V ⦿ BP.

The Oltrarno

$$$$ 🏨 **Lungarno.** Many rooms and suites here have private terraces that jut out over the Arno, affording sumptuous views of the palaces that line the river. Four suites in the 13th-century tower retain details like exposed stone walls and old archways; they face onto a little square with a medieval tower covered in jasmine. The very chic decor approximates a breezily wealthy home, with lots of crisp white fabrics with blue trim. A wall of windows and a sea of white couches make the lobby bar one of the nicest places in the city to stop for a drink. The Lungarno Suites, across the river, are apartment-like lodgings that have kitchens. ✉ Borgo San Jacopo 14, Lungarno South, 50125 ☎ 055/27261 🖷 055/268437 ⊕ www.lungarnohotels.com ⇨ 60 rooms, 13 suites ⚘ Restaurant, in-room fax, cable TV with movies, in-room data ports, Wi-Fi, bar, babysitting, dry cleaning, laundry service, concierge, meeting rooms, parking (fee) 🚫 AE, DC, MC, V ⦿ BP.

$$ 🏨 **Albergo La Scaletta.** For a tremendous view of the Boboli Garden, near the Ponte Vecchio and Palazzo Pitti, come to this exquisite pensione run by a mother-and-son team. It has simply furnished yet rather large rooms and a sunny breakfast room. In warm weather two flower-bedecked terraces are open, one with a stunning 360-degree view of Florence. ✉ Via Guicciardini 13, near Palazzo Pitti, 50125 ☎ 055/283028 🖷 055/289562 ⊕ www.hotellascaletta.it ⇨ 11 rooms, 10 with bath ⚘ Cable TV, parking (fee), some pets allowed 🚫 MC, V ⦿ BP.

Santa Croce

★ $$$$ 🏨 **Monna Lisa.** Housed in a 15th-century palazzo, with parts of the building dating from the 13th century, this hotel retains some of its original wood-coffered ceilings from the 1500s, as well as its original marble staircase. Though some rooms are small, they are tastefully decorated, each with different floral wallpaper. The public rooms retain a 19th-century aura, and the intimate bar, with its red velveteen wallpaper, is a good place to unwind. ⊠ *Borgo Pinti 27, near Santa Croce, 50121* ☎ *055/2479751* 🖷*055/2479755* ⊕*www.monnalisa.it* ↩*45 rooms* ⏆*In-room safes, minibars, cable TV, bar, babysitting, dry cleaning, laundry service, concierge, parking (fee), some pets allowed* ▤ *AE, DC, MC, V* ⫯◎⫯ *BP.*

$$$–$$$$ 🏨 **J&J.** Cavernous suites in the 16th-century convent are ideal for honeymooners, families, and small groups of friends. Some are bi-level, and many are imaginatively arranged around the central courtyard. The smaller rooms are more intimate, some opening onto a little shared courtyard. Some bathrooms have been refitted with pale travertine tiles. The gracious owners enjoy chatting in the light and airy lounge; breakfast is served in a glassed-in Renaissance loggia or in the central courtyard. ⊠ *Via di Mezzo 20, near Santa Croce, 50121* ☎ *055/26312* 🖷 *055/240282* ⊕ *www.cavalierehotels.com* ↩ *19 rooms, 7 suites* ⏆ *Cable TV, in-room data ports, bar, babysitting, dry cleaning, laundry service, parking (fee)* ▤ *AE, DC, MC, V* ⫯◎⫯ *BP.*

¢ 🏨 **Albergo Losanna.** Most major sights are within walking distance of this tiny pensione just within the Viale, the edge of the city center. Though dated and a little worn around the edges, the property is impeccably clean and the rooms have high ceilings; the mother and son who run the place are enthusiastic and cordial. Try to get a room facing away from the street; you won't have a view but you can get a quiet night's sleep. ⊠ *Via V. Alfieri 9, near Santa Croce, 50121* ☎🖷*055/245840* ⊕ *www.albergolosanna.com* ↩ *8 rooms, 3 with bath* ⏆ *Parking (fee); no a/c in some rooms, no room TVs* ▤ *AE, MC, V* ⫯◎⫯ *BP.*

¢ 🏨 **Istituto Oblate dell'Assunzione.** Twelve nuns run this perfectly situated convent just minutes from the Duomo. Rooms are spotless and simple; some of them have views of the cupola, and others look out onto a carefully tended garden where guests are encouraged to relax. Several rooms have three and four beds. Curfew is at 11:30 PM, and those of you who want to attend Mass can do so every morning at 7:30. The nuns will provide half or full pension for groups of 10 or more. ⊠ *Borgo Pinti 15, near Santa Croce, 501201* ☎ *055/2480582* 🖷 *055/2346291* ↩ *28 rooms, 22 with bath* ⏆ *Parking (fee); no a/c in some rooms, no room phones, no room TVs* ▤ *No credit cards* ⫯◎⫯ *EP.*

Outside the City

★ $$–$$$ 🏨 **Villa Poggio San Felice.** Livia Puccinelli Sannini, the descendant of a famed 19th-century Florentine hotelier, and her husband, Lorenzo Magnelli, have turned the family's former country villa (documented to the 15th century) into a lovely hotel 5 km (3 mi) southwest of the city limits. With only five rooms available, the villa still feels like a single-family dwelling. Some of the high-ceiling rooms have divine views of Brunelleschi's cupola below, others have working fireplaces. The landscaped gardens help make a stay here serene. Though there is daily shuttle service to the center of town, a car is vital. ⊠ *Via San Matteo in Arcetri 24, Lungarno South, 50125* ☎ *055/220016* 🖷 *055/2335388* ⊕ *www.*

villapoggiosanfelice.com 4 rooms, 1 suite Golf privileges, pool, wading pool, babysitting, laundry service, Internet room, free parking, some pets allowed = AE, MC, V Closed Jan. 10–Feb. 28 BP.

NIGHTLIFE & THE ARTS

The Arts

Florence is justifiably famous for its musical offerings. The annual Maggio Musicale attracts the best international talent. Theaters also host visiting American rock stars and cabaret performers. Opera, ballet, and concerts occur regularly throughout the year at different venues in town. Major traveling art exhibitions are mounted at Palazzo Strozzi throughout the year. There's a little publication available at bars and hotels called *Informacittà* (www.informacittafirenze.it): even though it's in Italian, it's pretty easy to read for event times and addresses.

Film

You can find movie listings in *La Nazione*, the daily Florentine newspaper. Note that most American films are dubbed into Italian rather than subtitled. The **Odeon** (Piazza Strozzi, near Piazza della Repubblica 055/214068 www.cinehall.it) shows first-run English-language films on Monday, Tuesday, and Thursday at its magnificent art deco theater.

Concerts & Operas

The **Teatro Comunale** (Corso Italia 16, Lungarno North 055/213535) hosts the opera season September–December, as well as concerts, festivals, and dance performances throughout the year.

Teatro della Pergola (Via della Pergola 18/32, box office Via Alamanni 39, near Santissima Annunziata 055/2264316 www.pergola.firenze.it) hosts classical concerts, Maggio Musicale events, and other dramatic performances.

★ The **Maggio Musicale Fiorentino** (055/213535 www.maggiofiorentino.com) is a series of internationally acclaimed concerts and dance, ballet, and opera performances running May and June in venues across the city. Tickets can be purchased online and at the Teatro Comunale box office.

October to April is the concert season for the **Orchestra della Toscana** (Via Alamanni 39, near Santa Croce 055/210804 www.orchestradellatoscana.it), with performances staged at the Teatro Verdi. **Amici della Musica** (055/210804 www.amicimusica.fi.it) organizes classical concerts at the Teatro della Pergola.

Nightlife

Florentines are rather proud of their nightlife. Most bars have some sort of happy hour, which usually lasts for many hours, often accompanied by substantial snacks. Dance clubs typically don't open until very late in the evening and don't get crowded until 1 or 2 in the morning. Cover charges are steep, but it's fairly easy to find free passes in trendier bars around town. Most clubs are closed either Sunday or Monday.

Bars

Zona 15 (✉ Piazza Brunelleschi, Via del Castellaccia 53–55/r, near Duomo ☎ 055/211678) is coolly chic with its pale interior, blond woodwork, and metallic surfaces. Lunch, dinner, cocktails, and brunch are on offer for Florentine cognoscenti and others. The oh-so-cool—bordering on pretentious—vibe at **La Dolce Vita** (✉ Piazza del Carmine 6/r, near Santo Spirito ☎ 055/284595) attracts Florentines and the occasional visiting American movie star.

Negroni (✉ Via dei Renai 17/r, near San Niccolò ☎ 055/243647) teems with well-dressed young Florentines at happy hour. **Zoe** (✉ Via dei Renai 13/r, near San Niccolò ☎ 055/243111) calls itself a café, and although coffee may indeed be served, twentysomething Florentines flock here for the fine (and expensive) cocktails.

i Visacci (✉ Borgo Albizi 80/r near Santa Croce ☎ 055/2001956) serves coffee and tasty panini throughout the day, and delivers cocktails with zing at aperitivo time.

Fusion Bar (✉ Vicolo dell'Oro 5, near Santa Maria Novella ☎ 055/27263) is the in-house bar of the Gallery Art Hotel. Beautiful folk come here to sip expensive cocktails and to snack on sushi. **Moyo** (✉ Via de'Benci 23/r, near Santa Croce ☎ 055/2479738) opened in December 2004; high ceilings, dramatic lighting, and superb aperitivi (with equally superb snacks) draw trendy Florentines. They also serve a respectable lunch until 5 PM. **Rex** (✉ Via Fiesolana 23–25/r, near Santa Croce ☎ 055/2480331) attracts a trendy, artsy clientele. **Sant'Ambrogio Caffè** (✉ Piazza Sant'Ambrogio 7–8/r, near Santa Croce ☎ 055/241035) has outdoor summer seating with a view of an 11th-century church (Sant'Ambrogio) directly across the street. When last call's come and gone and you're not finished with your evening, go where the bartenders unwind after their shift: **Loch Ness** (✉ Via de' Benci 19/r, near Santa Croce) pours drinks there until 5 AM. For a swanky experience lubricated with trademark Bellinis and fine martinis, head to **Harry's Bar** (✉ Lungarno Vespucci 22/r, Lungarno North ☎ 055/2396700).

Nightclubs

Yab (✉ Via Sassetti 5/r, near Piazza della Repubblica ☎ 055/215160) is one of the largest clubs; it attracts a young clientele. **Maracaná** (✉ Via Faenza 4, near Santa Maria Novella ☎ 055/210298) is a restaurant and pizzeria featuring Brazilian specialties; at 11 PM it transforms itself into a cabaret floor show and then it opens the floor to dancing. Book a table if you want to eat. If you had a transvestite grandmother, her home would look like **Montecarla** (✉ Via de' Bardi 2, near San Niccolò ☎ 055/2340259). On its two crowded floors people sip cocktails against a backdrop of exotic flowers, leopard-print chairs and chintz, and red walls and floors.

Jazz Club (✉ Via Nuova de' Caccini 3, at Borgo Pinti, near Santa Croce ☎ 055/2479700) puts on live music in a smoky basement.

SHOPPING

Since the days of the medieval guilds, Florence has been synonymous with fine craftsmanship and good business. Such time-honored Florentine specialties as antiques (and reproductions), bookbinding, jewelry, lace, paper products, leather goods, and silks attest to this. The various shopping areas are mostly a throwback to the Middle Ages, when each district supplied a different product. The Ponte Vecchio houses reputable but very expensive jewelry shops, as it has since the 16th century. The area around Santa Croce is the heart of the leather merchants' district. The fanciest clothing designers are mainly on Via Tornabuoni and Via della Vigna Nuova. There's a large concentration of antiques shops on Borgo Ognissanti and near Santo Spirito. Across the river in the Oltrarno, there's also a variety of artisans—goldsmiths, leather workers, and antique furniture restorers—plying their trade.

Shops are generally open 9–1 and 3:30–7:30 and are closed Sunday and Monday morning most of the year. Summer (June–September) hours are usually 9–1 and 4–8, and some shops close Saturday afternoon instead of Monday morning. When looking for addresses of shops, notice the two-color numbering system: the red numbers are commercial addresses; the blue or black numbers are residential.

Markets

Roam through the stalls under the loggia of the **Mercato Nuovo** (⊠ Via Por Santa Maria and Via Porta Rossa, near Piazza della Repubblica) for cheery, inexpensive trinkets. In the huge, two-story **Mercato Centrale** (⊠ Off Via Nazionale, near San Lorenzo ☉ Mon.–Sat. 7–2), food is everywhere, some of it remarkably exotic. The ground floor contains meat and cheese stalls, as well as some very good bars selling panini, and the second floor teems with vegetable stands. If you're looking for dill or mangoes in Florence, this is most likely where you'll find them. In the streets next to the church of San Lorenzo, shop for bargains at stalls full of clothing and leather goods that are part of the **Mercato di San Lorenzo**.

The flea market on **Piazza dei Ciompi** (⊠ Sant'Ambrogio, near Santa Croce) takes place on the last Sunday of the month. An open-air produce and flea market is held in **Le Cascine park** (⊠ Off Viale Fratelli Rosselli, near Santa Maria Novella), just before the Ponte della Vittoria, every Tuesday morning.

Specialty Stores

Antiques
Giovanni Pratesi (⊠ Via Maggio 13, near Santo Spirito ☎ 055/2396568) specializes in furniture, with some fine paintings, sculpture, and decorative objects turning up from time to time. Vying with Luigi Bellini as one of Florence's oldest antiques dealers, **Guido Bartolozzi** (⊠ Via Maggio 18/r, near Santo Spirito ☎ 055/215602) sells predominately period Florentine pieces. **Galleria Luigi Bellini** (⊠ Lungarno Soderini 5, Lungarno South ☎ 055/214031) claims to be Italy's oldest antiques dealer, which

may be true, since father Mario Bellini was responsible for instituting Florence's international antiques biennial.

Books & Paper
Libreria d'Arte Galleria degli Uffizi (⊠ Piazzale degli Uffizi 6, near Piazza della Signoria ☎☎ 055/284508) carries monographs on famous artists, some of whose work can be found in the Uffizi; it also carries scholarly works from both the Italian and anglophone worlds. Long one of Florence's best art-book shops, **Libreria Salimbeni** (⊠Via Matteo Palmieri 14–16/r, near Santa Croce ☎ 055/2340905) has an outstanding selection.

Alberto Cozzi (⊠ Via del Parione 35/r, near Santa Maria Novella ☎ 055/294968) keeps an extensive line of Florentine papers and paper products. On-site artisans rebind and restore books and works on paper. One of Florence's oldest paper-goods stores, **Giulio Giannini e Figlio** (⊠ Piazza Pitti 37/r ☎ 055/212621) is *the* place to buy the marbleized stock, which comes in many shapes and sizes, from flat sheets to boxes and even pencils. Photograph albums, frames, diaries, and other objects dressed in handmade paper can be purchased at **Il Torchio** (⊠ Via dei Bardi 17, San Niccolò ☎ 055/2342862 ⊕ www.legatoriailtorchio.com). The stuff is of high quality, and the prices are lower than usual. **La Tartaruga** (⊠ Borgo Albizi 60/r, Santa Croce ☎ 055/2340845) sells brightly colored, recycled paper in lots of guises (such as calendars and stationery), as well as toys for children.

Ceramics
The mother-daughter team of Antonella Chini and Lorenza Adami sell their Florentine-inspired ceramic designs, based on Antonella's extensive ceramics training in Faenza, at **Sbigoli Terrecotte** (⊠ Via Sant'Egidio 4/r, near Santa Croce ☎ 055/2479713). They carry traditional Tuscan terra-cotta and ceramic vases, pots, and cups and saucers. **Rampini Ceramiche** (⊠ Borgo Ognissanti 32/34, Lungarno North ☎ 055/219720) sells exquisitely crafted ceramics in various patterns, shapes, and sizes.

Clothing
The usual fashion gurus—such as Prada and Armani—all have shops in Florence; more and more of Via Tornabuoni resembles a giant *passarella* (catwalk). If you want to buy Florentine haute fashion while in Florence, stick to Pucci, Gucci, Ferragamo, and Roberto Cavalli, all of which call Florence home.

Florentine **Patrizia Pepe** (⊠ Piazza San Giovanni 12/r, near Duomo ☎ 055/2645056) has body-conscious clothes perfect for all ages, especially for women with a tiny streak of rebelliousness. For cutting-edge fashion, the fun and funky window displays at **Spazio A** (⊠ Via Porta Rossa 109–115/r, Piazza della Repubblica ☎ 055/212995 ⊕ www.aeffe.com) merit a stop. The shop carries such well-known designers as Alberta Ferretti and Narciso Rodriguez, as well as lesser-known Italian, English, and French designers. **Bernardo** (⊠ Via Porta Rossa 87/r, near Piazza della Repubblica ☎ 055/283333) specializes in men's trousers, cashmere sweaters, and shirts with details like mother-of-pearl buttons. At **L'essentiel** (⊠ Via del Corso 10/r, near Piazza della Signoria ☎ 055/294713) Lara Caldieron has spun her club-going years into fashion that also works well on the street and

VOICES OF ITALY

Valentino Adami
ceramics shop owner,
Santa Croce area

Since 1970, Valentino Adami, a native of southern Tuscany who has lived all over the world, and his wife, Antonella Chini, a Florentine, have been owners of the ceramics shop Sbigoli Terrecotte. The operation is a family affair: Antonella studied in Faenza, the ceramics center in Emilia-Romagna, and daughter Lorenza holds two certificates in ceramics. Most days, they can be found in the back of the shop, painting vases. Valentino and daughter Chiara run the front of the store, two plain rooms bursting with colorful objects—vases, espresso cups, plates, and patio tables.

Valentino explains what makes Italian ceramics distinctive: "First of all, it's the type of clay we use. The clay we find here is softer. We fire it at a lower temperature, 950°C. You

get better color if you fire it at a lower temperature."

The use of color is crucial. "The color of the sun, of the sea—it gives us confidence with color. Our colors are similar to what the Renaissance masters used, only we don't use lead. Like those Renaissance masters, we used to fire with wood. It would take three or four days. Now we use an electric kiln."

According to Valentino, works from major ceramics-making areas within Italy can be distinguished both by color and type of design. "The farther you go south, you'll find that the colors are stronger. Deruta [in Umbria] makes one kind of ceramics, and Montelupo [near Florence] another. The main difference in ceramics from Faenza is that they use faces and produce lots of hunting scenes. In Florence, it's more geometric. Our portraits are rougher compared to Faenza."

in the office. Though it may seem American, **Diesel** (⊠ Via dei Lamberti 13/r, near Piazza della Signoria ☎ 055/2399963) started in Vicenza; its gear is on the "must-have" list of many self-respecting Italian teens.

The aristocratic Marchese di Barsento, **Emilio Pucci** (⊠ Via Tornabuoni 20–22/r, near Santa Maria Novella ☎ 055/2658082), became an international name in the late 1950s when the stretch ski clothes he designed for himself caught on with the dolce vita crowd—his pseudopsychedelic prints and "palazzo pajamas" became all the rage. You can take home a custom-made suit or dress from **Giorgio Vannini** (⊠ Borgo Santi Apostoli 43/r, near Santa Maria Novella ☎ 055/293037), who also has a showroom for his prêt-à-porter designs. **Prada** (⊠ Via Tornabuoni 51–53/r, near Santa Maria Novella ☎ 055/267471 ⊠ Outlet ⊠ Levanella Spacceo, Estrada Statale 69, Montevarchi ☎ 055/91911) appeals to an exclusive clientele. Cognoscenti will drive or taxi about 45 minutes out of town to the Prada Outlet. Native son **Roberto Cavalli** (⊠ Via Tornabuoni 83/r, near Santa Maria Novella ☎ 055/2396226), whose outlandish designs appeal to Hollywood celebrities and those who want to look like more expensive versions of Britney Spears, has a corner shop with a trendy café attached.

Geraldine Tayar (✉ Sdrucciolo de Pitti 6/r, Palazzo Pitti ☎ 055/290405) makes clothing and accessories of her own design in eclectic fabric combinations. **Piccolo Slam** (✉ Via de'Neri 9/11r, near Santa Croce ☎ 055/214504) has classic styles for members of the junior set.

Embroidery & Linens

Sumptuous silks, beaded fabrics, lace, wool, and tweeds can be purchased at **Valli** (✉ Via Strozzi 4/r, near Piazza della Repubblica ☎ 055/282485). It carries fabrics created by Armani, Valentino, and other high-end designers.

Antico Setificio Fiorentino (✉ via Bartolini 4 Lungarno South ☎ 055/213 861) has been furnishing lavish silks to international royalty for years; a visit is well worth it, as is making an appointment beforehand.

Loretta Caponi (✉ Piazza Antinori 4/r, near Santa Maria Novella ☎ 055/213668) is synonymous with Florentine embroidery, and her luxury lace, linens, and lingerie have earned her worldwide renown.

Food

Conti (✉ Mercato Centrale, enter at Via Signa, near San Lorenzo ☎ 055/2398501) sells top-quality wines, olive oils, and dried fruits; they'll shrink-wrap the highest-quality dried porcini for traveling. **La Bottega dell'Olio** (✉ Piazza del Limbo 2/r, near Santa Maria Novella ☎ 055/2670468) sells a great collection of fine olive oil, as well as bath products made from olive oil. **Antico Salumificio Anzuini-Massi** (✉ Via de'Neri 84/r, near Santa Croce ☎ 055/294901) shrink-wraps their own pork products, making it a snap to take home some *salame di cinghiale* (wild boar salami).

Fragrances

Antica Officina del Farmacista Dr. Vranjes (✉ Borgo La Croce 44/r, near Santa Croce ☎ 055/241748 ✉ Via San Gallo 63/r, near San Marco ☎ 055/494537) makes aromatic oils and perfumes for people and for spaces. The essence of a Florentine holiday is captured in the sachets of the **Officina Profumo Farmaceutica di Santa Maria Novella** (✉ Via della Scala 16, near Santa Maria Novella ☎ 055/216276), a turn-of-the-19th-century emporium of herbal cosmetics and soaps that are made following centuries-old recipes created by friars.

> **WORD OF MOUTH**
>
> "Officina Profumo di Farmaceutica Santa Maria Novella is the grandest perfume salon in the world."
> –ThinGorjus

Jewelry

Carlo Piccini (✉ Ponte Vecchio 31/r, near Piazza della Signoria ☎ 055/292030) has sold antique jewelry as well as made pieces to order for several generations; you can also get old jewelry reset. **Cassetti** (✉ Ponte Vecchio 54/r, near Piazza della Signoria ☎ 055/2396028) combines precious and semiprecious stones and metals in contemporary settings.

Gatto Bianco (✉ Borgo Santi Apostoli 12/r, near Santa Maria Novella ☎ 055/282989) has breathtakingly beautiful jewelry worked in semiprecious and precious stones; the look is completely contemporary. **Gherardi** (✉ Ponte Vecchio 5/r, near Piazza della Signoria ☎ 055/211809), Florence's king of coral, has the city's largest selection of finely crafted pieces, as well as cultured pearls, jade, and turquoise.

Oro Due (✉ Via Lambertesca 12/r, near Piazza della Signoria ☎ 055/292 143) sells gold jewelry the old-fashioned way: beauteous objects are priced according to the level of craftsmanship and the price of gold bullion that day. **Studio Ballerino** (✉ Borgo Allegri 25/r, near Santa Croce ☎ 055/234 4658) has one-of-a-kind pieces crafted in semiprecious stone, gold, and silver. One of Florence's oldest jewelers, **Tiffany** (✉ Via Tornabuoni 25/r, near Santa Maria Novella ☎ 055/215506), has supplied Italian (and other) royalty with finely crafted gems for centuries. Its selection of antique-looking classics has been updated with a choice of contemporary silver.

Shoes & Leather Accessories

Furla (✉ Via Calzaiuoli 47/r, near Piazza della Repubblica ☎ 055/2382883) makes beautiful leather bags and wallets in up-to-the-minute designs. **Pollini** (✉ Via Calimala 12/r, near Piazza della Repubblica ☎ 055/214738) has beautifully crafted shoes and leather accessories for those willing to pay that little bit extra. For sheer creativity in both color and design, check out the shoes at **Sergio Rossi** (✉ Via Roma 15/r, near Duomo ☎ 055/294873) and fantasize about having a life to go with them.

Cellerini (✉ Via del Sole 37/r, near Santa Maria Novella ☎ 055/282533) is a Florentine institution in a city where it seems that nearly everybody is wearing an expensive leather jacket. Born near Naples, the late Salvatore **Ferragamo** (✉ Via Tornabuoni 2/r, near Santa Maria Novella ☎ 055/292123) earned his fortune custom-making shoes for famous feet, especially Hollywood stars'. The elegant store, in a 13th-century Renaissance palazzo, also displays designer clothing and accessories in addition to shoes. Though the Florentine family is no longer involved with the store that bears its name, **Gucci** (✉ Via Tornabuoni 73/r, near Santa Maria Novella ☎ 055/264011) still manages to draw a crowd. **Il Bisonte** (✉ Via del Parione 31/r, off Via della Vigna Nuova, near Santa Maria Novella ☎ 055/215722) is known for its natural-looking leather goods, all stamped with the store's bison symbol.

Madova (✉ Via Guicciardini 1/r, near Palazzo Pitti ☎ 055/2396526) has a rainbow of high-quality leather gloves. **Paolo Carandini** (✉ Via de' Macci 73/r, near Santa Croce ☎ 055/245397) works exclusively in leather, producing exquisite objects such as picture frames, jewelry boxes, and desk accessories. The **Scuola del Cuoio** (✉ Piazza Santa Croce 16 ☎ 055/244533 ⊕ www.leatherschool.com), in the former dormitory of Santa Croce, is a consortium for leather workers who ply their trade and sell their wares on the premises. **Giotti** (✉ Piazza Ognissanti 3–4/r, Lungarno North ☎ 055/294265) has a full line of leather goods and leather clothing.

SIDE TRIPS FROM FLORENCE

West of Florence, and easily accessible by car or train, is Pisa, the town known the world over for its great engineering mistake, the Leaning Tower. North of Pisa, and also a quick shot from Florence, is the relaxed, elegant town of Lucca, which feels like its own little world, surrounded by 16th-century ramparts that have been transformed into parklike promenades. Pisa's tower is definitely worth seeing—and there's more to see than just the tower—but ultimately Lucca has greater charms, making it a better choice if you're picking one for an overnight.

PISA

When you think Pisa, you think Leaning Tower. Its position as one of Italy's most famous landmarks is a heavy reputation to bear, and it comes accompanied by abundant crowds and kitschy souvenirs. But the building *is* interesting and novel, and even if it doesn't captivate you, Pisa has other treasures that make a visit worthwhile. Taken as a whole, the Campo dei Miracoli (Field of Miracles), where the Leaning Tower, Duomo, and Baptistery are located, is among the most dramatic architectural ensembles in Italy.

Pisa may have been inhabited as early as the Bronze Age. It was certainly populated by the Etruscans and, in turn, became part of the Roman Empire. In the early Middle Ages it flourished as an economic powerhouse—along with Amalfi, Genoa, and Venice, it was one of the maritime republics. The city's economic and political power ebbed in the early 15th century as it fell under the domination of Florence, though it enjoyed a brief resurgence under Cosimo I in the mid-16th century. Pisa endured heavy Allied bombing—miraculously, the Duomo and Leaning Tower, along with some other grand Romanesque structures, were spared, though the Camposanto sustained heavy damage.

Exploring Pisa

Pisa is 84 km (52 mi) west of Florence. Like many other Italian cities, the town is best seen on foot. The views along the Arno are particularly grand and shouldn't be missed—there's a sense of spaciousness here that the Arno in Florence lacks. You should weigh the different options for combination tickets to sights on the Piazza del Duomo when you begin your visit. Combination tickets are sold at each sight (one monument costs €5, two monuments €6, up to €10.50 for all the main sights, excluding the Leaning Tower).

The Main Attractions

② **Battistero.** The Gothic baptistery, which stands across from the Duomo's facade, is best known for the pulpit carved by Nicola Pisano in 1260. Ask one of the ticket takers if he'll sing for you inside the baptistery: the acoustics are remarkable (a tip of €3 is appropriate). ⊠ *Piazza del Duomo, Campo dei Miracoli* ☎ *050/3872210* ⊕ *www.opapisa.it* ☎ *€5* ⊙ *Apr.–Sept., daily 8–8; Oct., daily 9–7; Nov.–Feb., daily 10–5; Mar., daily 9–6.*

❸ **Duomo.** Pisa's cathedral was the first building to use the horizontal marble stripe motif (borrowed from Moorish architecture in the 11th century) common to Tuscan cathedrals. It's famous for the Romanesque panels depicting the life of Christ on the transept door facing the tower and for its expertly carved 14th-century pulpit by Giovanni Pisano. ⊠ *Piazza del Duomo, Campo dei Miracoli* ☎ *050/3872210* ⊕ *www.opapisa. it* ☎ *€2, Oct.–Mar. free* ⊙ *Apr.–Sept., daily 10–8; Oct., daily 10–7; Nov.–Feb., daily 10–1 and 3–5; Mar. daily 10–6.*

★ ☙ **❹** **Leaning Tower.** The final addition to the complex comprising the Duomo, Baptistery, and the Camposanto was what is today known as the Torre Pendente (Leaning Tower). Construction started in 1174, and the lopsided settling was evident by the time work began on the third story. The tower's architects attempted to compensate by making the remaining floors slightly taller on the tilting side, but the extra weight only made the problem worse. The settling continued, to a point that by the end of the 20th century many feared it would simply topple over, despite all efforts to prop the structure up. In early 2000 the final step of restoring the tower to its original tilt of 300 years ago was executed, and it appears to have been successful. It has been firmly anchored to the earth and after years of being closed is once again open to the public for climbing. Legend holds that Galileo conducted an experiment on the nature of gravity by dropping metal balls from the top of the 187-foot-high tower; historians say this legend has no basis in fact (which is not quite to say that it is false). If you're visiting in low season (November–March), it's pretty easy to climb the tower without a reservation; if you come in high season, by all means book in advance. English-language tours are of-

> **WORD OF MOUTH**
>
> "At Pisa we discovered a peaceful haven with relatively few tourists compared with Florence, and a magnificent lawn you could actually walk and sit on. I lay down in the lovely grass and slept in the sun until I was awakened by the cool shadow of the Leaning Tower. It was magic and peaceful and beautiful." –Jo

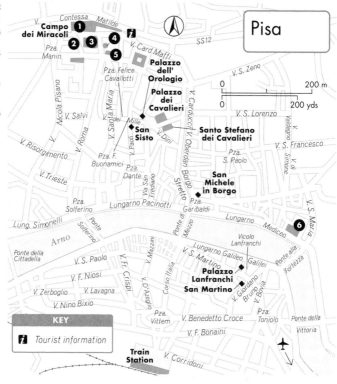

KEY

Tourist information

fered three times a day during high season. Tickets are available online 16–45 days in advance. ⊠ *Campo dei Miracoli* ☎ *050/3872210* ⊕ *www.opapisa. it* ✉ *€15* ⊘ *Mar. 21–Sept., daily 8:30–8:30; Oct., daily 9–7; Nov.–Feb., daily 9:30–5; Mar. 1–Mar. 13, daily 9–6; Mar. 14–Mar. 20, daily 10–7.*

Also Worth Seeing

① Camposanto. According to legend, this cemetery, a walled structure on the western side of the Campo dei Miracoli, is filled with earth from the Holy Land brought back by returning Crusaders. Contained within are numerous frescoes, notably the *Drunkenness of Noah* by Renaissance artist Benozzo Gozzoli and the disturbing *Triumph of Death* (14th century), whose authorship is disputed but whose subject matter shows what was on people's minds in a century that saw the ravages of the Black Death. ⊠ *Camposanto, Campo dei Miracoli* ☎ *050/3872210* ⊕ *www.opapisa.it* ✉ *€5* ⊘ *Apr.–Sept., daily 8–8; Oct., daily 9–7; Nov.–Feb., daily 10–5; Mar., daily 9–6.*

⑤ Museo dell'Opera del Duomo. At the southeast corner of the sprawling Campo dei Miracoli, a marginally interesting museum holds numerous medieval sculptures and the ancient Roman sarcophagi that inspired the figures of Nicola Pisano (circa 1220–84). ⊠ *Via Arcivescovado, Campo dei Miracoli* ☎ *050/3872210* ⊕ *www.opapisa.it* ✉ *€5* ⊘ *Apr.–Sept., daily 8–8; Oct., daily 9–7; Nov.–Feb., daily 10–5; Mar., daily 9–6.*

6 Museo Nazionale di San Matteo. On the north bank of the Arno, this museum contains wonderful early-Renaissance sculpture and a stunning reliquary by Donatello (circa 1386–1466). ⊠ *Lungarno Mediceo, Lungarni* ☎ *050/541865* 🏷 *€5* ☉ *Tues.–Sat. 8:30–7:30, Sun. 8:30–1.*

Where to Stay & Eat

$$ ✕ **La Mescita.** Tall, vaulted ceilings and stenciled walls lined with wine bottles provide the simple background at this trattoria. There's nothing basic, however, about the inventive Tuscan dishes that chef-owner Elisabetta Bauti turns out. She draws inspiration—and fresh produce—from the market outside the door. *Tagliolini al sugo e piccolo ragù di salsiccia toscano*, thin noodles with sausage and a red-wine sauce, is one option you might find on the constantly changing menu. Desserts are not to be missed, especially the *ricotta montata col cioccolato fuso* (fresh sheep's milk cheese topped with chocolate sauce). ⊠ *Via Cavalca 2, Santa Maria* ☎ *050/544294* 🖃 *AE, DC, MC, V* ☉ *Closed Mon., 3 wks in Jan., and last 3 wks in Aug. No lunch Tues.*

$–$$ ✕ **Osteria dei Cavalieri.** This charming white-wall *osteria* (a down-to-earth, tavernlike restaurant) has a versatile menu pleasing to carnivores and vegetarians alike. There are three reasonable, set-price menus—from the sea, garden, and earth—or you can order à la carte. *Piatti veloci* (fast plates) are available at lunch only. The kitchen reliably turns out grilled fish, and the *tagliata* (thin slivers of rare beef) is a treat. A lemon sorbet bathed in *prosecco* (a dry sparkling wine) or chilled vodka makes a perfect finish to your meal—even if service can be a bit rushed. ⊠ *Via San Frediano 16, off Piazza dei Cavalieri, Santa Maria* ☎ *050/580858* 🖃 *AE, DC, MC, V* ☉ *Closed Sun., July 25–Aug. 25, Dec. 29–Jan. 7. No lunch Sat.*

¢ ✕ **Vineria alla Piazza.** Translated, the name means "wine store on the square," and the food here is just as straightforward: a simple blackboard lists two or three *primi* (first courses) and secondi. When the kitchen runs out of something, a choice is erased and a new one chalked in—a sure sign the food is made-that-moment fresh. The polenta *gratinata al gorgonzola* (mixed with Gorgonzola and run briefly under the broiler) is light as a feather. ⊠ *Piazza delle Vettovaglie 13, Santa Maria* ☎ *No phone* 🕭 *Reservations not accepted* 🖃 *No credit cards* ☉ *Closed Sun.*

$$$$ 🏩 **Hotel Relais dell'Orologio.** What used to be a private family palace opened as an intimate hotel in spring of 2003. Eighteenth-century antiques fill the rooms and public spaces; some rooms have stenciled walls and wood-beam ceilings. On the third floor, sloped ceilings add romance. A large shared sitting room, complete with fireplace, provides a relaxing spot to read or sip a glass of wine. ⊠ *Via della Faggiola 12/14, off Campo dei Miracoli, Santa Maria, 56126* ☎ *050/830361* 📠 *050/ 551869* ⊕ *www.hotelrelaisorologio.com* ⇥ *16 rooms, 5 suites* ⚐ *Dining room, room service, in-room safes, minibars, refrigerators, cable TV, in-room data ports, bar, babysitting, dry cleaning, laundry service, concierge, business services, meeting rooms, parking (fee), some pets allowed, no-smoking rooms* 🖃 *AE, DC, MC, V* ❢❢ *EP.*

$–$$ 🏩 **Royal Victoria.** The Piegaja family has owned and operated the Royal Victoria since 1837—such dedication probably explains why Charles Dickens and Charles Lindbergh, among others, have stayed here in the past. The hotel faces the Arno, and though rooms are simply furnished and a bit dated, many have splendid river views. A fourth-floor terrace is a perfect spot for an *aperitivo* (aperitif) or postcard writing. The hotel's rental-car service helps provide easy access to beaches and points of interest outside town. From here it's a 10-minute walk to the Campo dei Miracoli. ⊠ *Lungarno Pacinotti 12, Lungarni, 56126* ☎ *050/940111* 🖷 *050/940180* ⊕ *www.royalvictoria.it* ⤳ *48 rooms, 40 with bath* ♤ *Room service, some fans, cable TV, in-room data ports, bicycles (fee), bar, babysitting, dry cleaning, laundry service, concierge, parking (fee), some pets allowed; no a/c in some rooms* ▭ *AE, DC, MC, V* ⅏*BP.*

Nightlife & the Arts

The **Luminaria** feast day on June 16 honors San Ranieri, the city's patron saint. Palaces along the Arno are lighted up, and there are plenty of fireworks; it's Pisa at its most beautiful.

Pisa has a lively performing arts scene, most of which happens at the 19th-century Teatro Verdi. Music and dance performances are presented from September through May. Contact **Fondazione Teatro di Pisa** (⊠ Via Palestro 40, Lungarni ☎ 050/941111 ⊕ www.teatrodipisa.pi. it) for schedules and information.

LUCCA

Ramparts built in the 16th and 17th centuries enclose a charming fortress town filled with churches (99 of them), terra-cotta-roof buildings, and narrow cobblestone streets, along which local ladies maneuver bikes to do their daily shopping. Here Caesar, Pompey, and Crassus agreed to rule Rome as a triumvirate in 56 BC. Lucca was later the first Tuscan town to accept Christianity, and it still has a mind of its own: when most of Tuscany was voting communist as a matter of course, Lucca's citizens rarely followed suit. The famous composer Giacomo Puccini (1858–1924) was born here; he is celebrated, along with his peers, during the summer Opera Theater and Music Festival of Lucca. The ramparts that circle the center city are the perfect place to take a stroll, ride a bicycle, kick a ball, or just stand and look down onto Lucca, both within and without.

Exploring Lucca

The historic center of Lucca, 51 km (31 mi) west of Florence, is walled, and motorized traffic is restricted. Walking and biking are the most efficient and most enjoyable ways to get around. You can rent bicycles, and the center is quite flat, so biking is easy. A combination ticket costing €6.50 gains you admission to both the Museo Nazionale di Villa Guinigi and the Pinacoteca Nazionale di Palazzo Mansi.

The Main Attractions

★ ❸ **Duomo.** The round-arched facade of the cathedral is an example of the rigorously ordered Pisan Romanesque style, in this case happily enlivened by a varied collection of small carved columns. Take a closer look at the decoration of the facade and of the portico below, which make for one of the most entertaining church exteriors in Tuscany. The Gothic in-

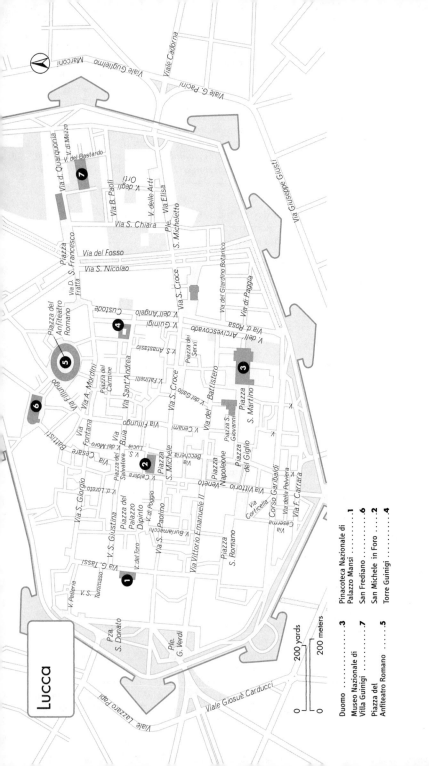

Lucca

Duomo **3**	Pinacoteca Nazionale di
Museo Nazionale di	Palazzo Mansi **1**
Villa Guinigi **7**	San Frediano **6**
Piazza del	San Michele in Foro **2**
Anfiteatro Romano **5**	Torre Guinigi **4**

0   200 yards
0   200 meters

terior contains a moving wood crucifix (called the *Volto Santo*, or Holy Face) brought here, legend has it, in the 8th century (though in fact it probably dates from between the 11th and early 13th centuries). The marble **tomb of Ilaria del Carretto** (1408) is the masterpiece of the Sienese sculptor Jacopo della Quercia (circa 1371–1438). ✉ *Piazza del Duomo* ☎*0583/490530* 🖃*Duomo free, tomb of Ilaria del Carretto €2* ☉*Duomo weekdays 7–5:30, Sat. 9:30–6:45, Sun. 11:30–11:50 and 1–5:30. Tomb Nov.–Mar., weekdays 9:30–4:45, Sat. 9:30–6:45, Sun. 11:30–11:50 and 1–5; Apr.–Oct., weekdays 9:30–5:45, Sat. 9–6:45, Sun. 9–10 and 1–5:45.*

★ ☾ **Passeggiata delle Mura** (Walk on the Walls). Any time of day when the weather is agreeable, you can find the citizens of Lucca cycling, jogging, strolling, or kicking a soccer ball in this large, unusual park atop the ring of ramparts that surrounds the city's *centro storico* (historic center). Sunlight streams through two rows of tall plane trees to dapple the walkway, a loop almost 5 km (3 mi) in length. Ten bulwarks are topped with lawns, many containing picnic tables, some with play equipment for children. One caution: there are no railings along the ramparts' edge and the drop to the ground is a precipitous 40 feet.

NEED A BREAK?

Gelateria Veneta (✉ Via V. Veneto ☎ 0583/467037 ✉ Via Beccheria ☎ 0583/496856) makes outstanding ice creams, sorbets, and ices (some sugar-free). The pièces de résistance are frozen fruits stuffed with their own creamy filling: don't miss the apricot-sorbet-filled apricot.

❺ **Piazza del Anfiteatro Romano.** A Roman amphitheater once stood on this spot; the medieval buildings constructed over the amphitheater retain its original oval shape and brick arches. It's a popular gathering place, with numerous cafés and some eclectic shops. ✉ *Off Via Fillungo.*

☾ ❻ **San Frediano.** The church contains a gorgeous sculpted polyptych by Jacopo della Quercia. The bizarrely lace-clad mummy of the patron saint of domestic servants, St. Zita, really seems to make kids shriek (usually in a good way) when they see her. ✉ *Piazza San Frediano, Anfiteatro* ☉ *Mon.–Sat. 8:30–noon and 3–5, Sun. 10:30–5.*

❷ **San Michele in Foro.** The facade of this church, slightly west of the centro storico, is even more fanciful than the Duomo's. Check out the superb panel painting of Sts. Girolamo, Sebastian, Rocco, and Helen by Filippino Lippi (1457/58–1504) in the right transept. ✉ *Piazza San Michele, San Michele* ☉ *Daily 7:40–noon and 3–6.*

☾ ❹ **Torre Guinigi.** The tower of the medieval palace contains one of the city's most curious sights: six ilex trees have established themselves at the top, and their roots have grown into the room below. From the tower there's a magnificent view of the city and the surrounding countryside. ✉ *Palazzo Guinigi, Via Sant'Andrea 42, Anfiteatro* ☎ *0583/583150* 🖃 *€3.50* ☉ *Mar. and Apr., daily 9:30–6; May–Sept., daily 9–midnight; Oct.–Feb., daily 9–5.*

Also Worth Seeing

❼ **Museo Nazionale di Villa Guinigi.** On the east end of the historic center, the museum houses an extensive collection of local Romanesque and

Renaissance art. ✉ *Villa Guinigi, Via della Quarquonia, Lucca East* ☎ *0583/496033* 🖂 *€4* ⊗ *Tues.–Fri. 9–7, Sun. 9–1.*

❶ Pinacoteca Nazionale di Palazzo Mansi. Highlights at this art museum are the brightly colored *Portrait of a Youth* by Pontormo and portraits of the Medici painted by Bronzino (1503–72) and others. ✉ *Palazzo Mansi, Via Galli Tassi 43, San Donato* ☎ *0583/55570* 🖂 *€4* ⊗ *Tues.–Sat. 9–7.*

Off the Beaten Path

Villa Reale. Napoléon's sister, Princess Elisa, once called Villa Reale home. Restored by the Counts Pecci-Blunt, the estate is celebrated for its spectacular gardens, which were originally laid out in the 16th century and redone in the middle of the 17th century. Gardening buffs adore the legendary **teatro di verdura,** a theater carved out of hedges and topiaries. The Lucca tourist office has information about the occasional concerts held here. ✉ *Villa Reale, Marlia, 8 km (5 mi) north of Lucca* ☎ *0583/30108* 🖂 *€6* ⊗ *Mar.–Nov., guided visits Tues.–Sun. at 10, 11, noon, 3, 4, 5, and 6; Dec.–Feb., by appointment.*

Where to Stay & Eat

$$ ✕ **Bucadisantantonio.** The staying power of Bucadisantantonio—it's
Fodor'sChoice   been around since 1782—is the result of superlative Tuscan food brought
★   to the table by waitstaff that doesn't miss a beat. The menu includes the simple-but-blissful, like *tortelli lucchesi al sugo* (meat-stuffed pasta with a tomato-and-meat-sauce), and more daring dishes such as roast *capretto* (kid) with herbs. A white-wall interior hung with copper pots and brass musical instruments creates a classy but comfortable dining space. ✉ *Via della Cervia 3, San Michele* ☎ *0583/55881* 🖐 *Reservations essential* 🖃 *AE, DC, MC, V* ⊗ *Closed Mon., 2 wks in Jan., and 2 wks in July. No dinner Sun.*

$$ ✕ **Il Giglio.** High ceilings, a large chandelier, and a big fireplace evoke the 19th century inside, and there is a terrace for dining outside in summer. Waiters in black double-breasted suits provide wise counsel on the wine choices, which complement the mostly Lucchesi dishes on the menu. Among the regional favorites are *farro garfagnino* (a thick soup made with emmer, a grain that resembles barley, and beans) and *coniglio con olive* (rabbit stew with olives). Save room for one of the desserts, such as *la frutta carmellata in forno con gelato di castagne* (caramelized fruit with chestnut ice cream)—wow! ✉ *Piazza del Giglio 2, off Piazza Napoleone, Duomo* ☎ *0583/494058* 🖃 *AE, DC, MC, V* ⊗ *Closed Wed. No dinner Tues.*

¢   ✕ **i Santi.** This intimate little wine bar, just outside the amphitheater, offers a perfect place to have a light meal and a fine glass of wine. The extensive wine list has first-rate local and foreign (French) selections, and the menu has tasty things to go with it, such as *carpaccio di manzo affumicato* (thin slices of smoked beef served with celery and a fresh cheese made of cow's milk). Specials include a pasta of the day. In summer it is open throughout the day, meaning if you're hungry at 4 in the afternoon or at 11:30 at night (when just about everywhere else is closed), you're in luck. ✉ *Via dell'Anfiteatro 29/a* ☎ *0583/496124* 🖃 *AE, DC, MC, V* ⊗ *Closed Wed. Nov.–Mar.*

$$$$ ✕⊡ **Locanda l'Elisa.** A stay here could evoke home for you—that is if home is a neoclassical villa with a lush garden and a caring staff that caters to your needs. Most rooms are suites, outfitted with fresh flowers, antiques, and fine fabrics. The restaurant il Gazebo is in a former Victorian conservatory. The Tuscan food-with-flair is deftly served by English-speaking waiters. Locanda l'Elisa is a short ride from the city. ⊠ *Via Nuova per Pisa 1952, 5 km (3 mi) southwest of town center, 55050* ☎ *0583/379737* 🖷 *0583/379019* ⊕ *www.locandalelisa.com* ➫ *3 rooms, 7 suites* ⚙ *Restaurant, in-room safes, minibars, cable TV, in-room data ports, pool, massage, bar, babysitting, dry cleaning, laundry service, concierge, Internet room, free parking* ▤ *AE, DC, MC, V* ☉ *Closed Jan. 7–Feb. 11* ¶❍¶ *EP.*

$$$$ ⊡ **Hotel Ilaria.** The former stables of the Villa Bottini have been transformed into a modern hotel within the historic center. A second-floor terrace, overlooking the villa, makes a comfortable place to relax. Rooms are done in a warm wood veneer. The availability of free bicycles is a great bonus in this bike-friendly city. Residenza dell'Alba, the hotel's annex across the street, was originally part of a 14th-century church; now it's a luxe accommodation with in-room hot tubs. ⊠ *Via del Fosso 26, Lucca East, 55100* ☎ *0583/47615* 🖷 *0583/991961* ⊕ *www.hotelilaria.com* ➫ *36 rooms, 5 suites* ⚙ *In-room safes, minibars, cable TV, bicycles, bar, babysitting, dry cleaning, laundry service, concierge, meeting room, free parking, some pets allowed (fee), no-smoking rooms* ▤ *AE, DC, MC, V* ¶❍¶ *BP.*

★ **$$$** ⊡ **Palazzo Alexander.** Lucchesi nobility would have felt at home at this small boutique hotel. The building, with its timbered ceilings and warm yellow walls, dates from the 12th century but has been completely restructured with 21st-century amenities. Brocade chairs adorn the public rooms, and the elegance is carried into the guest rooms, all of which have that same glorious damask upholstery and high ceilings. Top-floor suites have sweeping views of the town. The location is on a quiet side street, a stone's throw from San Michele in Foro. ⊠ *Via S. Giustina 48, San Michele, 55100* ☎ *0583/583571* 🖷 *0583/583610* ⊕ *www.palazzo-alexander.com* ➫ *9 rooms, 3 suites, 1 apartment* ⚙ *In-room safes, minibars, cable TV, in-room data ports, bicycles, wine bar, dry cleaning, laundry service, concierge, parking (fee), no-smoking rooms* ▤ *AE, DC, MC, V* ¶❍¶ *BP.*

$ ⊡ **Piccolo Hotel Puccini.** Steps away from the busy square and church of San Michele, this little hotel is quiet and calm—and a great deal. Wallpaper, hardwood floors, and throw rugs are among the handsome decorations. Paolo, the genial manager, speaks fluent English and dispenses great touring advice. ⊠ *Via di Poggio 9, San Michele, 55100* ☎ *0583/55421* 🖷 *0583/53487* ⊕ *www.hotelpuccini.com* ➫ *14 rooms* ⚙ *Fans, in-room safes, cable TV, bar, babysitting, dry cleaning, laundry service, parking (fee), some pets allowed, no-smoking floors; no a/c* ▤ *AE, DC, MC, V* ¶❍¶ *EP.*

Nightlife & the Arts

The **Opera Theater of Lucca Festival,** sponsored by Lucca's opera company and the school of music of the University of Cincinnati, runs from mid-June to mid-July; performances are staged in open-air venues.

Throughout summer there are jazz, pop, and rock concerts in conjunction with the **Estate Musicale Lucchese** music festival. The **Lucca Tourist Office** (⊠ Piazza Santa Maria Verdi 35, San Michele ☎ 0583/919931) has schedule and ticket information for many local events, including the Opera Theater and Estate Musicale Lucchese festivals.

From September through April you can see operas, plays, and concerts staged at the **Teatro del Giglio** (⊠ Piazza del Giglio, Duomo ☎ 0583/46531 ⊕ www.teatrodelgiglio.it).

Sports & the Outdoors

A splendid bike ride (rental about €12) may be had by circling the entire historic center along the top of the bastions—affording something of a bird's-eye view. **Barbetti Cicli** (⊠ Via dei Gaspari 83/r, Anfiteatro ☎ 0583/517073) rents bikes near the Piazza di Anfiteatro. **Poli Antonio Biciclette** (⊠ Piazza Santa Maria 42, Lucca East ☎ 0583/493787) is an option for bicycle rental on the east side.

Shopping

Lucca's justly famed olive oils are available throughout the city (and exported around the world). Look for those made by Fattoria di Fubbiano and Fattoria Fabbri—two of the best. On the second Sunday of the month there's a **flea market** in Piazza San Martino.

★ Chocoholics can get their fix at **Caniparoli** (⊠ Via S. Paolino 96, San Donato ☎ 0583/53456). They are so serious about their sweets here that they do not make them from June through August because of the heat. Bargain hunters won't want to miss **Benetton Stock Outlet** (⊠ Via Mordini 17/19, Anfiteatro ☎ 0583/464533), with its brightly colored garments at reduced prices.

FLORENCE ESSENTIALS

Transportation

BY AIR
Florence's Aeroporto A. Vespucci, commonly called Peretola, receives flights from Milan, Rome, London, and Paris. To get into the city center from the airport by car, take the A11. Tickets for the local bus service into Florence are sold at the airport's second-floor bar. Take Bus 62, which goes directly to the train station at Santa Maria Novella; the airport's bus shelter is beyond the parking lot.

Pisa's Aeroporto Galileo Galilei is the closest landing point with significant international service. It's relatively easy to get to Florence, as the SS67 leads directly there. For flight information, call the airport or Florence Air Terminal (which is an office at Santa Maria Novella, Florence's main train station). A train service connects Pisa's airport station with Santa Maria Novella, roughly a 1½-hour trip. Starting about 7 AM, several trains run from the airport and from Florence in the morning. Later service from both Pisa Aeroporto and Florence Santa Maria Novella is more sporadic, as only a handful of trains run from the late afternoon through the evening. You can check in for departing flights at the Florence Air Terminal, which is around the corner from train tracks 1 and 2.

⚡ Airport Information **Aeroporto Galileo Galilei** ✈ 12 km [7 mi] south of Pisa and 80 km [50 mi] west of Florence 📞 050/849300 ⊕ www.pisa-airport.it. **Florence Air Terminal** ✉ Stazione Centrale di Santa Maria Novella 📞 055/216073. **Peretola** ✈ 10 km [6 mi] northwest of Florence 📞 055/373498 ⊕ www.airport.florence.it.

BY BIKE & MOPED

Brave souls (cycling in Florence is difficult at best) may rent bicycles at easy-to-spot locations at Fortezza da Basso, the Stazione Centrale di Santa Maria Novella, and Piazza Pitti. Otherwise try Alinari. You'll be up against hordes of tourists and those pesky *motorini* (mopeds). Le Cascine, a former Medici hunting ground turned into a large public park with paved pathways, admits no cars. The historic center can be circumnavigated via bike paths lining the *viali,* the ring road surrounding the historic center. If you want to go native and rent a noisy motorino, you may do so at Maxirent. However unfashionable, helmets are mandatory by law and you must rent one.

⚡ Rentals **Alinari** ✉ Via Guelfa 85/r, San Marco 📞 055/280500 ⊕ www.alinarirental. com. **Maxirent** ✉ Borgo Ognissanti 155/r, Santa Maria Novella 📞 055/265420.

BY BUS

Long-distance buses provide inexpensive if somewhat claustrophobic service between Florence and other cities in Italy and Europe. Lazzi Eurolines and SITA are the major lines; they have neatly divided up their routes, so there's little overlap.

Maps and timetables for local bus service are available for a small fee at the ATAF (Azienda Trasporti Area Fiorentina) booth, or for free at visitor information offices. Tickets must be bought in advance at tobacco shops, newsstands, from automatic ticket machines near main stops, or at ATAF booths. The ticket must be canceled in the small validation machine immediately upon boarding.

You have several ticket options, all valid for one or more rides on all lines. A €1 ticket is valid for one hour from the time it is first canceled. A multiple ticket—four tickets, each valid for 60 minutes—costs €3.90. A 24-hour tourist ticket costs €4.50. Two-, three-, and seven-day passes are also available.

⚡ Bus Information **ATAF** ✉ Next to train station; Piazza del Duomo 57/r, Santa Maria Novella 📞 800/424500 ⊕ www.ataf.net. **Lazzi Eurolines** ✉ Via Mercadante 2, Santa Maria Novella 📞 055/363041 ⊕ www.lazzi.it. **SITA** ✉ Via Santa Caterina da Siena 17/r, Santa Maria Novella 📞 055/214721 ⊕ www.sita-on-line.it.

BY CAR

Florence is connected to the north and south of Italy by the Autostrada del Sole (A1). It takes about 1 hour of driving on scenic roads to get to Bologna (although heavy truck traffic over the Apennines often makes for slower going), about 3 hours to Rome, and 3–3½ hours to Milan. The Tyrrhenian Coast is an hour west on the A11. For help with car trouble, call the ACI (Automobile Club Firenze).

⚡ ACI ✉ Viale Amendola 36, outside town 📞 055/2486246.

BY TAXI

Taxis usually wait at stands throughout the city (in front of the train station and in Piazza della Repubblica, for example), or you can call for one. The meter starts at €2.30, with a €3.60 minimum and extra charges at night, on Sunday, and for radio dispatch.

🚹 Taxi Company **Taxis** ☎ 055/4390 or 055/4798.

BY TRAIN

Florence is on the principal Italian train route between most European capitals and Rome, and within Italy it is served frequently from Milan, Venice, and Rome by Intercity (IC) and nonstop Eurostar trains. Stazione Centrale di Santa Maria Novella, the main station, is in the center of town. Be sure to avoid trains that stop only at the Campo di Marte or Rifredi stations, which are not convenient to the center.

🚹 Train Information **Stazione Centrale di Santa Maria Novella** ☎ 892021 ⊕ www. trenitalia.com.

Contacts & Resources

EMERGENCIES

You can get a list of English-speaking doctors and dentists at the U.S. Consulate, or contact the Tourist Medical Service. If you need hospital treatment and an interpreter, you can call AVO, a group of volunteer interpreters; it's open Monday, Wednesday, and Friday 4–6 PM and Tuesday and Thursday 10–noon. Comunale No. 13, a local pharmacy, is open 24 hours a day, seven days a week. For a complete listing of other pharmacies that have late-night hours on a rotating basis, dial 192.

🚹 **AVO** ☎ 055/2344567. **Tourist Medical Service** ✉ Via Lorenzo il Magnifico 59 ☎ 055/475411. **U.S. Consulate** ✉ Lungarno Vespucci 38, Lungarno North ☎ 055/ 266951 ⊕ www.usembassy.it.

🚹 Emergency Services **Ambulance** ☎ 118. **Emergencies** ☎ 113. **Misericordia** (Red Cross) ✉ Piazza del Duomo 20 ☎ 055/212222. **Police** ✉ Via Zara 2, near Piazza della Libertà ☎ 055/49771.

🚹 24-Hour Pharmacy **Comunale No. 13** ✉ Stazione Centrale di Santa Maria Novella ☎ 055/289435.

TOURS

WALKING TOURS Licensed Abercrombie & Kent guides can take you to the highlights of Florence or create custom-tailored tours.

🚹 Company **Abercrombie & Kent** ✉ Via de' Fossi 13, near Santa Maria Novella ☎ 055/2648029.

VISITOR INFORMATION

The main Florence tourist office, APT, has locations next to the Palazzo Medici-Riccardi, in the main train station, and around the corner from the Basilica di Santa Croce. Its Web site is in Italian only. Fiesole's office is on the main piazza.

🚹 Tourist Information **Fiesole** ✉ Via Portigiani 3, 50014 ☎ 055/598720 ⊕ www.comune. fiesole.fi.it. **Florence** Agenzia Promozione Turistica (APT) ✉ Via Cavour 1/r, next to Palazzo Medici-Riccardi, near San Lorenzo, 50100 ☎ 055/290832 ✉ Stazione Centrale di Santa Maria Novella, 50100 ☎ 055/212245 ✉ Borgo Santa Croce 29/r ☎ 055/2340444 ⊕ www.comune.firenze.it.

Between Florence & Venice

HIGHLIGHTS OF EMILIA–ROMAGNA & THE VENETO

Palazzo Comunale (Town Hall) at Piazza Maggiore, Bologna

WORD OF MOUTH

"Ah, Bologna . . . one of Italy's truly underrated gems. Sitting in an outdoor café in Piazza Maggiore is a true Italian experience."
—HowardR

"Verona is genteel and upscale, with a handful of outstanding attractions. It's a very walkable city, and it has luxuriously rich food and wine."

—nessundorma

WELCOME TO EMILIA-ROMAGNA & THE VENETO

TOP REASONS TO GO

★ **The signature foods of Emilia-Romagna:** This region's food—the *prosciutto crudo*, the Parmigiano-Reggiano, the balsamic vinegar, and perhaps above all, the pasta—alone makes the trip to Italy worthwhile.

★ **Mosaics that take your breath away:** The intricate tile creations in Ravenna's Mausuleo di Galla Placidia, in brilliantly well-preserved primary colors, depict pastoral scenes that transport you to another age.

★ **The nightlife of Bologna:** Red-roofed, left-leaning Bologna has the oldest university in Europe, and a lively after-dark scene to go with it.

★ **Giotto's frescoes in the Capella degli Scrovegni:** At this chapel in Padua, Giotto's innovations in painting technique helped to launch the Renaissance.

★ **Opera in Verona's ancient arena:** Even if the music doesn't move you, the spectacle will.

1 **Bologna.** In Emilia-Romagna's cultural and intellectual center, rows of street arcades wind around ancient university buildings, grandiose towers—and some of the best restaurants in Italy.

2 **Ravenna.** It's worth a detour off the path between Florence and Venice to visit this well-preserved city with its remarkable mosaics—glittering treasures left from Byzantine rule.

3 **Ferrara.** This wonderfully characteristic medieval city north of Bologna is, among other things, home to the world's oldest wine bar, Osteria Al Brindisi, where they've been pouring since 1435.

4 **Padua.** Bustling with bicycles and lined with frescoes, Padua has long been a cultural center of northern Italy. It's home to Europe's second-oldest university (after the one in Bologna), and you can feel the youthful student energy everywhere.

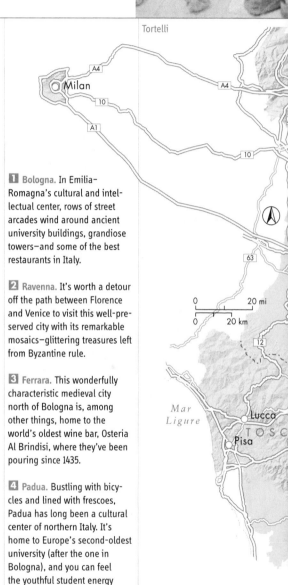

Vicenza

Verona

Padua

Venice

VENETO

A27

A4

A4

A13

E55

Po di Volano

Ferrara

Comacchio

Modena

A13

16

309

EMILIA-ROMAGNA

A1

Bologna

Ravenna

Pavullo

Imola

A14

Vado

Faenza

Cesenati

64

A1

Forli

9

Cesena

67

71

E74

Florence

A1

Empoli

GETTING ORIENTED

Stretching between Florence and Venice, the region of Emilia-Romagna is Italy's bread basket. The flat expanses of farmland can't compete with the spectacular natural beauty of Tuscany and Umbria; the appeal instead lies in its prosperous, highly cultured midsize cities, where the locals seem to have mastered the art of living—and especially eating—well. The same holds true when you enter the Veneto region: lined up in a row to the west of Venice are three beautiful, artistically rich cities that compete for your attention.

5 Vicenza. The elegant art city of Vicenza, nestled on the green plain reaching inland from Venice's lagoon, is most noted for its palaces designed by the great 16th-century architect Andrea Palladio.

6 Verona. Shakespeare placed Romeo, Juliet, and a couple of gentlemen in Verona, one of the oldest, best-preserved, and most beautiful cities in Italy. Try to catch *Aida* at the gigantic Roman arena.

Ravenna

EMILIA–ROMAGNA & THE VENETO PLANNER

Bologna

Making the Most of Your Time

Each city covered in this chapter has at least one truly world-class sight that's reason enough to merit a visit, but once you've arrived, you're likely to be won over by the cities as a whole. Many's the traveler who came to Italy to see Florence or Venice but ended up falling in love with Bologna or Vicenza.

Bologna makes sense as a base in Emilia-Romagna—there's a lot to do in the city, and you can make easy day trips east to Ravenna and west to the foodie havens of Emilia.

In the Veneto, Padua, Vicenza, and Verona are all within day-trip distance of Venice. Or, if the price and hassle of staying in Venice turn you off, you can make one of these cities your base and visit La Serenissima during the day.

Getting Around

The cities in these regions are connected by well-maintained highways and an efficient railway system. A car provides added freedom, but it's not essential, and it can be a headache. (See below.)

Going by Car: Italy's major north–south highway, A1, runs from Florence to Bologna, then makes a left and continues to Milan. From Bologna, A13 runs north through Ferrara to Padua. If you're driving from Florence to Venice and want to see the cities of the Veneto, continue on A1 past Bologna to A22 (just beyond Modena), which takes you north to Verona. From there A4 leads to Vicenza, Padua, and Venice.

Going by Train: There's frequent train service between the cities covered here. Travel times vary depending on the type of train: Eurostars are the fastest; avoid *regionale* trains, which stop at every town along the line.

For more information about getting around, see "Essentials" at the end of the chapter.

Sample Travel Times

	HOURS BY CAR/TRAIN
Florence–Venice	3:15/3:00
Florence–Bologna	1:30/1:00
Bologna–Ravenna	1:00/1:15
Venice–Bologna	2:15/2:00
Venice–Padua	1:15/0:30
Venice–Vicenza	1:30/0:45
Venice–Verona	2:00/1:30

The Challenges of City Driving

When deciding whether to rent a car, keep in mind that driving in Italian cities is a trial: streets are difficult to navigate, congestion can be fierce, and drivers aren't known for their patience. In addition, Padua, Vicenza, and Verona sporadically limit car access—sometimes permitting only cars with plates ending in an even number on even days, odd on odd, or prohibiting cars altogether on weekends. There's no central source for such information; the best strategy is to check with your hotel. In Emilia–Romagna, Bologna's historic center is closed to cars during the day, and the center of Ravenna is closed to cars at all times.

What's on the Menu

Emilia-Romagna's specialties are nothing new in name, they're just better here, where they were born—for example, Parma's world-famous prosciuttos and crumbly Parmigiano Reggiano cheese. Bologna's pasta (especially tagliatelle) *al ragú* is in a heavenly, slow-cooked sauce of onions, carrots, minced pork and beef, milk, and (sometimes) tomatoes. The rich, soft, garlicky mortadella has been reincarnated elsewhere to its detriment as "baloney."

Another specialty is stuffed pasta, which comes in a multitude of forms and is often filled with pumpkinlike squash or spinach and cheese. Stuffed pastas are generally served simply, with melted butter, sage, and (what else) Parmigiano-Reggiano cheese, or *in brodo* (in beef or chicken broth). Other dishes to keep an eye out for: *zampone* (a sausage made from pig's trotter); risotto *in padella* (with fresh herbs and tomatoes); *brodetto* (tangy seafood stew); *piadine* (chewy, flat griddle breads); *salama da sugo* (aged sausage); and the list goes on.

In the Veneto, the defining culinary elements are from the field and the forest: in spring, highlights include white asparagus and wild herbs; in autumn, chestnuts, radicchio, and wild mushrooms. For starches, the Veneto dines on *bigoli* (thick, whole wheat pasta), wine-saturated risotto, and polenta that varies from a stiff porridge topped with Gorgonzola to a patty grilled alongside meat. Pork and veal are the standard meats, supplemented by lamb and rabbit; goose, duck, and guinea fowl are poultry options.

Finding a Place to Stay

The hotels in these regions are run with uncommon efficiency. Many cater to the business traveler, but there are smaller, more intimate options as well. Though prices are relatively high, there are none of the manipulative pricing schemes that sometimes mar Italy's tourist meccas.

How's the Weather?

The ideal times to visit are late spring and early summer (May and June) and in early fall (September and October). Summers tend to be hot and humid—though if you're an opera buff, it's worth tolerating the heat in order to see a performance at the Arena di Verona (where the season runs from July through September).

Winter is a good time to avoid travel to these regions: although the dense fog can be beautiful, it makes for bad driving conditions, and wet, bone-chilling cold isn't unusual from November through March.

TOP PASSEGIATA

An evening walk along Via Mazzini between Piazza dei Signori and Piazza Bra captures the essence of Verona's appeal. On nights when there's a performance, you can sit in one of Piazza Bra's cafés and make out strains of opera coming from the arena next door.

Checking the prosciutto

DINING & LODGING PRICE CATEOGORIES (In Euros)

	$$$$	$$$	$$	$	¢
Restaurants	over €45	€35–45	€25–35	€15–25	under €15
Hotels	over €220	€160–220	€110–160	€70–110	under €80

Restaurant prices are for a first course (*primo*), second course (*secondo*), and dessert (*dolce*). Hotel prices are for two people in a standard double room in high season, including tax and service.

EMILIA–ROMAGNA

Updated by
Robin
Goldstein

THE REGION OF EMILIA–ROMAGNA, made up predominantly of the Po River plain, doesn't have the drop-dead good looks that you find in many Italian landscapes. Instead, it wins your heart through your stomach. Many of Italy's signature food products come from here, including Parmigiano-Reggiano cheese (aka Parmesan), prosciutto di Parma, and balsamic vinegar. The pasta is considered Italy's finest—a reputation the region's chefs earn every day. But food isn't Emilia–Romagna's be-all and end-all. Attractive cities dot the map: Bologna is the principal cultural and intellectual center, with rows of street arcades winding through grandiose towers. The mosaics in Ravenna are glittering treasures left from the era of Byzantine rule, and Ferrara is a meticulously maintained medieval city with a youthful spirit.

BOLOGNA

The centuries of wars, sackings, rebellions, and bombings that left such dramatic evidence in other cities of Emilia-Romagna have not taken their toll on Bologna's old city center. Narrow, cobblestone streets remain intact, as do the ancient churches, massive palaces, and medieval towers. Arcades line many of the main thoroughfares, shading the walkways to such an extent that you can stroll around town in a rainstorm for hours without feeling a drop.

Through its long history, first as an Etruscan city, then a Roman one, then as an independent city-state in the Middle Ages, and ultimately as an epicenter of industry—manufacturing goods from silk to motorcycles—Bologna has always played a significant role in the north of Italy. Over the centuries the city has acquired a number of nicknames: Bologna the Learned, in honor of its venerable university, the oldest in the world; Bologna the Red, for its rosy rooftops and communist leanings; Bologna the Turreted, recalling the forest of medieval towers that once rose from the city center (two remarkable examples survive); and Bologna the Fat, a tribute to its preeminent position in the world of cuisine, the birthplace of mortadella, tortellini, and ragù.

Today one might also be tempted to dub it Bologna the Hip, for its position at the cutting edge of Italian culture. Recent years have brought an explosion of trendy *newyorkese* bars and lounges with postmodern music and Germanic track lighting, American brunches and California construction cuisine, and pricey boutiques in primary colors. The result is a jarring juxtaposition of leaning medieval towers and towering modernist fashion billboards. Unfortunately, the influx of people and industry that has accompanied these changes has also brought air and noise pollution, a further distraction from the city's architectural and culinary gems.

to the baby Jesus. Within the church of **San Sepolcro** (12th century) is the **Cortile di Pilato** (Courtyard of Pilate), named for the basin in its center said to be where Pontius Pilate washed his hands after condemning Christ. Also in the building is a **museum** displaying various medieval religious works and with a shop where you can buy sundry items such as honey, shampoo, and jam made by the monks. ⊠ *Via Santo Stefano 24, Piazza Santo Stefano, University area* ☎ *051/223256* ☒ *Free* ⊙ *Daily 9–noon and 3:30–6.*

9 Università di Bologna. Take a stroll through the streets of the university area, a jumble of buildings, some dating as far back as the 15th century and most to the 17th and 18th. The neighborhood, as befits a college town, is full of bookshops, coffee bars, and cheap restaurants. None of them are particularly distinguished, but they're all characteristic of student life in the city. Try eating at the *mensa universitaria* (cafeteria) if you want to strike up a conversation with local students (most speak English). Political slogans and sentiments are scrawled on walls all around the university and tend to be ferociously leftist. Among the **university museums**, the most interesting are the **Musei di Palazzo Poggi**, which display scientific instruments and paleontological, botanical, and university-related artifacts. ⊠ *Via Zamboni 33, University area* ☎ *051/ 2099360* ⊕ *www.museopalazzopoggi.unibo.it* ☒ *Free* ⊙ *Weekdays 10–1 and 2–4.*

Also Worth Seeing

7 Museo Internazionale della Musica. The music museum in the spectacular old Palazzo Aldini Sanguinetti, with its 17th- and 18th-century frescoes, offers among its exhibits a 1606 harpsichord and a collection of beautiful musical manuscripts going back to the 1500s. ⊠ *Strada Maggiore 34, University area* ☎ *051/2757711* ⊕ *www.museomusicabologna. it* ☒ *€4* ⊙ *Jan.–May, Tues.–Sun. 10–5; June–July 14 and Sept. 16–Dec., Tues.–Thurs. 10–1:30, Fri.–Sun. 10–5.*

1 Palazzo Comunale. A mélange of building styles and constant modifications characterize this huge palace dating from the 13th to 15th century. When Bologna was an independent city-state, this was the seat of government, a function it still serves today. Over the door is a statue of Bologna-born Pope Gregory XIII, most famous for reorganizing the calendar. There

ᴋING UP AN APPETITE IN BOLOGNA

This tour through the heart of Bologna should take two or three hours. It's the perfect way to work up your appetite for an indulgent lunch–or to walk lunch off in the afternoon–while seeing some of the city's top sights. Start at the southern end of sprawling Piazza Maggiore

at the 14th-century **Basilica di San Petronio 4**. Its interior is stark and expansive, and the half-finished facade is interesting in its own right. On the west side of Piazza Maggiore is the **Palazzo Comunale 1**, and at the north end, in the adjoining Piazza Nettuno, is the **Palazzo del Podestà 2** and its Torre dell'Arengo. In Piazza Nettuno you'll also find the Fontana del Nettuno, aka Il Gigante, the city's informal nerve center and meeting place. To the left (west) is **Palazzo Re Enzo 3**, a palace with dark medieval associations. Toward the

EMILIA-ROMAGNA THROUGH THE AGES

Ancient History. Emilia-Romagna owes its beginnings to a road. In 187 BC the Romans laid out their Via Aemilia, a long highway running straight northwest from the Adriatic port of Rimini to the central garrison town of Piacenza, and it was along this central spine that the primary towns of the region developed.

Despite the unifying factor of what came to be known as the Via Emilia, the region has had a fragmented history. Its eastern portion, roughly the area from Faenza to the coast, known as Romagna, has looked first to the Byzantine east and then to Rome for art, political power, and, some say, national character. The western portion, Emilia, from Bologna to Piacenza, had a more northern, rather dour sense of self-government and dissent.

The principal city of Bologna was founded by the Etruscans and eventually came under the influence of the Roman Empire. The Romans established a garrison there, renaming the old Etruscan settlement Bononia. It was after the fall of Rome that the region began its fragmentation. Romagna, centered in Ravenna, was ruled from Constantinople. Ravenna eventually became the capital of the empire in the west in the 5th century, passing to papal control in the 8th century. Even today, the city is still filled with reminders of two centuries of Byzantine rule.

Family Ties. The other cities of the region, from the Middle Ages on, became the fiefs of important noble families—the Este in Ferrara and

Modena, the Pallavicini in Piacenza, the Bentivoglio in Bologna, and the Malatesta in Rimini. Today all these cities bear the marks of their noble patrons. When in the 16th century the papacy managed to exert its power over the entire region, some of these cities were divided among the papal families—hence the stamp of the Farnese family on Parma, Piacenza, and Ferrara.

A Leftward Tilt. Bologna and Emilia-Romagna have established a robust tradition of rebellion and dissent. The Italian socialist movement was born in the region, as was Benito Mussolini—in keeping with the political climate of his home state, he was a firebrand socialist during the early part of his career. Despite having Mussolini as a native son, Emilia-Romagna did not take to fascism: it was here that the antifascist resistance was born, and during World War II the region suffered terribly at the hands of the Fascists and the Nazis.

Despite a long history of bloodletting, turmoil, and rebellion, the arts have always flourished. The great families financed painters, sculptors, and writers. (Dante found a haven in Ravenna after being expelled from his native Florence.) In modern times Emilia-Romagna has given to the arts such famous figures as painter Giorgio Morandi, filmmakers Michelangelo Antonioni and Federico Fellini, and tenor Luciano Pavarotti. Even since Bologna's emergence as a major tourist destination, the city has not lost its liberal feel, and it has been a locus of anti–Iraq war protests.

4

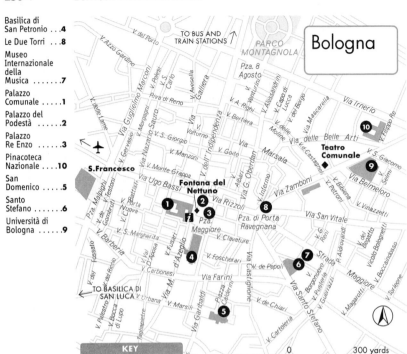

Although foreign tourists have lately begun to discover Bologna's special charm and arrive (along with Italians) in increasing numbers, the city's urban vitality still comes in large part from its student population. The university was founded in about the year 1088, and by the 13th century already had more than 10,000 students. It was a center for the teaching of law and theology, and it was ahead of its time in that many of the professors were women. Guglielmo Marconi, the inventor of the wireless telegraph, first formulated his groundbreaking theories in the physics labs of the university. Today the university has prominent business and medical faculties.

Exploring Bologna

Piazza Maggiore and the adjacent Piazza del Nettuno make up the core of the city. Arranged around these two squares are the imposing Basilica di San Petronio, the massive Palazzo Comunale, the Palazzo del Podestà, the Palazzo di Re Enzo, and the Fontana del Nettuno—one of the most visually harmonious groupings of public buildings in the entire country. From here, sights that aren't on one of the piazzas are but a short walk away, along delightful narrow cobbled streets or under the ubiquitous arcades that double as municipal umbrellas. Take at least a

full day to explore Bologna; it's compact an[?] ration, but there is plenty to see.

The Main Attractions

④ Basilica di San Petronio. Construction on this c[?] century, and work was still in progress on th[?] years later. It's not finished yet, as you can see[?] are missing and the facade is only partially d[?] the marble face the architects had intended. The [?] by the great Sienese master of the Renaissan[?] Above the center of the door is a Madonna an[?] Ambrose and Petronius, the city's patrons.

The interior of the basilica is huge: the Bologn[?] bigger church—you can still see the columns ere[?] church outside the east end—but had to tone [?] the university seat was established next door in[?] **Petronio** contains models showing how the c[?] tended to look. The most important artworks [?] left aisle, frescoes by Giovanni di Modena datin[?] the 1400s. ⊠ *Piazza Maggiore* 🕿 *051/2254*[?] *Apr.–Sept., daily 7:30–1:15 and 2:30–6; Oct.–*[?] *2:30–6. Museum Mon.–Sat. 9:30–12:30 and 2:3*[?]

Fontana del Nettuno. Sculptor Giambologna's e[?] monument to Neptune occupying Piazza Nettu[?] named *Il Gigante* (The Giant). Its exuberantly[?] undraped God of the Sea drew fire when it wa[?] enough, apparently, to dissuade the populace fr[?] as a public washing stall for centuries. It's also k[?] son: walk behind Neptune and to his right fo[?] angle on the statue. ⊠ *Piazza Nettuno, next to*[?] *Piazza Maggiore area.*

★ **⑧ Le Due Torri.** Two landmark towers, mentioned by[?] stand side by side in the compact Piazza di Porta R[?] ily of importance had a tower as a symbol of pr[?] as a potential fortress; only 60 remain out of mo[?] presided over the city. **Torre Garisenda** (from the l[?] ing 10 feet, was shortened to 165 feet for safety in[?] closed to visitors. **Torre degli Asinelli** (circa 1109) i[?] an alarming 7½ feet off perpendicular. If you're u[?] cal challenge—and you're not claustrophobic—yo[?] the 500 narrow, wooden steps to get to the view [?] *azza di Porta Ravegnana, east of Piazza Maggiore* [?] *Asinelli Apr.–Sept., daily 9–6; Oct.–Mar., daily 9–*[?]

⑥ Santo Stefano. This splendid and unusual basilica a[?] tween four and seven connected churches (authoriti[?] on this site there was a 4th-century pagan temple t[?] est remaining component is **Santi Vitale e Agricola**[?] the 8th century. It contains a 14th-century nativity[?] by Bologna's children, who come at Christmastime t[?]

Fodor$Choice

WOR

are good views from the upper stories of the palace. The first-floor **Sala Rossa** (Red Room) is open on advance request and during some exhibitions, and the **Sala del Consiglio Comunale** (City Council Hall) is open to the public during short hours in the late morning.

Within the palazzo there are also two museums. The **Collezioni Comunali d'Arte** exhibits paintings from the Middle Ages as well as some Renaissance works by Luca Signorelli (circa 1445–1523) and Tintoretto. The **Museo Morandi** is dedicated to the 20th-century still-life artist Giorgio Morandi; in addition to his paintings, there's a re-creation of his studio and living space. Underground caves and the foundations of the old cathedral can be visited by appointment made through the tourist office. ⊠ *Piazza Maggiore 6* ☎ *051/203111 Palazzo, 051/203526 Collezioni, 051/203332 Museo* ⊕ *www.museomorandi.it* 🖃 *Palace free, each museum €4, combined ticket €6* ☺ *Sala del Consiglio Comunale Tues.–Sat. 10–1; Collezioni Tues.–Fri. 9–3, weekends 10–6:30; Museo Tues.–Fri. 9–3, weekends 10–6:30.*

The **Biblioteca Sala Borsa,** connected to the Palazzo Comunale, has an impressive interior courtyard surrounded by the library. ⊠ *Entrance from Piazza Nettuno, Piazza Maggiore area* ☎ *051/204400* ⊕ *www. bibliotecasalaborsa.it* 🖃 *Free* ☺ *Mon. 2:30–8, Tues.–Fri. 10–8, Sat. 10–7.*

2 **Palazzo del Podestà.** This classic Renaissance palace facing the Basilica di San Petronio was erected in 1484, and attached to it is the soaring **Torre dell'Arengo.** The bells in the tower have rung whenever the city has celebrated, mourned, or called its citizens to arms since 1453. ⊠ *Piazza Nettuno, Piazza Maggiore area* ☎ *051/224500* ☺ *During exhibitions only.*

3 **Palazzo Re Enzo.** King Enzo of Sardinia was imprisoned in this 13th-century medieval palace for 23 years, until his death in 1272. He had waged war on Bologna and was captured after the fierce battle of Fossalta in 1249. The palace has other macabre associations: common criminals received the last rites of the Church in the tiny courtyard chapel before being executed in Piazza Maggiore. The courtyard is worth peeking into, but the palace merely houses government offices. ⊠ *Piazza Re Enzo, Piazza Maggiore area* ☎ *051/224500* ☺ *During exhibitions only.*

busy, chic Via Rizzoli, which runs east from Piazza Nettuno, is the gleaming glass tourist office complex, which has drawn mixed reviews from locals.
From this central piazza, follow Via Rizzoli directly into the medieval section of the city. At Piazza di Porta Ravegnana, if you're feeling courageous, you can climb the slightly off-kilter Torre degli Asinelli, the taller of **Le Due Torri** 🕗 , Bologna's two landmark towers. From Piazza di Porta Ravegnana, take Via Santo Stefano southeast and walk five minutes to the remarkable

Santo Stefano 🕕 , made up of seven connected churches. It's free, and it's one of Bologna's most impressive sights. Wander through the ancient chapels, mausoleums, and courtyards, and you'll eventually come upon the fountain where Pontius Pilate is said to have washed his hands after condemning Christ. From there, head west on Via Farini. Take a left on Via Garibaldi and another left two blocks down to reach the piazza and church of **San Domenico** 🕔 . By now, you're probably ready to make lunch your next stop.

⑩ Pinacoteca Nazionale. Bologna's principal art gallery contains many works by the immortals of Italian painting, including the famous *Ecstasy of St. Cecilia* by Raphael. There's also a beautiful multipanel painting by Giotto, as well as *Madonna and Saints* by Parmigianino. ⊠ *Via delle Belle Arti 56, University area* ☎ *051/4209411* ⊕ *www.pinacotecabologna.it* 🖾 €4 ☉ *Tues.–Sun. 9–7.*

❺ San Domenico. The tomb of St. Dominic, who died here in 1221, is called the **Arca di San Domenico** and is found in this church in the sixth chapel on the right. Many artists participated in its decoration, notably Niccolò di Bari, who was so proud of his contribution that he changed his name to Niccolò dell'Arca to recall this famous work. The young Michelangelo carved the angel on the right. In the right transept of the church is a tablet marking the last resting place of the hapless King Enzo, the Sardinian ruler imprisoned in the Palazzo Re Enzo. The attached **museum** displays religious relics and art. ⊠ *Piazza San Domenico 13, off Via Garibaldi, south of Piazza Maggiore* ☎ *051/6400411* ☉ *Church daily 7:30–1 and 3:30–7:30; museum weekdays 10–noon and 3:30–6, Sat. 9:30–noon and 3:30–5:30, Sun. 3:30–5:30.*

Bologna walking tours. English-language "Discover Bologna" walking tours (€13) run by the tourist office in Piazza Maggiore depart at 10:30 AM Wednesday, Saturday, and Sunday. Tours by affiliated organizations also depart the office Monday and Friday at 11 AM and Tuesday, Thursday, and Saturday at 3 PM, also at a cost of €13 per person; bike tours cost €18 and leave Wednesday at 10 AM. ⊠ *Tourist office, Piazza Maggiore 1* ☎ *051/246541* ⊕ *www.guidebologna.com.*

Off the Beaten Path

Basilica di San Luca. A spectacular one-hour walk (or 10-minute drive) leads uphill from Porta Saragozza to the Basilica di San Luca (follow Via Saragozza), an impressive church that has perched dramatically atop Monte della Guardia since 1160. The road is arcaded the entire way; you walk beneath 666 arches before arriving at the round basilica, which has a famous Madonna icon. But it's the sweeping views of the Emilian countryside and city from the 990-foot altitude that make the trip worthwhile—most of all in autumn, when the leaves of the hills on one side play off the blazing red rooftops of Bologna on the other. If

After your meal, consider spending some time in the university district. Return to the Piazza di Porta Ravegnana (home of the two towers), and head northeast along Via Zamboni. Continue along that street until you reach the **Università di Bologna** ⑨. Wander around the university and take in the student culture—lively cafés, outdoor bookstalls, and so on. The university spirit isn't limited to Via Zamboni—also check out Via delle Belle Arti, Via Mascarella, and Via delle Moline. True devotees of Italian painting will want to set aside some time for the **Pinacoteca Nazionale** ⑩, at the intersection of Bella Arti and Zamboni; it's a comprehensive collection, though it's short on true masterpieces. Linger long enough in the district, and you may be ready for a mid-afternoon coffee or beer at one of the cafés.

you go by car (or, better yet, scooter), it's possible to ask for directions at the church and take an unmarked route back through the hills, winding past rustic Emilian restaurants before reentering the city center through Porta San Mammolo. ☒ *Via Saragozza, 3½ km (2 mi) southwest of Bologna* ☎ *051/6142339* ☾ *Oct.–Feb., Mon.–Sat. 7–12:30 and 2:30–5, Sun. 7–5; Mar., Mon.–Sat. 7–12:30 and 2:30–6, Sun. 7–6; Apr.–Sept., 7–12:30 and 2:30–7, Sun. 7–7.*

Museo del Patrimonio Industriale. Offering a refreshing change from all the art museums, this museum's displays document the development of Bologna's industries and industrial technologies from the 16th to 21st century, including fascinating examples of antique machinery, scientific devices, and cars. ☒ *Via della Beverara 123, Northwest of the city center* ☎ *051/6356611* ⊕ *www.comune.bologna.it/patrimonioindustriale* ☒ *€4* ☾ *Jan.–Mar., Tues.–Thurs. 9–1, Fri. and Sat. 9–1 and 3–6, Sun. 3–6; Apr., May, and Oct.–Dec., Tues.–Fri. 9–1, Sat. 9–1 and 3–6, Sun. 3–6; June–Sept., weekdays 9–1.*

Where to Stay & Eat

$$$$ ✕ **Al Pappagallo.** The well-known restaurant steps from Le Due Torri has hosted just about everyone, including Alfred Hitchcock. Its long and storied past, which goes back to 1919, is documented in the many black-and-white photos that line the tall, white walls. Al Pappagallo is formal and expensive, but this is a classic Bologna experience. Menu options might include the region's famed *culatello di Zibello* (raw cured ham) wonderfully paired with a Parmesan mousse and tomato *mostarda* (like a chutney), a filled pasta in an impossibly rich sauce of foie gras and cheese, or an interesting plate of deep-fried meats and fruits. ☒ *Piazza della Mercanzia 3/c, Piazza Maggiore area* ☎ *051/231200* ⊕ *www.alpappagallo.it* ☖ *Reservations essential* ☐ *AE, DC, MC, V* ☾ *Closed Sun. and Aug., and Sat. June–July.*

★ $$–$$$ ✕ **Da Cesari.** It's the creative menu options—such as delicate squash gnocchi, or a slowly braised veal cheek—that make Da Cesari truly memorable. Area standards such as veal cutlet Bolognese (with ham and melted cheese) are also reasonably priced and well executed. Accompany your meal with wine made by the owner's brother: Cesari's Liano is excellent. The gentle romantic buzz in the dining room is warm and welcoming; the restaurant is in the very heart of the *centro storico* (historic center). ☒ *Via de' Carbonesi 8, south of Piazza Maggiore* ☎ *051/237710* ☖ *Reservations essential* ☐ *AE, DC, MC, V* ☾ *Closed Sun., Aug., and Jan. 1–7.*

★ $$–$$$ ✕ **Drogheria della Rosa.** This is not just a romantic little place to escape from the city bustle; it's a complete experience. In the atmospheric wine cellar below the restaurant, you can select from a large, uniformly excellent selection. If you want to try an old Barolo or Amarone, this is the place to do it—but tell the staff a few hours beforehand so they can let the wine breathe and prepare a meal to match. No matter what, you'll eat fabulously here; chef Emanuele Addone, who's a real character, focuses above all on beautifully simple local ingredients in season; he might prepare pasta with black truffle, or filet mignon with balsamic vinegar.

✉ *Via Cartoleria 10, University area* ☎ *051/222529* ⊕ *www. drogheriadellarosa.it* ⊟ *AE, DC, MC, V* ☉ *Closed Sun. No lunch.*

$$–$$$ ✗ **Godot Wine Bar.** The buzzing, modern, bi-level Godot (open until 2 AM, full dinner menu until midnight) is equally popular with students as with wine aficionados. This is the new face of Bologna. The extraordinary wine list is so diverse that you might be able to have, say, a scarce Pugliese bottle that is impossible to find in Puglia. Although the food may be the side attraction here, the basics are solid: they make a mean tagliatelle *al ragù* (with a slow-cooked, tomato-based meat sauce), for instance. ✉ *Via Cartoleria 12, University area* ☎ *051/226315* ⊕ *www. godotwine.it* ⊟ *AE, MC, V* ☉ *Closed Sun. and 3 wks in Aug.*

$$–$$$ ✗ **Scacco Matto.** This extremely popular yet intimate and dimly lit restaurant specializes in food from Lucania (the traditional name for the Basilicata region). That might mean *soppressata lucana* (a sausage from Basilicata); *cavatelli* (small, thick homemade pasta twists) with tomato and meatballs; or lamb with a wine sauce made from Aglianico, the typical grape from that region. ✉ *Via Broccaindosso 63/b, University area* ☎ *051/263404* ⊟ *AE, DC, MC, V* ☉ *Closed July 20–Sept. 1. No lunch Mon.*

$–$$ ✗ **Da Bertino.** Happy diners don't seem to mind the close quarters in the large, bustling space here. Maybe it's because of the low prices, or maybe it's because popularity hasn't spoiled this traditional neighborhood trattoria and its simple home-style dishes. Highlights are the homemade *paglia e fieno* (yellow and green, plain and spinach, pasta) with sausage and the choices on the steaming tray of *bollito misto* (boiled meats). Ask to be seated in the back, rather than the less-attractive room up front. ✉ *Via delle Lame 55, Porta San Felice* ☎ *051/522230* ⊟ *AE, DC, MC, V* ☉ *Closed Sun. and Aug. 5–Sept. 4. No dinner Sat. in July. No dinner Mon. Aug.–June.*

$ ✗ **Victoria.** It's not unusual for this unpretentious and charming trattoria-pizzeria off Via dell'Indipendenza to have lines, so reserve ahead. Locals come for the cheap pizzas, which are indisputably the highlight (*mozzarella di bufala*, buffalo mozzarella, is an excellent topping choice). Pastas and salads are less impressive. The back room has a lovely 17th-century painted wooden ceiling. ✉ *Via Augusto Righi 9/c, north of Piazza Maggiore* ☎ *051/233548* ⊟ *AE, DC, MC, V* ☉ *Closed Thurs.*

¢ ✗ **Cantina Bentivoglio.** This two-floor wine-jazz extravaganza is a classic place to relax by night. The ground floor is a dim, bottle-clad wine cellar; the cavernlike basement downstairs has live jazz. The extraordinarily reasonable wine list includes labels from many of Italy's lesser-known regions, and the menu lists pastas, meats, and interesting salads and lighter plates, such as *crostini* (toasted bread) with mozzarella, eggplant, tomato, and roasted peppers. Vegetarian options are plentiful. Doors stay open until 2 AM, and wine is also available to go. ✉ *Via Mascarella 4, University area* ☎ *051/265416* ⊕ *www.cantinabentivoglio.it* ⊟ *AE, DC, MC, V* ☉ *Closed Sun. Oct.–May. No lunch Sat.*

¢ ✗ **La Scuderia.** A bit of New York chic comes to Bologna via the cutting-edge café–wine bar–performance space in a stunning vaulted ballroom of an old palazzo. Next door to the university, La Scuderia serves as an informal meeting place for hip students and intellectuals. Salads, desserts, lunches, wines by the glass, and American-style Sunday brunch are options. You can just as easily drink coffee over a newspaper at breakfast as flirt over a piña colada in the evening. Many nights there's live jazz. ⊠ *Piazza G. Verdi 2, off Via Zamboni, University area* ☎ *051/6569619* ▤ *AE, DC, MC, V* ☉ *Closed Mon.*

¢ ✕ **Tamburini.** Smells of all that is good about Bolognese food waft through the room and out into the streets. Breads, numerous cheeses, salumi such as Parma and Bologna hams and prosciuttos, roasted peppers, inventive salads, balsamic vinegars, local olive oils, smoked salmon, and fresh pasta are among the delights. This upscale deli/self-service buffet is *the* lunch spot. Tamburini also vacuum-packs foods for shipping or air travel. ⊠ *Via Drapperie 1, Piazza Maggiore area* ☎ *051/234726* ▤ *AE, MC, V* ☉ *No dinner.*

★ $$$$ ▦ **Corona d'Oro 1890.** A medieval printing house in a former life, this hotel is delightful—lyrically art nouveau in its reception and atrium, with enough flowers for a wedding. Guest rooms make opulent use of original 15th- and 16th-century decorations such as painted wood ceilings and Gothic-vault windows. The morning English breakfast buffet is worth getting up for. ⊠ *Via Oberdan 12, north of Piazza Maggiore, 40126* ☎ *051/7457611* ◳ *051/7457622* ⊕ *www.bolognarthotels.it/corona* ◁ *35 rooms* ⊘ *In-room safes, minibars, cable TV, in-room broadband, bicycles, bar, Internet room, meeting room, parking (fee), some pets allowed* ▤ *AE, DC, MC, V* ☉ *Closed 1st 3 wks in Aug.* †⊚l *BP.*

★ $$$$ ▦ **Grand Hotel Baglioni.** Sixteenth-century paintings and frescoes by the Bolognese Carracci brothers are rarely seen outside a museum or church, but in this 15th-century palazzo they provide the stunning backdrop for the public rooms and restaurant of one of Italy's most glamorous—and pricey—hotels. Lady Di slept here, and you may feel no less royal in a handsome room with antique furniture and brocaded walls. The highly regarded I Carracci restaurant serves top-notch food in regal, formal surroundings. ⊠ *Via dell'Indipendenza 8, north of Piazza Maggiore, 40121* ☎ *051/225445* ◳ *051/234840* ⊕ *www.baglionihotels.com* ◁ *116 rooms, 11 suites* ⊘ *Restaurant, some in-room faxes, in-room safes, minibars, cable TV, in-room data ports, Wi-Fi, bar, babysitting, laundry service, business services, meeting room, parking (fee)* ▤ *AE, DC, MC, V* †⊚l *BP.*

$$$–$$$$ ▦ **Art Hotel Commercianti.** Rooms here were designed to retain the structural integrity of the 11th-century palace and tower the hotel occupies, and are therefore cozy and unique, with original wood beams built into the walls. Tower rooms and suites have balconies with magnificent views of San Domenico church; all are stylishly furnished with, among other things, Carrara marble desks custom-built following a 15th-century design. ⊠ *Via De' Pignattari 11, south of Piazza Maggiore, 40124* ☎ *051/7457511* ◳ *051/7457522* ⊕ *www.bolognarthotels.it/commercianti* ◁ *33 rooms, 2 suites* ⊘ *Dining room, in-room safes, minibars, in-room broadband, bicycles, bar, Internet room, parking (fee)* ▤*AE, DC, MC, V* †⊚l *BP.*

★ $$$–$$$$ ▦ **Art Hotel Novecento.** A design-oriented hotel inspired by 1930s Europe, Novecento is at its core modern, modern, modern. Clean lines and elegant restraint are the hallmarks of the rooms, the lobby, and even the elevators. Breakfast is great, and happy hour comes with free wine and snacks. The hotel is in the middle of everything in downtown Bologna. Call ahead if you need a parking space, and be advised that the garage closes for the night. ✉ *Piazza Gallilei, Piazza Maggiore area, 40126* ☎ *051/7457311* 🖷 *051/7457322* ⊕ *www.bolognarthotels.it/novecento* 🔖 *25 rooms* ♿ *Dining room, in-room safes, minibars, in-room broadband, bar, Internet room, parking (fee)* ▭ *AE, DC, MC, V* ⦿ *BP.*

$$$–$$$$ ⛫ **Art Hotel Orologio.** Although occupying an old palazzo, which was originally a public building, the Orologio achieves a contemporary effect. A mid-level lounge and Internet room is a pleasant place to relax, and top-floor rooms have good views of Bologna's skyline. Under the same ownership as the other Art Hotels and the Corona d'Oro, this hotel is in a quiet pedestrian zone off Piazza Grande—an ideal sightseeing location. Fax ahead or check the Web site for driving directions. ✉ *Via IV Novembre 10, Piazza Maggiore area, 40123* ☎ *051/7457411* 🖷 *051/ 7457422* ⊕ *www.bolognarthotels.it/orologio* 🔖 *33 rooms* ♿ *Dining room, in-room safes, minibars, cable TV, in-room broadband, bicycles, Internet room, parking (fee), some pets allowed* ▭ *AE, DC, MC, V* ⦿ *BP.*

$$ ⛫ **Accademia.** Looking for a mid-range, comfortable base for exploring the area? This small hotel is right in the center of the university quarter. The rooms are adequate, the staff friendly. Look for discounted prices on the Web site. A few more inexpensive rooms have a shared bath. ✉ *Via delle Belle Arti 6, at Via delle Moline, University area, 40126* ☎ *051/ 232318* 🖷 *051/263590* ⊕ *www.hotelaccademia.com* 🔖 *28 rooms, 24 with bath* ♿ *Minibars, cable TV, bar, parking (fee), some pets allowed* ▭ *MC, V* ⦿ *BP.*

$ ⛫ **San Vitale.** Modern furnishings and a garden distinguish this modest hostelry, about 1 km (½ mi) east of the center of town. The service is courteous, and rooms are clean and bright. There are private bathrooms, but facilities are very basic. ✉ *Via San Vitale 94, University area, 40125* ☎ *051/225966* 🖷 *051/239396* 🔖 *17 rooms* ♿ *Internet room, parking (fee)* ▭ *No credit cards* ⦿ *BP.*

Nightlife & the Arts

The Arts

Bologna's arts scene is one of the liveliest in Italy, reaching out not just to the traditional older crowds of operagoers and ballet fans, but also to younger generations and food lovers with regional festivals.

FESTIVALS   The first weekend in October crowds celebrate the **Festa di San Petronio** with bands, fireworks, and free mortadella sandwiches in Piazza Maggiore. Free movies are shown at the **Open-air Cinema** in the Arena Puccini, at Via Serlio near the train station, June–August. The tourist office has the schedule.

MUSIC & OPERA   The 18th-century **Teatro Comunale** (✉ Largo Respighi 1, University area ☎ 199/107070 ⊕ www.comunalebologna.it) presents concerts by Italian and international orchestras throughout the year, but is dominated by the highly acclaimed opera performances November–May. Reserve seats well in advance. The ticket office is open Tuesday–Saturday 11–6:30.

Nightlife

As a university town, Bologna has long been known for its hopping nightlife. As early as 1300 it was said to have had 150 taverns. Most of the city's current 200-plus pubs and lounges are frequented by Italian students, young adults, and the international study-abroad crowd, with the university district forming the epicenter. In addition to the university area, the pedestrian-only zone on Via del Pratello, lined with a host of pubs, is also a hopping night scene, as is Via delle Moline, with cutting-edge cafés and bars. A more upmarket, low-key evening experience can be had at one of Bologna's many wine bars that are also restaurants, such as Cantina Bentivoglio and Godot Wine Bar. And then there are the hypertrendy bar-lounges that represent the newest, and most newyorkese, of Bologna's many faces; some of these joints make even Milan look old-school.

With live jazz staged every night (€4 cover), **Cantina Bentivoglio** (✉ Via Mascarella 4/b, University area ☎ 051/265416) is one of Bologna's most appealing nightspots. You can order light meals and nibbles as well. At **Le Stanze** (✉ Via del Borgo di S. Pietro 1, University area ☎ 051/228767) you can sip an *aperitivo* (aperitif) or a late-night drink at a modern bar under 17th-century frescoes in what was the private chapel of the 1576 Palazzo Bentivoglio. The adjoining avant-garde restaurant serves modern Italian fusion cooking. **The Loft** (✉ Via delle Moline 16/d, University area ☎ 320/5610963), one of Bologna's most cutting-edge spaces for drinking and dancing, is in a 15th-century convent. Featuring DJs and wine, the place hops on most nights; on Tuesday there are Latin dance lessons, and Friday and Saturday bring live music.

Balmoral (✉ Via de' Pignattari 1, Piazza Maggiore area ☎ 051/228694), a restaurant right near Piazza Maggiore, has good live music most nights, and a vague Middle Eastern theme. The casually hip **Divinis** (✉ Via Battibecco 4/c, University area ☎ 051/2961502) wine bar has a remarkable, if pricey, selection by the glass (as well as high-end food) served in chichi surroundings until 1:30 AM. A wine bar with romantic ambient lighting and a good draft beer selection, **Contavalli** (✉ Via Belle Arti 2, University area ☎ 051/268395) is a relaxing choice.

The elegant and trendy **Bar Calice** (✉ Via Clavature 13/a, at Via Marchesana, Piazza Maggiore area ☎ 051/264508) runs an indoor-outdoor operation year-round (with heat lamps); it's a cocktail and wine bar that's extremely popular with the see-and-be-seen thirtysomethings. The loud, modern, haywire **Nu Bar Lounge** (✉ Off Buco San Petronio, Via de' Musei 6, Piazza Maggiore area ☎ 051/222532 ⊕ www.nu-lounge. com) hosts a cocktail-sipping crowd.

Shopping

Books

Next to the Due Torri is the best bookstore in the region, **Feltrinelli** (✉ Piazza Ravegnana 1, east of Piazza Maggiore ☎ 051/266891 ⊕ www. lafeltrinelli.it), which capitalizes on the university town setting. Look at **Feltrinelli International** (✉ Via Zamboni 7/b, east of Piazza Maggiore

☎ 051/268070), one of Italy's best selections of English and other for-eign-language books, and innumerable travel guides and maps.

Clothing

A host of small clothing and jewelry shops lines Via d'Azeglio in the center of town. For cheaper goods, Via dell'Indipendenza between the station and downtown is often lined with street vendors hawking bar-gain-basement clothing.

One of the most upscale malls in Italy, the **Galleria Cavour** (✉ Piazza Cavour, south of Piazza Maggiore) houses many of the fashion giants, including Gucci, Versace, and the jeweler and watchmaker Bulgari.

Wine & Food

Bologna is a good place to buy wine. Several shops have a bewilderingly large selection—to go straight to the top, ask the managers which wines were awarded the prestigious *Tre Bicchieri* (Three Glasses) award from Gambero Rosso's wine bible, *Vini d'Italia*.

Repeatedly recognized as one of the best wine stores in Italy, **Enoteca Italiana** (✉ Via Marsala 2/b, north of Piazza Maggiore ☎ 051/227132) lives up to its reputation with shelves lined with excellent selections from all over Italy at reasonable prices. Their delicious sandwiches with wine by the glass also make a great stand-up light lunch. Friendly owners run the midsize, down-to-earth **Scaramagli** (✉ Strada Maggiore 31/d, University area ☎ 051/227132) wine store.

For fresh produce, meats, and other foods sold in traditional Italian mar-kets, head to **Via Oberdan** (✉ Piazza Maggiore area), the street just off Via dell'Indipendenza downtown. The **Mercato di Mezzo** (✉ Via Peschiere Vecchie Piazza Maggiore area), which sells specialty foods, fruits, and vegetables, is an intense barrage of sights and smells; it's open daily 7–1 and 4:15–7:30, except on Thursday afternoons and Sunday. The **Mer-cato delle Erbe** (✉ Via Ugo Bassi Piazza Maggiore area) is an equally bustling food market, open Monday, Tuesday, Wednesday, and Friday 7–1:15 and 5–7:30, Thursday and Saturday 7–1:15. The gargantuan **La Piazzola** city market (✉ Piazza VIII Agosto off Via dell'Indipendenza, north toward the train station, Piazza Maggiore area) has vendors hawking wares of variable quality, including food, clothing, shoes, books, and every imaginable household necessity. It's open Friday and Saturday during daylight hours, and on some Sundays.

4 towns, dozens of foods, and a mouthful of flavors you'll never forget

Imagine biting into the silkiest prosciutto in the world or the most delectable homemade tortellini you've ever tasted. In Emilia, Italy's most acclaimed food region, you'll discover simple tastes that exceed all expectations. Beginning in Parma and moving eastward to Bologna, you'll find the epicenters of such world-renowned culinary treats as *prosciutto crudo*, Parmigiano-Reggiano, *aceto balsamico*, and tortellini. The secret to this region is not the discovery of new and exotic delicacies, but rather the rediscovery of foods you thought you already knew—in much better versions than you've ever tasted before.

TASTE 1 | PROSCIUTTO CRUDO

Quality testing

From Piacenza to the Adriatic, ham is the king of meats in Emilia-Romagna, but nowhere is this truer than in **Parma**.

Parma is the world's capital of *prosciutto crudo*, raw cured ham (*crudo* for short). Ask for *crudo di Parma* to signal its local provenance; many other regions also make their own crudo.

CRUDO LANGUAGE

It's easy to get confused with the terminology. Crudo is the product that Americans simply call "prosciutto" or the Brits might call "Parma ham." *Prosciutto* in Italian, however, is a more general term that means any kind of ham, including *prosciutto cotto*, or simply *cotto*, which means "cooked ham." Cotto is an excellent product and frequent pizza topping that's closer to (but much better than) what Americans would put in a deli sandwich.

Greasing the ham

Crudo is traditionally eaten in one of three ways: in a dry sandwich (*panino*); by itself as an appetizer, often with shaved butter on top; or as part of an appetizer or snack platter of assorted *salumi* (cured meats).

WHAT TO LOOK FOR

For the best crudo di Parma, look for slices, always cut to order, that are razor thin and have a light, rosy red color (not dark red). Don't be shy about going into a simple *salumeria* (a purveyor of cured meats) and ordering crudo by the pound. You can enjoy it straight out of the package on a park bench—and why not?

Fire branding

BEST SPOT FOR A SAMPLE

You can't go wrong with any of Parma's famed salumerie, but **Salumeria Garibaldi** (Via Farini 9) is one of the town's oldest and most reliable. You'll find not only spectacular prosciutto crudo, but also delectable cheeses, wines, porcini mushrooms, and more.

Quality trademark

LEARN MORE

For more information on crudo di Parma, contact the **Consorzio del Prosciutto di Parma** (Via Marco dell'Arpa 8/b, 0521/243987, www.prosciuttodiparma.com/eng).

Prosciutto di Parma

Warming milk in copper cauldrons

TASTE 2 | PARMIGIANO-REGGIANO

From Parma, it's only a half-hour trip east to **Reggio Emilia**, the birthplace of the crumbly and renowned Parmigiano-Reggiano cheese. Reggio (not to be confused with Reggio di Calabria in the south) is a cute and characteristic little Emilian town that has been the center of production for this legendary cheese for more than 70 years.

SAY CHEESE
Grana is the generic Italian term for hard, aged, full-flavored cheese that can be grated. Certain varieties of Pecorino Romano, for example, or Grana Padano, also fall under this term, but Parmigiano-Reggiano is the foremost example.

Breaking up the curds

NOT JUST FOR GRATING
In Italy, Parmigiano-Reggiano is not only grated onto pasta, but also often served by itself in chunks, either as an appetizer—perhaps accompanied by local salumi (cured meats)—or even for dessert, when it might be drizzled with honey or Modena's balsamic vinegar.

Placing cheese in molds

MEET THE MAKERS
If you're a cheese enthusiast, you shouldn't miss the chance to take a free two-hour guided tour of a Parmigiano-Reggiano–producing farm. You'll witness the entire process and get to meet the cheese makers. Tours can be arranged by contacting the **Consorzio del Formaggio Parmigiano-Reggiano** in Reggio Emilia (0522/506160, sezionere@parmigiano-reggiano.it, www.parmigiano-reggiano.it) at least 20 days in advance. (Ask specifically for an English-language tour if that's what you want.)

Aging cheese wheels

BEST SPOT FOR A SAMPLE
The production of Parmigiano-Reggiano is heavily controlled by the Consorzio del Formaggio, so you can buy the cheese at any store or supermarket in the region and be virtually guaranteed equal quality and price. For a more distinctive shopping experience, however, try buying Parmigiano-Reggiano at the street market on Reggio's central square. The market takes place on Tuesday and Friday from 8 AM to 1 PM year-round.

Parmigiano-Reggiano

TASTE 3 | ACETO BALSAMICO DI MODENA

Modena is home to *Aceto Balsamico Tradizionale di Modena*, a species of balsamic vinegar unparalleled anywhere else on Earth. The balsamic vinegar you've probably tried—even the pricier versions sold at specialty stores—may be good on salads, but it bears only a fleeting resemblance to the real thing.

Tasting tradizionale vinegar

HOW IS IT MADE?

The *tradizionale* vinegar that passes strict government standards is made with Trebbiano grape must, which is cooked over an open fire, reduced, and fermented from 12 to 25 or more years in a series of specially made wooden casks. As the vinegar becomes more concentrated, so much liquid evaporates that it takes more than 6 gallons of must to produce 1 quart of vinegar 12 years later. The result is an intense and syrupy concoction best enjoyed sparingly on grilled meats, strawberries, or Parmigiano-Reggiano cheese. The vinegar has such a complexity of flavor that some even drink it as an after-dinner liqueur.

Wooden casks for fermenting

BEST SPOT FOR A SAMPLE

The **Consorzio Produttori Aceto Balsamico Tradizionale di Modena** (Corso Cavour 60, 059/236981, www.balsamico.it) offers tours and tastings by reservation only. The main objective of the consortium is to monitor the quality of the authentic balsamic vinegar, made by only a few licensed restaurants and small producers.

The consortium also limits production, keeping prices sky high. Expect to pay €50 for a 100-ml (3.4 oz) bottle of tradizionale, which is generally aged 12 to 15 years, or €80 and up for the older tradizionale extra vecchio variety, which is aged 25 years.

OTHER TASTES OF EMILIA

❏ **Cotechino:** a sausage made from pork and lard, a specialty of Modena

❏ **Culatello de Zibello:** raw cured ham produced along the banks of the Po River, and cured and aged for more than 11 months

❏ **Mortadella:** soft, smoked sausage made with beef, pork, cubes of pork fat, and seasonings

❏ **Ragù:** a sauce made from minced pork and beef, simmered in milk, onions, carrots, and tomatoes

❏ **Salama da sugo:** salty, oily sausage aged and then cooked, a specialty of Ferrara

❏ **Tortelli and cappellacci:** pasta pillows with the same basic form as tortellini, but stuffed with cheese and vegetables

WHERE TO EAT

In Modena, it's hard to find a bad meal. Local trattorie do great versions of tortellini and other stuffed pasta. If you can find *zampone* (a sausage made from stuffed pig's trotter), don't miss it—it's an adventurous Modena specialty. **Hosteria Giusti** (Vicolo Squallore 46, 059/222533, www.giusti1605.com) is a particularly good place to try local specialties; the adjacent **Salumeria Giusti** is reputedly the world's oldest deli, founded in 1605.

TASTE 4 | TORTELLINI

The venerable city of **Bologna** is called "the Fat" for a reason: this is the birthplace of tortellini, not to mention other specialties such as mortadella and ragù. Despite the city's new reputation for chic nightclubs and flashy boutiques, much of the food remains as it ever was.

Making the dough

You'll find the many Emilian variations on stuffed pasta all over the region, but they're perhaps at their best in Bologna, especially the native tortellini.

INSPIRED BY THE GODS

According to one legend, tortellini was inspired by the bellybutton of Venus, goddess of love. As the story goes, Venus and some other gods stopped at a local inn for the night. A nosy chef went to their room to catch a glimpse of Venus. Peering through the keyhole, he saw her lying only partially covered on the bed. He was so inspired after seeing her perfect navel that he created a stuffed pasta, tortellini, in its image.

Stretching the dough

ON THE MENU

Tortellini is usually filled with beef (sometimes cheese), and is served two ways: *asciutta* is "dry," meaning it is served with a sauce such as ragù, or perhaps just with butter and Parmigiano. *Tortellini in brodo* is immersed in a lovely, savory beef broth.

Adding the filling

BEST SPOT FOR A SAMPLE

Don't miss **Tamburini** (Via Drapperie 1, 051/234726), Bologna's best specialty food shop, where smells of Emilia-Romagna's famous spoils waft out through the room and into the streets.

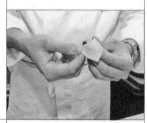
Shaping each piece

WHERE TO EAT

The classic art deco restaurant **Rosteria Luciano** (Via Nazario Sauro 19, 051/231249, www.rosterialuciano.it) is a great place to try tortellini in brodo, one of the best choices on their fixed menu. A changing list of daily specials augments the menu. For a meat course it's usually best to order whatever special the kitchen has that day. The selection of local cheeses is also good. Please note that the restaurant is closed on Wednesday, the whole month of August, and Sunday from June through September.

Tortellini di Bologna

RAVENNA

A small, quiet city, Ravenna has brick palaces, cobbled streets, magnificent monuments, and spectacular Byzantine mosaics to remind you of its storied past. The high point in Ravenna's history was 1,500 long years ago, when it became the capital of the Roman Empire. The honor was short-lived—the city was taken by the barbarian Ostrogoths in the 5th century; in the 6th century it was conquered by the Byzantines, who ruled it from Constantinople.

Because Ravenna spent much of its past looking to the East, its greatest art treasures show that influence. Churches and tombs with the most unassuming exteriors contain within them walls covered with tiny, glittering tiles. The beautifully preserved Byzantine mosaics put an emphasis on nature—green pastures, sheep, and starry skies, for instance—not found in Italy's other ancient artistic treasures. Outside Ravenna, the town of Classe hides even more mosaic gems.

Exploring Ravenna

A combination ticket (available at ticket offices of all included sights) admits you to six of Ravenna's important monuments: the Mausoleo di Galla Placidia, the Basilica di San Vitale, the Battistero Neoniano, Sant'Apollinare Nuovo, the church of Spirito Santo, and the Museo Arcivescovile e Cappella Sant'Andrea. Start out early in the morning to avoid lines (reservations are necessary for the Mausoleo and Basilica in May and June). A half day should suffice to walk the town alone; allow an hour each for the Mausoleo, the Basilica, and the Museo Nazionale. Ticket offices often close 15–30 minutes before the sights themselves.

> **WORD OF MOUTH**
>
> "Much of Ravenna is car-free, so we were on foot. Many local people rode bicycles; some of them smoked as they rode. Bikes for hire are parked in blue holders. One rents a key, and can take a bike from any holder and leave it at any holder, like luggage carts at an airport."   –smalti

The Main Attractions

❷ **Basilica di San Vitale.** The octagonal church of San Vitale was built in AD 547, after the Byzantines conquered the city, and its interior shows a strong Byzantine influence. In the area behind the altar are the most famous works in the church, accurate portraits of the Emperor of the East, Justinian, attended by his court and the bishop of Ravenna, Maximian. Notice how the mosaics seamlessly wrap around the columns and curved arches on the upper sides of the altar area. Reservations are recommended from March through mid-June. ⊠ *Via San Vitale off Via Salara* ☎ *0544/541688 reservations, 800/303999 information* ⊕ *www. ravennamosaici.it* ⊠ *Combination ticket €7.50* ⊙ *Nov.–Feb. daily 9:30–5; Mar. and Oct. daily 9–5:30; Apr.–Sept. daily 9–7; ticket office closes 15 mins earlier.*

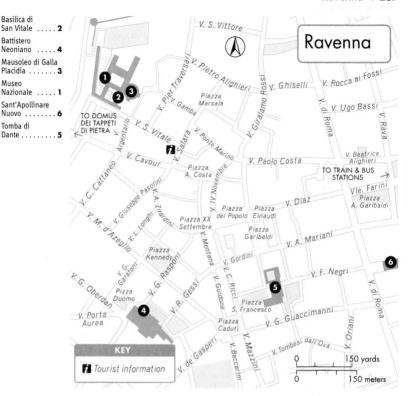

KEY

🛈 *Tourist information*

❹ **Battistero Neoniano.** The baptistry, next door to Ravenna's 18th-century cathedral, is one of the town's most important mosaic sights. In keeping with the building's role, the great mosaic in the dome shows the baptism of Christ, and beneath that scene are the Apostles. The lowest band of mosaics contains Christian symbols, the Throne of God, and the Cross. Note the naked figure kneeling next to Christ—he is the personification of the River Jordan. The Battistero building is said to have been a Roman bath dating from the 5th century AD. ⊠ *Via Battistero* ☎ *0544/541688 reservations, 800/303999 toll-free information* ⊕ *www. ravennamosaici.it* 🎟 *Combination ticket €7.50* ☉ *Nov.–Feb. daily 10–5; Mar. and Oct. daily 9:30–5:30; Apr.–Sept. daily 9–7; ticket office closes 15 mins earlier.*

❸ **Mausoleo di Galla Placidia.** The little tomb and the great church stand side by side, but the tomb predates the Basilica di San Vitale by at least a hundred years. These two adjacent sights are decorated with the best-known, and most elaborate, mosaics in Ravenna. Galla Placidia was the sister of Rome's emperor, Honorius, the man who moved the imperial capital to Ravenna in AD 402. She is said to have been beautiful and strong-willed, and to have taken an active part in the governing of the crumbling empire. This tomb, constructed in the mid-5th century, is her memorial.

Fodor'sChoice
★

Outside, the tomb is a small, unassuming redbrick building; the exterior's seeming poverty of charm only serves to enhance by contrast the richness of the interior mosaics, in deep midnight blue and glittering gold. The tiny, low central dome is decorated with symbols of Christ and the evangelists and striking gold stars. Over the door is a depiction of the Good Shepherd. Eight of the Apostles are represented in groups of two on the four inner walls of the dome; the other four appear singly on the walls of the two transepts. Notice the small doves at their feet, drinking from the water of faith. Also in the tiny transepts are some delightful pairs of deer (representing souls), drinking from the fountain of resurrection. There are three sarcophagi in the tomb, none of which are believed to contain the remains of Galla Placidia. She died in Rome in AD 450, and there is no record of her body having been transported back to the place where she wished to lie. Reservations are required for the Mausoleo from March through mid-June. ⊠ *Via San Vitale off Via Salara* ☎ *0544/ 541688 reservations, 800/303999 toll-free information* ⊕ *www. ravennamosaici.it* ⬚ *€2 supplement in addition to obligatory €7.50 combination ticket Mar. 1–June 15* ⊙ *Nov.–Feb. daily 9:30–5; Mar. and Oct. daily 9–5:30; Apr.–Sept. daily 9–7; ticket office closes 15 mins earlier.*

❻ **Sant'Apollinare Nuovo.** The mosaics displayed in this church date from the early 6th century, making them slightly older than the works in San Vitale. Since the left side of the church was reserved for women, it's only fitting that the mosaic decoration there is a scene of 22 virgins offering crowns to the Virgin Mary. On the right wall are 26 men carrying the crowns of martyrdom. They are approaching Christ, surrounded by angels. ⊠ *Via Roma at Via Guaccimanni* ☎ *0544/541688 reservations, 800/303999 toll-free information* ⊕ *www.ravennamosaici.it* ⬚ *Combination ticket €7.50* ⊙ *Nov.–Feb. daily 10–5; Mar. and Oct. daily 9:30–5:30; Apr.–Sept. daily 9–7; ticket office closes 15 mins earlier.*

Also Worth Seeing

Domus dei Tappeti di Pietra (Ancient Home of the Stone Carpets). This underground archaeological site was uncovered during the course of routine maintenance work by the city in 1993 and opened to the public in 2002. Below ground level (10 feet down) lie the remains of a 6th-century AD Byzantine palace, in which a beautiful and well-preserved network of floor mosaics display themes that are fascinatingly un-Christian. ⊠ *Via Barbiani; enter through Sant'Eufemia* ☎ *0544/32512* ⊕ *www. ravennantica.it* ⬚ *€3.50* ⊙ *Mar.–Oct., daily 10–6:30; Nov.–Feb., Mon.–Sat. 10–4:30, Sun. 10–6:30.*

❶ **Museo Nazionale.** The National Museum of Ravenna, next to the Church of San Vitale, contains artifacts from ancient Rome, Byzantine fabrics and carvings, and pieces of early Christian art. The collection is housed in a former monastery, but is well displayed and artfully lighted. ⊠ *Via Fiandrini* ☎ *0544/34424* ⬚ *€4* ⊙ *Tues.–Sun. 8:30–7:30.*

❺ **Tomba di Dante.** The tomb of Dante is in a small neoclassical building next door to the large church of St. Francis. Exiled from his native Florence, the author of *The Divine Comedy* died here in 1321. The Florentines have been trying to reclaim their famous son for hundreds of years, but the Ravennans refuse to give him up, arguing that since Florence did not welcome Dante in life it does not deserve him in death. The small **Museo Dantesco** has displays on the writer's life and the history of the tomb. ⊠ *Via Dante Alighieri 4 and 9* ☎ *0544/30252* 🖅 *Tomb free, museum €2* ⊙ *Tomb daily 9–noon and 2–5, museum Tues.–Sun. 9–noon.*

Off the Beaten Path

Sant'Apollinare in Classe. This church, about 5 km (3 mi) southeast of Ravenna, is landlocked now, but when it was built it stood in the center of the busy shipping port known to the ancient Romans as Classis. The arch above and the area around the high altar are rich with mosaics. Those on the arch, older than the ones behind it, are considered superior. They show Christ in Judgment and the 12 lambs of Christianity leaving the cities of Jerusalem and Bethlehem. In the apse is the figure of Sant'Apollinare himself, a bishop of Ravenna, and above him is a magnificent Transfiguration against blazing green grass, animals in skewed perspective, and flowers. ⊠ *Via Romea Sud, Classe* ☎ *0544/473569* 🖅 *€2* ⊙ *Mon.–Sat. 8:30–7:30, Sun. 1–7:30; ticket office closes ½ hr earlier.*

Where to Stay & Eat

$$ ✕ **Bella Venezia.** Graceful low archways lead into this attractive pink-and-white restaurant's two small, brightly lighted dining rooms. Try the beans with olive oil and *bottarga* (cured roe) or the owner's special risotto with butter, Parmesan, cured ham, mushrooms, and peas to start. For the second course, the *fegato alla Veneziana* (grilled liver with onions) is a good choice. The outdoor garden is quite pleasant in season. ⊠ *Via IV Novembre 16* ☎ *0544/212746* ⊕ *www.bellavenezia.it* ▭ *AE, DC, MC, V* ⊙ *Closed Sun. and 3 wks in Dec. and Jan.*

$–$$ ✕ **La Gardèla.** The kitchen seems to operate with an otherworldly efficiency, making this bright, bustling downtown restaurant extremely popular with the local business crowd—especially at lunch (always a good sign). The place is best for classics like tagliatelle al ragù and Adriatic fish, such as *sardoncini* (sardines, breaded and fried). ⊠ *Via Ponte Marino 3* ☎ *0544/217147* ▭ *AE, DC, MC, V* ⊙ *Closed Thurs. and 10 days in Jan.*

★ $–$$ ✕ **Locanda del Melarancio.** This contemporary establishment, on the second floor of a palazzo in the heart of the centro storico, is impossible not to like. Decor is minimalist without being stark, and modern artwork on the walls doesn't take away from the warm, traditional feeling. So, too, for the menu, which makes brilliant use of modern techniques to harness traditional Romagnan ingredients: *formaggio di fossa* (cheese aged in a cave) is made into a *sformato* (like a firm mousse) with julienned salami, honey, and balsamic vinegar, and cappellacci are filled with mascarpone and truffle under a sauce of porcini mushrooms. ⊠ *Via Mentana 33* ☎ *0544/215258* ⊕ *www.locandadelmelarancio.it* ▭ *AE, DC, MC, V.*

★ $ ✕ **Ca' de Ven.** A vaulted wine cellar in the heart of the old city, the Ca' de Ven is great for a hearty meal. You sit at long tables with other diners and feast on platters of delicious cold cuts, flat breads, and cold, heady white wine. The tortelli *di radicchio e pecorino* (stuffed with radicchio and goat cheese) makes the best first course. ⊠ *Via C. Ricci 24* ☎ *0544/ 30163* ⊟ *AE, DC, MC, V* ⊗ *Closed Mon., 3 wks in Jan. and Feb., and 1st wk of June.*

$$–$$$ ⊡ **Hotel Bisanzio.** Steps from San Vitale and the Tomb of Galla Placidia, this Best Western hotel is the most convenient lodging for mosaic enthusiasts. The exterior is drab, but rooms are comfortable and modern; the lobby's Florentine lamps add a touch of style. Ask to be on the top floor and you may get a view of the basilica. ⊠ *Via Salara 30, 48100* ☎ *0544/217111* 🖷 *0544/32539* ⊕ *www.bisanziohotel.com* ↳ *38 rooms* ♻ *Dining room, in-room safes, minibars, 2 bars, Internet room, meeting room, parking (fee)* ⊟ *AE, DC, MC, V* ❙❙❙ *BP.*

$$ ⊡ **Sant'Andrea.** This simple bed-and-breakfast opened in 2005 offers an absolutely prime location, steps away from the Basilica di San Vitale. It's like staying in a well-appointed house—rooms are big, bright, and clean, done up in primary colors. The lobby is decked out with homey furniture, and breakfast can be taken in the breakfast room, or in the garden in good weather. Bathrooms are spotless and modern. A suite only costs €20 extra and can accommodate a family of four or five. ⊠ *Via Cattaneo 33, 48100* ☎🖷 *0544/215564* ⊕ *www.santandreahotel.com* ↳ *12 rooms* ♻ *In-room safes, minibars, bar, parking (fee)* ⊟ *AE, DC, MC, V* ❙❙❙ *BP.*

$ ⊡ **Hotel Centrale Byron.** Tranquillity is assured here in the center of Ravenna's old town, because it's in a pedestrian zone. The old-fashioned, well-managed hotel has spotless if uninspired rooms. You can drop off your luggage at the door, but you have to park your car in one of the nearby garages or lots. ⊠ *Via IV Novembre 14, 48100* ☎ *0544/212225* 🖷 *0544/34114* ⊕ *www.hotelbyron.com* ↳ *54 rooms* ♻ *In-room safes, minibars, cable TV, bar, parking (fee)* ⊟ *AE, DC, MC, V* ❙❙❙ *BP.*

$ ⊡ **Hotel Ravenna.** A functional stopover near the train station, the Ravenna is still only a few minutes' walk from the center. This modern hotel has smallish rooms; two rooms are equipped for people with disabilities. Service is friendly and helpful. ⊠ *Via Maroncelli 12, 48100* ☎ *0544/212204* 🖷 *0544/212077* ⊕ *www.hotelravenna.ra.it* ↳ *26 rooms* ♻ *Bar, parking (fee); no a/c* ⊟ *MC, V* ❙❙❙ *BP.*

Nightlife & the Arts

Friday evenings in July and August bring **Mosaics by Night,** when the Byzantine mosaic masterpieces in town are illuminated. The event is also held on certain Tuesdays; to check, call the tourist office, which also offers guided tours.

The **Ravenna Festival** is a musical extravaganza, held every year in June and July. Orchestras from all over the world come to perform in Ravenna's mosaic-clad churches and theaters.

FERRARA

47 km (29 mi) northeast of Bologna, 74 km (46 mi) northwest of Ravenna.

Today you are likely to be charmed by Ferrara's prosperous air and meticulous cleanliness, its excellent local restaurants and fin-de-siècle coffee-houses, and its hospitable, youthful spirit: a boisterous mass of wine drinkers gathers outside the Duomo on even the foggiest of weekend evenings. Though Ferrara is a UNESCO World Heritage Site, the city still draws amazingly few tourists—which only adds to its appeal. The legendary Ferrarese filmmaker Michelangelo Antonioni called his beloved hometown "a city that you can see only partly, while the rest disappears to be imagined," and perhaps he was referring to the low-lying mist that rolls in off the Adriatic each winter and shrouds Ferrara's winding knot of medieval alleyways, turreted pleasure palaces, and ancient wine bars—once inhabited by the likes of Copernicus—in a ghostly fog. But perhaps Antonioni was also suggesting that Ferrara's striking beauty often conceals a dark and tortured past.

Although the site was first settled before the time of Christ and was once ruled by Ravenna, Ferrara's history really begins with an ominous event—the arrival of the Este in 1259. For more than three centuries the infamous dynasty ruled with an iron fist; brother killed brother, son fought father, husband murdered wife. The majestic castle with moat, which now guards the heart of Ferrara's old town in innocuous splendor, was originally built as a fortress to protect the ruthless Este dukes from their own citizens; deep within the castle's bowels the Este kept generations of political dissidents in dank cells barely larger than a human body. The greatest of the dukes, Ercole I (1433–1505), attempted to poison a nephew who challenged his power, and when that didn't work he beheaded him. Yet it is to this pitiless man that Ferrara owes its great beauty. In one of his more empathetic moments, Ercole invited Sephardic Jews exiled from Spain to settle in Ferrara, spawning half a millennium of Jewish history that came to a spectacular end as Italy succumbed to Axis ideology. The maze of twisting cobblestone streets that forms the old ghetto witnessed the persecution of its Jews once fascist Italy came under the spell of Nazi Germany, a tragedy documented in Giorgio Bassani's book and Vittorio De Sica's canonical neorealist film, *The Garden of the Finzi-Continis*.

If you plan to explore the city fully, consider buying a museum card (€14) at the Palazzo dei Diamanti or at one of the art museums around town; it grants admission to every museum, palace, and castle in Ferrara. The first Monday of the month is free at many museums.

The Main Attractions

Naturally enough, the building that was the seat of Este power dominates the town: the massive **Castello Estense** is a perfectly preserved castle in the center of the city in Piazza Castello. The building was a suitable symbol for the ruling family: cold and menacing on the outside, lavishly decorated within. The public rooms are grand, but deep in the bowels of the fortress are chilling dungeons where enemies of the state were held in wretched conditions—a function these quarters served as recently as 1943, when antifascist prisoners were detained there. In particular, the **Prisons of Don Giulio, Ugo, and Parisina** have some fascinating features, like 15th-century smoke graffiti protesting the imprisonment of the young lovers Ugo and Parisina, who were beheaded in 1425.

The castle was established as a fortress in 1385, but work on its luxurious ducal quarters continued into the 16th century. Representative of Este grandeur are the **Sala dei Giochi,** extravagantly painted with pagan athletic scenes, and the **Sala dell'Aurora,** decorated to show the times of the day. The tower, the terraces of the castle, and the hanging garden—once reserved for the private use of the duchesses—have fine views of the town and the surrounding countryside. You can cross the castle's moat, traverse its drawbridge, and wander through many of its arcaded passages at any time; in the still of a misty night, the experience is haunting. ⊠ *Piazza Castello* ☎ *0532/299233* 🖻 *Castle €6, tower €1 extra* ☽ *Castle Tues.–Sun. 9:30–5:30, tower Tues.–Sun. 10–4:45; ticket office closes at 4:45.*

★ The magnificent Gothic **Duomo,** a few steps away from the Castello Estense, has a three-tier facade of bony arches and beautiful carvings over the central door. It was begun in 1135 and took more than 100 years to complete. The interior was completely remodeled in the 17th century. ⊠ *Piazza Cattedrale* ☎ *0532/207449* ☽ *Mon.–Sat. 7:30–noon and 3–6:30, Sun. 7:30–12:30 and 3:30–7:30.*

The collection of ornate religious objects in the **Museo Ebraico** (Jewish Museum) bears witness to the long history of the city's Jewish community. This history had its high points—1492, for example, when Ercole I invited the Jews to come over from Spain—and its lows, notably 1624, when the papal government closed the **ghetto,** which was reopened only with the advent of a united Italy in 1859. The triangular warren of narrow, cobbled streets that made up the ghetto originally extended as far as Corso Giovecca (originally Corso Giudecca, or Ghetto Street); when it was enclosed, the neighborhood was restricted to the area between Via Scienze, Via Contrari, and Via di San Romano. The museum, in the center of the ghetto, was once Ferrara's synagogue. A guided tour is required to visit. ⊠ *Via Mazzini 95* ☎ *0532/210228* 🖻 *€4* ☽ *Guided tours Sun.–Thurs. at 10, 11, and noon.*

The **Palazzo dei Diamanti** (Palace of Diamonds) is so called because of the 12,600 small, pink-and-white marble pyramids ("diamonds") that stud the facade. The building was designed to be viewed in perspective—both faces at once—from diagonally across the street. Originally built in the 15th and 16th centuries, today the palazzo contains the **Pinacoteca Nazionale,** which has an extensive

art gallery and rotating exhibits. ⊠ *Corso Ercole I d'Este 19–21* ☎ *0532/ 205844* 🖻 *€4* ☽ *Tues., Wed., Fri., and Sat. 9–2; Thurs. 9–7; Sun. 9–1.*

The oldest and most characteristic area of Ferrara is to the south of the Duomo, stretching between the Corso Giovecca and the city's ramparts. Here various members of the Este family built pleasure palaces, the most famous of which is the **Palazzo Schifanoia** (*schifanoia* means "carefree" or, literally, "fleeing boredom"). Begun in the 14th century, the palace was remodeled in 1466 and was the city's first Renaissance palazzo. The interior is lavishly decorated, particularly the **Salone dei Mesi,** with an extravagant series of frescoes showing the months of the year and their mythological attributes. The adjacent **Museo Civico Lapidario,** on Via Camposabbionario, has a collection of coins, statuary, and paintings. ⊠ *Via Scandiana 23* ☎ *0532/244949* ⊕ *www.comune.fe.it/musei-aa/ schifanoia/skifa.html* 🎫 *€5* ⊙ *Tues.–Sun. 9–6.*

One of the streets most characteristic of Ferrara's past, the 2-km-long (1-mi-long) **Via delle Volte,** is also one of the oldest preserved medieval streets in Europe. The series of ancient *volte* (arches) along the narrow cobblestone alley once joined the merchants' houses on the south side of the street to their warehouses on the north side. The street ran parallel to the banks of the Po River, which was home to the busy port of ancient Ferrara.

Also Worth Seeing

One of the best-preserved of the Renaissance palaces along Ferrara's old streets is the charming **Casa Romei.** Downstairs are rooms with 15th-century frescoes and several sculptures collected from destroyed churches. The house stands not far from the Palazzo del Paradiso, in the area behind Ferrara's castle. The schedule varies with exhibits. ⊠ *Via Savonarola 30* ☎ *0532/240341* 🎫 *€2* ⊙ *Tues.–Sun. 8:30–7:30.*

On the busy Corso Giovecca is the **Palazzina di Marfisa d'Este,** a grandiose 16th-century home that belonged to a great patron of the arts. The house has painted ceilings, fine 16th-century furniture, and a garden containing a grotto and an outdoor theater. ⊠ *Corso Giovecca 170* ☎ *0532/ 244949* ⊕ *www.comune.fe.it/musei-aa/schifanoia/marfi.html* 🎫 *€3* ⊙ *Tues.–Sun. 9–1 and 3–6.*

The grand but unfinished courtyard is the most interesting part of the luxurious **Palazzo di Ludovico il Moro,** a magnificent 15th-century dwelling built for Ludovico Sforza, husband of Beatrice d'Este. The palazzo contains the region's **Museo Archeologico,** a repository of relics of early man, Etruscans, and Romans found in the country surrounding the city. ⊠ *Via XX Settembre 124, near Palazzo Schifanoia* ☎ *0532/66299* 🎫 *€4* ⊙ *Tues.–Sun. 9–2.*

Where to Stay & Eat

★ **\$\$\$\$** ✕ **Il Don Giovanni.** To find this elegant and secluded dining room, full of oranges, reds, yellows, and jazz vocals, is a challenge; look for the street sign that points you through a courtyard to the restaurant. Once inside, the high prices are justified by fireworks on the plate. Complex mozzarella di bufala is shockingly paired with raw shrimp so fruity it's like a dab of marmalade. Meltingly tender raw scallops reveal but a whisper of sweetness. Swallowing the raw, silver-skinned *sgombro,* like a smaller, milder version of mackerel, might remind you of the well-behaved dolphins at Sea World. Cooked fish is equally impressive: in an inspired combination, juicy, well-seasoned *branzino* (striped sea bass) sits daringly atop chili peppers. If you can't afford the restaurant, check out the less-expensive **La Borsa** wine bar, in the same complex (and with the same phone number), which has excellent cured meats, cheeses, sandwiches, and traditional dishes like *cappellacci di zucca* (squash-filled pasta pillows) and roast pork. ⊠ *Corso Ercole I d'Este 1* ☎ *0532/243363* ⊕ *www.ildongiovanni.com* ⩘ *Reservations essential* ☰ *AE, DC, MC, V* ☽ *Closed Mon. No lunch.*

★ **$$$–$$$$** ✕ **Max.** A modern, minimalist restaurant steps from the Castello Estense is quietly turning the Ferrara dining scene on its head. Exciting *alta cucina* (haute cuisine) dishes at Max include an absolutely spectacular plate of raw shellfish from the nearby Adriatic. In the deconstructed eggplant Parmigiana, pieces of eggplant are molded into an impossibly soft *sformatino* (soufflélike dish) with a béchamel sauce and sweet *scampi* (a Mediterranean shellfish); a whole crisped tomato sits off to the side. In spite of the restaurant's relative formality, the service is friendly. ⊠ *Piazza Repubblica 16* ☎ *0532/209309* ⩘ *Reservations essential* ☰ *AE, DC, MC, V* ☽ *Closed Mon. and Aug. 15–31. No lunch Sun.*

$–$$$ ✕ **Trattoria La Romantica.** The former stables of a 17th-century merchant's house have been transformed into this casually elegant, welcoming restaurant, which is a great favorite among well-fed locals. Although the decor (warm light and wood-beam ceilings, incongruous prints, and a piano) seems to be in perpetual transition, the haute-rustic food is fully realized. Ferrarese specialties like cappellacci di zucca are served side by side with French oysters. ⊠ *Via Ripagrande 36* ☎ *0532/765975* ☰ *AE, DC, MC, V* ☽ *Closed Wed., Jan. 7–17, and Aug. 1–15.*

$–$$ ✕ **Antica Trattoria Volano.** Local businessmen often fill this white-wall, traditional-to-the-core neighborhood trattoria. The decor is rustic and the food includes such local treats as cappellacci di zucca and a good version of *salama da sugo,* a salty and oily boiled sausage, served over mashed potatoes. *Tris* is a first-course sampler of three pastas that change nightly. ⊠ *Via Volano 20* ☎ *0532/761421* ☰ *AE, DC, MC, V* ☽ *Closed Fri.*

$–$$ ✕ **Osteria del Ghetto.** Though the casually elegant *osteria* (tavernlike restaurant) is buried deep in the old Jewish ghetto, its seasonal menu is anything but old-fashioned. Dishes here represent the cutting edge of Ferrarese cooking: basmati rice torte with Colonnata lard and boletus mushrooms; eggplant flan with cold *grana* (aged, granulated cheese) cream; a lukewarm pheasant salad with balsamic vinegar. The dining room is modern and relaxing, with wood-beamed ceilings, a no-smoking section, and tables on the street in summer. ⊠ *Via Vittorio 26* ☎ *0532/ 764936* ☰ *AE, DC, MC, V* ☽ *Closed Tues.*

★ **¢** ✕ **Osteria Al Brindisi.** Ferrara is a city of wine bars, beginning with this, Europe's oldest, which began pouring in 1435. This might just be the most perfect place to drink wine in Italy—Copernicus, who once lived upstairs, seemed to think so. Prices are low, the ambient lighting soft, and even the music (usually good jazz) somehow feels just right. There's a great selection by the glass, or you can choose from among the thousands of national and international bottles that line the ancient walls. A memorable spread of salumi and local cheeses is available, as well as tasty hot meals such as tortellini *in brodo* (in beef or chicken broth). ⊠ *Via degli Adelardi 11* ☎ *0532/209142* ☰ *AE, DC, MC, V* ☽ *Closed Mon.*

The **Prenotel hotel reservation hotline** (☎ *0532/462046*), run by the city, allows you to make reservations at any of the accommodations listed below, among many others.

CLOSE UP

Talking Politics

EMILIA-ROMAGNA MIGHT seem staid: city after city has immaculate streets filled with smartly dressed businessmen in impeccable shoes, covertly murmuring to each other through the winter fog over cups of coffee. But after dark, from Parma to Bologna, Piacenza to Ferrara, the middle managers are replaced on the streets by young, energetic would-be intellectuals, and the murmurs turn into impassioned political discussion—usually with a leftist slant—over jugs of table wine. If you enjoy this type of conversation, take time to stop for a drink after dinner in a student cafeteria, cozy café, or back-alley bar. Don't be afraid to join in—all ages are welcome, and divergent opinions, thoughtfully argued, are treated with respect. (Locals are usually happy to practice their English, which can often be quite good.) You'll experience another side of the region—a side that's important to understanding its culture and history.

4

$$$ **Annunziata.** The flower-covered minibalconies of this hotel could hardly be any closer to the castle and Ferrara's old town—this might just be the best location in the city. The building feels like an old private home, the lobby is inviting, and the pleasantly understated rooms have ceilings with old wooden beams. ⊠ *Piazza Repubblica 5, 44100* ☎ *0532/201111* 📠 *0532/203233* ⊕ *www.annunziata.it* ↘ *26 rooms* ♢ *Room service, in-room safes, minibars, cable TV, Wi-Fi, bicycles, bar, parking (fee)* ▤ *AE, DC, MC, V* ⌗ *BP.*

$$–$$$ **Hotel Ripagrande.** The courtyards, vaulted brick lobby, and breakfast
Fodor'sChoice room of this 15th-century noble's palazzo retain much of their lordly
★   Renaissance flair. Rooms are decidedly more down-to-earth, but standard doubles and some of the enormous bi- and tri-level suites have faux-Persian rugs, tapestries, and cozy antique furniture; top-floor rooms and suites resemble a Colorado ski lodge, with terraces, and are roomy—especially good for families. Everything here, including the room service, is impeccable. The location is quiet but fairly convenient. ⊠ *Via Ripagrande 21, 44100* ☎ *0532/765250* 📠 *0532/764377* ⊕ *www.ripagrandehotel.it* ↘ *20 rooms, 20 suites* ♢ *Restaurant, room service, in-room safes, minibars, cable TV, bar, meeting room, free parking* ▤ *AE, DC, MC, V* ⌗ *BP.*

$ **Hotel San Paolo.** On the edge of the old city, San Paolo is the best inexpensive choice in town. The 10-minute walk from the heart of Ferrara's medieval quarter is pleasant, and there are good restaurants in the vicinity. Singles are a particularly good value (about €65); triples are available. ⊠ *Via Baluardi 9, 44100* ☎ *0532/762040* 📠 *0532/ 762040* ⊕ *www.hotelsanpaolo.it* ↘ *29 rooms* ♢ *Cable TV, bicycles, some pets allowed; no a/c in some rooms* ▤ *AE, DC, MC, V* ⌗ *EP.*

$ **Locanda Borgonuovo.** This lovely bed-and-breakfast is in a 17th-century monastery on a quiet but central pedestrians-only street. It books up months in advance, partly because musicians and actors from the local theater make this their home away from home. Rooms are furnished with antiques, and one has its own kitchen for longer stays. Summer breakfasts are served in the leafy courtyard. ⊠ *Via Cairoli 29, 44100* ☏ *0532/211100* 🖷 *0532/246328* ⊕ *www.borgonuovo.com* ⤴ *4 rooms* ⚘ Dining room, in-room safes, some kitchens, minibars, bicycles, library, free parking ⊟ AE, MC, V ⦿| BP.

Nightlife

The dim, stylish **Enobar Estense** (⊠ Piazza Cattedrale 7 ☏ 339/4831510), right next to the cathedral, accompanies wines from all over Italy with endless plates of delightful free Italian tapas and soothing jazz. **Enoteca I Contrari** (⊠ Via Contrari 52, at Via Mazzini ☏ 0532/242422) has huge wooden beams, high ceilings, good music, and good feelings. They serve panini, plates of local salumi and cheeses, specialty rums and Scotches, and great wines by the glass.

For live jazz, check out the **Jazz Club Ferrara** (⊠ Torrione San Giovanni ☏ 0532/211573 ⊕ www.jazzclubferrara.com), which has a star-studded lineup.

Orsatti 1860 (⊠ Via Cortevecchia 33 ☏ 0532/207572) is one of the oldest and best places in town for local pastries and great espresso (standing at the bar, of course). The low-key **Leon d'Oro** (⊠ Piazza Cattedrale 2–10 ☏ 0532/209318) is a grand old café serving expensive drinks, coffee, and signature Ferrarese fruitcakes (as well as a few basic pasta dishes at lunchtime) in a truly regal environment. It's closed Wednesday.

Bicycling

Cycling is extremely popular in Ferrara. **Pirana e Bagni** (⊠ Piazzale Stazione 2 ☏ 0532/772190) rents bicycles. Call **Cicloclub Estense** (☏ 0532/900931) to arrange a guided bike trip.

THE VENETO

Updated by
Robin
Goldstein

THE GREEN PLAINS STRETCHING west of Venice hold three of northern Italy's most appealing midsize cities: Padua, Vicenza, and Verona. Each has notable artistic treasures and an attractive historic center; Padua is famous for its Giotto frescoes, Vicenza for its Palladian villas, and Verona for its ancient arena. All three were once under the control of Venice, and one of the pleasures of exploring them is discovering the traces of Venetian influence—still evident in everything from food to architecture.

PADUA

Bustling with bicycles and lined with frescoes, Padua has long been one of the major cultural centers in northern Italy. It's home to the peninsula's—and the world's—second-oldest university, founded in 1222, which attracted the likes of Dante (1265–1321), Petrarch (1304–74), and Galileo Galilei (1564–1642), thus earning the city the sobriquet *La Dotta* (The Learned). Padua's Basilica di Sant'Antonio, begun not long after the university in 1234, is dedicated to St. Anthony, the patron saint of lost-and-found objects, and attracts grateful pilgrims in droves, especially on his feast day, June 13. Three great artists—Giotto (1266–1337), Donatello (circa 1386–1466), and Mantegna (1431–1506)—left great works here, with Giotto's Scrovegni chapel one of the best-known, and most meticulously preserved, works of art in the country. Today, cycle-happy students rule the roost, flavoring every aspect of local culture. Don't be surprised if you spot a *laurea* (graduation) ceremony marked by laurel leaves, mocking lullabies, and X-rated caricatures.

Exploring Padua

Padua is a pedestrian's city, and you'll want to spend your time in the city on foot (or bike). If you arrive by car, leave your vehicle in one of the parking lots on the outskirts, or at your hotel. The *Padova Arte* ticket (€14), valid for 48 hours, is a good deal if you plan to visit several of the town's principal sights: it allows entry to the Cappella degli Scrovegni, Musei Civici degli Eremitani, Palazzo della Ragione, Battistero, Scoletta del Santo, Musei Antoniani, and the Orto Botanico. It is available from the tourist office and at some museums.

WORD OF MOUTH

"To me, Padua, even more than Venice, is evocative of the 'old' Italy. In the old city *(città vecchia)*, the maze of tiny streets is just the thing for wandering around and getting lost."   –Wayne

THE VENETO, PAST & PRESENT

THE WINGED LION of St. Mark, emblem of Venice, is very much in evidence in the Veneto, emblazoned on palazzos and standing atop lofty columns. It's a symbol of the strong influence Venice has had over the region's architecture, art, and way of life.

Middle Age Tyrants & Family Feuds. Long before Venice came to dominate, Ezzelino III da Romano (1194–1259), a larger-than-life scourge who was excommunicated by Pope Innocent IV and even had a crusade launched against him, laid claim to as much land as he could. He seized the cities of Verona, Padua, Este, Montagnana, and Monselice and their surrounding territory. After his fall, powerful families such as the Carrara in Padua and the della Scala (Scaligeri) from Verona vied with each other during the 14th century to annex these towns.

When not destroying each other, the noble families of the region bestowed on their progeny a rich legacy of architectural and artistic jewels, which are today the hallmark of Padua, Vicenza, and Verona. The characters of these cities, though sharing the Venetian influence, were well defined long before Venice arrived on the scene. Padua had established itself as a city-state during the 12th century. Its university, founded in 1222, counted Galileo among its teachers and drew the poets Dante and Petrarch into its orbit. In the 14th century, the cultural flowering found its most sublime expression in the frescoes of Giotto, a landmark in the history of art, and later in the painters and sculptors of the Renaissance, most notably Donatello and Mantegna.

Palladian Style. Vicenza lays claim to a scion who was to have a predominant influence on the course of Western architecture, Andrea di Pietro della Gondola— better known as Palladio, whose mark can be seen in practically every capitol in the United States. Not only did Palladio create new buildings, but he grafted his classically inspired designs on the existing Gothic palazzos; his spirit prevails also in numerous villas in the surrounding countryside. In Verona, on the other hand, there's no escaping a much earlier epoch, for this was once a city of ancient Rome, and its awe-inspiring arena is the third largest in Italy. Here "circuses" still astound audiences, though the spectacles have moved on from the gladiatorial to the operatic, in the form of large-scale productions complete with animals. Among the performances, there is an annual Shakespeare Festival— one more reminder that this is the home of that most fabled of love stories, *Romeo and Juliet*.

Venetian to a T. Once Venice had established its presence in the region, a time of relative peace ensued, exquisitely marked by the blooming of Venetian palazzos and the works of master artists. The three Ts—Titian, Tintoretto, and Tiepolo—have all contributed to the impressive heritage of the zone. When Venetians took vacations, they made sure they did it in style, their retreats designed by the best architects and decorated by the best painters of the day. Palladio was first choice for the job, and his work is nobly illustrated by the superlative Villa La Rotonda, near Vicenza.

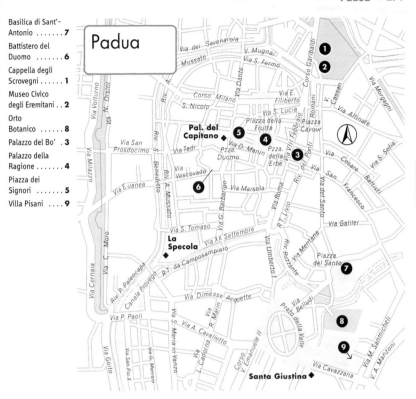

The Main Attractions

★ **❼ Basilica di Sant'Antonio.** Thousands of worshippers throng to Il Santo, a cluster of Byzantine domes and slender, minaret-like towers that gives this huge basilica an Asian-inspired style reminiscent of San Marco in Venice. The interior is sumptuous, too, with marble reliefs by Tullio Lombardo (1455–1532), the greatest in a talented family of marble carvers who decorated many churches in the area, among them Venice's Santa Maria dei Miracoli. The artistic highlights here, however, bear Donatello's name; the 15th-century Florentine master did the remarkable series of bronze reliefs illustrating the life of St. Anthony. The **Cappella del Santo** was built to house the green marble tomb of the saint and is now filled with votive offerings. Reconstructed in the 16th century, it shows Italian High Renaissance at its best. The **Cappella del Tesoro** (🕓 Daily 8–noon and 2:30–7) holds the not-so-pristine tongue of the saint in a 15th-century reliquary. In front of the church is Donatello's powerful statue of the *condottiere* (mercenary general) Erasmo da Narni, known by the nickname Gattamelata. Cast in bronze—a monumental technical achievement in 1453—the statue had an enormous influence on the development of Italian Renaissance sculpture. ⊠ *Piazza del Santo* ☎ *049/8789722* ⊕ *www.santantonio.org* 🕓 *Daily 6:30 AM–7 PM.*

❶ Cappella degli Scrovegni. This chapel, the second-most famous in Italy
Fodor'sChoice after the Sistine, was erected by wealthy Paduan Enrico Scrovegno to
★ atone for the usury practiced by his deceased father, Reginaldo. Giotto
and his assistants were commissioned to decorate the interior; they
worked from 1303 to 1305 on a magnificent fresco cycle illustrating
the lives of Mary and Christ. In typical medieval comic-strip fashion,
the 38 panels are arranged in tiers intended to be read from left to right.
Opposite the altar is a powerful *Last Judgment,* where Enrico offers his
chapel to the Virgin. The depth and perspective in these frescoes—
which include the first blue skies in Western painting—were revolutionary. Mandatory reservations, available by Web or phone, are for a
specific time and are nonrefundable. In order to preserve the artwork,
doors are opened only every 15 minutes. A maximum of 25 visitors at
a time must spend 15 minutes in an acclimatization room before making a 15-minute chapel visit. You can see fresco details as part of a virtual tour at Musei Civici degli Eremitani. A good place to get some
background before visiting the chapel is the multimedia room, which
offers films and interactive computer presentations. Entrance is only by
reservation, which you should make at least two days ahead. It is usually possible to buy your admission on the spot—although you might
have to wait a while until there's an opening. Visits are scheduled every
20 minutes, and punctuality is essential. Get to the chapel at least a half
hour before your reservation time. ⊠ *Piazza Eremitani 8* ☎ *49/2010020
for reservations* ⊕ *www.cappelladegliscrovegni.it* 🎟 *€12 including
Musei Civici, or €1 with Padova Card* ⊙ *Daily 9 AM–10 PM.*

★ ❹ Palazzo della Ragione. Also known as Il Salone, this spectacular, arcaded
palace, which divides the Piazza delle Frutta from the Piazza delle Erbe,
is the most memorable architectural image of the city. In the Middle Ages
the building was the seat of Padua's government; today, its street-level
arcades shelter shops and cafés. Art shows are often held upstairs in the
frescoed **Salone,** at 85 feet high one of the largest and most architecturally
pleasing halls in Italy, where there's an enormous 15th-century wooden
replica of Gattamelata's bronze steed sculpted by Donatello. ⊠ *Piazza
della Ragione* ☎ *049/8205006* 🎟 *Salone €8* ⊙ *Tues.–Sun. 9–7.*

❺ Piazza dei Signori. Some fine examples of 15th- and 16th-century buildings line this square. On the west side, the **Palazzo del Capitanio** has an
impressive **Torre dell'Orologio,** with an astronomical clock dating from
1344. The **Duomo,** just a few steps away, is not the most interesting church
in town.

☾ ❾ Villa Pisani. Extensive grounds with rare trees, ornamental fountains, and
garden follies surround this extraordinary 18th-century palace in Stra, 13
km (8 mi) southeast of Padua. It was one of the last of many stately residences constructed along the Brenta River from the 16th to 18th century
by wealthy Venetians for their *villeggiatura*—vacation and escape from
the midsummer humidity. Tiepolo's trompe-l'oeil frescoes on the ballroom
ceiling alone are worth the visit. If you have youngsters in tow surfeited
with old masters, explore the gorgeous **park** and **maze.** To get here from
Venice, you can take the Brenta River bus that leaves from Piazzale Roma.
⊠ *Via Doge Pisani 7, Stra* ☎ *049/502074* 🎟 *Villa, maze, and park €5;*

maze and park only €2.50 ⊙ Apr.–Sept., Tues.–Sun. 9–7; villa and park only Oct.–Mar., Tues.–Sun. 9–4; last entry 1 hr before closing.

Also Worth Seeing

❻ Battistero del Duomo (Cathedral Baptistery). The often-overlooked 12th-century baptistry contains mid-1370s frescoes depicting scenes from the Book of Genesis. They're the greatest work of Giusto de' Menabuoi, who further developed Giotto's style of depicting human figures naturally, using perspective and realistic lighting. The building is a refreshingly cool retreat from the city. ⊠ *Piazza Duomo* ☎ *049/656914* 🎫 *€2.50 or Padova Card* ⊙ *Daily 10–6.*

❷ Musei Civici degli Eremitani (Civic Museum). What was once a monastery now houses works of Venetian masters, as well as fine collections of archaeological pieces and ancient coins. Notable are the Giotto Crucifix, which was once in the Scrovegni Chapel, and the *Portrait of a Young Senator* by Bellini. ⊠ *Piazza Eremitani 10* ☎ *049/8204551* 🎫 *€10, €12 with Scrovegni Chapel, or Padova Card* ⊙ *Tues.–Sun. 9–7.*

❽ Orto Botanico (Botanical Garden). The Venetian Republic ordered the creation of Padua's botanical garden in 1545 to supply the university with medicinal plants. You can stroll the arboretum and wander through hothouses and beds of plants that were first introduced to Italy in this Renaissance garden, which still maintains its original layout. A St. Peter's palm, planted in 1585, stands protected in its own private greenhouse. ⊠ *Via Orto Botanico 15* ☎ *049/8272119* ⊕ *www.ortobotanico. unipd.it* 🎫 *€4 or Padova Card* ⊙ *Apr.–Oct., daily 9–1 and 3–6; Nov.–Mar., Mon.–Sat. 9–1.*

❸ Palazzo del Bo'. The University of Padua, founded in 1222, centers around this 16th-century palazzo with an 18th-century facade. It's named after the Osteria del Bo' (*bo'* means "ox"), an inn that once stood on the site. It's worth a visit to see the exquisite and perfectly proportioned anatomy theater and a hall with a lectern used by Galileo. You can enter only as part of a guided tour. Most guides speak English, but it is worth checking ahead by phone. ⊠ *Via VIII Febbraio* ☎ *049/ 8273044* 🎫 *€3* ⊙ *Mon., Wed., and Fri. at 3:15, 4:15, and 5:15; Tues., Thurs., and Sat. at 9:15, 10:15, and 11:15.*

Where to Stay & Eat

$$$$ ✕ **Antico Brolo.** In a 16th-century building not far from central Piazza dei Signori, charming Antico Brolo is one of Padua's top restaurants. The outdoor area has a simpler menu; the indoor restaurant is more elaborate. Pastas are uniformly excellent; seasonal specialties prepared with flair might include starters such as tiny flans with wild mushrooms and herbs or fresh pasta with zucchini flowers. The wine list doesn't disappoint. ⊠ *Corso Milano 22* ☎ *049/664555* ⊕ *www.anticobrolo.it* ▤ *AE, MC, V* ⊙ *No lunch Mon.*

$$$ ✕ **La Vecchia Enoteca.** The ceiling is mirrored, the shelves are filled with books and wine, the silver service on which your meal arrives once belonged to a shipping line, and the flower displays are extravagant. In this luxurious ambience enjoy *branzino in crosta di patate* (sea bass with a potato crust) or beef with rosemary and balsamic vinegar, followed by a homemade dessert such as *crema catalana* (cream caramel). Reservations are advised. ⊠ *Via Santi Martino e Solferino 32* ☎ 049/8752856 ☰ *MC, V* ⊗ *Closed Sun. and 1st 3 wks in Aug. No lunch Mon.*

$–$$$ ✕ **Bastioni del Moro.** The genial owner devises his own recipes according to season, with vegetarians and calorie watchers in mind, although carnivores are well cared for, too. Gnocchi, eggplant, artichokes, and pumpkin all appear on the menu in different guises. For starters, you could try *tagliolini gratinati con prosciutto* (thin ribbons of egg noodles with prosciutto) or *gnocchi con capesante e porcini* (gnocchi with scallops and porcini mushrooms). The garden is put to good use in summer. Reservations are recommended. ⊠ *Via Pilade Bronzetti 18* ☎ 049/8710006 ⊕ *www.bastionidelmoro.it* ☰ *AE, DC, MC, V* ⊗ *Closed Sun. and 2 wks in Aug.*

★ **$–$$** ✕ **L'Anfora.** Sometimes you stumble across an *osteria* (tavernlike restaurant) that is so infused with local character that you wonder why every meal can't be this atmospheric, this authentically local, this effortlessly delicious. With dark wooden walls and typically brusque service, L'Anfora, in Padua's old center, is just such a gem. Skip the fried appetizers, which can get soggy as they sit, and start with some cheese: a nearly perfect piece of *mozzarella di bufala campana* (water-buffalo mozzarella from the Campania region) or, even better, an impossibly creamy *burrata* (similar to mozzarella, wrapped in herbs). After that, you might move on to *tagliatelle* (flat noodles) with fresh seasonal mushrooms, or perhaps a plate of simply grilled artichokes and potatoes. The place is packed at lunchtime, so expect a wait. ⊠ *Via Soncin 13* ☎ 049/656629 ☰ *AE, V* ⊗ *Closed Sun. except Dec.; closed 1 wk in Aug.*

$ ✕ **Gigi Bar.** Simple and unpretentious: yellow walls and tablecloths brighten this inexpensive restaurant where high ceilings open up a second-floor seating area. The central kitchen is behind a counter low enough for the convivial owner-chef Ferruccio to see and supervise the equally friendly dining-room staff. The terrific and popular fish soup is one of the affordable seafood dishes that keep locals queuing up. There are also tasty steaks, salads, vegetable plates, and pizzas with a surprisingly light crust. ⊠ *Via Verdi 18/20* ☎ 049/8760028 ☰ *DC, MC, V* ⊗ *Closed Tues., 2 wks in July.*

¢–$ ✕ **Hostaria Ai Do Archi.** Frequented by an older neighborhood crowd, this is nothing more—or less—than a Padovan version of the *bacari* that are so typical of the Veneto: wine bars where people sit and stand all day long, sipping wine, tasting local snacks, and talking politics. It's a true experience. ⊠ *Via Nazario Sauro 23* ☎ 049/652335 ☰ *No credit cards* ⊗ *Closed Tues. No lunch.*

$$$ ▥ **Plaza.** In a town without many downtown hotels, this is one of the few comfortable options. Even if its design seems trapped in a 1960s modernist fantasy, that's not necessarily a bad thing; the giant globes that illuminate the sidewalk in front of the hotel add a little dreaminess to an otherwise nondescript block of apartments and office buildings. Rooms are spacious, modern, and comfortable, and it's only a five-minute walk to the city center. ⊠ *Corso Milano 40, 35139* ☎ 049/656822 ☈ 049/661117 ⊕ *www.plazapadova.it* ⇗ *130 rooms, 9 suites, 7 apartments*

⚴ *Restaurant, bar, WiFi, in-room safes, minibars, gym, meeting rooms, parking (fee)* ⊟ *AE, DC, MC, V* ❄ *BP.*

★ $$$ ⌂ **Villa Pisani.** The spacious high-ceiling rooms in this enormous 16th-century villa are furnished entirely with period pieces—some units even have fully frescoed walls. All rooms look out over stunning formal gardens and beyond to a 15-acre park with rare trees, a chapel, a theater, and a concealed swimming pool. You have access to three big *sale* (lounges), where you can chat with the few other lucky guests and Signora Scalabrin, who shares her patrician living areas, music, and books. With breakfast served on silver platters, this is a bed-and-breakfast that outstrips almost all the hotel competition. ⊠ *Via Roma 19, 35040 Vescovana, 30 km (19 mi) south of Padua, off Hwy. A13* ☎ *0425/920016* ⊕ *www.villapisani.it* ⇆ *7 rooms, 1 suite* ⚴ *Pool, horseback riding, convention center, free parking, some pets allowed, Internet room; no a/c in some rooms, no room phones, no TV in some rooms, no smoking* ⊟ *AE, DC, MC, V* ❄ *BP.*

★ $$–$$$ ⌂ **Majestic Toscanelli.** The elegant entrance, with potted evergreens flanking the steps, sets the tone in this stylish, central hotel close to the Piazza della Frutta. It's easily the best-located hotel in the city, but beside that the rooms and service justify the price. Plants feature strongly in the breakfast room, and the charming bedrooms are furnished in different styles from 19th-century mahogany and brass to French Empire. Your very welcoming hosts offer discounts to seniors, AAA members, and those carrying Fodor's guidebooks. ⊠ *Via dell'Arco 2, near Piazza della Frutta, 35122* ☎ *049/663244* ⊟ *049/8760025* ⊕ *www.toscanelli.com* ⇆ *26 rooms, 6 suites* ⚴ *Café, some in-room safes, minibars, cable TV with movies, in-room data ports, bar, meeting room, parking (fee), some pets allowed (fee), no-smoking floor, WiFi* ⊟ *AE, DC, MC, V* ❄ *BP.*

$ ⌂ **Al Fagiano.** Some rooms in this peaceful hotel have views of the spires and cupolas at Basilica di Sant'Antonio. Facilities are modest and rooms simply furnished, but an amiable staff and central location make this a pleasant and convenient place to stay. Breakfast is available for €6. ⊠ *Via Locatelli 45, 35100* ☎ *049/8750073* ⊟ *049/8753396* ⊕ *www.alfagiano.it* ⇆ *29 rooms* ⚴ *Restaurant, cable TV, in-room data ports, bar, parking (fee), some pets allowed* ⊟ *AE, DC, MC, V* ❄ *EP.*

Cafés & Wine Bars

Since 1831 **Caffè Pedrocchi** (⊠ Piazzetta Pedrocchi ☎ 049/8781231) has been a place to sip and snack while musicians play jazz and intellectuals debate. An innovative bistro menu means you can now enjoy coffee-flavor pasta, or share zabaglione made from Pedrocchi's 150-year-old recipe. This neoclassical cross between a museum and stage set is open Sunday–Wednesday 9–9, and until midnight Thursday–Saturday.

One of Padua's greatest traditions is the outdoor en-masse consumption, most nights in decent weather, of **aperitifs**: *spritz* (a mix of Aperol or Campari, soda water, and wine), *prosecco* (sparkling wine), or wine. It all happens in the Piazza delle Erbe and Piazza delle Frutta, where several bars provide drinks in plastic cups to masses of people, who then take the drinks outside and consume them standing up. The ritual begins at 6 PM or so, at which hour you can also get a snack from one of the outdoor seafood vendors; on weekends, the open-air revelry transitions from lively cocktail hour to wine-soaked bash.

VICENZA

Vicenza bears the distinctive signature of the 16th-century architect Andrea Palladio, whose name has been given to the "Palladian" style of architecture. He gracefully incorporated elements of classical architecture—columns, porticoes, and domes—into a style that reflected the Renaissance celebration of order and harmony. His elegant villas and palaces were influential in propagating classical architecture in Europe, especially Britain, and later in America—most notably at Thomas Jefferson's Monticello.

In the mid-16th century Palladio was commissioned to rebuild much of Vicenza, which had been greatly damaged during wars waged against Venice by the League of Cambrai, an alliance of the papacy, France, the Holy Roman Empire, and several neighboring city-states. He made his name with the Basilica in 1549 then embarked on a series of lordly buildings, all of which adhere to the same classicism.

Exploring Vicenza

Many of Palladio's works join the Venetian Gothic and baroque palaces that line Corso Palladio, an elegant shopping thoroughfare where Vicenza's status as one of Italy's wealthiest cities is evident.

The Main Attractions

★ ❷ **Teatro Olimpico.** Palladio's last, and perhaps most exciting, work was completed after his death by Vincenzo Scamozzi (1552–1616). Based closely on the model of an ancient Roman theater, it represents an important development in theater and stage design and is noteworthy for its acoustics and the cunning use of perspective in Scamozzi's permanent backdrop. The anterooms are frescoed with images of important figures in Venetian history. ⊠ *Piazza Matteotti* ☎ *0444/222800* 🖭 *€8, includes admission to Palazzo Chiericati* ⊘ *Sept.–June, Tues.–Sun. 9–5; July and Aug., Tues.–Sun. 9–7.*

Villa La Rotonda. ⇨ page 290 for details of one of Palladio's grandest buildings.

Also Worth Seeing

❸ **Palazzo Chiericati.** This exquisite and unmistakably Palladian palazzo houses Vicenza's **Museo Civico.** The museum's Venetian collection includes paintings by Tiepolo (1696–1770) and Tintoretto (1519–94). ⊠ *Piazza Matteotti* ☎ *0444/321348* 🖭 *€8, includes admission to Teatro Olimpico* ⊘ *Sept.–June, Tues.–Sun. 9–5; July and Aug., Tues.–Sun. 9–6.*

> ## WORD OF MOUTH
>
> Vicenza is fairly small and very quaint. I loved it as a base. We could walk to the train station to catch a train to Venice. We rented a car and that is how we explored some of the other cities in the area." —Eurotraveller

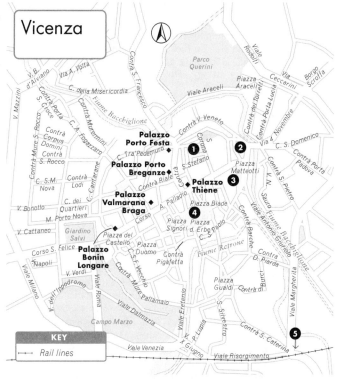

❶ Palazzo Leoni Montanari. In a city dominated by Palladio, this distinctly baroque building is often overlooked, as are its galleries. On display are more than 500 Orthodox icons dating back to the 13th century, making this one of the most significant such collections outside Russia. A second gallery of Veneto art includes paintings by Longhi (1702–85), Canaletto (1697–1768), and Francesco Guardi (1712–93). ⊠ *Contrà Santa Corona 25* ☎ *800/578875* ⊕ *www.palazzomontanari.com* 🎫 *€3.50* ☾ *Fri.–Sun. 10–6.*

❹ Piazza dei Signori. At the heart of Vicenza sits this square, which contains the **Palazzo della Ragione,** commonly known as Palladio's basilica, though it wasn't a church at all but originally a courthouse and public meeting hall. Palladio made his name by successfully modernizing the medieval building, grafting a graceful two-story exterior loggia onto the existing Gothic structure. Take a look also at the **Loggia del Capitaniato,** opposite, which Palladio designed but never completed. Note that the palazzo and its loggia are open to the public only when there's an exhibition: ask at the tourist office.

❺ Villa Valmarana ai Nani. Inside this 18th-century country house a series of frescoes by Tiepolo depict fantastic visions of a mythological world, including one of his most stunning works, the *Sacrifice of Iphigenia.* The neighboring *foresteria* (farmworkers' dormitory) is also part of the museum; it contains more frescoes showing 18th-century Veneto life at its most charming by Tiepolo's son Giandomenico (1727–1804). You can reach the villa on foot by following the same path that leads to Palladio's Villa la Rotonda. ⊠ *Via dei Nani 2/8* ☎ *0444/544546* ⊡€6 ⊙ *Mid-Mar.–Oct., Wed., Thurs., and weekends 10–noon and 3–6, Tues. and Fri. 10–noon.*

Where to Stay & Eat

$$$ ✕ **Antico Ristorante agli Schioppi.** Veneto country-style decor, with enormous murals, matches simple yet imaginative cuisine in this family-run restaurant established in 1897. Begin with the Parma ham served with eggplant mousse and Parmesan. The *baccalà* (salt cod) is a delicacy, as are the *petto d'anitra all'uva moscata e indivia* (duck breast with muscat grapes and endive) and *coniglio alle olive nere* (rabbit with black olives). Desserts include ever-so-light fruit mousse and a pear cake with red-wine sauce. ⊠ *Contrà del Castello 26* ☎ *0444/543701* ⊕ *www.ristoranteaglischioppi.com* ⊟ *AE, DC, MC, V* ⊙ *Closed Sun., last wk of July–mid-Aug., and Jan. 1–6. No dinner Sat.*

$$–$$$ ✕ **Dai Nodari.** Seven restaurant veterans—with a shared passion for good food and hard work—opened this exciting restaurant in January 2005. They must also share a flair for the dramatic: a silent film shows in the bar and Dante's *Inferno* plays in the men's room. Appetizers include interesting cheeses, such as *bastardo del drappa* (aged 60 days), and dishes like tuna marinated in orange. Move on to fish or steak, or try rabbit roasted with juniper berries. There are also several pasta and salad choices. ⊠ *Contrà do Rode 20* ☎ *0444/544085* ⊟ *AE, DC, MC, V.*

★ $–$$ ✕ **Ponte delle Bele.** With all the pine furniture and lacy lamps, you may feel like you've stumbled into an Alpine cabin, so it's no surprise when your homemade pasta resembles dumplings or spaetzle. At this friendly *Tyrolese* (Tirolean) restaurant, your prosciutto might be made from wild deer or boar, and venison in blueberry sauce is not usually found this far south of the mountains. Try guinea fowl roasted with white grapes, or the local cheese plate served with honey and preserves (but take care with the tough rye cracker-bread, which only a dentist could love). ⊠ *Contrà Ponte delle Bele 5* ☎ *0444/320647* ⊕ *www.pontedellebele.it* ⊟ *AE, DC, MC, V* ⊙ *Closed Sun. and 2 wks in mid–Aug.*

¢–$ ✕ **Righetti.** After staking out seats, line up (with elbows ready) at the self-service food counters here. There's a daily pasta, a risotto, and a hearty soup such as *orzo e fagioli* (barley and bean) on the menu. Vegetables, salads, and baccalà are standards; at dinner, meats are grilled to order. Once you have your meal on your tray, help yourself to bread, wine, and water. Sharing tables is the norm. After you've finished, tell the cashier what you had and he'll total your (very reasonable) bill. Low prices and simple, enjoyable food has generated a loyal following. ⊠ *Piazza Duomo 3* ☎ *0444/543135* ⊟ *No credit cards* ⊙ *Closed weekends and Aug.*

$$ ▥ **Giardini.** The hotel Giardini is in good company near Palladio's Teatro Olimpico and Palazzo Chiericati, off the central Piazza Matteotti. Rooms have a modern Italian style, with sleek, midtone wood floors

Continued on page 292

PALLADIO COUNTRY

They asked for a villa. Andrea Palladio gave them a lifestyle. Wealthy 16th-century Venetians by the score commissioned country houses from this architectural genius so they could pursue *la dolce vita*. Today, his Veneto villas are considered among the most beautiful structures ever conceived. When he managed to publish his designs in his *Four Books of Architecture* (1570), Palladio inspired a legion of wannabes that eventually spanned the globe. His influence was crucial in Thomas Jefferson's Monticello as well as, by unofficial count, half the state capitol structures in America. Jefferson wasn't lucky enough to visit the Veneto, but a tour of Palladio's finest buildings today will let you discover the seductions of *la dolce villa*.

TOWN & COUNTRY

Although the villa, or "country residence," was still a relatively new phenomenon in the 16th century, it quickly became all the rage once the great lords of Venice turned their eyes from the sea toward the fertile plains of the Veneto. They were forced to do this once their trade routes had faltered when Ottoman Turks conquered Constantinople in 1456 and Columbus opened a path to the riches of America in 1492. In no time, canals were built, farms were laid out, and the fashion for *villeggiatura*—the attraction of idyllic country retreats for the nobility—became a favored lifestyle. As a means of escaping an overheated

Rome, villas had been the original brainchild of the ancient emperors. But emperors, after all, required palatial, not rustic, lodgings—so it was no accident that Palladio zeroed in on this style of country residence. His process of evaluating the standards, and standbys, of ancient Roman life through the eye of the Italian Renaissance, combined with Palladio's innate sense of proportion and symmetry, became the lasting foundation of his art. In turn, Palladio threw out the jambalaya of styles prevalent in Venetian architecture—Oriental, Gothic, and Renaissance—for the pure, noble lines he had found in the buildings of the Caesars.

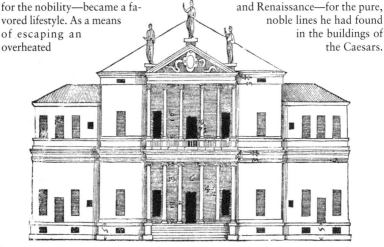

PALLADIO, STAR ARCHITECT

Andrea Palladio (1508–1580)

"Face dark, eyes fiery. Dress rich. His appearance that of a genius." So was Palladio described by his wealthy mentor, Count Trissino. In a brilliant bit of brand marketing, Trissino encouraged the young student to trade in his birth name, Andrea della Gondola, for the catchy Palladio, derived from Pallas, Greek deity of wisdom. He did, and it proved a wise move indeed. Born in Padua in 1508, Andrea moved to nearby Vicenza in 1524 and was quickly taken up

THE OLD BECOMES NEW

La Malcontenta

Studying ancient Rome with the eyes of an explorer, Palladio created a style that linked old with new—but often did so in unexpected ways. Just take a look at Villa Foscari, nicknamed "**La Malcontenta**" (Mira, 041/5470012, www. lamalcontenta.com € 5.15. Open May–Oct., Tues. and Sat. 9–noon; from Venice, take an ACTV bus from Piazzale Roma to Mira or opt for a boat ride up on the Burchiello). Shaded by weeping willows and mirrored by the Brenta Canal—the Beverly Hills of 16th-century Venice—"The Unhappy" was built for Nicolò and Alvise Foscari and is the quintessence of Palladian poetry. Its nickname was presumably coined for the recalcitrant wife of one of the original owners, as she had misbehaved so scandalously in Venice that she was kept locked up here. In revolutionary fashion, Palladio applied the ancient Roman public motif of a temple facade to a private, domestic dwelling, topped off by a pediment, a construct previously used exclusively for religious structures. Inside, he used the technique of vaulting seen in ancient Roman baths to enhance the spatial flow. With giant windows and immense white walls ready-made for the colorful frescoes painted by Zelotti, the resulting effect almost feels like a spacious New York City loft.

by the city's power elite. But he experienced a profound revelation on his first trip, in 1541, to Rome. Forgoing his earlier impulse to turn his adopted city, Vicenza, into a Gothic-mannered Venice, he decided instead to turn it into another Rome. This turnaround led to his spectacular conversion of the city's Palazzo della Ragione (1545) into a basilica modeled after the great meeting halls of antiquity. In years to come, after relocating to Venice, he created some memorable churches, such as S. Giorgio Maggiore (1564). Despite these varied projects, Palladio's unassailable position as one of the world's greatest architects is tied to the countryside villas, which he spread across the Veneto plains like a firmament of stars. Nothing else in the Veneto illuminates more clearly the idyllic beauty of the region than these elegant residences, their stonework now nicely mellowed and suntanned after five centuries.

VICENZA, CITY OF PALLADIO

Palazzo della Ragione

La Rotonda

To see Palladio's pageant of palaces, head for Vicenza, 53 km (33 mi) to the northwest of Mira's Malcontenta. His **Palazzo della Ragione**, or "Basilica," landmarks the city's heart, the Piazza dei Signori. This is where Palladio most brilliantly adopted the Serliana motif, an open arch framed by columns and circular windows. Across the way is his redbrick **Loggia dei Capitaniato**. One block past the Loggia is Vicenza's main street, appropriately named Corso Andrea Palladio. Just off this street is the Contrà Porti, where you'll find the **Palazzo Porto Barbaran** (1570) at No. 11, with its fabulously rich facade erupting with Ionic and Corinthian pillars. Today, this is the Centro Internazionale di Studi di Architettura Andrea Palladio (0444/323014, www.cisapalladio.org), a study center that mounts impressive temporary exhibitions. At No. 12 is Palladio's **Palazzo Thiene** (1558), and No. 21 is **Palazzo Porto Festa**, which he started. Contrà Reale leads to Corso A. Fogazzaro, where Palladio's **Palazzo Valmarana Braga** is found at No. 16, its grand facade ornamented with gigantic pilasters. A family cartouche once surmounted the roofline and was illuminated at night—à la Trump. Return to Corso Palladio and head left for five blocks to Piazza Mattotti and the **Palazzo Chiericati** (1550)—now the Museo Civico—Palladio's take on an imperial Roman loggia. Across the piazza the **Teatro Olimpico**, one of his final works (begun in 1579–80), reveals Palladio's knowledge of ancient Roman theaters. For a suitably grand finale, nothing will satisfy but a visit to one of the greatest buildings in all of Europe, **Villa La Rotonda** (Via della Rotonda 29, 0444/321793; villa €10, grounds €5. Villa open mid-Mar.–Oct., Wed. 10–noon and 3–6. Grounds mid-Mar.–Oct., Tues.–Sun. 10–noon and 3–6; Nov.–mid-Mar., Tues.–Sun. 10–noon and 2–5. Getting to the villa is a pleasant 20-minute walk from the city center, or take Bus 8 from Viale Roma. Created for papal prelate Paolo Almerico, La Rotonda seems less a villa than a Roman temple, which was precisely the architect's intention. Take sufficient time to admire it from all sides; you'll realize Palladio just repeated the temple portico on all four faces, to take advantage of the idyllic views. Inspired by the hillside site on Monte Berico and topped by a dome like Rome's Pantheon, La Rotonda is Palladio's only freestanding, centralized design, because it was intended to be a showplace, not a working farm. Still owned by the Counts Valmarana, La Rotonda's interior is rarely open. But it's no loss, as it's awash in florid frescoes Palladio would have detested.

THE "WINGED DEVICE"

Villa Barbaro

One of Palladio's most gracious Renaissance creations lies 48 km (30 mi) northeast of Vicenza: his **Villa Barbaro** (Via Cornuda 7, 0423/923004, www.villadimases.it, €5. Open Apr.–Oct., Tues. and weekends 3–6; Nov.–Mar., weekends 2:30–5; or by reservation; closed Dec. 24–Jan. 6). Near Asolo and built just outside the town of Maser in 1549 for the two Barbaro brothers, this villa spectacularly illustrates Palladio's famous "winged device"—using a villa's outlying wings, which often housed granaries, to frame the main building, and linking them together with graceful loggias (the 16th-century answer to air-conditioning). With this one stroke, he brought everything together, making the parts subservient to the whole. His dramatic frontal designs have led historians to compare these facades to theater stages and to term his sense of space scenographic. Inside the cool halls of the villa, painted courtiers provocatively peek out behind frescoed doors. Legend has it that these famous paintings of Paolo Veronese were the cause of a rift, since Palladio felt these trompe l'oeil scenes distorted the purity of his architectural design. Today, the villa is still owned by Barbaro descendants, and its enduring beauty ensures that future generations of architects will continue to shape and enrich the Palladian style.

ALONG THE BRENTA CANAL

During the 16th century the Brenta was transformed into a landlocked version of Venice's Grand Canal with the building of nearly 50 waterside villas. Back then, boating parties viewed them in *burchielli*—beautiful boats. Today, the Burchiello excursion boat (Via Orlandini 3, Padua, 049/8206910, www.ilburchiello.it) makes an all-day villa tour along the Brenta, from March to November, departing from Padua on Wednesday, Friday, and Sunday and from Venice on Tuesday, Thursday, and Saturday; tickets are €62 and can also be bought at American Express at Salizzada San Moisè in Venice. You visit three houses, including the Villas Pisani and Foscari, with a lunchtime break in Oriago. Another canal excursion is run by the Battelli del Brenta (www.battellidelbrenta.it). Note that most houses are on the left side coming from Venice, or the right from Padua.

and multicolor bedspreads; two rooms are equipped for guests with disabilities. ☒ *Viale Giurioli 10, 36100* ☎☎ *0444/326458* ⊕ *www. hotelgiardini.com* ⇨ *17 rooms* ⚲ *In-room safes, minibars, cable TV, bar, meeting room, free parking* ⊟ *AE, DC, MC, V* ⊘ *Closed Dec. 23–Jan. 2 and 3 wks in Aug.* ⓘ⊙ *BP.*

$ ⌧ **Due Mori.** Antiques fill the rooms at the 1883 hotel Due Mori, one of the oldest in the city. Loyal regulars favor the place because it's light and airy (with tall ceilings and pale walls), yet at the same time cozy (with substantial wood beds). This comfortable, convenient bargain is off the Piazza dei Signori. ☒ *Contrà Do Rode 24, 36100* ☎ *0444/ 321886* 🖷 *0444/326127* ⊕ *www.hotelduemori.com* ⇨ *30 rooms* ⚲ *Bar, some free parking, some pets allowed; no a/c, no room TVs* ⊟ *AE, MC, V* ⊘ *Closed last 2 wks in July* ⓘ⊙ *BP.*

Nightlife & the Arts

The **Teatro Olimpico** (☒ Piazza Matteotti ☎ 0444/222801 ⊕ www. comune.vicenza.it) hosts a jazz festival in May, classical concerts in June, and classical drama performances in September. Even if your Italian is dismal, it can be thrilling to see a performance in Palladio's magnificent theater.

VERONA

On the banks of the fast-flowing River Adige, 60 km (37 mi) west of Vicenza, enchanting Verona has timeless monuments, a picturesque town center, and a romantic reputation as the setting of Shakespeare's *Romeo and Juliet.* With its lively Venetian air and proximity to Lake Garda, it attracts hordes of tourists, especially Germans and Austrians. Tourism peaks during summer's renowned season of open-air opera in the Arena and during spring's Vinitaly, one of the world's most important wine expos. For five days you can sample the wines of more than 3,000 wineries from dozens of countries. (Book months in advance for hotels during approximately the second week in April.)

Verona grew to power and prosperity within the Roman Empire as a result of its key commercial and military position in northern Italy. After the fall of the Empire, the city continued to flourish under the guidance of barbarian kings such as Theodoric, Alboin, Pepin, and Berenger I, reaching its cultural and artistic peak in the 13th and 14th centuries under the della Scala dynasty. (Look for the *scala,* or ladder, emblem all over town.) In 1404 Verona traded its independence for security and placed itself under the control of Venice. (The other recurring architectural motif is the lion of St. Mark, symbol of Venetian rule.) Verona remained under Venetian protection until 1797, when Napoléon invaded. In 1814 the entire Veneto region was won by the Austrians. It wasn't reunited with Italy until 1866.

Exploring Verona

If you're going to visit more than a sight or two, it's worthwhile to purchase a Verona Card, available at museums, churches, and tobacconists

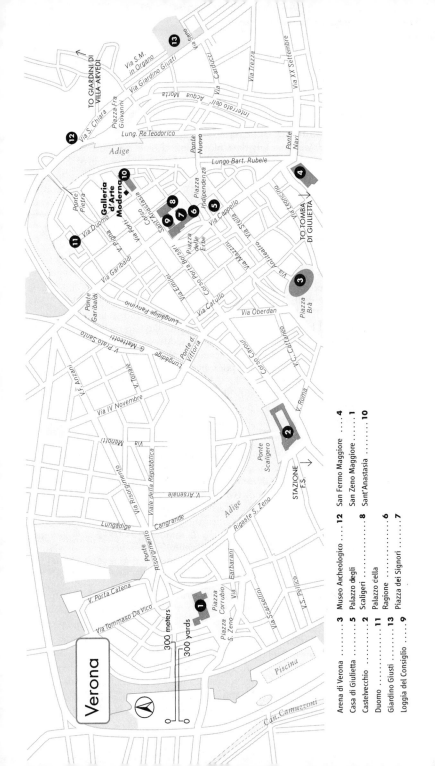

Verona

300 meters
300 yards

Arena di Verona **3**
Casa di Giulietta **5**
Castelvecchio **2**
Duomo **11**
Giardino Giusti **13**
Loggia del Consiglio **9**

Museo Archeologico **12**
Palazzo degli Scaligeri **8**
Palazzo della Ragione **6**
Piazza dei Signori **7**

San Fermo Maggiore **4**
San Zeno Maggiore **1**
Sant'Anastasia **10**

TO GIARDINI DI VILLA ARVEDI

TO TOMBA DI GIULIETTA

Galleria d'Arte Moderna

Adige

for €8 (one day) or €12 (three days). You get a single admission to most of the city's significant museums and churches, and you can ride free on city buses. A €5 Chiese Vive Card is sold at Verona's major churches and gains you entry to the Duomo, San Fermo Maggiore, San Zeno Maggiore, and Sant'Anastasia. Do note that Verona's churches strictly enforce their dress code: no sleeveless shirts, shorts, or short skirts.

The Main Attractions

⊙ ❸ **Arena di Verona.** Only the Colosseum in Rome and the arena in Capua
Fodor'sChoice can outdo this amphitheater in size. Just four arches remain of the arena's
★ outer arcade, but the main structure is so complete that it takes little imagination to picture it as the site of the cruel deaths of countless gladiators, wild beasts, and Christians. Today you can visit the arena year-round; in summer, audiences of up to 16,000 pack the stands for Verona's famously spectacular open-air opera productions. ⊠ *Arena di Verona, Piazza Brà 5* ☎ *045/8003204* ⊕ *www.arena.it* ✉ *€5 or VeronaCard, €1 1st Sun. of month* ☉ *Mon. 1:30–7:15, Tues.–Sun. 8:30–7:15, on performance days 8–3:30; last entry 45 mins before closing.*

❷ **Castelvecchio** (Old Castle). This crenellated, russet brick building with massive walls, towers, turrets, and a vast courtyard was built for Cangrande II della Scala in 1354. It presides over a street lined with attractive old buildings and palaces of the nobility. To really appreciate the massive castle complex, go inside the **Museo di Castelvecchio,** which gives you a good look at the vaulted halls and the collections of Venetian art and medieval weapons and jewelry. For the benefit of sightless visitors, some paintings have been rendered in plastic relief and have recorded explanations. Behind the castle is the Ponte Scaligero, a public walkway spanning the River Adige. ⊠ *Corso Castelvecchio 2* ☎ *045/ 8062611* ✉ *€4 or VeronaCard, free 1st Sun. of month* ☉ *Mon. 1:30–7:30, Tues.–Sun. 8:30–7:30; last entry 6:45.*

⓫ **Duomo.** Verona's cathedral is an amalgamation of religious buildings, the earliest dating back to 380; it's ornately Romanesque but also shows Venetian and even Byzantine influences. Noteworthy inside are carvings of Oliver and Roland, two of Charlemagne's knights, guarding the main entrance, and Titian's *Assumption* gracing the first chapel on the left. Unlike in most Italian cities, this Duomo is tucked off in one of the quieter parts of town. ⊠ *Via Duomo* ☎ *045/592813* ⊕ *www. chieseverona.it* ✉ *€2.50, €5 for combined churches ticket, or VeronaCard* ☉ *Nov.–Feb., Tues.–Sat. 10–4, Sun. 10–5; Mar.–Oct., Mon.–Sat. 10–5:30, Sun. 1:30–5:30.*

❾ **Loggia del Consiglio.** This graceful structure, built in the 12th century as a site for city council meetings, still serves as seat of the provincial government. ⊠ *Piazza dei Signori* ☉ *Closed to the public.*

❽ **Palazzo degli Scaligeri.** The iron-fisted della Scalas ruled Verona from this medieval stronghold. Though the palazzo is closed to the public, you can gaze into the adjacent **Arche Scaligere,** site of the suitably impressive marbled Gothic tombs of family members Cangrande I ("Big Dog"), Mastino II ("Mastiff"), and Cansignorio ("Top Dog"). ⊠ *Via Arche Scaligere* ✉ *€4* ☉ *Arche Scaligere visible at all times from the* *outside; inside open to walk among the tombs, Mon. 1:30–7:30, Tues.–Sun. 8:30–7:30; last entry 30 mins before closing.*

❻ Palazzo della Ragione. An elegant pink marble staircase leads up from the *mercato vecchio* (old market) courtyard to the magistrates' chambers in the 12th-century palace also known as the Palazzo del Comune. The building is undergoing renovation and will be turned into a conference center. You can get the highest view in town from atop the attached 270-foot-tall **Torre dei Lamberti,** which is open during reconstruction. Taking the elevator costs only slightly more than walking up the 368 steps for the panoramic view—but the burned calories are priceless. ⊠ *Piazza dei Signori* ☎ *045/8032726* ▧ *€2, €3 with elevator* ☼ *Mon. 1:30–7:30, Tues.–Sun. 8:30–7:30; last entry 6:45.*

★ Piazza delle Erbe. A Roman forum once bustled on this site and until recently it housed the daily fruit-and-vegetable market. Many of the stalls have now gone (you still have a wide choice of trinkets, postcards, and snacks), perhaps adding charm to the medieval square. The surrounding frescoed town houses, the fountains, and the buzz of people and vendors all combine to make this one of northern Italy's most memorable city squares.

❼ Piazza dei Signori. Verona's most impressive piazza, the center of things for more than 1,000 years, is today lorded over by a pensive statue of Dante, often as not with a pigeon on his head. His back is toward the Loggia del Consiglio and his left hand points toward the Palazzo degli Scaligeri. He faces Palazzo del Capitanio (to his left) and Palazzo della Ragione (to his right). All these buildings are closed to the public except those on government business.

❹ San Fermo Maggiore. From its humble Benedictine beginnings, San Fermo grew through the centuries, in part as a result of rebuilding after floods from the nearby River Adige. The tomblike lower church, dating from the 8th century, became usable again when the Adige was reengineered to stay within its banks. The mammoth upper church completed in the 14th century has the Veneto's oldest and perhaps finest ship's-keel ceiling, decorated with paintings of 400 saints. ⊠ *Stradone S. Fermo* ☎ *045/592813* ⊕ *www.chieseverona.it* ▧ *€2.50, €5 for combined churches ticket, or VeronaCard* ☼ *Nov.–Feb., Tues.–Sat. 10–1 and 1:30–4, Sun. 1–5; Mar.–Oct., Mon.–Sat. 10–6, Sun. 1–6.*

★ ❶ San Zeno Maggiore. Possibly Italy's finest Romanesque church, San Zeno stands between two medieval bell towers. A 13th-century rose window depicts the wheel of fortune, and bronze doors from the 11th and 12th centuries are decorated with scenes from the Bible and from the life of Verona's patron saint, Zeno, who's buried in the crypt. Look for the statue *San Zeno Laughing* to the left of the main altar—the unknown artist, or perhaps the saint himself, must have had a sense of humor. A *Madonna and Saints* triptych by Andrea Mantegna (1431–1506) hangs over the main altar, and a peaceful cloister lies to the north (left) of the nave. ⊠ *Piazza San Zeno* ☎ *045/592813* ⊕ *www.chieseverona.it* ▧ *€2.50, €5 for combined churches ticket, or VeronaCard* ☼ *Nov.–Feb., Tues.–Sat. 10–4, Sun. 1–5; Mar.–Oct., Mon.–Sat. 8:30–6, Sun. 1–6.*

⑩ Sant'Anastasia. Verona's largest church, completed in 1481, is a fine example of Gothic brickwork and has a grand doorway with elaborately carved biblical scenes. The finest of its numerous frescoes is the pastel *St. George and the Princess* by Pisanello (1377–1455) above the Pellegrini Chapel right off the main altar, where the saint appears more gentleman than warrior. As you come in, look for the *gobbi* (hunchbacks) supporting holy-water stoups. ⊠ *Vicolo Sotto Riva 4* ☎ *045/592813* ⊕ *www.chieseverona.it* ☑ *€2.50, €5 for combined churches ticket, or VeronaCard* ☉ *Nov.–Feb., Tues.–Sat. 10–4, Sun. 1–5; Mar.–Oct., Mon.–Sat. 9–6, Sun. 1–6.*

Also Worth Seeing

❺ Casa di Giulietta (Juliet's House). The small courtyard balcony evokes Shakespeare's play, even if it is part of a 20th-century remodel. Despite historians' belief that the famous lovers had no real-life counterparts, thousands of visitors refuse to let truth get in the way of a good story. ⊠ *Via Cappello 23* ☎ *045/8034303* ☑ *€4* ☉ *Mon. 1:30–7:30, Tues.–Sun. 8:30–7:30; last entry 6:45.*

⑬ Giardino Giusti. In 1570 Agostino Giusti designed these formal gardens on the hillside behind his villa. Though the toothy mask halfway up the hill no longer breathes flames, little has been changed of Giusti's maze, fountains, or stalactite grotto. And though Verona might no longer be recognizable to Johann Wolfgang von Goethe (1749–1832), you can still enjoy the terrace views that inspired this German poet and dramatist to record his impressions. ⊠ *Via Giardino Giusti 2* ☎ *045/8034029* ☑ *€5* ☉ *Apr.–Sept., daily 9–8; Oct.–Mar., daily 9–7.*

⑫ Museo Archeologico. The views of the city from this museum housed in an old monastery are even better than its archaeological exhibits. It sits high above the Teatro Romano, near the Arena di Verona. ⊠ *Rigaste del Redentore 2* ☎ *045/8000360* ☑ *€3, free 1st Sun. of month* ☉ *Mon. 1:30–7:30, Tues.–Sun. 8:30–7:30; last entry 6:45.*

Out of Town: Amarone & Valpolicella Wine Country

Touring wineries near Verona is a good way to see, and taste, the lush countryside of the Veneto. Be aware that at Italian wineries you need to call ahead to arrange a visit.

Allegrini, one of the top producers in the region, is also one of the friendliest; at their Fumane estate, less than half an hour's drive from downtown Verona, you can tour the facility and watch a video of their story, which goes back to 1854. Of course, you can also taste their wines, including an award-winning Amarone Classico and a spectacular, full-bodied wine, La Poja, made from 100% Corvina grapes. To get here from Verona, follow the *super strada* toward Sant'Ambrogio and San Pietro in Cariano, then head north on SP33 to reach Fumane. ⊠ *Via Giare 7, Fumane* ☎ *045/6832011* ⊕ *www.allegrini.it* ☑ *Free* ☉ *By appointment.*

Serègo Alighieri ages some of its wines in cherrywood, a virtually unheard-of practice. Wondering about that name? Legend has it that the poet Dante Alighieri finished his *Paradiso* while living out several years of his exile in the castle here. One of his direct descendents, a count, owns Castel dei Ronchi (now an inn and convention center) and makes delicious Amarone. He operates in partnership with Masi, another extremely important producer; at the shop you can taste Masi as well as Alighieri wines, and buy vintages going back to the 1980s. The winery is 20 km (12 mi) from Verona: take the super strada toward Sant'Ambrogio and head west on SP4. ⊠ *Gargagnano di Valpolicella* ☎ *045/7703622* ⊕ *www.seregoalighieri.it* ⊠ *Tours €8, wines €.50–€2.50 per taste* ⊗ Wine shop Mon.–Sat. 10 AM–6 PM; tours by appointment 3 days in advance.

Where to Stay & Eat

★ **$$$$** ✕ **Il Desco.** *Cucina dell' anima* (food of the soul) is how Chef Elia Rizzo describes his cuisine, which preserves natural flavors through quick cooking and a limit of three ingredients per dish. He spares no expense in selecting those ingredients, and you pay accordingly. Dishes like *petto di faraona con purea di topinambur, salsa al ll'aceto balsamico e cioccolato* (breast of guinea fowl with Jerusalem artichoke purèe and a chocolate and balsamic vinegar sauce) are standouts. For a real splurge, order the tasting menu (€110), which includes appetizers, two first courses, two second courses, and dessert. Decor is elegant, if overstated, with fine tapestries, paintings, and an impressive 16th-century lacunar ceiling. ⊠ *Via Dietro San Sebastiano 7* ☎ *045/595358* ⊲ *Reservations essential* ⊟ *AE, DC, MC, V* ⊗ *Closed Sun. and Mon., Dec. 25–Jan. 8, and June 6–25.*

$$$$ ✕ **Dodici Apostoli.** Vaulted ceilings, frescoed walls, and a medieval ambience make this an exceptional place to enjoy classic regional dishes. Near Piazza delle Erbe, it stands on the foundations of a Roman temple. Specialties include gnocchi *di zucca e ricotta* (with squash and ricotta cheese) and *vitello alla Lessinia* (veal with mushrooms, cheese, and truffles). ⊠ *Vicolo Corticella San Marco 3* ☎ *045/596999* ⊕ *www.12apostoli.it* ⊟ *AE, DC, MC, V* ⊗ *Closed Mon.; no dinner Sun. Closed Jan. 1–10 and June 15–30.*

★ **¢–$** ✕ **Antica Osteria al Duomo.** You'd think, from the name of the place, that this would be a tourist trap. Quite the contrary—the side-street eatery lined with old wooden walls and ceilings, and decked out with musical instruments, serves Veronese food to a Veronese crowd; they come to quaff the local wine (€1–€3 per glass) and to savor northern dishes like *canederli con speck, burro fuso, e rosmarino* (dumplings with bacon, melted butter, and rosemary) and *stracotto di cavallo con polenta* (horse meat with polenta). ⊠ *Via Duomo 7/a* ☎ *045/8004505* ⊟ *AE, MC, V* ⊗ *Closed Thurs. Oct.–Mar., Sun. Apr.–Sept.*

¢ ✕ **Du de Cope.** Il Desco's star chef decided to branch into pizza making and the result is four-star, wood-fired pizza at one-star prices. Toppings like buffalo mozzarella and Parmigiano-Reggiano cheese cover the lightest crust that ever hovered on a plate. Notice how well modern drop lighting merges with old-fashioned, blue-and-white tile walls; place mats quilt the hardwood tables and burlap tapestries decorate the walls. ⊠ *Galleria Pellicciai 10* ☎ *045/595562* ⊟ *AE, DC, MC, V* ⊗ *Closed Tues. No lunch Sun.*

★ ¢ ✕ **Osteria al Duca.** Folks jam this place at lunchtime, sharing tables, wine, and conversation in a building that legend claims to have been Romeo's birthplace. Beneath low-slung ceilings, generous portions of local specialties are served for a very reasonable fixed price along with a wine list that belies the simplicity of the surroundings. Try Gorgonzola served with polenta, vegetarian eggplant with mozzarella, or homemade *bigoli al torchio,* a thick spaghetti forced through a press. This may be some of the best food available for the price in town. ⊠ *Arche Scaligere 2* ☎ *045/594474* ⊟ *MC, V* ⊘ *Closed Sun. and mid-Dec.–mid-Jan.*

★ $$$$ ✕▦ **Villa del Quar.** Leopoldo and Evelina Montresor spared no expense when converting part of their 16th-century villa into a sophisticated luxury property with antiques and marble bathrooms. The Relais & Chateaux hotel is surrounded by gardens and vineyards, 15 minutes by car from Verona's city center. Service is both familiar and impeccable, whether at the poolside bar or in the acclaimed Arquade restaurant ($$$$). One of the top places to dine in northern Italy, it occupies a softly lighted converted chapel and a beautiful outdoor terrace. Chef Bruno Barbieri's creative menu might include inspired preparations of lobster, scampi, and foie gras, but simpler dishes, such as a platter of steamed fish, meet with equal success. The wine list, needless to say, is magnificent, and the hotel can help you organize a visit to some of Valpolicella's best wineries. ⊠ *Via Quar 12, 37020 Pedemonte di San Pietro in Cariano, 10 km (6 mi) northwest of Verona* ☎*045/6800681* 🖶*045/6800604* ⊕*www.hotelvilladelquar. it* ⇗ *18 rooms, 10 suites* ♿ *Restaurant, in-room safes, minibars, cable TV, in-room data ports, pool, health club, massage, 2 bars, meeting room, helipad, free parking, some pets allowed, no-smoking rooms, Internet room* ⊟*AE, DC, MC, V* ⊘*Closed Jan.–mid-Mar. Restaurant closed Mon. Oct.–May. No lunch Tues.* ⦿ *BP.*

$$ ▦ **Hotel Europa.** The third generation of this inn-keeping family, which has operated the Europa since 1956, welcomes you to a convenient downtown hotel. Expect hardwood floors and pastel *marmarino* (Venetian polished plaster) walls. Rooms are comfortable and up to date, and the breakfast room on the ground floor is exceptionally bright. ⊠ *Via Roma 8, 37121* ☎ *045/594744* 🖶 *045/8001852* ⊕ *www. veronahoteleuropa.com* ⇗ *46 rooms* ♿ *In-room safes, minibars, cable TV, parking (fee), no-smoking rooms* ⊟ *AE, DC, MC, V* ⦿ *BP.*

$ ▦ **Torcolo.** It may not look like much from the outside, but this hotel boasts several advantages: a warm welcome from owners Diana Castellani and Silvia Pomari, pleasant rooms decorated unfussily, and a central location close to Piazza Brà and the Arena. Breakfast, which costs an extra €7–€12, is served outside on the front terrace in summer. ⊠ *Vicolo Listone 3, 37121* ☎ *045/8007512* 🖶 *045/8004058* ⊕ *www. hoteltorcolo.it* ⇗ *19 rooms* ♿ *Breakfast room, in-room safes, minibars, cable TV, bar, parking (fee), some pets allowed* ⊟ *AE, DC, MC, V* ⊘ *Closed mid-Jan.–mid-Feb.* ⦿ *EP.*

Opera

Of all the venues for enjoying opera in the region, pride of place must go to the **Arena di Verona** (Box office ⊠ Via Dietro Anfiteatro 6/b ☎ 045/8005151 ⊕ www.arena.it ⊘ Box office weekdays 9–noon and 3:15–5:45, Sat. 9–noon. June 21–Aug. 31, 10–9 on performance days

FodorśChoice
★

and 10–5:45 on nonperformance days ✉ Tickets start at €22). During its summer opera season (July–September) audiences of as many as 16,000 sit on the original stone terraces or in the modern cushioned stalls. The best operas are the big, splashy ones, like *Aïda,* that demand huge choruses, lots of color and movement, and, if possible, camels, horses, or elephants. But the experience is memorable no matter what's playing. Order tickets by phone or online: if you book a place on the cheaper terraces, be sure to take or rent a cushion—four hours on a 2,000-year-old stone bench can be an ordeal. Sometimes you can even hear the opera from Piazza Brà cafés.

Shopping

Food & Wine
Salumeria Albertini (✉ Corso S. Anastasia 41 ☎ 045/8031074) is Verona's oldest delicatessen: look for the prosciutto and salami hanging outside. **De Rossi** (✉ Corso Porta Borsari 3 ☎ 045/8002489) sells baked bread and cakes, pastries, and biscotti that are lusciously caloric.

Markets
On the third Saturday of every month an antiques and arts-and-crafts market fills **Piazza San Zeno.** The city's main general market takes place at the **Stadio** on Saturday 8:30 AM–1 PM.

IN TRANSIT: MILAN

Updated by
Madeleine
Johnson

Milan isn't between Florence and Venice, but as Italy's transport hub, with the biggest international airport, it may well be your point of entry into the country. It's also Italy's business hub, serving as the capital of commerce, finance, fashion, and media. Leonardo da Vinci's *Last Supper* and other great works of art are here, as well as a spectacular Gothic Duomo, the finest of its kind. Milan even reigns supreme where it really counts (in the minds of many Italians), routinely trouncing the rest of the nation with its two premier soccer teams.

And yet, Milan hasn't won the battle for hearts and minds. Most tourists prefer Tuscany's hills and Venice's canals to Milan's hectic efficiency and wealthy indifference, and it's no surprise that in a country of medieval hilltop villages and skilled artisans, a city of grand boulevards and global corporations leaves visitors asking the real Italy to please stand up. They're right, of course. Milan is more European than Italian, a new buckle on an old boot, and although its old city can stand cobblestone for cobblestone against the best of them, seekers of Roman ruins and fairy-tale towns may pass. But Milan's new faces are hidden behind splendid Beaux-Arts facades and in luxurious 19th-century palazzi, and those lured by its world-class shopping and European sophistication enjoy the city's lively, cosmopolitan feel.

Virtually every invader in European history—Gaul, Roman, Goth, Longobard, and Frank—as well as a long series of rulers from France, Spain, and Austria, took a turn at ruling the city. After being completely sacked by the Goths in AD 539 and by the Holy Roman Empire under

COMING & GOING FROM MILAN

BY AIR

Aeroporto Malpensa (MXP), 50 km (31 mi) northwest of Milan, is the major northern Italian hub for intercontinental flights and also sees substantial European and domestic traffic. The smaller **Aeroporto Milano Linate** (LIN), 10 km (6 mi) east of Milan, handles additional European and domestic flights.

The **Malpensa Express Train** connects Malpensa airport to Cadorna station near downtown Milan. The 40-minute train ride costs €9 (€12 round-trip), leaving Cadorna every half hour from 5:50 AM to 8:20 PM and Malpensa every half hour 6:45 AM to 9:45 PM. **Malpensa Express Buses** make the trip outside of these hours. In addition, **Malpensa Shuttle Buses** (€5) go to and from Milan's central train station (Stazione Centrale). There are departures every half hour from about 5 AM to 10 PM, and the trip takes about 75 minutes. If you're connecting from a Malpensa flight to a train out of Stazione Centrale, you can also take the Malpensa Express to Cadorna station, then pick up the Milan subway green line from the Cadorna stop to the Centrale stop.

From Linate, the **Municipal Bus 73** runs every 10 minutes to Piazza San Babila in the heart of the city. The trip takes approximately 20 minutes. Tickets cost €1 and are sold at the Arrivals lounge newsstand (by the pharmacy). You can go from Linate to Stazione Centrale on the **STARFLY Bus,** which runs every half hour; tickets are €2.50 and are sold on board.

If you need to get from one airport to the other, you can take the shuttle bus **Airpullman** (€8), which runs every 90 minutes. The trip takes approximately 90 minutes.

The drive from Malpensa to Milan is about an hour; take Route S336 east to the A8 autostrada southeast. From Linate it's about 10 minutes into the central city; head west following the signs.

BY TRAIN

The massive **Stazione Centrale**, 3 km (2 mi) northwest of Milan's Duomo, is one of Italy's major passenger-train hubs, with service to destinations throughout Italy. Milan has several other railway stations; the one you're most likely to encounter is Cardorna, the central-city destination for the shuttle train from Malpensa airport.

For general information on trains and schedules, check with **FS−Trenitalia** (☎ 892021 ⊕ www. trenitalia.com), Italy's national railway system. The automated telephone line requires that you know Italian, but the Web site has an English version.

Frederick Barbarossa in 1157, Milan became one of the first independent city-states of the Renaissance. Its heyday of self-rule proved comparatively brief. From 1277 until 1500 it was ruled by the Visconti and subsequently the Sforza dynasties. These families were known, justly or not, for a peculiarly aristocratic mixture of refinement, classical learning, and cruelty, and much of the surviving grandeur of Gothic and Renaissance art and architecture is their doing. Be on the lookout in your wanderings for the Visconti family emblem—a viper, its jaws straining wide, devouring a child.

The city center is compact and walkable, and the efficient Metropolitana (subway), as well as buses and trams, provides access to locations farther afield. Driving the streets of Milan is difficult at best, and parking can be downright miserable, so leave the car behind. The **tourist office** (⊠ Via Marconi 1, near Piazza Duomo ☎ 02/72524301 ⊕ www. milanoinfotourist.com ⊙ Mon.–Sat. 8:45–1 and 2–6, Sun. 9–1 and 2–5) in Piazza Duomo is an excellent place to begin your visit. It's tucked under the arches of one of the twin buildings designed in 1939 to complement the facade of the Galleria across the piazza. Free maps on a variety of themes are available. There is also a good selection of brochures about smaller museums and cultural initiatives. Pick up a copy of the English-language *Hello Milano* (ask, if it is not on display). This monthly magazine includes a day-to-day schedule of events of interest to visitors and a comprehensive map.

The Duomo & Points North

Milan's main streets radiate out from the massive Duomo, a late-Gothic cathedral that was started in 1386. Leading north is the handsome Galleria Vittorio Emanuele, an enclosed walkway that takes you to the world-famous opera house known as La Scala. Beyond are the winding streets of the elegant Brera neighborhood, once the city's bohemian quarter. Here you'll find one of Italy's leading art galleries, as well as the academy of fine arts. Heading northeast from La Scala is Via Manzoni, which leads to the *quadrilatero della moda*, or fashion district. Its streets are lined with elegant window displays from the world's most celebrated designers—the Italians taking the lead, of course.

> ### WORD OF MOUTH
>
> "What I loved about Milan was: attending a concert at La Scala and taking their backstage tour; walking amidst the marble spires on the roof of the Duomo on a sunny day, gazing at the Dolomites in the distance (a definite wow!); window-shopping in the too-chic-for-words Via Montenapoleone area; and seeing the *Last Supper*."
>
> –Maribel

Leading northeast from the Duomo is Corso Vittorio Emanuele. Locals and visitors stroll along this pedestrians-only street, looking at the shop windows, buying ice cream, or stopping for a coffee at one of the sidewalk cafés. Northwest of the Duomo is Via Dante, at the top of which is the imposing outline of the Castello Sforzesco.

The Main Attractions

★ ❽ **Castello Sforzesco.** For the serious student of Renaissance military engineering, the Castello must be something of a travesty, so often has it been remodeled or rebuilt since it was begun in 1450 by the *condottiere* (hired mercenary) who founded the city's second dynastic family, Francesco Sforza, fourth duke of Milan. Though today the word *mercenary* has a pejorative ring, during the Renaissance all Italy's great

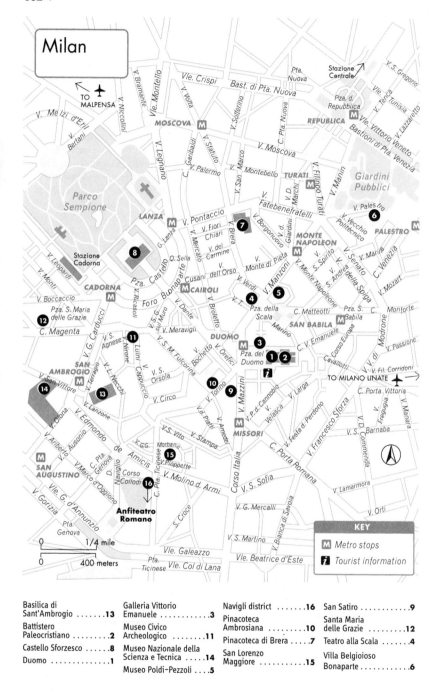

Milan

TO
MALPENSA

KEY

M Metro stops

i Tourist information

soldier-heroes were professionals hired by the cities and principalities that they served. Of them—and there were thousands—Francesco Sforza (1401–66) is considered one of the greatest, most honest, and most organized. It is said he could remember the names not only of all his men but of their horses as well. His rule signaled the enlightened age of the Renaissance, but preceded the next foreign rule by a scant 50 years.

Since the turn of the 20th century, the Castello has housed municipal museums devoted variously to Egyptian and other antiquities, musical instruments, paintings, and sculpture. Highlights include the **Sala delle Asse,** a frescoed room still sometimes attributed to Leonardo da Vinci (1452–1519). Michelangelo's unfinished *Rondanini Pietà* is believed to be his last work—an astounding achievement for a man nearly 90, and a moving coda to his life. Reopened in 2005, after a four-year restoration project, the *pinacoteca* (picture gallery) features paintings from medieval times to the 18th century. The 230 paintings on display include works by Antonello da Messina, Canaletto, Andrea Mantegna, and Bernardo Bellotto. ✉ *Piazza Castello, Brera* ☎ *02/88463700* ⊕ *www. milanocastello.it* 🖹 *€3, free Fri. 2–5* ☉ *Tues.–Sun. 9–5:30* Ⓜ *Cairoli.*

★ ❶ **Duomo.** This intricate Gothic structure has been fascinating and exasperating visitors and conquerors alike since it was begun by Galeazzo Visconti III (1351–1402), first duke of Milan, in 1386. Consecrated in the 15th or 16th century, it was not completed until just before the coronation of Napoléon as king of Italy in 1809. Whether or not you concur with travel writer H. V. Morton's 1964 assessment that the cathedral is "one of the mightiest Gothic buildings ever created," there is no denying that for sheer size and complexity it is unrivaled. It is the second-largest church in the world—the largest being St. Peter's in Rome. The capacity is reckoned to be 40,000. Usually it is empty, a sanctuary from the frenetic pace of life outside and the perfect place for solitary contemplation.

The building is adorned with 135 marble spires and 2,245 marble statues. The oldest part is the **apse.** Its three colossal bays of curving and counter-curved tracery, especially the bay adorning the exterior of the stained-glass windows, should not be missed. At the end of the southern transept down the right aisle lies the **tomb of Gian Giacomo Medici.** The tomb owes some of its design to Michelangelo but was executed by Leone Leoni (1509–90) and is generally considered to be his masterpiece; it dates from the 1560s. Directly ahead is the Duomo's most famous sculpture, the gruesome but anatomically instructive figure of **San Bartolomeo** (St. Bartholomew), whose glorious martyrdom consisted of being flayed alive. It is usually said the saint stands "holding" his skin, but this is not quite accurate. It would appear more that he is luxuriating in it, much as a 1950s matron might have shown off a new fur stole.

As you enter the apse to admire those splendid windows, glance at the **sacristy doors** to the right and left of the altar. The lunette on the right dates from 1393 and was decorated by Hans von Fernach. The one on the left also dates from the 14th century and is ascribed jointly to Giacomo da Campione and Giovanni dei Grassi. Don't miss the view from the Duomo's **roof;** walk out the left (north) transept to the stairs and elevator. Sadly, air pollution drastically reduces the view on all but the rarest days. As you stand among the forest of marble pinnacles, remember that virtually every inch of this gargantuan edifice, including the roof itself, is decorated with precious white marble dragged from quarries near Lake Maggiore by Duke Visconti's team along road laid fresh for the purpose and through the newly dredged canals.

Inspection and possible repair of 12 of the northern spires means the facade facing the piazza may be shrouded in scaffolding, although as individual sections are restored, some scaffolding comes down. The rest of the Duomo's intricate masonry and statuary, including the gleaming, emblematic **Madonnina** perched on the highest spire, remain unencumbered. ⊠ *Piazza del Duomo* ☎ *02/86463456* ⊕ *duomomilano. com* ✉ *Stairs to roof €3.50, elevator €5* ⊗ *Mid-Feb.–mid-Nov., daily 9–5:45; mid-Nov.–mid-Feb., daily 9–4:15* Ⓜ *Duomo.*

Exhibits at the **Museo del Duomo** shed light on the cathedral's history and include some of the treasures removed from the exterior for preservation purposes. ⊠ *Piazza del Duomo 14* ☎ *02/860358* ✉ *€6, €7 including ticket for elevator to Duomo roof* ⊗ *Daily 10–1:15 and 3–6.*

★ ❸ **Galleria Vittorio Emanuele.** This spectacular, late-19th-century glass-topped, barrel-vaulted tunnel is essentially one of the planet's earliest and most select shopping malls. Like its suburban American cousins, the Galleria Vittorio Emanuele fulfills numerous social functions. This is the city's heart, midway between the Duomo and La Scala. It teems with life, inviting people-watching from the tables that spill from the bars and restaurants, where you can enjoy an overpriced coffee. Books, records, clothing, food, pens, and jewelry are all for sale, and you'll also find here the venerable Savini restaurant.

The Galleria has undergone a refurbishment in recent years. Realizing that the quality of the stores (except the Prada flagship store) and restaurants was not what the city wanted in its "parlor," city government and merchants' groups evicted some longtime tenants who had enjoyed anomalously low rents, in favor of Gucci, Tod's and Louis Vuitton.

Like the cathedral, the Galleria is cruciform in shape. Even in poor weather the great glass dome above the octagonal center is a splendid sight. And the floor mosaics are a vastly underrated source of pleasure, even if they are not to be taken too seriously. They represent Europe, Asia, Africa, and the United States; those at the entrance arch are devoted to science, industry, art, and agriculture. Be sure to follow tradition and spin your heels once or twice on the more "delicate" parts of the bull beneath your feet in the northern apse; the Milanese believe it brings good luck. ⊠ *Piazza del Duomo* Ⓜ *Duomo.*

NEED A BREAK?

One thing has stayed constant in the Galleria: the **Caffè Zucca**, known by the Milanese as Camparino. Its inlaid counter, mosaics, and wrought-iron fixtures have been welcoming tired shoppers since 1867. Enjoy a Campari or Zucca *aperitivo* (aperitif) as well as the entire range of Italian coffees, served either in the Galleria or in an elegant upstairs room.

VOICES OF ITALY

Giampaolo Abbondio
Gallery owner, Milan

Giampaolo Abbondio is a rising star in Milan's contemporary art scene. His **Galleria Pack** (✉ Foro Buonaparte 60 ☎ 02/86996395 ⊕ www.galleriapack.com) has attracted a number of important young artists to its stable. Giampaolo is a Milanese by birth, and unabashedly proud of what he calls "the least Italian city in Italy."

Q: Giampaolo, what exactly do you mean when you call Milan the least Italian city in Italy?

A: Well, it's not, of course. We're still Italians. But Milan has been a crossroads for many years, a meeting place from which Italy can access the rest of Europe, and from which the rest of Europe can be introduced to Italy. I think that has made Milan a little more European than other parts of the country. Some of that is good: we have excellent public transportation, stores that are open all day, things like that. And some of that is not so good: they say we work too much, we don't take the time to enjoy life like they do in the rest of Italy. But I'm sure that's clearer to Italians than from a foreigner's point of view. I mean, we still make an excellent risotto . . .

Q: Most people don't think of Milan when they're thinking of great Italian art; they think of places like Rome, Florence, and Venice. Are they making a mistake?

A: Of course! I mean, it's true that Milan isn't the most "artistic" place in Italy. It has a very strong private sector but a weak public sector, meaning there is not a lot of money for museums and other public cultural works. But it also means that there's a lot of private investment in art. Rome may have the museums, but Milan has the more-fertile art scene.

Q: What features of Milan's contemporary art world should a visitor know about?

A: Well, the P.A.C., or **Padiglione di Arte Contemporanea** (✉ Via Palestro 14 ☎ 02/76009085 ⊕ www.comune.milano.it/pac). The P.A.C. is a public space that hosts a constantly changing series of temporary shows. It is a kind of city gallery that does four or five important shows a year. Another is the **Palazzo della Triennale** (✉ Via Alemagna 6 ☎ 02/724341 ⊕ www.triennale.it), which, like the Stazione Centrale, is interesting for its classic Fascist architecture no matter what's going on inside. And the Triennale is located in the middle of Parco Sempione, which has some important public artworks including a fountain by De Chirico and an amphitheater by Arman. And of course, at least as far as I'm concerned, no visit to Milan would be complete without a tour of the important contemporary art galleries! Besides my gallery, there are the **Emi Fontana** (✉ Viale Bligny 42 ☎ 02/58322237), **Salvatore & Carolina Ala** (✉ Via Monte di Pietà 1 ☎ 02/8900901), **Massimo De Carlo** (✉ Via Ventura 4 ☎ 02/70003987 ⊕ www.massimodecarlo.it), and **1,000 Eventi** (✉ Via Porro Lambertenghi 3 ☎ 02/45478297). This is the best way to avoid lines at the museums . . . you go see the art in a gallery before it gets too famous!

❺ Museo Poldi-Pezzoli. This exceptional museum, opened in 1881, was once a private residence and collection, and contains not only pedigreed paintings but also porcelain, textiles, and a cabinet with scenes from Dante's life. The gem is undoubtedly the *Portrait of a Lady* by Antonio Pollaiolo (1431–98), one of the city's most prized treasures and the source of the museum's logo. The collection also includes masterpieces by Botticelli (1445–1510), Andrea Mantegna (1431–1506), Giovanni Bellini (1430–1516), and Fra Filippo Lippi (1406–69). ✉ *Via Manzoni 12, Brera* ☎ *02/794889* ⊕ *www.museopoldipezzoli.it* 🎟 *€7* ⊙ *Tues.–Sun. 10–6* Ⓜ *Montenapoleone.*

★ ❼ Pinacoteca di Brera (Brera Gallery). The collection here is star-studded even by Italian standards. The entrance hall (Room I) displays 20th-century sculpture and painting, including Carlo Carrà's (1881–1966) confident, stylish response to the schools of cubism and surrealism. The museum has nearly 40 other rooms, arranged in chronological order—pace yourself.

The somber, moving *Cristo Morto* (*Dead Christ*) by Mantegna dominates Room VI, with its sparse palette of umber and its foreshortened perspective. Mantegna's shocking, almost surgical precision—in the rendering of Christ's wounds, the face propped up on a pillow, the day's growth of beard—tells of an all-too-human agony. It is one of Renaissance painting's most quietly wondrous achievements, finding an unsuspected middle ground between the excesses of conventional gore and beauty in representing the Passion's saddest moment.

Room XXIV offers two additional highlights of the gallery. Raphael's (1483–1520) *Sposalizio della Vergine,* with its mathematical composition and precise, alternating colors, portrays the betrothal of Mary and Joseph (who, though older than the other men gathered, wins her hand when the rod he is holding miraculously blossoms). *La Vergine con il Bambino e Santi* (*Madonna with Child and Saints*), by Piero della Francesca (1420–92), is an altarpiece commissioned by Federico da Montefeltro (shown kneeling, in full armor, before the Virgin); it was intended for a church to house the Duke's tomb. The ostrich egg hanging from the apse, depending on whom you ask, either commemorates the miracle of his fertility—Federico's wife died months after giving birth to a long-awaited male heir—or alludes to his appeal for posthumous mercy, the egg symbolizing the saving power of grace. ✉ *Via Brera 28* ☎ *02/722631* ⊕ *www.brera.beniculturali.it* 🎟 *€5* ⊙ *Tues.–Sun. 8:30–7:15; last admission 45 mins before closing* Ⓜ *Montenapoleone.*

❹ Teatro alla Scala. You need know nothing of opera to sense that, like Carnegie Hall, La Scala is closer to a cathedral than an auditorium. Here Verdi established his reputation and Maria Callas sang her way into opera lore. It looms as a symbol—both for the performer who dreams of singing here and for the opera buff who knows every note of *Rigoletto* by heart. Audiences are notoriously demanding and are apt to jeer performers who do not measure up. The opera house was closed after destruction by Allied bombs in 1943, reopened at a performance led by Arturo Toscanini in 1946, and closed again in 2002 for renovations. The massive reconstruction project, which left only the exterior shell standing, was completed in late 2004 and the opera house officially reopened on December 7, 2004—the traditional first night of the opera season, which coincides with the feast day of Saint Ambrose, Milan's patron saint.

If you are lucky enough to be here during the opera season, which runs for approximately six months, do whatever is necessary to attend. Tickets go on sale two months before the first performance and are usually sold out the same day. Hearing opera sung in the magical acoustic of La Scala is an unparalleled experience. ☒ *Piazza della Scala* ☎ *02/ 72003744* ⊕ *www.teatroallascala.org* Ⓜ *Duomo.*

At **Museo Teatrale alla Scala** you can admire librettos, posters, costumes, instruments, design sketches for the theater, curtains, and viewing box decorations, along with an explanation of the reconstruction project and several interactive exhibits. A highlight is the collection of antique gramophones and phonographs. ☒ *Piazza della Scala* ☎ *02/43353521* 🎫 *€5* 🕙 *Daily 9–noon and 1:30–5.*

Also Worth Seeing

❷ **Battistero Paleocristiano.** Beneath the Duomo's piazza lies this baptistery ruin dating from the 4th century. Although opinion remains divided, it is widely believed to be where Ambrose, Milan's first bishop and patron saint, baptized Augustine. Tickets are available at the kiosk inside the cathedral. ☒ *Piazza del Duomo, enter through Duomo* ☎ *02/ 86463456* 🎫 *€1.50* 🕙 *Daily 9:30–5:15* Ⓜ *Duomo.*

★ ❻ **Villa Belgioioso Bonaparte—Museo dell'Ottocento.** After three years of restoration, finished in March 2006, this museum, formerly known as the Galleria di Arte Moderna, is one of the city's most beautiful buildings. An outstanding example of neoclassical architecture, it was built between 1790 and 1796 as a residence for a member of the Belgioioso family. It later became known as the Villa Reale (royal) when it was donated to Napoléon, who lived here briefly with Empress Josephine. Its origins as residence are reflected in the elegance of its proportions and its private garden behind.

Likewise, the collection of paintings is domestic rather than monumental. There are many portraits, as well as collections of miniatures on porcelain. Unusual for an Italian museum, this collection derives from private donations from Milan's hereditary and commercial aristocracies. Among pieces on display are the collection left by prominent painter and sculptor Marino Marini and the immense *Quarto Stato* (Fourth Estate) which is at the top of the grand staircase. Completed in 1901 by Pellizza da Volpedo, this painting of striking workers is an icon of 20th-century Italian art and labor history, and as such it has been satirized almost as much as the Mona Lisa.

This collection will not satisfy museumgoers seeking major Italian art. No matter, the best part is the building itself, with its delightful shell-color stucco decorations, splendid neoclassical chandeliers, pastel taffeta curtains, and garden view. It offers a unique glimpse of the splendors that the city hides behind its discreet and often stern facades. ☒ *Via Palestro 16* ☎ *02/76340809* ⊕ *www.villabelgiojosobonaparte.it* 🕙 *Tues.–Sun. 9–1 and 2–5:30.*

The **Giardini Pubblici** (Public Gardens), across Via Palestro from the Villa Reale, were laid out by Giuseppe Piermarini, architect of La Scala, in 1770. They were designed as public pleasure gardens, and today they still are popular with families who live in the city center. Generations of Milanese have taken pony rides and gone on the miniature train and merry-go-round. The park also contains a small planetarium and the **Museo Civico di Storia Naturale** (The Municipal Natural History Museum).

Parents may want to visit the garden of the Villa Belgioioso-Bonaparte, on Via Palestro, which is entered from a gate to the building's left. Access to the garden, which has statuary and a water course designed in 1790 (the first English-style garden in Milan), is primarily for children accompanied by an adult. Adults without children wanting to see the garden are tolerated, as long as they do not linger in this protected area.

NEED A BREAK? If your energy is flagging after shopping or chasing children around the park, try some of Milan's best cappuccino and pastry at **Dolce In** (⊠ Via Turati 2/3 ⊙ Closed Mon.), which is equally close to Via della Spiga and the Giardini Pubblici. It's famous for its pastry and also serves sandwiches and cold plates at lunch. On Sunday mornings, classic-car enthusiasts meet informally here, parking their handsome machines out front while they have coffee.

South & West of the Duomo

If the part of the city to the north of the Duomo is dominated by its shops, the section to the south is famous for its works of art. The most famous is *Il Cenacolo*—known in English as *The Last Supper*. If you have time for nothing else, make sure you see this masterwork, which has now been definitively restored, after many, many, years of work. Reservations will be needed to see this fresco, housed in the refectory of Santa Maria delle Grazie. Make these before you depart for Italy, so you can plan the rest of your time in Milan.

There are other gems as well. Via Torino, the ancient road for Turin, leads to a half-hidden treasure: Bramante's Renaissance masterpiece, the church of San Satiro. At the intersection of Via San Vittore and Via Carducci is the medieval Basilica di Sant'Ambrogio, named for Milan's patron saint. Another lovely church southeast of Sant'Ambrogio along Via de Amicis is San Lorenzo Maggiore. It's also known as San Lorenzo alle Colonne because of the 16 columns running across the facade.

The Main Attractions

13 Basilica di Sant'Ambrogio (Basilica of St. Ambrose). Noted for its medieval architecture, the church was consecrated by St. Ambrose in AD 387 and is the model for all Lombard Romanesque churches. The church is often closed for weddings on Saturday. ⊠ *Piazza Sant'Ambrogio 15* ☎ *02/86450895* ⊙ *Mon.–Sat. 7–noon and 2:30–7, Sun. 3–8* Ⓜ *Sant'Ambrogio.*

NEED A BREAK? A bit overcrowded at night, the **Bar Magenta** (⊠ Via Carducci 13, at Corso Magenta, Sant'Ambrogio ☎ 02/8053808) can be a good stop en route during the day. Beyond coffee at all hours, lunch, and beer, the real attraction is its casual but civilized, quintessentially Milanese ambience. It's open until 2 AM.

⓾ **Pinacoteca Ambrosiana.** This museum, founded in the 17th century by Cardinal Federico Borromeo, is one of the city's treasures. Here you can contemplate works of art such as Caravaggio's *Basket of Fruit,* prescient in its realism, and Raphael's awesome preparatory drawing for *The School of Athens* that hangs in the Vatican, as well as paintings by Leonardo, Botticelli, Luini, Titian, and Brueghel. The adjoining library, the Biblioteca Ambrosiana, dates from 1609, and is thought to be the oldest public library in Italy. Admission to the library these days is limited to scholars. ⊠ *Piazza Pio XI 2, near Duomo* ☎ *02/806921* ⊕ *www.ambrosiana.it* 🗐 *€7.50* ⊙ *Tues.–Sun. 10–5:30* Ⓜ *Duomo.*

⓯ **San Lorenzo Maggiore.** Sixteen ancient Roman columns line the front of this sanctuary; 4th-century paleochristian mosaics survive in the Cappella di Sant'Aquilino (Chapel of St. Aquilinus). ⊠ *Corso di Porta Ticinese 39, Porta Ticinese* ☎ *02/89404129* 🗐 *Mosaics €2* ⊙ *Daily 8:30–12:30 and 2:30–6:30.*

★ ❾ **San Satiro.** First built in 876, this architectural gem was later perfected by Bramante (1444–1514), demonstrating his command of proportion and perspective, keynotes of Renaissance architecture. Bramante tricks the eye with a famous optical illusion that makes a small interior seem extraordinarily spacious and airy, while accommodating a beloved 13th-century fresco. ⊠ *Via Torino 9, near Duomo* ⊙ *Weekdays 7:30–11:30 and 3:30–6:30, weekends 9–noon and 3:30–7* Ⓜ *Duomo.*

★ ⓬ **Santa Maria delle Grazie.** Leonardo da Vinci's *The Last Supper,* housed in the church and former Dominican monastery of Santa Maria delle Grazie, has had an almost unbelievable history of bad luck and neglect—its near destruction in an American bombing raid in August 1943 was only the latest chapter in a series of misadventures, including, if one 19th-century source is to be believed, being whitewashed over by monks. Well-meant but disastrous attempts at restoration have done little to rectify the problem of the work's placement: it was executed on a wall unusually vulnerable to climatic dampness. Yet Leonardo chose to work slowly and patiently in oil pigments—which demand dry plaster—instead of proceeding hastily on wet plaster according to the conventional fresco technique. Novelist Aldous Huxley (1894–1963) called it "the saddest work of art in the world." After years of restorers' patiently shifting from one square centimeter to another, Leonardo's masterpiece is free of the shroud of scaffolding—and centuries of retouching, grime, and dust. Astonishing clarity and luminosity have been regained. *Reservations are required* to view the work; call several days ahead for weekday visits and several weeks in advance for a weekend visit. The reservations office is open 9 AM–6 PM weekdays and 9 AM–2 PM on Saturday. Viewings are in 15-minute slots.

Despite Leonardo's carefully preserved preparatory sketches in which the apostles are clearly labeled by name, there still remains some small debate about a few identities in the final arrangement. But there can be no mistaking Judas, small and dark, his hand calmly reaching forward to the bread, isolated from the terrible confusion that has taken the hearts of the others. One critic, Frederick Hartt, offers an elegantly terse explanation for why the composition works: it combines "dramatic confusion" with "mathematical order." Certainly, the amazingly skillful and unobtrusive repetition of threes—in the windows, in the grouping of the figures, and in their placement—adds a mystical aspect to what at first seems simply the perfect observation of spontaneous human gesture.

The painting was executed in what was the order's refectory, which is now referred to as the **Cenacolo Vinciano**. Take a moment to visit Santa Maria delle Grazie itself. It's a handsome church, with a fine dome, which Bramante added along with a cloister about the time that Leonardo was commissioned to paint *The Last Supper*. If you're wondering how two such giants came to be employed decorating and remodeling the refectory and church of a comparatively modest religious order, and not, say, the Duomo, the answer lies in the ambitious but largely unrealized plan to turn Santa Maria delle Grazie into a magnificent Sforza family mausoleum. Though Ludovico il Moro Sforza (1452–1508), seventh duke of Milan, was but one generation away from the founding of the Sforza dynasty, he was its last ruler. Two years after Leonardo finished *The Last Supper*, Ludovico was defeated by Louis XII and spent the remaining eight years of his life in a French dungeon. ⊠ *Piazza Santa Maria delle Grazie 2, off Corso Magenta, Sant'Ambrogio* ☎ *02/89421146 weekdays 9–6, Sat. 9–2* 🖃 *€6.50 plus €1.50 reservation fee* ⊗ *Tues.–Sun. 8–7:30; last entry 6:45* Ⓜ *Cadorna*.

Also Worth Seeing

⑪ **Museo Civico Archeologico** (Municipal Archaeological Museum). Housed in a former monastery, this museum has some enlightening relics from Milan's Roman past—from everyday utensils and jewelry to several fine examples of mosaic pavement. ⊠ *Corso Magenta 15, Sant'Ambrogio* ☎ *02/86450011* 🖃 *€2, free Fri. 2–5* ⊗ *Tues.–Sun. 9–5:30* Ⓜ *Cadorna*.

ⓒ ⑭ **Museo Nazionale della Scienza e Tecnica** (National Museum of Science and Technology). This museum houses an extensive, eccentric collection of engineering achievements, from metal-processing equipment to full-size locomotives. But the highlights are undoubtedly the exhibits based on the inventive technical drawings of Leonardo da Vinci. On the second floor a collection of models based on these sketches is artfully displayed, with Leonardo's paintings offering striking counterpoint overhead. Explanations are not offered in English, leaving you to ponder possible purposes for the contraptions. On the ground level—in the hallway between the courtyards—is a room featuring interactive, moving models of the famous *vita aerea* (aerial screw) and *ala battente* (beating wing), thought to be forerunners of the modern helicopter and airplane, respectively. ⊠ *Via San Vittore 21, Sant'Ambrogio* ☎ *02/48555200* ⊕ *www. museoscienza.org* 🖃 *€7* ⊗ *Tues.–Fri. 9:30–4:50, weekends 9:30–6:20* Ⓜ *Sant'Ambrogio*.

⑯ **Navigli district.** In medieval times, a network of *navigli,* or canals, crisscrossed the city. Almost all have been covered over, but two—Naviglio Grande and Naviglio Pavese—are still navigable. Once a down-at-theheels neighborhood, the Navigli district has been gentrified over the last 20 years. Humble workshops have been replaced by trendy boutiques, art galleries, cafés, bars, and restaurants. The Navigli at night is about as close as you will get to more-southern-style Italian street life in Milan.

On weekend nights, it is difficult to walk (and impossible to park) among the youthful crowds thronging the narrow streets along the canals. Check out the antiques fair on the last Sunday of the month. ⊠ *South of Corso Porta Ticinese, Porta Genova* Ⓜ *Porta Genova.*

Where to Eat

★ $$$$ ✕ **Antica Osteria del Ponte.** Rich, imaginative seasonal cuisine composed according to the inspired whims of chef Ezio Santin is reason enough to make your way 20 km (12 mi) southwest of Milan to one of Italy's finest restaurants. The setting is a traditional country inn, where a wood fire warms the rustic interior in winter. The menu changes regularly; in fall, wild porcini mushrooms are among the favored ingredients. Various fixed menus (at €110 and €145) offer broad samplings of antipasti, primi, and meat or fish; some include appropriate wine selections, too. ⊠ *Cassinetta di Lugagnano, 3 km (2 mi) north of Abbiategrasso* ☎ *02/ 9420034* ⊕ *www.anticaosteriadelponte.it* ⌂ *Reservations essential* 🖃 *AE, DC, MC, V* ⊗ *Closed Sun. and Mon., Dec. 25–Jan. 12, and Aug.*

★ $$$$ ✕ **Cracco-Peck.** When a renowned local chef (Carlo Cracco) joined forces with the city's top gourmet food store (Peck), the results were not long in coming. Within three years, Cracco-Peck boasted two Michelin stars. The dining room is done in an elegant style that favors cool earth tones. Specialties include Milanese classics revisited—Cracco's take on saffron risotto and breaded veal cutlet should not be missed. Be sure to save room for the light, steam-cooked tiramisu. If you can't decide, opt for the gourmet menu (€88 for six courses, excluding wine). ⊠ *Via Victor Hugo 4, near Duomo* ☎ *02/876774* ⊕ *www.peck.it* ⌂ *Reservations essential* 🖃 *AE, DC, MC, V* ⊗ *Closed Sun., 10 days in Jan., and 2 wks in Aug. No lunch Sat. No dinner Sat. in July and Aug.* Ⓜ *Duomo.*

★ $$$$ ✕ **Don Carlos.** One of the few restaurants open after La Scala lets out, Don Carlos, in the Grand Hotel et de Milan, is nothing like its indecisive operatic namesake (whose betrothed was stolen by his father). Flavors are bold, their presentation precise and full of flair: broiled red mullet floats on a lacy layer of crispy leek. Walls are blanketed with sketches of the theater, and the opera recordings are every bit as well chosen as the wine list, setting the perfect stage for discreet business negotiation or, better yet, refined romance. A gourmet menu costs €75 for six courses (two-person minimum), excluding wine. ⊠ *Grand Hotel et de Milan, Via Manzoni 29, Duomo* ☎ *02/723141* ⊕ *www. grandhoteletdemilan.it* ⌂ *Reservations essential* 🖃 *AE, DC, MC, V* ⊗ *Closed Aug. No lunch* Ⓜ *Montenapoleone.*

$$$$ ✕ **Joia.** At this haute-cuisine vegetarian restaurant near Piazza della Re-pubblica, delicious dishes are artistically prepared by chef Pietro Leemann. The ever-changing menu offers dishes such as ravioli with basil, potatoes, pine nuts, and crisp green beans. (Fish also makes an appearance.) The dishes all have creative names, such as the onomatopoeic soup called "blub." In the depths of this thick mushroom-and-asparagus soup is an air bubble that makes a distinctive sound when it comes to the surface. Multicourse menus range from €55 to €95, excluding wine. ⊠ *Via Panfilo Castaldi 18, Porta Venezia* ☎ *02/29522124* 🖃 *AE,*

4

DC, MC, V ⊘ *Closed Sun., 3 wks in Aug., and Dec. 24–Jan. 7. No lunch Sat.* Ⓜ *Repubblica.*

$$$$ ✕ **La Terrazza.** An office building at the edge of the fashion district is home to this stylish eatery where contemporary design dominates both food and decor. Well-dressed business executives dine on inventive "Mediterranean sushi," which uses pearl barley instead of rice and incorporates pesto, blood oranges, or olive tapenade. There is a fixed-price meal for €62. In warmer weather, the scene shifts to the terrace, where you can see the treetops of the nearby Giardini Pubblici. There's a "happy hour" every day except Sunday; on Sunday, brunch is served. Takeout is also available. ⊠ *Via Palestro 2, Quadrilatero* ☎ *02/76002277* ⊟ *AE, DC, MC, V* ⊘ *Closed last 3 wks in Aug.* Ⓜ *Turati, Palestro.*

$$$–$$$$ ✕ **Antica Trattoria della Pesa.** Fin-de-siècle furnishings, dark-wood paneling, and old-fashioned lamps still look much as they must have when this eatery opened 100 years ago. It's authentic Old Milan, and the menu is right in line, offering risotto, minestrone, and osso buco. Sample the *riso al salto con rognone trifolato,* which is fried rice with thinly sliced kidney. In winter, polenta is the best choice. ⊠ *Viale Pasubio 10, Porta Volta* ☎ *02/6555741* ⊟ *AE, DC, MC, V* ⊘ *Closed Sun., Aug., and Dec. 24–Jan. 6* Ⓜ *Porta Garibaldi.*

$$$–$$$$ ✕ **Boeucc.** Milan's oldest restaurant, opened in 1696, is on the same square as novelist Alessandro Manzoni's house, not far from La Scala. With stone columns, chandeliers, Oriental rugs, and a garden, it has come a long way from its basement origins (*boeucc,* pronounced "birch," is old Milanese for *buco,* or "hole"). You'll savor such dishes as penne *al branzino e zucchini* (with sea bass and zucchini). For dessert, try the *gelato di castagne con zabaglione caldo* (chestnut ice cream with hot zabaglione). ⊠ *Piazza Belgioioso 2, Scala* ☎ *02/76020224* ⟐ *Reservations essential* ⊟ *AE* ⊘ *Closed Sat., Easter Sun. and Mon., Aug., and Dec. 24–Jan. 4. No lunch Sun.* Ⓜ *Montenapoleone, Duomo.*

$$$–$$$$ ✕ **Nobu.** From a minimalist corner of the Armani minimall, Milan's Nobu serves the same delicious Japanese-Peruvian fusion as its siblings in the world's other culinary capitals. Cocktails, appetizers, and beautiful people can be found at the ground-floor bar, well worth a visit even if you're not dining upstairs. Dinner can be a scene here; at lunch there is a fixed-price "box" for €25. ⊠ *Via Pisoni, 1, corner of Via Manzoni 31, Quadrilatero* ☎ *02/72318645* ⟐ *Reservations essential* ⊟ *AE, DC, MC, V* ⊘ *No lunch Sun. and Mon.* Ⓜ *Montenapoleone.*

$$–$$$ ✕ **Il Brellin.** In front of this Milan classic is a sluice from the Naviglio (one of the canals that once crisscrossed the city) where the washerwomen who gave the street its name used to scrub the clothes of Milan's noble families. Now the Navigli area is filled with bars and restaurants, of which Il Brellin is one of the more serious. It offers a mix of homey classics, such as pasta rustica and rigatoni sautéed with pancetta, as well as new twists on typical ingredients—a pumpkin tart as an appetizer. With its several small rooms with exposed beams, Il Brellin is cozy in winter. But on a nice Sunday, enjoy the brunch buffet at an outside table. ⊠ *Vicolo dei Lavandai Navigli* ☎ *02/89402700* ⊟ *AE, DC, MC, V* ⊘ *No dinner Sun.*

$$–$$$ ✕ **La Libera.** Although this establishment in the heart of Brera calls itself a *birreria con cucina* (beer cellar with kitchen), locals come here for excellent evening meals in relaxed surroundings. A soft current of jazz and sylvan decor soothe the ripple of conversation. The creative cooking varies with the season, but could include linguine *al pescato* (with a fish sauce); *fritto di gamberi, zucchine e totanetti* (fried shrimp, zucchini, and baby squid); or *rognone alla senape* (veal kidneys cooked in mustard). ⊠ *Via Palermo 21, Brera* ☎ *02/8053603 or 02/86462773* ▤ *AE, DC, MC, V* ✸ *No lunch* Ⓜ *Moscova.*

$$–$$$ ✕ **Paper Moon.** Hidden behind Via Montenapoleone and thus handy to the restaurant-scarce Quadrilatero, Paper Moon is a cross between neighborhood restaurant and celebrity hangout. Clients include families from this wealthy area, professionals, football players, and television stars. What the menu lacks in originality it makes up for in consistency—reliable pizza and *cotoletta* (veal cutlet). Like any Italian restaurant, it's not child friendly in an American sense—no high chairs or children's menu—but children will find food they like. Open until 12:30 AM. ⊠ *Via Bagutta 1, Quadrilatero* ☎ *02/76022297* ▤ *AE, MC, V* ✸ *Closed Sun., 2 wks in Aug., and Dec. 25–Jan. 7* Ⓜ *San Babila.*

$$–$$$ ✕ **Trattoria Montina.** Twin brothers Maurizio and Roberto Montina have
Fodor'sChoice turned this restaurant into a local favorite. Don't be fooled by the "trat-
★ toria" name—Chef Roberto creates exquisite modern Italian dishes such as warmed bruschetta with Brie and prosciutto, while Maurizio moves around the restaurant chatting and taking orders. Try the *frittura impazzita,* a wild-and-crazy mix of delicately fried seafood. The warm chocolate-and-pear pie also comes highly recommended. ⊠ *Via Procaccini 54, Procaccini* ☎ *02/3490498* ▤ *AE, DC, MC, V* ✸ *Closed Sun., Aug., and Dec. 25–Jan. 7. No lunch Mon.* Ⓜ *Trams 1, 19, 29, 33.*

★ **$–$$** ✕ **Da Abele.** If you love risotto, then make a beeline for this neighborhood trattoria. The superb risotto dishes change with the season, and there may be just two or three on the menu at any time. It is tempting to try them all. The setting is relaxed, the service informal, the prices strikingly reasonable. Outside the touristy center of town but quite convenient by subway, this trattoria is invariably packed with locals. ⊠ *Via Temperanza 5, Loreto* ☎ *02/2613855* ▤ *AE, DC, MC, V* ✸ *Closed Mon., Aug., and Dec. 22–Jan. 7. No lunch* Ⓜ *Pasteur.*

$–$$ ✕ **La Bruschetta.** This tiny, bustling first-class pizzeria near the Duomo serves specialties from Tuscany and other parts of Italy. The wood oven is in full view, so you can see your pizza cooking in front of you, although there are plenty of nonpizza dishes available, too, such as spaghetti *alle cozze e vongole* (with clam and mussel sauce) and grilled and skewered meats. ⊠ *Piazza Beccaria 12, Duomo* ☎ *02/8692494* ▤ *AE, MC, V* ✸ *Closed Mon., 3 wks in Aug., and late Dec.–early Jan.* Ⓜ *Duomo.*

¢–$$ ✕ **Joia Leggero.** In the Porta Ticinese area, and near the Navigli district, Joia Leggero (light) is a lower-priced, more-informal initiative of innovative chef Pietro Leemann, the man behind Joia. With a pleasant view of the church of St. Eustorgio and a few tables outside, this airy restaurant serves haute vegetarian food. "Leggero" does not necessarily refer to the calorie content; the offerings—especially the excellent desserts— are often satisfyingly rich. This is not typical sprouts-and-grains health food. Try the well-priced set meals (vegetarian lunch is €11, €14 with fish), which are attractively presented on Japanese-inspired trays.

✉ *Corso di Porta Ticinese 106, Porta Ticinese* ☎ *02/89404134* ▭ *AE, MC, V* ⊘ *Closed Sun. and 3 wks in Aug. No lunch Mon.*

$–$$ ✕ **Al Rifugio Pugliese.** Just outside the center of town, this is a fun place to sample specialties from the Puglia region of southern Italy. These include homemade *orecchiette* (a small, ear-shape pasta) with a variety of sauces. There is a choice of 60 first courses, as well as plenty of vegetable and fish dishes. The lunch buffet is a good deal as are the fixed-price menus of €29 and €39 that can include wine, coffee, and after-dinner drinks. ✉ *Via Costanza 2, corner of Via Boni 16, Fiera* ☎ *02/ 48000917* ▭ *AE, DC, MC, V* ⊘ *Closed Sun., Aug. 5–25, and Dec. 25–Jan. 7* Ⓜ *Wagner.*

¢–$ ✕ **Pizza Ok.** Pizza is almost the only item on the menu at this popular spot near Corso Buenos Aires, but it's very good and the dining experience will be easy on your pocketbook. Possibilities for toppings seem endless. ✉ *Via Lambro 15, Porta Venezia* ☎ *02/29401272* ▭ *No credit cards* ⊘ *Closed Aug. and Dec. 24–Jan. 7. No lunch Sun.* Ⓜ *Porta Venezia.*

¢ ✕ **Bar Tempio.** This wine bar, not far from Giardini Pubblici and the shops of the Quadrilatero, was once so unprepossessing that it didn't have a name—but it turned out some of Milan's best panini. It's been renovated and given a name, but the same artist is still making the sandwiches. This is a lunch-only establishment, and you might have to wait your turn, as panini are made to order from a list (not in English, so bring your phrase book). They feature cured prosciutto *di praga, cipolle* (onions), and various cheeses (including easily recognizable Brie). ✉ *Piazza Cavour 5 (enter from Via Turati), near Quadrilatero* ☎ *02/6551946* ⊘ *No dinner* Ⓜ *Turati.*

¢ ✕ **Taverna Morigi.** This dusky, wood-panel wine bar near the stock exchange is the perfect spot to enjoy a glass of wine with cheese and cold cuts. At lunch, pasta dishes and select entrées are available; pasta is the only hot dish served in the evening. Platters of cheese and cold cuts are always available; if you're coming for a meal, a reservation is a good idea. ✉ *Via Morigi 8, Sant'Ambrogio* ☎ *02/86450880* ▭ *AE, DC, MC, V* ⊘ *Closed Sun. and Aug. No lunch Sat.* Ⓜ *Cairoli.*

Where to Stay

$$$$ 🏨 **Carlton-Baglioni.** If you're in Milan to shop in the fashion district, this hotel is an ideal base. It's light and airy, with double-glazed windows, a parking garage, and lots of little touches such as complimentary chocolates and liqueurs to make up for the rather functional rooms. Some have terraces large enough for a table, a chair, and a shrub in a pot. The highly rated Baretto restaurant is a haunt of Milan's business and cultural elite. ✉ *Via Senato 5, Quadrilatero, 20121* ☎ *02/77077* 🖷 *02/ 783300* ⊕ *www.baglionihotels.com* 🛏 *92 rooms* ⌖ *Restaurant, room service, minibars, cable TV, bar, laundry service, convention center, business services, parking (fee), no-smoking rooms* ▭ *AE, DC, MC, V* ⦿❙ *EP* Ⓜ *San Babila.*

$$$$ 🏨 **Four Seasons.** The Four Seasons has been cited more than once by the Italian press as the country's best city hotel—perhaps because once you're inside, the feeling is anything but urban. Built in the 15th century as a convent, the hotel surrounds a colonnaded cloister, and rooms added in a 2004 expansion have balconies giving onto a glassed-in courtyard. Everything about the place is standard Four Seasons (high) style, including a Brioni-decorated suite and a Royal Suite occupying its own floor. The Theater restaurant has some of Milan's best hotel dining. ⊠ *Via Gesù 6–8, Quadrilatero, 20121* ☎ *02/7708167* 🖷 *02/ 77085000* ⊕ *www.fourseasons.com* ↩ *77 rooms, 41 suites* ♨ *2 restaurants, room service, minibars, cable TV, Internet, bar, laundry service, business services, meeting rooms, no-smoking rooms, parking (fee), gym* ⊟ *AE, DC, MC, V* ⵏⵓ *EP* Ⓜ *Montenapoleone.*

$$$$ 🏨 **Grand Hotel et de Milan.** Only blocks from La Scala, this hotel, which opened in 1863, is sometimes called the "Hotel Verdi," because the composer lived here for 27 years. His apartment, complete with his desk, is now the Presidential Suite. In 2005 the entire hotel was refurbished. Moss-green and persimmon velvet enlivened the 19th-century look without sacrificing dignity and luxury. It's everything you hope for in a traditional European hotel; dignified but not stuffy, elegant but not ostentatious. The renovation also turned a former terrace into a small and airy glass-enclosed fitness center, which is a far cry from the usual, fluorescent-lighted basement den. The Don Carlos restaurant is one of Milan's best. ⊠ *Via Manzoni 29, Scala, 20121* ☎ *02/723141* 🖷 *02/86460861* ⊕ *www. grandhoteletdemilan.it* ↩ *87 rooms, 8 suites* ♨ *Restaurants, room service, minibars, cable TV, Wi-Fi, bar, laundry service, gym, parking (fee), no-smoking rooms* ⊟ *AE, DC, MC, V* ⵏⵓ *EP* Ⓜ *Montenapoleone.*

★ $$$$ 🏨 **The Gray.** At this small luxury hotel you get the best of everything, from location to amenities—all for a price. The interiors are decorated by famed Italian designer Guido Ciompi (who handles Gucci boutiques the world over). The atmosphere is trendy chic, from bottom-lighted tables in the hotel restaurant to patterns of laser light that play across the walls of the lobby. Rooms come equipped with everything from plasma TVs to specially designed oversize toiletries. The hotel does not have rooms with twin beds. Guests not staying in one of the two suites with private gyms may use the gym at sister Hotel de la Ville about three blocks away. ⊠ *Via San Raffaele 6, near Duomo, 20121* ☎ *02/7208951* 🖷 *02/ 866526* ⊕ *www.sinahotels.it* ↩ *21 rooms, 2 suites* ♨ *Restaurant, room service, minibars, cable TV, Wi-Fi, bar, laundry service, business services, no-smoking rooms* ⊟ *AE, DC, MC, V* ⵏⵓ *EP* Ⓜ *Duomo.*

★ $$$$ 🏨 **Principe di Savoia.** Milan's *grande dame* has all the trappings of an exquisite traditional hotel: lavish mirrors, drapes, and carpets, and Milan's largest guest rooms, outfitted with eclectic fin-de-siècle furnishings. Forty-eight "Deluxe Mosaic" rooms (named for the glass mosaic panels in their ample bathrooms) are even larger, and the three-bedroom presidential suite features its own marble pool. The Winter Garden is an elegant aperitivo spot, and the Acanto restaurant has garden seating. Lighter food is served in the Lobby Lounge. ⊠ *Piazza della Repubblica 17, Porta Nuova, 20124* ☎ *02/62301* 🖷 *02/653799* ⊕ *www.hotelprincipedisavoia.com* ↩ *269 rooms, 132 suites* ♨ *2 restaurants, room service, minibars, cable TV, Wi-Fi, health club, indoor pool, spa, bar, laundry service, business services, meeting rooms, convention center, no-smoking rooms* ⊟ *AE, DC, MC, V* ⵏⵓ *EP* Ⓜ *Repubblica.*

$$$–$$$$ 🏨 **Hotel Spadari al Duomo.** That this hotel is owned by an architect's family shows in the details, including architect-designed furniture and a fine collection of contemporary art. The owner's idea of creating a hotel/gallery extends to the guest rooms, where paintings by young Milanese artists are on rotating display. For all the artistic accents, this is still a comfortable, homey hotel, with an inviting frescoed breakfast room and many rooms with private terraces. Personal touches, such as a collection of short stories on the turned-downed beds, abound. ⊠ *Via Spadari 11, near Duomo, 20123* ☎ *02/72002371* 🖷 *02/861184* ⊕ *www.spadarihotel.com* 🖃 *40 rooms, 3 suites* ♻ *Minibars, cable TV, Wi-Fi, in-room broadband, bar, no-smoking rooms* ☱ *AE, DC, MC, V* ⦾ *BP* Ⓜ *Duomo.*

★ **$$–$$$** 🏨 **Antica Locanda dei Mercanti.** On a quiet side street off Via Dante, this 14-room hotel is minutes—and light-years—away from Milan's bustling downtown. Rooms are on the second and third floors (four have private terraces), but you check in at ground-floor reception and take breakfast in the dining room—both added in 2006. Despite the renovations, prices at this hidden jewel remain in the same category. Reserve early for the terrace rooms. ⊠ *Via San Tomaso 6, Duomo, 20121* ☎ *02/8054080* 🖷 *02/8054090* ⊕ *www.lalocanda.it* 🖃 *14 rooms* ♻ *Cable TV, Wi-Fi, bar* ☱ *MC, V* ⦾ *EP* Ⓜ *Cordusio.*

$$–$$$ 🏨 **Ariston.** "Bio-architectural" principles prevail at this hotel near the Duomo, which was built using natural materials and has ionized air circulating throughout. As you might expect from such a progressive-minded place, the buffet breakfast includes organic foods. There's Internet access for free in the lobby (and for a fee in the rooms), and bicycles are available in summer. The location is close to the lively Porta Ticinese shops and restaurants and the young people's fashion mecca, Via Torino. Although a longish walk from the nearest subway stop, the Duomo, it is well served by tram. ⊠ *Largo Carrobbio 2, Duomo, 20123* ☎ *02/72000556* 🖷 *02/72000914* ⊕ *www.aristonhotel.com* 🖃 *52 rooms* ♻ *Minibars, cable TV, in-room broadband, bicycles, bar, laundry service, parking (fee), no-smoking rooms* ☱ *AE, DC, MC, V* ⦾ *BP* Ⓜ *Duomo.*

$$–$$$ 🏨 **Hotel Gran Duca di York.** This small hotel has spare but classically elegant and efficient rooms—four with private terraces. Built around a courtyard, the 1890s building was originally a seminary and still belongs to a religious institution. With an ideal location a few steps west of the Duomo, it offers exceptional value for Milan. ⊠ *Via Moneta 1/a, Duomo, 20123* ☎ *02/874863* 🖷 *02/8690344* ⊕ *www.ducadiyork. com* 🖃 *33 rooms* ♻ *Minibars, cable TV, bar, laundry service, meeting rooms, parking (fee), no-smoking floor* ☱ *AE, MC, V* ☉ *Closed Aug.* ⦾ *EP* Ⓜ *Cordusio.*

$$ 🏨 **Antica Locanda Leonardo.** Convenient to the church where you'll find *The Last Supper* and near the city center, this small hotel is in an inner courtyard, making it one step removed from the traffic outside. It's been run by the same family for more than 40 years, and the staff is welcoming and helpful. The rooms overlook the courtyard or the garden, which was renovated in 2006. ⊠ *Corso Magenta 78, Sant'Ambrogio,*

20123 ☎ 02/463317 🖷 02/48019012 ⊕ *www.anticalocandaleonardo. com* ⇱ *20 rooms* ⚷ *Cable TV, Wi-Fi, bar, laundry service* 🖃 *AE, DC, MC, V* ⊘ *Closed Dec. 31–Jan. 7 and 3 wks in Aug.* ⵾◯╎ *BP* Ⓜ *Sant'Am-brogio.*

$–$$ 🎫 **Hotel Vittoria.** You'll forgive this hotel its baroque decor when you see how it reflects the owners' southern Italian approach to hospital-ity: they're eager to please, and they're proud of renovations that are bringing the telecommunications up to date and making rooms wheel-chair accessible. Although out of the central tourist area (on a quiet residential street), the Vittoria is on the bus line from Linate airport and on other major tram lines. It's about a 20-minute walk from the Duomo, and there's a good selection of restaurants nearby. English-speak-ing staff (not a given in smaller hotels) and spotless, comfortable rooms make this an attractive haven after a day out. ⊠ *Via Pietro Calvi 32, East Central Milan, 20129* ☎ 02/5456520 🖷 02/55190246 ⊕ *www. hotelvittoriamilano.it* ⇱ *40 rooms* ⚷ *In-room safes, minibars, cable TV, no-smoking rooms, parking (fee), meeting room* 🖃 *AE, DC, MC, V* ⵾◯╎ *EP.*

★ **$–$$** 🎫 **London.** On a quiet side street just round the corner from the Castello Sforzesco, the London offers a good value and convenient access to Milan's main sights. Well-appointed rooms are in a 1960s-era building. ⊠ *Via Rovello 3, Castello, 20121* ☎ 02/72020166 🖷 02/8057037 ⊕ *www. hotellondonmilano.com* ⇱ *29 rooms* ⚷ *Cable TV, bar, laundry serv-ice, Internet* 🖃 *MC, V* ⊘ *Closed Dec. 23–Jan. 6* ⵾◯╎ *EP* Ⓜ *Cairoli.*

$ 🎫 **Gritti.** The Gritti is a bright, cheerful hotel with adequate rooms and good views (from the inside upper floor) of tiled roofs and the gold Madon-nina statue on top of the Duomo, a few hundred yards away. ⊠ *Piazza Santa Maria Beltrade 4, north end of Via Torino, Duomo, 20123* ☎ 02/ 801056 🖷 02/89010999 ⊕ *www.hotelgritti.com* ⇱ *48 rooms* ⚷ *Mini-bars, cable TV, bar, laundry service, meeting room, parking (fee)* 🖃 *AE, DC, MC, V* ⵾◯╎ *BP* Ⓜ *Duomo.*

Nightlife & the Arts

The Arts

For events likely to be of interest to non-Italian speakers, see *Hello Milano* (www.hellomilano.it.), a monthly magazine available at the tourist office on Via Marconi, or *The American* (www.theamericanmag. com), which is available at international bookstores and newsstands, and which has a thorough cultural calendar. The tourist office pub-lishes the monthly *Milano Mese,* which also includes some listings in English.

MUSIC The two halls belonging to the **Conservatorio** (⊠ Via del Conservatorio 12, Duomo ☎02/7621101 Ⓜ San Babila) host some of the leading names in classical music. The modern **Auditorium di Milano** (⊠ Corso San Got-tardo, at Via Torricelli, Conchetta ☎ 02/83389201), known for its ex-cellent acoustics, is home to the **Orchestra Verdi,** founded by Milan-born conductor Richard Chailly. The season, which runs from September to June, includes many top international performers. The **Teatro Dal Verme**

(✉ Via San Giovanni sul Muro 2, Castello ☏ 02/87905201 Ⓜ Cairoli) stages frequent classical music concerts from October to May.

OPERA Milan's hallowed **Teatro alla Scala** (✉ Piazza della Scala ☏ 02/86077 ⊕ www.teatroallascala.org) has undergone a complete renovation, with everything refreshed, refurbished, or replaced except the building's exterior walls. Special attention was paid to the acoustics, which have always been excellent. The season runs from early December to mid-June. Plan well in advance, as tickets sell out quickly.

THEATER Milan's **Piccolo Teatro** (☏ 02/72333222 ⊕ www.piccoloteatro.org) is made up of three separate venues, each of which is noted for its excellent productions. The intimate **Teatro Paolo Grassi** (✉ Via Rovello 2, Castello) is the traditional headquarters of the theater, and is named after its founder. The spacious, modern **Teatro Giorgio Strehler** (✉Largo Greppi 1, east of Piazzo Castello, Brera) takes its name from a famous Italian theater director. It hosts dance and musical performances as well as plays. The horseshoe-shape **Teatro Studio** (✉ Via Rivoli 6, Castello) is a popular venue for experimental theater and music concerts.

Nightlife

BARS Milan has a bar somewhere to suit any style; those in the better hotels are respectably chic and popular meeting places for Milanese as well as tourists. The bar of the **Sheraton Diana Majestic** (✉ Viale Piave 42 ☏ 02/20581), which has a splendid garden, is a prime meeting place for young professionals and the fashion people from the showrooms of the Porta Venezia neighborhood. **El Brellin** (✉Vicolo Lavandai at Alzaia Naviglio Grande ☏ 02/58101351) is one of the many bars in the arty Navigli district. For a quiet drink in a sophisticated setting, try **Fiori Oscuri** (✉ Via Fiori Oscuri 3 ☏ 02/45477057), in the heart of Brera. If you decide to stay for dinner, chefs Giovanni Valsecchi and Luca Marongiu will wow you with their creative Italian cuisine, savored with a fine wine from their cellar. Also in Brera, check out the **Giamaica** (✉ Via Brera 32 ☏ 02/876723), a traditional hangout for students from the nearby Brera art school. On summer nights this neighborhood pulses with life; street vendors and fortune-tellers jostle for space alongside the outdoor tables.

For a break from the traditional, check out ultratrendy **SHU** (✉Via Molino delle Armi, Ticinese ☏ 02/58315720), whose gleaming interior looks like a cross between *Star Trek* and Cocteau's *Beauty and the Beast*. The **Trussardi Bar** (✉ Piazza della Scala 5 ☏ 02/80688295) has an enormous plasma screen that keeps hip barflies entertained with video art. Open throughout the day, it's a great place for coffee.

Blue Note (✉ Via Borsieri 37, Garibaldi ☏ 02/69016888 ⊕ www. bluenotemilano.com), the first European branch of the famous New York nightclub, features regular performances by some of the most famous names in jazz, as well as blues and rock concerts. There's a popular jazz brunch on Sunday. Monday evenings are reserved for Italian musicians. For an evening of live music—predominantly rock to jazz—head to perennial favorite **Le Scimmie** (✉ Via Ascanio Sforza 49, Navigli ☏ 02/

Calcio Crazy

FOR THE VAST MAJORITY of Italians, *il calcio* (soccer) is much more than a national sport—it's a way of life. The general level of passion for the game exceeds that expressed by all but the most die-hard sports fans in the United States. In 2005 there were no fewer than seven prime-time television shows and four major national newspapers dedicated to soccer—not to mention countless radio programs and local TV shows. In a country that's fine-tuned to nuance and inclined to see conspiracy around every corner, controversial referee calls can spark arguments that last weeks. In 2004, debate over questionable rulings in a match between Roma and Juventus (a perennial power from Turin) made it all the way to the floor of Parliament, where conflict between senators actually degenerated into a fistfight.

Nowhere is the passion more feverish than in big soccer cities, of which

Milan is the prime example. It's home to two of the country's dominant teams: AC Milan and F.C. Internazionale (aka, Inter Milan). On game days, it is not unusual to see boisterous bands of fans wandering the city center, team colors draped across their shoulders and rousing team choruses issuing from their mouths. At the stadium, even the most innocuous games are events where chants, insults, and creative banners make crowd-watching an appealing sideshow—especially the banners, which Italians affectionately refer to as *sfotto* ("razzings"). In the 2004 matchup between the Milanese teams, AC Milan fans silenced their rivals by unrolling an enormous banner that made fun of Internazionale's decade-long streak as runners-up, stating simply: "We live your dreams." Adding injury to insult, AC Milan took the game, three goals to one.

89402874 ⊕ www.scimmie.it). It features international stars, some of whom jet in to play here, while others, including Ronnie Jones, are long-time residents in Milan.

NIGHTCLUBS **La Banque** (⊠ Via Bassano Porrone 6, Scala ☎ 02/86996565 ⊕ www.labanque.it) is an exclusive and expensive bar, restaurant, and dance club, and is great for anything from an aperitivo to a night on the town. The dance floor starts hopping at 10:30 PM. The hip **Café l'Atlantique** (⊠ Viale Umbria 42, Porta Romana ☎ 02/55193906 ⊕ www.cafeatlantique. com) is a popular place for dancing the night away and enjoying a generous buffet brunch on Sunday afternoon. **C-Side** (⊠ Via Castelbarco 11, Porta Romana ☎02/58310682) is near Bocconi University. The music on the dance floor varies but includes Latin favorites.

Hollywood (⊠ Corso Como 15/c, Centro Direzionale ☎ 02/6598996 ⊕ www.discotecahollywood.com) continues to be one of the most popular places for the sunglasses set. **Magazzini Generali** (⊠ Via Pietrasanta 14, Porta Vigentina ☎ 02/55211313 ⊕ www.magazzinigenerali.it), in what was an abandoned warehouse, is a fun, futuristic venue for dancing and concerts.

Sports

Car Racing

Italy's Formula I fans are passionate about team Ferrari. Huge numbers of them converge on the second Sunday in September for the **Italian Grand Prix,** held 15 km (9 mi) northeast of Milan in Monza. The racetrack was built in 1922 within the **Parco di Monza** (⊕ www.monzanet.it).

Soccer

AC Milan and Inter Milan, two of the oldest and most successful teams in Europe, vie for the heart of soccer-mad Lombardy. For residents, the city is *Milano* but the teams are *Milan,* a vestige of their common founding as the Milan Cricket and Football Club in 1899. When an Italian-led faction broke off in 1908, the new club was dubbed Internazionale (or "Inter") to distinguish it from the bastion of English exclusivity that would become AC Milan (or simply "Milan"). Since then, the picture has become more clouded: although Milan prides itself as the true team of the city and of its working class, Inter can more persuasively claim pan-Italian support.

AC Milan and Inter Milan share the use of **San Siro Stadium (Stadio Meazza)** (✉ Via Piccolomini) during their August–May season. With more than 60,000 of the 85,000 seats appropriated by season-ticket holders and another couple of thousand allocated to visiting fans, tickets to the Sunday games can be difficult to come by, especially for high-profile matches. You can purchase advance AC Milan tickets at Cariplo bank branches, including one at Via Verdi 8, or at the club's **Web site** (⊕ www. acmilan.com). Inter tickets are available at Banca Popolare di Milano branches, including one at Piazza Meda 4, or at the club's **Web site** (⊕ www.inter.it). To reach San Siro, take subway Line 1 (red) toward Molino Dorino, exit at the Lotto station, and board a bus for the stadium. Alcohol is not sold inside, but beer poured into plastic cups by vendors outside is allowed past the gates.

If you're a soccer fan but can't get in to see a game, you might settle for a **stadium tour** (☎ 02/4042432 ⊕ www.sansirotour.com), which includes a visit to the Milan-Inter museum. Tours are available every half hour from Gate 21 from 10 AM to 5 PM, except on game Sundays; they cost €12.50. Call for reservations a few days before your visit.

Shopping

The heart of Milan's fashion scene is the **quadrilatero della moda** district north of the Duomo. Here the world's leading designers compete for shoppers' attention, showing off their ultrastylish clothes in stores that are works of high style themselves. You won't find any bargains, but regardless of whether you're making a purchase, the area is a great place for window-shopping and people-watching. But fashion is not limited to one neighborhood. Wander around the **Brera** to find smaller shops with lesser-known names but with some interesting and exciting offerings. The densest concentration is along Via Brera, Via Solferino, and Corso Garibaldi.

Corso Buenos Aires, which runs northeast from the Giardini Pubblici, is a wide boulevard lined with boutiques. It has the highest concentration of clothing stores in Europe, so be prepared to give up halfway. Avoid Saturday after 3 PM, when it seems the entire city is here looking for bargains.

Department Stores
Department stores, unlike all but the big Quadrilatero shops, are generally open all day and some evenings.

La Rinascente (⊠ Piazza del Duomo ☎ 02/88521) is Milan's most important department store, carrying everything from Armani cosmetics to Zegna men's suits over eight floors. An outstanding selection of household goods is found in the basement. Check out the restaurants on the top floor, where you can get everything from a quick sandwich to a gourmet meal, with prices to match.

The **Coin** stores, distributed around the city (⊠ Piazza Cinque Giornate 1/A, Piazza, Cantore 12, Corso Vercelli 30-32 and Piazzale Loreto 16 ☎ 02/55192083) have an impressive selection at moderate prices. Check out the handbags, accessories, and costume jewelry on the ground floor. The housewares in the basement are a good value. The eighth-floor Globe bar in the Cinque Giornate store is a fun place to have a drink.

Markets
Weekly open markets selling fruits and vegetables are still a common sight in Milan. Many also sell clothing and shoes. Bargains in designer apparel can be found at the huge **Mercato Papiniano** (⊠ Porta Genova) on Saturday and Tuesday from about 9 to 1. The stalls to look for are at the Piazza Sant'Agostino end of the market. It's very crowded—watch out for pickpockets.

Monday- and Thursday-morning markets in **Mercato di Via S. Marco** (⊠ Brera) cater to the wealthy residents of this central neighborhood. In addition to food stands where you can get cheese, roast chicken, and dried beans and fruits, there are several clothing and shoe stalls that are important stops for some of Milan's most elegant women. Check out the knitwear at Valentino, about midway down on the street side. Tasty french fries and potato croquettes are available from the chicken stand at the Via Montebello end.

If you collect coins, stamps, or postcards, or if you just want to see Italian collectors in action, go on Sunday morning to the market at **Via Armorari** (⊠ Off Piazza Cordusio, near Duomo). Milan's most comprehensive antiques market is the **Mercatone dell'Antiquario,** held on the last Sunday of each month along the Naviglio Grande. The third Saturday of every month there's a major antiques and flea market on **Via Fiori Chiari,** near Via Brera.

THE FASHIONISTA'S MILAN

Opera buffs and lovers of Leonardo's *Last Supper,* skip ahead to the next paragraph. No one else should be dismayed to learn that clothing is Milan's greatest cultural achievement. The city is one of the fashion capitals of the world and home base for practically every top Italian designer. The same way art aficionados walk the streets of Florence in a state of bliss, the style-conscious come here to be enraptured.

It all happens in the *quadrilatero della moda,* Milan's toniest shopping district, located just north of the Duomo. Along the cobblestone streets, Armani, Prada, and their fellow *stilisti* sell the latest designs from flagship stores that are as much museums of chic as retail establishments. Any purchase here qualifies as a splurge, but you can have fun without spending a euro—just browse, window-shop, and

> FLORENCE HAS THE *DAVID.*
>
> ROME HAS THE PANTHEON.
>
> MILAN HAS THE CLOTHES.

people-watch. Not into fashion? Think of the experience as art, design, and theater all rolled into one. If you wouldn't visit Florence without seeing the Uffizi, you shouldn't visit Milan without seeing the quadrilatero.

On these pages we give a selective, street-by-street list of stores in the area. Hours are from around 10 in the morning until 7 at night, Monday through Saturday.

VIA DELLA SPIGA
(east to west)

Prada (No. 1)
☎ 02/76014448
www.prada.com
lingerie: for down-to-the-skin Prada fans

Dolce & Gabbana (No. 2)
☎ 02/795747
www.dolcegabbana.it
women's accessories

Agnona (No. 3)
☎ 02/76316530
www.agnona.com

women's clothes:
Ermenegildo excellence
for women

Gio Moretti (No. 4)
☎ 02/76003186
women's and men's
clothes: many labels, as
well as books, CDs,
flowers, and an art
gallery

Sergio Rossi (No. 5)
☎ 02/76390927
www.sergiorossi.com
men's shoes

Bulgari Italia (No. 6)
☎ 02/777001
www.bulgari.com
jewelry, fragrances,
accessories

cross Via Sant'Andrea

Sergio Rossi (No. 15)
☎ 02/76002663
www.sergiorossi.com
women's shoes

Fay (No. 16)
☎ 02/76017597
www.fay.it
women's and men's
clothes, accessories: a
flagship store, designed
by Philip Johnson

Prada (No. 18)
☎ 02/76394336
www.prada.com
accessories

Giorgio Armani (No. 19)
☎ 02/783511
www.giorgioarmani.com
accessories

Tod's (No. 22)
☎ 02/76002423
www.tods.com
shoes and handbags:
the Tod's flagship store

Dolce & Gabbana (No. 26)
☎ 02 76001155
www.dolcegabbana.it
women's clothes, in a
baroque setting

✔ **Just Cavalli** (No. 30)
☎ 02/76390893
www.robertocavalli.net
**Women's and men's
clothes, plus a café
serving big salads and
carpaccio. It's the
offspring of the Just
Cavalli Café in Parco
Sempione, one of the
hottest places in town
for drinks (with or
without dinner).**

Moschino (No. 30)
☎ 02/76004320
www.moschino.it
women's, men's, and
children's clothes: Chic
and cheap, so they say

Roberto Cavalli (No. 42)
☎ 02/76020900
www.robertocavalli.net
women's and men's
clothes, accessories:
3,200 square feet of
Roberto Cavalli

4

Marni (No. 50)
☎ 02 76317327
www.marni.com
women's clothes

VIA MONTENAPOLEONE
(east to west)

Fratelli Rossetti (No. 1)
☎ 02/76021650
www.rossetti.it
shoes

Louis Vuitton (No. 2)
☎ 02/7771711
www.vuitton.com
leather goods, accessories, women's clothes

Armani Collezioni (No. 2)
☎ 02/76390068
www.giorgioarmani.com
women's and men's
clothes: the "white label"

Tanino Crisci (No. 3)
☎ 02/76021264
www.taninocrisci.com
women's and men's
shoes, leather goods

Etro (No. 5)
☎ 02/76005049
www.etro.it
women's and men's
clothes, leather goods,
accessories

Bottega Veneta (No. 5)
☎ 02/76024495
www.bottegaveneta.com
leather goods: signature
woven-leather bags

Gucci (No. 5/7)
☎ 02/771271
www.gucci.com
women's and men's
clothes

Prada (No. 6)
☎ 02/76020273
www.prada.com
men's clothes

Prada (No. 8)
☎ 02/7771771
www.prada.com
women's clothes

cross Via Sant'Andrea

Armani Junior (No. 10)
☎ 02/783196
www.giorgioarmani.com
children's clothes: for the
under-14 fashionista

Versace (No. 11)
☎ 02/76008528
www.versace.com
everything Versace,
except Versus and
children's clothes

Corneliani (No. 12)
☎ 02/777361
www.corneliani.com

Versace in
Via Montenapoleone

men's clothes: bespoke
tailoring excellence

Cartier
corner Via Gesù
☎ 02/3030421
www.cartier.com

**FASHION SHOPPING,
ACCESSORIZED**

Milan's most ambitious
shops don't just want to
clothe you– they want
to trim your hair, clean
your pores, and put a
cocktail in your hand.
Some "stores with
more" in and around
the quadrilatero are
indicated by a ✔.

jewelry: precious stones,
fine gifts

Valentino
corner Via Santo Spirito
☎ 02/76020285
www.valentino.it
women's clothes: elegant
designs for special
occasions

Loro Piana (No. 27c)
☎ 02/7772901
www.loropiana.it
women's and men's
clothes, accessories:
cashmere everything

REFUELING

If you want refreshments and aren't charmed by the quadrilatero's in-store cafés, try **Cova** (Via Montenapoleone 8, ☎ 02 76000578) or **Sant'Ambroeus** (Corso Matteotti 7, ☎ 02 76000540). Both serve coffee, tea, aperitifs, sandwiches, and snacks in an ambience of starched tablecloths and chandeliers.

Cova's courtyard café

When the hurlyburly's done, head for the **Bulgari Hotel** (Via Fratelli Gabba 7b, ☎ 02/8058051), west of Via Manzoni, for a quiet (if pricey) drink, In summer, the bar extends into a beautiful, mature garden over an acre in size.

VIA SAN PIETRO ALL'ORTO
(east to west)

Versus (No. 10)
☎ 02/76014722
www.versace.com
women's, men's, and children's clothes: Versace Jeans and Sport

Jimmy Choo (No. 17)
☎ 02/45481770
www.jimmychoo.com
women's and men's shoes

CORSO VENEZIA
(south to north)

Miu Miu (No. 3)
☎ 02/76001799
www.prada.com
women's clothes: Prada's playful line

D&G (No. 7)
☎ 02/76002450
www.dolcegabbana.it
swimwear, underwear, accessories: Dolce & Gabbana diffusion

✔ **Dolce & Gabbana** (No. 15)
☎ 02/76028485
www.dolcegabbana.it
Men's clothes, sold in a four-story, early-19th-century patrician home. Added features are a barbershop (☎ 02/76408881), a beauty parlor (☎ 02/76408888), and the

Martini Bar, which also serves light lunches.

Borsalino
corner Via Senato
☎ 02/76017072
www.borsalino.com
hats: for people who want to be streets ahead

VIA VERRI
(south to north)

Ermenegildo Zegna (No. 3)
☎ 02/76006437
www.zegna.com.
men's clothes, in the finest fabrics

Borsalino
Via Verri/corner Via Bigli
☎ 02/76398539
www.borsalino.com
hats

cross Via Bigli

Etro Profumi
corner Via Bigli
☎ 02/76005450
www.etro.it
fragrances

D&G in Via della Spiga

VIA SANT'ANDREA
(south to north)

✔ **Trussardi** (No. 5)
☎ 02/76020380
www.trussardi.com
Women's and men's clothes. The nearby flagship store (Piazza della Scala 5) includes the Trussardi Marino alla Scala Café (☎ 02 80688242), a fashion-forward bar done in stone, steel, slate, and glass. For a more substantial lunch, and views of Teatro alla Scala, head upstairs to the Marino alla Scala Ristorante (☎ 02 80688201), which serves creative Mediterranean cuisine.

Banner (No. 8/A)
☎ 02/76004609
women's and men's clothes: a multibrand boutique

Giorgio Armani (No. 9)
☎ 02/76003234
www.giorgioarmani.com
women's and men's clothes: the "black label"

Moschino (No. 12)
☎ 02/76000832
www.moschino.it
women's clothes: world-renowned window displays

BARGAIN-HUNTING AT THE OUTLETS

Milan may be Italy's richest city, but that doesn't mean all its well-dressed residents can afford to shop at the boutiques of the quadrilatero. Many pick up their designer clothes at outlet stores, where prices can be reduced by 50% or more.

Salvagente (Via Bronzetti 16, ☎ 02/76110328, www.salvagentemilano.it) is the top outlet for designer apparel and accessories from both large and small houses. There's a small men's department. To get there, take the 60 bus, which runs from the Duomo to the Stazione Centrale, to the intersection of Bronzetti and Archimede. Look for the green iron gate with the bronze sign, between the hairdressers and an apartment building. No credit cards.

DMagazine Outlet (Via Montenapoleone 26, ☎ 02/76006027, www.dmagazine.it) has bargains in the

✔ **Gianfranco Ferré**
(No. 15)
☎ 02/794864
www.gianfrancoferre.com
Everything Ferré, plus
a spa providing facials,
Jacuzzis, steam baths,
and mud treatments.
Reservations are
essential (☎
02/76017526), preferably
a week in advance.

Prada (No. 21)
☎ 02 76001426
www.prada.com
women's and men's
sportswear

VIA MANZONI
(south to north)

P-Box (No. 13)
☎ 02/89013000
www.aeffe.com
women's accessories,
shoes, bags: Aeffe group
labels, including Alberta
Ferretti, Philosophy, and
Narciso Rodriquez

Armani in Via Manzoni

✔ **Armani Megastore**
(No. 31)
☎ 02/72318600
www.giorgioarmani.com
The quadrilatero's most
conspicuous shopping
complex. Along with
many Armani fashions,
you'll find a florist, a
bookstore, a chocolate
shop (offering Armani
pralines), the Armani
Caffè, and Nobu (of the
upscale Japanese
restaurant chain). The
Armani Casa furniture
collection is next door at
number 37.

CORSO COMO
✔ **10 Corso Como**
☎ 02/29000727
www.10corsocomo.com
Outside the quadrilatero,
but it's a must-see for
fashion addicts. The
bazaar-like 13,000-
square-foot complex
includes women's and
men's boutiques, a bar
and restaurant, a
bookstore, a record shop,
and an art gallery
specializing in
photography. You can
even spend the night (if
you can manage to get a
reservation) at Milan's
most exclusive B&B,
Three Rooms (☎
02/626163). The
furnishings are a modern
design-lover's dream.

Prada store in the Galleria

GALLERIA VITTORIO EMANUELE
(not technically part of
the quadrilatero, but
nearby)

✔ **Gucci**
☎ 02/8597991
www.gucci.com
Gucci accessories, plus
the world's first Gucci
café. Sit outside behind
the elegant boxwood
hedge and watch the
world go by.

Prada (No. 63-65)
☎ 02/876979
www.prada.com
the original store: look

for the murals
downstairs.

Louis Vuitton
☎ 02/72147011
www.vuitton.com
accessories, women's
and men's shoes,
watches

Tod's
☎ 02/877997
www.tods.com
women's and men's
shoes, leather goods,
accessories

Borsalino (No. 92
☎ 02/804337
www.borsalino.com
hats

Galleria Vittorio Emanuele

midst of the quadrilatero. Names on sale include Armani, Cavalli, Gucci, and Prada.

DT-Intrend (Galleria San Carlo 6, ☎ 02/76000829) sells last year's Max Mara, Max & Co, Sportmax, Marella, Penny Black, and Marina Rinaldi. It's just 300 meters from the Max Mara store located on Corso Vittorio Emanuele at the corner of Galleria de Cristoforis.

At the **10 CorsoComo** outlet (Via Tazzoli 3, ☎ 02/29015130, www.10corsocomo.com) you can find clothes, shoes, bags, and accessories.

Fans of **Marni** who have a little time on their hands will want to check out the outlet (Via Tajani 1, ☎ 02/70009735 or 02/71040332, www.marni.com). Take the 61 bus to the terminus at Largo Murani, from which it's about 200 meters on foot.

Giorgio Armani has an outlet, but it's way out of town—off the A3, most of the way to Como. The address is Strada Provinciale per Bregnano 13, in the town of Verte-mate (☎ 031 887373, www.giorgioarmani.com).

EMILIA–ROMAGNA & THE VENETO ESSENTIALS

Transportation

BY AIR

Bologna is an important business and convention center, well served by European airlines linking it with Italian cities and European capitals, including Rome and Milan (on Alitalia), Paris (on Air France), London (on British Airways and easyJet), Barcelona (on Iberia), Amsterdam (on KLM), and Frankfurt (on Lufthansa)—among others. Start-up airline EuroFly introduced the first nonstop service to the United States from Emilia-Romagna, with a direct New York (JFK)–Bologna route. At this writing, the service is limited to two days a week, and only operates May–October; check with the airline for the latest information.

Bologna's airport, Guglielmo Marconi, is 10 km (6 mi) northwest of town. Aerobus service (Bus 54, €5) connects Guglielmo Marconi with Bologna's central train station and also has a downtown stop. It runs every half hour from 6 AM to 11:30 PM.

The main airport serving the Veneto is Venice's Aeroporto Marco Polo, which you can read more about in the Essentials section of the Venice chapter. Aeroporto Catullo di Verona–Villafranca, 11 km (7 mi) southwest of Verona, is served by European and domestic airlines such as Alitalia, Alpi Eagles, Air Dolomiti, Iberia, Air France, British Airways, Meridiana, and Lufthansa. A regular bus service connects the airport with Verona's Porta Nuova railway station.

🛈 Airport Information **Aerobus** ☎ 051/290290 ⊕ www.atc.bo.it. **Aeroporto Catullo di Verona–Villafranca** ☎ 045/8095666 ⊕ www.aeroportoverona.it. **Aeroporto Guglielmo Marconi di Bologna** ✉ Via Triumvirato 84, Bologna ☎ 051/6479615 ⊕ www.bologna-airport.it. **Aeroporto Marco Polo di Venezia** ☎ 041/2606111 ⊕ www.veniceairport.it.

BY BUS

There's little reason to travel by bus in Emilia-Romagna. Trains are fast, efficient, and relatively inexpensive; they run frequently and connect most towns in the region.The same holds true in the Veneto, though if you prefer going by bus, there are numerous interurban and interregional connections you can choose from. Local tourist offices may be able to provide details of timetables and routes; otherwise contact the local bus station or, in some cases, the individual bus companies operating from the station, listed below.

🛈 Bus Information **ACTV buses** ✉ Piazzale Roma, Venice ☎ 041/24240 buses to Brenta Riviera ⊕ www.actv.it. **AMT buses** ✉ Via Torbido 1, Verona ☎ 045/8871111 ⊕ www.amt.it. **APTV buses** ✉ Autostazione di Verona Porta Nuova, Piazzale XXV Aprile, Verona ☎ 045/8057911 ⊕ www.aptv.it. **ATVO buses** ✉ Piazzale Roma, Venice ☎ 0421/383671 ⊕ www.atvo.it. **FTV buses** ✉ Piazzale della Stazione near Campo Marzio, Vicenza ☎ 0444/223115 ⊕ www.ftv.vi.it. **SITA buses** ✉ Piazzale Boschetti, Padua ☎ 049/8206844 ⊕ www.sita-on-line.it.

BY CAR

Getting around by car in these two regions is a breeze. All of the cities covered in this chapter are reachable by Italy's well-maintained autostrada network. The Autostrada del Sole (A1) runs from Florence to Bologna, then makes a left and continues through western Emilia–Romagna and on to Milan. For a more scenic, more historic (but slower) trip, spend some time on the Via Emilia (SS9), one of the oldest roads in the world. It parallels the A1 and the A14 through the heart of the region. From Bologna the A14 takes you east to Ravenna, and the A13 runs north through Ferrara, culminating in Padua. The A4, the primary autostrada east from Milan, runs through the Veneto, linking Verona, Vicenza, Padua, and Venice.

Note that much of the historic center of Bologna is closed off to cars daily 7 AM–8 PM. The centers of Verona, Vicenza, and Padua also sometimes have limited car access, but regulations fluctuate. The best strategy is to check with your hotel before arriving to find out the current status.

BY TRAIN

Bologna is an important rail hub for the entire northern part of Italy and has frequent, fast service to Milan, Florence, Rome, and Venice. Within the region, the railway line follows the Via Emilia (SS9). Trains run frequently, and connections are easy. Ferrara is half an hour from Bologna on the train, and Ravenna is just over an hour.

Heading into the Veneto, trains on the main routes from the south stop almost hourly in Verona, Padua, and Venice. From northern Italy and the rest of Europe, trains usually enter via Milan or through Porta Nuova station in Verona. To the west of Venice, the main line running across the north of Italy stops at Padua (30 minutes from Venice), Vicenza (1 hour), and Verona (1½ hours)

Visit the Web site of FS, the Italian State Railway, for schedules and booking. Note that the FS automated telephone line requires that you understand Italian.

Train Information FS ☎ 892021 ⊕ www.trenitalia.com.

Contacts & Resources

EMERGENCIES

For first aid, dial the general emergency number (118), which is the same throughout Italy, and ask for *pronto soccorso* (first aid). Be prepared to give your address. If you can find a concierge or some other Italian-speaker to call on your behalf, do so, as not all operators speak English. All pharmacies post signs on the door with addresses of pharmacies that stay open in off-hours (at night, on Saturday afternoon, and on Sunday).

For car emergencies, call ACI for towing and repairs—you can ask to be transferred to an English-speaking operator; be prepared to tell the operator which road you're on, the direction you're going (e.g., "*verso* [in the direction of] Padua") and the *targa* (license plate number) of your car. The great majority of Italians carry cellular phones, so if you don't have one, for help, flag down someone who does.

🚗 ACI ☎ 803/116. **Medical emergencies** ☎ 118. **Police** ☎ 113. **Fire** ☎ 115.

VISITOR INFORMATION

🛈 Tourist Information Offices, Emilia-Romagna **Bologna** ✉ Guglielmo Marconi airport ☎ 051/246541 ✉ Stazione Centrale, 40121 ☎ 051/246541 ✉ Piazza Maggiore 1, 40124 ☎ 051/246541 ⊕ www.bolognaturismo.info. **Ferrara** ✉ Castello Estense, 44100 ☎ 0532/299303 ⊕ www.ferrarainfo.com ✉ Piazza Municipale 11, 44100 ☎ 0532/419474. **Ravenna** ✉ Via Salara 8, 48100 ☎ 0544/35755 ⊕ www.turismo.ravenna.it.

🛈 Tourist Information Offices, the Veneto **Padua** ✉ Padova Railway Station, 35100 ☎ 049/8752077 ✉ Galleria Pedrocchi, 35135100 ☎ 049/8767927 ⊕ www.turismopadova. it. **Verona** ✉ Piazza Brà, 37100 ☎ 045/8068680 ✉ Porta Nuova Railway Station ☎ 045/8000861 ⊕ www.tourism.verona.it. **Vicenza** ✉ Piazza Giacomo Matteotti 12, 36100 ☎ 0444/320854 ✉ Piazza dei Signori 8 ☎ 0444/544122 ⊕ www.vicenza.org.

Venice

Gondola

WORD OF MOUTH

"There's no way to adequately describe the uniqueness, the beauty, and the charm that is Venice. It's like the Grand Canyon. It doesn't matter how many pictures you've seen, until you've come face to face with her, you can't begin to imagine her splendor."

—dcd

WELCOME TO VENICE

Gondola navigating a side canal

TOP REASONS TO GO

★ **Basilica di San Marco:** Whether its opulence seduces you or overwhelms you, it's a sight to be seen.

★ **Gallerie dell'Accademia:** It only makes sense that you find the world's best collection of Venetian painting here.

★ **Santa Maria Gloriosa dei Frari:** Of Venice's many gorgeous churches, this one competes with San Marco for top billing.

★ **Cruising the Grand Canal:** Whether seen by gondola or by water bus, Venice's Main Street is something from another world.

★ **Snacking at a bacaro:** The best way to sample genuine Venetian cuisine is to head for one of the city's classic wine bars.

1 The Grand Canal is Venice's major thoroughfare, lined with grand palazzos that once housed the city's richest families.

2 Piazza San Marco, called by Napoleon "the world's most beautiful drawing room," is the heart of Venice and the location of its two most distinctive sights, the **Basilica di San Marco** and the **Palazzo Ducale.**

3 The sestiere of San Marco, in the city's center, is one of Italy's most expensive neighborhoods. Its streets are lined with fashion boutiques, art galleries, and grand hotels.

4 The neighboring sestieri of Santa Croce and San Polo are largely commercial districts, with many shops, several major sights, and the Rialto fish and produce markets.

5 Dorsoduro is an elegant residential area that's home to the **Gallerie dell'Accademia** and the **Peggy Guggenheim Collection.** The Zattere promenade is one of the best spots to stroll with a gelato or linger at an outdoor café.

6 Cannaregio is short on architectural splendor, but it provides some of the prettiest canal-side walks in town. **The Fondamenta della Misericordia** is a nightlife center, and the **Jewish Ghetto** has a fascinating history and tradition all its own.

7 Castello, along with Cannaregio, is home to most of the locals. It's the sestiere that's least influenced by Venice's tourist culture—except when the Biennale art festival is on.

GETTING ORIENTED

5

Seen from the window of an airplane, central Venice looks like a fish laid out on a blue platter. The train station at the western end is the fish's eye, and the Castello sestiere (neighborhood) is the tail. In all, the "fish" consists of six sestieri—Cannaregio, Santa Croce, San Polo, Dorsoduro, San Marco, and Castello. More sedate outer islands swim around them— San Giorgio Maggiore and the Giudecca just to the south, beyond them the Lido, and to the east Murano, Borano, and Torcello.

CANNAREGIO

6 Fond. d. Misericordia

THE JEWISH GHETTO

Canal Grande

Ca' d'Oro

SAN POLO

4

1

CIMITERO SAN MICHELE

Campo Santi Giovanni e Paolo

7

Ruga Giuffa

3 SAN MARCO

Basilica di San Marco

2

Piazza San Marco

Palazzo Ducale

CASTELLO

Gallerie dell' Accademia

Santa Maria della Salute

Peggy Guggenheim Collection

DORSODURO

Zatterre Promenade

5

SAN GIORGIO MAGGIORE

0		1/4 mile
0		400 meters

Santa Maria della Salute

Getting Around

It's true: there are no cars whatsoever in Venice. You get around primarily on foot, with occasional trips by boat on the famous canals that lace through the city. These are your basic boat-going options:

■ **Vaporetto.** Water buses run up and down the Grand Canal, around the city, and out to the surrounding islands. They're Venice's primary means of public transportation.

■ **Gondola.** Traveling by gondola is a romantic, pricey joy ride (rather than a way to get from one place to another). You pay by the hour. Be sure to agree on the fare before boarding, and ask to be taken down smaller side canals.

■ **Traghetto.** There are only three bridges across the Grand Canal. Traghetti are gondola-like ferries (rowed by gondoliers in training) that fill in the gaps, going from one bank to the other in eight spots. They can save a lot of walking, and they're a cheap (€0.50), quick taste of the gondola experience.

■ **Water taxi.** A more accurate name might be "water limousine"—sky-high fares make taxis an indulgent way to get from place to place.

For details on getting around, see "Essentials" at the end of this chapter.

Making the Most of Your Time

A great introduction to Venice is a ride on vaporetto (water bus) Line 1 from the train station all the way down the Grand Canal. If you've just arrived and have luggage in tow, you'll need to weigh the merits of taking this trip right away versus getting settled at your hotel first. (Crucial factors: your mood, the bulk of your bags, and your hotel's location.)

Seeing Piazza San Marco and the sights bordering it can fill a day, but if you're going to be around awhile, consider holding off on your visit there—the crowds can be overwhelming, especially when you're fresh off the boat. Instead, spend your first morning at Santa Maria Gloriosa dei Frari and the Scuola Grande di San Rocco, then wander through the Dorsoduro sestiere, choosing between visits to Ca' Rezzonico, the Gallerie dell'Accademia, the Peggy Guggenheim Collection, and Santa Maria della Salute—all A-list attractions. End the afternoon with a gelato-fueled stroll along the Zattere boardwalk. Then tackle San Marco on day two.

If you have more time, make these sights your priorities: the Rialto fish and produce markets; Ca' d'Oro and the Jewish Ghetto in Cannaregio; Santa Maria dei Miracoli and Santi Giovanni e Paolo in Castello; and, across the water from Piazza San Marco, San Giorgio Maggiore. (In Venice, there's a spectacular church for every day of the week, and then some.) A day on the outer islands of Murano, Burano, and Torcello is good for a change of pace.

KNOWING WHERE YOU'RE GOING

Be sure to arrive in Venice with precise directions to your hotel (usually available on the hotel Web site). Getting lost in Venice can be a charming adventure, but the charm level drops to zero when you're hauling around luggage.

Festivals to Build a Trip Around

■ Venice's most famous festival is **Carnevale**, drawing revelers from all over the world. For 10 days leading up to Ash Wednesday, it takes over the city—think Mardi Gras meets Casanova.

■ The prestigious **Biennale** is a century-old international art festival held in late summer and early fall of odd-numbered years. It's spawned several other festivals, including the Biennale Danza, Biennale Musica, and, most famously, Biennale Cinema, also known as the Venice Film Festival, held every year at the end of August.

■ The **Festa Redentore** (Feast of the Redeemer), on the third Sunday in July, is the biggest celebration of the year among locals, who float out in boats on Bacino San Marco and watch midnight fireworks displays.

■ There are three noteworthy annual contests of Venetian-style rowing: the **Regata delle Bafane**, on January 6; **Vogalonga** (long row), on a Sunday in May; and **Regata Storica**, on the first Sunday in September.

How's the Weather?

One thing Venice has in common with much of Italy: spring and fall are the best times to visit. Summers are hot, sticky, and crowded.

Winters are relatively mild and tourist-free, but there are frequent rainy spells, and at the beginning and end of the season there's the threat of acqua alta, when tides roll in and flood low-lying parts of the city, including Piazza San Marco.

TOP PASSEGGIATA

With its streets given over to pedestrians, all of Venice is in a state of perpetual passeggiata, but Fondamenta delle Zattere, along the southern end of Dorsoduro, is a particularly prime spot.

Venetian Vocabulary

Venetians use their own terms to describe their unique city. In fact, they have their own dialect; if you have an ear for Italian, you'll notice a distinct difference in the language. Here are some key words to know:

Sestiere: A neighborhood in central Venice. (There are six of them.)

Rio: A small canal.

Riva: A street running along a canal.

Fondamenta: Another name for a riva.

Calle: A street not running along a canal.

Campo: A square—what elsewhere in Italy would be called a piazza. (The only piazza in Venice is Piazza San Marco.)

Bacaro: A wine bar.

Ombra: A glass of wine served at a bacaro.

Cicchetto (pronounced "chick-ay-toh"): A snack served at a bacaro—roughly the Venetian equivalent of tapas.

Zattere

IT'S CALLED LA SERENISSIMA, "the most serene," a reference to the majesty, wisdom, and monstrous power of this city that was for centuries the unrivaled mistress of trade between Europe and the Orient and the bulwark of Christendom against the tides of Turkish expansion. "Most serene" could also describe the way lovers of this miraculous city feel when they see it, imperturbably floating on its calm blue lagoon.

Built entirely on water by men who defied the sea, Venice is unlike any other town. No matter how many times you've seen it in movies or on TV, the real thing is more dreamlike than you could ever imagine. Its landmarks, the Basilica di San Marco and the Palazzo Ducale, seem hardly Italian: delightfully idiosyncratic, they are exotic mixes of Byzantine, Gothic, and Renaissance styles. Shimmering sunlight and silvery mist soften every perspective here, and you understand how the city became renowned in the Renaissance for its artists' rendering of color. It's full of secrets, inexpressibly romantic, and at times given over entirely to pleasure.

You'll see Venetians going about their daily affairs in *vaporetti* (water buses), aboard the *traghetti* (traditional gondola ferries) that carry them across the Grand Canal, in the *campi* (squares), and along the *calli* (narrow streets). They are nothing if not skilled—and remarkably tolerant—in dealing with the veritable armies of tourists from all over the world who fill the city's streets for most of the year.

EXPLORING VENICE

Updated by
Pamela Santini

Many of Venice's major churches and museums are organized into two groups that coordinate hours and admissions fees. Fifteen art-filled churches are known as the **Chorus churches** (☎ 041/2750462 ⊕ www. chorusvenezia.org): Santa Maria del Giglio, Santo Stefano, Santa Maria Formosa, Santa Maria dei Miracoli, Santa Maria Gloriosa dei Frari, San Polo, San Giacomo dell'Orio, San Stae, Sant'Alvise, Madonna dell'Orto, San Pietro di Castello, Santissimo Redentore, San Sebastiano, Gesuati, and San Giovanni Elemosinario. They're open to visitors all day except Sunday morning, and usually someone there can provide information and a free leaflet in English. Postcards and booklets about the sights are on sale. Single church entry costs €2.50, or you can visit them all with an €8 Chorus pass. The price of the pass includes audio guides except in the Frari, where they cost an additional €1.60. The artwork in Chorus churches is labeled, and the staff can show you where to switch on lighting for selected paintings.

Eleven museums make up Venice's **Musei Civici** (☎ 041/2715911 ⊕ www. museiciviciveneziani.it). A museum pass costing €18 and valid for three months lets you make one visit to each museum. A Museum Card, good only at the Piazza San Marco museums—Palazzo Ducale, Museo Correr, Museo Archeologico, and Biblioteca Nazionale Marciana—costs €12.

CRUISING THE GRAND CANAL

THE BEST INTRODUCTION TO VENICE IS A TRIP DOWN MAIN STREET

Venice's Grand Canal is one of the world's great thoroughfares. It winds its way in the shape of a backward "S" from Ferrovia (the train station) to Piazza San Marco, passing 200 palazzos born of a culture obsessed with opulence and fantasy. There's a theatrical quality to a boat ride on the canal: it's as if each pink- or gold-tinted façade is trying to steal your attention from its rival across the way.

The palaces were built from the 12th to 18th century by the city's richest families. A handful are still private residences, but many have been converted to other uses, including museums, hotels, government offices, university buildings, a post office, a casino, and even a television station.

It's romantic to see the canal from a gondola, but the next best thing, at a fraction of the cost, is to take the Line 1 *vaporetto* (water bus) from Ferrovia to San Marco. The ride costs €5 and takes about 35 minutes. Invest in a Travel Card (€12 buys 24 hours of unlimited passage) and you can spend the better part of a day hopping on and off at the vaporetto's 16 stops, visiting the sights along the banks. Either way, keep your eyes open for the highlights listed here; those with numbered bullets have fuller descriptions later in this chapter.

FROM FERROVIA TO RIALTO

Santa Maria di Nazareth

Ponte di Scalzi

R. DI BIASI

FERROVIA

Stazione Ferrovia Santa Lucia

As you head out from Ferrovia, the baroque church immediately to your left is **Santa Maria di Nazareth**. Its shoeless friars earned it the nickname Chiesa degli Scalzi (Church of the Barefoot).

The first of only three bridges over the Grand Canal is the **Ponte di Scalzi**. The original version was built of iron in 1858; the existing stone bridge dates from 1934.

After passing beneath the Ponte di Scalzi, ahead to the left you'll spy **Palazzo Labia** ㉒, one of the most imposing buildings in Venice, looming over the bell tower of the church of San Geremia.

A hundred yards or so farther along on the left bank, the uncompleted façade of the church of **San Marcuola** gives you an idea of what's behind the marble decorations of similar 18th-century churches in Venice. Across the canal, flanked by two *torricelle* (side wings in the shape of small towers) and a triangular

merlatura (crenellation), is the **Fondaco dei Turchi**, one of the oldest Byzantine palaces in Venice; it's now a natural history museum. Next comes the plain brick **Depositi del Megio**, a 15th-century granary—note the lion marking it as Serenissima property—and beyond it the obelisk-topped **Ca' Belloni-Battagia**. Both are upstaged by the **Palazzo Vendramin-Calergi** ㉔ on the opposite bank: this Renaissance gem was built in the 1480s, at a time when late-Gothic was still the prevailing style. A gilded banner identifies the palazzo as the site of Venice's casino.

Palazzo Vendramin-Calergi

The German composer Richard Wagner died in Palazzo Vendramin-Calergi in 1883, soon after the success of his opera *Parsifal*. His room has been preserved—you can visit it on Saturday mornings by appointment.

Ca' d'Oro

Ca' d'Oro means "house of gold," but the gold is long gone—the gilding that once accentuated the marble carvings of the façade has worn away over time.

Church of San Marcuola

S. MARCUOLA ▲

Ca' Belloni-Battagia

S. STAE ▲

Ca' Pesaro

Fondaco dei Turchi

Depositi del Megio

San Stae Church

▲ CA' D'ORO

Ca' Corner della Regina

Pescheria

The pescheria has been in operation for over 1,000 years. Stop by in the morning to see the exotic fish for sale—one of which may wind up on your dinner plate. Produce stalls fill the adjacent *fondamenta*, and butchers and cheesemongers occupy the surrounding shops.

Fondaco dei Tedeschi

Ca' dei Camerlenghi

▲ RIALTO

The white, whimsically baroque church of **San Stae 🏛** on the right bank is distinguished by a host of marble saints on its façade. Farther along the bank is another baroque showpiece, **Ca' Pesaro 🏛**, followed by the tall, balconied **Ca' Corner della Regina**. Next up on the left is the flamboyant pink-and-white **Ca' d'Oro 🏛**, arguably the finest example of Venetian Gothic design.

Across from Ca' d'Oro is the loggia-like, neo-Gothic **pescheria**, Venice's fish market, where boats dock in the morning to deliver their catch.

The canal narrows as you approach the impressive Rialto Bridge. To the left, just before the bridge, is the **Fondaco dei Tedeschi**. This was once the busiest trading center of the republic—German, Austrian, and Hungarian merchants kept warehouses and offices here;

today it's the city's main post office. Across the canal stands the curiously angled **Ca' dei Camerlenghi**. Built in 1525 to accommodate the State Treasury, it had a jail for tax evaders on the ground floor.

FROM RIALTO TO THE PONTE DELL' ACCADEMIA

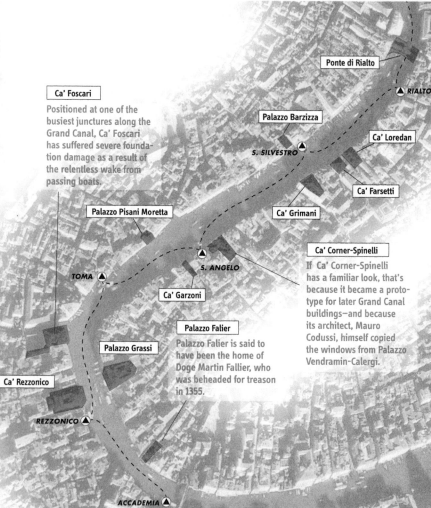

Ponte di Rialto

▲ RIALTO

Ca' Foscari

Positioned at one of the busiest junctures along the Grand Canal, Ca' Foscari has suffered severe foundation damage as a result of the relentless wake from passing boats.

Palazzo Barzizza

Ca' Loredan

S. SILVESTRO

Ca' Farsetti

Palazzo Pisani Moretta

Ca' Grimani

Ca' Corner-Spinelli

If Ca' Corner-Spinelli has a familiar look, that's because it became a prototype for later Grand Canal buildings—and because its architect, Mauro Codussi, himself copied the windows from Palazzo Vendramin-Calergi.

S. ANGELO

TOMA ▲

Ca' Garzoni

Palazzo Falier

Palazzo Falier is said to have been the home of Doge Martin Fallier, who was beheaded for treason in 1355.

Palazzo Grassi

Ca' Rezzonico

REZZONICO ▲

ACCADEMIA ▲

Gallerie dell'Accademia

Until the 19th century, the shop-lined **Ponte di Rialto**  was the only bridge across the Grand Canal.

Rialto is the only point along the Grand Canal where buildings don't have their primary entrances directly on the water, a consequence of the two spacious *rive* (waterside paths) once used for unloading two Venetian staples: coal and wine. On your left along Riva del Carbon stand **Ca' Loredan** and **Ca' Farsetti**, 13th-century Byzantine palaces that today make up Venice's city hall. Just past the San Silvestro vaporetto landing on Riva del Vin is the 12th- and 13th-century facade of **Palazzo Barzizza**, an elegant example of Veneto-Byzantine architecture that managed to survive a complete renovation in the 17th century. Across the water, the sternly Renaissance

Ca' Grimani has an intimidating presence that seems appropriate for today's Court of Appeals. At the Sant'Angelo landing, the vaporetto passes close to another massive Renaissance palazzo, **Ca' Corner-Spinelli**.

Back on the right bank, in a salmon color that seems to vary with the time of day, is elegant **Palazzo Pisani Moretta**, with twin water entrances. To your left, four-storied **Ca' Garzoni**, part of the Universita di Venezia Ca' Foscari, stands beside the San Toma *traghetto* (gondola ferry), which has operated since 1354. The boat makes a sharp turn and, on the right, passes one of the city's tallest Gothic palaces, **Ca' Foscari**.

The vaporetto passes baroque **Ca' Rezzonico**  so closely that you get to look inside one of the most fabulous entrances along the canal. Opposite stands the

Grand Canal's youngest palace, **Palazzo Grassi**, commissioned in 1749. Just beyond Grassi and Campo San Samuele, the first house past the garden was once Titian's studio. It's followed by **Palazzo Falier**, identifiable by its twin loggias (windowed porches).

Approaching the canal's third and final bridge, the vaporetto stops at a former church and monastery complex that houses the world-renowned **Gallerie dell'Accademia** .

> The wooden pilings on which Venice was built (you can see them at the bases of the buildings along the Grand Canal) have gradually hardened into mineral form.

ARCHITECTURAL STYLES ALONG THE GRAND CANAL

BYZANTINE: 12th and 13th centuries.
Distinguishing characteristics: high, rounded arches, relief panels, multicolored marble.
Examples: Fondaco dei Turchi, Ca' Loredan, Ca' Farsetti, Palazzo Barzizza (and, off the canal, Basilica di San Marco).

GOTHIC: 14th and 15th centuries.
Distinguishing characteristics: Pointed arches, high ceilings, and many windows.
Examples: Ca' d'Oro, Ca' Foscari, Ca' Franchetti, Palazzo Falier (and, off the canal, Palazzo Ducale).

RENAISSANCE: 16th century.
Distinguishing characteristics: classically influenced emphasis on order, achieved through symmetry and balanced proportions.
Examples: Palazzo Vendramin-Calergi, Ca' Grimani, Ca' Corner-Spinelli, Ca' dei Camerlenghi (and, off the canal, Libreria Sansoviniana on Piazza San Marco and the church of San Giorgio Maggiore).

BAROQUE: 17th century.
Distinguishing characteristics: Renaissance order wedded with a more dynamic style, achieved through curving lines and complex decoration.
Examples: churches of Santa Maria di Nazareth and San Stae, Ca' Pesaro, Ca' Rezzonico (and, off the canal, the church of Santa Maria della Salute).

Ca' Franchetti

Until the late 19th century, Ca' Franchetti was a *squero* (gondola workshop). A few active squeri remain, though none are on the Grand Canal. The most easily spotted is Squero di San Trovaso, in Dorsoduro on a small canal near the Zattere boat landing.

Ca' Barbaro

Monet, Henry James, and Cole Porter are among the guests who have stayed at Ca' Barbaro. Porter later lived aboard a boat in Giudecca Canal.

Ponte dell' Accademia

ACCADEMIA ▲

Casetta Rossa

Ca' Pisani-Gritti

S. M. DEL GIGLIO ▲

Ca' Barbarigo

Palazzo Venier dei Leoni

Palazzo Salviati

SALUTE ▲

Ca' Dario

S. Maria della Salute

The wooden Ponte dell'Accademia, like the Eiffel Tower (with which it shares a certain structural grace), wasn't intended to be permanent. Erected in 1933 as a quick replacement for a rusting iron bridge built by the Austrian military in 1854, it was so well liked by Venetians that they kept it. (A perfect replica, with steel bracing, was installed in 1986.)

You're only three stops from the end of the Grand Canal, but this last stretch is packed with sights. The lovely **Ca' Franchetti**, with a central balcony made in the style of Palazzo Ducale's loggia, dates from the late Gothic period, but its gardens are no older than the cedar tree standing at their center.

When she was in residence at Palazzo Venier dei Leoni, Peggy Guggenheim kept her private gondola parked at the door and left her dogs standing guard (in place of Venetian lions).

Ca' Barbaro, next door to Ca' Franchetti, was the residence of the illustrious family who rebuilt the church of Santa Maria del Giglio.

Farther along on the left bank, a garden, vibrant with flowers in summer, surrounds **Casetta Rossa** (small red house) as if it were the centerpiece of its bouquet. Across the canal, bright 19th-century mosaics on **Ca' Barbarigo** give you some idea how the frescoed facades of many Venetian palaces must have looked in their heyday. A

However tilted Dario might be, it has outlasted its many owners, who seem plagued by misfortune. They include the Italian industrialist Raul Gardini, whose 1992 suicide followed charges of corruption and an unsuccessful bid to win the America's Cup.

few doors down are the lush gardens within the walls of the unfinished **Palazzo Venier dei Leoni,** which holds the **Peggy Guggenheim Collection** 12 of contemporary art.

Lovely, leaning **Ca' Dario** on the right bank is notable for its colorful marble façade.

Past the landing of Santa Maria del Giglio stands the

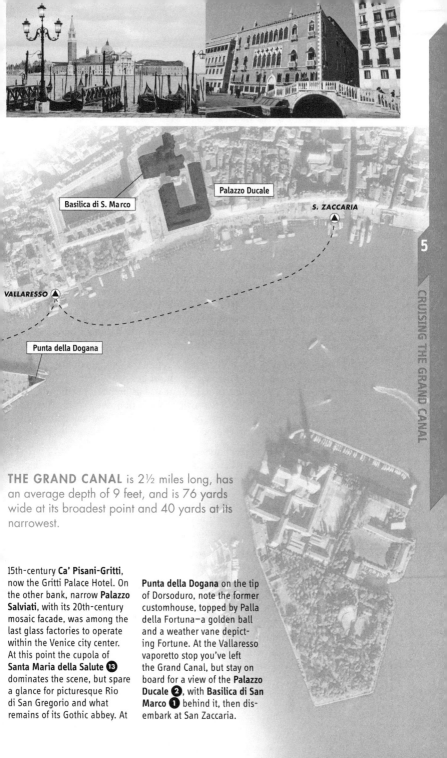

Basilica di S. Marco

Palazzo Ducale

S. ZACCARIA

VALLARESSO

Punta della Dogana

THE GRAND CANAL is 2½ miles long, has an average depth of 9 feet, and is 76 yards wide at its broadest point and 40 yards at its narrowest.

15th-century **Ca' Pisani-Gritti**, now the Gritti Palace Hotel. On the other bank, narrow **Palazzo Salviati**, with its 20th-century mosaic facade, was among the last glass factories to operate within the Venice city center. At this point the cupola of **Santa Maria della Salute** ⑬ dominates the scene, but spare a glance for picturesque Rio di San Gregorio and what remains of its Gothic abbey. At

Punta della Dogana on the tip of Dorsoduro, note the former customhouse, topped by Palla della Fortuna–a golden ball and a weather vane depicting Fortune. At the Vallaresso vaporetto stop you've left the Grand Canal, but stay on board for a view of the **Palazzo Ducale** ❷, with **Basilica di San Marco** ❶ behind it, then disembark at San Zaccaria.

Piazza San Marco

One of the world's most evocative squares, Piazza San Marco (St. Mark's Square) is the heart of Venice, a vast open space bordered by an orderly procession of arcades marching toward the fairy-tale cupolas and marble lacework of the Basilica di San Marco. Perpetually packed by day with people and fluttering pigeons, it can be magical at night, especially in winter, when mists swirl around the lampposts and the Campanile.

If you face the basilica from in front of the Correr Museum, you'll notice that rather than being a strict rectangle, this square opens wider at the basilica end, creating the illusion that it's even larger than it is. On your left, the long, arcaded building is the Procuratie Vecchie, built in the early 16th century as offices and residences for the powerful procurators (magistrates) of San Marco.

On your right is the Procuratie Nuove, built half a century later in a more-grandiose classical style. It was originally planned by Venice's great Renaissance architect, Sansovino, to carry on the look of his Libreria Sansoviniana (Sansovinian Library), but he died before construction on the Nuove had begun. Vincenzo Scamozzi (circa 1552–1616), a neoclassicist pupil of Andrea Palladio (1508–80), completed the design and construction. Still later, the Procuratie Nuove was modified by architect Baldassare Longhena (1598–1682), one of Venice's baroque masters.

When Napoléon (1769–1821) entered Venice with his troops in 1797, he called Piazza San Marco "the world's most beautiful drawing room"— and promptly gave orders to redecorate it. His architects demolished a 16th-century church with a Sansovino facade in order to build the Ala Napoleonica (Napoleonic Wing), or Fabbrica Nuova (New Building), which linked the two 16th-century procuratie and effectively enclosed the piazza.

Piazzetta San Marco, the "little square" leading from Piazza San Marco to the waters of Bacino San Marco (St. Mark's Basin), is a *molo* (landing) that was once the grand entryway to the republic. It's distinguished by two columns towering above the waterfront. One is topped by the winged lion, a traditional emblem of St. Mark that became the symbol of Venice itself; the other supports St. Theodore, the city's first patron, along with his dragon. Between these columns the republic traditionally executed convicts.

Timing

It takes a full day to take in everything on the piazza thoroughly; so if time is limited you'll have to prioritize. Plan on 1½ hours for the basilica and its Pala d'Oro, Galleria, and Museo di San Marco. You'll want at least two hours to appreciate the Palazzo Ducale. Do take time to enjoy the piazza itself from a café table, or on a clear day, from atop the Campanile.

The Main Attractions

① **Basilica di San Marco.** An opulent synthesis of Byzantine and Romanesque
FodorśChoice styles, Venice's gem is laid out in a Greek-cross floor plan and topped
★ with five plump domes. It didn't become the cathedral of Venice until 1807, but its role as the Chiesa Ducale (doge's private chapel) gave it

immense power and wealth. The original church was built in 828 to house the body of St. Mark the Evangelist. His remains, filched from Alexandria by the doge's agents, were supposedly hidden in a barrel under layers of pickled pork to sneak them past Muslim guards. The escapade is depicted in the 13th-century mosaic above the door farthest left of the front entrance, one of the earliest mosaics on the heavily decorated facade; look closely to see the church as it appeared at that time.

A 976 fire destroyed most of the original church. It was rebuilt and reopened in 1094, and for centuries it would serve as a symbol of Venetian wealth and power, endowed with all the riches admirals and merchants could carry off from the Orient, to the point where it earned the nickname Chiesa d'Oro (Golden Church). The four bronze horses that prance and snort over the doorway are copies of sculptures that victorious Venetians took from Constantinople in 1204 after the fourth crusade (the originals are in the Museo di San Marco). The rich, colorful exterior decorations, including the numerous different marble columns, all came from the same source. Look for a medallion of red porphyry in the floor of the porch inside the main door. It marks the spot where, in 1177, Doge Sebastiano Ziani orchestrated the reconciliation between Barbarossa—the Holy Roman Emperor—and Pope Alexander III. Dim lighting, galleries high above the naves—they served as the *matroneum* (women's gallery)—the *iconostasis* (altar screen), and the single massive Byzantine chandelier all seem to wed Christianity with the Orient, giving San Marco its exotic blend of majesty and mystery.

The basilica is famous for its 43,055 square feet of mosaics, which run from floor to ceiling thanks to an innovative roof of brick vaulting. Many of the original windows were filled in to make room for even more artwork. At midday, when the interior is fully illuminated, the mosaics truly come alive, the shimmer of their tiny gold tiles becoming nothing short of magical. The earliest mosaics are from the 11th and 12th centuries, and the last were added in the early 1700s. One of the most recent is the *Last Judgment,* believed to have been designed by Tintoretto (1518–94), on the arch between the porch and the nave. Inside the main entrance, turn right on the porch to see the Book of Genesis depicted on the ceiling. Ahead through a glass door, 13th-century mosaics depict St. Mark's life in the **Cappella Zen** (Zen Chapel). The **Cappella della Madonna di Nicopeia,** in the left transept, holds the altar icon that many consider Venice's most powerful protector. In nearby **Cappella della Madonna dei Mascoli** the life of the Virgin Mary is depicted in fine 15th-century mosaics, believed to be based on drawings by Jacopo Bellini (1400–71) and Andrea Mantegna (1431–1506).

In the **Santuario** (Sanctuary), the main altar is built over the tomb of St. Mark, its green marble canopy lifted high on carved alabaster columns. Perhaps even more impressive is the **Pala d'Oro,** a dazzling gilt silver screen encrusted with 1,927 precious gems and 255 enameled panels. Originally commissioned in Constantinople by Doge Orseolo I (976–978), it was enlarged and embellished over four centuries by master craftsmen and wealthy merchants. The bronze door leading from the sanctuary into the sacristy is by Jacopo Sansovino (1486–1570). In the top left corner the artist included a self-portrait, and above that, he pictured friend and fellow artist Titian (1485–1576). The **Tesoro** (Treasury), entered from the right transept, contains many treasures carried home from conquests abroad.

Climb the steep stairway to the **Galleria** and the **Museo di San Marco** for the best overview of the basilica's interior. From here you can step outdoors for a sweeping panorama of Piazza San Marco and out over the lagoon to San Giorgio. The displays focus mainly on the types of mosaic and how they have been restored over the years. But the highlight is a close-up view of the original gilt bronze horses that were once on the outer gallery. The four were most probably cast in Rome and taken to Constantinople, where the Venetians pillaged them after sacking that city. When Napoléon sacked Venice in 1797, he took them to Paris. They were returned after the fall of the French Empire, but came home "blind"—their big ruby eyes had been sold.

Be aware that guards at the basilica door turn away anyone with bare shoulders or knees; no shorts, short skirts, or tank tops are allowed. If you want a free guided tour in English during summer months (less certain in winter, as the guides are volunteers), look for groups forming on the porch inside the main door. You may also arrange tours by appointment. ⊠ *Piazza San Marco* ☎ *041/5225205 basilica, 041/*

2702421 for free tours Apr.–Oct. (call Tues. or Thurs. morning)
🔲 *Basilica free, Tesoro €2, Santuario and Pala d'Oro €1.50, Galleria and Museo di San Marco €3* ⊙ *May–Sept., Mon.–Sat. 9:45–5:30, Sun. 2–4; Oct.–Apr., Mon.–Sat. 9:45–4:30, Sun. 2–4; last entry ½ hr before closing* Ⓥ *Vallaresso/San Zaccaria.*

★ ❷ **Palazzo Ducale** (Doge's Palace). Rising above the Piazzetta San Marco, this Gothic-Renaissance fantasia of pink-and-white marble is a majestic expression of the prosperity and power attained during Venice's most glorious period. Some architectural purists find the building top-heavy—its hulking upper floors rest upon a graceful ground-floor colonnade—but the design is what gives the palace its distinctive identity; it's hard to imagine it any other way. Always much more than a residence, the palace was Venice's White House, Senate, torture chamber, and prison rolled into one.

Though a fortress for the doge stood on this spot in the early 9th century, the building you see today was begun in the 12th century, and like the basilica next door was continually remodeled over the centuries. Near the basilica you'll see the ornately Gothic **Porta della Carta** (Gate of the Paper), where official decrees were traditionally posted, but visitors enter under the portico facing the water. You'll find yourself in an immense courtyard with the **Scala dei Giganti** (Stairway of the Giants) directly ahead, guarded by Sansovino's huge statues of Mars and Neptune. Though ordinary mortals must use the central interior staircase, its upper flight is the lavishly gilded **Scala d'Oro** (Golden Staircase), also by Sansovino. It may seem odd that you have to climb so many steps to reach the government's main council rooms and reception halls, but imagine how this extraordinary climb must have impressed, and perhaps intimidated, foreign emissaries.

The palace's sumptuous chambers have walls and ceilings covered with works by Venice's greatest artists. Visit the **Anticollegio,** a waiting room outside the Collegio's chamber, where you'll see the *Rape of Europa* by Veronese (1528–88) and Tintoretto's *Bacchus and Ariadne Crowned by Venus.* Veronese also painted the ceiling of the adjacent **Sala del Collegio.** The ceiling of the **Sala del Senato** (Senate Chamber), featuring *The Triumph of Venice* by Tintoretto, is magnificent, but it's dwarfed by his masterpiece *Paradise* in the **Sala del Maggiore Consiglio** (Great Council Hall). A vast work commissioned for a vast hall, this dark, dynamic piece is the world's largest oil painting (23 by 75 feet). The room's carved, gilt ceiling is breathtaking, especially with Veronese's majestic *Apotheosis of Venice* filling one of the center panels. Around the upper walls, study the portraits of the first 76 doges, and you'll notice one picture is missing near the left corner of the wall opposite *Paradise.* A black painted curtain, rather than a portrait, marks Doge Marin Falier's fall from grace; he was beheaded for treason in 1355, which the Latin inscription bluntly explains.

A narrow canal separates the palace's east side from the cramped cell blocks of the **Prigioni Nuove** (New Prisons). High above the water arches the enclosed marble **Ponte dei Sospiri** (Bridge of Sighs), which earned its name from the sighs of those being led to their fate. Look out its windows to see the last earthly view these prisoners beheld.

VENICE THROUGH THE AGES

Up from the Muck. Venice was founded in the 5th century when the Veneti, inhabitants of the mainland region roughly corresponding to today's Veneto, fled their homes to escape invading Lombards. The unlikely city, built atop wooden posts driven into the marshes, would evolve into a great maritime republic. Its fortunes grew as a result of its active role in the Crusades, beginning in 1095 and culminating in the Venetian-led sacking of Constantinople in 1204. The defeat of rival Genoa in the Battle of Chioggia (1380) established Venice as the dominant sea power in Europe.

Early Democracy. As early as the 7th century, Venice was governed by a participatory democracy, with a ruler, the doge, elected to a lifetime term. Beginning in the 12th century, the doge's power was increasingly subsumed by a growing number of councils, commissions, and magistrates. In 1268 a complicated procedure for the doge's election was established to prevent nepotism, but by that point power rested foremost with the Great Council, which at times numbered as many as 2,000 members.

Laws were passed by the Senate, a group of 200 elected from the Great Council, and executive powers belonged to the College, a committee of 25. In 1310 the Council of Ten was formed to protect state security. When circumstances dictated, the doge could expedite decision making by consulting only the Council of Ten. To avoid too great a concentration of power, these 10 served only one year and belonged to different families.

A Long Decline. Venice reached its height of power in the 15th and 16th centuries, during which time its domain included all of the Veneto region and part of Lombardy. But beginning in the 16th century, the tide turned. The Ottoman Empire blocked Venice's Mediterranean trade routes, and newly emerging sea powers such as Britain and the Netherlands ended Venice's monopoly by opening oceanic trading routes. The republic underwent a slow decline. When Napoleon arrived in 1797, he took the city without a fight, eventually delivering it to the Austrians, who ruled until 1848. In that tumultuous year throughout Europe, the Venetians rebelled, an act that would ultimately lead to their joining the Italian Republic in 1866.

Art Stars. In the 13th through 15th century the influence of Gothic architecture resulted in palaces in the Florid Gothic style, for which the city is famous. Renaissance sensibilities arrived comparatively late. Early Venetian Renaissance artists—Carpaccio, Giorgione, and the Bellini brothers, Giovanni and Gentile—were active in the late 15th and early 16th century. Along with the stars of the next generation—Veronese, Titian, and Tintoretto—they played a key role in the development of Western art, and their best work remains in the city.

Like its dwindling fortunes, Venice's art and culture underwent a prolonged decline, leaving only the splendid monuments to recall a fabled past. The 18th-century paintings of Canaletto and Tiepolo were a glorious swan song.

The palazzo's "Secret Itinerary" tour takes you to the doge's private apartments, through hidden passageways to the interrogation (torture) chambers, and into the rooftop *piombi* (lead) prison, named for its lead roofing. Venetian-born writer and libertine Giacomo Casanova (1725–98), along with an accomplice, managed to escape from the piombi in 1756, the only men ever to do so. ⊠ *Piazzetta San Marco* ☎ *041/2715911, 041/5209070 "Secret Itinerary" tour* ✉ *Piazza San Marco museum card €12, Musei Civici museum pass €18, "Secret Itinerary" tour €12.50* ⊙ *Apr.–Oct., daily 9–7; Nov.–Mar., daily 9–5; last tickets sold 1 hr before closing. English "Secret Itinerary" tours in morning; reservations advisable* Ⓥ *Vallaresso/San Zaccaria.*

NEED A BREAK?

Caffè Florian (☎ 041/5205641), located in the Procuratie Nuove, has served coffee to the likes of Casanova, Charles Dickens, and Marcel Proust. It's Venice's oldest café, continuously in business since 1720 (though you'll find it closed Wednesday in winter). Counter seating is less expensive than taking a table, especially when there's live music. In the Procuratie Vecchie, **Caffè Quadri** (☎ 041/5289299) exudes almost as much history as Florian across the way, and is similarly pricey. It was shunned by 19th-century Venetians when the occupying Austrians made it their gathering place. In winter it closes Monday.

Also Worth Seeing

(ᐂ ❸ **Campanile.** Venice's famous brick bell tower (325 feet tall, plus the angel) had been standing nearly 1,000 years when in 1902, practically without warning, it collapsed, taking with it Jacopo Sansovino's 16th-century marble loggia at the base. The crushed loggia was promptly restored, and the new tower, rebuilt to the old plan, reopened in 1912. In the 15th century, clerics found guilty of immoral behavior were suspended in wooden cages from the tower. Some were forced to subsist on bread and water for as long as a year, and others were left to starve. The stunning view from the tower on a clear day includes the Lido, the lagoon, and the mainland as far as the Alps but, strangely enough, none of the myriad canals that snake through the city. ⊠ *Piazza San Marco* ☎ *041/5224064* ✉ *€6* ⊙ *Apr.–Sept., daily 9:30 AM–5:30; Oct.–Mar., daily 9:30–4:30; last entry ½ hr before closing* Ⓥ *Vallaresso/San Zaccaria.*

❹ **Museo Correr.** Exhibits in this museum of Venetian art and history range from the absurdly high-soled shoes worn by 16th-century Venetian ladies (who walked with the aid of a servant) to the huge *Grande Pianta Prospettica* by Jacopo de' Barbari (circa 1440–1515), which details in carved wood every nook and cranny of 16th-century Venice. The city's proud naval history is evoked in several rooms through highly descriptive paintings and numerous maritime objects, including ships' cannons and some surprisingly large iron mast-top navigation lights. The Correr has a room devoted entirely to antique games, and its second-floor **Quadreria** (Picture Gallery) has works by Venetian, Greek, and Flemish painters. The Correr exhibition rooms lead directly into the **Museo Archeologico** and the **Stanza del Sansovino,** the only part of the **Biblioteca Marciana** open to visitors. ⊠ *Piazza San Marco, Ala Napoleonica* ☎ *041/2405211* ✉ *Piazza San Marco museum card €12, Musei Civici*

Wading Through the Acqua Alta

CLOSE UP

YOU HAVE TO WALK almost everywhere in Venice, and where you can't walk, you go by water. Occasionally you walk *in* water, when normally higher fall and spring tides are exacerbated by falling barometers and southeasterly winds. The result is *acqua alta*—flooding in the lowest parts of town, especially Piazza San Marco, which lasts a few hours, until the tide recedes.

Work has begun on the Moses Project, a plan that would close off the lagoon when high tides threaten, but it's a much-debated response to an emotionally charged problem. Protecting Venice and its lagoon from high tides—as well as high use and the damaging wave action caused by powerboats—is among the city's most contentious issues.

museum pass €18 ⊗ Apr.–Oct., daily 9–7; Nov.–Mar., daily 9–5; last tickets sold 1 hr before closing Ⓥ *Vallaresso/San Zaccaria.*

NEED A BREAK?

If you'd like to attend happy hour with the ghosts of Ernest Hemingway, Aristotle Onassis, and Orson Welles, head to **Harry's Bar** (☎ 041/5285777). Walk out Piazza San Marco near the Correr Museum and turn left at Calle Vallaresso; you'll find the legendary hangout right at the vaporetto landing. Harry's still boasts Venice's driest martinis and freshest Bellinis (white peach juice and sparkling *prosecco* wine).

❺ **Torre dell'Orologio.** Five hundred years ago, when this enameled clock was built, twin Moor figures would strike the hour, and three wise men with an angel would walk out and bow to the Virgin Mary on Epiphany (January 6) and during Ascension Week (40 days after Easter). An inscription on the tower reads HORAS NON NUMERO NISI SERENAS ("I only count happy hours"); if that's true, perhaps happy hours will return to Venice when they finally fix the clock. It's been under restoration for years and may resume functioning sometime in 2007. You can visit the three wise men in the Palazzo Ducale, where they are on display. ⊠ *North side of Piazza San Marco.*

Dorsoduro

The sestiere Dorsoduro (named for its "hard back" solid clay foundation) is across the Grand Canal to the south of San Marco. It is a place of monumental churches, meandering canals, the city's finest art museums, and a boardwalk called the Zattere, where on sunny days you'll swear half the city is out for a *passeggiata*, or stroll. The eastern point of the peninsula, Punta della Dogana, has one of the best views in town. The Stazione Marittima, where in summer cruise ships line the dock, lies at the western end. Midway between these two points, just off the Zattere, is the Squero di San Trovaso, where gondolas have been built and repaired for centuries.

Dorsoduro is also home to the Gallerie dell'Accademia, which has an unparalleled collection of Venetian painting, and Ca' Rezzonico, the

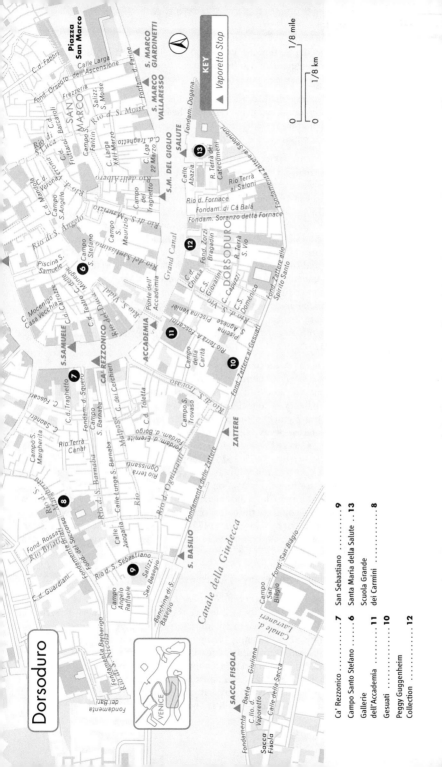

Dorsoduro

KEY

▲ Vaporetto Stop

| 0 | | 1/8 km |
| 0 | | 1/8 mile |

Museo del Settecento Veneziano. Another of its landmark sites, the Peggy Guggenheim Collection, has a fine selection of 20th-century art.

Timing

The Gallerie dell'Accademia demands a few hours, but if time is short an audio guide can help you cover the highlights in about an hour. Give yourself at least 1½ hours for the Guggenheim Collection. Ca' Rezzonico deserves a couple of hours.

The Main Attractions

★ **❼ Ca' Rezzonico.** Designed by Baldassare Longhena in the 17th century, this palace was completed nearly 100 years later by Giorgio Massari and became the last home of English poet Robert Browning (1812–89). Elizabeth Taylor and Richard Burton danced in the baroque ballroom in the 1960s. Today Ca' Rezzonico is the home of the **Museo del Settecento** (Museum of Venice in the 1700s). Its main floor is packed with period furniture and tapestries in gilded salons (note the four Tiepolo ceiling frescoes) and successfully retains the feel of an old Venetian palazzo. Upper floors contain hundreds of paintings, most from Venetian schools of artists. There's even a restored apothecary, complete with powders and potions. ✉ *Fondamenta Rezzonico, Dorsoduro 3136* ☎ *041/2410100* 🖅 *€6.50; museum card €8, includes Palazzo Mocenigo and Casa Goldoni; Musei Civici museum pass €18* ⊙ *Apr.–Oct., daily 10–6; Nov.–Mar., daily 10–5; last entry 1 hr before closing* Ⓥ *Ca' Rezzonico.*

★ **⓫ Gallerie dell'Accademia.** Napoléon founded these galleries in 1807 on the site of a religious complex he'd suppressed, and what he initiated now amounts to the world's most extraordinary collection of Venetian art. Jacopo Bellini is considered the father of the Venetian Renaissance, and in Room 2 you can compare his *Madonna and Child with Saints* with such later works as *Madonna of the Orange Tree* by Cima da Conegliano (circa 1459–1517) and *Ten Thousand Martyrs of Mt. Ararat* by Vittore Carpaccio (circa 1455–1525). Jacopo's son Giovanni (circa 1430–1516) draws your eye not with his subjects but with his rich color. Rooms 4 and 5 are full of his Madonnas; note the contrast between the young Madonna and Child and the neighboring older Madonna after the crucifixion—you'll see the colors of dawn and dusk in Venice. Room 5 contains *Tempest* by Giorgione (1477–1510), a work that was revolutionary in its time and has continued to intrigue viewers and critics over the centuries. It depicts a storm approaching as a nude woman nurses her child and a soldier looks on. The overall atmosphere that Giorgione creates is as important as any of his figures.

In Room 10, *Feast in the House of Levi*, commissioned as a Last Supper, got Veronese dragged before the Inquisition over its depiction of dogs, jesters, and German (therefore Protestant) soldiers. The artist saved his neck by simply changing the title, so that the painting represented a different biblical feast. Titian's *Presentation of the Virgin* (Room 24) is the collection's only work originally created for the building in which it hangs. Don't miss Rooms 20 and 21, with views of 15th- and 16th-century Venice by Carpaccio and Gentile Bellini (1429–1507), Giovanni's brother—you'll see how little the city has changed.

Booking tickets in advance isn't essential but helps during busy seasons and costs only an additional €1. Booking is necessary to see the **Quadreria,** where additional works art and artists, and the bookshop sells a more informative English-language booklet. In the main galleries a €4 audio guide saves reading but adds little to each room's excellent annotation. ✉ *Campo della Carità, Dorsoduro 1050* ☎ *041/5222247, 041/5200345 reservations* ⊕ *www.artive.arti.beniculturali.it* ✉ *€6.50, €11 includes Ca' d'Oro and Museo Orientale* ☉ *Tues.–Sun. 8:15–7:15, Mon. 8:15–2* Ⓥ *Accademia.*

NEED A BREAK? There's no sunnier spot in Venice than **Fondamenta delle Zattere,** along the southern edge of Dorsoduro. It's the city's gigantic public terrace, with bustling bars and gelato shops; come here to stroll, read in the open air, and play hooky from sightseeing. The Zattere's most decadent treat is found at **Gelateria Nico** (✉ Dorsoduro 922 ☎ 041/5225293)—order their famous *gianduiotto,* a nutty slab of chocolate ice cream floating on a cloud of whipped cream, and relax on the big, welcoming deck.

☉ ⑫ **Peggy Guggenheim Collection.** A small but choice selection of 20th-century painting and sculpture is on display at this gallery in the heiress Guggenheim's former Grand Canal home. Through wealth and social connections, Guggenheim (1898–1979) became a serious art patron, and her collection here in Palazzo Venier dei Leoni includes works by Picasso, Kandinsky, Pollock, Motherwell, and Ernst (at one time her husband). The museum serves beverages, snacks, and light meals in its refreshingly shady, artistically sophisticated garden. On Sunday at 3 PM the museum offers a free tour and art workshop for children 12 and under. ✉ *Fondamenta Venier dei Leoni, Dorsoduro 701* ☎ *041/2405411* ⊕ *www.guggenheim-venice.it* ✉ *€10* ☉ *Wed.–Mon. 10–6* Ⓥ *Accademia.*

> ## WORD OF MOUTH
>
> "Personally, I liked the garden and the villa itself at the Peggy Guggenheim museum better than the art."
>
> –Dayle

⑬ **Santa Maria della Salute.** The view of La Salute (as this church is commonly called) from the Riva degli Schiavoni at sunset or from the Accademia Bridge by moonlight is unforgettable. Baldassare Longhena was 32 years old when he won a competition to design a shrine honoring the Virgin Mary for saving Venice from a plague that killed 47,000 residents. Outside, this simple white octagon is adorned with a colossal cupola lined with snail-like buttresses and a Palladian-style facade; inside are a polychrome marble floor and six chapels. The Byzantine icon above the main altar has been venerated as the Madonna della Salute (of health) since 1670, when Francesco Morosini brought it here from Crete. Above it is a sculpture showing Venice (left) on her knees while the plague (right) is driven from the city. The **Sacrestia Maggiore** contains a dozen works by Titian, including his *San Marco Enthroned with Saints* altarpiece. You'll also see Tintoretto's *The Wedding at Canaan,* and on special occasions the altar displays a 15th-century tapestry depicting the Pentecost. For the Festa della Salute, held November 21, Venetians make a pilgrimage here and light candles in thanksgiving for another year's health. ⊠ *Punta della Dogana, Dorsoduro* ☎ *041/5225558* ☎ *Church free, sacristy €1.50* ☉ *Apr.–Sept., daily 9–noon and 3–6:30; Oct.–Mar., daily 9–noon and 3–5:30* Ⓥ *Salute.*

Also Worth Seeing

❻ **Campo Santo Stefano.** In Venice's most prestigious residential neighborhood, you'll find one of the city's busiest crossroads just over the Accademia bridge; it's hard to believe this square once hosted bullfights, with bulls (or oxen) tied to a stake and baited by dogs. For centuries the campo was grass except for a stone avenue called the *liston.* It was so popular for strolling that in Venetian dialect *"andare al liston"* still means "go for a walk." A sunny meeting spot popular with Venetians and visitors alike, the campo also hosts outdoor fairs during Christmas and Carnevale seasons. Check out the 14th-century **Chiesa di Santo Stefano** and its ship's-keel roof, created by shipbuilders. You'll see works by Tintoretto and the tipsiest bell tower in town—best appreciated from nearby Campo San Angelo. ⊠ *Campo Santo Stefano, San Marco* ☎ *041/2750462 Chorus* ☎ *€2.50, Chorus pass €8* ☉ *Mon.–Sat. 10–5, Sun. 1–5* Ⓥ *Accademia.*

❿ **Gesuati.** When the Dominicans took over the church of Santa Maria della Visitazione from the suppressed order of Gesuati laymen in 1668, Giorgio Massari was commissioned to build this structure. It has a score of works by Giambattista Tiepolo (1696–1770), Giambattista Piazzetta (1683–1754), and Sebastiano Ricci (1659–1734). ⊠ *Zattere, Dorsoduro* ☎ *041/2750462 Chorus* ☎ *€2.50, Chorus pass €8* ☉ *Mon.–Sat. 10–5, Sun. 1–5* Ⓥ *Zattere.*

❾ **San Sebastiano.** Paolo Veronese (1528–88) established his reputation while still in his twenties with the frescoes at this, his parish church, and for decades he continued to embellish them with amazing trompel'oeil scenes. Don't miss his altarpiece *Madonna in Glory with Saints.* Veronese is buried beneath his bust near the organ. ⊠ *Campo San Sebastiano, Dorsoduro* ☎ *041/2750462 Chorus* ☎ *€2.50, Chorus pass €8* ☉ *Mon.–Sat. 10–5, Sun. 1–5* Ⓥ *San Basilio.*

❽ **Scuola Grande dei Carmini.** When the order of Santa Maria del Carmelo commissioned Baldassare Longhena to build Scuola Grande dei Carmini in the late 1600s, their brotherhood of 75,000 members was the largest in Venice and one of the wealthiest. Little expense was spared in the decorating of stuccoed ceilings and carved ebony paneling, and the artwork was choice, even before 1739, when Tiepolo painted the **Sala Capitolare.** In what many consider his best work, Tiepolo's nine great canvases vividly transform some rather unpromising religious themes into flamboyant displays of color and movement. ⊠ *Campo dei Carmini, Dorsoduro 2617* ☏ *041/5289420* 🖘 *€5* ☉ *Daily 10–5* Ⓥ *Ca' Rezzonico.*

San Polo & Santa Croce

The two smallest of Venice's six sestieri, San Polo and Santa Croce were named after their main churches, though the Chiesa di Santa Croce was demolished in 1810. The city's most famous bridge, the Ponte di Rialto, unites sestiere San Marco (east) with San Polo (west). San Polo has two other major sites, Santa Maria Gloriosa dei Frari and the Scuola Grande di San Rocco, as well as some worthwhile but lesser-known churches.

Shops abound in the area surrounding the Rialto Bridge. On the San Marco side you'll find fashions, on the San Polo side food. Chiesa di San Giacometto, where you see the first fruit vendors as you come off the bridge on the San Polo side, was probably built in the 11th and 12th centuries, about the time the surrounding market came into being. Public announcements were traditionally read in the church's campo; its 24-hour clock, though lovely, has rarely worked.

Timing

To do the area justice requires at least half a day. If you want to take part in the food shopping, come early to beat the crowds. Bear in mind that a *metà kilo* is about a pound and an *etto* is a few ounces. The campo of San Giacomo dell'Orio, west of the main thoroughfare that takes you from the Ponte di Rialto to Santa Maria Gloriosa dei Frari, is a peaceful place for a drink and a rest. The museums of Ca' Pesaro are a time commitment—you'll want at least two hours to see them both.

The Main Attractions

★ ⓮ **Ponte di Rialto** (Rialto Bridge). The competition to design a stone bridge across the Grand Canal (replacing earlier wooden versions) attracted the late 16th century's best architects, including Michelangelo, Palladio, and Sansovino, but the job went to the less-famous but appropriately named Antonio da Ponte. His pragmatic design featured shop space and was high enough for galleys to pass beneath; it kept decoration and cost to a minimum at a time when the republic's coffers were low due to continual wars against the Turks and the opening of oceanic trade routes. Along the railing you'll enjoy one of the city's most famous views: the Grand Canal vibrant with boat traffic. Ⓥ *Rialto.*

⓴ **Santa Maria Gloriosa dei Frari.** This
FodorsChoice immense Gothic church of russet-
★ color brick, completed in the 1400s after more than a century of work, is deliberately austere, befitting the Franciscan brothers' insistence on spirituality and poverty. However, *I Frari* (as it's known locally) contains some of the most brilliant paintings in any Venetian church. Visit the sacristy first, to see Giovanni Bellini's 1488 triptych

WORD OF MOUTH

"Scuola Grande di San Rocco is absolutely mind-boggling. It is near Santa Maria Gloriosa dei Frari—also well worth a visit. The bonus is that in the small street between these two places is Millevoglie, a sandwich/pizza shop with *the best* gelato."

–Rosemary

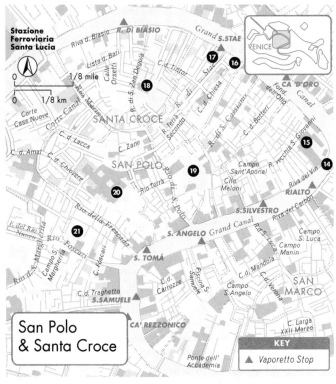

San Polo
& Santa Croce

Madonna and Child with Saints in all its mellow luminosity, painted for precisely this spot. The Corner Chapel on the other side of the chancel is graced by Bartolomeo Vivarini's (1415–84) 1474 altarpiece *St. Mark Enthroned and Saints John the Baptist, Jerome, Peter, and Nicholas,* of similar exquisite detail and color. There is also a fine sculpture of St. John the Baptist here by Jacopo Sansovino. You can see the rapid development of Venetian Renaissance painting by contrasting Bellini and Vivarini with the heroic energy of Titian's *Assumption,* over the main altar, painted only 30 years later. Unveiled in 1518, this work was not initially accepted by the church, precisely because of the innovative style and bright colors, especially Titian's trademark red, which would make it famous.

Titian's beautiful *Madonna di Ca' Pesaro,* in the left aisle, was modeled after his wife, who died in childbirth. The painting took almost 10 years to complete, and in it Titian totally disregarded the conventions of his time by moving the Virgin out of center frame and making the saints active participants. On the same side of the church look at the spooky, pyramid-shape monument to the sculptor Antonio Canova (1757–1822). Across the nave is a neoclassical 19th-century monument to Titian, executed by two of Canova's pupils. ✉ *Campo dei Frari, San Polo* ☎ *041/2728618, 041/2750462 Chorus* ✉ *€2.50, Chorus pass €8* ☉ *Mon.–Sat. 9–6, Sun. 1–6* Ⓥ *San Tomà.*

Venice's Scuola Days

CLOSE UP

AN INSTITUTION you'll inevitably encounter from Venice's glory days is the *scuola* (plural *scuole*). These weren't schools, as the word today translates, but an important network of institutions established by different social groups—enclaves of foreigners, tradesmen, followers of a particular saint, and parishioners.

For the most part secular despite their devotional activities, the scuole concentrated on charitable work, either helping their own membership or assisting the city's neediest citizens. The tradesmen's and servants' scuole formed social security nets for elderly and disabled members. Wealthier scuole assisted orphans or provided dowries so poor girls could marry. By 1500 there were more than 200 major and minor scuole in Venice, some of which contributed substantially to arts and crafts guilds. The republic encouraged their existence—the scuole kept strict records of the names and professions of contributors to the brotherhood, which helped when it came time to collect taxes.

NEED A BREAK?

On a narrow passage between the Frari and San Rocco, **Gelateria Millevoglie** ([Thousand Desires]; ☎ 041/5244667) has pizza slices, calzones, and gelato so popular it backs up traffic. It's closed December and January, but it's open seven days a week—10 AM to midnight in summer and until 9 PM October–March.

Just off of Campo San Tomà is the decadent **Vizio Virtù** (☎ 041/2750149). If it's too cold for a gelato, have a hot chocolate to go or choose from a selection of gourmet chocolate creations.

㉑ **Scuola Grande di San Rocco.** St. Rocco's popularity stemmed from his miraculous recovery from the plague and his care for fellow sufferers. Throughout the plague-filled Middle Ages, followers and donations abounded, and this elegant example of Venetian Renaissance architecture was the result. Although it is bold and dramatic outside, its contents are even more stunning—a series of more than 60 paintings by Tintoretto. In 1564 Tintoretto edged out competition for a commission to decorate a ceiling by submitting not a sketch, but a finished work, which he moreover offered free of charge. *Moses Striking Water from the Rock, The Brazen Serpent,* and *The Fall of Manna* represent three afflictions—thirst, disease, and hunger—that San Rocco and later his brotherhood sought to relieve. ⊠ *Campo San Rocco, San Polo 3052* ☎ *041/5234864* ⊕ *www. scuolagrandesanrocco.it* ⊠ *€5.50; students up to 26 €4; children up to 18 free if accompanied by parent* ☉ *Apr.–Oct., daily 9–5:30; Nov.–Mar., daily 10–5; last entry ½ hr before closing* Ⓥ *San Tomà.*

NEED A BREAK?

The bridge behind Scuola Grande di San Rocco leads to a bustling little student area of bars and restaurants. **Café Noir** (⊠ Calle Crosera, Dorsoduro 3805 ☎ 041/710925) has a good selection of sandwiches. It's open until 2 AM but closed Sunday morning.

Pasticceria Tonolo (⊠ Calle Crosera, Dorsoduro 3764 ☎ 041/5237209) has been fattening up Venetians since 1886. During Carnevale it's still the best place in town for *fritelle*, fried doughnuts (traditional raisin or cream-filled); during *acqua alta* flooding, the staff dons rubber boots and keeps working. The place is closed Monday, and there's no seating anytime.

Also Worth Seeing

⑲ Campo San Polo. Only Piazza San Marco is larger than this square, where not even the pigeons manage to look cozy, and the echo of children's voices bouncing off the surrounding palaces makes the space seem even more cavernous. Not long ago Campo San Polo hosted bull races, fairs, military parades, and packed markets, but now it only really comes alive on summer nights, when it hosts the city's outdoor cinema. The **Chiesa di San Polo** has been restored so many times that little remains of the original 9th-century church, and sadly, 19th-century alterations were so costly that the friars sold off many great paintings to pay bills. Though Giambattista Tiepolo is represented here, his work is outdone by 16 paintings by his son Giandomenico (1727–1804), including the *Stations of the Cross* in the oratory to the left of the entrance. The younger Tiepolo also created a series of expressive and theatrical renderings of the saints. Look for altarpieces by Tintoretto and Veronese that managed to escape auction. San Polo's bell tower remained unchanged through the centuries—don't miss the two lions guarding it, playing with a disembodied human head and a serpent. ⊠ *Campo San Polo* ☎ *041/ 2750462 Chorus* 🖃 *€2.50, Chorus pass €8* ⊙ *Mon.–Sat. 10–5, Sun. 1–5* Ⓥ *San Tomà.*

⑯ Ca' Pesaro. Baldassare Longhena's grand baroque palace is the beautifully restored home of two impressive collections. The **Galleria Internazionale d'Arte Moderna** has works by 19th- and 20th-century artists such as Klimt, Kandinsky, Matisse, and Miró. It also has a collection of representative works from Venice's Biennale art show that amounts to a panorama of 20th-century art. The **Museo Orientale** has a small but striking collection of Oriental porcelains, musical instruments, arms, and armor. ⊠ *San Stae, Santa Croce 2076* ☎ *041/5240662 Galleria, 041/ 5241173 Museo Orientale* 🖃 *€5.50 includes both museums* ⊙ *Apr.–Sept., Tues.–Sun. 10–6; Oct.–Mar., Tues.–Sun. 10–5* Ⓥ *San Stae.*

⑱ San Giacomo dell'Orio. It was named after a laurel tree *(orio)*, and today trees give character to this square. Add benches and a fountain (with a drinking bowl for dogs), and the pleasant, oddly shaped campo becomes a welcoming place for friendly conversation, picnics, and neighborhood kids at play. Legend has it the **Chiesa di San Giacomo dell'Orio** was founded in the 9th century on an island still populated by wolves. The current church dates from 1225; its short unmatched Byzantine columns survived renovation during the Renaissance, and the church never lost the feel of an ancient temple sheltering beneath its 15th-century ship's-keel roof. In the sanctuary, large marble crosses are surrounded by a bevy of small medieval Madonnas. The altarpiece is *Madonna with Child and Saints* (1546) by Lorenzo Lotto (1480–1556), and the sacristies contain works by Palma il Giovane (circa 1544–1628).

✉ *Campo San Giacomo dell'Orio, Santa Croce* ☎ *041/2750462 Chorus* 🎟 *€2.50, Chorus pass €8* ⊗ *Mon.–Sat. 10–5, Sun. 1–5* Ⓥ *San Stae.*

⑮ San Giovanni Elemosinario. Storefronts make up the facade, and the altars were built by market guilds—poulterers, messengers, and fodder merchants—at this church intimately bound to the Rialto Market. It's as rich inside as it is simple outside. During San Giovanni Elemosinario's restoration, workers stumbled upon a frescoed cupola by Pordenone (1484–1539) that had been painted over centuries earlier. Don't miss Titian's *St. John the Almsgiver* and Pordenone's *Sts. Catherine, Sebastian, and Roch,* which in 2002 were returned after 30 years by the Gallerie dell'Accademia, a rare move for an Italian museum. ✉ *Rialto Ruga Vechia San Giovanni, Santa Croce* ☎ *041/2750462 Chorus* 🎟 *€2.50, Chorus pass €8* ⊗ *Mon.–Sat. 10–5, Sun. 1–5* Ⓥ *San Silvestro/Rialto.*

⑰ San Stae. The most renowned Venetian painters and sculptors of the early 18th century—known as the Moderns—decorated this church with the legacy left by Doge Alvise Mocenigo II, who's buried in the center aisle. A broad sampling of these masters includes works by Tiepolo, Ricci, Piazzetta, and Lazzarini. ✉ *Campo San Stae, Santa Croce* ☎ *041/2750462 Chorus* 🎟 *€2.50, Chorus pass €8* ⊗ *Mon.–Sat. 9–5, Sun. 1–5* Ⓥ *San Stae.*

Castello & Cannaregio

Twice the size of tiny San Polo and Santa Croce, Castello and Cannaregio combined spread east to west from one end of Venice to the other. From working-class shipbuilding neighborhoods to the world's first ghetto, here you see a cross section of city life that's always existed beyond the palace walls. There are churches that could make a Renaissance pope jealous and one of the Grand Canal's prettiest palaces, Ca' d'Oro, as well as detour options for leaving the crowds behind.

Timing

Visiting both sestieri involves a couple of hours of walking, even if you never enter a building, and there are few chances to hop a boat and save your legs. Some sights have restricted hours, making it virtually impossible to see everything even in a full day. Your best bet is to choose a few sights as priorities, time your tour around their open hours, and then drop in at whatever others happen to be open as you're passing by. If you're touring on Friday, keep in mind that synagogues close at sunset.

The Main Attractions

㉞ Arsenale. The Venetian Republic never could have thrived without the Arsenale shipyard. Today it belongs to the Italian Navy and isn't regularly open to the public, but it opens for the Biennale and for Venice's festival of traditional boats, held every May. If you're here during those times, don't miss the chance for a look inside. At other times, it's still worthwhile to walk by and observe the place from the outside.

The Arsenale is said to have been founded in 1104 on twin islands. The immense facility that evolved was given the old Venetian dialect name *arzanà,* borrowed from the Arabic *darsina'a,* meaning "workshop." At

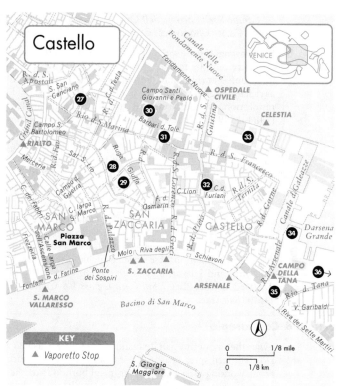

times it employed as many as 16,000 *arsenalotti,* workers who were among
the most respected shipbuilders in the world. (Dante immortalized these
sweating men armed with pitch and boiling tar in his *Inferno.*) Their
diligence was confirmed time and again—whether building 100 ships
in 60 days to battle the Turks in Cyprus (1597) or completing one perfectly armed warship—start to finish—while King Henry III of France
attended a banquet.

The Arsenale's impressive Renaissance **gateway** (1460) is guarded by
four lions, war booty of Francesco Morosini, who took the Pelopon-
nese from the Turks in 1687. The 10-foot-tall lion on the left stood sen-
tinel more than 2,000 years ago near Athens, and experts say its
mysterious inscription is runic "graffiti" left by Viking mercenaries
hired to suppress 11th-century revolts in Piraeus. If you look at the winged
lion above the doorway, you'll notice that the Gospel at his paws is open
but lacks the customary *Pax* inscription; praying for peace perhaps
seemed inappropriate above a factory that manufactured weapons.
⊠ *Campo dell'Arsenale, Castello* Ⓥ *Arsenale.*

★ ㉕ **Ca' d'Oro.** This exquisite Venetian Gothic palace was once literally a
"Golden House," when its marble traceries and ornaments were embellished with pure gold. Created in 1434 by the enamored patrician

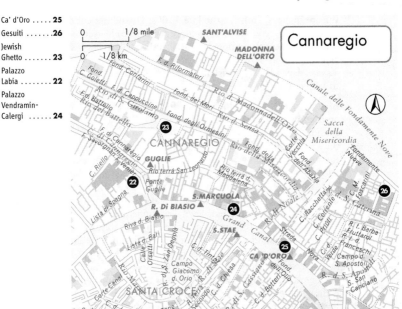

Marino Contarini for his wife, Ca' d'Oro became a love offering a second time when a 19th-century Russian prince gave it to Maria Taglioni, a celebrated classical dancer who collected palaces along the Grand Canal. The last proprietor, perhaps more taken with Venice than with any of his lovers, left Ca' d'Oro to the city, after having had it carefully restored and filled with antiquities, sculptures, and paintings that today make up the **Galleria Franchetti.** Besides Andrea Mantegna's celebrated *St. Sebastian* and other first-rate Venetian works, the Galleria Franchetti contains the type of fresco that once adorned the exteriors of Venetian buildings (commissioned by those who could not afford a marble facade). One such detached fresco displayed here was made by a young Titian for the (now grayish-white) facade of the Fondaco dei Tedeschi, now the main post office. ⊠ *Calle Ca' d'Oro, Cannaregio 3933* ☎ *041/ 5200345* 🖃 *€5, €11 includes Gallerie dell'Accademia and Museo Orientale* 🕙 *Tues.–Sun. 8:15–7, Mon. 8:15–1; last entry ½ hr before closing* Ⓥ *Ca' d'Oro.*

㉓ **Jewish Ghetto.** The neighborhood that gave the world the word *ghetto* is today a quiet warren of backstreets that is still home to Jewish institutions, a kosher restaurant, a rabbinical school, and five synagogues. Though Jews may have arrived earlier, the first synagogues weren't built and a cemetery wasn't founded until the Askenazim, or Eastern

European Jews, came in the late 1300s. Dwindling coffers may have prompted the republic to sell temporary visas to Jews, but over the centuries they were alternately tolerated and expelled. The Rialto commercial district, as vividly recounted in Shakespeare's *The Merchant of Venice,* depended on Jewish merchants and moneylenders for trade, and to help cover ever-increasing war expenses.

In 1516 relentless local opposition forced the Senate to confine Jews to an island in Cannaregio, named for its *geto* (foundry), which produced cannons. Gates at the entrance were locked at night, and boats patrolled the surrounding canals. The German accents of early residents changed the soft g sound of "geto" (zheto) into the hard g in "ghetto." Jews were allowed only to lend money at low interest, operate pawnshops controlled by the government, trade in textiles, or practice medicine. Jewish doctors were highly respected and could leave the ghetto at any hour when on duty. Though ostracized, Jews were nonetheless safe in Venice, and in the 16th century the community grew considerably, with refugees from the Near East, southern and central Italy, Spain, and Portugal. The ghetto was allowed to expand twice, but it still had the city's densest population and consequently ended up with the city's tallest buildings (nine stories); notice the slanting apartment blocks on Campo del Ghetto Nuovo. Although the gates were pulled down after Napoléon's 1797 arrival, the Jews realized full freedom only in the late 19th century with the founding of the Italian state. On the eve of World War II there were about 1,500 Jews left in the ghetto: 247 were deported by the Nazis; 8 returned.

The area has Europe's highest density of Renaissance-era synagogues, and visiting them is a unique cross-cultural experience. Though each is marked by the tastes of its individual builders, Venetian influence is evident throughout. Women's galleries resemble those of theaters from the same era, and some synagogues were decorated by artisans who were simultaneously active in local churches.

The small but well-arranged **Museo Ebraico** highlights centuries of Jewish culture with splendid silver Hanukkah lamps and torahs, and handwritten, beautifully decorated wedding contracts in Hebrew. Tours of the ghetto in Italian and English leave hourly from the museum. ⊠ *Campo del Ghetto Nuovo, Cannaregio 2902/b* ☎ *041/715359* ⊕ *www. museoebraico.it* 🖅 *Museum €3, museum and synagogues €8.50* ☉ *June–Sept., Sun.–Fri. 10–7, last tour 5:30; Oct.–May, Sun.–Fri. 10–5:30, last tour 4:30* Ⓥ *San Marcuola/Guglie.*

You might complete your circuit of Jewish Venice with a visit to the **Antico Cimitero Ebraico** (Ancient Jewish Cemetery) on the Lido, full of fascinating old tombstones half hidden by ivy and grass. The earliest grave dates from 1389; the cemetery remained in use until the late 18th century. ⊠ *Via Cipro, Lido* ☎ *041/715359* 🖅 *€8.50* ☉ *Tours Apr.–Oct., Sun. 2:30; call for arrangements* Ⓥ *Lido–S.M.E.*

★ ㉗ **Santa Maria dei Miracoli.** Tiny yet perfectly proportioned, this early Renaissance gem is sheathed in marble and decorated inside with exquisite marble reliefs. Architect Pietro Lombardo (circa 1435–1515) miraculously compressed the building into its confined space, then created the illusion of greater size by varying the color of the exterior, adding extra pilasters on the building's canal side, and offsetting the arcade windows to make the arches appear deeper. The church was built in the 1480s to house *I Miracoli,* an image of the Virgin Mary that is said to perform miracles—look for it on the high altar. ⊠ *Campo Santa Maria Nova, Cannaregio* ☎ *041/2750462 Chorus* 🎟 *€2.50, Chorus pass €8* ◷ *Mon.–Sat. 10–5, Sun. 1–5* Ⓥ *Rialto.*

★ ㉚ **Santi Giovanni e Paolo.** This massive Dominican church, commonly called San Zanipolo, contains a wealth of art. The 15th-century stained-glass window near the side entrance is breathtaking for its brilliant colors and beautiful figures, made from drawings by Bartolomeo Vivarini and Gerolamo Mocetto. The second official church of the republic after San Marco, San Zanipolo is the Venetian equivalent of London's Westminster Abbey, with a great number of important people, including 25 doges, buried here. Artistic highlights include an outstanding polyptych by Giovanni Bellini (right aisle, second altar); Alvise Vivarini's *Christ Carrying the Cross* (sacrestia); and Lorenzo Lotto's *Charity of St. Antonino* (right transept). Don't miss the *Cappella del Rosario* (Rosary Chapel), off the left transept, built in the 16th century to commemorate the 1571 victory of Lepanto, in western Greece, when Venice led a combined European fleet to defeat the Turkish navy. The chapel was devastated by a fire in 1867 and restored in the early years of the 20th century with works from other churches, among them the sumptuous Veronese ceiling paintings. However quick your visit, don't miss the Pietro Mocenigo tomb to the right of the main entrance, a monument built by the ubiquitous Pietro Lombardo and his sons. ⊠ *Campo dei Santi Giovanni e Paolo, Castello* ☎ *041/5235913* 🎟 *€2.50* ◷ *Mon.–Sat. 9–6, Sun. 1–6* Ⓥ *Fondamente Nuove/Rialto.*

NEED A BREAK?
To satisfy your sweet tooth head for Campo Santa Marina and the family-owned and -operated **Didovich Pastry Shop** (☎ 041/5230017). It's a local favorite, especially for Carnevale-time *fritelle* (fried doughnuts). There is limited seating inside, but in the warmer months you can sit outside. **Bar ai Miracoli** (☎ 041/5231515) in Campo Santa Maria Nova is a good place to grab a quick bite and gaze across the canal at Maria dei Miracoli, Lombardo's miracle in marble.

Also Worth Seeing

㉖ **Gesuiti.** Extravagantly baroque, this 18th-century church completely abandons classical Renaissance straight lines in favor of flowing, twisting forms. Its interior walls resemble brocade drapery, and only touching them will convince skeptics that rather than paint, the green-and-white walls are inlaid marble. Over the first altar on the left the *Martyrdom of St. Lawrence* is a dramatic example of Titian's feeling for light and movement. ⊠ *Campo dei Gesuiti, Cannaregio* ☎ *041/5286579* ◷ *Daily 10–noon and 4–6* Ⓥ *Fondamente Nuove.*

㉟ **Museo Storico Navale** (Museum of Naval History). The boat collection here includes scale models such as the doges' ceremonial *Bucintoro,* and full-size boats such as Peggy Guggenheim's private gondola complete with romantic *felze* (cabin). There's a range of old galley and military pieces, and also a large collection of seashells. ⊠ *Campo San Biagio, Castello 2148* ☎ *041/5200276* 🖼 *€1.55* ⊙ *Weekdays 8:45–1:30, Sat. 8:45–1* Ⓥ *Arsenale.*

③ **Ospedaletto.** This 16th-century "little hospital" was one of four church foundling homes that each had an orchestra and choir of orphans. Entering through **Santa Maria dei Derelitti** (St. Mary of the Destitute) you'll see a large gallery built for the young musicians. The orphanage is now a home for the elderly; its beautiful 18th-century **Sala della Musica** (Music Room) is the only one of its kind to survive. On the far wall the fresco by Jacopo Guarana (1720–1808) depicts Apollo, god of music, surrounded by the orphan musicians and their maestro, Pasquale Anfossi. ⊠ *Calle Barbaria delle Tole, Castello 6691* ☎ *041/2719012* 🖼 *€2* ⊙ *Thurs.–Sat. 3:30–6:30* Ⓥ *Fondamente Nuove/Rialto.*

㉒ **Palazzo Labia.** Once the home of 18th-century Venice's showiest family, this palace is now the Venetian headquarters of the Italian media giant RAI—modern broadcasting goes baroque. In the **Tiepolo Room,** the Labia's gorgeous ballroom, the final flowering of Venetian painting is seen in Giambattista Tiepolo's playful frescoes of Antony and Cleopatra among dwarfs and Barbary pirates. You have to call ahead to arrange a visit here. ⊠ *Campo San Geremia, Cannaregio 275* ☎ *041/781277* 🖼 *Free* ⊙ *Wed.–Fri. 3–4, by appointment* Ⓥ *Ferrovia.*

㉔ **Palazzo Vendramin-Calergi.** This Renaissance classic with an imposing carved frieze is the work of Mauro Codussi (1440–1504). You can see some of its interior by dropping into the **Casinò di Venezia.** Fans of Richard Wagner (1813–83) might enjoy visiting the **Sala di Wagner,** the room (separate from the casino) in which the composer died. Though rather plain, it's loaded with music memorabilia. ⊠ *Cannaregio 2040* ☎ *041/ 5297111, 041/2760407 Fri. AM to reserve Wagner Room tours* 🖼 *Casino €10, tour €5 suggested donation* ⊙ *Slots 2:45 PM–2:30 AM, tables 3:30 PM–2:30 AM, Wagner Room Sat. AM by appointment* Ⓥ *San Marcuola.*

㉙ **Querini-Stampalia.** The art collection at this Renaissance palace includes Giovanni Bellini's *Presentation in the Temple* and Sebastiano Ricci's triptych *Dawn, Afternoon, and Evening.* Portraits of newlywed Francesco Querini and Paola Priuli were left unfinished on the death of Giacomo Palma il Vecchio (1480–1528); note the groom's hand and the bride's dress. Original 18th-century furniture and stuccowork are a fitting background for Pietro Longhi's portraits. Nearly 70 works by Gabriele Bella (1730–99) capture scenes of Venetian street life. Admission Friday and Saturday includes concerts with antique instruments at 5 and 8:30. ⊠ *Campo Santa Maria Formosa, Castello 5252* ☎ *041/2711411* ⊕ *www.querinistampalia.it* 🖼 *€8* ⊙ *Tues.–Thurs. and Sun. 10–6, Fri. and Sat. 10–10* Ⓥ *San Zaccaria.*

㉝ **San Francesco della Vigna** (St. Francis of the Vineyard). Legend says this is where an angel awakened St. Mark the Evangelist with the famous words, "Pax tibi Marce Evangelista meus" (Peace to you, Mark, my Evangelist), which became the motto of the Venetian Republic. The land was given in 1253 to the Franciscans, who kept the vineyard but replaced the ancient church. Bring some €0.20 coins to light up the Antonio Vi-

Let's Get Lost

GETTING AROUND VENICE presents some unusual problems: the city's layout has few straight lines; house numbering seems nonsensical; and the *sestieri* (six districts) of San Marco, Cannaregio, Castello, Dorsoduro, Santa Croce, and San Polo all duplicate each other's street names. The numerous vaporetto lines can be bewildering, and often the only option for getting where you want to go is to walk. Yellow signs, posted on many busy corners, point toward the major landmarks—San Marco, Rialto, Accademia, etc.—but don't count on finding such markers once you're deep into residential neighborhoods. Even buying a good map at a newsstand—the kind showing all street names and vaporetto routes—won't necessarily keep you from getting lost.

Fortunately, as long as you maintain your patience, getting lost in Venice can be a pleasure. For one thing, being lost is a sign that you've escaped the tourist throngs. And although you might not find the Titian masterpiece you'd set out to see, instead you could wind up coming across an ageless bacaro or a quirky shop that turns out to be the highlight of your afternoon. Opportunities for such serendipity abound. Keep in mind that the city is nothing if not self-contained: sooner or later, perhaps with the help of a patient native, you can rest assured you'll regain your bearings.

varini (circa 1415–84) triptych of Sts. Girolamo, Bernardino da Siena, and Ludovico, which hangs to your right as you enter the main door, and Giovanni Bellini's *Madonna with Saints* inside the Cappella Santa. Antonio da Negroponte's glittering gold *Madonna Adoring the Child,* near the side door, is an inspiring work of the late 15th century. Here you'll see the transition from formal Gothic rigidity to naturalistic Renaissance composition and detailed decoration. Two cloisters open out from the left aisle, paved entirely with VIP tombstones. ⊠ *Campo San Francesco della Vigna, Castello* ☎ *041/5206102* 🎫 *Free* ☉ *Daily 8–12:30 and 3–7* Ⓥ *Celestia.*

❸❻ **San Pietro di Castello.** This church's stark campanile, the first in Venice built from marblelike Istrian stone, stands out against the picturesque, workaday slips along the Canale di San Pietro and the Renaissance cloister, which for years was a squatters' colony. The Veneti settled on the island where the church is located years before Venice was officially founded, but today it's a sleepy, almost forgotten place, with little to suggest that for 1,000 years the church was Venice's cathedral—until the Basilica di San Marco superseded it in 1807. The interior has some minor 17th-century art and San Pietro's ancient *cattedra* (throne). ⊠ *Campo San Pietro, Castello* ☎ *041/2750462 Chorus* 🎫 *€2.50, Chorus pass €8* ☉ *Mon.–Sat. 10–5, Sun. 1–5* Ⓥ *San Pietro di Castello/Giardini.*

❷❽ **Santa Maria Formosa.** Guided by his vision of a beautiful Madonna, 7th-century St. Magno is said to have followed a small white cloud and built a church where it settled. Gracefully white, the marble building you see today dates from 1492, built by Mauro Codussi on an older foundation. The interior is a blend of Renaissance decoration, a Byzantine cupola, barrel vaults, and narrow-columned screens. Of interest are two fine paintings: *Our Lady of Mercy* by Bartolomeo Vivarini and *Santa Barbara* by Palma il Vecchio. The surrounding square bustles

with sidewalk cafés and a produce market on weekday mornings. ⊠ *Campo Santa Maria Formosa, Castello* ☎ *041/5234645, 041/2750462 Chorus* ⌦ *€2.50, Chorus pass €8* ☉ *Mon.–Sat. 10–5, Sun. 1–5* Ⓥ *Rialto.*

🞉 **Scuola di San Giorgio degli Schiavoni.** Founded in 1451 by the Dalmatian community, this small scuola was, and still is, a social and cultural center for migrants from what is now Croatia. It's dominated by one of Italy's most beautiful rooms, lavishly yet harmoniously decorated with the *teleri* (large canvases) of Vittore Carpaccio. A lifelong Venice resident, Carpaccio painted legendary and religious figures against backgrounds of Venetian architecture. Here he focused on saints especially venerated in Dalmatia: St. George, St. Tryphone, and St. Jerome. He combined observation with fantasy, a sense of warm color with a sense of humor (don't miss the priests fleeing St. Jerome's lion, or the body parts in the dragon's lair). ⊠ *Calle dei Furlani, Castello 3259/a* ☎ *041/5228828* ⌦ *€3* ☉ *Apr.–Oct., Tues.–Sat. 9:30–12:30 and 3:30–6.30, Sun. 9:30–12:30; Nov.–Mar., Tues.–Sat. 10–12:30 and 3–6, Sun. 10–12:30; last entry ½ hr before closing* Ⓥ *Arsenale/San Zaccaria.*

San Giorgio Maggiore & the Giudecca

Beckoning travelers across St. Mark's Basin, sparkling white through the mist, is the island of San Giorgio Maggiore, separated by a small channel from the Giudecca. A tall brick campanile on that distant bank perfectly complements the Campanile of San Marco. Beneath it looms the stately dome of one of Venice's greatest churches, San Giorgio Maggiore, the creation of Andrea Palladio.

You can reach San Giorgio Maggiore via vaporetto Line 82 from San Zaccaria. The next three stops on the line take you to the Giudecca. The island's past may be shrouded in mystery, but today it's about as down to earth as you can get and one of the city's few remaining neighborhoods that feels truly Venetian.

Timing

A half day should be plenty of time to visit the area. Allow about a half hour to see each of the churches, and an hour or two to look around the Giudecca.

The Main Attractions

Giudecca. The island's name is something of a mystery. It may come from a possible 14th-century Jewish settlement, or because 9th-century nobles condemned to *giudicato* (exile) were sent here. It became a pleasure garden for wealthy Venetians during the republic's long and luxurious decline, but today, like Cannaregio, it's largely working class. The Giudecca provides spectacular views of Venice and is becoming increasingly gentrified. While here, visit the **Santissimo Redentore** church, designed by Palladio and built to commemorate a plague. The third weekend in July it's the site of the Venetians' favorite festival, Redentore, featuring boats, fireworks, and outdoor feasting. Thanks to several bridges, you can walk the entire length of the Giudecca's promenade, relaxing at one of several restaurants or just taking in the lively atmosphere. Accommodations run the gamut from youth hostels to the city's most exclusive hotel, Cipriani. ⊠ *Fondamenta San Giacomo, Giudecca* ☎ *041/5231415, 041/2750462 Chorus* ◈ *€2.50, Chorus pass €8* ◷ *Mon.–Sat. 10–5, Sun. 1–5* Ⓥ *Redentore.*

San Giorgio Maggiore. There's been a church on this island since the 8th century, with a Benedictine monastery added in the 10th century (closed to the public). Today's refreshingly airy and simply decorated church of brick and white marble was begun in 1566 by Palladio and displays his architectural hallmarks of mathematical harmony and classical influence. *The Last Supper* and the *Gathering of Manna,* two of Tintoretto's later works, line the chancel. To the right of the entrance hangs *The Adoration of the Shepherds* by Jacopo Bassano (1517–92); his affection for his foothills home, Bassano del Grappa, is evident in the bucolic subjects and terra-firma colors he chooses. The monks are happy to show Carpaccio's *St. George and the Dragon,* hanging in a private room, if they have time. The campanile is so tall that it was struck by lightning in 1993. Take the elevator to the top for some of the finest views in town. ⊠ *Isola di San Giorgio Maggiore* ☎ *041/5227827* ◈ *Church free, campanile €3* ◷ *Daily 9–12:30 and 2:30–6* Ⓥ *San Giorgio.*

Islands of the Lagoon

The perfect vacation from your Venetian vacation is an escape to Murano, Burano, and sleepy Torcello, the islands of the northern lagoon. Torcello offers greenery, breathing space, and picnic opportunities (remember to pack lunch). Burano is a toy town of houses painted in a riot of colors—blue, yellow, pink, ocher, and dark red. Visitors still love to shop here for "Venetian" lace, even though the vast majority of it is machine-made in Taiwan. Murano is renowned for its glass, but also notorious for the high-pressure sales on its factory tours, even those organized by top hotels. Vaporetto connections to Murano aren't difficult, and for the price of a boat ticket you'll buy your freedom and more time to explore. The Murano "guides" herding new arrivals follow a rotation so that factories take turns giving tours, but you can avoid the hustle by just walking away.

Timing
Hitting all the sights on all the islands takes a full day. If you limit yourself to Murano and San Michele, a half day will suffice. In summer San Zaccaria is connected to Murano by express vaporetto Line 5; the trip takes 25 minutes. In winter the local Line 41 takes about 45 minutes.

The boat leaves San Zaccaria (in front of the Savoia e Jolanda hotel) every 20 minutes, circling the east end of Venice and stopping at Fondamente Nuove before making the 5-minute hop to the San Michele island cemetery and then heading on to Murano. To see glassblowing, get off at Colonna; the Museo stop will put you near the Museo Vetrario.

Line LN goes from Fondamente Nuove direct to Murano, Burano, and Torcello every 30 minutes, and the full trip takes 45 minutes each way. To get to Burano and Torcello from Murano, pick up Line LN at the Faro stop (Murano's lighthouse), which runs to Burano before continuing on to Torcello, only five minutes away.

The Main Attractions

★ ❸❾ **Burano.** Cheerfully painted houses line the canals of this quiet village where lace making rescued a faltering fishing-based economy centuries ago. As you walk the 100 yards from the dock to Piazza Galuppi, the main square, you pass stall after stall of lace vendors. These good-natured ladies won't press you with a hard sell, but don't expect precise product information or great bargains—real handmade Burano lace costs $1,000 to $2,000 for a 10-inch doily.

The **Museo del Merletto** (Lace Museum) lets you marvel at the intricacies of Burano's lace making. It's also a skills center—more sewing circle than school—where on weekdays you'll usually find women carrying on the tradition. They

> **WORD OF MOUTH**
>
> "A ferry ride (cheap) to Burano is a great way to see how the average person outside the city lives and works. Yes, lace is very expensive, but you can always just look, and you can even watch a woman making it by hand in a store window. Pretty, colorful homes, more canals. Have lunch on a canal. It's laid back and just darn nice."
> –Carole

sometimes have authentic pieces for sale privately. ✉ *Piazza Galuppi 187* ☎ *041/730034* 🎫 *€4, €6 with Museo Vetrario; Musei Civici pass €18* ☉ *Apr.–Oct., Wed.–Mon. 10–5; Nov.–Mar., Wed.–Mon. 10–4* Ⓥ *Burano.*

☾ ❸❽ **Murano.** As in Venice, bridges here link a number of small islands, which are dotted with houses that once were workmen's cottages. In the 13th century the republic, concerned about fire hazard, moved its glassworks to Murano, and today you can visit the factories and watch glass being made. Many of them line the Fondamenta dei Vetrai, the canal-side walkway leading from the Colonna vaporetto landing.

Before you reach Murano's Grand Canal (a little more than 800 feet from the landing) you'll pass **Chiesa di San Pietro Martire.** Reconstructed in the 16th century, it houses Giovanni Bellini's *Madonna and Child* and Veronese's *St. Jerome.* ✉ *Fondamenta dei Vetrai* ☎ *041/739704* ☉ *Mon.–Sat. 9–noon and 3–6, Sun. 3–6* Ⓥ *Colonna.*

The collection at the **Museo Vetrario** (Glass Museum) ranges from priceless antiques to only slightly less-expensive modern pieces. You'll see authentic Venetian styles and patterns, including the famous Barovier wedding cup (1470–80). ✉ *Fondamenta Giustinian 8* ☎ *041/739586*

Venetian Lagoon

Mestre
A27
A4
S14
S245
S11
A4
S11
S309
S309

Aeroporto
Marco Polo

Torcello
40

39 Burano

38 Murano

PUNTA SABBIONI
Cavallino

37
Punta Sabbioni

Malcontenta

San Michele

S.M. ELISABETTA

Venice

Lido

Malamocco

Alberoni

Golfo di Venezia

Laguna Veneta

Pellestrina

Chioggia

0   4 miles
0   6 km

5

📷 *€4, €6 with Museo del Merletto; Musei Civici pass €18 🕐 Apr.–Oct., Thurs.–Tues. 10–5; Nov.–Mar., Thurs.–Tues. 10–4; last tickets sold ½ hr before closing* **V** *Museo.*

The **Basilica dei Santi Maria e Donato,** just past the glass museum, is among the first churches founded by the lagoon's original inhabitants. The elaborate mosaic pavement includes the date 1140; its ship's-keel roof and Veneto-Byzantine columns add to the semblance of an ancient temple. ✉ *Fondamenta Giustinian* ☎ *041/739056* 📷 *Free* 🕐 *Mon.–Sat. 8–noon and 4–6, Sun. 2–6* **V** *Museo.*

★ **40** **Torcello.** In their flight from barbarians 1,500 years ago, the first Venetians landed here, prospering even after many left to found the city of Venice. As malaria took its toll and the island's wool manufacturing was priced out of the market, Torcello became a ghost town. In the 16th century there were 10 churches and 20,000 inhabitants; today you'll be lucky to see one of the island's 16 permanent residents.

Santa Maria Assunta was built in the 11th century, and Torcello's wealth at the time is evident in the church's high-quality Byzantine mosaics. The massive *Last Judgment* shows sinners writhing in pain, while opposite, above the altar, the Madonna looks calmly down from her field of gold. Ask to see the inscription dated 639 and a sample of mosaic pavement from the original church. The adjacent **Santa Fosca** church, added when the body of the saint arrived in 1011, is still used for religious services. It's worth making the climb up the adjacent **Campanile** for an incomparable view of the lagoon wetlands. ✉ *Torcello* ☎ *041/730119* 🎫 *Santa Maria Assunta €3, Campanile €3* 🕐 *Basilica Mar.–Oct., daily 10:30–6; Nov.–Feb., daily 10–5. Campanile Mar.–Oct., daily 10:30–5:30; Nov.–Feb., daily 10–4:30. Last entry ½ hr before closing* Ⓥ *Torcello.*

NEED A BREAK?

Locanda Cipriani (☎ 041/730150), closed Tuesday and January, is famous for good food and its connection to Ernest Hemingway, who often came to Torcello seeking solitude. Today the restaurant (not to be confused with the Giudecca's Cipriani hotel) is busy, with well-heeled customers speeding in for lunch (dinner also on weekends). Dining is pricey, but you can relax in the garden with just a glass of prosecco.

Also Worth Seeing

㊲ San Michele. This cypress-lined island is home to the pretty Renaissance church of **San Michele in Isola**—and to some of Venice's most illustrious deceased. The church was designed by Codussi; the graves include those of poet Ezra Pound (1885–1972), impresario and art critic Sergey Diaghilev (1872–1929), and composer Igor Stravinsky (1882–1971). Surrounded by the living sounds of Venice's lagoon, this would seem the perfect final resting place. However, these days newcomers are exhumed after 10 years and transferred to a less-grandiose location. ☎ *041/7292811* 🎫 *Free* 🕐 *Apr.–Sept., daily 7:30–6; Oct.–Mar., daily 7:30–4* Ⓥ *San Michele.*

WHERE TO EAT

Updated by
Jeff Booth

The catchword in Venice, at both fancy restaurants and holes-in-the-wall, is fish, often at its tastiest when it looks like nothing you've seen before. How do you learn firsthand about the catch of the day? An early-morning visit to the Rialto's *pescheria* (fish market) is more instructive than any book.

There's no getting around the fact that Venice has more than its share of overpriced, mediocre eateries that prey on tourists. Avoid places with cajoling waiters standing outside, and beware of restaurants that don't display their prices. At the other end of the spectrum, showy *menu turistico* (tourist menu) boards make offerings clear in a dozen languages, but for the same 15–20 euros you'd spend at such places you could do better at a *bacaro* (the local version of a wine bar) making a meal of *cicchetti* (savory snacks).

Dining options in Venice range from the ultrahigh end, where jackets and ties are required, to the supercasual, where the clientele (almost all of them tourists) won't notice if you're wearing shorts. Some of Venice's swankiest restaurants—the ones that usually have only male waiters wearing white jackets and bow ties—trade on long-standing reputations and might seem a little stuffy and faded. The food at such places tends toward interpretations of international cuisine and, though often expertly prepared, can seem as old-fashioned as the waiters who serve it. On the other hand, mid-range restaurants are often more willing to break from tradition, incorporating ingredients such as ginger and wasabi in their creations.

Budget-conscious travelers, and those simply looking for a good meal in unpretentious surroundings, might want to stick to trattorias and bacari. Trattorias often serve less-highfalutin versions of classic Venetian dishes at substantially reduced prices; bacari offer lighter fare, usually eaten at the bar (though sometimes tables are available), and wine lists that offer lots of choices by the glass.

WHAT IT COSTS In euros					
	$$$$	$$$	$$	$	¢
AT DINNER	over €45	€35–€45	€25–€35	€15–€25	under €15

Prices are for a first course *(primo)*, second course *(secondo)*, and dessert *(dolce)*.

Cannaregio

$$–$$$ ✕ **A la Vecia Cavana.** The young, talented kitchen staff here creates a highly refined menu of Italian and Venetian dishes. Look for *filetti di pesce a cottura differenziata* (fish fillet, cooked on one side and quickly seared on the other), tender baby cuttlefish, and, among desserts, *gelato al basilico* (basil ice cream). The 18th-century *cavana* (boathouse) maintains its original low columns, arches, and brick walls, but has been decorated with contemporary flair. ⊠ *Rio Terà SS. Apostoli, Cannaregio 4624* ☎ *041/5287106* ⊟ *AE, DC, MC, V* ⊗ *Closed Mon., 2 wks in Jan., and Aug.* Ⓥ *Rialto/Ca' d'Oro.*

★ **$$–$$$** ✕ **Vini da Gigio.** A friendly, family-run trattoria on the quay side of a canal just off the Strada Nova, da Gigio is very popular with Venetians and other visiting Italians. They appreciate the affable service; the well-prepared homemade pasta, fish, and meat dishes; the imaginative and varied wine cellar; and the high-quality draft wine. It's good for a simple lunch at the tables in the barroom. ⊠ *Fondamenta de la Chiesa, Cannaregio 3628/a* ☎ *041/5285140* ⊟ *DC, MC, V* ⊗ *Closed Mon. and Tues., 2 wks in Jan., and 3 wks in Aug.* Ⓥ *Ca' d'Oro.*

$–$$$ ✕ **Algiubagiò.** A waterfront table is still relatively affordable here on Venice's northern Fondamente Nuove, where you can gaze out toward San Michele and Murano—on a clear day, you can even see the Dolomites. Algiubagiò has a dual personality: pizzas and big, creative salads at lunch; elegant secondi such as Angus fillets and duck with prunes and rosemary at dinner. (There are no fish on the dinner menu.) The young, friendly staff also serves ice cream, drinks, and *tramezzini* (sandwiches) all day. A table here is worth the walk. ⊠ *Fondamente Nuove, Cannaregio 5039* ☎ *041/5236084* ⊟ *MC, V* Ⓜ *Fondamente Nuove.*

$$ ✕ **Anice Stellato.** Hidden away on one of the most romantic fondamente of Cannaregio, this family-run bacaro-trattoria is the place to stop for fairly priced, great-tasting food in a part of town that doesn't teem with restaurants. The space has plenty of character: narrow columns rise from the colorful tile floor, dividing the room into cozy booths. Traditional Venetian fare is enriched with such offerings as *carpacci di pesce* (thin

EATING WELL IN VENICE

VENETIAN CUISINE is based on seafood—*granseola* (crab), *moeche* (soft-shell crab), and *seppie* or *seppioline* (cuttlefish) are all prominently featured, and trademark dishes include *sarde in saor* (fried sardines with olive oil, onions, pine nuts, and raisins) and *baccalà mantecato* (cod creamed with milk and olive oil). When served whole, fish is usually priced by the *etto* (100 grams, about ¼ pound) and can be quite expensive. Antipasti may take the form of a seafood salad, prosciutto, or pickled vegetables. As a first course, Venetians favor risotto, the creamy rice dish, prepared with vegetables or shellfish. Pasta, too, is paired with seafood sauces: *pasticcio di pesce* is pasta baked with fish, usually baccalà, and *bigoli* is a strictly local pasta shaped like short, thick spaghetti, usually served with *nero di seppia* (squid-ink sauce). A classic first course is pasta *e fagioli* (thick bean soup with pasta). Polenta (creamy cornmeal) is another pillar of regional cooking;

it's often served with *fegato alla veneziana* (calf's liver and onions).

Though it originated on the mainland, tiramisu is Venice's favorite dessert, a heavenly concoction of mascarpone (a rich, soft double-cream cheese), espresso, chocolate, and *savoiardi* (ladyfingers). Local wines are the dry white tocai and pinot grigio from the Friuli region and bubbly white prosecco, a naturally fermented sparkling wine that is a shade less dry. Popular red wines include merlot, cabernet, raboso, and refosco. You can sample all of these in Venice's *bacari* (little watering holes), a great Venetian tradition. For centuries, locals have gathered at these neighborhood spots to chat and have a glass of wine (known as an *ombra* in Venetian dialect) accompanied by *cicchetti* (snacks such as marinated fish, deep-fried vegetables, and meatballs), often substantial enough for a light meal.

slices of raw tuna, swordfish, or salmon dressed with olive oil and fragrant herbs), tagliatelle with king prawns and zucchini flowers, and several tasty fish stews. Meat dishes are also served, including a tender beef fillet stewed in Barolo wine with potatoes. ✉ *Fondamenta de la Sensa, Cannaregio 3272* ☎ *041/720744* ▬ *MC, V* ⊘ *Closed Mon., Tues., and Aug.* Ⓥ *S. Alvise.*

★ $ ✕ **Alla Vedova.** This warm trattoria not far from the Ca' d'Oro (it's also known as Trattoria Ca' d'Oro) was opened as a bacaro by the owner's great-grandparents. A Venetian terrazzo floor, old marble counter, and rustic furnishings lend a pleasant authenticity that's matched by the food and service. Cicchetti include tender *seppie roste* (grilled cuttlefish), *polpette* (meatballs), and *baccalà mantecato* (cod creamed with milk and olive oil). The house winter pasta is the *pastisso de radicio rosso* (lasagna with sausage, radicchio, and béchamel sauce). In spring the chef switches to pastisso *de asparagi* (with asparagus). ✉ *Calle del Pistor, Cannaregio 3912* ☎ *041/5285324* ▬ *No credit cards* ⊘ *Closed Thurs. No lunch Sun.* Ⓥ *Ca' d'Oro.*

Castello

★ $$$$ ✕ **Alle Testiere.** A strong local following can make it tough to get one of the 22 seats at this tiny trattoria near Campo Santa Maria Formosa. With its decidedly unglamorous ceiling fans, the place feels as informal as a bistro (or a saloon); the food, however, is much more sophisticated. Chef Bruno Gavagnin's dishes stand out for lightness and balance: try the *gnocchetti con moscardini* (little gnocchi with tender baby octopus) or the linguine with *coda di rospo* (monkfish), or inquire about the carpaccio of the day. The well-assembled wine list is particularly strong on local whites. ⊠ *Calle del Mondo Novo, Castello 5801* ☎ *041/5227220* ⚱ *Reservations essential* ▤ *MC, V* ⊘ *Closed Sun. and Mon., 3 wks in Jan. and Feb., and 4 wks in July and Aug.* Ⓥ *Rialto/San Zaccaria.*

$$$$ ✕ **Do Leoni.** The Two Lions, in the Hotel Londra Palace, is a sumptuous candlelit setting in which to sample Venetian and other Italian cuisine. The kitchen turns out creative dishes like millet soup with bacon; the seven-course €85 tasting menu utilizes such non-Italian ingredients as vanilla and ginger. The summer terrace occupies a good portion of the Riva. ⊠ *Riva degli Schiavoni, Castello 4171* ☎ *41/2700680* ⚱ *Reservations essential* ▤ *AE, DC, MC, V* Ⓥ *San Zaccaria.*

★ $–$$ ✕ **Corte Sconta.** You're close to seafood heaven at this firm favorite on the Venetian dining scene. Simple wooden tables are arranged around an open courtyard with outdoor seating in summer. You could make a meal of the seafood antipasti alone, but you'd miss out on such delights as spaghetti *neri alle capesante e zucchine* (cuttlefish-ink pasta with scallops and zucchini) and *vongole veraci spadellate allo zenzero* (clams sautéed in ginger). The house dessert is a warm zabaglione with Venetian cookies, and the house pour is a smooth, still prosecco, backed up by a good range of bottled wines. ⊠ *Calle del Pestrin, Castello 3886* ☎ *041/5227024* ⚱ *Reservations essential* ▤ *MC, V* ⊘ *Closed Sun. and Mon., 4 wks in Jan. and Feb., and 4 wks in July and Aug.* Ⓥ *Arsenale.*

$–$$ ✕ **Da Remigio.** Locals almost always fill this place, especially on the weekend (you'll need to book ahead), and it's easy to see why: the food is good, the service prompt (if sometimes rushed), and the atmosphere lively. The *canocchio bollite* (boiled, then chilled mantis shrimp) is a perfect starter, particularly when paired with an effervescent local white wine. Though the menu is strong on fish (fish risotto for two is particularly creamy), Da Remigio also turns out respectable alternatives such as the spaghetti *con porcini* (with mushrooms) and grilled meats. ⊠ *Salizzada dei Greci, Castello 3416* ☎ *041/5230089* ⚱ *Reservations essential* ▤ *AE, DC, MC, V* ⊘ *Closed Tues., 2 wks in July and Aug., and 4 wks in Dec. and Jan. No dinner Mon.* Ⓥ *Arsenale.*

Dorsoduro

$$$–$$$$ ✕ **Ai Gondolieri.** If you're tired of fish, this is the place to come—meat and food of the mainland are menu mainstays. Despite the tourist-trap name, it's a favorite with Venetians. Feast on *filetto di maiale con castraure* (pork fillet with baby artichokes), duck breast with apple and sweet onion, or more-traditional dishes from the Veneto hills such as horse meat and game, gnocchi, and polenta. The wine list is above average in

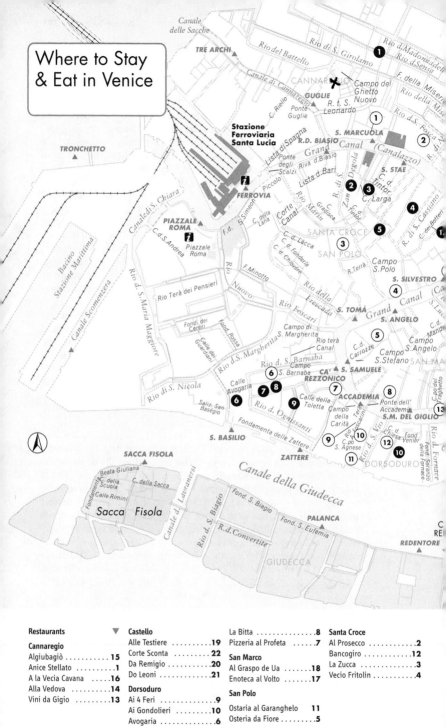

Where to Stay & Eat in Venice

Stazione Ferroviaria Santa Lucia

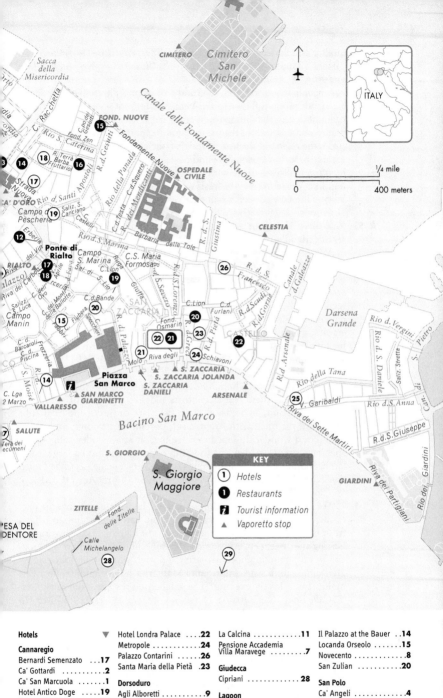

quality and variety. ⊠ *Fondamenta dell'Ospedaletto, Dorsoduro 366* ☎ *041/5286396* ⊟ *AE, DC, MC, V* ☉ *Closed Tues. No lunch in July and Aug.* Ⓥ *Accademia.*

★ **$$$–$$$$** ✕ **Avogaria.** In terms of both food and architecture, ultrafashionable Avogaria lends modern flavor to the Venice restaurant scene. The clean, elegant design of the dining room and garden leaves no doubt that here, you're in the Venice of the present, not the past. The cuisine is Pugliese (from the region in the heel of Italy's boot); highlights among the primi include *orecchiette* (small, round pasta) with turnip tops, and zucchini *involtini* (roll-ups) made with fresh stracciatella cheese. Pugliese cooking, like Venetian, reveres fresh seafood, and you can taste this sensibility in the slow-cooked, sesame-encrusted tuna steak. ⊠ *Calle Avogaria, Dorsoduro 1629* ☎ *041/2960491* ⊟ *AE, DC, MC, V* ☉ *Closed Tues.*

★ **$$** ✕ **La Bitta.** The decor is more discreet, the dining hours longer, and the service friendlier and more efficient here than in many small restaurants in Venice—and the creative nonfish menu is a temptation at every course. You can start with a light salad of Treviso radicchio and crispy bacon, followed by smoked-beef carpaccio or *gnocchetti ubriachi al Montasio* (small marinated gnocchi with Montasio cheese). Then choose from secondi such as lamb chops with thyme, *anatra in pevarada* (duck in a pepper sauce), or Irish Angus fillet steak. Secondi are served with vegetables, which helps bring down the price. The restaurant is open only for dinner, but serves much later than most, continuously from 6:30 to 11. ⊠ *Calle Lunga San Barnaba, Dorsoduro 2753/A* ☎ *041/5230531* ⊟ *No credit cards* ☉ *Closed Sun. No lunch* Ⓥ *Ca' Rezzonico.*

$–$$ ✕ **Pizzeria al Profeta.** Though Pizzeria al Profeta offers more than 100 types of pizza, their real strength is massive portions of roast and grilled meats and, on occasion, fresh fish. Two or three people can split the baked pie filled with Angus beef, porcini mushrooms, and radicchio. For a wonderfully medieval feeling, sit at a wooden table in the spacious, simple garden and use both hands to tear into a large leg of lamb. Sharing an ample dish can make this a great value. ⊠ *Calle Lunga San Barnaba, Dorsoduro 2671* ☎ *041/5237466* ⊟ *AE, DC, MC, V* ☉ *Closed Tues. in winter.*

$ ✕ **Ai 4 Feri.** The paper tablecloths and cozy, laid-back ambience are part of this small restaurant's charm. The menu varies according to what's fresh that day; imaginative combinations of ingredients in the primi— herring and sweet peppers, salmon and radicchio, giant shrimp and broccoli (with pumpkin gnocchi)—are the norm. A meal here followed by after-dinner drinks at Campo Santa Margarita, a five-minute walk away, makes for a lovely evening. The kitchen closes early on weekdays. ⊠ *Calle Lunga San Barnaba, Dorsoduro 2754/a* ☎ *041/5206978* ⊟ *No credit cards* ☉ *Closed Sun. and June* Ⓥ *Ca' Rezzonico.*

San Marco

$$$$ ✕ **Al Graspo de Ua.** Opened in the 19th century as a small osteria, the "Bunch of Grapes" became the meeting place of artists and movie stars back in the 1960s. Today it serves a faithful clientele of wealthy Italians. The decor is a miscellany of plants, sculpture, candlelight, and paintings set against brick and white-stucco walls. The owner, Lucio Zanon,

VOICES OF ITALY

Lino & Sandra Gastaldi
bacaro owners, Dorsoduro

Husband and wife Lino and Sandra Gastaldi run the *bacaro* (wine bar) Cantinone Già Schiavi, on Fondamenta Nani, across from the *squero* (gondola workshop), in Dorsoduro. Following the bacaro tradition, they serve *cicchetti*–distinctly Venetian snacks–with their wine. Lino pours and handles distribution, while Sandra makes exquisite panini and crostini. The couple works seven days a week, with assistance from three sons.

All in the family. "We have been here since 1949," Lino explains. "My father took over from the Schiavi family–we kept the name. Soon I'll retire and my sons will take over. It's always been a family-run business, and I hope it stays that way. Over the years we've continued to grow, and we have a wide range of customers–regulars who come in every day at the same time, university students who stop in for a bite before class, as well as an increasing number of foreign visitors."

Cicchetti and ombre. "I love bacari and fight to keep the tradition alive," Sandra says. "There aren't many left in Venice that still follow the tradition of cicchetti and ombre, which has been around for more than 500 years. *Il cicchetto* was the typical break taken by Venetians at about 10 o'clock in the morning. In past centuries, workers would stop and have a sandwich or piece of cheese with a small glass of wine in the shade of the bell tower in Piazza San Marco. The term *ombra*, which means "shade" or "shadow" in Italian, is the name for a glass of

wine in Venetian dialect. Nowadays people come in throughout the day–it's busiest at lunchtime and early in the evening.

"Some typical Venetian cicchetti are *baccalà mantecato*, whipped codfish served on bread, chunks of *mortadella* or salted pork meat with peppers, hard-boiled eggs served with onion, *folpeti*–tiny octopus–and *polpette*, which are deep-fried meatballs. And I love creating new cicchetti–like my tuna-and-leek spread or crostini with cheese and figs."

The bacaro state of mind. Sandra surveys Cantinone and declares, "*This* is bacaro." Her husband and sons hustle at the counter; behind them, the wall is lined with wine bottles. Customers sip, snack, and chat, creating a pleasant buzz. "People come to socialize. That's the real bacaro–you come in, have a cicchetto, and talk. It's like you're part of the family."

Despite the sociable atmosphere, bacari aren't meant for lingering–they're places for a quick bite, taken standing at the counter. "Many visitors don't understand this, and they go all the way to our storage room at the back looking for a table, or sit outside on the steps of the San Trovaso bridge. This is a definite faux pas."

But as the population of native Venetians declines, such bacaro traditions are slowly eroding. Few places meet Sandra's standards. "The only traditional bacaro is Do Mori, near the Rialto market. It's run by the Schiavi family who used to own Cantinone. The bacaro there dates back to the 15th century."

5

speaks fluent English and will introduce you to a wide-ranging menu of fresh pastas, seasonal risottos, and meat and seafood. A treat in late spring is the thick white asparagus from Bassano, which, with a couple of fried eggs, is eaten as a main course. Desserts are all homemade. ⊠ *Calle dei Bombaseri, San Marco 5094* ☎ *041/5223647* ⊟ *AE, DC, MC, V* ⊗ *Closed Mon. and 1 wk in Jan.* Ⓥ *Rialto.*

¢–$ ✕ **Enoteca al Volto.** A short walk from the Rialto Bridge, this bar has been around since 1936; the fine cicchetti and primi have a lot to do with its staying power. Two small, dark rooms with wooden tables and chairs are the backdrop for the enjoyment of simple fare. The place prides itself on its considerable wine list of both Italian and foreign vintages; if you stick to the *panini* (sandwiches) and a cicchetto or two, you'll eat well for relatively little. If you opt for one of the primi of the day, the price category goes up a notch. ⊠ *Calle Cavalli, San Marco 4081* ☎ *041/5228945* ⊟ *No credit cards* ⊗ *Closed Sun.* Ⓥ *Rialto.*

San Polo

★ $$$$ ✕ **Osteria da Fiore.** Tucked away on a little calle off the top of Campo San Polo, Da Fiore is a favorite among high-end diners for its superbly prepared Venetian cuisine and refined yet relaxed atmosphere. A superlative seafood lunch or dinner here might include delicate hors d'oeuvres of soft-shell crab, scallops, and tiny octopus, followed by a succulent risotto or pasta *con scampi e radicchio* (with shrimp and radicchio), and a perfectly cooked main course of *rombo* (turbot) or *tagliata di tonno* (tuna steak). A jacket is not required, but is highly recommended. ⊠ *Calle del Scaleter, San Polo 2202* ☎ *041/721308* ◿ *Reservations essential* ⊟ *AE, DC, MC, V* ⊗ *Closed Sun. and Mon., Aug., and Dec. 24–Jan. 15* Ⓥ *San Silvestro/San Stae.*

$–$$ ✕ **Ostaria al Garanghelo.** Superior quality, competitive prices, and great ambience means this place is often packed with Venetians, especially for lunch and an after-work *ombra* (small glass of wine) and cicchetti. Chef Renato takes full advantage of the fresh ingredients from the Rialto market, located a few steps away, and prefers cooking many dishes *al vapore* (steamed). The spicy *fagioli al uciletto* (literally beans, bird-style) has an unusual name and Tuscan origins; it's a perfect companion to a plate of fresh pasta. Don't confuse this centrally located restaurant with one of the same name in Via Garibaldi. ⊠ *Calle dei Boteri, San Polo 1570* ☎ *041/721721* ⊟ *MC, V* ⊗ *Closed Sun.*

Santa Croce

$$$ ✕ **Vecio Fritolin.** At this tidy bacaro *con cucina* (with kitchen) you can have a traditional meal featuring such dishes as *bigoli in salsa* (thick spaghetti with anchovy sauce), baked fish with herbs, and ravioli with scampi and chicory. The name, which translates as "Old Fry Shop," refers to a bygone Venetian tradition of shops selling fried fish "to go," like in London, except paired with polenta rather than chips. For €8, you can still get a paper cone of *fritto* here. ⊠ *Calle della Regina, Santa Croce 2262* ☎ *041/5222881* ⊟ *AE, DC, MC, V* ⊗ *Closed Mon.* Ⓥ *San Stae.*

$–$$$ ✕ **Bancogiro.** Come to this casual spot in the heart of the Rialto market
Fodor'sChoice in a 15th-century loggia for a change from standard Venetian food. Yes,
★ fish is on the menu, but offerings such as mousse *di gamberoni con salsa
di avocado* (shrimp mousse with an avocado sauce) and Sicilian-style
sarde incinte (stuffed, or "pregnant," sardines) are far from typical
fare—though portions can be small. The wine list and cheese plate are
both divine. There are tables upstairs in a carefully restored room with
a partial view of the Grand Canal; when it's warm you can sit outdoors
and get the full canal view. ⊠ *Campo San Giacometto, Santa Croce 122
(under the porch)* ☎ *041/5232061* ⊟ *No credit cards* ⊙ *Closed Mon.
No dinner Sun.* Ⓥ *Rialto.*

$–$$ ✕ **La Zucca.** The simple place settings, latticed-wood walls, canal window, and mélange of languages make this place feel as much like a typ-
ical vegetarian restaurant as you could expect to find in Venice. Though
the menu does have superb meat dishes such as the *piccata di pollo ai
caperi e limone con riso* (sliced chicken with capers and lemon served
with rice), more attention is paid to dishes from the garden: try the *radicchio di Treviso con funghi e scaglie di Montasio* (radicchio with mushrooms and shavings of Montasio cheese) or the *finocchi piccanti con
olive* (fennel in a spicy tomato-olive sauce). ⊠ *Calle del Tintor, Santa
Croce 1762* ☎ *041/5241570* ⚔ *Reservations essential* ⊟ *AE, DC,
MC, V* ⊙ *Closed Sun. and 1 wk in Aug.* Ⓥ *San Stae.*

¢–$$ ✕ **Al Prosecco.** Locals stream into this place, down an order of "spritz
bitter" (a combination of white wine, Campari, and seltzer water), and
continue on their way. Or they linger over a glass of one of the nu-
merous wines on offer, perhaps also tucking into a tasty panino, such
as the *porchetta romane verdure* (roasted pig, Roman style, with
greens). Proprietors Davide and Stefano preside over a young and
friendly staff who reel off the day's specials with ease. There are a few
tables in the enticing back room, and when the weather's warm you
can eat outside on the beautiful campo. ⊠ *Campo San Giacomo del-
l'Orio, Santa Croce 1503* ☎ *041/5240222* ⊟ *No credit cards* ⊙ *Closed
Sun.* Ⓥ *San Stae.*

WHERE TO STAY

Most of Venice's hotels are in renovated palaces, but space is at a pre-
mium—and comes for a price—with all Venice lodging. The most ex-
clusive hotels are indeed palatial, although even they may have some
small, dowdy rooms. In lower-price categories rooms may be cramped,
and not all hotels have lounge areas. Because of preservation laws,
some hotels are not allowed to have elevators. In summer you might
suffer the heat but unless specified otherwise, all hotels listed here have
air-conditioning. Although the city has no cars, it does have boats ply-
ing the canals and pedestrians chattering in the streets, even late at night,
so ask for a quiet room if noise bothers you. In summer don't leave your
room lights on at night *and* your window wide open: mosquitoes can
descend en masse. If you find that these creatures are a problem, ask at
your hotel's desk for a Vape, a plug-in antimosquito device.

It is *essential* to know how to get to your hotel when you arrive, as transport can range from arriving in a very expensive water taxi or gondola to wandering alleys and side streets—luggage in hand—with relapses of déjà vu. Many hotels accept reservations online; the handy Web site ⊕ www.veniceinfo.it offers free information (with photographs) about most hotels in town. It's advisable to book well in advance. If you don't have reservations, try **Venezia Si** (☎ 39/0415222264 from abroad, 199/173309 from Italy, Mon.–Sat. 9 AM–11 PM ☎ 041/5221242 ⊕ www.veneziasi.it), which offers a free reservation service over the phone. It's the public relations arm of **AVA** (Venetian Hoteliers Association) and has booths where you can make same-day reservations at **Piazzale Roma** (☎ 041/5231397 ☉ Daily 9 AM–10 PM), **Santa Lucia train station** (☎ 041/715288 or 041/715016 ☉ Daily 8 AM–9 PM), and **Marco Polo Airport** (☎ 041/5415133 ☉ Daily 9 AM–10 PM).

Prices

Venetian hotels cater to all tastes and come in all price ranges. Rates are about 20% higher than in Rome and Milan, but can be reduced by as much as half off-season (November–March, excluding Christmas and Carnevale, and also to some degree in August).

WHAT IT COSTS In euros				
$$$$	**$$$**	**$$**	**$**	**¢**
FOR 2 PEOPLE over €290	€210–€290	€140–€210	€80–€140	under €80

Prices are for two people in a standard double room in high season.

Cannaregio

★ **$$$–$$$$** 🏨 **Hotel Antico Doge.** The delightful palazzo that was once home to Doge Marino Falier has been completely modernized in elegant Venetian style, with a wealth of textiles and some fine original furnishings. Some rooms have *baldacchini* (canopied beds) and views; all have fabric walls and hardwood floors. The location is only minutes away from San Marco and the Rialto Bridge. An ample buffet breakfast is served in a room with a frescoed ceiling and a Murano chandelier. ⊠ *Campo SS. Apostoli, Cannaregio 5643, 30131* ☎ *041/2411570* ☎ *041/2443660* ⊕ *www.anticodoge.com* ⤳ *20 rooms, 1 suite* ⚡ *In-room safes, minibars, cable TV, in-room data ports, bar* ▭ *AE, DC, MC, V* ☉ *Closed 3 wks in Jan.* ⟲ *BP* Ⅴ *Ca' d'Oro.*

$$$–$$$$ 🏨 **Palazzo Abadessa.** At this palace dating to the late 16th century, you sense the passion for precious materials and luxury that's part of Venice's heritage. You ascend a majestic staircase to enter rooms decorated with antique furniture, frescoed ceilings, original stuccoes, paintings, and silk fabrics. In summer breakfast is served in the garden. ⊠ *Calle Priuli off Strada Nova Cannaregio 4011, 30131* ☎ *041/2413784* ☎ *041/5212236* ⊕ *www.abadessa.com* ⤳ *6 rooms, 7 suites* ⚡ *Cable TV, minibars, in-room safes, Wi-Fi, laundry, dry cleaning* ▭ *DC, MC, V* ⟲ *BP* Ⅴ *Ca' d'Oro.*

★ **$$** 🏨 **Ca' Gottardi.** Ca' Gottardi is one of a new generation of small hotels that dusts off traditional Venetian style and mixes in some contemporary design. The entrance, on the second floor of a Renaissance palace, is done in white marble and glass, making a graceful contrast to the Murano chandeliers and wall brocades of the guest rooms. Bathrooms are large and modern, and a rich breakfast is served in a salon that's pleasantly full of light. Location is another plus: it's just off the Grand Canal, near the Ca' d'Oro and across the canal from the Rialto markets. ⊠ *Strada Nova, Cannaregio 2283, 30121* ☎ *041/2759333* 🖨 *041/2759421* ⊕ *www. cagottardi.com* ⇄ *10 rooms, 1 suite* ⚭ *Minibars, in-room data ports, cable TV, Internet, bar, babysitting* ☰ *DC, MC, V* ¶⊙¶ *BP* Ⓥ *Ca' d'Oro.*

$ 🏨 **Bernardi Semenzato.** This is a particularly inviting little place just off Strada Nova and near the gondola ferry to the Rialto market. Some rooms have exposed ceiling beams, and some have rooftop or garden views. Practical pluses include in-room coffee- and tea-making facilities. All rooms are very basic, but those in the nearby *dipendenza* (annex) are larger with newer amenities. ⊠ *Calle dell'Oca, Cannaregio 4366, 30121* ☎ *041/ 5211052* 🖨 *041/5222424* ⊕ *www.hotelbernardi.com* ⇄ *24 rooms, 20 with bath* ⚭ *In-room safes, cable TV, Internet, some pets allowed, no-smoking rooms* ☰ *AE, DC, MC, V* ⊗ *Closed Jan.* ¶⊙¶ *BP* Ⓥ *Ca' d'Oro.*

$ 🏨 **Ca' San Marcuola.** Opened in 2002 in a busy area of shops, trattorias, and wine bars frequented by Venetians and tourists alike, this family-owned hotel stands out for its relaxed and familiar atmosphere. The comfortable rooms, all full of light and with spacious bathrooms, are furnished in a quiet Venetian mode with delicate pastel colors. An elevator that provides access to all floors and a very convenient location close to a water-bus stop on the Grand Canal make this a good choice for those with limited mobility. ⊠ *Campo San Marcuola, Cannaregio 1763, 30121* ☎ *041/716048* 🖨 *041/2759217* ⊕ *www.casanmarcuola. com* ⇄ *14 rooms* ⚭ *In-room safes, minibars, in-room data ports, cable TV, bar, Internet, concierge* ☰ *AE, DC, MC, V* ⊗ *Closed 4 wks in Dec. and Jan.* ¶⊙¶ *BP* Ⓥ *San Marcuola.*

Castello

$$$$ 🏨 **Danieli.** You'll feel like a doge in Venice's largest luxury hotel, a complex of newer buildings and a 14th-century palazzo. Sumptuous Venetian decor prevails from the moment you set foot in the soaring atrium with its sweeping staircase. Long favored by world leaders and movie stars, Danieli is predictably expensive and very elegant. The rooftop terrace restaurant has a heavenly view but unexceptional food. May through October, you have access to the pool, tennis courts, and beach of the Hotel Excelsior on the Lido via a private (free) launch running on the hour. ⊠ *Riva degli Schiavoni, Castello 4196, 30122* ☎ *041/ 5226480, 041/2961222 reservations in English* 🖨 *041/5200208* ⊕ *www. starwoodhotels.com/danieli* ⇄ *221 rooms, 12 suites* ⚭ *Restaurant, room service, in-room safes, minibars, cable TV, in-room data ports, bar, babysitting, dry cleaning, laundry service, concierge, Internet, business services, meeting rooms, some pets allowed, no-smoking rooms* ☰ *AE, DC, MC, V* ¶⊙¶ *EP* Ⓥ *San Zaccaria.*

$$$$ 🏨 **Hotel Londra Palace.** A wall of windows overlooking the lagoon and the island of San Giorgio makes this the hotel of choice for soaking up that extraordinary lagoon view—sweeping all the way from the Salute to the Lido. The downstairs restaurant is all glass, light, and water views,

and 34 rooms offer the same spectacle. The view must have been pleasing to Tchaikovsky, who wrote his 4th Symphony here in 1877. Neoclassical public rooms, with splashes of blue-and-green glass suggesting the sea, play nicely off guest rooms, which have fine fabric, damask drapes, Biedermeier furniture, and Venetian glass. The staff is top-notch, as are the restaurant and the bar. ⊠ *Riva degli Schiavoni, Castello 4171, 30122* ☎ *041/5200533* 🖷 *041/5225032* ⊕ *www.hotelondra.it* ⤴ *36 rooms, 17 suites* ⚒ *Restaurant, room service, in-room fax, in-room safes, minibars, cable TV, in-room data ports, Wi-Fi, piano bar, wine bar, babysitting, dry cleaning, laundry service, concierge, Internet, business services, meeting room* ⊟ *AE, DC, MC, V* ⍾ *BP* Ⓥ *San Zaccaria.*

$$$$ 🖾 **Metropole.** Eccentrics, eclectics, and fans of Antonio Vivaldi (who taught music here) love the Metropole, a labyrinth of unusual spaces furnished with antiques and jammed with cabinets displaying some very unusual collections indeed. The owner, a lifelong collector of odd objects, displays enough antiques to fill a dealer's shop—some of which furnish the beautifully appointed rooms. The best rooms here are up in the roof— two with spacious rooftop terraces—but only six of the standard double rooms offer lagoon views. The restaurant receives high accolades. ⊠ *Riva degli Schiavoni, Castello 4149, 30122* ☎ *041/5205044* 🖷 *041/ 5223679* ⊕ *www.hotelmetropole.com* ⤴ *43 rooms, 26 suites* ⚒ *Restaurant, room service, in-room safes, minibars, cable TV, in-room data ports, bar, babysitting, dry cleaning, laundry service, concierge, meeting room, some pets allowed* ⊟ *AE, DC, MC, V* ⍾ Ⓥ *San Zaccaria.*

$$$$ 🖾 **Palazzo Contarini della Porta di Ferro.** Formerly the residence of the Contarinis, one of the most powerful families of Venice, this late-14th-century palace has been a hotel since 2001. The building's aristocratic past shows in the elegant inner courtyard with a majestic marble staircase. All differently furnished, the spacious, light-filled rooms have high wood-beamed ceilings, and the apartments include a kitchen, dining room, and open mezzanine. The large Torcello Suite also has a wooden roof terrace from which you can take in a spectacular view of the city. On the *piano nobile* (main floor) is a large, well-appointed hall overlooking the garden; private dinners, meetings, and small conferences are sometimes held here. In sunny weather breakfast is served in the small garden. The hotel has an elevator and a private dock for boats. ⊠ *Salizzada S. Giustina, Castello 2926, 30122* ☎ *041/2770991* 🖷 *041/2777021* ⊕ *www.palazzocontarini.com* ⤴ *9 apartments* ⚒ *In-room safes, minibars, cable TV, in-room data ports, room service, babysitting, dry cleaning, Internet, concierge, some pets allowed* ⊟ *AE, MC, V* ⍾ *BP.*

$$–$$$ 🖾 **Ca' Formenta.** You're in residential rather than tourist Venice here, but the front rooms still have a wonderful lagoon view. Dating from the 15th century, the simple building underwent a complete makeover before opening in 2003 as a hotel with high-quality services, an elevator, and a canal-side entrance for guests arriving by water taxi. The 15-minute stroll along the waterfront between Piazzo San Marco and this friendly gem of a hotel is through a genuinely "local" part of the city, with plenty of cafés and restaurants. One of the rear rooms has direct access to a pleasant rooftop terrace with tables. ⊠ *Via Garibaldi, Castello 1650, 30122* ☎ *041/5285494* 🖷 *041/5204633* ⊕ *www.hotelcaformenta.it* ⤴ *14 rooms* ⚒ *In-room safes, minibars, cable TV, in-room data ports,* *laundry service, some pets allowed* ⊟ *AE, DC, MC, V* |❍| *BP* Ⓥ *Arsenale/Giardini.*

$ Ⓗ **Santa Maria della Pietà.** There's more space—both public and private—in this *casa per ferie* (vacation house) than in many four-star hotels in Venice. It occupies two historic palaces and opened as a hotel in 1999. Completely restored with Venetian terrazzo floors throughout, it has big windows and a huge rooftop terrace with a coffee shop, a bar, and unobstructed lagoon views. On top of all this, it is excellently situated—just 100 yards from the main waterfront and about 10 minutes' walk from St. Mark's—meaning you'll have to book early to stay here. The spartan rooms have only beds and wardrobes, but the shared bathrooms are plentiful, spacious, and scrupulously clean. Some family rooms with up to six beds are available. ⊠ *Calle della Pietà, Castello 3701, 30122* ☎ *041/2443639* 📠 *041/2411561* ⤳ *15 rooms* ♿ *Coffee shop, bar, lounge; no room phones, no room TVs* ⊟ *No credit cards* |❍| *BP* Ⓥ *San Zaccaria/Arsenale.*

Dorsoduro

$$$$ Ⓗ **Ca' Maria Adele.** Venice's most elegant small hotel is a mix of classic
Fodor'sChoice   style—terrazzo floors, dramatic Murano chandeliers, antique furnish-
★   ings—and touches of modern design, found in the African-wood reception area and breakfast room. Five "concept rooms" take on themes from Venetian history; the Doge's Room is draped in deep red brocades, and the Oriental Room is inspired by the travels of Marco Polo. Ca' Maria Adele's location is a quiet spot near the church of Santa Maria della Salute. ⊠ *Campo Santa Maria della Salute, Dorsoduro 111, 30123* ☎ *041/5203078* 📠 *041/5289013* ⊕ *www.camariaadele.it* ⤳ *12 rooms, 2 suites* ♿ *Bar, room service, cable TV, in-room data ports, in-room safes, minibars, babysitting, laundry service, dry cleaning, some pets allowed* ⊟ *AE, DC, MC, V* |❍| *BP* Ⓥ *Salute.*

$$$$ Ⓗ **Ca' Pisani.** Here's a breath of fresh air: a Venetian hotel with no brocades and chandeliers to be found. Instead there's a tasteful mix of modern design and well-chosen antique pieces. The entrance hall has marble floors and an interesting play of colors and lights; the rooms contain original art deco pieces from the 1930s and '40s (every bed is different). The no-smoking wine bar La Rivista serves light meals all day, and upstairs are a Turkish bath and a wooden rooftop terrace where you can take the sun. ⊠ *Rio Terà Antonio Foscarini, Dorsoduro 979/a, 30123* ☎ *041/2401411* 📠 *041/2771061* ⊕ *www.capisanihotel.it* ⤳ *25 rooms, 4 suites* ♿ *Restaurant, room service, in-room safes, minibars, cable TV with movies, in-room data ports, Turkish bath, wine bar, dry cleaning, laundry service, concierge, Internet, some pets allowed, no-smoking floor* ⊟ *AE, DC, MC, V* |❍| *BP* Ⓥ *Accademia.*

$$$–$$$$ Ⓗ **American–Dinesen.** This quiet, family-run hotel has a yellow stucco facade typical of Venetian houses. A hall decorated with reproduction antiques and Oriental rugs leads to a breakfast room reminiscent of a theater foyer, with red velvet chairs and gilt wall lamps. Rooms are spacious and tastefully furnished in sage-green and delicate pink fabrics, with lacquered Venetian-style furniture throughout. Some front rooms have terraces with canal views. A 2002 overhaul has made the place sparkle, though the four-story building still has no elevator. ⊠ *San Vio, Dorso-*

duro 628, 30123 ☎*041/5204733* 🖷*041/5204048* ⊕*www.hotelamerican. com* 🗲 *28 rooms, 2 suites* ♧ *In-room safes, minibars, cable TV, in-room data ports, babysitting, Internet, no-smoking rooms, laundry service, some pets allowed* ⊟ *AE, MC, V* ⦿❘ *BP* Ⓥ *Accademia/Salute.*

$$–$$$ 🏨 **Hotel Pausania.** From the moment you ascend the grand staircase rising above the fountain of this 14th-century palazzo, you sense the combination of good taste and modern comforts that characterizes Hotel Pausania. Light-colored rooms are spacious, with comfortable furniture and carpets strewn with rugs. Some rooms face the small canal (which can become a bit noisy early in the morning) in front of the hotel, whereas others look out over the large garden courtyard. ⊠ *Fondamenta Gherardini, Dorsoduro 2824, 30123* ☎ *041/5222083* 🖷 *041/5222989* ⊕ *www.hotelpausania.it* 🗲 *26 rooms* ♧ *Minibars, cable TV, Internet, bar, babysitting, dry cleaning, concierge, some pets allowed* ⊟ *AE, MC, V* ⦿❘ *BP* Ⓥ *Ca' Rezzonico.*

$$–$$$ 🏨 **Pensione Accademia Villa Maravege.** A secret garden awaits just be-
Fodor'sChoice yond an iron gate, complete with a mini Palladian-style villa, flower beds,
★ stone cupids, and verdant trees—all rarities in Venice. Aptly nicknamed "Villa of the Wonders," this patrician retreat once served as the Russian embassy and was the residence of Katharine Hepburn in the movie *Summertime.* Conservative rooms are outfitted with Venetian-style antiques and fine tapestry. The location is on a promontory where two side canals converge with the Grand Canal, which can be seen from the garden. Book well in advance. ⊠ *Fondamenta Bollani, Dorsoduro 1058, 30123* ☎ *041/5210188* 🖷 *041/5239152* ⊕ *www.pensioneaccademia. it* 🗲 *27 rooms* ♧ *In-room safes, minibars, cable TV, bar, babysitting, dry cleaning, laundry service* ⊟ *AE, DC, MC, V* ⦿❘ *BP* Ⓥ *Accademia.*

$$ 🏨 **Agli Alboretti.** The Alboretti is one of the many hotels clustered at the foot of the Ponte dell'Accademia. Its unpretentious, rather small rooms are blessed with plenty of light. Their nautical decor, with original pieces taken from old ships' cabins, goes well with the cries of seagulls living along the nearby Giudecca Canal. In warm weather, breakfast is served in an inner courtyard under a rose bower and a small terrace with potted plants is open. The elevator is a welcome convenience for weary travelers. ⊠ *Rio Terà Foscarini, Dorsoduro 884, 30123* ☎ *041/5230058* 🖷 *041/5210158* ⊕ *www.aglialboretti.com* 🗲 *23 rooms* ♧ *Restaurant, cable TV, Wi-Fi, bar, laundry service, concierge, some pets allowed, no-smoking rooms* ⊟ *AE, MC, V* ⦿❘ *BP* Ⓥ *Accademia.*

★ **$–$$** 🏨 **La Calcina.** The Calcina sits in an enviable position along the sunny Zattere, with front rooms offering views across the wide Giudecca Canal. You can sunbathe on the *altana* (wooden roof terrace) or enjoy an afternoon tea in one of the reading corners of the lounge with flickering candlelight and barely perceptible classical music. A stone staircase (no elevator) leads to the rooms upstairs, which have parquet floors, original art deco furniture and lamps, and firm beds. Besides full meals at lunch and dinner, the Piscina bar and restaurant offers drinks and freshly made snacks all day in the elegant dining room or on the wooden waterside terrace out front. ⊠ *Zattere, Dorsoduro 780, 30123* ☎ *041/5206466* 🖷 *041/5227045* ⊕ *www.lacalcina.com* 🗲 *27 rooms, 26 with bath; 5 suites* ♧ *Restaurant, in-room safes, minibars, cable TV* ⊟ *AE, DC, MC, V* ⦿❘ *BP* Ⓥ *Zattere.*

Giudecca

$$$$ 🏨 **Cipriani.** It's impossible to feel stressed in this oasis of stunning rooms and suites, some with garden patios. The hotel launch whisks you to Giudecca from San Marco and back at any hour; those dining at the exceptional restaurants can use it as well. Rooms of extraordinary luxury are available both in the main building and in the adjoining 16th-century-style annexes, Palazzo Vendramin and Palazzetto, which offers view across to Piazza San Marco. Prices are high even by Venetian standards, but this is the only place in town with such extensive facilities and services, from an Olympic-size pool and tennis courts to cooking courses, a beauty-and-wellness center, fitness programs, and even a vineyard. ✉ *Giudecca 10, 30133* ☎ *041/5207744* 🖷 *041/5207745* ⊕ *www.hotelcipriani.it* ↪ *46 rooms, 58 suites* ⚒ *4 restaurants, room service, in-room safes, minibars, cable TV, Wi-Fi, Internet, tennis court, saltwater pool, health club, massage, sauna, spa, bar, babysitting, dry cleaning, laundry service, concierge, meeting room* ▤ *AE, DC, MC, V* ⊗ *Main hotel closed Nov.–Mar.; Palazzo Vendramin and Palazzetto closed 4 wks in Jan. and Feb.* ¶◎¶ *BP* Ⓥ *Zitelle.*

Lagoon

$$$$ 🏨 **San Clemente Palace.** If you prefer wide-open spaces to the intimacy of Venice, this is your hotel. It occupies an entire island, about 15 minutes from Piazza San Marco by (free) shuttle launch, with acres of parkland, a swimming pool, tennis courts, a wellness center, and three restaurants. The 19th-century buildings are on the site of a 12th-century monastery, of which only the chapel remains. They form a large quadrangle and contain spacious, modern rooms. The view back to Venice with the Dolomites behind on a clear day is stunning. This hotel, opened in 2003, offers all the five-star comforts: it even has three holes of golf. ✉ *Isola di San Clemente 1, San Marco, 30124* ☎ *041/2445001* 🖷 *041/2445800* ⊕ *www.sanclemente.thi.it* ↪ *107 rooms, 96 suites* ⚒ *3 restaurants, coffee shop, in-room safes, minibars, cable TV, in-room data ports, 3-hole golf course, 2 tennis courts, pool, exercise equipment, health club, hair salon, hot tub, massage, sauna, spa, bars, shop, laundry service, convention center, meeting rooms, some pets allowed, no-smoking rooms* ▤ *AE, DC, MC, V* ¶◎¶ *BP.*

San Marco

$$$$ 🏨 **Gritti Palace.** Queen Elizabeth, Greta Garbo, and Winston Churchill all made this their Venetian address. The feeling of being in an aristocratic private home pervades this legendary hotel replete with fresh flowers, fine antiques, sumptuous appointments, and old-style service. The dining terrace on the Grand Canal is best enjoyed in the evening, when the boat traffic dies down. May through October you have access to the pool, tennis courts, and beach of the Hotel Excelsior on the Lido via a private (free) launch. ✉ *Campo Santa Maria del Giglio, San Marco 2467, 30124* ☎ *041/794611* 🖷 *041/5200942* ⊕ *www.starwoodhotels.com/grittipalace* ↪ *84 rooms, 6 suites* ⚒ *Restaurant,* *room service, in-room safes, minibars, cable TV with movies, in-room data ports, bar, babysitting, dry cleaning, laundry service, concierge, Internet, Wi-Fi, business services, meeting rooms, some pets allowed, no-smoking rooms* ⊟ *AE, DC, MC, V* ⦿ *BP* ☑ *Giglio.*

$$$$ 🏨 **Il Palazzo at the Bauer.** Il Palazzo, under the same management as the larger Bauer Hotel, is the ultimate word in luxury. Bevilacqua and Rubelli fabrics cover the walls, and no two rooms are decorated the same. What they have in common, however, are high ceilings, Murano glass, marble bathrooms, and damask drapes. Many have sweeping views. Breakfast is served on Venice's highest terrace, appropriately named Il Settimo Cielo (Seventh Heaven). The outdoor hot tub, also on the 7th floor, offers views of La Serenissima that won't quit. ⊠ *Campo San Moisè, San Marco 1413/d, 30124* ☎ *041/5207022* 🖷 *041/5207557* ⊕ *www.ilpalazzovenezia.com* 🛏 *36 rooms, 40 suites* ⚘ *Restaurant, room service, in-room fax, in-room safes, some in-room hot tubs, minibars, cable TV with movies, in-room data ports, golf privileges, health club, outdoor hot tub, massage, sauna, Turkish bath, dock, bar, babysitting, dry cleaning, laundry service, concierge, Wi-Fi, some pets allowed, no-smoking rooms* ⊟ *AE, DC, MC, V* ⦿ *EP* ☑ *Vallaresso.*

$$$ 🏨 **Locanda Orseolo.** This small hotel just behind Piazza San Marco has a friendly staff and comfortable, well-appointed rooms. Classic Venetian design is given a Carnevale theme, with each room dedicated to a traditional mask. The friendly atmosphere pervades at breakfast, where it's common to get engrossed in conversation with the other guests. ⊠ *Corte Zorzi (off Campo San Gallo), San Marco 1083, 30124* ☎ *041/5204827* 🖷 *041/5235586* ⊕ *www.locandaorseolo.com* 🛏 *15 rooms* ⚘ *In-room safes, minibars, cable TV, in-room data ports, Wi-Fi, babysitting, dry cleaning, some pets allowed* ⊟ *AE, DC, MC, V* ⦿ *BP* ☑ *Vallaresso.*

★ $$$ 🏨 **San Zulian.** A minimalist entrance hall leads to rooms that are a refined variation on the Venetian theme, with lacquered 18th-century-style furniture and parquet floors. Room 304 is on two levels and has its own delightful covered veranda. Two ground-floor rooms have bathrooms equipped for people with disabilities. The handy location near San Marco and the Rialto and the top-notch staff make a stay here eminently enjoyable. ⊠ *Campo della Guerra, San Marco 534/535, 30124* ☎ *041/5225872 or 041/5226598* 🖷 *041/5232265* ⊕ *www.hotelsanzulian.com* 🛏 *22 rooms* ⚘ *In-room safes, minibars, cable TV, some pets allowed* ⊟ *AE, DC, MC, V* ⦿ *BP* ☑ *Vallaresso/San Zaccaria.*

$$-$$$ 🏨 **Novecento.** In a quiet street just a 10-minute walk from St. Mark's Square is this small family-run hotel, opened in 2002. Inspired by the style of Mariano Fortuny, the early-1900s artist and fashion designer, the intimate rooms are a surprisingly elegant mélange of multiethnic and exotic furnishings. The Mediterranean, Indian, and Venetian fabrics, silverware, chandeliers, and furniture create a sensual turn-of-the-20th-century atmosphere. In fine weather breakfast is served in the inner courtyard. ⊠ *Calle del Dose (Campo San Maurizio), San Marco 2683/84, 30124* ☎ *041/2413765* 🖷 *041/5212145* ⊕ *www.novecento.biz* 🛏 *9 rooms* ⚘ *In-room safes, minibars, cable TV, in-room data ports,*

bar, dry cleaning, laundry service, Wi-Fi ⊟ *AE, DC, MC, V* |○| *BP* ⓥ *Santa Maria del Giglio.*

$ 🏨 **Albergo San Samuele.** Near the Grand Canal and Palazzo Grassi, this friendly hotel has clean, sunny rooms in surprisingly good shape for the price. Five of the bathrooms are relatively new, with white-and-gray-blue tiles, and the walls are painted in crisp, pleasant shades of pale pink or blue. Curtains and bedspreads are made from antique-looking fabrics, and although the furniture is of the boxy modern kind, the owners are gradually adding more-interesting-looking pieces. ⊠ *Salizzada San Samuele, San Marco 3358, 30124* ☎ *041/5228045* ⇆ *10 rooms, 7 with bath* ♿ *Fans, some pets allowed, no-smoking rooms; no a/c, no room TVs* ⊟ *No credit cards* |○| *EP* ⓥ *San Samuele.*

San Polo

$$–$$$$ 🏨 **Oltre il Giardino—Casaifrari.** It's easy to overlook (and a challenge to find) this quiet house, sheltered by a brick wall near the Frari church. Especially in high season, the six-room hotel with a pleasant garden is an oasis of peace. The prevalent white-and-pastel color scheme and elegant, understated decor contribute to the relaxed environment. The house was once the residence of Alma Mahler, widow of composer Gustav Mahler and a fascinating woman in her own right; today it still conveys her style and charm. ⊠ *San Polo 2542, 30125* ☎ *041/2750015* 🖷 *041/795452* ⊕ *www.oltreilgiardino-venezia.com* ⇆ *6 rooms* ♿ *Cable TV, minibars, safes, in-room data ports, babysitting* ⊟ *DC, MC, V* |○| *BP* ⓥ *San Tomà.*

$$$ 🏨 **Sturion.** At the end of the 13th century this building housed foreign merchants selling their wares at the Rialto, and the painter Vittore Carpaccio depicted it in his 1494 *Miracle of the Cross* (on view at the Accademia). Now it's decorated in 18th-century Venetian style and run with great care by a Venetian family. Rooms (two with views of the Grand Canal) are done in red-and-gold brocade; there's also a small but inviting breakfast room. Two rooms comfortably sleep four and are perfect for families. All rooms have tea- and coffeemakers, an uncommon feature for Italy. Be warned that the stairs are steep here (the hotel is on the 4th and 5th floors), and there's no elevator. ⊠ *Calle del Sturion, San Polo 679, 30125* ☎ *041/5236243* 🖷 *041/5228378* ⊕ *www. locandasturion.com* ⇆ *11 rooms* ♿ *In-room safes, minibars, Internet, some pets allowed, no-smoking rooms* ⊟ *MC, V* |○| *BP* ⓥ *San Silvestro/Rialto.*

$$–$$$ 🏨 **Ca' Angeli.** The former residence of a Venetian architect, located on the top floor of a palace along the Grand Canal, has been transformed by his heirs into a small, elegant hotel. It retains the classic style of its former owner—most of the furniture was his, including an 18th-century briar-wood bureau, an original icon, and 18th- and 19th-century art. A rich breakfast, including select cheese and ham from local producers, is served in a room overlooking the Grand Canal. ⊠ *Calle del Tragheto della Madoneta 1434, 30125, San Polo* ☎ *041/5232480* 🖷 *041/2417077* ⊕ *www.caaangeli.net* ⇆ *7 rooms* ♿ *In-room safes, minibars, in-room data ports, babysitting* ⊟ *DC, MC, V* |○| *BP* ⓥ *San Silvestro.*

NIGHTLIFE & THE ARTS

The Arts

A Guest in Venice, a monthly bilingual booklet free at most hotels, is your most accessible, up-to-date guide to Venice happenings. It also includes information about pharmacies, vaporetto and bus lines, and the main trains and flights. You can visit their Web site, ⊕ www. aguestinvenice.com, for a preview of musical, artistic, and sporting events. *Venezia News,* available at newsstands, has similar information but also includes in-depth articles about noteworthy events. The tourist office publishes *Leo* and *Bussola,* bimonthly brochures in Italian and English listing events and updated museum hours. *Venezia da Vivere* is a seasonal guide listing nightspots and live music. Several Venice Web sites allow you to scan the cultural horizon before you arrive; try ⊕ www.ombra.net (which has a fantastic map function to find any address in Venice), ⊕ www.veniceonline.it, and ⊕ www.venicebanana.com. Last but not least, don't ignore the posters you see everywhere in the streets. They're often the most up-to-date information you can find.

Carnevale

The first historical evidence of Carnevale (Carnival) in Venice dates from 1097, and for centuries the city marked the days preceding *quaresima* (Lent, the 40 days of abstinence leading up to Palm Sunday) with abundant feasting and wild celebrations. The word *carnival* is derived from the words for meat (*carne*) and to remove (*levare*), as eating meat was prohibited during Lent. Venice earned its international reputation as the "city of Carnevale" in the 18th century, when partying would begin right after Epiphany (January 6) and the city seemed to be one continuous decadent masquerade. With the republic's fall in 1797, the city lost a great deal of its vitality, and the tradition of Carnevale celebrations was abandoned.

Carnevale was revived in the 1970s when residents began taking to the calli and campi in their own impromptu celebrations. It didn't take long for the tourist industry to embrace the revival as a means to stimulate business during low season. The efforts were successful. Each year over the 10- to 12-day Carnevale period (ending on the Tuesday before Ash Wednesday) more than a half million people attend concerts, theater and street performances, masquerade balls, historical processions, fashion shows, and contests. *A Guest in Venice* (⊕ www.aguestinvenice.com) gives free advertising to public and private event festivities and is therefore one of the most complete Carnevale guides. For general Carnevale information, contact **Consorzio Comitato per il Carnevale di Venezia** (✉ Santa Croce 1714, 30135 ☎ 041/717065, 041/2510811 during Carnevale 🖷 041/5200410 ⊕ www.carnevale.venezia.it). The **Tourist Office** (☎ 041/5298711) has detailed information about daily events.

If you're not planning on joining in the revelry, you'd be wise to choose another time to visit Venice. Enormous crowds clog the streets (which become one-way, with police directing foot traffic), bridges are designated "no-stopping" zones to avoid gridlock, and prices absolutely skyrocket.

Festivals

The **Biennale** (⊕ www.labiennale.org) cultural institution organizes events year-round, including the Venice Film Festival, which begins the last week of August. The Biennale international exhibition of contemporary art is held in odd-numbered years, usually from mid-June to early November, at the Giardini della Biennale, and in the impressive Arsenale.

The third weekend of July, the **Festa del Redentore** (Feast of the Redeemer) commemorates the end of a 16th-century plague that killed about 47,000 city residents. Just as doges have done annually for centuries, you too can make a pilgrimage across the temporary bridge connecting the Zattere to the Giudecca. Venetians take to the water to watch fireworks at midnight, but if you can't find a boat, the Giudecca is the best place to be. Young people traditionally greet sunrise on the Lido beach while their elders attend church.

Music

Although there are occasional jazz and Italian pop concerts in clubs around town, the vast majority of music you'll hear is classical, with Venice's famed composer, Vivaldi, frequently featured. A number of churches and palazzi regularly host concerts, as do the Ca' Rezzonico and Querini-Stampalia museums. You'll find these events listed in publications such as *A Guest in Venice*; also try asking the tourist information office or your concierge. The **Vela Call Center** (☎ 041/2424 ☉ Daily 8–8) has information about musical events, and you can buy tickets at Vela sales offices in Piazzale Roma, Ferrovia, and Calle dei Fuseri (a 10-minute walk from San Marco). (When busy, the Vela Call Center number doesn't give a signal, but instead is silent.)

The travel agency **Kele & Teo** (✉ Ponte dei Bareteri, San Marco 4930 ☎ 041/5208722) has tickets for a number of venues and is conveniently located midway between Rialto and San Marco.

Opera

Teatro La Fenice (✉ Campo San Fantin, San Marco ☎ 041/786511 ⊕ www.teatrolafenice.it), one of Italy's oldest opera houses, has witnessed many memorable premieres, including the 1853 first-night flop of Verdi's *La Traviata*. It's also had its share of disasters, the most recent being a terrible fire, deliberately set in January 1996. It was completely and luxuriously restored, and reopened to great fanfare in 2004. Visit the Fenice Web site for a schedule of performances and to buy tickets.

Nightlife

Piazza San Marco is a popular meeting place in nice weather, when the cafés stay open late and all seem to be competing to offer the best live music. The younger crowd, Venetians and visitors alike, tends to gravitate toward the area around Rialto Bridge, with Campi San Bartolomeo and San Luca on one side and Campo Rialto Nuovo on the other. Especially popular with university students are the bars along Cannaregio's Fondamenta della Misericordia and around Campo Santa Margarita and San Pantalon. Pick up a booklet of *2Night* or visit their Web site ⊕ www.2night.it for nightlife listings and reviews.

Bars

L'Olandese Volante (⊠ Campo San Lio near Rialto ☎ 041/5289349) is a popular hangout for many young Venetians. Nothing special by day, **Bar Torino** (⊠ Campo San Lucaz ☎ 041/5223914) is one of Venice's liveliest nightspots, open late and spilling out onto the campo in summer. **Bácaro Jazz** (⊠ Across from Rialto Post Office ☎ 041/5285249) has music (not usually live) and meals until 2 AM, and its gregarious staff is unlikely to let you feel lonely. The **Martini Scala Club** (⊠ Campo San Fantin, San Marco 1983 ☎ 041/5224121), the Antico Martini restaurant's elegant bar, has live music from 10 PM to 3:30 AM. Full meals are served until 2 AM.

> ### WORD OF MOUTH
>
> "Piazza San Marco is a unique and romantic experience at night—with the beautiful architecture and orchestras playing, it's like traveling back in time a few centuries. The cost is free—unless you want to sit outside at one of the famous and historic cafés, in which case you will pay a hefty price for a drink."
>
> –Nicole

One of the newest and hippest bars for the late-night chill-out crowd, **Centrale** (⊠ Piscina Frezzeria, San Marco 1659/B ☎ 041/2960664) is in a former movie theater—and the crowd does look more Hollywood than Venice. Excellent mojitos and other mixed drinks, black-leather couches, and dim lighting strike a loungey note, and the DJ keeps the beats cool.

Campo Santa Margarita is a student hangout all day and late into the night. Try **Orange** (⊠ Campo Santa Margarita, Dorsoduro 3054/a ☎ 041/5234740) for sandwiches, drinks, and soccer games on a massive screen. The bohemian **Il Caffè** (⊠ Campo Santa Margarita, Dorsoduro 2963 ☎ 041/5287998), also known as Caffè Rosso for its red exterior, is especially popular in nice weather.

Casinos

The city-run gambling casino in the splendid **Palazzo Vendramin-Calergi** is a classic scene of well-dressed high-rollers playing French roulette, Caribbean poker, chemin de fer, 30–40, and slots. You must be 18 to enter, and men must wear jackets; no tennis shoes allowed. ⊠ *Cannaregio 2040* ☎ *041/5297111* 🎫 *€10 entry includes €10 in chips* ⊙ *Slots 2:45 PM–2:30 AM, tables 3:30 PM–2:30 AM* Ⓥ *San Marcuola.*

Mestre's **Ca' Noghera** casino, near the airport, has slots, blackjack, craps, poker, and roulette. Minimum age is 18. There's a free shuttle bus from Piazzale Roma from 4:05 PM until closing. ⊠ *Via Triestina 222, Tessera, Mestre* ☎ *041/5297111* 🎫 *€10 entry includes €10 in chips* ⊙ *Slots 11 AM–3:30 AM, tables 3:30 PM–3:30 AM.*

Nightclubs

Dancing and clubbing is a hard find on the Venetian islands, so your best bets are on the *terra firma*. **Magic Bus** (⊠ Via delle Industrie, 118, 2nd Industrial Zone, Marcon ☎ 041/5952151) is an alternative rock club with pop art walls and zebra-stripe floors. It showcases new and established European acts every weekend.

Claiming to be Venice's only "real" disco club, **Casanova** (✉ Lista di Spagna, Cannaregio 158/a ☎ 041/2750199) undeniably has the largest dance floor. With Internet points, student-night specials, and no cover charge, it attracts mostly foreign students and some young Venetians.

SPORTS

Beaches
Those looking for a cooling break in summer should head for the **Lido** (🅥 S. M. Elisabetta). Large sections of the long, narrow beach are private, renting chairs and umbrellas and offering toilets, showers, and restaurants. If your hotel has no beach rights, you can pay for entry. The free beach areas, with no facilities, are generally crowded unless you head south by bus toward Malamocco and Alberoni.

Running
The most scenic running route (6–7 km [4–4½ mi] long) heads east from Piazza San Marco and skirts the lagoon along the Riva degli Schiavoni to the pinewood of Sant'Elena. You can return by way of the picturesque neighborhood of Castello and the island of San Pietro di Castello. This route can get packed with pedestrians from spring through fall, so if you don't want to run a slalom course, try the Lido beach or the area around the Zattere.

SHOPPING

Updated by
Pamela Santini

Alluring shops abound in Venice. You'll find countless vendors of trademark Venetian wares such as glass and lace; the authenticity of some goods can be suspect, but they're often pleasing to the eye regardless of their place of origin. For more-sophisticated tastes (and deeper pockets), there are jewelers, antiques dealers, and high-fashion boutiques on a par with those in Italy's larger cities but often maintaining a uniquely Venetian flair. There are also some interesting craft and art studios, where you can find high-quality, one-of-a-kind articles, from handmade shoes to decorative lamps and mirrors.

It's always a good idea to mark on your map the location of a shop that interests you; otherwise you may not be able to find it again in the maze of tiny streets. Regular store hours are usually 9–12:30 and 3:30 or 4–7:30; some stores are closed Saturday afternoon or Monday morning. Food shops are open 8–1 and 5–7:30, and are closed Wednesday afternoon and all day Sunday. Many tourist-oriented shops are open all day, every day. Some shops close for both a summer and a winter vacation.

Food Markets

The morning open-air fruit-and-vegetable market at **Rialto** offers animated local color and commerce. On Tuesday through Saturday mornings the **fish market** (adjacent to the Rialto produce market) provides an impressive lesson in ichthyology, with species you've probably never seen before. In the Castello district you'll find a lively food market weekday mornings on **Via Garibaldi**.

Shopping Districts

The **San Marco** area is full of shops and couture boutiques such as Armani, Missoni, Valentino, Fendi, and Versace. **Le Mercerie,** along with the Frezzeria and Calle dei Fabbri, leading from Piazza San Marco, are some of Venice's busiest shopping streets. Other good shopping areas surround Calle del Teatro and Campi San Salvador, Manin, San Fantin, and San Bartolomeo. Less-expensive shops are between the Rialto Bridge and San Polo.

Specialty Stores

Glassware

Glass, most of it made in Murano, is Venice's number one product, and you'll be confronted by mind-boggling displays of traditional and contemporary glassware, much of it kitsch. Take your time and be selective. You will probably find that prices in Venice's shops and the showrooms of Murano's factories are pretty much the same. However, because of competition, shops in Venice with wares from various glassworks may charge slightly less.

Domus (⊠ Fondamenta dei Vetrai, Murano 82 ☎ 041/739215) has a selection of smaller objects and jewelry from the best glassworks.

For chic, contemporary glassware, Carlo Moretti is a good choice; his designs are on display at **L'Isola** (⊠ Campo San Moisè, San Marco 1468 ☎ 041/5231973 ⊕ www.carlomoretti.com). **Marina Barovier** (⊠ Calle delle Botteghe off Campo Santo Stefano, San Marco 3216 ☎ 041/5236748 ⊕ www.barovier.it) has an excellent selection of contemporary collectors' glass.

Go to Michel Paciello's **Paropàmiso** (⊠ Frezzeria, San Marco 1701 ☎ 041/5227120) for stunning Venetian glass beads and traditional jewelry from all over the world. **Pauly** (⊠ Piazza San Marco 73, 77, and 316; Ponte dei Consorzi ☎ 041/5209899 ⊕ www.paulyglassfactory.com) has four centrally located shops with an impressive selection of glassware at better prices than for Murano. **Venini** (⊠ Piazzetta dei Leoncini 314, San Marco ☎ 041/5224045 ⊕ www.venini.com) has been an institution since the 1930s, attracting some of the foremost names in glass design.

Lace & Fabrics

Much of the lace and embroidered linen sold in Venice and on Burano is really made in China or Taiwan. However, at **Il Merletto** (⊠ Sotoportego del Cavalletto, under the Procuratie Vecchie, Piazza San Marco 95 ☎ 041/5208406), you can ask for the authentic, handmade lace kept in the drawers behind the counter. This is the only place in Venice connected with the students of the Scuola del Merletto in Burano, who, officially, do not sell to the public. Hours of operation are daily 10 to 5. A top address for linen is **Jesurum** (⊠ Cannaregio 3219, Fondamenta della Sensa ☎ 041/5242540 ⊕ www.jesurum.it).

Go to **Lorenzo Rubelli** (⊠ Palazzo Corner Spinelli, San Marco 3877 ☎ 041/5284411 ⊕ www.rubelli.it) for the same brocades, damasks, and cut velvets used by the world's most prestigious decorators. **Venetia**

Venetian Masks Revealed

IN THE TIME OF THE REPUBLIC, the mask trade was vibrant—Venetians wore masks all year to go about town incognito. Napoléon suppressed their use, a by-product of his effort to end Carnevale, and when Carnevale was revived in the late 1970s, mask making returned as well. Though many workshops use centuries-old techniques, none has been in business for more than 30 years.

A landmark date in the history of Venetian masks is 1436, when the *mascareri* (mask makers) founded their guild, but masks were popular well before then. Laws regulating their use appeared as early as 1268, intended to prevent wearers from carrying weapons and masked men disguised as women from entering convents to seduce nuns.

In the 18th century, masks started being used by actors playing the traditional roles of the commedia dell'arte. Inexpensive papier-mâché versions of these masks can be found everywhere. The character Arlecchino has the round face and surprised expression, Pantalone is the one with the curved nose and long mustache, and Pulcinella has the protruding nose.

The least-expensive mask is the white Bauta, smooth and plain with a short, pointed nose intended to disguise the wearer's voice; in the 18th century it was commonly accompanied by a black three-cornered hat and a black cloak. The pretty Gnaga, which resembles a cat's face, was used by gay men to "meow" proposals to good-looking boys. The basic Moretta is a black oval with eyeholes. The Medico della Peste (the Plague Doctor) has a beaklike nose and glasses; during the plague of 1630 and 1631, doctors wore masks with herbs inside the nose intended to filter infected air and glasses to protect the eyes.

5

Studium (⊠ Calle Larga XXII Marzo, San Marco 2403 ☎ 041/5229281 ⊠ Calle Larga XXII Marzo, San Marco 723 ☎ 041/5229859 ⊕ www. venetiastudium.com) sells silk scarves, bags, and cushion covers, as well as the famous Fortuny lamps.

Lamps

The studio **A Mano** (⊠ Rio Terà, San Polo 2616 ☎ 041/715742), near the Frari, is worth hunting down. Alessandro Savadori makes imaginative table, wall, and ceiling lamps that may well cross the boundary from craft into art.

Masks

Guerrino Lovato, proprietor of **Mondonovo** (⊠ Rio Terà Canal, Dorsoduro 3063 ☎ 041/5287344 ⊕ www.mondonovomaschere.it) is one of the most respected mask makers in town. He was called on to oversee reconstruction of reliefs and sculptures in Teatro La Fenice after it burned to the ground in 1996.

Shoes

Fine shoes and boots are handmade to order at **Daniela Ghezzo, Segalin a Venezia** (⊠ Calle dei Fuseri, San Marco 4365 ☎ 041/5222115), operated by one of the city's two female shoemakers. Ghezzo carries on the tradition established by the renowned Rolando Segalin.

Giovanna Zanella (✉ Calle Carminati, Castello 5641 ☎ 041/5235500) creates custom-made footwear with daring color combinations and unique styles. Her accessories make a statement as well.

VENICE ESSENTIALS

Transportation

BY AIR

Venice's Aeroporto Marco Polo is served by domestic and international flights, including connections from 21 European cities, plus direct flights from Moscow and New York's JFK. In addition, Treviso Airport, some 32 km (20 mi) north of Venice, receives daily arrivals from London's Stansted Airport.

A shuttle bus or 10-minute walk takes you from Marco Polo's terminal to a dock where public and private boats are available to deliver you directly to Venice's historic center. For €10 per person, including bags, Alilaguna operates regularly scheduled service from predawn until nearly midnight. It takes about an hour to reach the landing near Piazza San Marco, stopping at the Lido on the way. A *motoscafo* (water taxi) carries up to four people and four bags to the city center in a sleek, modern powerboat. The base cost is €80, and the trip takes about 25 minutes. Each additional person, bag, and stop costs extra, so it's essential to agree on a fare before boarding.

Blue ATVO buses take 20 minutes to make the nonstop trip from the airport to Piazzale Roma; from here you can get a vaporetto to the landing nearest your hotel. The ATVO fare is €3, and tickets are available on the bus when the airport ticket booth (open daily 9 to 7:30) is closed. Orange ACTV local buses (Line 5) leave for Venice at 10 and 40 minutes past every hour (hourly service after 11:10 PM) and take 30 minutes; before boarding, you must buy a €2 ticket at the airport tobacconist-newsstand, open daily 6:30 AM to 9 PM, or from the ATVO/ACTV booth in the arrivals hall on the ground floor. During rush hour, luggage can be a hassle on the local bus. A land taxi from the airport to Piazzale Roma costs about €40.

🚹 **Airport Information Aeroporto Marco Polo** ✉ Tessera, 10 km (6 mi) north of the city on the mainland ☎ 041/2609260 ⊕ www.veniceairport.it.

🚹 **Taxis & Shuttles Alilaguna** ☎ 041/5235775 ⊕ www.alilaguna.it. **ATVO** ☎ 0421/383672 ⊕ www.atvo.it. **Motoscafo** ☎ 041/5222303 airport transfers. **Radio Taxi** ☎ 041/5952080.

BY BOAT & FERRY

BY GONDOLA It's hard to believe that Venice could get any more beautiful, but as your gondola glides away from the fondamenta, a magical transformation takes place—you've left the huddled masses behind to marvel at the city as visitors have for centuries before you. To some it feels like a Disney ride, and some complain about flotsam, jetsam, and less-than-pleasant odors, but if you insist that your gondolier take you winding through the tiny side canals, you'll get out of the city's main sa[...] intimate chambers, where only private boats can go. [...] loaded with gondola stations, but to get off the circuit, a[...] have a canal to yourself, try the San Tomà or Santa Sofia ([...]) stations. The price of a 40-minute ride is supposed to b[...] for up to six passengers, rising to €95 between 7:30 PM and 8 AM, but these are minimums and you may have difficulty finding a gondolier who will work for that unless the city is empty. Bargaining can help, but in any case come to terms on cost and duration before you start, and make it clear that you want to see more than just the Grand Canal.

BY TRAGHETTO Many tourists are unaware of the two-man gondola ferries that cross the Grand Canal at numerous strategic points. At €0.50, they're the cheapest and shortest gondola ride in Venice, and they can save a lot of walking. Look for TRAGHETTO signs and hand your fare to the gondolier when you board.

BY VAPORETTO ACTV water buses serve several routes daily and after 11 PM provide limited service through the night. Some routes cover the length of the Grand Canal, and others circle the city and connect Venice with the lagoon islands. Landing stages are clearly marked with name and line number, but check before boarding to make sure the boat is going in your direction.

Line 1 is the Grand Canal local, calling at every stop and continuing via San Marco to the Lido. The trip takes about 35 minutes from Ferrovia to Vallaresso, San Marco. Circular Line 41 (the odd number indicates it goes counterclockwise) will take you from San Zaccaria to Murano, and Line 42 (clockwise) makes the return trip. Likewise, take Line 42 from San Zaccaria to Giudecca's Redentore, but Line 41 to return. Line 51 (counterclockwise) runs from the station to San Zaccaria via Piazzale Roma, then continues to the Lido. From the Lido, Line 52 circles clockwise, stopping at San Zaccaria, the Zattere, Piazzale Roma, the station, Fondamente Nuove (connect to northern lagoon islands), San Pietro di Castello, and back to the Lido. From San Zaccaria, Line 82 (same number both directions) loops past Giudecca and the Zattere, then stops at Tronchetto (parking garage) on the way to Piazzale Roma and the station. From the station, Line 82 becomes the Grand Canal express to Rialto, with some boats continuing to Vallaresso (San Marco) and in summer going all the way to the Lido beaches. Line N runs from roughly midnight to 6 AM, stopping at the Lido, Vallaresso, Accademia, Rialto, the train station, Piazzale Roma, Giudecca, and San Zaccaria, then returning in the opposite direction.

BY WATER TAXI A motoscafo (water taxi) isn't cheap; you'll spend about €60 for a short trip in town, €65 to the Lido, and €85 per hour to visit the outer islands. The fare system is convoluted, with luggage handling, waiting time, early or late hours, and even ordering a taxi from your hotel adding expense. Always agree on the price first.

FARES & SCHEDULES An ACTV water bus ticket for all lines costs €5 one-way. (Children under four ride free.) Another option is Travel Cards: €12 buys 24 hours and €25 buys 72 hours of unlimited travel on ACTV boats and buses. For travelers between 14 and 29, the 72-hour pass is €15 with the Rolling

Venice card. Ask for the card (€4) before buying your tickets. A shuttle ticket allows you to cross a canal, one stop only, for €2.

Line information is posted at each landing, and complete timetables for all lines are available for €0.60 at ACTV/Vela ticket booths, located at most major stops. Buy tickets before getting on the boat and remember to validate them in the yellow time-stamp machines. Tickets are also sold on the boat; you must ask to buy one immediately upon boarding, which can be a hassle. When inspectors come aboard, ticketless riders are fined, as are those who haven't validated their tickets. Ignorance will not spare you; the fine is €25, and getting fined can be embarrassing. The law says you must also buy tickets for dogs, baby strollers left unfolded, and bags more than 28 inches long (there's no charge for your bag if you have a Travel Card), but this is generally enforced only for very bulky bags. The telephone number for ferry information listed below has assistance in English.

🚢 **Boat & Ferry Information ACTV** ☎ 041/2424 ⊕ www.hellovenezia.it or www.actv. it. **Water taxi** ☎ 041/5415084 or 041/5222303.

BY BUS
From Venice's Piazzale Roma terminal, buses connect with Mestre, the Brenta Riviera, Padua, Treviso, Cortina d'Ampezzo, and other regional destinations as well as many major European cities.

FARES & ACTV buses to Mestre (€1) are frequent, and there's night service;
SCHEDULES ACTV buses to Padua (€3.80) leave at 25 and 55 minutes past each hour and stop along the Brenta River. ATVO has daily buses to Cortina (€11) June–September and throughout the Christmas–New Year holidays. Buses leave Venice at 7:50 AM and depart from Cortina at 3:15 PM. Service is available only on weekends September–May.

🚌 **Bus Information ACTV** ☎ 041/2424 ⊕ www.actv.it. **ATVO** ☎ 0421/383671 ⊕ www. atvo.it. **Bus Terminal** ✉ Piazzale Roma across Grand Canal from train station, Santa Croce.

BY CAR
Venice is on the east–west A4 autostrada, which connects with Padua, Verona, Brescia, Milan, and Turin. If you bring a car to Venice, you will have to pay for a garage or parking space.

You can take your car to the Lido; the car ferry (Line 17) makes the half-hour trip about every 50 minutes from a landing at Tronchetto, but in summer there can be long lines. It costs €10–€20, depending on the size of the car.

PARKING Warning: don't be waylaid by illegal touts, often wearing fake uniforms, who may try to flag you down and offer to arrange parking and hotels; drive on to one of the parking garages. Parking at Autorimessa Comunale costs €20 for 24 hours. The private Garage San Marco costs €20 for up to 12 hours and €26 for 12–24 hours. You can reserve a space in advance at either of these garages; you'll come upon both immediately after crossing the bridge from the mainland. Another alternative is Tronchetto parking (€20 for 1–24 hours); watch for signs for it coming over the bridge—you'll have to turn right before you get to Piazzale Roma. Many hotels have negotiated guest discounts with San

Marco or Tronchetto garages; get a voucher when you check in at your hotel and present it when you pay the garage. Line 82 connects Tronchetto with Piazzale Roma and Piazza San Marco and also goes to the Lido in summer. When there's thick fog or extreme tides, a bus runs to Piazzale Roma instead. Avoid private boats—they're a rip-off. There's a luggage-check office, open daily 6 AM–9 PM, next to the Pullman Bar on the ground floor of the municipal garage at Piazzale Roma.

🚗 Garages **Autorimessa Comunale** ⊠ Piazzale Roma, Santa Croce, End of S11 road ☎ 041/2727211 ⊕ www.asmvenezia.it. **Garage San Marco** ⊠ Piazzale Roma 467/f, Santa Croce, Turn right into bus park ☎ 041/5232213 ⊕ www.garagesanmarco.it. **Tronchetto** ☎ 041/5207555.

BY TRAIN

Venice has rail connections with every major city in Italy and Europe. Some Continental trains do not enter Venice but stop only at the mainland Mestre station. All trains traveling to and from Venice Santa Lucia stop at Mestre, and it's just a 10-minute hop on the next passing train. If you change from a regional train to an Intercity or Eurostar, you'll need to upgrade with a *supplemento* (extra charge) or be liable for a hefty fine. You'll also be fined if before boarding you forget to validate your train ticket in one of the yellow machines found on or near platforms.

🚆 Train Information **Stazione Ferroviaria Santa Lucia** ⊠ Grand Canal, northwest corner of the city, Cannaregio ☎ 041/785670, 892021 Trenitalia train information ⊕ www. trenitalia.com. **Stazione Ferroviaria Venezia-Mestre** ⊠ Mestre, 12 km [7 mi] north-west of Venice ☎ 041/784498, 892021 Trenitalia train information ⊕ www.trenitalia.com.

Contacts & Resources

EMERGENCIES

The U.K. Consulate can recommend doctors and dentists, as can your hotel or any pharmacy. The nearest pharmacy is never far, and they take turns staying open nights, Saturday afternoons, and Sunday; the list of after-hours pharmacies is posted on the front of every pharmacy and appears in daily newspapers.

🚑 Emergency Services **General Emergencies** ☎ 113. **Ambulance** ☎ 118. **Carabinieri** ☎ 112. **U.K. Consulate** ⊠ Piazza Donatori di Sangue 2, Mestre ☎ 041/5055990.

TOURS

BOAT TOURS Boat tours to the islands of Murano, Burano, and Torcello, organized by Serenissima Motoscafi and Bucintoro Viaggi, leave from various docks around Piazza San Marco daily. The 3½-hour trip costs €19 per person with Serenissima Motoscafi. Bucintoro Viaggi charges €20 for a four-hour boat ride. Both can be annoyingly commercial, often emphasizing glass-factory showrooms and pressuring you to buy at prices even higher than normal. Trips depart at 9:30 and 2:30 April–October, at 2:30 November–March.

More than a dozen major travel agents in Venice have grouped together to provide frequent, good-quality tours of the city. Serenaded gondola trips, with or without dinner (€74, €36), can be purchased at any of their offices or at American Express. Nightly tours leave at 7:30 and

8:30 April–September, at 7:30 only in October, and at 3:30 November–March.

🅸**American Express** ✉ Salizzada San Moisè, San Marco 1471 ☎ 041/5200844 🖷 041/5229937. **Bucintoro Viaggi** ✉ Campo San Luca 4267 ☎ 041/5210632 🖷 041/2411619 ⊕ www.bucintoroviaggi.com. **Serenissima Motoscafi** ☎ 041/5224281.

PRIVATE GUIDES Cooperativa Guide Turistiche Autorizzate has a list of more than 100 licensed guides. Tours lasting about two hours with an English-speaking guide start at €124 for up to 30 people. Agree on a total price before you begin, as there can be some hidden extras. Guides are of variable quality.

🅸**Cooperativa Guide Turistiche Autorizzate** ✉ San Marco 750, near San Zulian ☎ 041/5209038 🖷 041/5210762.

TOURS OF THE REGION Various agencies offer several excursions in the Veneto region of the Venetian Arc. A boat trip to Padua along the Brenta River with Il Burchiello makes stops at three Palladian villas, and you return to Venice by bus. The tours run three times a week (Tuesday, Thursday, and Saturday) from March to October and cost €62 per person (€86 with lunch); bookings need to be made a few days in advance.

Bassani offers excursions as well as personalized travel through the Veneto and other Italian cities.

🅸**Fees & Schedules Avventure Bellissime** ✉ San Marco 2442/A ☎ 041/5208616 🖷 041/2960282 ⊕ www.tours-italy.com. **Bassani** ✉ San Basilio, Santa Marta, Fab. 17 ☎ 041/5203644 🖷 041/5204009 ⊕ www.bassani.it. **Il Burchiello** ✉ Via Orlandini 3 ☎ 049/8206910 🖷 049/8206923 ⊕ www.ilburchiello.it

WALKING TOURS More than a dozen major travel agents offer a two-hour walking tour of the San Marco area (€30), which ends with a glassblowing demonstration daily (no Sunday tour in winter). From April to October there's also an afternoon walking tour that ends with a gondola ride (€40). Venicescapes, an Italo-American cultural association, offers several themed itineraries focusing on history and culture as well as tourist sights. Their three- to seven-hour tours are private, and groups are small (generally six to eight people). Reservations are recommended during busy seasons, and prices start at €240 for two people. Walks Inside Venice also does several themed tours for small groups starting at €70 per hour and lasting up to three hours.

🅸 **Fees & Schedules Alba Travel** ✉ Calle del Magazin, San Marco 4538 ☎ 041/5210123 🖷 041/5200781 ⊕ www.albatravel.it. **Oltrex Viaggi** ✉ Castello 4192 ☎ 041/5242840 🖷 041/5221986 ⊕ www.oltrex.it. **Venicescapes** ✉ Campo San Provolo, Castello 4954 ☎☎ 041/5206361 ⊕ www.venicescapes.org. **Walks Inside Venice** ☎☎ 041/5202434 ⊕ www.walksinsidevenice.com.

VISITOR INFORMATION

The train-station branch of the Venice Tourist Office is open daily 8–6:30; other branches generally open at 9:30.

The Rolling Venice pass, costing €4 and valid throughout a calendar year, buys visitors ages 14–29 discounts on 72-hour vaporetto passes and admission to lots of museums, and at assorted hotels, restaurants, and shops. Just show your passport or ID at Vela ticket offices (major vaporetto stops), at the Assessorato alla Gioventù (weekdays 9:30–1, plus Tuesday and Thursday afternoons 3–5), or at the Associazione Italiana Alberghi per la Gioventù (Monday through Saturday 8–2). The Rolling Venice card allows you to avoid lines at city museums and prepays for vaporetti and municipal toilets. Order online or by phone and pay cash when you pick up the card. Price depends on how many days you're staying; though convenient, it's not a significant discount.

⛵ **Assessorato alla Gioventù** ✉ Corte Contarina, San Marco 1529, behind Piazza San Marco post office ☎ 041/2747651. **Associazione Italiana Alberghi per la Gioventù** ✉ Calle Castelforte, San Polo 3101, near San Rocco ☎ 041/5204414. **Rolling Venice** ☎ 041/5298711 or 041/2424 ⊕ www.venicecard.it.

Venice Tourist Offices ☎ 041/5298711 ⊕ www.turismovenezia.it ✉ Marco Polo Airport ✉ Train Station, Cannaregio ✉ Procuratie Nuove, San Marco 71/f, near Museo Correr ✉ Venice Pavilion, near Giardini Reali, San Marco ✉ Garage Comunale, Piazzale Roma ✉ S. Maria Elisabetta 6/a, Lido ⊙ Summer only.

5

ITALIAN VOCABULARY

English	Italian	Pronunciation
Basics		
Yes/no	Sí/No	see/no
Please	Per favore	pear fa-**vo**-ray
Yes, please	Sí grazie	see **grah**-tsee-ay
Thank you	Grazie	**grah**-tsee-ay
You're welcome	Prego	**pray**-go
Excuse me, sorry	Scusi	**skoo**-zee
Sorry!	Mi dispiace!	mee dis-spee-**ah**-chay
Good morning/ afternoon	Buongiorno	bwohn-**jor**-no
Good evening	Buona sera	**bwoh**-na **say**-ra
Good-bye	Arrivederci	a-ree-vah-**dare**-chee
Mr. (Sir)	Signore	see-**nyo**-ray
Mrs. (Ma'am)	Signora	see-**nyo**-ra
Miss	Signorina	see-nyo-**ree**-na
Pleased to meet you	Piacere	pee-ah-**chair**-ray
How are you?	Come sta?	**ko**-may **stah**
Very well, thanks	Bene, grazie	**ben**-ay **grah**-tsee-ay
And you?	E lei?	ay **lay**-ee
Hello (phone)	Pronto?	**proan**-to

Numbers

English	Italian	Pronunciation
one	uno	**oo**-no
two	due	**doo**-ay
three	tre	tray
four	quattro	**kwah**-tro
five	cinque	**cheen**-kway
six	sei	say
seven	sette	**set**-ay
eight	otto	**oh**-to
nine	nove	**no**-vay
ten	dieci	dee-**eh**-chee
eleven	undici	**oon**-dee-chee
twelve	dodici	**doe**-dee-chee
thirteen	tredici	**tray**-dee-chee

fourteen	quattordici	kwa-**tore**-dee-chee
fifteen	quindici	**kwin**-dee-chee
sixteen	sedici	**say**-dee-chee
seventeen	diciassette	dee-cha-**set**-ay
eighteen	diciotto	dee-**cho**-to
nineteen	diciannove	dee-cha-**no**-vay
twenty	venti	**vain**-tee
twenty-one	ventuno	vain-**too**-no
twenty-two	ventidue	vain-tee-**doo**-ay
thirty	trenta	**train**-ta
forty	quaranta	kwa-**rahn**-ta
fifty	cinquanta	cheen-**kwahn**-ta
sixty	sessanta	seh-**sahn**-ta
seventy	settanta	seh-**tahn**-ta
eighty	ottanta	o-**tahn**-ta
ninety	novanta	no-**vahn**-ta
one hundred	cento	**chen**-to
one thousand	mille	**mee**-lay
ten thousand	diecimila	dee-eh-chee-**mee**-la

Useful Phrases

Do you speak English?	Parla inglese?	**par**-la een-**glay**-zay
I don't speak Italian	Non parlo italiano	non **par**-lo ee-tal-**yah**-no
I don't understand	Non capisco	non ka-**peess**-ko
Can you please repeat?	Può ripetere?	pwo ree-**pet**-ay-ray
Slowly!	Lentamente!	**len**-ta-men-tay
I don't know	Non lo so	non lo **so**
I'm American/ British	Sono americano(a)	**so**-no a-may-ree-**kah**-no(a)
	Sono inglese	**so**-no een-**glay**-zay
What's your name?	Come si chiama?	**ko**-may see kee-**ah**-ma
My name is . . .	Mi chiamo . . .	mee kee-**ah**-mo
What time is it?	Che ore sono?	kay **o**-ray **so**-no
How?	Come?	**ko**-may
When?	Quando?	**kwan**-doe
Yesterday/today/ tomorrow	Ieri/oggi/domani	**yer**-ee/**o**-jee/ do-**mah**-nee

This morning/ afternoon	Stamattina/Oggi pomeriggio	sta-ma-**tee**-na/**o**-jee po-mer-**ee**-jo
Tonight	Stasera	sta-**ser**-a
What?	Che cosa?	kay **ko**-za
What is it?	Che cos'è?	kay ko-**zay**
Why?	Perché?	pear-**kay**
Who?	Chi?	kee
Where is . . .	Dov'è . . .	doe-**veh**
the bus stop?	la fermata dell'autobus?	la fer-**mah**-ta del ow-toe-**booss**
the train station?	la stazione?	la sta-tsee-**oh**-nay
the subway station?	la metropolitana?	la may-tro-po-lee-**tah**-na
the terminal?	il terminale?	eel ter-mee-**nah**-lay
the post office?	l'ufficio postale?	loo-**fee**-cho po-**stah**-lay
the bank?	la banca?	la **bahn**-ka
the . . . hotel?	l'hotel . . .?	lo-**tel**
the store?	il negozio?	eel nay-**go**-tsee-o
the cashier?	la cassa?	la **kah**-sa
the . . . museum?	il museo . . .?	eel moo-**zay**-o
the hospital?	l'ospedale?	lo-spay-**dah**-lay
the first-aid station?	il pronto soccorso?	eel **pron**-to so-**kor**-so
the elevator?	l'ascensore?	la-shen-**so**-ray
a telephone?	un telefono?	oon tay-**lay**-fo-no
Where are the restrooms?	Dov'è il bagno?	do-**vay** eel **bahn**-yo
Here/there	Qui/là	kwee/la
Left/right	A sinistra/a destra	a see-**neess**-tra/ a **des**-tra
Straight ahead	Avanti dritto	a-**vahn**-tee **dree**-to
Is it near/far?	È vicino/lontano?	ay vee-**chee**-no/ lon-**tah**-no
I'd like . . .	Vorrei . . .	vo-**ray**
a room	una camera	**oo**-na **kah**-may-ra
the key	la chiave	la kee-**ah**-vay
a newspaper	un giornale	oon jor-**nah**-lay
a stamp	un francobollo	oon frahn-ko-**bo**-lo
I'd like to buy . . .	Vorrei comprare . . .	vo-**ray** kom-**prah**-ray
a cigar	un sigaro	oon see-**gah**-ro
cigarettes	delle sigarette	**day**-lay see-ga-**ret**-ay
some matches	dei fiammiferi	**day**-ee **fee**-ah-**mee**-fer-ee
some soap	una saponetta	**oo**-na sa-po-**net**-a
a city plan	una pianta della città	**oo**-na **pyahn**-ta day-la chee-**tah**

a road map of . . .	una carta stradale di . . .	**oo**-na **cart**-a stra-**dah**-lay dee
a country map	una carta geografica	**oo**-na **cart**-a jay-o-**grah**-fee-ka
a magazine	una rivista	**oo**-na ree-**veess**-ta
envelopes	delle buste	**day**-lay **booss**-tay
writing paper	della carta da lettere	**day**-la **cart**-a da let-air-ay
a postcard	una cartolina	**oo**-na car-toe-**lee**-na
a guidebook	una guida turistica	**oo**-na **gwee**-da too-**reess**-tee-ka
How much is it?	Quanto costa?	**kwahn**-toe **coast**-a
It's expensive/ cheap	È caro/economico	ay **car**-o/ay-ko-**no**-mee-ko
A little/a lot	Poco/tanto	**po**-ko/**tahn**-to
More/less	Più/meno	pee-**oo**/**may**-no
Enough/too (much)	Abbastanza/troppo	a-bas-**tahn**-sa/**tro**-po
I am sick	Sto male	sto **mah**-lay
Call a doctor	Chiama un dottore	kee-**ah**-mah oon doe-**toe**-ray
Help!	Aiuto!	a-**yoo**-toe
Stop!	Alt!	ahlt
Fire!	Al fuoco!	ahl **fwo**-ko
Caution/Look out!	Attenzione!	a-ten-**syon**-ay

Dining Out

A bottle of . . .	Una bottiglia di . . .	**oo**-na bo-**tee**-lee-ah dee
A cup of . . .	Una tazza di . . .	**oo**-na **tah**-tsa dee
A glass of . . .	Un bicchiere di . . .	oon bee-key-**air**-ay dee
Bill/check	Il conto	eel **cone**-toe
Bread	Il pane	eel **pah**-nay
Breakfast	La prima colazione	la **pree**-ma ko-la-**tsee**-oh-nay
Cocktail/aperitif	L'aperitivo	la-pay-ree-**tee**-vo
Dinner	La cena	la **chen**-a
Fixed-price menu	Menù a prezzo fisso	may-**noo** a **pret**-so **fee**-so
Fork	La forchetta	la for-**ket**-a
I am diabetic	Ho il diabete	o eel dee-a-**bay**-tay
I am vegetarian	Sono vegetariano/a	**so**-no vay-jay-ta-ree-**ah**-no/a
I'd like . . .	Vorrei . . .	vo-**ray**

I'd like to order	Vorrei ordinare	vo-**ray** or-dee-**nah**-ray
Is service included?	Il servizio è incluso?	eel ser-**vee**-tzee-o ay een-**kloo**-zo
It's good/bad	È buono/cattivo	ay **bwo**-no/ka-**tee**-vo
It's hot/cold	È caldo/freddo	ay **kahl**-doe/**fred**-o
Knife	Il coltello	eel kol-**tel**-o
Lunch	Il pranzo	eel **prahnt**-so
Menu	Il menù	eel may-**noo**
Napkin	Il tovagliolo	eel toe-va-lee-**oh**-lo
Please give me . . .	Mi dia . . .	mee **dee**-a
Salt	Il sale	eel **sah**-lay
Spoon	Il cucchiaio	eel koo-kee-**ah**-yo
Sugar	Lo zucchero	lo **tsoo**-ker-o
Waiter/Waitress	Cameriere/ cameriera	ka-mare-**yer**-ay/ ka-mare-**yer**-a
Wine list	La lista dei vini	la **lee**-sta **day**-ee **vee**-nee

MENU GUIDE

English	Italian
Set menu	Menù a prezzo fisso
Dish of the day	Piatto del giorno
Specialty of the house	Specialità della casa
Local specialties	Specialità locali
Extra charge	Extra . . .
In season	Di stagione
Cover charge/Service charge	Coperto/Servizio

Breakfast

Butter	Burro
Croissant	Cornetto
Eggs	Uova
Honey	Miele
Jam/Marmalade	Marmellata
Roll	Panino
Toast	Pane tostato

Starters

Assorted cold cuts	Affettati misti
Assorted seafood	Antipasto di pesce
Assorted appetizers	Antipasto misto
Toasted rounds of bread, fried or toasted in oil	Crostini/Crostoni
Diced-potato and vegetable salad with mayonnaise	Insalata russa
Eggplant parmigiana	Melanzane alla parmigiana
Fried mozzarella sandwich	Mozzarella in carrozza
Ham and melon	Prosciutto e melone
Cooked sausages and cured meats	Salumi cotti
Filled pastry shells	Vol-au-vents

Soups

"Angel hair," thin noodle soup	Capelli d'angelo
Cream of . . .	Crema di . . .
Pasta-and-bean soup	Pasta e fagioli
Egg-drop and Parmesan cheese soup	Stracciatella

Pasta, Rice, and Pizza

Filled pasta	Agnolotti/ravioli/tortellini
Potato dumplings	Gnocchi

Semolina dumplings	Gnocchi alla romana
Pasta	Pasta
with four cheeses	*al quattro formaggi*
with basil/cheese/pine nuts/ garlic sauce	*al pesto*
with tomato-based meat sauce	*al ragù*
with tomato sauce	*al sugo* or *al pomodoro*
with butter	*in bianco* or *al burro*
with egg, Parmesan cheese, and pepper	*alla carbonara*
green (spinach-based) pasta	*verde*
Rice	Riso
Rice dish	Risotto
with mushrooms	*ai funghi*
with saffron	*alla milanese*
Noodles	Tagliatelle
Pizza	Pizza
Pizza with seafood, cheese, artichokes, and ham in four different sections	Pizza quattro stagioni
Pizza with tomato and mozzarella	Pizza margherita
Pizza with oil, garlic, and oregano	Pizza marinara

Fish and Seafood

Anchovies	Acciughe
Bass	Persico
Carp	Carpa
Clams	Vongole
Cod	Merluzzo
Crab	Granchio
Eel	Anguilla
Lobster	Aragosta
Mackerel	Sgombro
Mullet	Triglia
Mussels	Cozze
Octopus	Polpo
Oysters	Ostriche
Pike	Luccio
Prawns	Gamberoni
Salmon	Salmone
Shrimp	Scampi
Shrimps	Gamberetti
Sole	Sogliola
Squid	Calamari
Swordfish	Pescespada

Trout	Trota
Tuna	Tonno

Methods of Preparation

Baked	Al forno
Cold, with vinegar sauce	In carpione
Fish stew	Zuppa di pesce
Fried	Fritto
Grilled (usually charcoal)	Alla griglia
Seafood salad	In insalata
Smoked	Affumicato
Stuffed	Ripieno

Meat

Boar	Cinghiale
Brain	Cervella
Braised meat with wine	Brasato
Chop	Costoletta
Duck	Anatra
Lamb	Agnello
Baby lamb	Abbacchio
Liver	Fegato
Pheasant	Fagiano
Pork roast	Arista
Rabbit	Coniglio
Steak	Bistecca
Sliced raw steak with sauce	Carpaccio
Mixed boiled meat	Bollito misto

Methods of Preparation

Battered with eggs and crumbs and fried	. . . alla milanese
Grilled	. . . ai ferri
Grilled (usually charcoal)	. . . alla griglia
Raw, with lemon/egg sauce	. . . alla tartara
Roasted	. . . arrosto
Very rare	. . . al sangue
Well done	. . . ben cotta
With ham and cheese	. . . alla valdostana
With Parmesan cheese and tomatoes	. . . alla parmigiana

Vegetables

Artichokes	Carciofi
Asparagus	Asparagi
Beans	Fagioli

Brussels sprouts	Cavolini di Bruxelles
Cabbage	Cavolo
Carrots	Carote
Cauliflower	Cavolfiore
Cucumber	Cetriolo
Eggplants	Melanzane
Green beans	Fagiolini
Leeks	Porri
Lentils	Lenticchie
Lettuce	Lattuga
Mushrooms	Funghi
Onions	Cipolle
Peas	Piselli
Peppers	Peperoni
Potatoes	Patate
Roasted potatoes	*Patate arroste*
Boiled potatoes	*Patate bollite*
Fried potatoes	*Patate fritte*
Small, roasted potatoes	*Patatine novelle*
Mashed potatoes	*Purè di patate*
Radishes	Rapanelli
Salad	Insalata
vegetable	*mista*
green	*verde*
Spinach	Spinaci
Tomatoes	Pomodori
Zucchini	Zucchini

Sauces, Herbs, and Spices

Basil	Basilico
Bay leaf	Lauro
Chervil	Cerfoglio
Dill	Aneto
Garlic	Aglio
Hot dip with anchovies (for vegetables)	Bagna cauda
Marjoram	Maggiorana
Mayonnaise	Maionese
Mustard	Mostarda *or* senape
Oil	Olio
Parsley-based sauce	Salsa verde
Pepper	Pepe
Rosemary	Rosmarino
Tartar sauce	Salsa tartara
Vinegar	Aceto
White sauce	Besciamella

Cheeses

Fresh:	Caprino fresco
	Mascarpone
	Mozzarella
	Ricotta
Mild:	Caciotta
	Caprino
	Fontina
	Grana
	Provola
	Provolone dolce
	Robiola
	Scamorza
Sharp:	Asiago
	Gorgonzola
	Groviera
	Pecorino
	Provolone piccante
	Taleggio
	Toma

Fruits and Nuts

Almonds	Mandorle
Apple	Mela
Apricot	Albicocca
Blackberries	More
Black currant	Ribes nero
Blueberries	Mirtilli
Cherries	Ciliege
Chestnuts	Castagne
Coconut	Noce di cocco
Dates	Datteri
Figs	Fichi
Green grapes	Uva bianca
Black grapes	Uva nera
Grapefruit	Pompelmo
Hazelnuts	Nocciole
Lemon	Limone
Melon	Melone
Nectarine	Nocepesca
Orange	Arancia
Pear	Pera
Peach	Pesca
Pineapple	Ananas
Plum	Prugna/Susina
Prune	Prugna secca

Raisins	Uva passa
Raspberries	Lamponi
Red currant	Ribes
Strawberries	Fragole
Tangerine	Mandarino
Walnuts	Noci
Watermelon	Anguria/Cocomero
Dried fruit	Frutta secca
Fresh fruit	Frutta fresca
Fruit salad	Macedonia di frutta

Desserts

Custard-filled pastry, with candied fruit	Cannoli
Ricotta-filled pastry shells with sugar glaze	Cannoli alla siciliana
Ice cream with candied fruit	Cassata
Ricotta-filled cake with sugar glaze	Cassata siciliana
Chocolate	Cioccolato
Cup of ice cream	Coppa gelato
Caramel custard	Crème caramel
Pie	Crostata
Fruit pie	Crostata di frutta
Ice cream	Gelato
Flaked pastry	Millefoglie
Chestnuts and whipped-cream cake	Montebianco
Whipped cream	Panna montata
Pastries	Paste
Sherbet	Sorbetto
Chocolate-coated ice cream	Tartufo
Fruit tart	Torta di frutta
Apple tart	Torta di mele
Ice-cream cake	Torta gelata
Vanilla	Vaniglia
Egg-based cream with sugar and Marsala wine	Zabaione
Ice-cream-filled cake	Zuccotto

Alcoholic Drinks

On the rocks	Con ghiaccio
Straight	Liscio
With soda	Con seltz
Beer	Birra
light/dark	*chiara/scura*

Bitter cordial	Amaro
Brandy	Cognac
Cordial	Liquore
Aniseed cordial	Sambuca
Martini	Cocktail Martini
Port	Porto
Vermouth	Vermut/Martini
Wine	Vino
blush	*rosé*
dry	*secco*
full-bodied	*corposo*
light	*leggero*
red	*rosso*
sparkling	*spumante*
sweet	*dolce*
very dry	*brut*
white	*bianco*
Light wine	Vinello
Bottle	Bottiglia
Carafe	Caraffa
Flask	Fiasco

Nonalcoholic Drinks

Mineral water	Acqua minerale
carbonated	*gassata*
still	*non gassata*
Tap water	Acqua naturale
Tonic water	Acqua tonica
Coffee with steamed milk	Cappuccino
Espresso	Caffè espresso
with milk	*macchiato*
decaffeinated	*decaffeinato*
lighter espresso	*lungo*
with cordial	*corretto*
Fruit juice	Succo di frutta
Lemonade	Limonata
Milk	Latte
Orangeade	Aranciata
Tea	Tè
with milk/lemon	*col latte/col limone*
iced	*freddo*

SMART TRAVEL TIPS

There are planners and there are those who, excuse the pun, fly by the seat of their pants. We happily place ourselves among the planners. Our writers and editors try to anticipate all the issues you may face before and during any journey, and then they do their research. This section is the product of their efforts. Use it to get excited about your trip to Italy, to inform your travel planning, or to guide you on the road should the seat of your pants start to feel threadbare.

ADDRESSES

Addresses in Italy are fairly straightforward: the street is followed by the building number. However, you might see an address with a number plus "bis" or "A"; for instance, "Via Verdi 3/bis" or "Via Mazzini 8/A." This indicates that 3/bis and 8/A are the next doors down from Via Verdi 3 and Via Mazzini 8. In Rome, street numbers flow down one side of a street and back up the other. In central Florence, the letter "r" following an address (e.g., Via Santo Spirito 35/r) refers to "rosso" (red), the color of the number painted on the wall. Red addresses are commercial; blue or black numbers are residential. (Many hotels have blue or black street numbers.)

Venice addresses consist of the name of one of the city's six neighborhoods and a number. The hitch is that the numbers don't go in any sequential order, so San Marco 3672 and 3673 might well be several narrow winding streets away from each other. When helpful, the Venetian addresses in this book include the nearest *campo*, bridge, or *calle*.

In rural areas some addresses give only the route name or the distance in kilometers along a major road (e.g., Via Fabbri, Km 4.3), or sometimes only the name of the nearest small village.

AIR TRAVEL
CARRIERS
When flying internationally, you must usually choose between a domestic carrier, the national flag carrier of the country you are visiting (Alitalia for Italy), and a foreign

carrier from a third country. National flag carriers have the greatest number of non-stops. Domestic carriers may have better connections to your hometown and serve a greater number of gateway cities. Third-party carriers may have a price advantage.

On flights from the United States, Alitalia and Delta Air Lines serve Rome, Milan, and Venice. The major international hubs in Italy, Milan and Rome, are also served by Continental Airlines and American Airlines, and US Airways serves Rome. From April through October, the Italy-based EuroFly has nonstop flights from New York to Rome, Naples, Bologna, and Palermo.

Alitalia and British Airways have direct flights from London to Milan, Venice, Rome, and 10 other locations in Italy. Smaller, no-frills airlines also provide service between Great Britain and Italy. EasyJet connects Gatwick with Milan, Venice, Rome, and Bologna. British Midland connects Heathrow and Milan (Linate), Naples, and Venice. Ryanair, departing from London's Stansted Airport, flies to Milan, Rome, Pisa, and Venice. Meridiana has flights between Gatwick and Olbia on Sardinia in summer, and flights to Rome and Florence throughout the year.

FLIGHTS WITHIN ITALY

Tickets for flights within Italy, on Alitalia and small carriers such as EuroFly, Meridiana, and Air One, cost less when purchased from agents within Italy. Tickets are frequently sold at discounted prices, so check the cost of flights, even one-way, as an alternative to train travel. When weighing the cost of train versus plane, be sure to factor in the expense of getting to and from the airport. When flying out of Italian airports, always check with the airport or tourist agency about upcoming strikes, which are frequent in Italy and often affect air travel.

⚹ International Carriers Alitalia ☎ 800/223-5730 in U.S., 06/65641 in Rome, 848/865641 elsewhere in Italy ⊕ www.alitalia.it. **American Airlines** ☎ 800/433-7300 in U.S., 02/69682464 in Milan ⊕ www.aa.com. **British Airways** ☎ 800/403-0882 in U.S. and Canada, 0870/850-9850 in U.K., 06/52492800 in Italy ⊕ www.britishairways.com. **British Midland** ⊕ www.flybmi.com **Continental** ☎ 800/231-0856 in U.S., 02/69633256 in Milan,

800/296230 elsewhere in Italy ⊕ www.flycontinental.com. **Delta** ☎ 800/241-4141 in U.S., 06/65954406 in Italy ⊕ www.delta.com. **EasyJet** ☎ 0870/607-6543 in U.K., 848/887766 in Italy ⊕ www.easyjet.com. **EuroFly** ☎ 800/459-0581 in U.S., 199/509960 in Italy ⊕ www.euroflyusa.com, www.eurofly.it. **Ryanair** ☎ 08701/569569 in U.K., 199/114114 in Italy ⊕ www.ryanair.com. **US Airways** ☎ 800/428-4322 in U.S., 848/813177 in Italy ⊕ www.usairways.com.

⚹ Carriers within Italy Air One ☎ 06/488800 in Rome, 800/900966 elsewhere in Italy ⊕ www.flyairone.it. **Meridiana** ☎ 199/111333 in Italy ⊕ www.meridiana.it.

CHECK-IN & BOARDING

Double-check your flight times, especially if you made your reservations far in advance. Airlines change their schedules, and alerts may not reach you. Always **bring a government-issued photo I.D. to the airport** (even when it's not required, a passport is best), and **arrive when you need to and not before.** Check in usually at least an hour before domestic flights and two to three hours for international flights. But many airlines have more stringent advance check-in requirements at some busy airports. The TSA estimates the waiting time for security at most major airports and publishes the information on its Web site. Note that if you aren't at the gate at least 10 minutes before your flight is scheduled to take off (sometimes earlier), you won't be allowed to board.

Minimize the time spent standing in line. Buy an e-ticket, check in at an electronic kiosk, or—even better—check in on your airline's Web site before you leave home. These days, most domestic airline tickets are electronic; international tickets may be either electronic or paper. Also, pack light and limit carry-on items to only the essentials.

You usually pay a surcharge (up to $50) to get a paper ticket, and its sole advantage is that it may be easier to endorse over to another airline if your flight is canceled and the airline with which you booked can't accommodate you on another flight. With an e-ticket, you receive an e-mailed receipt citing your itinerary and reservation and ticket numbers. You should bring the receipt with you to the airport, though if you lose it you can simply present ID when checking in. If your airline allows you to check in on the Web, that means you can print your boarding pass at home as well; if you're not checking luggage, you can then bypass the check-in counter and go directly to your gate.

Particularly during busy travel seasons and around holiday periods, if a flight is over-sold, the gate agent will usually ask for volunteers and will offer some sort of compensation if you are willing to take a different flight. **Know your rights.** If you are bumped from a flight *involuntarily,* the airline must give you some kind of compensation if an alternate flight can't be found within one hour. If your flight is de-layed because of something within the air-line's control (so bad weather doesn't count), then the airline has a responsibility to get you to your destination on the same day, even if they have to book you on an-other airline and in an upgraded class if necessary. Read your airline's Contract of Carriage; it's usually buried somewhere on the airline's Web site.

Be prepared to quickly adjust your plans by programming a few numbers into your cell: your airline, an airport hotel or two, your destination hotel, your car service, and/or your travel agent.

CUTTING COSTS

It's always good to **comparison shop.** Web sites (aka consolidators) and travel agents can have different arrangements with the airlines and offer different prices for ex-actly the same flight and day. Certain Web sites have tracking features that will e-mail you immediately when good deals are posted. Other people prefer to stick with one or two frequent-flier programs, rack-ing up free trips and accumulating perks that can make trips easier. On some air-lines, perks include a special reservations number, early boarding, access to up-grades, and more roomy economy-class seating.

Check early and often. Start looking for cheap fares up to a year in advance, and keep looking until you see something you can live with; you never know when a

good deal may pop up. That said, **jump on the good deals.** Waiting even a few min-utes might mean paying more. For most people, saving money is more important than flexibility, so the more affordable nonrefundable tickets work. Just remem-ber that you'll pay dearly (often as much as $100) if you must change your travel plans. Check on prices for departures at different times of the day and to and from alternate airports, and look for departures on Tuesday, Wednesday, and Thursday, typically the cheapest days to travel. Re-member to **weigh your options,** though. A cheaper flight might have a long layover rather than being nonstop, or landing at a secondary airport might substantially in-crease your ground transportation costs.

Note that many airline Web sites—and most ads—show prices *without* taxes and surcharges. Don't buy until you know the full price. Government taxes add up quickly. Also **watch those ticketing fees.** Surcharges are usually added when you buy your ticket anywhere but on an air-line's own Web site. (By the way, that in-cludes on the phone—even if you call the airline directly—and for paper tickets re-gardless of how you book.)

Look into air passes. Many airlines, singly or in collaboration, offer discount air passes that allow foreigners to travel eco-nomically in a particular country or re-gion. These visitor passes usually must be reserved and purchased before you leave home. Information about passes often can be found on most airlines' international Web pages, which tend to be aimed at travelers from outside the carrier's home country. Also, try typing the name of the pass into a search engine, or search for "pass" within the carrier's Web site.

🔃 Online Consolidators **AirlineConsolidator.com** ⊕ www.airlineconsolidator.com; for international tickets. **Best Fares** ⊕ www.bestfares.com; $59.90 annual membership. **Cheap Tickets** ⊕ www.cheaptickets.com. **Expedia** ⊕ www.expedia.com. **Hotwire** ⊕ www.hotwire.com is a discounter. **last-minute.com** ⊕ www.lastminute.com specializes in last-minute travel; the main site is for the U.K., but it has a link to a U.S. site. **Luxury Link** ⊕ www.luxurylink.com has auctions (surprisingly good deals) as well as offers at the high-end side of travel. **Onetravel.com** ⊕ www.onetravel.com. **Orbitz** ⊕ www.orbitz.com. **Priceline.com** ⊕ www.priceline.com is a discounter that also allows bidding. **Travel.com** ⊕ www.travel.com allows you to compare its rates with those of other booking engines. **Travelocity** ⊕ www.travelocity.com charges a booking fee for airline tickets but promises good problem resolution.

ENJOYING THE FLIGHT

Get the seat you want. Avoid those on the aisle directly across from the lavatories. Most frequent fliers say those are even worse than the seats that don't recline (e.g., those in the back row and those in front of a bulkhead). For more legroom, you can request emergency-aisle seats, but do so only if you're capable of moving the 35- to 60-pound airplane exit door—a Federal Aviation Administration requirement of passengers in these seats. Seats behind a bulkhead also offer more legroom, but they don't have under-seat storage. Often, you can pick a seat when you buy your ticket on an airline's Web site. But it's not always a guarantee, particularly if the airline changes the plane after you book your ticket; check back before you leave. SeatGuru.com has more information about specific seat configurations, which vary by aircraft.

Fewer airlines are providing free food for passengers in economy class. **Don't go hungry.** If you're scheduled to fly during mealtimes, verify if your airline offers anything to eat; even when it does, be prepared to pay. If you have dietary concerns, request special meals. These can be vegetarian, low-cholesterol, or kosher, for example.

Ask the airline about its children's menus, activities, and fares. On some lines infants and toddlers fly for free if they sit on a parent's lap, and older children fly for half price in their own seats. Also inquire about policies involving car seats; having one may limit where you can sit. While you're at it, ask about seat-belt extenders for car seats. And note that you can't count on a flight attendant to automatically produce an extender; you may have to inquire about it again when you board.

FLYING TIMES

Flying time to Milan or Rome is approximately 2½ hours from London, 8–8½ hours from New York, 10–11 hours from Chicago, 11½ hours from Los Angeles, and 23½ hours from Sydney.

HOW TO COMPLAIN

If your baggage goes astray or your flight goes awry, complain right away. Most carriers require that you **file a claim immediately.** The Aviation Consumer Protection Division of the Department of Transportation publishes *Fly-Rights,* which discusses airlines and consumer issues and is available online. You can also find articles and information on mytravelrights.com, the Web site of the nonprofit Consumer Travel Rights Center.

🛈 Airline Complaints **Office of Aviation Enforcement and Proceedings** (Aviation Consumer Protection Division) ☎ 202/366-2220 ⊕ airconsumer.ost.dot.gov. **Federal Aviation Administration Consumer Hotline** ☎ 866/835-5322 ⊕ www.faa.gov.

RECONFIRMING

Confirm flights within Italy the day before travel. Labor strikes are frequent in Italy and can affect air and train travel. Your airline will have information about strikes directly affecting its flight schedule. If you are taking a train to get to the airport, check with the local tourist agency or rail station about upcoming strikes.

AIRPORTS

The major gateways to Italy are Rome's **Aeroporto Leonardo da Vinci,** better known as **Fiumicino** (FCO), and Milan's **Aeroporto Malpensa 2000** (MXP). There are direct connections from both airports to Florence and Venice. For information about regional airports, *see* the Essentials sections at the end of each chapter.

🛈 Airlines & Airports **Airline and Airport Links.com** ⊕ www.airlineandairportlinks.com has links to many of the world's airlines and airports. **Aeroporto Leonardo da Vinci** ✉ 35 km [20 mi] southeast of Rome ☎ 06/5951 ⊕ www.adr.it. **Aeroporto Malpensa** ✉ 45 km [28 mi] north of Milan ☎ 02/74852200 ⊕ www.sea-aeroportimilano.it.

🛈 Airline Security Issues **Transportation Security Administration** ⊕ www.tsa.gov/public has answers for almost every question that might come up.

BUSINESS HOURS

Religious and civic holidays are frequent in Italy. Depending on the holiday's local importance, businesses may close for the day. Businesses do not close on a Friday or Monday when the holiday falls on the weekend.

BANKS & POST OFFICES

Banks are open weekdays 8:30 to 1:30 and for an hour in the afternoon, depending on the bank. Most post offices are open Monday through Saturday 9 to 12:30; central post offices are open 9 to 6:30 weekdays, 9 to 12:30 on Saturday. On the last day of the month all post offices close at midday.

MUSEUMS & SIGHTS

Most churches are open from early morning until noon or 12:30, when they close for three hours or more; they open again in the afternoon, closing at about 6 PM. A few major churches, such as St. Peter's in Rome and San Marco in Venice, remain open all day. Walking around during services is discouraged. Many museums are closed one day a week, often Monday. During low season, museums often close early; during high season, many stay open until late at night.

PHARMACIES

Pharmacies are generally open weekdays 8:30 to 1 and 4 to 8, and Saturday 9 to 1. Local pharmacies cover the off-hours in shifts: on the door of every pharmacy is a list of which pharmacies in the vicinity will be open late.

SHOPS

Most shops are open Monday through Saturday 9 to 1 and 3:30 or 4 to 7:30. Clothing shops are generally closed Monday mornings. Barbers and hairdressers, with some exceptions, are closed Sunday and Monday. Some bookstores and fashion and tourist-oriented shops in places such as Rome and Venice are open all day, as well as Sunday. Large chain supermarkets such as Standa, COOP, and Eselunga do not close for lunch and are usually open Sunday; smaller *alimentari* (delicatessens) and other food shops are usually closed one evening during the week (it varies according to the town) and are almost always closed Sunday.

BUS TRAVEL

Italy's bus network is extensive, although buses are not as attractive an option as in other European countries, partly because of cheap, convenient train travel. In some areas buses are faster, so **compare bus and train schedules.** To reach some smaller towns, a bus may be your only option.

CUTTING COSTS

Bus service is provided by regional companies, some of which run day trips from their base of operations. Children under two usually ride for free, and children under eight travel at half price. If you need a car seat for your child, it's best to bring your own.

FARES & SCHEDULES

Unlike city buses, for which you must buy your ticket from a machine, newsstand, or tobacco shop and stamp it after you board, private bus lines usually have a ticket office in town or allow you to pay when you board.

🚌 Bus Information Eurolines ✉ 52 Grosvenor Gardens, London SW1W 0AU ☎ 020/7730-8235 or 020/7730-3499 ⊕ www.eurolines.com.

CAR RENTAL

Renting a car in Italy is essential for exploring the countryside, but not if you plan to stick to the cities. Signage on country roads is usually good, but be prepared for fast and impatient fellow drivers.

Hiring a car with a driver can come in handy, particularly if you plan to do some wine tasting or drive along the Amalfi Coast. Ask at your hotel for recommended drivers, or inquire at the local tourist office. Drivers are paid by the day, and are usually rewarded with a tip of about 15% upon completion of the journey.

Fiats and Fords in a variety of sizes are the most typical rental cars. Remember that most Italian cars have standard transmissions. **If you want to rent an automatic, be specific when you reserve the car.** Higher rates will apply.

In Italy an American, Canadian, or U.K. driver's license is acceptable. However, a universally recognized International Driver's Permit may make things easier if you have to deal with the local authorities. Permits are available from the American or Canadian Automobile Association and, in the United Kingdom, from the Automobile Association or Royal Automobile Club.

In Italy you must be 21 to rent a car, and most companies require those under 23 to pay by credit card.

Children under three are required to ride in a car seat, which must be booked in advance. The cost ranges from €26 to €40 for the duration of the rental.

Request car seats and extras such as GPS when you book, and make sure that a confirmed reservation guarantees you a car. Agencies sometimes overbook, particularly for busy weekends and holiday periods. Rates are sometimes—but not always—better if you book in advance or reserve through a rental agency's Web site. There are other reasons to book ahead, though: for popular destinations, during busy times of the year, or to ensure that you get a certain type of car (vans, SUVs, exotic sports cars).

CUTTING COSTS

Really weigh your options. Find out if a credit card you carry or organization or frequent-renter program to which you belong has a discount program. And check that such discounts really are the best deal. You can often do better with special weekend or weekly rates offered by a rental agency. (And even if you want to rent for only five or six days, ask if you can get the weekly rate; it may very well be cheaper than the daily rate for that period of time.)

Price local car-rental companies as well as the majors. Also investigate wholesalers, which don't own fleets but rent in bulk from those that do and often offer better rates (note you must usually pay for such rentals before leaving home). Consider adding a car rental onto your air/hotel vacation package; the cost will often be cheaper than if you had rented the car separately on your own.

When traveling abroad, **look for guaranteed exchange rates,** which protect you against a falling dollar. With your rate locked in, you won't pay more, even if the price goes up in the local currency. (Note to self: not the best thing if the dollar is surging rather than plunging.)

Beware of hidden charges. Those great rental rates may not be so great when you add in taxes, surcharges, cancellation penalties, taxes, drop-off charges (if you're planning to pick up the car in one city and leave it in another), and surcharges (for being under or over a certain age, for additional drivers, or for driving over state or country borders or out of a specific radius from your point of rental).

Note that airport rental offices often add supplementary surcharges that you may avoid by renting from an agency whose office is just off airport property. Don't buy the tank of gas that's in the car when you rent it unless you plan to do a lot of driving. Avoid hefty refueling fees by filling the tank at a station well away from the rental agency (those nearby are often more expensive) just before you turn in the car.

Most American chains have affiliates in Italy, but the rates are usually lower if you book a car before you leave home. A company's rates are the same throughout the country: you will not save money, for example, if you pick up a vehicle in a city rather than at an airport.

🚗 Automobile Associations **U.S.: American Automobile Association** (AAA) ☎ 315/797-5000 ⊕ www.aaa.com; most contact with the organization is through state and regional members. **National Automobile Club** ☎ 650/294-7000 ⊕ www.thenac.com; membership is open to California residents only.

🚗 Major Agencies **Alamo** ☎ 800/522-9696 ⊕ www.alamo.com. **Avis** ☎ 800/331-1084 ⊕ www.avis.com. **Budget** ☎ 800/472-3325 ⊕ www.budget.com. **Hertz** ☎ 800/654-3001 ⊕ www.hertz.com. **National Car Rental** ☎ 800/227-7368 ⊕ www.nationalcar.com.

🚗 Wholesalers **Auto Europe** ☎ 888/223-5555 ⊕ www.autoeurope.com. **Europe by Car** ☎ 212/581-3040 in New York or 800/223-1516 ⊕ www.europebycar.com. **Eurovacations** ☎ 877/471-3876

⊕ www.eurovacations.com. **Kemwel** ☎ 877/820–0668 ⊕ www.kemwel.com.

INSURANCE

Everyone who rents a car wonders about whether the insurance that the rental companies offer is worth the expense. No one—not even us—has a simple answer. This is particularly true abroad, where laws are different than at home.

If you own a car, your personal auto insurance may cover a rental to some degree, though not all policies protect you abroad; always read your policy's fine print. If you don't have auto insurance, then seriously consider buying the collision- or loss-damage waiver (CDW or LDW) from the car-rental company, which eliminates your liability for damage to the car. Some credit cards offer CDW coverage, but it's usually supplemental to your own insurance and rarely covers SUVs, minivans, luxury models, and the like. If your coverage is secondary, you may still be liable for loss-of-use costs from the car-rental company. But no credit-card insurance is valid unless you use that card for *all* transactions, from reserving to paying the final bill. All companies exclude car rental in some countries, so be sure to find out about the destination to which you are traveling.

Some countries require you to purchase CDW coverage or require car-rental companies to include it in quoted rates. Ask your rental company about issues like these in your destination. In most cases, it's cheaper to add a supplemental CDW plan to your comprehensive travel-insurance policy than to purchase it from a rental company. That said, you don't want to pay for a supplement if you're required to buy insurance from the rental company.

Note that you can decline the insurance from the rental company and purchase it through a third-party provider such as Travel Guard (www.travelguard.com)—$9 per day for $35,000 of coverage. That's sometimes just under half the price of the CDW offered by some car-rental companies. Also, Diners Club offers primary

CDW coverage on all rentals reserved and paid for with the card. This means that Diners Club's company—not your own car insurance—pays in case of an accident. It *doesn't* mean your car-insurance company won't raise your rates once it discovers you had an accident.

CAR TRAVEL

Italy has an extensive network of *autostrade* (toll highways), complemented by equally well-maintained but free *superstrade* (expressways). Save the ticket you are issued at an autostrada entrance, as you need it to exit; on some shorter autostrade, you pay the toll when you enter. Viacards, on sale for €25 at many autostrada locations, allow you to pay for tolls in advance. At special lanes you simply slip the card into a designated slot.

An *uscita* is an "exit." A *raccordo* is a ring road surrounding a city. *Strade regionale* and *strade provinciale* (regional and provincial highways, denoted by *S, SS, SR,* or *SP* numbers) may be two-lane roads, as are all secondary roads; directions and turnoffs aren't always clearly marked.

EMERGENCY SERVICES

Automobile Club Italiano offers 24-hour road service. English-speaking operators are available. Your rental-car company may also have an emergency tow service with a toll-free call. Be prepared to tell the operator which road you're on, the *verso* (direction) you're headed, and your *targa* (license-plate number).

When you're on the road, always carry a good road map, a flashlight, and, if possible, a cellular phone for emergencies. On the autostrade and superstrade, emergency phones are available. To find the nearest one, look on the pavement for painted arrows and the term "SOS."

🚗 **Automobile Club Italiano** ☎ 803/116.

GASOLINE

Gas stations are located along the main highways. Those on autostrade are open 24 hours. Otherwise, gas stations generally are open Monday through Saturday 7 to 7, with a break at lunchtime. At self-service gas stations the pumps are operated by a central machine for payment, which doesn't take credit cards; accepts only bills in denominations of 5, 10, 20, and 50 euros; and does not give change. Those with attendants accept cash and credit cards. It's not customary to tip the attendant.

Gasoline (*benzina*) costs, as of this writing, about €1.40 per liter and is available in unleaded (*verde*) and super-unleaded (*super*). **Many rental cars in Italy use diesel** (*gasolio*), which costs about €1.10 per liter.

PARKING

Parking is at a premium in most towns, especially in the *centri storici* (historic centers). Fines for parking violations are high, and towing is common. Don't think about tearing up a ticket, as car-rental companies may use your credit card to be reimbursed for any fines you incur. It's a good idea to park in a designated (and preferably attended) lot. And **don't leave valuables in your car,** as thieves often target rental cars.

In congested cities like Rome and Florence, indoor parking costs €23 to €30 for 12 to 24 hours; outdoor parking costs about €10 to €20. Parking in an area signposted ZONA DISCO (disk zone) is allowed for short periods (from 30 minutes to two hours or more—the time is posted); if you don't have a cardboard disk (get one at the tourist office or car-rental company) to show what time you parked, you can use a piece of paper. The *parcometro,* a central parking meter that, after coins are inserted, prints a ticket that you leave on your dashboard, has been introduced in most metropolitan areas.

ROAD CONDITIONS

Autostrade are generally well maintained, well marked, and easy to navigate, as are most regional roads. The condition of smaller roads varies, but road maintenance is generally good in Italy.

RULES OF THE ROAD

Driving is on the right. Regulations are largely the same as in Britain and the United States, except that the police have the power to levy on-the-spot fines. Using handheld mobile phones while driving is illegal; fines can exceed €100. In most Italian towns the use of the horn is forbidden

in many areas; a large sign, ZONA DI SILENZIO, indicates a no-honking zone. Speed limits are 130 kph (80 mph) on autostrade and 110 kph (70 mph) on state and provincial roads, unless otherwise marked.

The blood-alcohol content limit for driving is 0.5 gr (stricter than U.S. limits) with fines up to €5,000 for surpassing the limit and the possibility of six months' imprisonment. Although enforcement of laws varies depending on region, fines for speeding are uniformly stiff: 10 kph over the speed limit can warrant a fine of up to €500; greater than 10 kph, and your license could be taken away from you.

Nonetheless, Italians drive fast and are impatient with those who don't. Tailgating is the norm here—the only way to avoid it is to get out of the way. Right turns on red lights are forbidden. Headlights are not compulsory in cities when it rains or snows, but it's a good idea to turn them on. However, you must **turn on your headlights** outside city limits at all hours. You must **wear seat belts** and **strap young children into car seats** at all times.

COMPUTERS ON THE ROAD

Getting online in Italian cities isn't difficult. Internet cafés, some open 24 hours a day, are common. Prices differ, so **shop for the best deal.** Some hotels have in-room modems, but using the hotel's line is usually expensive. Always check the rates before plugging in. You may need an adapter for your computer for the European-style plugs. As always, if you are traveling with a laptop, carry a spare battery and an adapter. Wireless Internet is available in high-end hotels, airports, train stations, and shopping centers.

CUSTOMS & DUTIES

You're always allowed to bring goods of a certain value back home without having to pay any duty or import tax. There's also a limit on the amount of tobacco and liquor you can bring back duty-free, and some countries have separate limits for perfumes; for exact figures, check with your customs department. The values of so-called "duty-free" goods are included in these amounts. When you shop abroad, save all your receipts, as customs inspectors may ask to see them as well as the items you purchased. If the total value of your goods is more than the duty-free limit, then you'll have to pay a tax (most often a flat percentage) on the value of everything beyond that limit.

🔃 Information in Italy **Ministero delle Finanze, Direzione Centrale dei Servizi Doganali, Divisione I** ⊠ Via Carucci 71, 00143 Rome 🖷 06/50242117 ⊕ www.finanze.it. **Dogana Sezione Viaggiatori** ⊠ Customs, Aeroporto Leonardo da Vinci, Fiumicino, 00054 Rome 🖷 06/65954343 ⊕ www.agenziadogane.it.

🔃 U.S. Information **U.S. Customs and Border Protection** ⊕ www.cbp.gov.

EATING OUT

A few pointers on Italian dining etiquette: menus are posted outside most restaurants (in English in tourist areas); if not, you might step inside and ask to take a look at the menu, but don't ask for a table unless you intend to stay. Italians take their food as it is listed on the menu, seldom making special requests such as "dressing on the side" or "hold the olive oil." If you have special dietary needs, though, make them known, and they can usually be accommodated. Although mineral water makes its way to almost every table, you can always order a carafe of tap water (*acqua di rubinetto* or *acqua semplice*). Doing this, however, will mark you as a tourist.

Spaghetti should be eaten with a fork rolled against the side of the dish, although a little help from a spoon will not horrify the locals the way cutting spaghetti into little pieces might. Wiping your bowl clean with a (small) piece of bread is fine in less-formal eateries. Order your espresso (Italians almost never drink a cappuccino after breakfast) after dessert, not with it. You usually have to ask for *il conto* (the bill). Unless it's well past closing time, no waiter will put a bill on your table until you ask him to do so. Don't ask for a doggy bag.

MEALS & MEALTIMES

Unless otherwise noted, the restaurants listed in this guide are open daily for lunch and dinner.

What's the difference between a ristorante and a trattoria? Can you order food at an enoteca? Can you go to a restaurant just for a snack, or order just a salad at a pizzeria? The following definitions should help.

Not too long ago, restaurants tended to be more elegant and expensive than trattorias and osterie, which served more traditional, home-style fare in an atmosphere to match. But the distinction has blurred considerably, and an osteria in the center of town might be far fancier (and pricier) than a ristorante across the street. In all these types of places you are generally expected to order at least a two-course meal, such as a *primo* (first course) and a *secondo* (main course) or a *contorno* (vegetable side dish); an antipasto (starter) followed by either primo or secondo; or a secondo and a *dolce* (dessert).

In an *enoteca* (wine bar) or pizzeria it's common to order just one dish. An enoteca menu is often limited to a selection of cheese, cured meats, salads, and desserts, but if there's a kitchen you'll also find soups, pastas, and main courses. The typical pizzeria fare includes *affettati misti* (a selection of cured pork), simple salads, various kinds of bruschetta, crostini (similar to bruschetta, sometimes topped with cheese and broiled) and, in Rome, *fritti* (deep-fried finger food) such as *olive ascolane* (green olives with a meat stuffing) and *supplì* (rice balls stuffed with mozzarella). All pizzerias serve fresh fruit, ice cream, and simple desserts.

Throughout the country the handiest and least expensive places for a quick snack between sights are probably bars, cafés, and pizza *al taglio* (by the slice) spots. Bars in Italy are primarily places to get a coffee and a bite to eat rather than drinking establishments. Most have a selection of *panini* (sandwiches) warmed up on the griddle (*piastra*) and *tramezzini* (sandwiches made of untoasted white bread triangles). In larger cities, bars also serve vegetable and fruit salads, cold pasta dishes, and yogurt around lunchtime. Most bars offer beer and a variety of alcohol as well as wines by the glass (sometimes good but more often mediocre). A café (*caffè* in Italian) is like a bar but usually with more tables. Pizza at a café should be avoided—it's usually heated in a microwave. If you place your order at the counter, ask if you can sit down: some places charge for table service, others do not. In self-service bars and cafés it's good manners to clean your table before you leave. Note that in some places you have to pay a cashier, then place your order and show your *scontrino* (receipt) at the counter. Pizza al taglio shops sell pizza by weight: just point out which kind you want and how much. Very few pizza al taglio shops have seating.

Italian cuisine is still largely regional. Ask what the local specialties are: by all means, have spaghetti *alla carbonara* (with bacon and egg) in Rome, pizza in Rome or Naples, *bistecca alla fiorentina* (steak) in Florence, *chingale* (wild boar) in Tuscany, truffles in the Piedmont, and risotto *alla milanese* in Milan.

Breakfast (*la colazione*) is usually served from 7 to 10:30, lunch (*il pranzo*) from 12:30 to 2:30, dinner (*la cena*) from 7:30 to 10. Peak times are usually 1:30 for lunch and 9 for dinner. Enoteche and *bacari* (wine bars) are open also in the morning and late afternoon for a snack at the counter. Most pizzerias open at 8 PM and close around midnight—later in summer and on weekends. Most bars and cafés are open from 7 AM until 8 or 9 PM; a few stay open until midnight.

PAYING
For guidelines on tipping *see* Tipping *below*.

Most restaurants charge a "cover" charge per person, usually listed at the top of the check as "*coperto*" or "*pane e coperto.*" It should be a modest charge (€1 to €2.50 per person) except at the most expensive restaurants. Whenever in doubt, ask before you order to avoid unpleasant discussions later. It is customary to leave a small tip (around 10%) in appreciation of good service. If *servizio* is included at the bottom of the check, no tip is necessary. Tips are always given in cash.

The price of fish dishes is often given by weight (before cooking), so the price you

see on the menu is for 100 grams of fish, not for the whole dish. An average fish portion is about 350 grams. In Tuscany, *bistecca alla fiorentina* (florentine steak) is also often priced by weight.

Major credit cards are widely accepted in Italy, though cash is usually preferred. More restaurants take Visa and Master-Card than American Express.

CATEGORY	COST
$$$$	over €45
$$$	€35–€45
$$	€25–€35
$	€15–€25
¢	under €15

Prices are for a first course (primo), *second course* (secondo), *and dessert* (dolce) *and are given in euros.*

RESERVATIONS & DRESS
Reservations are always a good idea; we mention them only when they're essential or not accepted. Book as far ahead as you can, and reconfirm as soon as you arrive. (Large parties should always call ahead to check the reservations policy.) Pizzerias and enoteche usually accept reservations only for large groups.

We mention dress only when men are required to wear a jacket or a jacket and tie. But unless they're dining outside or at an oceanfront resort, Italian men never wear shorts or running shoes in a restaurant. The same applies to women: no casual shorts, running shoes, or plastic sandals when going out to dinner. Shorts are acceptable in pizzerias and cafés.

WINES, BEER & SPIRITS
If you're in a restaurant or trattoria, ask your waiter about the house wine; sometimes it's very good indeed, sometimes it isn't. Wine in Italy is considerably less expensive than almost anywhere else. Beer can be more expensive than a glass of wine, and though Italy does produce beer it's not nearly as notable as its wine.

Beer, wine, and spirits can be purchased in any bar, grocery store, or enoteca, any day of the week. There's no minimum drinking age in Italy. Italian children begin drinking wine mixed with water at mealtimes when they are teenagers or even younger.

Many bars have their own *aperitivo della casa* (house aperitif). Italians are most imaginative with their mixed drinks—usually shaken, rarely blended.

Was the service stellar or not up to snuff? Did the food give you shivers of delight or leave you cold? Did the prices and portions make you happy or sad? Rate restaurants and write your own reviews in "Travel Ratings" or start a discussion about your favorite places in "Travel Talk" on www.fodors.com. Your comments might even appear in our books. Yes, you, too, can be a correspondent!

ELECTRICITY

The electrical current in Italy is 220 volts, 50 cycles alternating current (AC); wall outlets take Continental-type plugs, with two or three round prongs.

Consider making a small investment in a universal adapter, which has several types of plugs in one lightweight, compact unit. Most laptops and cell-phone chargers are dual voltage (i.e., they operate equally well on 110 and 220 volts) and so require only an adapter. These days the same is true more of small appliances such as hair dryers. Always check labels and manufacturer instructions to be sure, though. Don't use 110-volt outlets marked FOR SHAVERS ONLY for high-wattage appliances such as hair dryers. **Steve Kropla's Help for World Traveler's** ⊕ www.kropla.com has information on electrical and telephone plugs around the world. **Walkabout Travel Gear** ⊕ www.walkabout-travelgear.com has a good discussion about electricity under "adapters."

EMERGENCIES

No matter where you are in Italy, you can **dial 113 in case of emergency.** Not all 113 operators speak English, so you may want to ask a local person to place the call. Asking the operator for *"pronto soccorso"* (first aid) should get you an *ambulanza* (ambulance). If you just need a doctor, ask for *"un medico."*

Italy has the *carabinieri* (national police force) as well as the *polizia* (local police force). Both are armed and have the power to arrest and investigate crimes. Always **report the loss of your passport** to the police as well as to your embassy. When reporting a crime, you'll be asked to fill out an *una denuncia* (official report); keep a copy for your insurance company.

Local traffic officers, known as *vigili,* are responsible for, among other things, giving out parking tickets. They wear white (in summer) or black uniforms. Should you find yourself involved in a minor car accident, contact the vigili.

🛈 **Embassies** **Australian Embassy** ⊠ Via Alessandria 215, 00198 Rome ☎ 06/852721 ⊕ www.australian-embassy.it. **British Embassy** ⊠ Via XX Settembre 80A, 00187 Rome ☎ 06/42200001 ⊕ www.britain.it. **Canadian Embassy** ⊠ Via G. B. de Rossi 27, 00161 Rome ☎ 06/445981 ⊕ www.dfait-maeci.gc.ca/canadaeuropa/italy. **New Zealand Embassy** ⊠ Via Zara 28, 00198 Rome ☎ 06/4417171.
🛈 **General Emergency Contacts** **Emergencies** ☎ 113. **National police** ☎ 112.

ETIQUETTE & BEHAVIOR

Be sure to **dress appropriately** when visiting a church in Italy. Shorts, tank tops, and sleeveless garments are taboo in most churches throughout the country. In summer carry a sweater or other item of clothing to wrap around your bare shoulders before entering a church. You should **never bring food into a church,** and do not sip from your water bottle while inside. And **never enter a church when a service is in progress,** especially if it is a private affair such as a wedding or baptism.

Italians who are friends greet each other with a kiss, usually first on the right cheek, then on the left. When you meet a new person, shake hands.

HOLIDAYS

If you can avoid it, don't travel through Italy in August, when much of the population is on vacation. Most cities are deserted (except for foreign tourists) and many restaurants and shops are closed.

National holidays in 2007 include January 1 (New Year's Day); January 6 (Epiphany); April 8 and April 9 (Easter Sunday and Monday); April 25 (Liberation Day); May 1 (Labor Day or May Day); June 2 (Festival of the Republic); August 15 (Ferragosto); November 1 (All

Saints' Day); December 8 (Immaculate Conception); December 25 and 26 (Christmas Day and the feast of St. Stephen).

Feast days of patron saints are observed locally. Many businesses and shops may be closed in Florence, Genoa, and Turin on June 24 (St. John the Baptist); in Rome on June 29 (SS. Peter and Paul); in Palermo on July 15 (St. Rosalia); in Naples on September 19 (San Gennaro); in Bologna on October 4 (San Petronio); in Trieste on November 3 (San Giusto); and in Milan on December 7 (St. Ambrose). Venice's feast of St. Mark is April 25, the same as Liberation Day, so the Madonna della Salute on November 21 makes up for the lost holiday.

INSURANCE

What kind of coverage do you honestly need? Do you even need trip insurance at all? Take a deep breath and read on.

We believe that comprehensive trip insurance is especially valuable if you're booking a very expensive or complicated trip (particularly to an isolated region) or if you're booking far in advance. Who knows what could happen six months down the road? But whether or not you get insurance has more to do with how comfortable you are assuming all that risk yourself.

Comprehensive travel policies typically cover trip-cancellation and interruption, letting you cancel or cut your trip short because of a personal emergency, illness, or, in some cases, acts of terrorism in your destination. Such policies also cover evacuation and medical care. Some also cover you for trip delays because of bad weather or mechanical problems as well as for lost or delayed baggage. Another type of coverage to look for is financial default—that is, when your trip is disrupted because a tour operator, airline, or cruise line goes out of business. Generally you must buy this when you book your trip or shortly thereafter, and it's available to you only if your operator isn't on a list of excluded companies.

If you're going abroad, consider buying medical-only coverage at the very least. Neither Medicare nor some private insurers cover medical expenses anywhere outside of the United States besides Mexico and Canada (including time aboard a cruise ship, even if it leaves from a U.S. port). Medical-only policies typically reimburse you for medical care (excluding that related to preexisting conditions) and hospitalization abroad and provide for evacuation. You still have to pay the bills and await reimbursement from the insurer, though.

Emergency Room (Pronto Soccorso) care is free for tourists in Italy. If you need an ambulance, call the nationwide general emergency number 113 (no charge). You should first consult with personnel in their hotel about local medical assistance, and if no easy option is available, the next stop should be the nearest hospital emergency room.

Expect comprehensive travel-insurance policies to cost about 4% to 7% of the total price of your trip (it's more like 12% if you're over age 70). A medical-only policy may or may not be cheaper than a comprehensive policy. Always read the fine print of your policy to make sure that you are covered for the risks that are of the most concern to you. Compare several policies to make sure you're getting the best price and range of coverage available.

Just as an aside: You know you can save a bundle on trips to warm-weather destinations by traveling in rainy season. But there's also a chance that a severe storm will disrupt your plans. The solution? Look for hotels and resorts that offer storm/hurricane guarantees. Although they rarely allow refunds, most guarantees do let you rebook later if a storm strikes.

🔁 Insurance-Comparison Sites **Insure My Trip. com** ⊕ www.insuremytrip.com. **Square Mouth.com** ⊕ www.quotetravelinsurance.com.

🔁 Comprehensive Travel Insurers **Access America** ☎ 866/807-3982 ⊕ www.accessamerica.com. **CSA Travel Protection** ☎ 800/873-9855 ⊕ www. csatravelprotection.com. **HTH Worldwide** ☎ 610/ 254-8700 or 888/243-2358 ⊕ www.hthworldwide. com. **Travelex Insurance** ☎ 888/457-4602 ⊕ www.travelex-insurance.com. **Travel Guard International** ☎ 715/345-0505 or 800/826-4919 ⊕ www.travelguard.com. **Travel Insured International** ☎ 800/243-3174 ⊕ www.travelinsured.com. 🔁 Medical-Only Insurers **International Medical Group** ☎ 800/628-4664 ⊕ www.imglobal.com. International SOS ☎ 215/942-8000 or 713/521-7611 ⊕ www.internationalsos.com. **Wallach & Company** ☎ 800/237-6615 or 504/687-3166 ⊕ www.wallach. com.

LANGUAGE

In larger cities such as Venice, Rome, and Florence, language is not a big problem. Most hotels have English speakers at their reception desks, and if not, they can always find someone who speaks at least a little English. You may have trouble communicating in the countryside, but a phrase book and expressive gestures will go a long way. Try to **master a few phrases for daily use** and familiarize yourself with the words you'll need for deciphering signs and menus. A phrase book and language tape set can help get you started. *Fodor's Italian for Travelers* (available at bookstores everywhere) is excellent.

LODGING

Did the hotel look as good in real life as it did in the photos? Did you sleep like a baby, or were the walls paper thin? Did you get your money's worth? Rate hotels and write your own reviews in "Travel Ratings" or start a discussion about your favorite places in "Travel Talk" on www. fodors.com. Your comments might even appear in our books. Yes, you, too, can be a correspondent!

Most hotels and other lodgings require you to give your credit-card details before they will confirm your reservation. If you don't feel comfortable e-mailing this information, ask if you can fax it (some places even prefer faxes). However you book, get confirmation in writing and have a copy of it handy when you check in. If you book through an online travel agent, discounter, or wholesaler, you might even want to confirm your reservation with the hotel before leaving home—just to be sure everything was processed correctly.

Be sure you understand the hotel's cancellation policy. Some places allow you to cancel without any kind of penalty—even if you prepaid to secure a discounted rate—if you cancel at least 24 hours in advance. Others require you to cancel a week in advance or penalize you for the

cost of one night. Small inns and bed-and-breakfasts are most likely to require you to cancel far in advance. Most hotels allow children under a certain age to stay in their parents' room at no extra charge, but others charge for them as extra adults; find out the cutoff age for discounts.

Hotels with the designation **BP** (for Breakfast Plan) at the end of their listing include breakfast in their rate; offerings can vary from coffee and a roll to an elaborate buffet. Those designated **EP** (European Plan) have no meals included; **MAP** (Modified American Plan) means you get breakfast and dinner; **FAP** (Full American Plan) includes all meals.

CATEGORY	MAIN CITIES	ELSEWHERE
$$$$	over € 290	over € 220
$$$	€ 210–€ 290	€ 160–€ 220
$$	€ 140–€ 210	€ 110–€ 160
$	€ 80–€ 140	€ 70–€ 110
¢	under € 80	under € 70

Prices are for two people in a standard double room in high season, including tax and service, and are given in euros. "Main cities" are Florence, Milan, Rome, and Venice.

APARTMENT & VILLA RENTALS

In the capital, *Wanted in Rome* is a bimonthly magazine with extensive listings for short-term rentals all over the country. Another good source for rentals is *EYP*, available at English-language bookstores. 🏠 **At Home Abroad** ☎ 212/421-9165 ⊕ www. athomeabroadinc.com. **Barclay International Group** ☎ 516/364-0064 or 800/845-6636 ⊕ www. barclayweb.com. **Drawbridge to Europe** ☎ 541/482-7778 or 888/268-1148 ⊕ www. drawbridgetoeurope.com. **Homes Away** ☎ 416/920-1873 or 800/374-6637 ⊕ www.homesaway. com. **Hometours International** ☎ 865/690-8484 ⊕ thor.he.net/~hometour/. **Interhome** ☎ 954/791-8282 or 800/882-6864 ⊕ www.interhome.us. **Suzanne B. Cohen & Associates** ☎ 207/622-0743 ⊕ www.villaeurope.com. **Vacation Home Rentals Worldwide** ☎ 201/767-9393 or 800/633-3284 ⊕ www.vhrww.com. **Villanet** ☎ 206/417-3444 or 800/964-1891 ⊕ www.rentavilla.com. **Villas & Apartments Abroad** ☎ 212/213-6435 or 800/433-3020 ⊕ www.vaanyc.com. **Villas of Distinction** ☎ 707/778-1800 or 800/289-0900 ⊕ www. villasofdistinction.com. **Villas International** ☎ 415/

499-9490 or 800/221-2260 🌐 www.villasintl.com. **Wimco** ☎ 800/449-1553 🌐 www.wimco.com.

Local Agents **Homes International** ✉ Via Bissolati 20, 00187 Rome ☎ 06/4881800 📠 06/4881808 🌐 www.homeinternational.it. **Property International** ✉ Viale Aventino 79, 00153 Rome ☎ 06/5743170 📠 06/5743182 🌐 www.propertyint.net.

Roman Publications ***EYP English Yellow Pages*** 🌐 www.intoitaly.it. ***Wanted in Rome*** ✉ Via dei Delfini 17, 00186 Rome, Italy ☎ 06/6790190 📠 06/6783798 🌐 www.wantedinrome.com.

FARM HOLIDAYS & AGRITOURISM

Staying on working farms or vineyards, often in old stone farmhouses that accommodate a number of guests, has become more and more popular. Contact local tourist offices or consult *Agriturism* (🌐 www.agriturismo.com) for more than 1,600 farms in Italy. Although it's in Italian, the publication has photos and descriptions that make it a useful resource.

Agency **Italy Farm Holidays** ✉ 547 Martling Ave., Tarrytown, NY 10591 ☎ 914/631-7880 📠 914/631-8831 🌐 www.italyfarmholidays.com.

HOME EXCHANGES

With a direct home exchange, you stay in someone else's home while they stay in yours. Some outfits also deal with vacation homes, so you're not actually staying in someone's full-time residence, just their vacant weekend place.

Exchange Clubs **Home Exchange.com** ☎ 800/877-8723 🌐 www.homeexchange.com; $59.95 for a one-year online listing. **HomeLink International** ☎ 800/638-3841 🌐 www.homelink.org; $80 yearly for Web-only membership; $125 with Web access and two directories. **Intervac U.S.** ☎ 800/756-4663 🌐 www.intervacus.com; $78.88 for Web-only membership; $126 includes Web access and a catalog.

HOSTELS

Hostels offer bare-bones lodging at low, low prices—often in shared dorm rooms with shared baths—to people of all ages, though the primary market is young travelers, especially students. Most hostels serve breakfast; dinner and/or shared cooking facilities may also be available. In some hostels, you aren't allowed to be in your room during the day, and there may be a curfew at night. Nevertheless, hostels provide a sense of community, with public rooms where travelers often gather to share stories. Many hostels are affiliated with Hostelling International (HI), an umbrella group of hostel associations with some 4,500 member properties in more than 70 countries. Other hostels are completely independent and may be nothing more than a really cheap hotel.

Membership in any HI association, open to travelers of all ages, allows you to stay in HI-affiliated hostels at member rates. One-year membership is about $28 for adults; hostels charge about $10 to $30 per night. Members have priority if the hostel is full; they're also eligible for discounts around the world, even on rail and bus travel in some countries.

Hostelling International–USA ☎ 301/495-1240 🌐 www.hiusa.org.

HOTELS

Weigh all your options (we can't say this enough). Join "frequent-guest" programs. You may get preferential treatment in room choice and/or upgrades in your favorite chains. Check general travel sites and hotel Web sites, as not all chains are represented on all travel sites. Always research or inquire about special packages and corporate rates. If you prefer to book by phone, note you can sometimes get a better price if you call the hotel's local toll-free number (if one is available) rather than the central reservations number.

If your destination's high season is December through April and you're trying to book, say, in late April, you might save considerably by changing your dates by a week or two. Note, though, that many properties charge peak-season rates for your entire stay even if your travel dates straddle peak and nonpeak seasons. High-end chains catering to businesspeople are often busy only on weekdays and often drop rates dramatically on weekends to fill up rooms. **Ask when rates go down.**

Watch out for hidden costs, including resort fees, energy surcharges, and "convenience" fees for such things as unlimited local phone service you won't use and a free newspaper—possibly written in a language you can't read. Always verify whether local hotel taxes are or are not included in the rates you are quoted, so that you'll know the real price of your stay. In some places, taxes can add 20% or more to your bill. If you're traveling overseas **look for price guarantees,** which protect you against a falling dollar. With your rate locked in, you won't pay more, even if the price goes up in the local currency.

All hotels listed have private bath unless otherwise noted.

All Italian hotels are graded on a star scale, from five stars for the most deluxe hotels to one star for the most modest. This system can be misleading, as it reflects a hotel's facilities, not how well it is maintained. Some four- or five-star accommodations are past their prime, and some two- and three-star places might be sparkling. Except in the most expensive hotels, rooms may be very small by U.S. standards.

The quality of rooms in older hotels may be very uneven; if you don't like the room you're given, request another. A front room may be larger or have a view, but it also may have a lot of street noise. If you're a light sleeper, **request a quiet room** when making a reservation. Rooms in lodgings listed in this guide have a shower and/or tub unless noted otherwise. (Hotels with three or more stars always have private bathrooms.) Remember to **specify whether you prefer to have a bathtub or shower.**

In all hotels there will be a card inside the door of your room stating the basic rate (which often varies according to the location and size of the room). Any discrepancy between the posted rate and what you are charged is cause for complaint to the manager and to the police. By law, breakfast is supposed to be optional, but most hotels quote room rates including breakfast. When you book a room, **ask whether the rate includes breakfast.** You are under no obligation to take *colazione* (breakfast) at your hotel, and can have the charge removed from your bill if you decide to eat elsewhere.

You'll find some familiar chains, such as Best Western and Sheraton. Other chains include Atahotels, with mostly four- and five-star hotels; Agip, which has four-star motels along main highways; Jolly, which has four-star hotels; Space Hotels, which has 80 independently owned four- and three-star hotels; and Starhotels, which has mainly four-star lodgings.

🔢 **Discount Hotel Rooms Accommodations Express** 🕾 800/444-7666 or 800/277-1064. **Hotels. com** 🕾 800/219-4606 or 800/364-0291 ⊕ www. hotels.com. **International Marketing & Travel Concepts** 🕾 800/790-4682 ⊕ www.imtc-travel.com. **Steigenberger Reservation Service** 🕾 800/223-5652 ⊕ www.srs-worldhotels.com. **Turbotrip.com** 🕾 800/473-7829 ⊕ w3.turbotrip.com.

RESERVING A ROOM

High season in Italy generally runs from Easter through the beginning of November, and then for two weeks at Christmas. During low season, many hotels reduce their prices. Always **inquire about special rates.** It's always a good idea to **confirm your reservation** by e-mail or fax. If you need to cancel your reservation, do so by e-mail or fax and keep a record of the transmission. If you don't have a reservation, most cities have reservation booths in train stations.

Useful terms to know when booking a room are *aria condizionata* (air-conditioning), *bagno in stanza* (private bath), *letto matrimoniale* (double bed), *letti singoli* (twin beds), and *letti singoli uniti* (twin beds pushed together). Italy does not really have queen- or king-size beds, but larger beds are sometimes available in four- and five-star accommodations.

Other useful phrases include *una camera su un piano alto e con vista* (a room on a high floor with a view), *una camera a un piano basso* (a room on a low floor), and *una camera silenziosa* (a quiet room).

MAIL & SHIPPING

The Italian mail system is notoriously slow. Allow up to 15 days for mail to get to the United States, Canada, Australia, and New Zealand. It takes about a week to the United Kingdom and within Italy. Posta Prioritaria (for Italy only) and

Postacelere (for Italy and abroad) are special-delivery services from the post office that guarantee delivery within 24 hours in Italy and within three to five days abroad.

Most post offices are open Monday through Saturday 9 to 12:30; central post offices are open weekdays 9 to 6:30, Saturday 9 to 12:30. On the last day of the month, post offices close at midday. You can buy stamps at tobacco shops as well as post offices.

POSTAL RATES

Airmail letters and postcards sent *ordinaria* to the United States and Canada cost €0.65 for up to 20 grams, €1 for 21 to 50 grams, and €1.30 for 51 to 100 grams. Always stick the blue airmail tag on your mail, or write AIRMAIL in big, clear letters beside the address. Mail sent *ordinaria* to Italy, the United Kingdom, and other EU countries costs €0.45 for the first 20 grams.

For faster service, use priority delivery *Posta Prioritaria* (for small letters and packages), which guarantees delivery within Italy in three to five business days and abroad in five to six working days. The more expensive express delivery, *Postacelere* (for larger letters and packages), guarantees one-day delivery to most places in Italy and three- to five-day delivery abroad.

Mail sent as Posta Prioritaria to the United States and Canada costs €0.80 for up to 20 grams, €1.50 for 21 to 50 grams, and €1.80 for 51 to 100 grams; to Italy, the United Kingdom, and other EU countries it costs €0.62. Mail sent as Postacelere to the United States and Canada costs €35.05 for up to 500 grams. If you're shipping to the United Kingdom or elsewhere in Europe, the cost is €28.15.

Other package services to check are Quick Pack Europe, for delivery within Europe; and EMS ExpressMail Service, a global three- to five-day service for letters and packages that can be less expensive than Postacelere.

RECEIVING MAIL

Correspondence can be addressed to you in care of any Italian post office. Letters should be addressed to your name, C/O UF-FICIO POSTALE CENTRALE, followed by FERMO POSTA on the next line, and the name of the city (preceded by its postal code) on the next. You can **collect it at the central post office** by showing your passport or photo-bearing ID and paying a small fee. American Express also has a general-delivery service. There's no charge for cardholders, holders of American Express traveler's checks, or anyone who booked a vacation with American Express.

SHIPPING PACKAGES

You can ship parcels via air or surface. Air takes about two weeks, and surface anywhere up to three months to most countries. If you have purchased antiques, ceramics, or other objects, **ask if the vendor will do the shipping** for you; in most cases, this is a possibility. If so, ask if the article will be insured against breakage.

Overnight mail is generally available during the week in all major cities and at popular resorts. Service is reliable; a Federal Express letter to the United States costs about €30, to the United Kingdom, €51, and to Australia and New Zealand, €33. Overnight delivery usually means 24 to 36 hours.

If your hotel can't assist you, try an Internet café, many of which also offer overnight mail services using major carriers at reasonable rates.

🚩 Express Services **DHL** ☎ 199-199-345 ⊕ www. dhl.it. **Federal Express** ☎ 800/123800 ⊕ www. fedex.com. **SDA** ☎ 800/016027 ⊕ www.sda.it.

MONEY MATTERS

Banks rarely have every foreign currency on hand, and it may take as long as a week to order. If you're planning to exchange funds before leaving home, don't wait until the last minute.

Prices vary from region to region and are substantially lower in the country than in the cities. Of Italy's major cities, Venice and Milan are by far the most expensive. Resorts such as the Costa Smeralda, Portofino, and Cortina d'Ampezzo cater to wealthy people and charge top prices. Good values can be had in the scenic Trentino–Alto Adige region and the Dolomites and in Umbria and the

Marches. With a few exceptions, southern Italy, Sicily, and Sardinia also offer good values.

Prices throughout this guide are given for adults. Substantially reduced fees are almost always available for children, students, and senior citizens from the EU; citizens of non-EU countries rarely get discounts. For information on taxes, *see* Taxes.

ATMS & BANKS

Your own bank will probably charge a fee for using ATMs abroad; the foreign bank you use may also charge a fee. Nevertheless, you'll usually get a better rate of exchange via an ATM than you will at a currency-exchange office or even when changing money in a bank. And extracting funds as you need them is a safer option than carrying around a large amount of cash. Note that PIN numbers with more than four digits are not recognized at ATMs in many countries.

An ATM (*bancomat* in Italian) is the easiest way to get euros in Italy. There are numerous ATMs in large cities and small towns, as well as in airports and train stations. They are not common in places such as grocery stores. Be sure to **memorize your PIN number,** as ATM keypads in Italy don't always display letters.

CREDIT CARDS

MasterCard and Visa are preferred by Italian merchants, but American Express is usually accepted in tourist spots. Credit cards aren't accepted everywhere; if you want to pay with a credit card in a small shop, hotel, or restaurant, it's a good idea to make your intentions known early on. Throughout this guide, the following abbreviations are used: **AE,** American Express; **DC,** Diners Club; **MC,** MasterCard; and **V,** Visa.

It's a good idea to inform your credit-card company before you travel, especially if you're going abroad and don't travel internationally very often. Otherwise, the credit-card company might put a hold on your card owing to unusual activity—not a good thing halfway through your trip. Record all your credit-card numbers—as well as the phone numbers to call if your cards are lost or stolen—in a safe place so you're prepared should something go wrong. Both MasterCard and Visa have general numbers you can call (collect if you're abroad) if your card is lost, but you're better off calling the number of your issuing bank since MasterCard and Visa usually just transfer you to your bank; your bank's number is usually printed on your card.

If you plan to use your credit card for cash advances, you'll need to apply for a PIN at least two weeks before your trip. Although it's usually cheaper (and safer) to use a credit card abroad for large purchases (so you can cancel payments or be reimbursed if there's a problem) note that some credit-card companies *and* the banks that issue them add substantial percentages to all foreign transactions, whether they're done in a foreign currency or not. Check on these fees before leaving home so that there won't be any surprises when you get the bill.

Before you charge something, ask the merchant whether or not he or she plans to do a dynamic currency conversion (DCC). In such a transaction the credit-card *processor* (shop, restaurant, or hotel, not Visa or MasterCard) converts the currency and charges you in dollars. In most cases you'll pay the merchant a 3% fee for this service in addition to any credit-card company and issuing-bank foreign-transaction surcharges.

DCC programs are becoming increasingly widespread. Merchants who participate in them are supposed to ask whether you want to be charged in dollars or the local currency, but they don't always do so. And even if they do offer you a choice, they may well avoid mentioning the additional surcharges. The good news is that you *do* have a choice. And if this practice really gets your goat, you can avoid it entirely thanks to American Express; with its cards, DCC simply isn't an option.

🖪 **Reporting Lost Cards American Express**
☎ 800/992-3404 in U.S. or 336/393-1111 collect from abroad ⊕ www.americanexpress.com. **Diners Club** ☎ 800/234-6377 in U.S. or 303/799-1504 col-

lect from abroad ⊕ www.dinersclub.com. **Master-Card** ☎ 636/722–7111 collect from abroad, 800/870866 toll-free in Italy ⊕ www.mastercard.com. **Visa** ☎ 410/581–9994 collect from abroad, 800/877232 toll-free in Italy ⊕ www.visa.com.

CURRENCY & EXCHANGE

Even if a currency exchange booth has a sign promising no commission, rest assured that there's some kind of huge, hidden fee. (Oh . . . that's right. The sign didn't say no *fee*.) And, in terms of rates, you're almost always better off getting foreign currency through an ATM or exchanging money at a bank.

Post offices also exchange currency at good rates.

The euro is the main unit of currency in Italy, as well as in 11 other European countries. Under the euro system there are 100 *centesimi* (cents) to the euro. There are coins valued at 1, 2, 5, 10, 20, and 50 cents, as well as 1 and 2 euros. There are seven notes: 5, 10, 20, 50, 100, 200, and 500 euros.

At this writing, the exchange rate was about 0.76 euros to the U.S. dollar; 0.70 euros to the Canadian dollar; 1.47 euros to the pound sterling; 0.60 euros to the Australian dollar; and 0.49 euros to the New Zealand dollar.

🖪 **Exchange-Rate Information Oanda.com** ⊕ www.oanda.com also allows you to print out a handy table with the current day's conversion rates. **XE.com** ⊕ www.xe.com. **Yahoo Finance** ⊕ http://finance.yahoo.com/currency.

TRAVELER'S CHECKS & CARDS

Some consider this the currency of the caveman, and it's true that fewer establishments accept traveler's checks these days. Nevertheless, they're a cheap and secure way to carry extra money, particularly on trips to urban areas. Both Citibank (under the Visa brand) and American Express issue traveler's checks in the United States, but AmEx is better known and more widely accepted; you can also avoid hefty surcharges by cashing AmEx checks at AmEx offices. Whatever you do, keep track of all the serial numbers in case the checks are lost or stolen.

American Express now offers a stored-value card called a Travelers Cheque Card, which you can use wherever American Express credit cards are accepted, including ATMs. The card can carry a minimum of $300 and a maximum of $2,700, and it's a very safe way to carry your funds. Although you can get replacement funds in 24 hours if your card is lost or stolen, it doesn't really strike us as a very good deal. In addition to a high initial cost ($14.95 to set up the card, plus $5 each time you "reload"), you still have to pay a 2% fee for each purchase in a foreign currency (similar to that of any credit card). Further, each time you use the card in an ATM you pay a transaction fee of $2.50 on top of the 2% transaction fee for the conversion— add it all up and it can be considerably more than you would pay for simply using your own ATM card. Regular traveler's checks are just as secure and cost less.

🖪 **American Express** ☎ 888/412–6945 in U.S., 801/945–9450 collect outside of U.S. to add value or speak to customer service ⊕ www.americanexpress.com.

PACKING

Why do some people travel with a convoy of suitcases the size of large-screen TVs and yet never have a thing to wear? How do others pack a toaster-oven-size duffel with a week's worth of outfits *and* supplies for every possible contingency? We realize that packing is a matter of style—a very personal thing—but there's a lot to be said for traveling light. The tips in this section will help you win the battle of the bulging bag.

Make a list. In a recent Fodor's survey, 29% of respondents said they make lists (and often pack) at least a week before a trip. Lists can be used at least twice—once to pack and once to repack at the end of your trip. You'll also have a record of the contents of your suitcase, just in case it disappears in transit.

Think it through. What's the weather like? Is this a business trip or a cruise or resort vacation? Going abroad? In some places and/or sights, traditions of dress may be more or less conservative than you're used to. As your itinerary comes together, jot activities down and note possible outfits next to each (don't forget those shoes and accessories).

Edit your wardrobe. Plan to wear everything twice (better yet, thrice) and to do laundry along the way. Stick to one basic look—urban chic, sporty casual, etc. Build around one or two neutrals and an accent (e.g., black, white, and olive green). Women can freshen looks by changing scarves or jewelry. For a week's trip, you can look smashing with three bottoms, four or five tops, a sweater, and a jacket you can wear alone or over the sweater.

Be practical. Put comfortable shoes at the top of your list. (Did we need to tell you this?) Pack items that are lightweight, wrinkle resistant, compact, and washable. (Or this?) Stack and then roll your clothes when packing; they'll wrinkle less. Unless you're on a guided tour or a cruise, select luggage that you can readily carry. Porters, like good butlers, are hard to find these days.

Check weight and size limitations. In the United States you may be charged extra for checked bags weighing more than 50 pounds. Abroad some airlines don't allow you to check bags weighing more than 60 to 70 pounds, or they charge outrageous fees for every pound your luggage is over. Carry-on size limitations can be stringent, too.

Check carry-on restrictions. Research restrictions with the TSA. Rules vary abroad, so check them with your airline if you're traveling overseas on a foreign carrier. Consider packing all but essentials (travel documents, prescription meds, wallet) in checked luggage. This leads to a "pack only what you can afford to lose" approach that might help you streamline.

Lock it up. If you must pack valuables, use TSA-approved locks (about $10) that can be unlocked by all U.S. security personnel.

Tag it. Always put tags on your luggage with some kind of contact information; use your business address if you don't want people to know your home address. Put the same information (and a copy of your itinerary) inside your luggage, too.

Rethink valuables. On U.S. flights, airlines are only liable for about $2,800 per person for bags. On international flights, the liability limit is around $635 per bag. But items like computers, cameras, and jewelry aren't covered, and as gadgetry regularly goes on and off the list of carry-on no-no's, you can't count on keeping things safe by keeping them close. Although comprehensive travel policies may cover luggage, the liability limit is often a pittance. Your home-owner's policy may cover you sufficiently when you travel—or not.

Report problems immediately. If your bags—or things in them—are damaged or go astray, file a written claim with your airline *before you leave the airport*. If the airline is at fault, it may give you money for essentials until your luggage arrives. Most lost bags are found within 48 hours, so alert the airline to your whereabouts for two or three days. If your bag was opened for security reasons in the United States and something is missing, file a claim with the TSA.

WHAT YOU'LL NEED IN ITALY

The weather is considerably milder, in winter at least, in Italy than in the north and central United States or Great Britain. At the height of summer stick with very light clothing, as it can get steamy. But even during summer months a sweater may be necessary for cool evenings, especially in the mountains and on the islands. Sunglasses, a hat, and sunblock are essential. Brief summer afternoon thunderstorms are common in Rome and inland cities, so a small umbrella will come in handy. In winter bring a medium-weight coat and a raincoat for Rome and farther south. Northern Italy calls for heavier coats, gloves, hats, scarves, and boots. Bring sturdy shoes for winter and comfortable walking shoes in any season.

Living up to their reputation, Italians dress exceptionally well. Men aren't required to wear ties or jackets to dinner, except in some of the grander hotel dining rooms and top-level restaurants, but are expected to look reasonably sharp—and they do.

For sightseeing **pack a pair of binoculars;** they will help you get a good look at painted ceilings and domes. If you stay in budget hotels **take your own soap and towel.** Many such hotels either do not provide soap or give guests only one tiny bar per room, and towels are often small and thin.

PASSPORTS & VISAS

Citizens of Australia, Canada, New Zealand, and the United States need only a valid passport to enter Italy for stays of up to 90 days. Citizens of the United Kingdom need only a valid passport to enter Italy for an unlimited stay.

PASSPORTS

We're always surprised at how few Americans have passports—only 25% at this writing. This number is expected to grow in coming years, when it becomes impossible to reenter the United States from trips to neighboring Canada or Mexico without one. Remember this: A passport verifies both your identity and nationality—a great reason to have one.

U.S. passports are valid for 10 years. You must apply in person if you're getting a passport for the first time; if your previous passport was lost, stolen or damaged; or if your previous passport has expired and was issued more than 15 years ago or when you were under 16. All children under 18 must appear in person to apply for or renew a passport. Both parents must accompany any child under 14 (or send a notarized statement with their permission) and provide proof of their relationship to the child.

There are 13 regional passport offices, as well as 7,000 passport acceptance facilities in post offices, public libraries, and other governmental offices. If you're renewing a passport, you can do so by mail. Forms are available at passport acceptance facilities and online.

The cost to apply for a new passport is $97 for adults, $82 for children under 16; renewals are $67. Allow six weeks to process the paperwork for either a new or renewed passport. For an expediting fee of $60, you can reduce the time to about two weeks. If your trip is less than two weeks away, you can get a passport even more

rapidly by going to a passport office with the necessary documentation. Private expediters can get things done in as little as 48 hours but charge hefty fees for their services.

Before your trip, make two copies of your passport's data page (one for someone at home and another for you to carry separately). Or scan the page and e-mail it to someone at home and/or yourself.

VISAS

Visas are essentially formal permissions to travel to a country. They allow countries to keep track of you and other visitors and to generate revenue (from visa fees). You *always* need a visa to enter a foreign country; however, many countries routinely issue tourist visas on arrival, particularly to U.S. citizens. When your passport is stamped or scanned in the immigration line, you're actually being issued a visa. Sometimes you have to stand in a separate line and pay a small fee to get your stamp before going through immigration, but you can still do this at the airport on arrival. Getting a visa isn't always that easy. Some countries require you to arrange for one in advance of your trip. There's usually—but not always—a fee involved, and said fee may be nominal ($10 or less) or substantial ($100 or more).

If you must apply for a visa in advance, you can usually do it in person or by mail. When you apply by mail, you send your passport to a designated consulate, where your passport will be examined and the visa issued. Expediters—usually the same ones who handle expedited passport applications—can do all the work to obtain your visa for you; however, there's always an additional cost (often more than $50 per visa).

Most visas limit you to a single trip—basically during the actual dates of your planned vacation. Other visas allow you to visit as many times as you wish for a specific period of time. Remember that requirements change, sometimes at the drop of a hat, and the burden is on you to make sure that you have the appropriate visas. Otherwise, you'll be turned away at the airport or, worse, deported after you arrive in the country. No company or travel insurer gives refunds if your travel plans are disrupted because you didn't have the correct visa.

🔳 U.S. Passport Information **U.S. Department of State** ☎ 877/487-2778 ⊕ http://travel.state.gov/ passport.

🔳 U.S. Passport & Visa Expediters **A. Briggs Passport & Visa Expeditors** ☎ 800/806-0581 or 202/464-3000 ⊕ www.abriggs.com. **American Passport Express** ☎ 800/455-5166 or 603/559-9888 ⊕ www.americanpassport.com. **Passport Express** ☎ 800/362-8196 or 401/272-4612 ⊕ www. passportexpress.com. **Travel Document Systems** ☎ 800/874-5100 or 202/638-3800 ⊕ www. traveldocs.com. **Travel the World Visas** ☎ 866/ 886-8472 or 301/495-7700 ⊕ www.world-visa.com.

PHONES

The good news is that you can now make a direct-dial telephone call from virtually any point on earth. The bad news? You can't always do so cheaply. Calling from a hotel is almost always the most expensive option; hotels usually add huge surcharges to all calls, particularly international ones. In some countries, you can phone from call centers or even the post office. Calling cards usually keep costs to a minimum, but only if you purchase them locally. And then there are cell phones (⇨ *below*), which are sometimes more prevalent—particularly in the developing world—than land lines; as expensive as cell-phone calls can be, they are still usually a much cheaper option than calling from your hotel.

Italy's telephone system is quite reliable. Remember that telephone numbers do not have a standard number of digits (they can range anywhere from four to seven) and that the entire area code must be included even when calling a number in the same city.

The country code for Italy is 39. Here are the area codes for major cities: Bologna 051; Brindisi 0831; Florence 055; Genoa 010; Milan 02; Naples 081; Palermo 091; Perugia 075; Pisa 050; Rome 06; Siena 0577; Turin 011; Venice 041; Verona 045. A call from the United States to Rome would be dialed as 011 + 39 + 06 + phone number.

The country code is 1 for the United States and Canada, 61 for Australia, 64 for New Zealand, and 44 for the United Kingdom.

CALLING WITHIN ITALY

Public pay phones may take coins, but usually require a *carta telefonica* (phone card) purchased at newsstands and tobacco shops. There are national cards and international cards, so make sure to specify which you want.

For general information in English, dial 4176. To place international calls through an operator, dial 170.

For all calls within Italy, whether local or long-distance, dial the area code followed by the number. Rates for long-distance calls vary according to the time of day; it's cheaper to call before 9 AM and after 7 or 8 PM.

Public pay phones are scarce, although they can be found at train and subway stations, post offices, in hotel lobbies, and in some bars. In rural areas, town squares usually have a pay phone. Some accept coins, but most use only prepaid phone cards.

CALLING OUTSIDE ITALY

The country code is 1 for the United States.

Since hotels charge exorbitant rates for long-distance and international calls, it's best to call from public phones using telephone cards. You can **make collect calls from any phone by dialing 170,** which will get you an English-speaking operator. Rates to the United States are lowest all day Sunday and 10 PM to 8 AM the rest of the week.

🔳 Access Codes **AT&T Direct** ☎ 800/172-444. **MCI WorldPhone** ☎ 800/172-401 or 800/172-404. **Sprint International Access** ☎ 800/172-405.

CALLING CARDS

Prepaid *carte telefoniche* (phone cards) are available throughout Italy. Cards in different denominations are sold at post offices, newsstands, tobacco shops, and bars. For local or national cards, tear off the corner of the card and insert it in the slot. When you dial, its value appears in the window. After you hang up, the card is returned.

International calling cards are different; you must call a toll-free number and dial a code number on the back of the card. The best card to use when calling North America or Europe is the €5 or €10 Europa card, which gives you a local number to dial and 180 minutes and 360 minutes of calling time.

CELL PHONES

If you have a multiband phone (some countries use different frequencies than what's used in the United States) and your service provider uses the world-standard GSM network (as do T-Mobile, Cingular, and Verizon), you can probably use your phone abroad. Roaming fees can be steep, though: 99¢ a minute is considered reasonable. And overseas, you normally pay the toll charges for incoming calls. It's almost always cheaper to send a text message than to make a call since text messages have a very low set fee (often less than 5¢).

If you just want to make local calls, consider buying a new SIM card (note that your provider may have to unlock your phone for you to use a different SIM card) and a prepaid service plan in the destination. You'll then have a local number and can make local calls at local rates. If your trip is extensive you could also simply buy a new cell phone in your destination, as the initial cost will be offset over time.

If you travel internationally frequently, save one of your old cell phones or buy a cheap one on the Internet; ask your cell-phone company to unlock it for you, and take it with you as a travel phone, buying a new SIM card with pay-as-you-go service in each destination.

Cell phones are widely used by Italians, so there are fewer public pay phones. If you need to make a lot of calls, consider renting or even buying a cell phone. Renting one costs about €20 per week plus the cost of a calling card, and a €100 deposit is normal. Buying a basic phone runs between €80 and €125.

⚡ **Cellular Abroad** ☎ 800/287-5072 ⊕ www.cellularabroad.com rents and sells GMS phones and sells SIM cards that work in many countries. **Mobal** ☎ 888/888-9162 ⊕ www.mobalrental.com rents

mobiles and sells GSM phones (starting at $49) that will operate in 140 countries. Per-call rates vary throughout the world. **Planet Fone** ☎ 888/988-4777 ⊕ www.planetfone.com rents cell phones, but the per-minute rates are expensive.

RESTROOMS

Public restrooms are rather rare in Italy. Pay toilets are the exception, not the rule. In Rome, Florence, and Venice, a few public pay toilets costing €0.50 are strategically located in the city centers. Although private businesses can refuse to make their toilets available to the passing public, some bars will allow you to use the restroom if you ask politely. Alternatively, it is not uncommon to pay for a little something—a mineral water or coffee, for example—to get access to the facilities. Standards of cleanliness and comfort vary greatly. In cities, restaurants, hotel lobbies, and high-end department stores such as La Rinascente and Coin tend to have the cleanest restrooms. Pubs and bars rank among the worst. In general, it's in your interest to carry some toilet paper with you. There are bathrooms in museums and in airports and train stations (in major train stations you'll also find well-kept pay toilets for €0.50–€1). There are also bathrooms at highway rest stops and gas stations: a small tip (€0.25–€0.50) to the attendant is always appreciated. There are no bathrooms at churches, post offices, subway stations, or public beaches.

The Bathroom Diaries is a Web site that's flush with unsanitized info on restrooms the world over—each one located, reviewed, and rated.

⚡ **Find a Loo The Bathroom Diaries** ⊕ www.thebathroomdiaries.com.

SAFETY

The best way to protect yourself against purse snatchers and pickpockets is to wear a concealed money belt or a pouch on a string around your neck. Be on your guard when in buses and subways, when making your way through crowded trains, and in busy piazzas and other tourist spots. Distribute your cash, credit cards, IDs, and other valuables between a deep front pocket, an inside jacket or vest pocket, and a hidden money pouch. Don't reach for the money pouch once you're in public.

GOVERNMENT ADVISORIES

As different countries have different world views, look at travel advisories from a range of governments to get more of a sense of what's going on out there. And be sure to parse the language carefully. For example, a warning to "avoid all travel" carries more weight than one urging you to "avoid nonessential travel," and both are much stronger than a plea to "exercise caution." A U.S.–government travel warning is more permanent (though not necessarily more serious) than a so-called public announcement, which carries an expiration date.

The U.S. Department of State's Web site has more than just travel warnings and advisories. The consular information sheets issued for every country have general safety tips, entry requirements (though be sure to verify these with the country's embassy), and other useful details.

Consider registering online with the state department (https://travelregistration.state.gov/ibrs/), so the government will know to look for you should a crisis occur in the country you're visiting. If you travel frequently also look into the Registered Traveler program of the Transportation Security Administration (TSA; www.tsa.gov). The program, which is still being tested in five U.S. airports, is designed to cut down on gridlock at security checkpoints by allowing prescreened travelers to pass quickly through kiosks that scan an iris and/or a fingerprint. How sci-fi is that?

🔒 **General Information & Warnings** Australian Department of Foreign Affairs & Trade ⊕ www.smartraveller.gov.au. Consular Affairs Bureau of Canada ⊕ www.voyage.gc.ca. U.K. Foreign & Commonwealth Office ⊕ www.fco.gov.uk/travel. U.S. Department of State ⊕ www.travel.state.gov.

LOCAL SCAMS

In larger cities, some children have been trained to be adept pickpockets. One tactic is to proffer a piece of cardboard with writing on it. While you attempt to read the message *on* it, the children's hands are busy *under* it, trying to make off with purses or valuables. If you see such a group, avoid them—they are quick and know more tricks than you do. If traveling in a rental car, have someone remain near the car when you stop at rest areas. Thieves often target rental cars.

WOMEN IN ITALY

Purse-snatching is not uncommon, and thieves operate on foot as well as on *motorini* (mopeds). The difficulties encountered by women traveling alone in Italy are often overstated. Younger women have to put up with much male attention, but it is rarely dangerous or hostile. Ignoring whistling and questions is the best response; a firm *no, vai via* ("no, go away") usually works, too.

SIGHTSEEING GUIDES

Every province in Italy has tour guides licensed by the government. Some are eminently qualified in relevant fields such as architecture and art history; others have simply managed to pass the test. Tourist offices can provide the names of knowledgeable guides and the rates for certain services. Before you hire a guide, ask about their background and qualifications and make sure you can understand each other. Tipping is appreciated but not obligatory.

SMOKING

In 2005, smoking was banned in many public places, including bars and restaurants. Although Italians are for the most part unrepentant smokers, they are begrudgingly obeying the law. Always check to see if there's a VIETATO FUMARE (no-smoking) sign before lighting up. All Italian trains are smoke-free.

TAXES

The V.A.T. is 20% on clothing, wine, and luxury goods. On consumer goods it's already included in the amount shown on the price tag, whereas on services it may not be. If your purchases total more than €155 you may be entitled to a refund of the V.A.T.

A 9% V.A.T. (value-added tax) is included in the rate at all hotels except those at the upper end of the range. At luxury hotels a 12% tax is added to the bill.

No tax is added to the bill in restaurants. A service charge of approximately 10% to 15% is often added to your check; in some cases a service charge is included in the prices.

When making a purchase, ask for a V.A.T. refund form and find out whether the merchant gives refunds—not all stores do, nor are they required to. Have the form stamped like any customs form by customs officials when you leave the country or, if you're visiting several European Union countries, when you leave the EU. After you're through passport control, take the form to a refund-service counter for an on-the-spot refund (which is usually the quickest and easiest option), or mail it to the address on the form (or the envelope with it) after you arrive home. You receive the total refund stated on the form, but the processing time can be long, especially if you request a credit-card adjustment.

Global Refund is a Europe-wide service with 225,000 affiliated stores and more than 700 refund counters at major airports and border crossings. Its refund form, called a Tax Free Check, is the most common across the European continent. The service issues refunds in the form of cash, check, or credit-card adjustment.

V.A.T. Refunds **Global Refund** ☎ 800/566-9828 in U.S., 800/566-9828 in Canada ⊕ www.globalrefund.com.

TIME

Italy is 6 hours ahead of eastern standard time, 1 hour ahead of Great Britain, 10 hours behind Sydney, and 12 hours behind Auckland. Like the rest of Europe, Italy uses the 24-hour (or "military") clock, which means that after noon you continue counting forward: 13:00 is 1 PM, 23:30 is 11:30 PM.

TIPPING

In restaurants a service charge of 10% to 15% may appear on your check. If so, it's not necessary to leave an additional tip. If service is not included, leave a tip of up to 10%. Tip checkroom attendants €1 per person and restroom attendants €0.50 (more in expensive hotels and restaurants). In major cities tip €0.50 or more for table

service in cafés. At a hotel bar tip €1 and up for a round or two of drinks.

Italians rarely tip taxi drivers, which is not to say that you shouldn't do it. A euro or two, depending on the length of the journey, is appreciated, particularly if the driver helps with luggage. Service-station attendants are tipped only for special services; give them €1 for checking your tires. Railway and airport porters charge a fixed rate per bag. Tip an additional €0.25 per person, more if the porter is helpful. Give a barber €1 to €1.50 and a hairdresser's assistant €1.50 to €4 for a shampoo or cut, depending on the type of establishment.

On sightseeing tours, tip guides about €1.50 per person for a half-day group tour, more if they are especially knowledgeable. In monasteries and other sights where admission is free, a contribution (€0.50 to €1) is expected.

In hotels give the *portiere* (concierge) about 10% of his bill for services, or €2.50 to €5 for help with dinner reservations and such. For two people in a double room leave the chambermaid about €0.75 per day, or about €4.50 to €5 a week in a moderately priced hotel; tip a minimum of €1 for valet or room service. Double these amounts in an expensive hotel. In expensive hotels tip doormen €0.50 for calling a cab and €1.50 for carrying bags to the check-in desk, bellhops €1.50 to €2.50 for carrying your bags to the room, and €2 to €2.50 for room service.

TOURS & PACKAGES

GUIDED TOURS

Guided tours are a good option when you don't want to do it all yourself. You travel along with a group (sometimes large, sometimes small), stay in prebooked hotels, eat with your fellow travelers (sometimes included in the price of your tour, sometimes not), and follow a schedule. But not all guided tours are a "If This Is Tuesday, It Must Be Belgium" kind of experience. A knowledgeable guide can take you places that you might never discover on your own, and you may be pushed to see more than you would have otherwise.

Tours aren't for everyone, but they can be just the thing for trips to places where making travel arrangements is difficult or time-consuming (particularly when you don't speak the language). Whenever you book a guided tour, find out what's included and what isn't. A "land-only" tour includes all your travel (by bus, in most cases) in the destination, but not necessarily your flights to or even within it. Also, in most cases, prices in tour brochures don't include fees and taxes. And remember that you'll be expected to tip your guide (in cash) at the end of the tour.

VACATION PACKAGES

Packages *are not* guided tours. Packages combine airfare, accommodations, and perhaps a rental car or other extras (theater tickets, guided excursions, boat trips, reserved entry to popular museums, transit passes), but they let you do your own thing. During busy periods, packages may be your only option because flights and rooms may be otherwise sold out. Packages will definitely save you time. They can also save you money, particularly in peak seasons, but—and this is a really big "but"—you should price each part of the package separately to be sure. And be aware that prices advertised on Web sites and in newspapers rarely include service charges or taxes, which can up your costs by hundreds of dollars.

Note that local tourism boards can provide information about lesser-known and small-niche operators that sell packages to just a few destinations. And don't always assume that you can get the best deal by booking everything yourself. Some packages and cruises are sold only through travel agents.

Each year consumers are stranded or lose their money when packagers—even large ones with excellent reputations—go out of business. How can you protect yourself? First, always pay with a credit card; if you have a problem, your credit-card company may help you resolve it. Second, buy trip insurance that covers default. Third, choose a company that belongs to the United States Tour Operators Association, whose members must set aside funds ($1 million) to cover defaults. Finally choose a company that also participates in the Tour Operator Program of the American Society of Travel Agents (ASTA), which will act as mediator in any disputes. You can also check on the tour operator's reputation among travelers by posting an inquiry on one of the Fodors.com forums.

🔃 Organizations **American Society of Travel Agents (ASTA)** ☎ 703/739-2782 or 800/965-2782 24-hr hotline ⊕ www.astanet.com. **United States Tour Operators Association (USTOA)** ☎ 212/599-6599 ⊕ www.ustoa.com.

TRAIN TRAVEL

In Italy traveling by train is simple and efficient. Service between major cities is frequent, and trains usually arrive on schedule. You can either purchase your tickets in advance (all major credit cards are accepted online at ⊕ www.raileurope.com) or after you arrive at any train station or travel agency. If you are considering using a Eurailpass or any of its variations, you must **buy the pass before leaving your home country,** as they are not sold in Italy.

You must **validate your ticket before boarding** the train by punching it at a yellow box located in the waiting area of smaller train stations or at the end of the track in larger stations. Always **purchase tickets before boarding the train,** as you can no longer purchase one from a conductor. Fines are steep for passengers without tickets.

The fastest trains on the *Trenitalia,* the Italian State Railways, are the Eurostar trains that run between major cities. You will be assigned a specific seat in a specific coach. To avoid having to squeeze through narrow aisles, board only at your designated coach (the number on your ticket matches the one on near the door of each coach). The next-fastest trains are the *Intercity* (IC) trains. Reservations, required for some IC trains, are always advisable. *Diretto* and *Interregionale* trains make more stops and are a little slower. *Regionale* and *locale* trains are the slowest; many serve commuters. There are refreshments on all long-distance trains, purchased from a mobile cart or a dining car.

Traveling by night is a good deal, as you do not pay extra for a bed. More comfortable trains run on the longer routes (Sicily–Rome, Sicily–Milan, Sicily–Venice, Rome–Turin, Lecce–Milan); ask for the good-value T3, Intercity Notte, and Carrozza Comfort. The Vagone Letto Excelsior has private bathrooms, coffee machines, microwave ovens, refrigerators, and a suite with a double bed and TV.

Some cities—Milan, Turin, Genoa, Naples, Florence, and Rome included—have more than one train station, so be sure you get off at the right place. When buying train tickets be particularly aware that in Rome and Florence some trains do not stop at all of the cities' train stations and may not stop at the main central station. This is a common occurrence with regional and some intercity trains. When scheduling train travel on the Internet or through a travel agent, be sure to request a train that goes to the train station closest to your destination in Rome and Florence.

Except for Pisa and Rome, none of the major cities have trains that go directly to the airports, but there are commuter bus lines connecting train stations and airports.

Train strikes of various kinds are also common, so it's a good idea to make sure your train is running.

CLASSES

Most Italian trains have first and second classes. On local trains a first-class fare gets you little more than a clean doily on your headrest, but on long-distance trains you get wider seats, more legroom, and better ventilation and lighting. At peak travel times, a first-class fare is worth the price, as the coaches are less crowded. In Italian, *prima classe* is first class; second is *seconda classe.*

CUTTING COSTS

To save money, **look into rail passes.** But be aware that if you don't plan to cover many miles, you may come out ahead by buying individual tickets. If Italy is your only destination, consider an Italian Flexi Rail Card Saver. Over the course of a month you can travel on 4 days ($239 first class, $191 second class), 8 days ($334 first class, $268 second class), or 12 days ($429 first class, $343 second class). These tickets are sold only outside Italy.

The *Carta d'Argento* (Silver Card), for seniors, *Cartaverde* (Green Card), for those under 26, and *Comitive Ordinarie,* for groups, have been discontinued. They have been replaced with the *Railplus* card, which is used for the purchase of international tickets (25% reduction on international tickets from Italy to Austria, Germany, and France and 25% on internal ticket prices when combined with an international ticket). The *Railplus* card is purchased upon arrival in Italy and costs €45 for adults and €20 for seniors over 60 and youths under 26.

Italy is one of 17 countries that accept Eurailpass, which allows unlimited first-class travel. If you plan to rack up the miles, get a standard pass. Passes are available for 15 days ($605), 21 days ($785), one month ($975), two months ($1,378), and three months ($1,703). You also get free or discounted fares on some ferry lines. The Eurail Selectpass allows for travel in three to five contiguous countries. Five days of first-class travel in three countries is $383, four countries $428, five countries $473.

In addition to standard Eurailpasses, **ask about special plans.** Among these are the Eurail Youthpass (for those under 26), the Eurail Flexipass (which allows a certain number of travel days within a set period), the Eurail Saver Flexipass (which gives a discount for two or more people traveling together), and the EurailDrive Pass (which combines travel by train and rental car). All Eurailpasses must be purchased before you leave home. Order them on the Rail Europe Web site.

Remember that you need to reserve seats even if you are using a rail pass.

ℹ Information & Passes **CIT Rail** ✉ 15 W. 44th St., New York, NY 10036 ☎ 800/248-7245. **DER Tours** ☎ 800/782-2424 🖷 800/282-7474. **Rail Europe** ✉ 44 S. Broadway, White Plains, NY 10601 ☎ 800/438-7245 or 877/257-2887 ⊕ www.raileurope.com.

PAYING

You can pay for your train tickets in cash or with a major credit card such as American Express, Diners Club, MasterCard, and Visa.

RESERVATIONS

Trains can be very crowded, so it's always a good idea to make a reservation. You can reserve seats up to two months in advance at the train station or at a travel agent. Simply holding a train ticket does not guarantee a seat. In summer it's fairly common to see people standing for part of the journey.

🚆 **Train Information Trenitalia** ☎ 892021 in Italy ⊕ www.trenitalia.com.

TRAVEL AGENTS

If you use an agent—brick-and-mortar or virtual—you'll pay a fee for the service. And know that the service you get from some online agents isn't comprehensive. For example Expedia and Travelocity don't search for prices on budget airlines like JetBlue, Southwest, or small foreign carriers. That said, some agents (online or not) *do* have access to fares that are difficult to find otherwise, and the savings can more than make up for any surcharge.

A knowledgeable brick-and-mortar travel agent can be a godsend if you're booking a cruise, a package trip that's not available to you directly, an air pass, or a complicated itinerary including several overseas flights. What's more, travel agents who specialize in a destination may have exclusive access to certain deals and insider information on things such as charter flights. Agents who specialize in types of travelers (senior citizens, gays and lesbians, naturists) or types of trips (cruises, luxury travel, safaris) can also be invaluable. Complain about the surcharges all you like, but when things don't work out the way you'd hoped, it's nice to have an agent to put things right.

🚆 **Agent Resources American Society of Travel Agents** ☎ 703/739-2782 ⊕ www.travelsense.org. 🚆 **Online Agents Expedia** ⊕ www.expedia.com. **Onetravel.com** ⊕ www.onetravel.com. **Orbitz** ⊕ www.orbitz.com. **Priceline.com** ⊕ www. priceline.com. **Travelocity** ⊕ www.travelocity.com.

VISITOR INFORMATION

🚆 **Tourist Information Italian Government Tourist Board** ⊠ 630 5th Ave., Suite 1565, New York, NY 10111 ☎ 212/245-4822 🖷 212/586-9249 ⊠ 500 N. Michigan Ave., Chicago, IL 60611 ☎ 312/644-0996

☎ 312/644-3019 ⊠ 12400 Wilshire Blvd., Suite 550, Los Angeles, CA 90025 ☎ 310/820-1898 🖷 310/820-6357 ⊠ 175 Bloor St. E, Suite 907, South Tower, Toronto, Ontario M4W 3R8 ☎ 416/925-4882 🖷 416/925-4799 ⊠ 1 Princes St., London W1B 2.8AY ☎ 020/7408-1254 🖷 020/73993567 ⊕ www.italiantourism.com.

🚆 **Regional Offices Florence** ⊠ Via Cavour 1/r, next to Palazzo Medici-Riccardi, 50129 ☎ 055/290832 ⊕ www.comune.firenze.it. **Milan** ⊠ Stazione Centrale, 20121 ☎ 02/72524370 ⊕ www.milanoinfotourist.com. **Rome** ⊠ Via Parigi 5, 00185 ☎ 06/36004399 ⊕ www.romaturismo.it. **Venice** ⊠ Stazione Ferroviaria Santa Lucia ☎ 041/5298727 ⊕ www.turismovenezia.it.

WEB SITES

We're really proud of our Web site: Fodors.com is a great place to begin any journey. Scan "Travel Wire" for suggested itineraries, travel deals, restaurant and hotel openings, and other up-to-the-minute info. Check out "Booking" to research prices and book plane tickets, hotel rooms, rental cars, and vacation packages. Head to "Talk" for on-the-ground pointers from travelers who frequent our message boards. You can also link to loads of other travel-related resources.

After your trip, be sure to rate the places you visited and share your experiences and travel tips with us and other Fodorites in "Travel Ratings" and "Talk" on www.fodors.com.

🚆 **Currency Conversion Google** ⊕ www.google.com does currency conversion. Just type in the amount you want to convert and an explanation of how you want it converted (e.g., "14 Swiss francs in dollars"), and then voilà. **Oanda.com** ⊕ www.oanda.com also allows you to print out a handy table with the current day's conversion rates. **XE.com** ⊕ www.xe.com is a good currency conversion Web site. 🚆 **Time Zones Timeanddate.com** ⊕ www.timeanddate.com/worldclock can help you figure out the correct time anywhere in the world. 🚆 **Weather Accuweather.com** ⊕ www.accuweather.com is an independent weather-forecasting service. **Weather.com** ⊕ www.weather.com is the Web site for the Weather Channel. 🚆 **Other Resources CIA World Factbook** ⊕ www.odci.gov/cia/publications/factbook/index.html has profiles of every country in the world. It's a good source if you need some quick facts and figures.

INDEX

NOTES

ABOUT OUR WRITERS

After completing his master's degree in art history, Peter Blackman settled permanently in Italy in 1986. Since then he's worked as a biking and walking tour guide, managing to see more of Italy than most of his Italian friends. When he's not leading a trip, you'll find Peter at home in Chianti, listening to opera and planning his next journey.

While doing physics research in the same tower where Galileo once worked, Jeff Booth felt the gravitational pull of Venice. After two years of learning to row gondolas and raise a Venetian daughter, he hasn't fallen into the Grand Canal, yet. Jeff writes for *National Geographic Traveler* and *New York* magazine, among other publications.

Although Robin S. Goldstein is trained in philosophy at Harvard and law at Yale, his heart has always been in his travel writing. His credits include not only his home base of Italy but also Spain, Mexico, Ecuador, and the Galapagos Islands. Once a resident of Genoa, he now spends most of his time in the *mezzogiorno* and along the Sicilian coast.

Cristina Gregorin has worked as a guide in Venice since 1991. She's the author of *Venice Master Artisans,* a study of the city's traditional arts and crafts.

After many years of practicing law, Denise Hummel took up a career in journalism and now freelances for many U.S.-based newspapers and magazines. She lives in Varese, between Lake Como and Lake Maggiore, where she runs a public relations and communications firm.

Madeleine Johnson is an unrepentant Midwesterner who has lived in Italy—with a two-year break in Paris—since 1988. She has degrees in art history from Wellesley College and U.C. Berkeley, and her writing has appeared in *Connoisseur, The Journal of Art,* and *The American*—where she has a monthly column about life in Milan.

Dana Klitzberg studied at the Institute of Culinary Education and worked as a chef at the renowned Manhattan restaurant San Domenico. After a stint cooking in a restaurant in Rome, she decided to make the Eternal City home. Now she runs her own company, through which she caters, gives cooking classes, and conducts culinary tours of the city.

Florence resident Patricia Rucidlo holds master's degrees in Italian Renaissance history and art history. When she's not extolling the virtues of a Pontormo masterpiece or angrily defending the Medici, she's leading wine tours in Chianti and catering private dinner parties.

California native Pamela Santini came to study art history 15 years ago at Venice's Ca' Foscari University, where she currently teaches. She's also a writer and translator, and enjoys traveling with her husband and son.

Megan K. Williams is a Rome-based writer and correspondent, covering Italy and Africa in print for many newspapers and magazines, as well as on the radio for the CBC, Marketplace, NPR, and Deutsche Welle. Her collection of short stories about life in in her adopted hometown, *Saving Rome,* was published in 2006 to rave reviews.